Innovative Methods and Technologies for Electronic Discourse Analysis

Hwee Ling Lim
The Petroleum Institute, UAE

Fay Sudweeks
Murdoch University, Australia

A volume in the Advances in Human and
Social Aspects of Technology Book Series
(AHSAT)

Managing Director:	Lindsay Johnston
Editorial Director:	Joel Gamon
Production Manager:	Jennifer Yoder
Publishing Systems Analyst:	Adrienne Freeland
Development Editor:	Monica Speca
Assistant Acquisitions Editor:	Kayla Wolfe
Typesetter:	Erin O'Dea
Cover Design:	Jason Mull

Published in the United States of America by
Information Science Reference (an imprint of IGI Global)
701 E. Chocolate Avenue
Hershey PA 17033
Tel: 717-533-8845
Fax: 717-533-8661
E-mail: cust@igi-global.com
Web site: http://www.igi-global.com

Library of Congress Cataloging-in-Publication Data

Innovative methods and technologies for electronic discourse analysis / Hwee Ling Lim and Fay Sudweeks, editors.
    pages cm
 Includes bibliographical references and index.
 Summary: "This book highlights research, applications, frameworks, and theories of online communication to explore recent advances in the manipulation and shaping of meaning in electronic discourse"--Provided by publisher.
 ISBN 978-1-4666-4426-7 (hardcover) -- ISBN 978-1-4666-4427-4 (ebook) -- ISBN 978-1-4666-4428-1 (print & perpetual access) 1. Online chat groups. 2. Discourse analysis. 3. Communication--Technological innovations. I. Lim, Hwee Ling, 1964- II. Sudweeks, Fay.
 HM1169.I56 2014
 004.693--dc23
                                     2013014318

This book is published in the IGI Global book series Advances in Human and Social Aspects of Technology Book Series (AHSAT) (ISSN: Pending; eISSN: Pending)

British Cataloguing in Publication Data
A Cataloguing in Publication record for this book is available from the British Library.

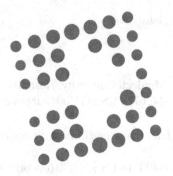

Advances in Human and Social Aspects of Technology Book Series (AHSAT)

Ashish Dwivedi
The University of Hull, UK

ISSN: Pending
EISSN: pending

MISSION

In recent years, the societal impact of technology has been noted as we become increasingly more connected and are presented with more digital tools and devices. With the popularity of digital devices such as cell phones and tablets, it is crucial to consider the implications of our digital dependence and the presence of technology in our everyday lives.

The **Advances in Human and Social Aspects of Technology (AHSAT) Book Series** seeks to explore the ways in which society and human beings have been affected by technology and how the technological revolution has changed the way we conduct our lives as well as our behavior. The AHSAT book series aims to publish the most cutting-edge research on human behavior and interaction with technology and the ways in which the digital age is changing society.

COVERAGE

- Activism & ICTs
- Computer-Mediated Communication
- Cultural Influence of ICTs
- Cyber Behavior
- End-User Computing
- Gender & Technology
- Human-Computer Interaction
- Information Ethics
- Public Access to ICTs
- Technoself

IGI Global is currently accepting manuscripts for publication within this series. To submit a proposal for a volume in this series, please contact our Acquisition Editors at Acquisitions@igi-global.com or visit: http://www.igi-global.com/publish/.

Titles in this Series

For a list of additional titles in this series, please visit: www.igi-global.com

Innovative Methods and Technologies for Electronic Discourse Analysis
Hwee Ling Lim (The Petroleum Institute-Abu Dhabi, UAE) and Fay Sudweeks (Murdoch University, Australia)
Information Science Reference • copyright 2014 • 368pp • H/C (ISBN: 9781466644267) • US $175.00 (our price)

Advanced Research and Trends in New Technologies, Software, Human-Computer Interaction, and Communicability
Francisco Vicente Cipolla-Ficarra (Alaipo, Italy)
Information Science Reference • copyright 2014 • 361pp • H/C (ISBN: 9781466644908) • US $175.00 (our price)

New Media Influence on Social and Political Change in Africa
Anthony A. Olorunnisola (Pennsylvania State University, USA) and Aziz Douai (University of Ontario Institute of Technology, Canada)
Information Science Reference • copyright 2013 • 373pp • H/C (ISBN: 9781466641976) • US $175.00 (our price)

Cases on Usability Engineering Design and Development of Digital Products
Miguel A. Garcia-Ruiz (Algoma University, Canada)
Information Science Reference • copyright 2013 • 362pp • H/C (ISBN: 9781466640467) • US $175.00 (our price)

Human Rights and Information Communication Technologies Trends and Consequences of Use
John Lannon (University of Limerick, Ireland) and Edward Halpin (Leeds Metropolitan University, UK)
Information Science Reference • copyright 2013 • 324pp • H/C (ISBN: 9781466619180) • US $175.00 (our price)

Collaboration and the Semantic Web Social Networks, Knowledge Networks, and Knowledge Resources
Stefan Brüggemann (Astrium Space Transportation, Germany) and Claudia d'Amato (University of Bari, Italy)
Information Science Reference • copyright 2012 • 387pp • H/C (ISBN: 9781466608948) • US $175.00 (our price)

Human Rights and Risks in the Digital Era Globalization and the Effects of Information Technologies
Christina M. Akrivopoulou (Democritus University of Thrace, Greece) and Nicolaos Garipidis (Aristotle University of Thessaloniki, Greece)
Information Science Reference • copyright 2012 • 363pp • H/C (ISBN: 9781466608917) • US $180.00 (our price)

Technology for Creativity and Innovation Tools, Techniques and Applications
Anabela Mesquita (ISCAP/IPP and Algoritmi Centre, University of Minho, Portugal)
Information Science Reference • copyright 2011 • 426pp • H/C (ISBN: 9781609605193) • US $180.00 (our price)

www.igi-global.com

701 E. Chocolate Ave., Hershey, PA 17033
Order online at www.igi-global.com or call 717-533-8845 x100
To place a standing order for titles released in this series, contact: cust@igi-global.com
Mon-Fri 8:00 am - 5:00 pm (est) or fax 24 hours a day 717-533-8661

Traian Rebedea, *University Politehnica of Bucharest, Romania*

Kate Thompson, *The University of Sydney, Australia*

Stefan Trausan-Matu, *University Politehnica of Bucharest, Romania*

Patrick Wessa, *Leuven Institute for Research on Information Systems, Belgium*

Asta Zelenkauskaite, *Drexel University, USA*

Table of Contents

Section 1
Electronic Educational Discourse: Developments in Theory, Methods, and Applications

Chapter 1
Divonna M. Stebick, Gettysburg College, USA
Mary L. Paxton, Shippensburg University, USA

Chapter 2
P. Wessa, Leuven Institute for Research on Information Systems, K.U.Leuven, Belgium
S. Poelmans, Leuven Institute for Research on Information Systems, K.U.Leuven, Belgium &
    Faculty of Economics Management, HUB, Brussels, Belgium
I. E. Holliday, Aston Brain Centre, Aston University, Aston Triangle, Birmingham, UK

Chapter 3
Stefania Cucchiara, University of Bari, Italy
M. Beatrice Ligorio, University of Bari, Italy
Nobuko Fujita, University of Windsor, Canada

Chapter 4
Traian Rebedea, University Politehnica of Bucharest, Romania
Stefan Trausan-Matu, University Politehnica of Bucharest, Romania
Costin Chiru, University Politehnica of Bucharest, Romania

Section 3
Future Trends: Emergent Methods for the New Media

Chapter 20

Carlos Baladrón, Universidad de Valladolid, Spain
Javier M. Aguiar, Universidad de Valladolid, Spain
Lorena Calavia, Universidad de Valladolid, Spain
Belén Carro, Universidad de Valladolid, Spain
Antonio Sánchez-Esguevillas, Universidad de Valladolid, Spain

Detailed Table of Contents

Section 1
Electronic Educational Discourse: Developments in Theory, Methods, and Applications

This case study in teacher education demonstrates how conversation evolves within a social media platform. The researchers analyzed online discussions and face-to-face dialogues between teacher educators and pre-service teachers in order to identify the affordances and constraints of each platform on perceived understanding. Findings from discourse analysis indicate the presence of metacognitive growth when comparing the initial reciprocal conversations with the final conversations. The chapter concludes that social media can be considered an effective strategy for fostering high levels of inquiry, peer-to-peer collaboration, and concrete reflection based on theory and practice through an investigative discourse analysis.

This chapter proposes a new approach to discourse analysis which is based on meta data from social networking behavior of learners who are submerged in a socially constructivist e-learning environment. Within the setting of a constructivist statistics course, the chapter illustrates what network-based discourse analysis is about from a methodological point of view, how it is implemented in practice, and why it is relevant for researchers and educators. Through the use of innovative, educational technology, the authors found that the macro structure of social networking and collaboration can be measured and used to improve the discourse analysis of learners. Also, the results imply that "deep" constructivism occurs when people advance the knowledge in their community. The chapter concludes that traditional data modeling techniques can be combined with social network analysis – an approach that promises to yield new insights into the largely uncharted domain of network-based discourse analysis.

Chapter 3

Stefania Cucchiara, University of Bari, Italy
M. Beatrice Ligorio, University of Bari, Italy
Nobuko Fujita, University of Windsor, Canada

Assessing the development of students' knowledge building discourse can be simplified with the availability of clear indicators of such discourse that signal if and how it is developing. Hence, this chapter seeks to identify indicators that can monitor how the knowledge building process develops during online discussions. The authors analyzed university students' discourse in an online setting oriented to knowledge building with an innovative mixed-method analysis approach that combines qualitative content analysis and Strategy Network Analysis. Findings from the study show the most often used strategies in the knowledge process and suggest that the organization of the course and online activities students are required to perform, have an effect on the interactive strategies used during the online discussions.

Chapter 4

Traian Rebedea, University Politehnica of Bucharest, Romania
Stefan Trausan-Matu, University Politehnica of Bucharest, Romania
Costin Chiru, University Politehnica of Bucharest, Romania

With the wide adoption of instant messaging, online discussion forums, blogs and social networks, online communication has shifted from narration to highly collaborative discussions with multiple authors and discussion threads. However, the theories and methodologies for analyzing this new type of discourse which is different from narration, but also from dialogue, have remained mostly the same. This chapter proposes a new discourse analysis method designed especially for multi-party chat conversations where parallel discussion floors and threads exist at the same time. The theoretical underpinning of the inter-animation framework is the detection of links between utterances in order to build a conversation graph that can be used to discover the discussion threads. With this new discourse analysis method, the authors analyzed chat conversations of students in Computer Science in order to assess the involvement of each student, the inter-animation of the conversation and the degree of collaborative discourse. The chapter concludes that the inter-animation framework has many benefits for processing online textual interactions because it exploits the links between utterances that enable a better understanding of the context of each utterance.

Chapter 5

Shannon Kennedy-Clark, Australian Catholic University, Australia
Kate Thompson, University of Sydney, Australia

This chapter proposes that through the combined use of group function analysis and discourse analysis perspectives, a deeper understanding of how learners interact on both macro and micro levels can be gained. This multimodal discourse analysis approach enables analyses that move beyond code and count resulting in an understanding of learner collaboration and group problem solving processes from multiple viewpoints. The findings show clear patterns of successful and non-successful problem solving. The chapter concludes with a discussion on factors that can impact goal attainment and suggests that for genuine learning to occur, participants need support beyond the task that includes their mastery of the environment.

Chapter 6

Studying the Suitability of Discourse Analysis Methods for Emotion Detection and
Interpretation in Computer-Mediated Educational Discourse 119

Thanasis Daradoumis, Open University of Catalonia, Spain & University of Aegean, Greece
Marta María Arguedas Lafuente, Open University of Catalonia, Spain

Conversation analysis (CA) and discourse analysis (DA) methods are widely used to analyze interaction in conventional and e-learning environments. However, CA and DA methods seem to ignore emotion detection and interpretation when analyzing learners' interaction in online environments. Yet effective regulation of emotion, motivation and cognition in social interaction are crucial in achieving problem-solving goals. This chapter is an in-depth study on the application of discourse analysis methods in e-learning contexts with implications for emotion detection, interpretation and regulation. The results reveal the presences of positive and negative emotions at different phases of a collaborative group learning activity. The findings on the emotional structure of discourse have implications for helping teachers to better understand the role and influences of emotions in teaching processes, and for enabling students to develop greater awareness of the group affective state.

Chapter 7

Social Networks and Creative Writing in EFL 144

Reima Al-Jarf, King Saud University, Riyadh, Saudi Arabia

The study identifies the types of creative text genres, themes and discoursal features of Facebook English creative texts posted by non-native writers in Saudi Arabia. The study also surveys Arab Facebook creative writers who are non-native speakers of English on the personal, social and cultural factors that impact their creativity in English as a foreign language. The author used content analysis to analyze creative texts posted on the Facebook wall for the characteristics of creative online discourse. The findings suggest that all people have creative potential, and that the right environment with prompts and encouragement can elicit creative work to a degree. Although talent, motivation and desire play an important role in creative writing, creative writing also involves tools, techniques and concepts. Hence, novice writers need to acquire those tools and techniques in order to experiment, practice, and master them.

Chapter 8

Second Language Learners' Spoken Discourse: Practice and Corrective Feedback Through
Automatic Speech Recognition.. 169

Catia Cucchiarini, Radboud University, The Netherlands
Helmer Strik, Radboud University, The Netherlands

Developing Computer Assisted Language Learning (CALL) systems for practice and feedback in second language (L2) spoken discourse is complex and challenging because L2 speech is highly variable and substantially differs from standard speech. With current state-of-the-art technology, it is possible to develop useful CALL systems, but this clearly requires a combination of expertise. This chapter describes the use of Automatic Speech Recognition (ASR) technology in the context of Computer Assisted Language Learning and language learning and teaching research. While most CALL systems focus on pronunciation, this chapter demonstrates that it is possible to develop systems for practicing grammar in spoken discourse and providing useful feedback. The authors explain how such systems can be used to the benefit of discourse analysis research. The chapter concludes with a discussion of possible perspectives for future research and development of ASR-based CALL systems.

Section 2
Electronic Discourse Analysis: Innovations in Theory, Methods, and Applications in Research on Society and Culture

Chapter 9

This chapter investigates and endorses the integration of two existing research traditions, electronic discourse analysis (EDA) and critical discourse analysis (CDA), into a more powerful and comprehensive form of analysis of electronic discourses, Critical Electronic Discourse Analysis (CEDA). It sets this analytic project against the massive, unpredictable changes in culture and society which are associated with the electronic media revolution. It argues for innovative forms of analysis, in which 'electronic discourse analysis' acquires two over-lapping interpretations: electronically enabled analysis of discourses in all media; and all forms of analysis of electronic discourses and the social forms they express. It uses McLuhan and multi-modality theory to argue that powerful innovations in analysis and technology need to recognize and incorporate the two fundamental semiotic modes, digital and analogue, and not seek to replace one with the other.

Chapter 10

After ten years, Internet dating has become mainstreamed with members producing and consuming a great deal of written text before meeting face-to-face. This chapter provides an in-depth case study of four participants in their rhetorical processes of writing profiles, interpreting others' profiles, and exchanging emails to facilitate courtship. Using the combinatory methods of discourse analysis and ethnography, the author analyzed the discourse of participants' self-presentations in comparison with their reported self-perceptions and impression management strategies. The findings suggest that the more effective members compose their e-texts after a methodical process of understanding the communication genre, the expectations and behaviors of their target audiences, and their own relationship objectives. Moreover, participants with greater experience with cyber dating have more positive experiences, which led to positive attitudes and greater satisfaction with e-dating. The chapter concludes with a set of rhetorical heuristics that can be adopted by e-daters to engage online with greater self-awareness, genre-based efficacy, context-informed deliberation, and rhetorical sophistication.

Chapter 11

The weblog incorporates technical capabilities which facilitate interaction and make it easy to exchange information and engage in discussion about controversial issues. This chapter presents a methodological framework to study how both allegiance and conflict are expressed and constructed in scientific controversies in science blogs. The study is based on the exploration of three controversies, related with global warming, the effects of vaccination and the role of women in science. The author analyzed a corpus of weblog comments to six posts which triggered off a dispute over these controversial issues for indicators both of social behaviour and of rude or verbally offensive behaviour. The findings show how blog comments are used by participants to signal their allegiance to a particular group within the disciplinary community, their ideological commitments, and their rejection of opposing standpoints and competing claims.

Patricia Mayes, University of Wisconsin – Milwaukee, USA

Recent attempts to theorize identity using sociolinguistic, discourse analysis, and conversation analysis frameworks have focused on the discursive constructions of speakers' identities, with particular focus on the point that identities are constructed moment by moment through social interaction. Although such frameworks are designed with face-to-face, synchronous interaction in mind, other types of discourse, traditionally thought of as distant, asynchronous, and solitary (or non-interactive), are being used in new ways, due to rapid developments in technology. These developments suggest that all language use is inherently interactive, if not interactional (i.e., synchronous). This chapter uses insights from social semiotics and frameworks grounded in the analysis of spoken interaction to analyze a commercial posted on YouTube in conjunction with unelicited comments from people who viewed the commercial on You-Tube. The analysis focuses on the multimodal expression of meaning potentials as well as their uptake and the stances displayed in response. The findings show how people who viewed the commercial and posted comments on YouTube displayed various stances concerning the commercial. Whether theses stances were positive, negative, or somewhere in between with regard to the commercial, they provided evidence that the posters had interpreted the meaning potentials of the commercial as suggested in the social semiotic analysis.

Ming Ming Chiu, University at Buffalo, State University of New York, USA
Gaowei Chen, University of Pittsburgh, USA

Educators are increasingly using electronic discourse for student learning and problem solving, given its time and space flexibility and greater opportunities for information processing and higher order thinking. However, when researchers try to statistically analyze the relationships among electronic discourse messages, they often face difficulties regarding the data, dependent variables and explanatory variables. Statistical discourse analysis (SDA) addresses all of these difficulties as shown in analyses of social cues in 894 messages posted by 183 students during 60 online asynchronous discussions. The results show that disagreements increased negative social cues, supporting the hypothesis that these participants did not save face during disagreements, but attacked face. Using these types of analyses and results, researchers can inform designs and uses of electronic discourse.

In recent years, mass media content has undergone a blending process with social media. Large amounts of text-based social media content have not only shaped mass media products, but also provided new opportunities to access audience behaviors through these large-scale datasets. Yet, evaluating a plethora of audience contents can be methodologically challenging. This chapter introduces a mixed-method approach that includes quantitative computer-mediated discourse analysis (CMDA) and automated analysis of content frequency. The author analyzed audience comments in the form of Facebook posts and SMS mobile texts to an Italian radio-TV station. This new approach uses blended media content and computer-mediated discourse analysis which expands the horizons of theoretical and methodological audience analysis research compared to conventional audience analysis metrics. The chapter describes the combinatory use of analytical tools such as word-frequency, word cluster analysis, and addressee analysis on large datasets. The findings show that communication occurred not only with the radio station, but audiences were involved in interpersonal communication.

Emails are a central genre in business communication, reflecting both how people communicate and how they go about their professional practices. This chapter examines embedded business emails as reflections of the professional practices of the regulatory and policy department of a multinational based in London, UK. It argues that the nature of online communication in international organizations, with its high levels of intertextuality and interdiscursivity, requires multidimensional analytical approaches that are capable of capturing its complexity and dynamics. Hence, the chapter introduces electronic discourse analysis networks (EDANs) as one example of such approaches. Through the use of embedded emails and a number of networked data sets, the chapter demonstrates how EDANs can be used to further our understanding of professional online communication.

This chapter describes a new method of Computer-Aided Deductive Critical Discourse Analysis (CDA) with ATLAS-ti 6.2 using a case study on eco-social work research from Mauritius. The author analyzed digital audio data from eight focus group discussions and three semi-structured interviews based on a newly developed eco-social work conceptual/theoretical framework. The chapter demonstrates the three steps of CDA using ATLAS-ti: (1) construction of a theoretical framework for guiding the deductive CDA; (2) selection of quotations and coding of gathered data based on the developed theoretical framework; and (3) deductive CDA of the data. The chapter concludes that ATLAS-ti offers a number of possibilities for undertaking a computer-based CDA but such a process can be very challenging due to the limitations of ATLAS-ti and the limited literature on how computer programmes can be used for CDA.

Section 3
Future Trends: Emergent Methods for the New Media

Chapter 17

Conversation Analysis and Electronic Interactions: Methodological, Analytic and
Technical Considerations 370

Joanne Meredith, Loughborough University, UK
Jonathan Potter, Loughborough University, UK

This chapter proposes that data from electronic communication should be analyzed as social practice. It should not be regarded as a way of getting to the participant behind the screen, but rather as a way of understanding the actions that discourse does in that particular interactional context. The chapter introduces an approach informed by both Conversation Analysis (CA) and Discursive Psychology (DP) for explicating participants' orientations and revealing the way in which the varied affordances of specific technology and software are relevant to interaction. The data used in this study includes both asynchronous and synchronous discourse in the forms of a corpus of quasi-synchronous instant messaging chats, screen capture data as well as timed transcripts. The chapter demonstrates, using empirical evidence, how the adoption of such an approach requires data to be collected in a certain way. By collecting transcripts and screen capture data, the analyst is able to gain a better understanding of how participants use the Internet in their everyday lives, and how this is oriented to in their interactions.

Chapter 18

Positioning Goes to Work: Computer-Aided Identification of Stance Shifts and Semantic
Themes in Electronic Discourse Analysis.. 394

Boyd Davis, University of North Carolina – Charlotte, USA
Peyton Mason, Next-Generation Marketing Insights, USA

This chapter presents two specific computer-aided techniques derived from corpus analysis, and grounded in positioning theory that allow researchers to combine quantitative and qualitative approaches to the discourse analysis of electronically-searchable text. The first technique is stance-shift analysis that is a software-based analysis keyed to tagged parts of speech that can identify when speakers/writers shift among evaluative and affective stances to topic, to prompts, and to other participants in communicative interactions. The second technique is semantic domain analysis using WMatrix® that is an online corpus analysis package including UCREL Semantic Analysis System, which tags words by semantic domains, and uses a log-likelihood calculator to identify significant semantic relationships across texts. The chapter illustrates the application of these techniques and their supporting tools to a range of online interactions, including entries in online tourism blogs and Facebook comments, to provide nuanced interpretations of electronic discourse.

Chapter 19

Textuality on the Web: A Focus on Argumentative Text Types 414

Chiara Degano, Università degli Studi di Milano, Italy

Central features in the construction of texts are the notions of cohesion and coherence, originally tailored for linear time-based modes of communication, where both the elements and their sequentiality contribute to meaning making. In light of the disruption of linear sequentiality brought by the space-based logic of the hypertext, this chapter aims to understand how cohesion and coherence work in the website environment, with specific regard to genres characterised by an argumentative drive, which potentially suffer more than other text types from the loss of the author's control on the linear dispositio of arguments.

The analysis identifies different patterns for the construction of cohesion and coherence in argumentative websites, which accommodate traditional standards of textuality into the new environment. The chapter concludes that the mechanisms at work for the construction of coherence on a website are not qualitatively different from those for the construction of coherence in traditional texts. However, the difference lies in the intensity of relevance ties between physically adjacent contents which tends to be significantly looser on the web.

This closing chapter provides an analysis of the current technological landscape in the m-learning world, studying some of the most prominent initiatives and solutions reported in the literature. It is clear that the paradigm is not yet fully adopted by the society but the paradigm has proven to be a useful tool for increasing motivation and interest in learners, and facilitating life-long education to those who are not full-time students. M-learning has potential benefits to the learning and academic communities, and even the entire society interested in collaborative and life-long learning. For the paradigm to progress and be more widely adopted, the chapter argues that the m-learning community needs to produce unified and/or standardized tools that are be perceived by potential adopters as viable, beneficial and easy to deploy solutions.

Preface

Discourse analysis (DA) is the study of language in use with descriptions of language forms and patterns of interaction taking into account the contexts in which they occur. The application of discourse analysis in research involves the examination of textual data and the general principles of interpretation by which people normally make sense of interactions.

Within the framework of DA, there is a typology of approaches for examining different discourse aspects: contextual, critical, linguistic, and interactional. The *contextual* approach examines language use in specific social or cultural contexts. The *critical* approach studies language patterns and related social institutional practices that empower and/or limit what people do and say. The *linguistic* approach studies language itself and variations in language systems in different settings. The *interactional* approach focuses on the activity of language use and the impact of context on shaping meaning and patterns of use. The context includes the immediate in-text situation of utterances as well as the technology medium and environment.

The advent of computer-mediated communication (CMC) technologies prompted research in computer-mediated discourse (CMD) or electronic discourse which is the communication product of human interaction via networked computer systems. The study of CMD is located in the field of CMC and distinguished by its focus on language and language use in computer networked environments, and by its use of DA methods to address that focus.

The emergence and rapid acceptance of Web 2.0 technologies present challenges in terms of understanding the new communicative contexts and the interaction of various media in shaping meaning and patterns of use. Moreover, CMC research in education, culture and society that utilize DA methods reflect a concentration on descriptive studies of the structural features of computer-mediated language while the implications of language change for theory and practice can be developed further. Also, current research has focus on the analyses of discursive products from a single communication technology while CMC increasingly co-exist on a single platform as convergent media computer-mediated communication (CM-CMC).

In response to such changes, many advances in DA methodology have been made in terms of data gathering, transcription techniques, data interpretation and ethical considerations in the new media and multimode contexts. At this point in time, there is a need to critically reflect on the recent advances in the theory and application of electronic DA methods from empirical studies, consolidate the methodological innovations that had emerged from the new communication contexts and identify what works and what does not.

The purpose of this book is to disseminate the challenges and successes in the search for innovative and effective methods of DA for understanding the new communicative contexts and the interaction of various media in shaping meaning and patterns of language use. Hence, this edited book showcases empirical studies, using qualitative, quantitative and mixed methodologies, where the application of DA methods to electronic discourse is rigorously grounded in theoretical frameworks and highlights research on the application of DA methods to electronic discourse from new media that consider implications for theory and practice, hence going beyond structural descriptions of language.

The book is organized into three sections with 20 chapters. The first section – *Electronic Educational Discourse: Developments in Theory, Methods and Applications* - consolidates studies on the application of DA methods in e-learning contexts with implications for constructivist theory, online pedagogy, instructional design and collaborative learning.

The second section - *Electronic Discourse Analysis: Innovations in Theory, Methods and Applications in Research on Society and Culture* - present cases where DA methods were applied in research on society and culture with implications for issues of power, identity and gender. In the final section – *Future Trends: Emergent Method for the New Media*, readers are presented with particular examples of innovative methodological advances in DA and the experimental use of Web 2.0 tools in educational and social research that outline emerging trends. The chapters provide suggestions for future research within this rapidly changing discipline.

This book is distinguished from other publication available on DA. For instance, Crystal's (2001) *Language and the Internet* provides a broad background to Internet language use and change. It focuses on language structure description hence more appropriate for a readership of applied linguists. The discourse data in the examples were products from early, well-established CMC technologies such as email, MUDs, MOOs, chat groups. In contrast, this book showcases research on application of DA methods to data from new media that go beyond structural description of language. Hardy and Bryman's (2004) *Handbook of Data Analysis* focused on approaches used in qualitative data analysis such as content analysis, conversation analysis, discourse analysis, grounded theory. The forms of discourse data, procedures for data gathering, processing and transcription were based mainly on data from face-to-face social interactions. However, this edited book includes research cases on electronic discourse, treatment of online interactional contexts and methods for handling such data that were not covered in Hardy and Bryman.

In addition, van Leeuwen's (2008) *Discourse and Practice: New Tools for Critical Analysis* focuses on only one method in analysis of discourse - critical discourse analysis (CDA) - but this approach has very distinct ideological assumptions and is mainly adopted for examining written texts and spoken words to reveal issues of power relations and redressing power imbalances. In comparison, this edited book is broader in the treatment of methods and encompasses educational and social research where other DA methods were applied.

This book can certainly be differentiated from available published works in this field since the contributions in this edited book represent the cutting edge of current research in the theory and application of electronic discourse analysis in the fields of education, society and culture. This collection of empirical studies introduces innovative methodological advances in DA that outline areas for future work for academics, students and researchers in the fields of human computer interaction, linguistics, education, sociology and organizational communication.

Finally, the book includes recent research and application of DA methods in educational and social contexts that will appeal to professionals working in the field of technology supported work groups and the management of organizational communication. We hope that this publication will inspire researchers to push the boundaries in the field of electronic discourse analysis.

Hwee Ling Lim
The Petroleum Institute, UAE

Fay Sudweeks
Murdoch University, Australia

REFERENCES

Crystal, D. (2001). *Language and the Internet*. Port Chester, NY: Cambridge University Press. doi:10.1017/CBO9781139164771.

Hardy, M., & Bryman, A. (2004). *Handbook of data analysis*. London, Thousand Oaks: Sage Publications.

van Leeuwen, T. (2008). *Discourse and practice: New tools for critical analysis*. NY: Oxford University Press. doi:10.1093/acprof:oso/9780195323306.001.0001.

Acknowledgment

We wish to thank all the authors who responded to our call for proposals. The authors whose proposals were accepted after a peer review process embarked on a long, and at times, arduous journey with us. We acknowledge their hard work as they took time from their demanding work schedules to draft and re-draft their chapters which ultimately culminated in the successful completion of this edited book. A number of authors also volunteered as reviewers and we thank them for their constructive feedback that enhanced the quality of the contributions to this book.

We would like to acknowledge the assistance provided by Mohamed Abdulrahman Othman and Lyas Ait Tayeb (research students from The Petroleum Institute) in the final stages of this edited book project. Special thanks go to the editorial advisory board members who were invaluable as reviewers and helped to shape the orientation of this book. We would like to thank the publishing team at IGI Global who provided much guidance in the production of the book; in particular, Monica Speca and Jan Travers.

Section 1
Electronic Educational Discourse:
Developments in Theory, Methods, and Applications

Chapter 1
Bridging the Gap:
21ˢᵀ Century Media Meets Theoretical Pedagogical Literacy Practices

Divonna M. Stebick
Gettysburg College, USA

Mary L. Paxton
Shippensburg University, USA

ABSTRACT

In this chapter, the researchers used an ethnographic stance to demonstrate how conversation evolved within a social media platform. They investigated the online discussions and face-to-face dialogues between teacher educators and pre-service teachers. They compared the participants' reciprocal conversations within this case study to analyze patterns in the language used in each forum in order to identify the affordances and constraints of perceived understanding. Through this discourse analysis the authors sought to identify indicators of each participant's metacognitive development while engaging in an online book discussion through a social media platform. Data analysis indicated that there was metacognitive growth when comparing the initial reciprocal conversations with the final conversations.

INTRODUCTION

Conversation is an aspect of a social setting that reflects the verbalized interactions of the participants. The study of the interactions within that reconstruction is useful in ethnography. Ethnography is defined as the analytic descriptions or reconstructions of intact cultural groups (Spradley & McCurdy, 1972). Educational ethnographers often assume the stance of participant-observer, becoming a member of the group who collects

data that occur within the group in an identified setting (LeCompte & Preissle, 2003). One way the conversation within a group can be examined is through the use of some type of discourse analysis. In this chapter, the researchers will use an ethnographic stance to demonstrate how conversation developed within social media can be used as a base for discourse analysis.

One intention of this study, utilizing the examination of the flow of conversation, was to determine the social structure existing within the

DOI: 10.4018/978-1-4666-4426-7.ch001

group. Since the group would consist of students, an instructor and the author of the text under discussion, the researchers hypothesized the initial conversations might reflect the students presuming they had less power due to less expertise and assuming the stance of being expected to respond to directions. They were interested in evaluating any identifiable shifts in perceived power based on changes in turn taking in subsequent group discussions.

As teacher-researchers, they utilized these theoretical underpinnings to develop a study that would examine the reciprocal social interactions between the invited members of a book study group. Using a social networking platform, the group had conversations based on a shared understanding of a text. Those conversations were collected and analyzed for perceived shifts of power from teacher to students as their level of expertise evolved.

BACKGROUND

In an educational setting, teachers often make use of a reciprocal teaching model. The concept of reciprocal teaching (Palinscar & Brown, 1984) is grounded in the use of a conversation between teacher and students to come to a shared understanding of a text. It is the use of conversation that allows for interactive teaching of strategies for predicting, questioning and clarification, modeled first by the teacher and then transferred to the students as they take on the role of "teacher" to lead discussions. Teachers become adept at monitoring the flow of the conversation in order to understand when the students are ready to assume the leadership role. It was this type of conversation monitoring that provided the foundation for this work. As the researchers examined the research on the use of conversation analysis as an ethnographic means of discourse analysis, they were led to a broader view. Gee (2004) posited that critical approaches to discourse analysis

treat social interactions in terms of "implication for things like, status, solidarity, distribution of social goods, and power" (p. 33).

Likewise, Sharrock (1989) suggested that the flow of conversation within a social structure can be used to examine who is in charge, or has the most perceived power, based on turn taking. The flow between participants who perceived themselves as equals tended to be a balance in turn taking. However, between participants who see one as having more power, the turn taking is disproportionately as response to the person with more perceived expertise. Sharrock (1989) likened this to air-traffic control, one is in charge and the others respond to directions.

By its very nature, conversation develops a detectable flow. Blimes (1988) theorized that conversation analysis should not evaluate meaning as inherent; it is not "fixed at the moment of production" (p. 162). Instead, the participants negotiate it over the natural course of the conversation. In fact, the conversation, produced by and for the participants, forms its own social structure. The participants create the structure and its features through their own interactions. As such, it doesn't fit in a pre-designed format.

The quality of discourse within a group interaction can be analyzed. That analysis provides an opportunity to consider both the sociolinguistic and ethnographic aspects of discourse and the cognitive aspects of peer learning (Chinn, O'Donnell, & Jinks, 2000). It is possible to consider the changing patterns of self-efficacy and building of knowledge through analyzing the types of utterances within the group. To consider the uses of response patterns, one must look at the level of explanations, elaborations, and clarifications. To consider how peer discourse supports learning, one must look at individual student's talk during interactions. "Peer discourse provides speakers with an opportunity to integrate their ideas while speaking, and listeners may receive new information that helps them construct new ideas" (Chinn et al., 2000, p. 78).

MAIN FOCUS OF THE CHAPTER

Social Networking, Online Chats, and Discussions

There appears to be a clear connection between social networking applications and discourse analysis of group conversations. In fact, social networking can be considered as the use of collective intelligence tools to develop a product or for collaborative knowledge creation through group conversations (Gunawardena, Hermans, Sanchez, Richmond, Bohley, & Tuttle, 2009). The group uses a socio-cultural context that moves through forms of discourse, action, reflection, and reorganization toward a socially mediated metacognition. Gunawardena et al. (2009) suggested that social networking is the practice of expanding knowledge by making connections with individuals of similar interests. Sites, such as Facebook, provide a virtual environment where users interact. In fact, reciprocal conversations within the group build a group zone of proximal development, the juncture where new learning can take place (Vygotsky, 1978).

Gee (1996) defined discourse as the artifacts of thinking, feeling, believing, valuing and acting that a member of a community uses within a social network. Group members bring with them their own understanding, perceptions, voice and their own view of themselves as a member of various social networks.

Goos, Galbraith, and Renshaw (2002) delineated expert-novice interactions and interaction between members of similar status within a community. Peer collaboration is built on a mutually developed understanding that includes the reasoning and viewpoints of all group members. In juxtaposition with that concept is Bandura's (1997) position that the individual sense of perceived abilities shapes his behavior as a reflection of self-efficacy. The more confident the individual of her own ability to perform or respond, the more likely she is to engage in that behavior. It would follow

that, within a group of peers who perceive their own abilities to be equal, the interactions between group members related to a topic would increase.

If metacognition is viewed as a social collaborative process (Goos et al., 2002), it should include reciprocal collaborative interactions. A balance of interactions that include self-discourse, feedback request, and the monitoring of the metacognition of others reflect a sense of mutuality. This creates a collective intelligence by the shared and overlapping knowledge of the group.

Virtual group interaction analysis must be done in a way that considers if there is a difference in the amount of knowledge one has with which to explain one's own behavior compared with other's behaviors. By interacting with several members of the group, a member is able to observe multiple sources of group behaviors and responses (Bazarova & Walther, 2008). Thus, in considering peer mediated learning, it is important to consider both the content of the individual student's comments and the overall structure of the discourse within the interaction (Chinn et al., 2000).

As a foundation for this study, the researchers considered several factors when selecting a social networking platform. The participants were young adult college students who were frequent users of Facebook. Their status was reflected in data included in the Pew Institute Research Report (2010) on social media use among young adults. The Pew report indicated that 72% of online 18-29 year olds use social networking websites. Another Pew Institute Research Report (2011) on social networking indicated that on an average day, 15% of Facebook users update their own status, 22% comment on another's post or status, 20% comment on another user's photos, 26% "like" another user's content, and 10% send another user a private message. Furthermore, users received a wide range of support from their social networks, including advice, information and understanding.

The researchers took into consideration that they were selecting a platform that the students, while very comfortable in this network and fairly adept at using it, considered its use a leisure and entertainment venue. Misztal (2001) noted that literacy is used to render transactions in virtual words as "predictable, reliable, and legible" (p. 313). These same practices are important in the construction and maintenance of social groups. While participating in online forums and groups may sometimes be viewed as a frivolous use of time, the underlying reasons for participating in the group is what determines its importance, not the format.

In order to clarify the underlying reasons for participating, they developed a structure for the online discussions. To foster collaboration and a feedback cycle, they used a teacher directed inquiry stance that would support the online conversation. These areas were selected as extensions of inter-action, collaboration, and contribution identified by Gunawardena et al. (2009) as needed for the construction of the collaborative understanding and thinking of a group.

Within inquiry, they identified a goal of exam-ining classroom contexts through ongoing reflec-tion. In the centralized environment of Facebook, there was an opportunity for reflection in that archived posts were displayed in reverse chrono-logical order. The participants were able to look back at the end of the group meeting, as well as the semester, and observe their own growth over time. This provided an expanded opportunity for metacognition, or, thinking about one's thinking (Bransford, Brown, & Cocking, 1999), in which students could reread their posts and literally reflect on their reflections.

Within collaboration, they identified a goal of socially mediated learning through social inter-face. The participants engaged in conversations based on their peers' reflections. This feature al-lowed them to operate in an online professional community, giving and receiving feedback from peers, an instructor and the author of the text under discussion. The feedback was quickly available, permitting participants to use it almost immedi-ately in their classroom pre-service placement, a critical feature to support theory-into-practice.

Finally, the individualized and interactive nature of each discussion allowed the participants to direct the conversation to their own situation.

Within feedback, they identified a goal of providing multiple levels of feedback, with partici-pants constantly receiving a stream of responses from their peers, an instructor and the author about specific, practice-based instances from their own classroom experiences. The online forum provided a safe space for real-time conversations.

Using these goals, the researchers would be able to analyze the conversations for the genera-tion of content that "enables sharing, co-creating, co-editing, and construction of knowledge" (Gunawardena et al., 2009, p. 12). This, in turn, allowed for consideration of whether or not the social networking platform was creating a place for the mediation between knowledge of the individual and their contribution to knowledge building in the community.

A final consideration of the group conversa-tions would be the effectiveness of the selected platform. Conole, Galley, and Culver (2011) chose Facebook as the platform to examine the development of academic practice. They reported that the initial conversation centered on the need for the participants to be come adept at using the tool. However, over time, members were able to gain proficiency in using the platform, personalize the use of the tool, and see ways the tool could replace their standard form of group interaction. The researchers were interested in examining if the participants would become able to see Facebook as a way to support a community that included a cognitive presence, a teaching presence, and a social presence.

Theoretical Framework

The researchers revised the theoretical framework created by Gunawardena et al. (2009) to capture collaborative learning within social networking as they investigated inquiry, reflection, collaboration, and feedback. They discussed the skills that were used to build the foundation of a pedagogically sound literacy environment and then identified the five phases in the learning process: context, discourse, action, reflection, and reorganization (Gunawardena et al., 2009, p. 13). These phases progressed as users contributed more thoughtful, less teacher-directed responses (see Figure 1).

As shown online discussions provide a setting for collaborative learning and group inquiry without the need to travel and schedule face to face discussions. Looking at the learning wheel, the spokes emanate from the Facebook conversation. These spokes represent the knowledge and tools that students needed to use when participating in the process of an online book discussion.

Questioning the Author is a protocol of inquires that students can make about the content they are reading. This strategy encourages students to think beyond the text and to consider the author's intent for the selection and his or her success at communicating it (Beck, McKeown, Hamilton, & Kucan, 1997).

Metacognition refers to one's knowledge concerning one's own cognitive processes or anything related to them, e.g., the learning-relevant properties of information or data. For example,

"I am engaging in metacognition if I notice that I am having more trouble learning A than B; if it strikes me that I should double check C before accepting it as fact" (Flavell, 1976, p. 232).

Gradual Release of Responsibility Instructional Model requires that the teacher, by design, transition from assuming "all the responsibility for performing a task . . . to a situation in which the students assume all of the responsibility" (Duke & Pearson, 2002, p. 211). This gradual release may occur over a day, a week, or a semester. Stated another way, the gradual release of responsibility "emphasizes instruction that mentors student into becoming capable thinkers and learners when handling the tasks with which they have not yet developed expertise" (Buehl, 2001, p. 67). This gradual release of responsibility model of instruction has been documented as an effective approach for improving reading comprehension (Lloyd, 2004).

Teacher Inquiry focuses on the concerns of teachers (not outside researchers) and engages teachers in the design, data collection, and interpretation of data around their question.

Figure 1. Social networking conversational flow

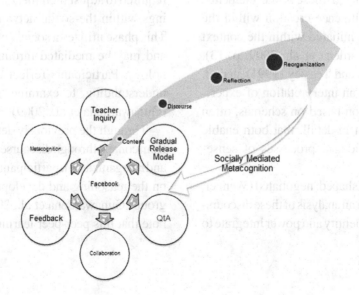

There are many benefits:

(1) Theories and knowledge are generated from research grounded in the realities of educational practice;

(2) Teachers become collaborators in educational research by investigating their own problems; and

(3) Teachers play a part in the research process, which makes them more likely to facilitate change based on the knowledge they create" (Dana, 2009, p. 4).

Collaboration occurs when educators come together to collaborate and put forth an intellectual effort to better themselves in order to benefit their students' learning (DuFour, DuFour, Eaker, & Many, 2009).

Feedback was captured within the context of the discussion and offered in "real-time" during the instructor – student discussions. Feedback was provided by author after discussion and was available for students to refer to and reflect on at any time.

Since Gunawardena et al. (2009) identified a process of context, discourse, action, reflection, reorganization, and socially mediated metacognition to emanate from a strong conversation, the researchers included these same elements. "The collective intelligence creation within the social networking is initiated within the context of the site" (Gunawardena et al., 2009, p. 13). As Resnick, Levine, and Teasley (1991) shared, "most knowledge is an interpretation of experience, an interpretation based on schemas, often idiosyncratic at least in detail, that both enable and constrain individuals' processes of sense-making" (p. 1).

Each discourse is shaped, negotiated (Wenger, 1998, p. 52). Through an analysis of these discourses, one can see how identity and power integrate to

negotiate meaning (Barton & Tusting, 2005). As an online book study, the group developed their own way of using language to convey meaning. A sub-culture formed as participants brought their life experiences, knowledge from other courses, questions for the author, and insights for future classroom implications to the group through discourse (Gunawardena et al., 2009). Negotiation of meaning reinforced the strength of the interaction as a foundation formed and members developed rapport among one another.

Participants shared insights, questions, opinions, and personal experiences in order to connect with one another. Some of these interactions were teacher to student, others were peer to peer, and others were author to students. Gunawardena et al. (2009) suggested that an action phase can be used to initiate the "process of socially mediated cognition" (p. 13).

This led to the reflection phase, characterized by the interaction of personal experience and group thinking and questioning. Again, Gunawardena et al. (2009) posited the reflection phase could be used to focus on "the consideration and integration of unfamiliar points of view" (p. 13).

The final stage would be the reorganization phase that utilizes the reflective process as members synthesize their new understanding and insight to reach a common goal. Participants are required to adjust their meanings and understandings within the social networking environment. This phase utilizes a social constructivist process and may be mediated through interactive technology. Participants reflect on and adjust their understanding, to examine their understanding (Gunawardena et al., 2009).

Through the previously described five phases, from context through discourse to action, reflection, and reorganization, participants mutually reflected on the reasoning and developmental process as a group (Gunawardena et al., 2009). It is critical to note that this peer-peer learning was the result of reciprocity, where participants could individually and collectively share and respond. It would appear that this made a connection between peer-to-peer mentoring and "a collaborative zone of proximal development" (Goos et al., 2002, p. 207). Further, a "collaborative metacognitive activity proceeds through offering one's thoughts to others for inspection, and acting as a critic of one's partner's thinking" (Goos et al., 2002, p. 207). The group generated reflective feedback through the Facebook discussions in order to capture the group's metacognitive monitoring and regulation as they embarked on the reflective process in an online forum.

Research Design

The researchers studied the implementation of using online discussions via a social networking site during an outside of class book study group. They used a qualitative case study methodology, selected for its ability to look closely at bounded situations of interest (Stake, 1995). The idealized instructional context certainly created a situation of interest because it allowed them to look past issues of implementation yet began to provide an opportunity for them to take an initial look at the growth of pre-service teachers through reflective, online discussions. They specifically focused on understanding the ways in which online discussions outside of class assignments facilitated inquiry, collaboration, and reflection. They collected and analyzed data in a variety of forms, including regular online discussion threads from the social media platform, as well as, field notes from face-to-face communications.

Context

This case study focused on an out of class book study discussion with invited participants. Once again, this ideal situation allowed researchers to develop close instructor-student-author relationships and avoid some of the implementation issues faced by other teacher educators. Because of the constraints inherent in this, and any methodology, findings from this study are not intended be generalized to the larger population. However, the researchers hope they can provide insight transferable to educators of all forms looking to integrate instructional technology into higher education classrooms (Donmoyer, 1990). They focused on the relationship between reciprocal socially mediated conversations, and the outcomes as mediated by one particular technology, Facebook discussions. Lessons from their critical case study can be translated to a variety of teaching and learning contexts using information technology as a pedagogical tool.

Participants

The researchers worked with three pre-service teacher candidates during the spring semester of 2010 (see Table 1).

All students' names were replaced with pseudonyms in order to maintain confidentiality and to mitigate researcher bias during the coding process. All students were education majors at one university, two females and one male. Data from all three participants were used for analysis. The pre-study face-to-face conversations indicated

Table 1. Characteristics of students using discussions on Facebook and study participants

Student Name	Gender	Prior Facebook Experience	Year	Major/Concentration
Stacy Lynn	Female	Yes	Junior	Reading
Kerry	Female	Yes	Senior	Early Childhood
Jack	Male	Yes	Senior	Reading

that, while all students were familiar with a variety of forms of information technology, including email, internet, and social networking, they had never participated in an academic discussion on Facebook. Two of the three had previously used Facebook discussions for other, social reasons. None of the participants had used Facebook for any academic reasons. Despite this inexperience regarding using Facebook for academic purposes, students generally found the Facebook discussion thread easy to navigate and reported no substantial technical difficulties.

The book, *Comprehension Strategy Instruction for Your K-6 Literacy Classroom: Thinking Before, During, and After Reading* (Stebick & Dain, 2007), integrated theory and practice in relation to effective comprehension instruction. Expectations for the book study included reading assigned chapters, taking notes to prepare for scheduled synchronous Facebook discussions, and participating in each Facebook discussion. The notes included the pre-service teachers' questions for the author but also future classroom implications and connections to current field experiences.

Procedure

As instructor and author, the researchers invited the pre-service teachers to read a theoretically grounded, pedagogically sound textbook that was written to be accessible to beginning teachers. They explained that this online discussion opportunity would provide a method to express their questions, insights, and confusions and an opportunity to apply theory to practice. Student participation in the group was voluntary. They would not receive any extra class credit and it was not tied to a grade in any of their courses. This group was strictly a professional development opportunity in which they were welcome to participate, but not required to join. Group members would be required to join a designated private group created in Facebook by the instructors.

In order to develop collegial relationships with peers and the instructors, the book study began with a face-to-face meeting and the distribution of the textbook, expectations, and questions for discussion regarding the logistics of the discussion. After the initial group meeting, the remaining group discussions occurred through the online platform, with meeting times scheduled in advance. Each group meeting lasted for no more than one hour.

Instruments

The researchers collaborated to develop a rubric specifically designed to interpret student responses. The rubric took into account the informal language used in social networking discussion threads, while attempting to identify the deeper meaning and ideas being shared among the participants. Close attention was paid to identifying and interpreting reciprocal conversations. They analyzed the data using the categories of inquiry, collaboration, and reflection. In order to better understand the development of inquiry abilities over time, they coded the Facebook entries using a rubric that captured the depth of the discussion and the synthesis the participants were able to create (Table 2).

The rubric provided clear standards to allow for consistency when evaluating discussion threads, comments, and questions. The rubric captured individual levels of inquiry as well as change in inquiry over time and according to topic.

Table 2. Discussion initiation and synthesis of ideas

Rating	Description
Low	Conversational – not related to topic
Mid	Related to topic but simple, surface reply
High	Reply shows evaluation of topic under discussion and examples from beyond the text synthesize topic.

The researchers initially scored the responses in isolation, and then compared findings to ensure inter-rater reliability at ninety percent. They scored the responses between one and three, with one indicating low inquiry and three indicating high inquiry. We agreed a level one inquiry consisted primarily of non-related conversation:

Stacy Lynn: I was very excited and honored to be asked to be a part of the group (not to mention to be included with the 3 Amigos!) I was worried about adding the extra work but decided to look at is as another career move and then it didn't seem to be as threatening.

Furthermore, they agreed a level two inquiry identified a conversation related to the topic, but the engagement into the topic remained at the surface level:

Kerry: Also, I thought that the organizer about: "I Do, We Do, and You Do" was AWESOME. It clearly lays out the responsibilities of teacher and student in each section of the literacy block, before, during, and after. It shows how much support the student should be given and how much independence the students should have.

Finally, the researchers identified the highest level of engagement, level three, to include an evaluation and synthesis of the topic being discussed. MuManych of the students' questions, thoughts, and confusions were anchored in theory. In this example, the student linked her experiences from the field to the apprehensions she felt as a result of the assigned reading and began to ask synthesis-type questions:

Kerry: I think ideas about conferencing with students: like questions or what we should be looking for would be good. I like the idea of meeting with students on a weekly basis to get a picture of where each individual is,

but how do we as teachers make the time to fit this into our literacy block? Between modeling, working in small groups, assessing individual practice, we must spread ourselves very thin. How do we make sure we meet with each student and ask the "right" questions and still are thorough in all areas? I 'm an all or nothing kinda girl, and my worst nightmare would be doing all of these jobs halfway. I want to be sure that I am thorough in all activities. A few suggestions on how to do that would be great.

Using these benchmarks, the researchers categorized initial discussion threads and their change over time.

Researchers concurred that student-to-student comments on discussions in order to better understand the nature of collaboration taking place. Initially, they coded these comments as superficial versus constructive with theory. This analytical process helped us to better understand the content as well as the structure of peer collaboration in each discussion. Superficial feedback was largely descriptive in nature, praising the students' ideas without offering concrete suggestions for improvement or making connections to theory:

Kerry: There is nothing more rewarding than opening the world of books to a child and instilling the love for reading in them. Jack, you gave me chills!!!! I whole-heartedly agree. Reading is an escape from the world. When times get tough, kids can escape to their special place and the characters in books become their friends. If only all children would turn to books instead of drugs, violence, etc.... the world would be a much brighter place.

On the other hand, constructive feedback analyzed the initial post and offered questions or suggestions to enhance understanding:

Kerry: That's a great idea Jack! I do that all the time to kind of skim and get an idea of what I should be thinking of. It sort of allows me to get my schema prepped and ready to read. It's like doing mind stretches before stretching, learning, and reading . . .

Some of these responses even included theory and methods drawn from the text and other education courses. The following comment connected to the gradual release model using in reading classes:

Kerry: The guided reading group that I'm working with has the above benchmark students in it. When I ask them to make connections to their own lives and other texts or the world, they are able to do that. When they struggle I give them a scaffold by providing an example from my own life and then they build off of that or off of one another.

Finally, they analyzed student responses from the field notes from face-to-face meetings using the same categories as previously mentioned, to integrate student feedback into their analysis and examine student growth in inquiry, collaboration, and reflection. These data provided students' perceptions of the process as they experienced it and supported the desire to integrate student feedback into the analysis.

In investigating the use of Facebook discussions in this pre-service teacher book study, the researchers worked together as teacher educa-

tors and author. They saw this study as a co-construction of knowledge, with blurred lines between investigators and participants. Although the teacher educators were primarily responsible for designing and implementing the books study and the pre-service teachers coming prepared to the book study, they worked together to analyze their experiences. They saw this collaboration as an extension of, rather than a departure from the constructivist approach they took in other courses. They also saw this collaborative self-study as enhancing, rather than detracting from the validity of the research (Lather, 2001).

Results

The data from this study supported the use of social networking in a constructivist-oriented pre-service teacher education sequence. The data showed that pre-service teachers improved their reflection abilities on an online discussion over the course of four months and most reached a high level of self-reflection. The researchers' data also indicate that the feedback among peers was supportive and helpful. They found the interaction among peers as overwhelmingly constructive and traced the development of some lessons directly to student-initiated posts. Data from surveys however, suggested that online discussions via a social networking site, Facebook, should does not meet all students' needs.

Figure 2. Graph showing student collaboration and inquiry level as measured by the rubric over the four months of the book discussion

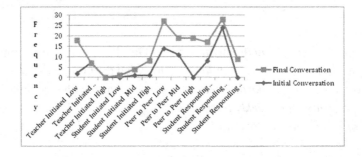

Inquiry

Scored student discussions (see Figure 2) showed the discourse analysis that collaborative abilities and levels of inquiry, as demonstrated in the discussion, consistently improved over time.

Even though students started out on different levels, all students continually advanced in their collaborative abilities propelling the conversation to deepen and develop into an effective inquiry book study. In the initial book discussion, there were nine teacher-initiated responses, only two student initiated responses, 25 peer to peer responses, and thirty-two student responses to the teacher. Of these, only one response rated as a high level of inquiry, forty-three were within the middle level of inquiry, and twenty-four were rated as low level inquiries. In the final book discussion, there were sixteen teacher-initiated responses, ten student initiated responses, forty peer to peer responses, and twenty-two student responses to the teacher. Of these, thirty-five responses included high levels of inquiry, fourteen responses were middle levels of inquiry, and twenty-six responses were low levels of inquiry.

Kerry: In the beginning, students shared descriptive, surface level ideas, reluctant to commit to an opinion through a synthesis of information:
It's basically what we're doing here at times. As we read the text, we're pretending that the authors are here with us and we're challenging what they are saying and asking questions about what we've read. As teachers, we'll be listening to our students to see if they can come up with the questions and how they respond to the questions. They need to be a higher level of questioning, literal questions would worry me. Yes and no questions would also be of concern. We would need things like "what does the author mean ..." "What are they referring to?"

A later post within the same discussion thread illustrates a bit more depth:

Kerry: It's important for us to teach our students to QtA so that they prove for deeper understanding. Also, they challenge the facts that don't correlate with their beliefs or schema. It pushes them to read on and grab a deeper understanding of what they are reading. Also, it requires students to use a higher level of thinking.

In this post, Kerry referred to the Questioning the Author (QtA) instructional strategy they learned about in class. However, the group was also implementing the QtA strategy through this book discussion as well. However, through further discourse analysis, the authors identified that Kerry simply mentioned a lot of education jargon, but did not synthesize this new knowledge to demonstrate her own higher-level thinking.

By the end of the semester, Kerry demonstrated much stronger responses to show her inquiry and collaborative thinking skills:

We were reading a book that had bears as characters in it, but the main topic was Mother Earth preparing for the different seasons. It was sort of abstract and I was questioning whether the kids would be able to see the main idea. They were though. They were able to connect the bears hibernating to winter and how Mother Earth sleeps... they connected hibernation to other animals that hibernate like our class turtles. Also, they saw how the different seasons change Mother Nature and the bears' activities. They linked this information to how the season cycle influences our own lives. It was an amazing week! Connections!!

The most growth was apparent when looking at a series of responses in a discussion thread. Sifting deeper into the discourse analysis of the Facebook discussion the authors identified a rich data set. After the instructor posed thought provoking questions, based on student responses, Stacy Lynn, Kerry, and Jack participated in a collaborative inquiry discussion:

Instructor: *Do you see that all of you are talking about gradual release in teaching, too? We (your profs) tell you how good teaching happens, we practice it in class when you do the demo lessons, but when you work with kids, you are in the I Do stage of teaching. This is the place where we see if you are ready to do it independently. Talk about a CONNECTION!*

Jack: *Yea, I think what everyone is saying teach the student in a different way. It is a waste of time to go back and do the same exact thing over again if the student didn't understand the first approach they likely won't understand the same thing the second go around we have to modify our teaching to fit each individual student.*

Kerry: *I feel like I should have a soapbox made to stand on about reflecting . . . I don't know if I ever realized how important reflecting is until I started to teach. Yeah, we did reflections on what we saw others do, but that just gave us the knowledge. Now that I'm teaching, I reflect and change my behavior to match what I know how a lesson just went with this particular class and lesson.*

Jack: *Yea Kerry, and it takes a lot more maturity to see what we have done wrong or what we could do better than not give someone else feedback.*

Stacy Lynn: *I don't usually watch Dancing with the Stars, but my daughter had it on one night and I heard Kate G. talking to her partner. She said something along the lines of "I understand and appreciate that you know how to teach me and that you are comfortable with your style but you're not asking me how I learn so that I understand you." It made me think of students and reading*

right away! It may be the most insightful thing I've ever heard her say!

Kerry: *So true Jack!!! The students only become frustrated when we try multiple times to teach them one way, and we become frustrated too. We understand the concept so we have the ability to change our perception and take it from a different angel. How is it even possible to believe that a child who has no understanding of the concept can change their perception to match how we are trying to teach them? Sort of insane if you ask me, but I've seen so many teachers try to teach one concept one way over and over . . . it's really sad.*

This discussion thread illustrated improvement in the collaborative inquiry and a stronger grounding of practice in theory over the course of the book study.

Future Trends

The researchers also envision future possibilities in which online book discussion use can be extended beyond the higher education context to bring in valued professionals from the field. This integration of authentic, real-world connections into the college classroom is supportive of the constructivist ideal of learning from experience (Dewey, 1938). In the context of teacher education, these online discussions could be expanded to incorporate individuals from the K-12 school setting, such as student teaching supervisors or cooperating teachers. In an even more elaborate form, the online book discussions could connect pre-service teachers with other beginning or veteran educators nationally or even internationally, providing a far-reaching professional network. Although issues of student confidentiality, pre-service teacher comfort, and commitment to the online environment would have to be addressed in order for these models to succeed, they see broad possibilities for using and even expanding this model of information technology in teacher education. Technological refinements such as integrated university-school networks, increased sophistication of video streaming, and enhanced online artifact display would facilitate the achievement of these greater constructivist goals.

FUTURE RESEARCH DIRECTIONS

This case study had a number of limitations, including its small scale, idealized instructional environment, and absence of implementation challenges. However, the in-depth examples of student inquiry, collaboration, and reflection offered a rich context for understanding the types of student learning which took place in an online book study. Further research on this topic should expand upon the findings to investigate an ideal combination of instructional methods for pre-service teacher education. The researchers acknowledge that the instrument they developed was specifically designed for this limited population and it would require adaptation before transferring it to another or larger population. Perhaps the trends that emerge using the instrument would yield different results if used with a larger population, as the coding requirement would be more intricate.

More broadly, it should also consider the integration of inquiry, collaboration, and reflection through online discussions with fields outside of teacher education. Finally, it should investigate the possibilities inherent in a more inclusive online discussion context, one that brings together individuals from higher education, K-12 schools, and beyond. Information technology has been used successfully to promote constructivist principles in teacher education, future research should move toward a more nuanced understanding of its use in supporting pre-service teachers and educators in general.

CONCLUSION

The researchers used a social media tool, Facebook discussions, in the context of an outside of class book study designed around reciprocal conversations in order to navigate through a discourse analysis using an ethnographic lens. They chose Facebook because the participants were comfortable using this social media platform and it allowed the author of the text to participate, where as, the university's discussion forum was only available to university students and the university's faculty. Further, they selected Facebook because there was no implementation learning curve for all participants and the reciprocal conversations commenced immediately as online discussions. In addition, the platform Facebook archives discussion threads allowing each of them asynchronous access to the data for coding purposes. In particular, they wanted pre-service teachers to learn to think like a teacher (Crowe & Berry, 2007) and designed a variety of online and face-to-face experiences in support of that goal. The in-depth case study of student experience in this book study investigated the ways in which social media fostered inquiry, collaborating and reflection among teacher educators, author, and pre-service teachers. They found that student inquiry and collaboration increased in sophistication over the four months, from mainly descriptive to more theory-based. They also found that student collaboration within the discussion was overwhelmingly constructive and at times spontaneously linked theory to practice. However, one important pedagogical drawback to Facebook discussions did emerge. The pre-service teachers felt that the Facebook discussions was a critical element in learning through the text, however, they preferred face-to-face discussions which allowed for more group analysis and synthesis of ideas.

At the completion of the book study sessions, the researchers convened an informal, face-to-face meeting. During this meeting, the researchers sought evaluative comments and feedback from the participants about the effectiveness of the experience. In this setting, the pre-service teachers openly shared high-level satisfaction with the hybrid characteristics of the book study. Their satisfaction was the direct result of the convenience, flexibility and the discourse during each book study session. They indicated the negotiated understandings that developed through the discussion fortified their personal schema for learning and teaching. This conclusion allowed the pre-service teachers to synthesize the theoretical learning with their practical experiences in a timely, supportive manner. Furthermore, the pre-service teachers shared that they were especially motivated to engage in an ongoing conversation with the actual author of the book being studied. This brought a sense of vitality to the text that they had not experienced previously in assigned readings in textbooks required in their teacher preparation programs. In fact, they hoped that Stebick would write another book, but beyond that, they requested a second online book study experience during the subsequent semester.

Based on this case study, the researchers concluded that social media could be considered an effective strategy for fostering high levels of inquiry, peer-to-peer collaboration, and concrete reflection based on theory and practice through an investigative discourse analysis. In doing so, online discussions supported general constructivist principles of student participation and interaction in learning. This case study in teacher education strengthened earlier work by Gomez et al. (2008), indicating a role for information technology in building social relationships and encouraging reflective teaching. It also exemplified the framework suggested by Garrison and Anderson (2003), in which information technology can be used in higher education for sense-making and community building.

This case study, together with earlier research (Kuzu, 2007), indicated that online book studies could be used successfully in teacher education. The researchers' experiences indicated however, that the key to effective use in the college classroom

is not only thoughtful implementation (Makri & Kynigos, 2007) but also a purposeful design combining online discussions with more conventional instructional methods. For example, each of the participants preferred face-to-face discussions. This reflected findings by Dickey (2004) indicating that while online book studies are successful on the whole, they may pose serious challenges for particular students. They suggest that future teacher education courses using online book discussions carefully consider the most effective combination of methods in order to achieve the best possible educational experience for students.

REFERENCES

Bandura, A. (1997). *Self-efficacy: The exercise of control*. New York: Freeman.

Barton, D., & Tusting, K. (2005). *Beyond communities of practice: Language, power, and social context*. New York: Cambridge University Press. doi:10.1017/CBO9780511610554.

Bazarova, N., & Walther, J. B. (2008). Attributions in virtual groups: Distances and behavioral variations in computer-mediated discussions. *Small Group Research*, *40*(2), 138–162. doi:10.1177/1046496408328490.

Beck, I. L., McKeown, M. G., Hamilton, R. L., & Kucan, L. (1997). *Questioning the author: An approach for enhancing student engagement in text*. Newark, DE: International Reading Association.

Blimes, J. (1988). The concept of preference in conversation analysis. *Language in Society*, *17*(2), 161–181. doi:10.1017/S0047404500012744.

Bransford, J. D., Brown, A. L., & Cocking, R. R. (1999). *How people learn: Brain, mind, experience, and school*. Washington, DC: National Academy Press.

Buehl, D. (2001). *Classroom strategies for interactive learning*. Newark, DE: International Reading Association.

Chinn, C. A., O'Donnell, A. M., & Jinks, T. S. (2000). The structure of discourse in collaborative learning. *Journal of Experimental Education*, *69*(1), 77–97. doi:10.1080/00220970009600650.

Conole, G., Galley, R., & Culver, J. (2011). Frameworks for understanding the nature of interactions, networking, and community in a social networking site for academic practice. *International Review of Research in Open and Distance Learning*, *12*(3), 119–138.

Crowe, A. R., & Berry, A. (2007). Teaching prospective teachers about learning to think like a teacher: Articulating *our* principles of practice. In Russell, T., & Loughran, J. (Eds.), *Enacting a pedagogy of teacher education: Values, relationships, and practices* (pp. 153–189). London: Routledge.

Dana, N. F., & Yendol-Hoppey, D. (2009). *The reflective educator's guide to classroom research: Learning to teach and teaching to learn through practitioner inquiry*. Thousand Oaks, CA: Corwin Press.

Dewey, J. (1938). *Experience and education*. New York: Simon & Schuster.

Dickey, M. D. (2004). The impact of web-logs (blogs) on student perceptions of isolation and alienation in a web-based distance-learning environment. *Open Learning*, *19*(3), 279–291. doi:10.1080/0268051042000280138.

Donmoyer, R. (1990). Generalizability and the single-case study. In Eisner, E., & Peshkin, A. (Eds.), *Qualitative inquiry in education: The continuing debate* (pp. 175–200). New York: Teachers College Press.

DuFour, R., Dufour, R., Eaker, R., & Many, T. W. (2009). *Collaborative teams in professional learning communities at work: Learning by doing*. Bloomington, MA: Solution Tree.

Duke, N., & Pearson, P. D. (2002). Effective practices for developing reading comprehension. In Farstrup, A. E., & Samuels, S. J. (Eds.), *What research has to say about reading instruction* (pp. 205–242). Newark, DE: International Reading Association.

Flavell, J. H. (1976). Metacognitive aspects of problem solving. In Resnick, L. B. (Ed.), *The nature of intelligence* (pp. 231–236). Hillsdale, NJ: Erlbaum.

Garrison, D. R., & Anderson, T. (2003). [*st century: A framework for research and practice*. London: Routledge Falmer.]. *E-learning*, 21.

Gee, J. P. (1996). *Social linguistics and literacies: Ideology in discourses*. New York: Routledge Falmer Press.

Gee, J. P. (2004). What is critical about critical discourse analysis? In Roger, R. (Ed.), *An introduction to critical analysis* (pp. 19–50). Mahwah, NJ: Lawrence Erlbaum.

Gomez, L. M., Sherin, M. G., Griesdorn, J., & Finn, L.-E. (2008). Creating social relationships: The role of technology in preservice teacher preparation. *Journal of Teacher Education*, *59*(2), 117–131. doi:10.1177/0022487107314001.

Goos, M., Galbraith, P., & Renshaw, P. (2002). Socially mediated metacognition: Creating collaborative zones of proximal development in small group problem solving. *Educational Studies in Mathematics*, *49*(2), 193–223. doi:10.1023/A:1016209010120.

Gunawardena, C. N., Hermans, M. B., Sanchez, D., Richmond, C., Boley, M., & Tuttle, R. (2009). A theoretical framework for building online communities of practice with social networking tools. *Educational Media International*, *46*(1), 3–16. doi:10.1080/09523980802588626.

Kuzu, A. (2007). Views of pre-service teachers on blog use for instruction and social interaction. *Turkish Online Journal of Education*, *8*(3), 34–51.

Lather, P. (2001). Validity as an incitement to discourse: Qualitative research and the crisis of legitimation. In Richardson, V. (Ed.), *Handbook of research on teaching* (4th ed., pp. 241–250). Washington, DC: American Educational Research Association.

LeCompte, M. D., & Preissle, J. (2003). *Ethnography and qualitative design in educational research* (2nd ed.). San Diego, CA: Academic Press.

Lloyd, S. L. (2004). Using comprehension strategies as a springboard for student talk. *Journal of Adolescent & Adult Literacy*, *48*(4), 114–124. doi:10.1598/JAAL.48.2.3.

Makri, K., & Kynigos, C. (2007). The role of blogs in studying the discourse and social practices of mathematics teachers. *Journal of Educational Technology & Society*, *10*(1), 73–84.

Misztal, J. (2001). Young children's literacy practices in a virtual world: Establishing an inline interaction order. *Reading Research Quarterly*, *46*(2), 101–118.

Palincsar, A. S., & Brown, A. L. (1984). Reciprocal teaching of comprehension-fostering, comprehension-monitoring activities. *Cognition and Instruction*, *1*(2), 117–175. doi:10.1207/s1532690xci0102_1.

Pew Institute. (2010). *Social media and internet use among teens and young adults*. Retrieved June 10, 2012, from http://pewinternet.org/Reports/2010/Social-Media-and-Young-Adults.aspx

Pew Institute. (2011). *Social networking and our lives*. Retrieved June 10, 2012, from http://pewinternet.org/Reports/2011/Technology-and-social-networks.aspx

Resnick, L. B., Levine, J. M., & Teasley, S. D. (1991). *Perspectives on socially shared cognition*. Washington, DC: American Psychological Association. doi:10.1037/10096-000.

Sharrock, W. (1989). Ethnomethodology. *The British Journal of Sociology*, *40*(4), 657–677. doi:10.2307/590893.

Spradley, J. P., & McCurdy, D. W. (Eds.). (1972). *The cultural experience: Ethnography in complex society*. Chicago, IL: Science Research Associates.

Stake, R. E. (1995). *The art of case study research*. Thousand Oaks, CA: Sage Publications.

Stebick, D. M., & Dain, J. M. (2007). *Comprehension strategies for your K-6 literacy classroom: Thinking before, during, and after reading*. Thousand Oaks, CA: Corwin Press.

Vygotsky, L. A. (1978). *Mind in society: The development of higher psychological processes*. Cambridge, MA: Harvard University Press.

Wenger, E. (1998). *Communities of practice: Learning, meaning, and identity*. Cambridge, UK: Cambridge University Press.

ADDITIONAL READING

Alvermann, D. (2008). Why bother theorizing adolescents' online literacies for classroom practice and research? *Journal of Adolescent & Adult Literacy*, *52*(1), 8–19. doi:10.1598/JAAL.52.1.2.

Ball, D. L., & Cohen, D. K. (1999). Developing practice, developing practitioners: Toward a practice-based theory of professional education. In Darling-Hammond, L., & Sykes, G. (Eds.), *Teaching as the learning profession: Handbook of policy and practice* (pp. 3–32). San Francisco: Jossey-Bass.

Bartu, H. (2001). Can't I read without thinking? *Reading in a Foreign Language, 13*(2), 593–614.

Cazden, C. (2001). *Classroom discourse: The language of teaching and learning* (2nd ed.). Cambridge, MA: Harvard University Press.

Cochran-Smith, M., & Lytle, S. (1993). *Inside outside: Teacher research and knowledge*. New York: Teachers College Press.

Cochran-Smith, M., & Lytle, S. (1999a). Relationships of knowledge and practice: Teacher learning in communities. In Iran-Nejad, A., & Pearson, P. D. (Eds.), *Review of research in education* (*Vol. 24*, pp. 249–305). Washington, DC: American Educational Research Association. doi:10.2307/1167272.

Frey, N., Fisher, D., & Gonzalez, A. (2010). *Literacy 2.0*. Bloomington, IN: Solution Tree.

Friedman, T. L. (2006). *The world is flat: A brief history of the twenty-first century*. New York, NY: Farrar, Straus, and Giroux.

Gee, J. P. (1999). *An introduction to discourse analysis*. New York: Routledge.

Grimshaw, A. D. (1982). Comprehensive discourse analysis: An instance of professional peer interaction. *Language in Society, 11*(1), 15–47. doi:10.1017/S0047404500009027.

Grossman, P., Wineburg, S., & Woolworth, S. (2001). Toward a theory of teacher community. *Teachers College Record, 103*(6), 942–1012. doi:10.1111/0161-4681.00140.

Lemke, J. (1992). Intertextuality and educational research. *Linguistics and Education, 4*(3), 257–268. doi:10.1016/0898-5898(92)90003-F.

Lerner, G. H. (2003). Selecting next speaker: The context-sensitive operation of a context-free organization. *Language in Society, 32*(2), 177–201. doi:10.1017/S004740450332202X.

Leu, D. J., Kinzer, C. K., Coiro, J. L., & Cammack, D. W. (2004). Toward a theory of new literacies emerging from the Internet and other information and communication technologies. In Ruddell, R. B., & Unrau, N. (Eds.), *Theoretical models and processes of reading* (5th ed., pp. 1570–1613). Newark, DE: International Reading Association.

Levin, B. B., & Rock, T. C. (2003). The effects of collaborative action research on preservice and experienced teacher partners in professional development schools. *Journal of Teacher Education, 54*(2), 135–149. doi:10.1177/0022487102250287.

Liang, L. L., Ebenezer, J., & Yost, D. S. (2010). Characteristics of pre-service teachers' online discourse: The study of local streams. *Journal of Science Education and Technology, 19*(1), 69–79. doi:10.1007/s10956-009-9179-x.

Moody, A. (2010). Using electronic books in the classroom to enhance emergent literacy skills in young children. *Journal of Literacy and Technology, 11*(4), 22–52.

Rhodes, J. A., & Milby, T. M. (2007). Teacher-created electronic books: Integrating technology to support readers with disabilities. *The Reading Teacher, 61*, 255–259. doi:10.1598/RT.61.3.6.

Richardson, J. S., Morgan, R. F., & Fleener, C. (2009). *Reading to learn in the content areas*. Belmont, CA: Wadsworth.

Rogers, R. (2002). "That's what you're here for, you're supposed to know.": Teaching and learning critical literacy. *Journal of Adolescent & Adult Literacy, 45*(8), 772–787.

Rogers, R., Malanchruvil-Berkes, Mosley, M., Hui, D., & Joseph, G. O. (2005). Critical discourse analysis in education: A review of the literature. *Review of Educational Research, 75*(3), 365–416. doi:10.3102/00346543075003365.

Schegloff, E. A. (2000). Overlapping talk and the organization of turn-taking for conversation. *Language in Society*, *29*(1), 1–63. doi:10.1017/S0047404500001019.

Valli, L., van Zee, E. H., Rennert-Ariev, P., Mikeska, J., Catlett-Muhammad, S., & Roy, P. (2006). Initiating and sustaining a culture of inquiry in a teacher leadership program. *Teacher Education Quarterly*, *33*(3), 97–114.

Wang, Z., Walther, J. B., & Hancock, J. T. (2009). Social identification and interpersonal communication in computer-mediated communication: What you do versus who you are in virtual groups. *Human Communication Research*, *35*, 59–85. doi:10.1111/j.1468-2958.2008.01338.x.

Zambo, D., & Zambo, R. (2006). Action research in an undergraduate teacher education program: What promises does it hold? *Action in Teacher Education*, *28*(4), 62–74. doi:10.1080/01626620.2007.10463430.

KEY TERMS AND DEFINITIONS

Collaboration: The process of working with other individuals in order to achieve the same goal.

Constructivist Theory: People construct their own understanding and knowledge of the world through experiences and reflections upon the experiences.

Gradual Release: Learning model where the responsiblitiy for task completion shifts gradually over time from the teacher to the student.

Inquiry: Seeking information by questioning.

Metacognition: Knowing about knowing.

Modeling: Instructional strategy where students imitate the behavior that is reinforced and demonstrated by the teacher.

Reflection: Challenging and testing out what you do as a teacher and being prepared to act on the results.

Schema: A cognitive framewok or concept that helps organize and interpret information.

Social Networking: Web-based services that allow individuals to construct a public or private profile within a bounded system where they share information and make connections Ethnographic.

Chapter 2
Analysis of Constructivist, Network-Based Discourses:
Concepts, Prospects, and Illustrations

P. Wessa
Leuven Institute for Research on Information Systems, K.U.Leuven, Belgium

S. Poelmans
Leuven Institute for Research on Information Systems, K.U.Leuven, Belgium & Faculty of Economics Management, HUB, Brussels, Belgium

I. E. Holliday
Aston Brain Centre, Aston University, Aston Triangle, Birmingham, UK

ABSTRACT

The authors propose a new approach to discourse analysis which is based on meta data from social networking behavior of learners who are submerged in a socially constructivist e-learning environment. It is shown that traditional data modeling techniques can be combined with social network analysis – an approach that promises to yield new insights into the largely uncharted domain of network-based discourse analysis.

The chapter is treated as a non-technical introduction and is illustrated with real examples, visual representations, and empirical findings. Within the setting of a constructivist statistics course, the chapter provides an illustration of what network-based discourse analysis is about (mainly from a methodological point of view), how it is implemented in practice, and why it is relevant for researchers and educators.

DOI: 10.4018/978-1-4666-4426-7.ch002

INTRODUCTION

Discourse Analysis (DA) is often considered to be situated within a socially constructivist setting, drawing loosely on Vygotsky's theoretical framework which interprets human inquiry within culturally mediated social interactions and the larger set of practices of learner communities (Imm & Stylianou, 2012). In this respect, it is interesting to note that, according to Scardamalia and Bereiter (2003), constructivism "is a term whose vagueness beclouds important distinctions" between shallow and deep forms of constructivism. They argue that "the shallowest forms engage students in tasks and activities in which ideas have no overt presence but are entirely implicit. Students describe the activities they are engaged in (e.g., planting seeds, measuring shadows) and show little awareness of the underlying principles that these tasks are to convey. In the deepest forms of constructivism, people are advancing the frontiers of knowledge in their community" (Scardamalia & Bereiter, 2003, pp. 1370-1373).

In particular, discourse analysis of mathematics discussions has shown that mathematical knowledge creation (i.e. "deep constructivism") can be facilitated by encouraging learners to "justify their ideas, evaluate one another's ideas carefully, and ask questions" (Chen, Chiu, & Wang, 2012, p. 868). This finding is consistent with our previous empirical research which was based on peer reviewing-based learning, facilitated by e-learning technology, such as the Compendium Platform (Poelmans, Wessa, Milis, & van Stee, 2009), that we developed over the last few years to organize statistical courses (Wessa, De Rycker, & Holliday, 2011).

Notwithstanding the widespread adoption of computer-assisted learning approaches, there seem to be only few studies in which computer mediated communication is actually studied in terms of structure, content, and quality of learner messages (Lu, Chiu, & Law, 2011). The chapter attempts to fill some of the gaps in the literature and discusses

three important aspects of DA based on social learning networks in statistics education: (a) the provisioning of innovative e-learning technology encompassing reproducible statistical computations, collaborative writing, and peer reviewing; (b) the capturing and use of objectively measured meta information about student discourses and associated social interaction networks using the e-learning technology; (c) several methodological concepts that allow researchers and educators to better understand the discourses and underlying social dynamics in collaborative, constructivist learning.

BACKGROUND

Towards a New Methodological Approach

According to Matsuzawa, Oshima, Oshima, Niihara, and Saki (2011, p. 199) there are traditional methodological approaches in educational DA: "Thus far, researchers have applied three methodological approaches to capture the nature of knowledge building. The first approach establishes the rubrics of content knowledge that researchers expect the learners to acquire following their learning. ... The second approach involves researchers in analyzing the process of learning by breaking it into small units to categorize into different cognitive actions. ... The third approach is fine-grained discourse analysis performed as a case study, which helps researchers describe what is happening in students' collaborative learning."

However, the authors continue to argue that:

Although the three approaches are appropriate to discuss well-structured collaborative learning, none of them are sufficient to capture collective knowledge advancement. Regarding the content of knowledge, we are not only concerned with deep comprehension of domain-specific knowledge but also epistemic operation by learners to advance their collective knowledge. Since the epistemic operation is a process, a static evaluation of knowledge will not capture its dynamics. Categorization of the cognitive processes that learners engage in might capture the epistemic operation, but it is so content-free that we cannot describe what knowledge learners actually develop. Consequently, fine-grained discourse analysis with narratives would be the last option. Although the microscopic view of discourse analysis provides us with details about how learners develop their collective knowledge within a period of time, we also need to describe its macroscopic view so that we can verify why the detected microscopic discourse should be important to argue and how the detected pieces of discourses are placed in the macro structure of collaboration. (Matsuzawa et al., 2011, p. 199)

Similarly, Nilsson, van Laere, Susi, and Ziemke (2012, p. 65) describe socially Distributed Cognition as "a theoretical framework that seeks to understand cognition as a distributed process" which is believed to "emerge from interactions between different components" such as "the brain, the body, and the social or material world." The perspective of Distributed Cognition can be applied to the study of Computer Supported Collaborative Learning and as an "analytical tool for capturing the interaction between humans and technology in various contexts" which can be illustrated, for instance, by "the cognitive process of solving a problem such as a mathematical equation, by using pen and paper, or by discussing it with others. The artefacts in use, or the involved people, are considered part of the cognitive process of problem solving, and the process itself is distributed across the system – the person/s and the artefacts s/he uses – rather than being merely an internal process" (Nilsson et al., 2012, p. 65).

The theoretical frameworks of collective knowledge advancement and distributed cognition, allow us to conclude that "deep" constructivist education involves cognitive processes that are

inherently social and dynamic. As a consequence, and in line with the arguments of Matsuzawa et al. (2011) we may conclude that any static type of DA would fail to capture some of the essential ingredients of socially constructivist learning processes.

The only way to solve this problem is to use meta data about the "macro structure of collaboration" – in other words, the properties of the social networks that emerge when students engage in collaborative types of learning activities. The macroscopic view provides us with a social framework that has the potential to solve the semantic problem of associating a theoretically founded meaning to the results of the DA.

Technological Developments

During the past few years, we developed several educational technologies to support students in their struggle to learn and truly understand statistical concepts. The development of our new Virtual Learning Environment (VLE) was based on a content-based design (rather than a design that primarily focuses on course and student administration) which was shown to improve the efficiency of constructivist learning activities by a factor greater than two (Wessa et al., 2011). We were also able to demonstrate, based on a randomized experiment, that repetitive rounds of Peer Review (as implemented in our computer-supported collaborative statistics courses) had beneficial causal effects in terms of attitudes, non-rote learning, and actual behavior (Wessa & Holliday, 2012).

Some of the key-technologies that we developed and implemented, constitute solutions to the fundamental problem of reproducibility as was described by many influential authors from a wide variety of scientific fields (de Leeuw, 2001; Peng, Dominici, Zeger, 2006; Schwab, Karrenbach, Claerbout, 2000; Green, 2003; Gentleman, 2005; Koenker & Zeileis, 2007; Donoho & Huo, 2005; Leisch, 2003). The concept of reproducibility is clearly illustrated by what is known as Claerbout's principle (Wessa, 2009b, p. 86): "An article about computational science in a scientific publication is not the scholarship itself, it is merely advertising of the scholarship. The actual scholarship is the complete software development environment and that complete set of instructions that generated the figures." In a comment about this principle, de Leeuw (2001) adds the requirement that: (a) any type of statistical computation should be fully reproducible, (b) it applies to any type of document we produce (this includes teaching materials), and (c) the software environment should be freely available to the reader.

Within the context of our statistics courses, it is of utmost importance to ensure effortless reproducibility of statistical computations (so-called Reproducible Computing as described in Wessa, 2009 and 2009b) and the ability to precisely reproduce the writing efforts of students when working on assignment papers (Reproducible Writing). Indeed, collaborative work and social constructivism (based on Peer Reviews), is impossible if students are not able to investigate the computations and writings of their peers.

Reproducible Computing allows students to simply click on a picture, table or associated hyperlink that is contained in the assignment paper under review to obtain full access to the computational results, the data, the constraining parameters, and the full source code that was used by the original author. In addition, Reproducible Computing allows any reader or reviewer to have the computation reproduced (in real time) without the need to download or install any software on the client machine (all computations are performed on a network of computational servers). It is even possible to re-compute the analysis with changed data values (e.g. outliers are removed) or different constraining parameters. There are several facilities that support Reproducible Computing and have made freely available for educational and research purposes. For instance, the use of the statistical computations website at http://

www.wessa.net and the archive system at http://www.freestatistics.org allow anyone to use this technology and to collect the associated social networking data in educational research (Wessa & Baesens, 2009; Wessa, 2009c).

Reproducible Writing allows us to identify each keystroke of the written assignment paper, even if there are multiple authors who edit a document simultaneously. In addition, it permits us to track the evolution of changes that are made over time. More importantly, Reproducible Writing allows to re-create the circumstances that were present at the time of writing. This implies that it is possible to relate the changes that are made to all the other information that was available at that time (including the statistical computations and social interactions of co-authors). This enables us to study the learning activities and related discourses within the relevant social context.

Research Questions and Hypotheses

The remainder of the book chapter provides an empirical view of the macroscopic approach of Network-Based DA (NBDA). At the same time, we introduce several research questions and hypotheses to investigate whether our position is confirmed empirically. In other words, the goal is to test the following list of research questions:

1. Is the quality of a submitted assignment paper reflected in the feedback scores and in the language of the paper and associated feedback?
2. Does good social behavior among co-authors improve the quality of submitted papers? Does this also affect the language that is used in the papers and associated peer review feedback?
3. Does negative social behavior among co-authors (such as free-riding) have negative effects on quality, feedback scores, and language use?

4. Is there an effect of paper language on the language of feedback from peers? Does it also affect the feedback scores?

5. Is the language of feedback related to the feedback scores that are assigned?

These research questions do not exist as separate questions but are, in fact, mutually dependent. Therefore we need to test them with a modeling approach that encompasses all simultaneous relationships. The Partial Least Squares-Path Model (PLS-PM) allows us to achieve this goal without relying on strong statistical assumptions (Tenenhaus, Vinzi, Chatelin, & Lauro, 2005). Furthermore, PLS-PM has become an established methodology in the field of DA which helps us overcome several limitations of traditional methods (Paus, Werner, & Jucks, 2012).

The first research question is related to the impact of the quality (as defined by objectively measured, quantitative properties) of weekly assignment papers on the feedback that is written by peers. Formally we can write the alternative hypothesis as follows: *submitted assignment papers of high quality have higher feedback scores than papers with low quality (H1b)*. The relationship described in this hypothesis is of crucial importance because it establishes a link between the authors of the original paper and the peer reviewers who write feedback about it – the role and impact of social networking may be perceived differently depending on the role that is played by the student. For instance, social collaboration may lead to positive experiences among co-authors, while the reviewers may view collaboration as something negative if the main author's contribution falls below expectations. However, if social collaboration among co-authors is constructive (i.e. positive) then it is likely to increase the quality of the paper. The negative, direct impact of social collaboration (among co-authors) on the assessment of the reviewer may be compensated by the higher quality of paper under review. If the quality improvement is weighted more highly than the

fact that the author collaborated with co-authors then the total (net) effect of social collaboration could become positive.

Authors who write high quality papers tend to use a richer and more academic language than authors of low quality papers. Therefore, we introduce two additional alternative hypotheses: *higher quality in submitted papers leads to a higher usage of academic vocabulary in submitted papers (H1c) and has an impact (either positive or negative) on academic vocabulary in the peer reviews of such papers (H1d)*.

Following the reasoning behind the previous hypotheses we describe the positive impact of good social behavior (as is implied in social constructivism) on paper quality and peer feedback (research question 2). Both relationships are expected to be positive (at least if we are interested in the total or net effects). Formally we can write the following: *good social behavior leads to high paper quality (H2a) and more positive peer feedback (H2b)*. Again, it is possible to explain the use of academic language by the exogenous variable: *positive social behavior increases the use of academic words in papers (H2c) and changes the use of academic vocabulary in their peer reviews (H2c)*.

Students who are allowed (and stimulated) to engage in collaborative learning activities do not always behave honestly. Free riding behavior is not only unfair towards students who make an honest attempt at solving the assignment problems but it also undermines the student's ability to gain a true understanding of statistical concepts and underlying principles as opposed to rote learning. We formulate four statistical hypotheses (corresponding to research question 3) as follows: *negative social behavior decreases paper quality (H3a), decreases peer feedback scores (H3b), decreases the use of academic language in papers (H3c) and changes academic language use in their peer reviews (H3d)*.

Papers written in academic language are more likely to receive favorable feedback (research question 4). Indeed, in previous (unpublished) research, we found that student assessments depended on: paper quality, information about the authors, language (spelling, vocabulary and grammar), and the presentation of the paper. We were able to largely eliminate the presentation effect by requiring students to use the web-based text processor that is embedded in our VLE. This text processor provides collaborative features (such as Reproducible Writing), but is otherwise very simple, without features that allow authors to embellish the presentation of their discourse. In other words, there are only three aspects that might influence peer feedback: author information (H2b and H3b), paper quality (H1b), and paper language (H4b). We formulate hypothesis H4b as follows: *the use of academic language in papers leads to better feedback scores.*

The hypotheses H1d, H2d, H3d, H4d, and H5d are two-sided tests because there is no theoretical reason to expect either a positive or negative parameter. On the one hand, reviewers may want to mimic the language of the authors (Ireland & Pennebaker, 2010) on the other hand critical reviewers may want to strengthen the trustworthiness of negative feedback about poorly written papers by using academic language. The last argument is an important one because our students are not graded according to the feedback they receive – rather, their grades depend on the quality of the feedback messages that are written. Therefore, it is plausible (though not certain) that reviewers might want to make a good impression by using

academic language, especially when they write negative comments about a paper.

The structure of the entire PLS-PM is displayed in Table 1 and demonstrates that the relationships are limited to the lower triangular region of the table – this is a necessary condition to ensure that the system equations are exactly identified. In addition, Table 1 provides a summary of all hypotheses with an indication of the expected sign of the relationship. A question mark (?) is used when the sign of the relationship cannot be determined theoretically. Note that the endogenous variables are displayed in rows (the columns represent exogenous variables).

NETWORK-BASED DISCOURSE ANALYSIS

Social Networks in a Socially Constructivist Statistics Course

Beyond any doubt, the pedagogical paradigm of social constructivism plays a dominant role in the pedagogical research literature in general and educational statistics/mathematics papers in particular. Therefore, it is not surprising that social constructivism also plays an important role in educational DA (Imm et al., 2012). On the other hand, scientists seem to have only recently started to develop technologies that are capable of capturing social interactions that are related to

Table 1. Lower triangular PLS-PM relationships between latent variables (endogenous variables are displayed in rows). The signs represent expected total (net) effects.

	Positive Social Behavior	Negative Social Behavior	Paper Quality	Paper Language	Peer Feedback	Feedback Language
Positive Social Behavior						
Negative Social Behavior						
Paper Quality	H2a: +	H3a: -				
Paper Language	H2c: +	H3c: ?	H1c: +			
Peer Feedback	H2b: +	H3b: -	H1b: +	H4b: +		
Feedback Language	H2d: ?	H3d: ?	H1d: ?	H4d: ?	H5d: ?	

learning processes as is illustrated in the work of Matsuzawa et al. (2011).

Based on our innovative educational technology, we have been able to capture detailed and dynamic information about the social interactions of students that emerge during learning activities. Our first reports of such interactions were based on collaborative Reproducible Computing which allowed students to improve on the analyses that were generated by their peers (Wessa, 2009c).

Since 2011, however, we have also been able to accurately measure social interactions occurring in collaborative writing efforts. The technology that allows us to achieve this, is based on some of the libraries that have recently been published by Google under the Apache license: "Most recently, ... Google... shut down ... the Etherpad service in December of 2009. Due to the outcry from the existing user-base, the source code behind Etherpad has been released as an open source project" (Katz, 2011, p. 63).

We used the underlying libraries to build a comprehensive, collaborative writing system which could be integrated into our VLE. We added new features that are important for the purpose of integrating and displaying statistical results in the documents and we built a meta-database that seamlessly connects to the unstructured data that is produced by Etherpad. The key problem in creating Reproducible Writing technology is not the editor but the subsystem that allows us to track and adequately store the dynamic data about social interactions.

In the online transactional database (containing data about the keystrokes or changes in documents), there are more than 15 million records that are related to the statistics course under study. This database, however, is meaningless if one is interested in DA because of its unstructured nature. Therefore, we had to build several systems to extract the data from the transactional database to generate analytical data which are meaningful for the purpose of quality control and scientific research. The analytical data are stored in a Data Warehouse which can be queried by research-

ers. For a good understanding, it is important to emphasize that the Data Warehouse does not only host meaningful information about the discourses in the statistics course – several other types of VLE-based data are available: more than 1.2 million transactions in the VLE, more than 25000 feedback items, and thousands of statistical computations. This implies that it is now possible to analyze the discourses with a very large set of meta data items.

The illustrations and analyses in this chapter are based on a small subset of the Data Warehouse: we extracted a data set which contains detailed information about each feedback item that was written by reviewers in the advanced, undergraduate statistics course for 126 psychology students at Aston University (academic year 2011-2012). In other words, every record identifies a feedback score (e.g. a 5-point Likert score) and associated text message that was generated for each (of an average of 5) rubric items for each assignment paper that was reviewed in the statistics course at Aston University. For the sake of illustration we mention three examples of feedback items:

- The rubric question "Did the author correctly report the mean and the standard deviation which was calculated for the sample?" has a binary feedback score (1 = yes and 0 = no) which can be selected from a drop down list by the reviewer. In addition, the reviewer writes (if necessary) a feedback text to explain why a certain score was given. It is possible to leave the feedback score blank (for instance, if it is not possible to answer the question with yes or no).
- The rubric question "Comment on the whether the author was able to provide a complete and accurate interpretation of the ANOVA output. Have they also reported Tukey-HSD results and accurately interpreted these?" was not associated with a feedback score because there was another rubric item which allowed the reviewer to

grade the quality of the submitted paper. In this case, the reviewer is required to write a detailed, meaningful, and constructive feedback message to the author(s).

- The rubric item "Overall Assessment of Quality: Here you need to assess the quality of the responses in terms of accuracy and professionalism of the finished report." was graded with a 5-point Likert score (ranging from 1=bad to 5=excellent). In this case, the reviewer selects the feedback score from a drop down list and provides a written feedback message which provides details about the feedback score that was given.

Every student submitted a collaborative workshop paper on a weekly basis. In addition, every student wrote 4-5 peer reviews (per week) about randomly assigned papers from the previous assignment. In other words, every student plays the role of co-author and reviewer – this yields a total of 25419 records and 48 fields which are contained in this data set. For obvious reasons, the data set was carefully cleaned by removing records about incomplete assignments: as a result 24741 records were available for analysis.

Even though there is much more data available (about other courses), we limited our focus to this particular course because it simplifies the interpretation of the findings that are presented – these are the most important reasons:

- The student population is mainly female. There are only few male students in this course which makes the interpretation of social interactions (almost) independent of gender differences. Based on explorative data analysis we didn't find any evidence that the male students behaved differently, in terms of social interactions and writing, than the majority of female students.
- Most students are regular, undergraduate students, with approximately the same age,

and roughly the same background. There are only few "diploma" students who might have a different background.

- All students are native English speakers. This simplifies the interpretation considerably because all course materials and discourses are in English, unlike some of the other courses we are monitoring at this moment.

More detailed information about this particular statistics course is available in Holliday (2011). In addition, the extracted data set and accompanying software will be available at http://www.freestatistics.org/index.php?action=10.

Figure 1 displays a so-called Sociogram that was computed for the statistics course under study. The student population is predominantly female (male students are displayed in light grey). The position of the vertices was computed with the Fruchterman-Reingold algorithm (Fruchterman & Reingold, 1991).

The Sociogram provides a visualization of the social interactions that occur when students work on their weekly assignments. Every student is represented by a vertex (dark colored circle) with a size that corresponds to the amount of time that was spent during the writing process. All vertices belong to active students because dropouts were removed from the dataset. When a student A "shares" her document with student B, a so-called edge (arrow) is drawn going from A to B. The sharing relationship is initiated by student A which implies that student B has full read and write access to the document of student A.

During the actual writing process, it is possible (as is illustrated in Figure 2) for students A and B (or even more) to simultaneously edit the document that is shared. This implies that we can build Sociograms that are not only based on "sharing" documents but use the actual discourse contributions of each co-author in a document. This can not only be done for any of the more than 1500 documents in this course but it is also possible to

Figure 1. Sociogram of collaborative writing in an undergraduate statistics course

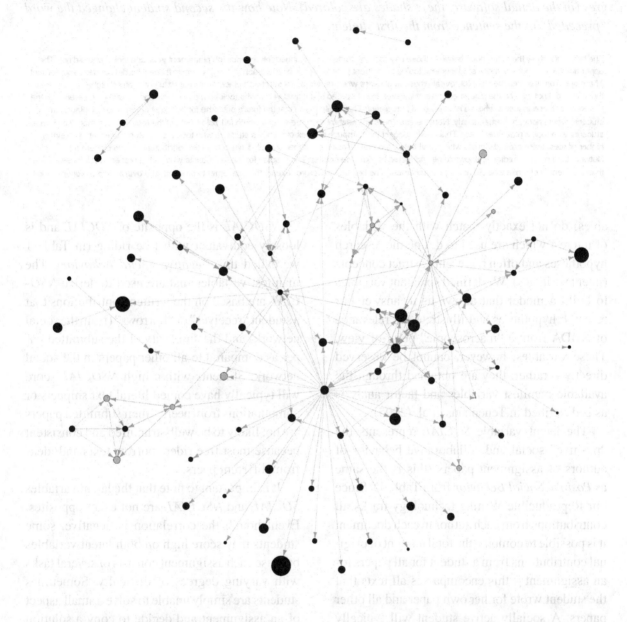

create "movies" of Sociograms that provide us with information about how social interactions evolve over time and how this impacts discourses.

Keeping in mind the goals of this chapter, it makes sense to limit the analysis and compute averaged statistics about the dynamical behavior of student contributions. Rather than simply using the total amount of contributed tokens or changes, we can use a *contribution index* that is standardized and averaged over all possible contribu-

tions when considering all papers that are submitted in a weekly assignment. This index is contained in the interval [0, 1] and has an easy interpretation because it represents the degree of social contributions in assignment paper writing.

Solving the Semantic Problem

One of the fundamental problems in DA is the fact that the observed variables (manifest vari-

Figure 2. Example of collaborative writing. The contributions of every author have a different shade of grey (in the actual software, these shades are colored). Note how the second student changed the word "preceded" in the sentence from the first student.

The box plots show the differences between those psychology students who undertook a sandwich placement year and those who did not. The upper and lower hinges of those students who took a placement year is higher on the graph in comparison to those who did not take a placement. Therefore, from the data the box plot reveals those final years who preceded in a sandwich placement year actually attained higher grades then those who did not take on the placement year. However, the H-spread of the final years who took on a placement has no drastic difference to the H-spread of those students who did not take on a placement. This could mean that the future outcome for both placement and non placement students would not vary tremendously. Nonetheless, there are several extreme values which fall below both of the lower hinges more so on those students who took a placement year. This could suggest that although the box plot shows students who took a sandwich placement achieving higher grades, there are individuals who do fall below the majority and so higher grades is not completely attributable to the placement. Notwithstanding, the median is known to be unaffected by extreme scores. The median for those students who took a placement is indeed higher than the median of those who did not take a placement. The box plot therefore reveals that placements students still overall attain higher grades

ables) do not exactly match with the variables of interest which are used to define the research hypotheses and often represent abstract concepts (latent variables). We defined six latent variables to build a model that allows us to answer our research hypotheses and illustrate the relevance of NBDA from a "macroscopic" point of view. These variables, however, cannot be observed directly – rather, they are obtained through the available manifest variables and factor analysis as is described in Tenenhaus et al. (2005).

The latent variable *SOCIAL* represents the "positive" social and collaborative behavior of authors of assignment papers (this is the same as *Positive Social Behavior* from Table 1). Since our Reproducible Writing technology tracks all contributions from each author in each document it is possible to compute the total amount of original contributions from a student for all papers for an assignment – this encompasses all texts that the student wrote for her own paper and all other papers. A socially active student will typically make several original contributions to different papers and receive contributions from peers. The variable *SOCIAL* is linked to two manifest variables: a measure for the contributions made by the student in the social network (*contribution index*) and a measure that takes into account the dissimilarity of the submitted paper as compared to all other papers in the social network.

NSOCIAL is the opposite of *SOCIAL* and is loosely equivalent with free riding (in Table 1 we called this *Negative Social Behavior*). The manifest variables that are used to derive *NSO-CIAL* are based on the written contributions that a student "receives" or "borrows" (from the social network) and the similarity of the submitted paper as compared to all other papers in the social network. Students with a high *NSOCIAL* score will typically have copied literal text snippets or computations from peers – their submitted papers are not likely to be well-structured and consistent because most free riders borrow texts and ideas from different peers.

It is important to note that the latent variables *SOCIAL* and *NSOCIAL* are not exact opposites. Even though the correlation is negative, some students may score high on both latent variables because each assignment consists of several tasks with varying degrees of difficulty. Sometimes students are simply unable to solve a small aspect of an assignment and decide to copy a solution from a friend.

The third latent variable represents the *QUALITY* of the submitted paper which is based on the objectively measured effort level that is associated with the paper. In principle there are an unlimited number of possible measures that could be used to quantify the quality of a paper. Through explorative data analysis in previous research, however, we have found that the number of revisions is one of the key factors that is highly correlated with the quality assessment by instructors. A revision is simply any token that is written, deleted or over-written during a writing session. Students who make a lot of revisions in their papers tend to have higher scores from reviewers. Another key factor that is highly correlated with instructor assessments is the time that is spent during the writing process. The time measurement that is obtained through our Reproducible Writing technology is accurate (to the nearest second) and includes the time that is used to generate the computations that are included in the paper.

There are many ways to incorporate meaningful, task-specific vocabularies in DA – this would certainly make sense in a more "microscopic" type of analysis. Within the context of this chapter however, there is no need to unnecessarily complicate the model. Hence, we introduce a generic vocabulary-based property which represents the use of academic language that is used in the submitted papers. Each of the ten divisions of the well-known Academic Word List (Coxhead, 2000) was used as a manifest variable to build up the latent variable *CAWL*. It is plausible to assume that papers with a high *QUALITY* tend to have higher *CAWL* values because all students in our data set are native English speakers.

The fifth latent variable, *FEEDBACK*, embodies the assessment that is provided by the reviewer about the submitted paper. The first manifest variable of this assessment consists of an actual grade (if available) which may be either qualitative or a quasi-ratio variable (e.g. a 4 or 5-point Likert scale). Each assessment grade was converted to a 5-point scale which allows us to compute an overall assessment grade for each reviewer and for each reviewed paper. This conversion required us to make a priori judgments about the importance of certain rubric scales (such as in binary scales with Yes/No options). All empty or missing grades were simply coded as a neutral

score of 3. While this procedure requires us to make quite a few implicit assumptions it seems to produce reasonable values for the "grade" of each paper. An analysis based on individual rubric grades provided by different reviewers about the same papers provides fairly strong evidence that reviewer assessments are (at least) consistent. For instance, in some assignments reviewers were asked to grade specific qualities of a paper and to determine an overall grade as well. It turns out that the overall grades correspond quite well with averages of individual, transformed rubric scores.

Nevertheless, we used a second manifest variable which is purely based on the feedback texts that were written by reviewers. In these feedback messages, we counted word frequencies that can be associated with negative and positive assessments of the paper. Obviously, the word lists used were different for each assignment and rubric. The assessment grade that is obtained through this procedure is used together with the previous manifest variable to estimate the latent variable *FEEDBACK*. In other words, even if one or both of the assessment grades would be nonsensical, this would merely be reflected by a low factor loading – by eliminating manifest variables that do not have a factor loading that is significantly larger than zero, we reduce the probability that nonsensical manifest variables remain in the final model.

Finally, we introduce the latent variable *AWL* which is the degree of academic language used in feedback messages that were generated by reviewers. The manifest variables that are used to determine this latent variable are the same as for *CAWL* which does not necessarily imply that all ten sub lists of academic words are contained in both cases.

Underlying Assumptions

Table 2 shows a summary of all latent variables, the number of manifest variables and the corresponding eigenvalues that were computed. Most importantly, Table 2 allows us to assess whether the so-called unidimensionality assumption is satisfied. The manifest variables that are retained in each latent variable must represent exactly one dimension. We don't use the traditional Cronbach alpha statistic to assess this assumption because it "has several limitations" and "wrongly assumes that all items contribute equally to reliability" (Assaker, Vinzi, & O'Connor, 2010, p. 15) – we prefer to base our assessment on the Dillon-Goldstein statistic and the first two eigenvalues (from each factor) as explained in Tenenhaus et al. (2005). As can be observed from the table, the Dillon-Goldstein values are all above 0.7 (which is the rule of thumb that is suggested in Tenenhaus et al. 2005). Most importantly, all first eigenvalues are larger than one, while all second eigenvalues are smaller than one. This last criterion provides us with a clear-cut and robust way to determine whether the unidimensionality assumption is satisfied.

As can be observed from Table 2, we had to eliminate four manifest variables from *AWL* (there are only six manifest variables instead of ten) in order to meet the assumption of unidimensionality. The difference between the so-called formative and reflective types of latent variables is important in theory, but in the computations of this model it doesn't make much difference. For the sake of brevity, it suffices to mention the fact that manifest variables in a formative construct do not need to be highly correlated. In fact, they are considered to "form" or "cause" the latent variable as opposed to the reflective constructs where the manifest variables are seen as instances of the same theoretical concept (i.e the latent variable).

The reason why *QUALITY* is treated as a formative construct can be argued by the fact that the associated manifest variables have low mutual correlations. For instance, the number of revisions that are made does not necessarily correlate with the total time that the author spends during the writing process. Some students need a lot of time thinking about the appropriate way to describe their findings while other students just start writing and make improvements afterwards.

Another important assumption to be checked is related to the cross loadings (correlations) between the manifest variables and the latent variables. Each manifest variable must have a positive correlation with its predetermined latent variable which must be higher than with any other latent variable. At the same time it is a good idea to check whether these loadings are significantly larger than zero. Due to the nature of the PLS-PM methodology this is only possible through a technique called bootstrapping which simulates the distribution of the parameters and the loadings.

DISCUSSION OF RESULTS

The results of the PLS-PM analysis can be summarized and visualized with graphs: each vertex embodies a latent variable and the edges represent the relationships from one latent variable to the other. Only those relationships which have a statistically significant parameter are displayed in the graph – therefore it is easy to interpret the results in terms of our research hypotheses.

Panel 1 of Figure 3 shows the Semantic Model for all 24741 feedback cases that were observed. Panel 2 exhibits the results when only long feedback messages about sizable papers are considered – this corresponds to 12396 cases or roughly 50% of the total set. In order to illustrate how the hypothesized relationships depend on the actual workshop assignments, we selected two examples (WS4 and WS8) – the results are shown in Panels 3 and 4 respectively.

The total effect parameters of Hypotheses H1 (which examine the effect of *QUALITY* on *CAWL*, *FEEDBACK*, and *AWL*) are all significant at the 5% level with the exception of the impact on feedback language (H1d) in Panel 2. This implies

Table 2. Unidimensionality of PLS-PM latent variables

Latent Variable	Type	MVs	Dillon-Goldstein	1st eigenvalue	2nd eigenvalue
SOCIAL	Reflective	2	0.937	1.762967	0.23703260
NSOCIAL	Reflective	2	0.975	1.901474	0.09852649
QUALITY	Formative	4	--	3.203811	0.45634884
CAWL	Reflective	10	0.832	3.409465	0.99547732
FEEDBACK	Reflective	2	0.717	1.118749	0.88125079
AWL	Reflective	6	0.808	2.486455	0.87123308

Figure 3. PLS-PM total effects of latent variables (displayed parameters are significant at the 5% type I error level)

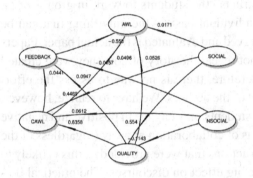

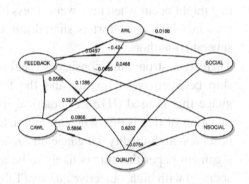

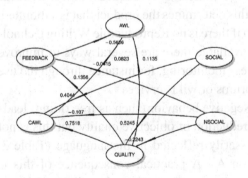

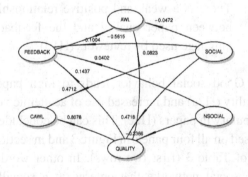

that submitted assignment papers of high quality have higher feedback scores than papers with low quality (H1b). On top of that, high quality leads to a higher usage of academic vocabulary in sub-

mitted papers (H1c) and in corresponding peer reviews (H1d). It is convenient to summarize the H1 Hypotheses and present the corresponding coefficients from all models in one overview (section B of Table 3). As we can observe, eleven out of twelve parameters are positive and significantly different from zero. As a consequence there are three conclusions from this result:

- There is a semi-strong but clearly positive relationship between the effort levels of authors and how the reviewers perceive the quality of the assignment papers (H1b). This means that the collaborative writing of papers improves the objectively measured quality and the perception of quality by reviewers. In this course, this effect is definitely larger than the negative effect that might occur when reviewers assess papers in which the effort is shared among several co-authors.
- There is a strong and consistent relationship between paper quality and the language that is used (H1c). A practical implication of this is that when an instructor observes high-quality language in an assignment paper that this is likely to be associated with high, objective quality (Table 3, section B). However, this is not true for the perceived quality by reviewers because it is not always associated with language quality (Figure 3, panels 3 and 4).
- There is a weak and positive relationship between paper quality and the feedback language used by reviewers (H1d).

Good social behavior leads to high paper quality (H2a) and increased use of academic vocabulary in papers (H2c). This can be concluded based on all four panels in Figure 3 and in section A of Table 3 (first two rows). In other words, the social networks that emerge in a socially constructivist setting play an important role in written discourses. Therefore we might interpret "good" social behavior as being "constructive" in the linguistic and in the pedagogical sense. The parameters of the *SOCIAL* variable are not only statistically significant but also among the most

substantial of all estimated relationships (as is measured by the total effect sizes; see first two rows in section A of Table 3). This constitutes strong evidence that DA of educational paper assignments has to take into account the macro structure that emerges through social networking among students – hence, the NBDA research paradigm that we suggested seems to make a lot of sense. This result may also have far reaching consequences for practitioners, even if they are not involved in constructive types of education. The reason for this is that the social context of collaborative writing practices is, in practice, not observed. It doesn't matter whether the educator "instructs" the students to work in groups or on an individual basis – the only thing that can be observed and evaluated is the actual paper. Papers do not reveal the story of how they were created – therefore, there is no way to assess the effort level of the authors. We have to realize, however, that students may engage in positive and negative forms of collaboration anyway (regardless of the instructions that were provided) – this is likely to have big effect on discourses. The practical bottom line is that instructors should carefully reflect about ways to monitor and assess the process of writing (not just the product). The process of writing is inherently embedded in social networks and this determines the product that is submitted. Even if there is no Reproducible Writing technology available there are several ways to improve process monitoring, for instance through the use of forums or wiki services.

Negative behavior (such as free riding) leads to a reduction of objective quality but this is not necessarily reflected in the language (Table 3, section A). A practical consequence of this is that peer review is not a good grading technique. This is one of the reasons why we don't use peer reviews to grade students (the peer review scores that are received do not count towards the final result of the reviewee). On the other hand, in previous experimental research we have shown that peer review is an excellent learning

Table 3. Summary of hypothesis tests (H4b and H4d were excluded)

Predictive relationships	All Feedback Messages	Long Feedback Messages	WS4 Feedback Messages	WS8 Feedback Messages
Section A: does social behavior predict discourses?				
Positive Social Behavior → Paper Quality	0.5540	0.6202	0.5245	0.4718
Positive Social Behavior → Paper Language	0.4469	0.5279	0.4044	0.4712
Positive Social Behavior → Peer Feedback	---	0.0497	---	0.1004
Positive Social Behavior → Feedback Language	0.0171	0.0188	---	-0.0472
Negative Social Behavior → Paper Quality	-0.1143	-0.0754	-0.2243	-0.2366
Negative Social Behavior → Paper Language	0.0612	0.0986	-0.1070	---
Negative Social Behavior → Peer Feedback	-0.0157	-0.0265	-0.0415	0.0402
Negative Social Behavior → Feedback Language	---	---	---	---
Section B: does objective paper quality (as measured by effort levels) predict discourses?				
Paper Quality → Paper Language	0.6358	0.5866	0.7518	0.8078
Paper Quality → Peer Feedback	0.4469	0.1386	0.1356	0.1437
Paper Quality → Feedback Language	0.0526	---	0.1135	0.0823
Section C: does perceived paper quality predict feedback language?				
Peer Feedback → Feedback Language	-0.5580	-0.4240	-0.5636	-0.5615

activity (Wessa et al., 2012) which causes deep, constructivist learning. Therefore, our practical suggestion is to grade the quality of peer reviews that are written (grading the reviewers rather than the reviewees) – if the reviewing process is randomized then there is a good chance that this reviewing process (and the associated evaluation of these reviews) is not (or only slightly) burdened by free riding problems. Rather than giving too much weight on the actual assignment papers we grade our students for active participation (requiring them to submit collaboratively written papers) and (more heavily) for the peer reviews that are written. Even if we wouldn't observe the social context we would still have the benefit of giving a fair score which is not (or only slightly) biased by negative social behavior.

If we examine the effect of good social behavior on feedback assessments (H2b and H2d) then the results seem to be inconclusive at first sight. This, however, is not surprising because we have to take into account the fact that reviewers have

information about the collaborative nature of the writing efforts (even though student names have been anonymized). It turns out that the negative, direct impact of social collaboration (of co-authors) on the assessment of the reviewer is often compensated by the higher quality of the paper which is under review. If we compute the PLS-PM for every assignment individually (not shown), it turns out that the total impact of SOCIAL on FEEDBACK (H2b) is positive (and significant) for all workshop assignments after the first five weeks. The most plausible explanation for this is that the effect starts to emerge as soon as the assignments become more complicated and the benefits of social networking are more relevant. As suggested before, social networks cause relationships to evolve over time because the networks themselves change or become more important. The effect of positive social behavior on feedback language (H2d) is inconclusive (sometimes positive and sometimes negative), but this may be caused by direct effects that have opposite signs.

From a practical point of view, these results imply that the process of collaborative writing has a learning curve – the associated collaboration effects only emerge over time and increase with complexity. Hence, if collective knowledge building is desirable, we would advise against using only one paper which is due by the end of the term. Instead, it makes sense to split the assignment into sub-tasks, which are submitted on regular time intervals (in our course we have used a weekly interval). Of course, this is only possible if the reviews are done by peers (otherwise the workload for the instructors would become unbearable). If, at the same time, the grading of peer reviews is based on the performance of reviewers (not the reviewees) then we may obtain the increasing effect of socially Distributed Cognition and social knowledge advancement ("deep" constructivism). On the other hand, the traditional approach of grading one single paper as an end product is not likely to stimulate the evolution of social/collaborative networks and their associated learning.

The PLS-PM results provide compelling evidence that bad social behavior (such as free riding) always results in decreased quality (H3a). The effect is fairly strong because the free riders spend less time, make fewer revisions, and make much smaller contributions to their own papers than other students. There were no blatant cases of "pure plagiarism" but occasionally students tried to avoid making an honest attempt to write their assignment papers or to borrow ideas and texts from peers (without making any revisions or improvements). In any case, free riding seems to, generally speaking, improve academic language (H3c: Figure 3, Panels 1-2) except in a few cases (WS4 and WS8 are exceptions). It is interesting to see that free riding, even though it always decreases objectively measured quality of the paper, sometimes pays off in terms of more favorable feedback assessments (H3b). For

instance, in workshop 8 (Figure 3, Panel 4) there is a positive relationship between *NSOCIAL* and *FEEDBACK*. In most other cases, however, the effect is negative (Figure 3, Panels 1-3). Clearly, reviewers do not like free riders, but sometimes it seems to be difficult to detect them. The practical consequence of this result is that we shouldn't rely on peer reviews to detect cheaters – this result is entirely consistent with a previous study that focused exclusively on fraud detection based on Reproducible Computing (Wessa et al., 2009).

The effect of bad social behavior on academic language use (H3c and H3d) is uncertain and depends on the actual assignment. Even though the sign is not determined, the effect is significant in most cases (Table 3, section A). This implies that social behavior is a potentially important co-factor when one engages in DA from a microscopic point of view. This seems to be confirmed, by our preliminary and explorative analyses of detailed properties of written discourses. For instance, it is interesting to see how the use of specific vocabulary (not just academic words) seems to propagate through the student population along the routes of the social networks that occur. Especially, in non-English speaking countries, the use of specific English jargon may be determined by social interactions of students (as was observed in one of our statistics courses in Belgium). Another remark needs to be made about the effect sizes that are computed – based on our (yet unpublished) exploration of various courses there seems to be preliminary evidence that the effect size of social interaction on discourse properties may increase as soon as the point of view becomes microscopic.

The analyses, based on all workshop assignments (Figure 3, Panels 1-2), provide strong evidence that the use of academic language in papers leads to better feedback scores (H4b) and more academic feedback language (H4d). There are a few exceptions however, as can be seen in Figure 3, Panels 3-4. However, based on our preliminary results about various courses, microscopic analysis promises to yield much stronger effects than those displayed in Figure 3.

Finally, hypothesis H5d yields very strong and interesting results (Table 3, section C). It turns out that *FEEDBACK* has a negative relationship with *AWL* in all workshops. As explained before, the sign could be negative or positive (depending on whether the mimicking effect or the grading of peer reviews is dominant). The results clearly indicate that negative review messages are formulated with a higher degree of academic language than positive review messages. Students may want to strengthen the trustworthiness of their negative feedback messages (and the impression this makes on the instructors) by using academic language. The practical implication of this result is that students tend to use more sophisticated language when correcting mistakes. This may imply that the verbalization of constructive feedback (about mistakes made by peers) involves higher order cognitive thinking. If this is true, then the practical implication is that we should not be worried about the fact that students make mistakes in their weekly papers because these mistakes are opportunities to learn, by carefully conceptualizing and deeply reflecting about the subject under review.

FUTURE RESEARCH DIRECTIONS

We believe that there are three major research areas that will play an important role in future development of NBDA. These areas are challenging because they require innovative solutions which cross the boundaries of several academic disciplines such as Psychology, Linguistics, Statistics, and Software Engineering.

The first area of future research is related to the development of educational technology which supports social networking, student-centered learning, and content-based course design (Wessa

et al., 2011). The homepage of our VLE (http://rfc.wessa.net) contains a couple of video podcasts which might be useful to get a first visual impression of how network-based, educational technology could evolve in the future. Another illustration of this is the Knowledge Building Discourse Explorer (KBDeX) which is currently under development (Matsuzawa et al., 2011) and promises to provide researchers with a tool to engage in explorative NBDA.

Future research will also have to deal with the methodological problem of analyzing discourses from a social networking point of view. Statisticians have created many methodologies for DA, Data Mining, Explorative Data Analysis, and various types of Social Network Analysis – however, there is currently no comprehensive statistical framework available which encompasses every aspect of NBDA in a unified and unambiguous way. In the statistical analysis that was described in the previous sections, we first computed the properties from the Sociograms and used those results as "deterministic" manifest variables in the PLS-PM. It would be much better if we could design a methodology that extracts the most predictive properties from the Sociogram and simultaneously computes the path model. Another problem is that the paths themselves will probably change over time due to the dynamics in the social learning networks. There are currently no methodologies that allow us to estimate such changes in the parameters – a comparative analysis of static models is all we can do at the moment.

The third area of future research is related to the theoretical, psychological underpinnings of social learning behavior and its impact on discourses. While there are many theoretical concepts that "vaguely" relate social networking to discourses and learning (such as social constructivism), there is currently no theory available that makes "detailed" predictions that can be tested in an empirical setting. In other words, NBDA is likely to become an "explorative" field in which empirical findings precede the development of theories. One of the key-aspects that might be discovered through explorative NBDA is the structure of the underlying dynamics: if we know how discourses (and their associated social networks) evolve over time then we might be in a better position to formulate detailed, predictive theories of social learning dynamics.

CONCLUSION

There is compelling evidence that educational discourses should be analyzed within the framework that is created by the collaborative social networks that emerge in socially constructivist course settings. Whether social networks are also relevant in the context of traditional (i.e. non constructivist) courses remains to be investigated in future research – however, it is our assertion that it is highly likely that discourses are dependent of social networking among students in traditional courses too. Indeed, social networking and collaborative learning is not solely observed in constructivist courses – students have many ways to communicate, share documents and engage in collaborative writing, even if this is not supported by the instructor or the VLE. Of course, there are also courses where little or no discourse efforts are required – in these cases, the relevance of social networks might be limited.

The PLS-PM results in this chapter do not only constitute strong support for NBDA, but also highlight the fact that cognition is, indeed, a distributed process which emerges from interactions between different components such as the students, the social networks among co-authors, the assignment papers, and the associated peer reviews. In other words, we have presented empirical evidence that cognitive processes that are related to academic discourses are strongly consistent with the theoretical framework of socially

Distributed Cognition, rather than being merely internal processes.

In addition, our results confirm that the ideas proposed by Matsuzawa et al. (2011) make a lot of sense. The approach that we presented effectively solves the problem of capturing collective knowledge advancement. Through the use of innovative, educational technology, we were able to demonstrate that the macro structure of social networking and collaboration can be measured and used to improve the discourse analysis of learners. On top of that, our results imply that "deep" constructivism occurs when people advance the knowledge in their community as was proposed by Scardamalia and Bereiter (2003).

Even if NBDA seems to make a lot of sense this does not mean that we expect to see many researchers adopt this approach in the near future. There are several reasons that might delay or even obstruct the adoption of our suggested approach. Most importantly, the available technology might not feature reproducibility of statistical computations, paper writings, or other collaborative learning activities. As a consequence, it may prove difficult to objectively measure discourse processes, Sociograms, and other meta data that is necessary to approach the DA from a social context. On top of that, there are other obstacles that may exist, such as lack of management support to dedicate resources to analyze discourses from a network-based perspective, no permission to use social networking data for analysis, insufficient methodological knowledge to combine social networking analysis and traditional DA, etc.

On the other hand, NBDA promises to yield scientific results that are of interest to a broad audience because it allows us to study old and new hypotheses in ways that have never been possible before. The good news is that the academic community has started to develop several projects which, slowly but surely, are released under open source or open access license models. At the moment of writing, it is already possible to use most of the Reproducible Computing technology free of charge. Some aspects, such as the archiving system of statistical computations and the associated R package, are available under the General Public License. In time, all of our components will be publicly available for the purpose of academic education and research – this includes all components of Reproducible Computing, Reproducible Writing, the content-based Virtual Learning Environment that we have used to develop our courses, and the Data Warehouse systems that allow us to collect NBDA data.

REFERENCES

Assaker, G., Vinzi, V.E., & O'Connor, P. (2010). Structural equation modeling in tourism demand forecasting: A critical review. *Journal of Travel and Tourism Research*, Spring/Fall 2010, 1-27.

Chen, G., Chiu, M. M., & Wang, Z. (2012). Social metacognition and the creation of correct, new ideas: A statistical discourse analysis of online mathematics discussions. *Computers in Human Behavior*, *28*(3), 868–880. doi:10.1016/j.chb.2011.12.006.

Coxhead, A. (2000). A new academic word list. *TESOL Quarterly*, *34*(2), 213–238. doi:10.2307/3587951.

de Leeuw, J. (2001). Reproducible research: The bottom line. *Department of Statistics Papers*. Department of Statistics, UCLA. Retrieved September 14, 2011, from http://repositories.cdlib.org/uclastat/papers/2001031101

Donoho, D. L., & Huo, X. (2005). BeamLab and reproducible research. *International Journal of Wavelets, Multresolution, and Information Processing*, *2*(4), 391–414. doi:10.1142/S0219691304000615.

Fruchterman, T. M., & Reingold, E. M. (1991). Graph drawing by force-directed placement. *Software, Practice & Experience*, *21*(11), 1129–1164. doi:10.1002/spe.4380211102.

Gentleman, R. (2005). Applying reproducible research in scientific discovery. *BioSilico*, Retrieved September 14, 2011, from http://web.archive.org/web/20090530044050/http://gentleman.fhcrc.org/Fld-talks/RGRepRes.pdf

Green, P. J. (2003). Diversities of gifts, but the same spirit. [The Statistician]. *Journal of the Royal Statistical Society: Series D*, *52*(4), 423–438. doi:10.1046/j.1467-9884.2003.02060.x.

Imm, K., & Stylianou, D. A. (2012). Talking mathematically: An analysis of discourse communities. *The Journal of Mathematical Behavior*, *31*(1), 130–148. doi:10.1016/j.jmathb.2011.10.001.

Ireland, M. E., & Pennebaker, J. W. (2010). Language style matching in writing: Synchrony in essays, correspondence, and poetry. *Journal of Personality and Social Psychology*, *99*(3), 549–571. doi:10.1037/a0020386 PMID:20804263.

Katz, J. L. (2010). *Comparing and contrasting web services and open source*. (Unpublished doctoral dissertation). Massachusetts Institute of Technology, US.

Koenker, R., & Zeileis, A. (2007). Reproducible econometric research (A Critical Review of the State of the Art). In Research Report Series, 60, Department of Statistics and Mathematics, Wirtschaftsuni-versität Wien.

Leisch, F. (2003). Sweave and beyond: Computations on text documents. In K. Hornik, F. Leisch, & A. Zeileis (Eds.), *Proceedings of the 3rd International Workshop on Distributed Statistical Computing* (pp. 1-15). Technische Universität Wien, Austria.

Lu, J., Chiu, M. M., & Law, N. W. (2011). Collaborative argumentation and justifications: A statistical discourse analysis of online discussions. *Computers in Human Behavior, 27*(2), 946–955. doi:10.1016/j.chb.2010.11.021.

Matsuzawa, Y., Oshima, J., Oshima, R., Niihara, Y., & Saki, S. (2011). KBDeX: A platform for exploring discourse in collaborative learning. *Procedia: Social and Behavioral Sciences, 26*(1), 198–207. doi:10.1016/j.sbspro.2011.10.576.

Nilsson, M., van Laere, J., Susi, T., & Ziemke, T. (2012). Information fusion in practice: A distributed cognition perspective on the active role of users. *Information Fusion, 13*(1), 60–78. doi:10.1016/j.inffus.2011.01.005.

Paus, E., Werner, C. S., & Jucks, R. (2012). Learning through online peer discourse: Structural equation modeling points to the role of discourse activities in individual understanding. *Computers & Education, 58*(4), 1127–1137. doi:10.1016/j.compedu.2011.12.008.

Peng, R. D., Dominici, F., & Zeger, S. L. (2006). Reproducible epidemiologic research. *American Journal of Epidemiology, 163*(9), 783–789. doi:10.1093/aje/kwj093 PMID:16510544.

Poelmans, S., Wessa, P., Milis, K., & van Stee, E. (2009). Modeling educational technology acceptance and satisfaction. In L. Gómez Chova, D. Martí Belenguer, & I. Candel Torres (Eds.), *Proceedings of EDULEARN09 Conference* (pp. 5882-5889). US: IATED.

Scardamalia, M., & Bereiter, C. (2003). Knowledge building. In Encyclopedia of Education (2nd ed., pp. 1370-1373). New York: Macmillan Reference, USA.

Schwab, M., Karrenbach, N., & Claerbout, J. (2000). Making scientific computations reproducible. *Computing in Science & Engineering, 2*(6), 61–67. doi:10.1109/5992.881708.

Tenenhaus, M., Vinzi, V. E., Chatelin, Y., & Lauro, C. (2005). PLS path modeling. *Computational Statistics & Data Analysis, 48*(1), 159–205. doi:10.1016/j.csda.2004.03.005.

Wessa, P. (2009a). A framework for statistical software development, maintenance, and publishing within an open-access business model. *Computational Statistics, 24*(2), 183–193. doi:10.1007/s00180-008-0107-y.

Wessa, P. (2009b). Reproducible computing: A new technology for statistics education and educational research. In Ao, S. (Ed.), *IAENG transactions on engineering technologies* (pp. 86–97). American Institute of Physics. doi:10.1063/1.3146201.

Wessa, P. (2009c). Exploring social networks in reproducible computing and collaborative assignments. In F. Salajan (Ed.), *Proceedings of the 4th International Conference on E-Learning* (pp. 486-492). University of Toronto, Canada.

Wessa, P., & Baesens, B. (2009). Fraud detection in statistics education based on the compendium platform and reproducible computing. In *Proceedings of the 2009 WRI World Congress on Computer Science and Information Engineering* (pp. 50-54). IEEE Computer Society.

Wessa, P., De Rycker, A., & Holliday, I. E. (2011). Content-based VLE designs improve learning efficiency in constructivist statistics education. *PLoS ONE, 6*(10), e25363. doi:10.1371/journal.pone.0025363 PMID:21998652.

Wessa, P., & Holliday, I. E. (2012). Does reviewing lead to better learning and decision making? Answers from a Randomized Stock Market Experiment. *PLoS ONE*, *7*(5), e37719. doi:10.1371/journal.pone.0037719 PMID:22666385.

ADDITIONAL READING

Asterhan, C. S. C., & Schwarz, B. B. (2009). Argumentation and explanation in conceptual change: Indications from protocol analyses of peer-to-peer dialog. *Cognitive Science: A Multidisciplinary Journal, 33*(3), 374–400.

Bereiter, C. (2002). *Education and mind in the knowledge age*. Mahwah, NJ: Lawrence Erlbaum Associates.

Boland, R. J. J., Tenkasi, R. V., & Te'en, D. (1994). Designing information technology to support distributed cognition. *Organization Science*, *5*(3), 456–475. doi:10.1287/orsc.5.3.456.

Carrington, P. J., Scott, J., & Wasserman, S. (2005). *Models and methods in social network analysis*. Cambridge, England: Cambridge University Press. doi:10.1017/CBO9780511811395.

Chiu, M. (2008). Effects of argumentation on group micro-creativity: Statistical discourse analyses of algebra students' collaborative problem solving. *Contemporary Educational Psychology*, *33*(3), 382–402. doi:10.1016/j.cedpsych.2008.05.001.

Csomay, E. (2006). Academic talk in American university classrooms: Crossing the boundaries of oral-literate discourse? *Journal of English for Academic Purposes*, *5*(2), 117–135. doi:10.1016/j.jeap.2006.02.001.

Daniel, B., McCalla, G., & Schwier, R. (2008). Social network analysis techniques: Implications for information and knowledge sharing in virtual learning communities. *International Journal of Advanced Media and Communication, 2*(1), 20–34. doi:10.1504/IJAMC.2008.016212.

Edmondson, W. J., & Beale, R. (2008). Projected cognition – Extending distributed cognition for the study of human interaction with computers. *Interacting with Computers*, *20*(1), 128–140. doi:10.1016/j.intcom.2007.10.005.

Gress, C. L. Z., Fior, M., Hadwin, A. F., & Winne, P. H. (2010). Measurement and assessment in computer-supported collaborative learning. *Computers in Human Behavior*, *26*(5), 806–814. doi:10.1016/j.chb.2007.05.012.

Hazlehurst, B., McMullen, C. K., & Gorman, P. N. (2007). Distributed cognition in the heart room: How situation awareness arises from coordinated communications during cardiac surgery. *Journal of Biomedical Informatics*, *40*(5), 539–551. doi:10.1016/j.jbi.2007.02.001 PMID:17368112.

Hogan, D. M., & Tudge, J. R. H. (1999). Implications of Vygotsky's theory for peer learning. In O'Donnell, A. M., & King, A. (Eds.), *Cognitive perspectives on peer learning* (pp. 39–65). Mahwah, NJ: Erlbaum.

Hogan, K., Nastasi, B. K., & Pressley, M. (1999). Discourse patterns and collaborative scientific reasoning in peer and teacher-guided discussions. *Cognition and Instruction, 17*(4), 379–432. doi:10.1207/S1532690XCI1704_2.

Holliday, I. E. (2011). *Teaching statistics to psychology students using reproducible computing package RC and supporting peer review framework*. Paper presented at the UseR! Conference 2011, University of Warwick, UK.

Hutchins, E. (1995). How a cockpit remembers its speeds. *Cognitive Science: A Multidisciplinary Journal, 19*(3), 265–288.

Kline, R. B. (2010). *Principles and practice of structural equation modeling* (3rd ed.). New York, NY: Guilford Press.

Kruger, A. C. (1993). Peer collaboration: Conflict, cooperation, or both? [Empirical study]. *Social Development, 2*(3), 165–182. doi:10.1111/j.1467-9507.1993.tb00012.x.

Leifeld, P., & Haunss, S. (2010). A comparison between political claims analysis and discourse network analysis: The case of software patents in the European Union. *MPI Collective Goods Preprint*, No. 2010/21.

Lockyer, L., & Patterson, J. (2008, July). Integrating social networking technologies in education: A case study of a formal learning environment. In *Advanced Learning Technologies*, 2008. ICALT'08. Eighth IEEE International Conference on (pp. 529-533). IEEE.

Luppicini, R. (2006). Review of computer mediated communication research for education. *Instructional Science, 35*(2), 141–185. doi:10.1007/s11251-006-9001-6.

Mäkitalo, K., Weinberger, A., Häkkinen, P., Järvelä, S., & Fischer, F. (2005). Epistemic cooperation scripts in online learning environments: Fostering learning by reducing uncertainty in discourse. *Computers in Human Behavior, 21*(4), 603–622. doi:10.1016/j.chb.2004.10.033.

Ryve, A. (2011). Discourse research in mathematics education: A critical evaluation of 108 journal articles. *Journal for Research in Mathematics Education, 42*(2), 167–199.

Scardamalia, M. (2002). Collective cognitive responsibility for the advancement of knowledge. In Smith, B. (Ed.), *Liberal education in a knowledge society* (pp. 67–98). Chicago: Open Court.

Scardamalia, M., Bereiter, C., & Lamon, M. (1994). The CSILE Project: Trying to bring the classroom into World 3. In McGilley, K. (Ed.), *Classroom lessons: Integrating cognitive theory and classroom practice* (pp. 201–228). Cambridge, MA: Massachusetts Institute of Technology Press.

Shea, P., Hayes, S., Vickers, J., Gozza-Cohen, M., Uzuner, S., & Mehta, R. et al. (2010). A re-examination of the community of inquiry framework: Social network and content analysis. *The Internet and Higher Education, 13*(1), 10–21. doi:10.1016/j.iheduc.2009.11.002.

Van Boxtel, C., & Roelofs, E. (2001). Investigating the quality of student discourse: what constitutes a productive student discourse? *Journal of Classroom Interaction, 36*(2), 55–62.

Wessa, P. (2009). How reproducible research leads to non-rote learning within socially constructivist statistics education. *Electronic Journal of e-Learning, 7*(2), 173-182.

Wessa, P., & De Rycker, A. (2010). Reviewing peer reviews - A rule-based approach. In *Proceedings of the 5th International Conference on E-Learning* (pp. 408-418). Universiti Sains Malaysia, Penang, Malaysia.

Wessa, P., & Van Stee, E. (2009). *The reproducible computing package*. Paper presented at the UseR! conference. Rennes, France.

Wheeler, S., Yeomans, P., & Wheeler, D. (2008). The good, the bad and the wiki: Evaluating student-generated content for collaborative learning. *British Journal of Educational Technology, 39*(6), 987–995. doi:10.1111/j.1467-8535.2007.00799.x.

KEY TERMS AND DEFINITIONS

Collaborative Writing: Is the practice of sharing and co-authoring documents with the purpose to solve a (scientific) problem. The authors engage in knowledge building and are able to contribute to the written work through the use of *Reproducible Writing* technology. The contribution of each author is transparently reported and can be improved over time.

Constructivism: Constructivism is a theory that claims that deep learning takes place during a learner's active involvement in guided learning activities and with a certain degree of freedom and self-control. Knowledge is not the result of rote memorization but "constructed" from individual and social experiences which are triggered by guided learning activities that stimulate interaction, communication, experimentation, discovery, organizing, and conceptualization. In this sense the educator plays an active role as coach and facilitator, and the learner is expected to take up responsibility for the learning process.

Latent Variable: A conceptual construct which cannot be directly observed but is important from a theoretical point of view. Latent Variables are commonly used to describe the research hypotheses of interest and to communicate the research results in human language (rather than with formulas).

Manifest Variable: An observable or measurable property which is used as a proxy for a Latent Variable. In practice, we always use more than one Manifest Variable to construct a Latent Variable – this process is closely related to what is called Factor Analysis in statistics.

Network-Based Discourse Analysis (NBDA): A scientific approach to investigate written or vocal language based on the information that is contained in the social network structures that emerge when people communicate with each other. Many types of "traditional" Discourse Analysis assume that the social context is important – the emphasis in Network-Based Discourse Analysis, however, is the fact that Sociograms and related statistics from Social Network Analysis can be used as predictive co-factors for the structural properties of the discourses and their evolution in time.

Partial Least Squares-Path Model (PLS-PM): Is a statistical methodology which was conceived and proposed by Herman Wold more than 40 years ago. The methodology computes multiple, structural equations between Latent Variables which are simultaneously constructed through Factor Analysis on Manifest Variables.

Reproducible Computing: Is a technology which allows anyone to create statistical computations that can be reproduced and re-used by the reader through freely available web-based computing services (Wessa 2009a).

Reproducible Writing: Is a technology which allows authors to collaboratively and simultaneously write and edit documents which are hosted in a cloud computing environment. Each key stroke is associated with a co-author and can be traced back in time. *Reproducible Writing* is more than just a Wiki because it records changes at the key stroke level and it encompasses the statistical analyses that have been generated by any author through *Reproducible Computing*.

Social Constructivism: This refers to "Constructivism" with an emphasis on the social interactions and experiences (as opposed to individual learning). For instance, in our statistics courses we allow students to collaborate during the writing process (of their assignment papers). In addition, students are required to engage in Peer Reviewing which is also a "social" activity because students have to write constructive feedback messages for other students.

Sociogram: Is a visual representation of a social network based on graph theory. Each node (vertex) corresponds to a person and each arrow (edge) represents a relationship. Sociograms can be very complex and are often accompanied by several statistics from Social Network Analysis. Sometimes, Sociograms can be used in explorative ways to reveal structures in social networks. The positioning of the vertexes can be determined manually or through an algorithm (Fruchterman et al. 1991) – in explorative analysis this is often a decisive factor for revealing hidden structures.

Chapter 3
Understanding Online Discourse Strategies for Knowledge Building Through Social Network Analysis

Stefania Cucchiara
University of Bari, Italy

M. Beatrice Ligorio
University of Bari, Italy

Nobuko Fujita
University of Windsor, Canada

ABSTRACT

Assessing the development of students' knowledge building discourse is difficult. It would be beneficial to have clear indicators of such discourse to understand if and how it is developing. The aim of this research is to identify indicators that can monitor how the knowledge building process develops during online discussions. In particular, we analyzed university students' discourse in an online setting oriented to knowledge building. An innovative mixed-method analysis approach was used. First, a qualitative content analysis was conducted to detect students' discussion strategies; second, an innovative version of Social Network Analysis (SNA), called Strategy Network Analysis was applied to analyze the relations among discursive strategies and to identify the most typical ones. Results showed that the most often used strategies in the knowledge process were "developing hypothesis" and "asking questions or problems of investigation." These were also the most effective strategies together with "expressing agreement or disagreement."

DOI: 10.4018/978-1-4666-4426-7.ch003

INTRODUCTION

Educational theories assign a crucial role to peer interaction as an important source of learning. By talking to each other, students can engage in non-conformist and non-rhetorical argumentation, genuine questioning and answering, and be very motivated to participate in discussion (Blumenfeld, Marx, Soloway, & Krajcik, 1996). Nevertheless, understanding whether a discussion is proceeding in a productive direction is very complex even for experienced researchers and teachers. Students would benefit from real-time feedback and scaffolding to optimize their learning through discourse. Online environments such as web forums may offer benefits of written communication by supporting student reflection on the contribution to the discussion before making it public. This could improve the metacognitive skills of the students, but it does not help us understand when a discussion is fulfilling its instructional goals. Web forums automatically record the discussions, offering the possibility to read and re-read the entries. This may facilitate the task of assessing the quality of discussions, because it can be analyzed post hoc, but usually not while the discussion is taking place. Thus, conceptual and methodological tools are needed to understand when the discussion is actually moving toward the desired direction in situ. This task is particularly important when students' discussion is considered the vehicle of learning, as in theories such as Knowledge Building (Scardamalia & Bereiter, 2003).

THEORETICAL BACKGROUND

Knowledge Building (KB) theory, pedagogy, and technology are attempts to reform education in a fundamental way to enculturate students into a knowledge creating culture (Scardamalia & Bereiter, 2006). Knowledge Building is a socio-constructivist framework defined as "the produc-tion and continual improvement of valuable ideas for a community" (Bereiter & Scardamalia, 2003, p. 1370).

According to KB, ideas are considered as real objects of inquiry and improvement (Scardamalia, 2002). This means that ideas can be revised, discussed, interconnected, corrected, and if necessary, replaced. This way of handling ideas represents a challenge to educate people to develop the capacity to create and innovate upon the knowledge of the community through the creation of new theories. Each contribution to the community is useful for creating a shared understanding and for giving ideas a life that goes beyond the transitory nature of the conversation. The developments in understanding a phenomenon or a theory produce conceptual artifacts that serve, in turn, to achieve further individual progress in a dynamic virtuous circle. This process will lead people to the advancement not only of their personal knowledge but also of the collective knowledge.

From this perspective, the difference between learning and KB becomes crucial. Learning is an internal psychological process that is not directly observable, results in lasting change of beliefs, attitudes and skills, and occurs as a result of experience; in contrast, KB is the result of the creation or modification of knowledge that depends on the active and collaborative participation in discussion, sharing, negotiation and integration of ideas (Bereiter & Scardamalia, 2003). Thus, in KB students should not only pursue a good individual performance, but also they should build and improve ideas that will be available and useful to the community. Individual learning is, however, functional for the advancement of knowledge in a community and, at the same time, it is a direct consequence of such advancement.

To guide the KB process, Scardamalia (2002) proposes a set of twelve principles or "socio-cognitive determinants of Knowledge Building" (p. 9) that act jointly with each other. The starting point of the KB process is the effort to understand the world around us. Issues and questions should arise from students' needs and curiosity, so they are "real ideas, authentic problems" of understanding for students. Subsequently, students are required to contribute ideas and theories to solve these problems collaboratively and create the best explanation for the observed phenomena. "Idea diversity" is essential to the advancement of knowledge because it creates a rich environment where theories can evolve into new directions. All ideas are considered "improvable ideas" so all members of the learning community work with the aim of increasing the quality, consistency, and usefulness of ideas. The goal of knowledge building is to reach a higher level of understanding and more coherent theories, in order to achieve the so called "rise above," which is a new idea that all participants can recognize as an advancement over their previous ideas (Bereiter & Scardamalia, 2003). This happens through "knowledge building discourse" within a community: knowledge is refined and transformed through discursive practices of the community members.

If ideas and theories are improvable, all the information that we come in contact with through books, encyclopedias and means of communication should not be passively accepted as "true" (Scardamalia, 2002; Scardamalia & Bereiter, 2006), but rather combined with a critical stance toward them. Therefore, on one hand students should not passively accept statements that are considered authoritative; but on other hand, it is necessary to learn how to handle a large amount of information from different sources. The only way out of this dilemma is to teach students how to develop skills in "constructive uses of authoritative sources."

Interactivity in online discussion is undoubtedly necessary to obtain such results. According to Rafaeli (1986; 1988), interactivity could be defined as the degree to which messages in a sequence relate to each other, and the extent to which later messages refer to earlier messages. Interactivity is essential for group communication. It is possible, but not always realized, particularly online and in large groups. One postulated outcome of interactivity is engagement, which is another relevant dimension in the learning context. Interactivity is not a characteristic of the medium. It is a process-related construct about communication, about the purpose of interaction, the shared interpretation of contexts and the iterative process leading to jointly produced meaning. Interactivity merges *speaking* with *listening*. Many authors consider interactivity as a useful concept for mapping group interactions in online discussion (e.g., Pawan, Paulus, Yalcin, & Chang, 2003; Schrire, 2004; 2006). Nevertheless, KB interactivity is not enough to explain how students become knowledge builders. It is, instead, essential to develop a sense of self-regulation, motivation and responsibility that lead to exercising of "epistemic agency," which refers to the active and intentional effort of each member to improve and construct new theories. Thus, each student is responsible for both his/her own learning and at the same time for the knowledge advancement. Members of a KB community share "collective cognitive responsibility" for the overall advancement of knowledge and contributions to shared, higher level goals of the community are accorded as much value as individual achievements. In this sense, not only the outcomes, i.e. ideas and theories developed, but also the processes through which students construct such products become important.

When all participants in a KB community contribute to the negotiation and sharing of the community goals, the "democratizing knowledge" occurs. In this case members help and support each other and take part in the process of constructing knowledge, developing a strong sense of community. In this way, the process becomes "pervasive knowledge building" that is not confined to a particular occasion or subject, and the members' expertise is distributed within and among communities through "symmetric knowledge advancement."

Last but not least, "embedded and transformative assessment" is a part of the effort to advance knowledge; it is used to identify problems and to monitor the daily work within the community. Therefore, is not only the teacher that should evaluate students, but all members are engaged in their own evaluation, as well as peer-assessment.

To summarize, several conditions are necessary for the KB process to occur. First, students should work on real problems that arise when trying to understand the world around them. Second, students should work with the aim of improving the consistency, quality, and usefulness of ideas. Third, the students should negotiate and compare their own ideas with those of others and use differences to advance knowledge, taking a critical stance when using authoritative sources of information. In addition, students must share the cognitive responsibility for the success of the community effort. Finally, knowledge building discourse is not just an exchange of information, but it involves the construction, redefinition and transformation of knowledge by the students.

To achieve KB, group activities are structured so that the responsibility for learning is shared, expertise is distributed and building on each other's ideas is the norm (Palincsar & Herrenkohl, 2002; Zhang, Scardamalia, Reeve, & Messina, 2009). Students, therefore, need to work collaboratively to problematize the content and take responsibility for advancing the collective knowledge. The persuasive speech occurring in the mutual exchange of questions, statements and other interactive strategies to enhancing knowledge construction requires students to work with significant problems, and help them to work critically and constructively with authoritative resources (Bereiter & Scardamalia, 2003). The discussion among community members is central to progressive

KB, and it occurs when everybody is actively involved and takes responsibility for their own and others' learning (Rogoff, Matusov, & White, 1996). Therefore, a fundamental matter emerges: the role that discourse plays in the construction of knowledge.

The Function of Discourse in Knowledge Building

Discourse has a great importance in KB because it allows going beyond the simple sharing of information. Bereiter (1994; 2002) argues that the process of KB is a discourse activity aimed at improving the collective understanding, through the continuous improvement of ideas and theories.

It is possible to distinguish the discourse aimed at KB from other forms of everyday conversation. During discourses aimed at KB, participants uphold commitments (Scardamalia & Bereiter, 2006):

- To *progress,* condition that usually does not characterizes the daily conversations, often dedicated to share information or express opinions;
- To seek a common understanding rather than a simple agreement;
- To expand the base of accepted facts.

The discourse aimed at KB has a constructive, progressive nature (Bereiter, Scardamalia, Cassells, & Hewitt, 1997) and occurs when all the participants are actively involved in deep discussions centered on knowledge (Cornelius & Herrenkohl, 2004; Engle & Conant, 2002). The literature (Burbules, 1993; Pontecorvo, 1997) points to two main discursive strategies that facilitate the development of KB.

The first one is "Asking questions." Questions serve to start a dialogue and direct the discourse toward a higher level. Moreover, questions help to frame goals, guide cognitive processes such as recalling important information, focusing on relevant aspects, and promoting the monitoring of discursive activities (Burbules, 1993). Teachers often use this strategy in order to: a) coordinate the interactions among participants, to enable effective collaboration and support the community in maintaining an effective dialogue; b) support metacognitive processes to keep the group focused on the goal; c) assist members of the community to express thoughts to be discussed and negotiated in order to reach a common and shared understanding (King, 1999). In KB, not only teachers but also students take on cognitive responsibility for asking questions to seek information, to cope with a lack of knowledge, or to monitor shared understanding. Different types of questions can stimulate different types of reasoning, and questions requiring a deep and complex reasoning are usually associated with better learning outcomes (Graesser & Person, 1994; King, 1999; Webb & Farivar, 1999). Emerging answers help to clarify thoughts and allow restatement of the concepts and move toward a clearer articulation of the discussed content.

The second strategy is "Making statements," i.e. claims challenging the ideas proposed or supporting the development or reformulation of an idea. This strategy can include identifying assumptions, ideas and theories shared by participants; moreover, all participants can initiate the discussion or contribute a different point of view. Any time an elaboration of a new theory is reached, there is an enrichment of knowledge for the whole community, due to the collaborative work of all members that, start from their initial knowledge, build new levels of explanation.

These discursive strategies facilitate argumentation, comparison and progression of ideas in the process of KB during which participants play an active role in identifying problems and improving collective theories.

The Use of Web Forums in the Knowledge Building Practice

In KB, the use of technology is emphasized because a virtual environment makes it possible to keep a persistent record of a community's progressive improvement of ideas. The virtual space enables students to work collaboratively with ideas, considered as conceptual artifacts, and to create new knowledge through a process of explanatory coherence (Thagard, 1989) to develop better theories that explain more facts.

Likewise, the Internet can play an important role in the process of KB, because it can support collaboration among students. The Internet is not only capable of conveying information, but it is also an artifact that mediates cognitive, social, and cultural processes (Cole, 1996).

In virtual environments a special kind of discourse is produced. It shares some characteristics with both oral and written communication (Ong, 1988), but ultimately online discourse constitutes a particular way of communication because of the specific tempo and the affordance of the tools available. Students using asynchronous tools, such as web forums, have the opportunity to read the same message several times, reflect on the text they want to produce, read what they wrote and modify it as necessary, before publishing it (Shana, 2009). While composing text, students can develop their ideas without conforming to the temporality of oral language. Furthermore, students are forced to make explicit their reasoning to avoid ambiguities; in this way, they develop cognitive skills and strategies that play an important role in the processes of KB (Ligorio, 2001). Moreover, before the posts are made public, participants can read their own and others' notes, consider all the ideas appearing on the screen, find information and monitor the discussion, and finally become aware of the ongoing process. Therefore, processes of collaboration and KB are visible to everyone in the community, motivating further student reflection and facilitating teachers in the analysis of the KB carried out by the group.

The technology supports the reconsideration of the learning process. Learning is no longer conceptualized as an abstract and individual activity, where isolated individuals engage in memorizing established theories, but rather considered a social process, taking place through communication exchanges between distributed participants with access to a wealth of information. Written computer-mediated communication facilitates critical thinking (Bullen, 1997; Newman, Johnson, Cochrane, & Webb, 1996), active learning, discourse processes, interaction and collaboration among students (Garrison, Anderson, & Archer, 2001; Harasim, Hiltz, Teles, & Turoff, 1995). Discussions in web forums can support and foster these kinds of desirable skills.

Many empirical studies (Caswell & Bielaczyc, 2002; Lee, Chan, & van Aalst, 2006; Philip, 2010; Scardamalia & Bereiter, 1994; Zhang et al., 2009) have shown that specially-designed web forums such as CSILE/Knowledge Forum can support KB. In these environments ideas are contributed, discussed, reviewed and organized. Online discussion in virtual spaces like these fosters idea advancement in which problems are constantly reformulated at a more complex level, leading to deeper understanding and knowledge building (Bereiter & Scardamalia, 2003). Thus far, we briefly reviewed the dynamics and dimensions involved in KB. In the next section we outline assessment of KB and argue that it requires novel concepts and tools.

Assessment in Knowledge Building Communities

Assessment has a very different connotation in KB than what it usually does in traditional assessment of learning. First of all, as Scarda-

malia argues (2002), assessment is part of KB, embedded in the process, and does not represent the final step. For this reason, assessment in KB involves a continuous process of transformation, essential in monitoring the ongoing activities. The community engages in its own internal assessment practices to constantly improve ideas. Second, assessment is an integrated and situated process, as it is closely related to the context in which knowledge is constructed and intrinsically linked to the processes, products and relationships developed in the community (Gipps, 2002). Furthermore, the assessment should be considered a co-constructed and distributed activity within the community. All members are invited to define the internal criteria for evaluation, asked to use them, and share responsibility for this process. Managing the negotiation of the criteria, their use for internal evaluation and monitoring the whole process may remain primarily the teacher's responsibility in most formal educational settings. Nevertheless, the active involvement of any participant implies a leveling of the power difference between the evaluator (teacher) and the evaluated (students). Therefore, the emphasis of assessment is not a final summative evaluation, but an ongoing formative assessment *for* learning. As all members are involved in defining the criteria for evaluation, the distinction between teacher and students is blurred. Over time, the object of the assessment and the practices of the entire assessment process should radically change.

As the goal of KB is to improve ideas and theories, the purpose of assessment is to monitor the progress of idea improvement and development of shared understanding. Considering the complexity of KB, the assessment should take into account at least three dimensions: Content, process, and relationship.

The first dimension, content, refers to the ideas and theories that are being improved. This type of assessment answers questions such as, "What is this idea is good for?," "What does it do and fail to do?" and "How can it be improved?" (Bereiter & Scardamalia, 2006, p. 701). The focus of this assessment is on examining the quality of the content of the ideas and on the contribution they make to the creation of knowledge. In this case, ongoing assessment allows for the monitoring of the progressive refinement of theories and explanations in discourse. A teacher can see in the student's discourse if there is a transition from simple theories to complex theories, but may lack tools to assess it in a timely way.

In terms of the second dimension, process, assessment focuses on the analysis of the work performed by the community. It tries to answer questions about strategies that students employ to build knowledge, and their role in improving ideas. This specific dimension of assessment can be analyzed through metacognitive reflection at both individual and group levels.

Finally, the third dimension concerns the relationship among the members of the community. The assessment covers all those aspects occurring in social and interactive exchanges among students, such as modalities of collaboration, leadership, and reciprocal support. Given KB theory and the importance of discourse and collaboration, the assessment should not be an individual assessment, but rather one that takes into account the community as a whole. Such as assessment should consider the quality of interaction as well as the quantity, particularly measuring the relationships between students working together to build knowledge. Consequently, it is necessary to use various tools and different methods for the analysis and the assessment of those diverse and complementary three dimensions of the KB process.

The application of the KB model requires, therefore, new tools to be put into practice, analyze, and assess the learning process (Martinez, Dimitriadis, Gomez, Jorrin, Rubia, & Marcos, 2006; Scardamalia, Bransford, Kozma, & Quellmalz, 2010; Teplovs & Scardamalia, 2007; Teplovs, 2008). Tutors and teachers need information

on different aspects of the assessment, including both individual and group levels (Chan & van Aalst, 2004). Furthermore, the information gathered should be used to improve the discursive practices (Sha & van Aalst, 2003) and intervene when needed, to obtain the active participation of students, in order to better support KB.

Given that learning is a socially constructed outcome and the development of new ideas and theories is collaborative work that involves group cognition among members (Stahl, 2006), it is necessary to find ways to take into account and assess the social aspects of this group process.

Teachers often are not able to develop appropriate conceptual tools to assess the discourse in its progression (Sha & van Aalst, 2003). Therefore, it is necessary to provide means to support teachers in assessing students' collaborative activities (Dimitracopoulou, 2005; Law & Wong, 2013). The outcomes of the evaluation procedures should help teachers and students to reflect on the discourse aimed at KB, in order to understand the ongoing process and to find out the next steps or possible changes to reach the goal.

Tracking interactions among students is one possible way to estimate the quality of learning, to monitor and support the process of KB, and to assess both individual and collaborative performances. We developed a new method of analysis that has the potential to give teachers and tutors some useful feedback, as described in a later section. We now turn to the research questions and methods used in this study.

Aims and Methods

The research questions that guided this study are:

1. How can the development of KB process be assessed through the discourse?
2. What are the discursive strategies most effective in developing and supporting the process of KB?

In order to identify indicators able to monitor the KB process occurring during online discussions, we designed a assessment method of online discourse based on the combination of content analysis and an innovative version of the Social Network Analysis, called Strategy Network Analysis. This analysis combines the following three steps. First, a content analysis was carried out to identify the discursive strategies that the students used (Stahl, 2006; Wegerif, 2006). To perform such analysis, eight categories, validated in a previous study and with high inter-rater reliability (Cacciamani & Ferrini, 2007), were used:

1. **Asking questions or posing problems to be investigated:** We consider as markers of this category questions explicitly targeting the content of the course; e.g.: "I wonder how the attachment bond develops" or "According to you, what is the relationship between learning and digital identities in online courses?"

2. **Developing hypothesis:** In this case, markers are concepts or opinions and possible explanations of the content covered during the discussion, as well as regulatory statements; e.g.: "This fact could be explained..." or "According to me..."

3. **Expressing agreement or disagreement:** Markers of this category are positive or negative comments on what expressed by another participant; e.g. "I think what you said is very useful" or "I do not agree with you."

4. **Metacognitive reflections:** This category is based on markers about explicit reference to evaluations and reflections on the cognitive activities; e.g. "I would like to focus on..." or "This note made me think..."

5. **Making examples:** Statements here included contain practical examples based on personal experience; e.g. "It happened to me that" or "The activities of this course are an example..."

6. **Sharing information from reliable sources:** As markers we used information students report from referenced sources or from scientific studies; e.g. "I read in the book that..." or "As Cole demonstrated in his work..."

7. **Repeating another member's idea:** In this category markers are reformulation of concepts with explicit reference to ideas of other students; e.g. "As you said before..." or "I had in mind the note you wrote in the previous module, when you said..."

8. **Providing a summary of ideas from different participants:** When students make a collection of several ideas or theories, even as a list; e.g. "To summarize..." or "In the discussion we focused on some aspects that I would like to resume."

The data was first categorized by two independent researchers who compared their results. The reported 20% disagreement was resolved through discussion with a third researcher.

Subsequently, the second step calculated the frequency and percentage of each category and observed when these categories occurred during the online discussions. Finally, the third step concerned the tabulation of these results into matrices to be imported into NetMiner 3, the software used to run the Social Network Analysis.

From Social Network Analysis to Strategy Network Analysis

Social Network Analysis (SNA) is a method of analysis that uses a variety of techniques to study the exchange of information, focusing on the relationships among actors (Haythornwaite, 1996). This approach can be defined as a quantitative analysis of relational data, based on the concept of a network; statistical analyses are carrying out on data concerning the relationships or ties that characterizes a group of persons. SNA focuses on the relationships between people and within communities looking at the interdependence among individuals. SNA employs an adjacency matrix of exchanges occurring within a community (Reffay & Chanier, 2002). Based on this matrix, it is possible to understand the socio-relational dynamics and a graphical representation composed by nodes and lines connecting the points makes it possible to reproduces the relational structure of the network. Then, SNA is a valuable tool, useful to analyze the complexity of social relations (Scott, 1997; Wasserman & Faust, 1994).

In the context of computer-supported collaborative learning (CSCL), SNA has been proved to be a powerful methodology, through which it is possible to measure levels and patterns of interaction in virtual learning environments, especially when used in combination with other methods such as content analysis (Daradoumis, Martinez-Mones, & Xhafa, 2004; De Laat et al., 2007; Martinez et al., 2006; Zhu, 2006). Indeed, combining SNA with a qualitative analysis allows implementing a process of content interpretation in order to catch the complexity of communication patterns. For these reasons, we use both content analysis and SNA to identify the links among the interactive strategies students used in discussion. This way, we coded for each message - or better for each meaningful segment of the message published on the web forum - the source of the origin (a previous message) and the communication strategy used in it. We called this strategy the "eliciting strategy" for its activation function, and the "elicited strategy" when referring to all the strategies activated by previous strategies. "Eliciting strategies" and "elicited strategies," therefore, could be considered senders and recipients in a communicative exchange, and the use of SNA can help in understanding what are the strategies able to activate other strategies.

In order to understand the relation among strategies, we focus on two different indexes available in NetMiner 3, software designed for SNA: a) neighbor analysis, with the corresponding index

of density; and b) centrality analysis, with the corresponding index of centralization.

The neighbor analysis considers all of the repertoire of interactive strategies used by the community during the discussion, marking the degree of use of each and their relevance. Indeed, the density describes the level of cohesion among the nodes examined, taking into account the number of lines (links) reported in the outcome (Scott, 1997; Wasserman & Faust, 1994). The centrality analysis, on the other hand, identifies critical strategies that elicited or were able to elicit the highest number of strategies; in this kind of analysis the focus is on individual nodes and their role within the network. The centrality analysis describes and measures the properties of the position of the actor (a strategy, in our case) within a social network (Wasserman & Faust, 1994). In other words, the analysis of the centrality identifies the nodes that are more central and strategic in the network through various indices which detect different aspects of their prestige and significance in the interactions of the entire community. The index of centralization, therefore, highlights how important an actor – in our new analysis, a strategy- is based on its involvement in the analyzed trade. This index varies from 0 to 1 and it is calculated on the basis of the nodal degree of each node, so the amount of bonds, both incoming (IN) and outbound (OUT), will identify the most central nodes, those able to activate a greater number of connections.

We re-named this innovative way of using SNA as "Strategy Network Analysis" because it enables us to understand what interactive strategies are most effective in supporting online discussions.

Context, Participants and Corpus of Data

Such procedure for data analysis was applied to several online discussions carried out by students in an undergraduate course called Educational

Psychology and e-Learning at the University of Bari. The course lasted 13 weeks and was offered in blended mode, integrating online and offline activities to those students that volunteered to use this option. The blended version of the course was attended by 16 students (average age=24), about half of the total number of students in the course. These students were exposed to exactly the same curricular content of other students who decided to participate only in the face-to-face course.

A two-hour, face-to-face session was held once a week, and alternated with the online activities based on the KB principles: web-forum discussion based on questions concerning the content of the course, as suggested by the Progressive Inquiry Model (Hakkarainen, Lipponen, & Järvelä, 2002); reciprocal reading of reviews - posted online - about the educational material read; collaborative building of artifacts such as synthesis and/ or conceptual maps of the content discussed; and role-taking based on competences the course aims to develop (Ligorio & Cucchiara, 2011; Ligorio, Loperfido, Sansone, & Spadaro, 2010).

The platform used for online activities is called Synergeia (http://bscl.fit.fraunhofer.de). It provides basic functionalities such as the ability to create folders, web forums, wikis, and concept maps. Like many other platforms, Synergeia also offers inquiry tools to check users' participation and monitor who posted, read, and/or modified each item. Students worked on five different modules: the first four modules pertained to specific content (1. Relationship between technology and learning; 2. Content of e-learning; 3. Online identity; and 4. New trends), while the last module was devoted to the preparation of a collective product, a grid to guide observational activities of a wide range of e-learning courses.

We analyzed seven discussions, all of which were content-related discussions comprising the course. A total amount of 511 student notes were contributed to the discussions.

Results of the Content Analysis

As mentioned earlier, we analyzed the students' notes in the web forum through a content analysis based on the eight categories described in the "Aims and method" section.

First, we counted the frequencies of the categories on the whole data set. This first analysis showed that the most used strategies were: "Developing and sharing hypothesis on contents" (22.3% of note segments); "Ask questions or problems of investigation" (13.9%); and "Share information from reliable sources" (12.6%).

This result is in line with the objective of the web-forum discussions students participated, aimed to develop an answer to content-based questions. The high frequency of the first two strategies is consistent with the previous references: regulatory statements and questions are useful strategies in sustaining a discussion focused on KB. Moreover, sharing information from authoritative sources is a strategy used to create a common repertoire of shared knowledge. This strategy is also useful to fulfill students' need to mention, during discussions, existing theories considered as a starting point for the formulation of new explanations or to better ground their positions.

However, as can be seen from the Figure 1, the distribution of frequencies indicates that also other interactive strategies were used in the web-forum discussion, outlining a quiet balanced use of all the discursive strategies.

Looking at this distribution, we wondered if the interactive strategies changed during the development of the discussions. To find out this information, we compared two discussions occurring at two different times: one at the beginning of the course (T1) and the second one at the end of the course (T2). Results reported in Figure 2 show that the use of some strategies, such as "Developing hypothesis on content" and "Meta-cognitive reflection" tended to increase over time;

Figure 1. Percentage distribution of frequencies of categories in content analysis

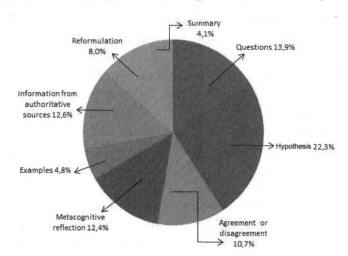

Figure 2. Percentage distribution of interactive strategies at T1 and T2

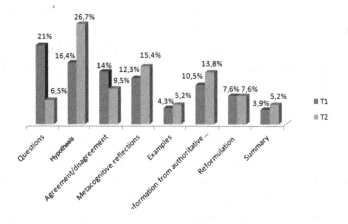

while other strategies, such as "Asking questions" and "Expressing agreement or disagreement" tended to fade.

The interactive strategy "Asking questions," used most by students during the first discussion, seems to be useful in involving students in the development of the content-based questions. Students use this strategy to be attuned to the understanding of content and to coordinate the production of hypotheses. Thus, this strategy became less important at the end of the course and its use decreased.

The use of "Developing hypothesis on contents" answers a content-based question. Increase in its frequency of use, therefore, seems to be the most functional way to produce theories and explanations.

Even "Expressing agreement or disagreement" is a useful strategy for the development of the discussion, as it is used to link together different notes and it allowed the progress of the discourse even in the absence of the strategy "Asking questions." This strategy, however, was rarely used alone in the discussions. It was often accompanied by strategies such as "Formulating questions" and

"Use of reliable information;" when combined with these two strategies, "Expressing agreement or disagreement" reached a high percentage of frequency.

The strategy "Metacognitive reflection" tended to increase from T1 to T2 of the course. The skills implied in this category developed as the discussions proceeded. The request to make explicit the processes of thought, such as finding connections between contents, reflecting on the content, and explaining ideas and positions to the peers emphasized in the course may have contributed to this finding.

Similarly, the "Synthesis of several ideas" seems to be a skill that students developed as the course proceeded. The progressive increase of the frequency of this category relates to the students' ability to include new elements in the discussion, which allows processing articulated concepts and complex theories. It is clear, however, that to propose a summary the concepts discussed, these should be already acquired, so it is reasonable to see this strategy appearing at a more mature stage of the course (T2). Moreover, when students dealt with complex contents, they felt the need to synthesize them. Therefore, students use their metacognitive skills to clarify the reasoning that led them to reflection, in order to make it visible also to the other participants.

"Making examples" drawn from the participants' personal experience is a strategy not very much used at T1 of the course, but it increased in T2, perhaps because this strategy helped participants to argue the content produced better by providing evidence.

The strategy "Sharing information from reliable sources" also increased at T2. This may be because students needed to make explicit the information they were discussing as the discussion proceeded.

Finally, "Repeating another member's idea" appeared to be a very useful strategy for students. This strategy allowed them to handle the content

efficiently because it allowed to check simultaneously their personal and a shared understanding.

In conclusion, this analysis allows us to understand:

1. What strategies students use while discussing online in a course based on KB activities;
2. The frequency each strategy appears;
3. If and how the frequency of these strategies evolve during the course (comparing T1 to T2).

It was found that students use interactive strategies mainly to formulate questions and hypotheses on the content; they use many strategies at the same time; and the number of simultaneous strategies increases during the course. Moreover, as the course proceeded, some strategies increased, as in the case of metacognitive reflections and the production of summary of many ideas, suggesting that these skills are learned through participation.

Furthermore, while looking at the content of the notes, we found that it was possible to recognize a consistent structure in such notes. Notes frequently included the following elements: an introduction, for example a "Metacognitive reflection" explaining why the information is reported in the note and anticipating the content; then, information was reported, using the strategy "Share information from reliable sources;" subsequently, students provided their personal opinions or elaborated on the content, coded as "Developing hypothesis on content;" finally, students augmented their thought through "Making examples" taken from their personal experiences.

Results of the Strategy Network Analysis

The centrality analysis from SNA showed that strategies were able to trigger many outbound connections. Those that elicit most other interactive strategies (out degree) were: "Developing

Figure 3. Degree of centrality (in and out)

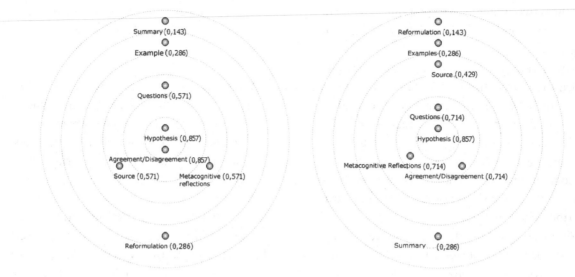

hypothesis on contents" (score = 0.857), "Asking questions" (0.714), "Explicit metacognitive reflections" (0.714), and "Express agreement or disagreement" (0.714). In contrast, the strategies that were elicited the most (in degree) by other strategies were: "Developing hypothesis on content" (0.857) and "Express agreement or disagreement" (0.857). Considering that the index values vary from 0 to 1, we consider these results as showing that all the strategies are interconnected to each other. In particular, the discussion seems centered on the use of: a) hypothesis on content; b) questions; and c) agreement or disagreement.

The strategies that were less effective in opening a discussion and supporting it (out degree) were: "Repetitions of another member's idea" (0.143); "Make examples" (0.286); "Summary of several ideas" (0.286). These three categories did not elicit any other strategies. Similarly, these strategies were not elicited (in degree) by any other strategies, pointing out that in the majority of cases these strategies did not emerge in response to other interactive modes.

However, as Figure 3 shows, the network of strategies looks balanced because there was no specific central node, as demonstrated by the low percentage of the index of centralization (network degree centralization index: 38.776% (in degree) and 38.776% (out degree).

The index of density related to neighbor analysis reported a value of 0.518, highlighting that the network was moderately cohesive. Figure 4 shows the graph about the index of density. Looking at this figure it is possible to see that the most central strategies were "Express agreement or disagreement" and "Developing hypothesis or opinion on contents." The first one was able to elicit any of the other strategies, except "Making examples" and "Summary of several ideas" were elicited by any other strategy except "Repetitions of another member's idea." The second one was able to elicit and to be elicited by any strategy, except that "Providing of a summary of more ideas," not directly connected to it. This latter strategy was elicited only by the "Metacognitive reflection" strategy. Furthermore, we see how "Asking questions" elicited five strategies: "De-

Figure 4. Graph of index of density

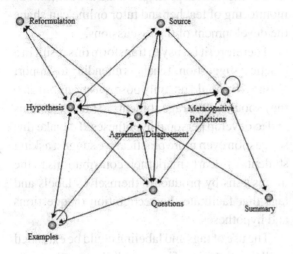

velopment of hypothesis on contents," "Sharing of information from reliable sources," "Making examples," "Express agreement or disagreement," and "Metacognitive reflection." All these strategies were used by students to support their answers, argue their points of views and to provide evidences for their thoughts.

Given these results, it should be possible to infer that "Developing hypothesis or opinion on content," "Express agreement or disagreement," and "Asking questions" are the strategies most successful at eliciting and being elicited in the discussions, so maybe they are the most effective strategies in supporting the development of the dialogue.

The purpose of using the Strategy Network Analysis was to understand in detail what are the most effective strategies to support and enhance online discussions. We that the strategies used the most were also the most effective. For example, the strategies reporting the highest frequency were "Developing hypotheses," "Asking questions," and "Sharing information from reliable sources." The Strategy Network Analysis confirmed that the first two strategies are also very effective for the progression of the discussion.

Both the students participating in the blended option and those participating only face-to-face were all assessed through oral colloquium – which is the standard assessment procedure in Italian university contexts. The students from the blended course scored as well as the students in the face-to-face course. There was a tendency towards a higher score in the blended course, but the difference in scores was not indicative. One explanation for this finding may be that most of the activities implemented within the blended course were more concerned with supporting students in acquiring interactive strategies focused on KB than on supporting content learning.

FUTURE REASEARCH DIRECTION

Considering the novel tool for analysis - the Strategy Network Analysis – used and the exploratory nature of this study, it would be desirable to replicate the research by expanding the sample to a larger number of discussions and notes. It would also be interesting to compare different type of courses, with variation in terms of structures and number of students to understand if and how these differences impact the discussion strategies and the students' participation patterns.

Moreover, it would be useful to focus on the role of the teacher when intervening online, to understand how they model the discursive activities of students. This would be particularly helpful in designing and planning the type of guidance needed to develop discussions aimed at building knowledge.

Another interesting direction for research could be to compare the discursive strategies of younger students rather than those adopted by adults – for instance, to compare high school students versus university students or professionals undertaking job training. This type of study would allow to better understand how interaction modes change at different ages and in contexts with different degree of formality.

Finally, we expect that additional studies in this field will advance the understanding of educational innovation and KB processes, both at a theoretical and a practical level.

CONCLUSION

The first aim of this study was to understand how to assess the development of KB process through the discourse. To achieve this aim, we integrate a content analysis and the SNA in an attempt to find an instrument to facilitate the evaluation process.

Our second aim was to investigate the interactive strategies students use the most when discussing online and which are the most effective in developing and supporting the process of KB in blended university courses. We found that in the course, students preferred to use strategies such as "Developing and sharing hypothesis on contents," "Asking questions or problems of investigation," and "Sharing information from reliable sources," although overall all the strategies examined were used by students. At the same time, the strategies that seem to be more promising in facilitating the development of Knowledge Building Discourse are "Developing hypothesis or opinion on contents," "Asking questions or problems of investigation," and "Expressing agreement or disagreement," consistent with the literature on the most effective interactive strategies and enriching the discursive repertoire with a new one.

Moreover, results demonstrate that the organization of the course and the online activities students are required to perform, have an effect on the interactive strategies used during the web-forum discussions. Specifically, having a goal (i.e. being required to answer to a content-based question) gives students a direction for the discussion that guides the development of the interaction. Indeed, the course structure and goals, the adher-

ence to theoretical principles, and the continuous monitoring of teacher and tutor online can shape the development of the discussions.

Therefore, it is easy to transform this result in a practical suggestion. Teachers intending to support online KB should not only pose questions but also they should encourage students to raise questions and to develop personal hypotheses. To make this suggestion even more practical we suggest asking students to clearly mark their contributions to the discussions by producing themselves labels and tags that facilitate the recognition of questions and hypotheses.

The use of tags and labeling could be extended to all the strategies. This would allow teachers and tutors to easily monitor the discussions. We also found that some strategies needed to be learned through the participation in the discussion. Practically this means teachers and tutors could encourage the use of these more reflective strategies to sustain the learning process.

Finally, in this study we attempted to simplify and operationalize some of the dimensions involved in the KB process to make it accessible for teachers and educators. This aspect is particularly relevant for assessment that should not be confined to the content knowledge that students acquire, but rather it should be extended to assessing the ongoing process of how students acquire such knowledge and how they use it to build knowledge collaboratively. This type of assessment is possible only when the online activities are designed with these assessments in mind; furthermore it implies a deep rethinking of the structure of the online activities and a redefinition of the parameters towards Knowledge Building.

REFERENCES

Bereiter, C. (1994). Implications of postmodernism for science, or, science as progressive discourse. *Educational Psychologist, 29*(1), 3–12. doi:10.1207/s15326985ep2901_1.

Bereiter, C. (2002). *Education and mind in the knowledge age*. Hillsdale: LEA.

Bereiter, C., & Scardamalia, M. (2003). Learning to work creatively with knowledge. In De Corte, E., Verschaffel, L., Entwistle, N., & van Merriënboer, J. (Eds.), *Powerful learning environments: Unravelling basic components and dimension* (pp. 55–68). Oxford: Elsevier Science.

Bereiter, C., & Scardamalia, M. (2006). Education for the knowledge age: Design-centered models of teaching and instruction. In Alexander, P. A., & Winne, P. H. (Eds.), *Handbook of educational psychology* (2nd ed., pp. 695–713). Mahwah, NJ: Lawrence Erlbaum.

Bereiter, C., Scardamalia, M., Cassells, C., & Hewitt, J. (1997). Postmodernism, knowledge building, and elementary science. *The Elementary School Journal, 97*, 329–340. doi:10.1086/461869.

Blumenfeld, P. C., Marx, R. W., Soloway, E., & Krajcik, J. (1996). Learning with peers: From small group cooperation to collaborative communities. *Educational Research, 25*(8), 37–40.

Bullen, M. (1997). *A case study of participation and critical thinking in a University-level course delivered by computer conferencing*. (Unpublished doctoral dissertation). University of British Columbia, Vancouver, Canada.

Burbules, N. C. (1993). *Dialogue in teaching: Theory and practice*. New York: Teachers College Press.

Cacciamani, S., & Ferrini, T. (2007). Costruire conoscenza in un corso universitario on line: è davvero possibile? [Knowledge building in an online university course: Is it really possible?] In *Tecnologie didattiche, 40*, 28-35.

Caswell, B., & Bielaczyc, K. (2002). Knowledge forum: Altering the relationship between students and scientific knowledge. *Education Communication and Information, 1*(3), 281–305. doi:10.1080/146363102753535240.

Chan, C. K. K., & Van Aalst, J. (2004). Learning, assessment, and collaboration in computer-supported collaborative learning. In Strijbos, J. W., Kirschner, P., & Martens, R. (Eds.), *What we know about CSCL: And implementing it in higher education* (pp. 87–112). Kluwer Academic Publishers. doi:10.1007/1-4020-7921-4_4.

Cole, M. (1996). *Cultural psychology*. Cambridge, MA.

Cornelius, L. L., & Herrenkohl, L. R. (2004). Power in the classroom: How the classroom environment shapes students' relationships with each other and with concepts. *Cognition and Instruction, 22*, 467–498. doi:10.1207/s1532690Xci2204_4.

Daradoumis, T., Martinez-Mones, A., & Xhafa, F. (2004). In De Vreede, G., Guerrero, L. A., & Raventós, G. M. (Eds.), *An integrated approach for analyzing and assessing the performance of virtual learning groups* (pp. 289–304). Lecture notes in computer science New York: Springer, Berlin Heidelberg. doi:10.1007/978-3-540-30112-7_25.

De Laat, M. F., Lally, V., Lipponen, L., & Simons, R. J. (2007). Investigating patterns of interaction in networked learning and computer-supported collaborative learning: A role for social network analysis. *International Journal of Computer-Supported Collaborative Learning, 2*, 87–103. doi:10.1007/s11412-007-9006-4.

Dimitracopoulou, A. (2005). Designing collaborative learning systems: Current trends and future research agenda. In T. Koschmann, D. Suthers, & T. Chan (Eds.), *Computer supported collaborative learning. The next 10 years! Proceedings of CSCL 2005* (pp. 115-124). Mahwah, NJ: Lawrence Erlbaum Associates.

Engle, R. A., & Conant, F. R. (2002). Guiding principles for fostering productive disciplinary engagement: Explaining an emergent argument in a community of learners classroom. *Cognition and Instruction, 20*, 399–484. doi:10.1207/S1532690XCI2004_1.

Garrison, D. R., Anderson, T., & Archer, W. (2001). Critical thinking, cognitive presence and computer conferencing in distance education. *American Journal of Distance Education*, *15*(1), 7–23. doi:10.1080/08923640109527071.

Gipps, C. (2002). Socio-cultural perspectives on assessment. In Wells, G., & Claxton, G. (Eds.), *Learning for life in the 21st century* (pp. 73–83). Malden, MA: Blackwell Publishers. doi:10.1002/9780470753545.ch6.

Graesser, A. C., & Person, N. (1994). Question asking during tutoring. *American Educational Research Journal*, *31*, 104–137.

Hakkarainen, K. (2012 in press). Expertise, collective creativity, and shared knowledge practices. In Gaunt, H., & Westerlund, H. (Eds.), *Collaborative learning in higher music education: Why, what, and how*. Ashgate.

Hakkarainen, K., Lipponen, L., & Järvelä, S. (2002). Epistemology of inquiry and computer supported collaborative learning. In Koschmann, T., Miyake, N., & Hall, R. (Eds.), *CSCL2: Carrying forward the conversation* (pp. 129–156). Mahwah, NJ: Erlbaum.

Harasim, L., Hiltz, R. S., Teles, L., & Turoff, M. (1995). *Learning network: A field guide to teaching and learning online*. Cambridge: The MIT Press.

Haythornthwaite, C. (1996). Social network analysis: An approach and technique for the study of information exchange. *Library & Information Science Research*, *18*(4), 323–342. doi:10.1016/S0740-8188(96)90003-1.

King, A. (1999). Discourse patterns for mediating peer learning. In O'Donnell, A. M., & King, A. (Eds.), *Cognitive perspectives on peer learning* (pp. 87–117). Mahwah, NJ: Erlbaum.

Law, N., & Wong, O.-W. (2013). Exploring pivotal moments in students' knowledge building progress using participation and discourse marker indicators as heuristic guides. In Suthers, D., Lund, K., Rosé, C., Law, N., & Teplovs, C. (Eds.), *Productive multivocality in the analysis of group interactions*. New York: Springer.

Lee, E. Y. C., Chan, C. K. K., & van Aalst, J. (2006). Students assessing their own collaborative knowledge building. *International Journal of Computer-Supported Collaborative Learning*, *1*, 103–125.

Ligorio, M. B. (2001). Integrating communication formats: Synchronous versus asynchronous and text-based versus visual. *Computers & Education*, *37*(2), 103–125. doi:10.1016/S0360-1315(01)00039-2.

Ligorio, M. B., & Cucchiara, S. (2011). Blended Collaborative Constructive Participation (BCCP): A model for teaching in higher education. In eLearning Papers 27th Edition "Transforming education through technology" (pp. 1-9). Barcelona, Spain: elearningeuropa.info.

Ligorio, M. B., Loperfido, F. F., Sansone, N., & Spadaro, P. F. (2010). Blending educational models to design blended activities. In Persico, D., & Pozzi, F. (Eds.), *Techniques for fostering collaboration in online learning communities: Theoretical and practical perspectives* (pp. 64–81). Hershey, PA: IGI Global. doi:10.4018/978-1-61692-898-8.ch005.

Martinez, A., Dimitriadis, Y., Gomez, E., Jorrin, I., Rubia, B., & Marcos, J. A. (2006). Studying participation networks in collaboration using mixed methods. *International Journal of Computer-Supported Collaborative Learning*, *1*(3), 383–408. doi:10.1007/s11412-006-8705-6.

Newman, D. R., Johnson, C., Webb, B., & Cochrane, C. (1996). Evaluating the quality of learning in Computer Supported Co-operative Learning. *Journal of the American Society for Information Science American Society for Information Science*, *48*(6), 484–494. doi:10.1002/(SICI)1097-4571(199706)48:6<484::AID-ASI2>3.0.CO;2-Q.

Ong, W. (1988). *Orality and literacy: The technologizing of the Word*. New York: Methuen.

Palincsar, A. S., & Herrenkohl, L. (2002). Designing collaborative learning contexts. *Theory into Practice*, *41*, 26–32. doi:10.1207/s15430421tip4101_5.

Pawan, F., Paulus, T. M., Yalcin, S., & Chang, C.-F. (2003). Online learning: Patterns of engagement and interaction among in-service teachers. *Language Learning & Technology*, *7*(3), 119–140.

Philip, D. N. (2010). Social network analysis to examine interaction patterns in knowledge building communities. *Canadian Journal of Learning and Technology*, *36*(1), 1–19.

Pontecorvo, C. (1997). Classroom discourse for the facilitation of learning. Encyclopedia of language and education, 3, 169-178.

Rafaeli, S. (1986). The electronic bulletin board: A computer driven mass medium. *Computers and the Social Sciences*, *2*(3), 123–136. doi:10.1177/089443938600200302.

Rafaeli, S. (1988). Interactivity: From new media to communication. In Hawkins, R. P., Wiemann, J. M., & Pingree, S. (Eds.), *Sage annual review of communication research: Advancing communication science* (Vol. *16*, pp. 110–134). Beverly Hills, CA: Sage.

Reffay, C., & Chanier, T. (2002). Social network analysis used for modelling collaboration in distance learning groups. In S. A. Cerri, G. Guarderes, & F. Paraguaco (Eds.), Lecture Notes in Computer Science (LNCS), 2363, 31-40.

Rogoff, B., Matusov, E., & White, C. (1996). Models of teaching and learning: Participating in a community of learners. In Olson, D. R., & Torrance, N. (Eds.), *Handbook of education and human development* (pp. 338–414). Malden, MA: Blackwell Publishing.

Scardamalia, M. (2002). Collective cognitive responsibility for the advancement of knowledge. In Smith, B. (Ed.), *Liberal education in a knowledge society* (pp. 76–98). Chicago: Open Court.

Scardamalia, M., & Bereiter, C. (1994). Computer support for knowledge-building communities. *Journal of the Learning Sciences*, *3*(3), 265–283. doi:10.1207/s15327809jls0303_3.

Scardamalia, M., & Bereiter, C. (2003). Knowledge building. In J. W. Guthrie (Ed.), Encyclopedia of education, (2nd ed., pp. 1370–1373). New York: Macmillan Reference, USA.

Scardamalia, M., & Bereiter, C. (2006). Knowledge building: Theory, pedagogy, and technology. In Sawyer, K. (Ed.), *Cambridge handbook of the learning sciences* (pp. 97–118). New York: Cambridge University Press.

Scardamalia, M., Bransford, J., Kozma, B., & Quellmalz, E. (2012). New assessments and environments for knowledge building. In Griffin, P., McGaw, B., & Care, E. (Eds.), *Assessment & Teaching of 21ˢᵗ Century Skills* (pp. 231–300). New York: Springer. doi:10.1007/978-94-007-2324-5_5.

Schrire, S. (2004). Interaction and cognition in asynchronous computer conferencing. *Instructional Science*, *32*(6), 475–502. doi:10.1007/s11251-004-2518-7.

Schrire, S. (2006). Knowledge building in asynchronous discussion groups: Going beyond quantitative analysis. *Computers & Education*, *46*, 49–70. doi:10.1016/j.compedu.2005.04.006.

Scott, J. (1997). *Social network analysis*. Newbury Park, CA: Sage.

Sha, L., & Van Aalst, J. (2003). *An application of social network analysis to knowledge building*. Paper presented at the American Educational Research Association, Chicago, April 21-25, 2003.

Shana, Z. (2009). Learning with technology: Using discussion forums to augment a traditional-style class. *Journal of Educational Technology & Society*, *12*(3), 214–228.

Stahl, G. (2006). *Group cognition: Computer support for building collaborative knowledge*. Cambridge, MA: The MIT Press.

Teplovs, C. (2008). The knowledge space visualizer: A tool for visualizing online discourse. In G. Kanselaar, V. Jonker, P. A. Kirschner, & F. J. Prins (Eds.), *Proceedings of the International Conference of the Learning Sciences 2008: Cre8 a learning world* (pp.1-12). Utrecht, NL: International Society of the Learning.

Teplovs, C., & Scardmalia, M. (2007). *Visualizations for knowledge building assessment*. Paper presented at the AgileViz workshop, Computer-Supported Collaborative Learning Conference 2007. New Brunswick, NJ.

Thagard, P. (1989). Explanatory coherence. *The Behavioral and Brain Sciences*, (12): 435–502. doi:10.1017/S0140525X00057046.

Wasswerman, S., & Faust, K. (1994). *Social network analysis. Methods and applications*. Cambridge: Cambridge University Press. doi:10.1017/CBO9780511815478.

Webb, N. M., & Farivar, S. (1999). Developing productive group interaction in middle-school mathematics. In O'Donnell, A. M., & King, A. (Eds.), *Cognitive perspectives on peer learning* (pp. 117–150). Mahwah, NJ: Erlbaum.

Wegerif, R. (2006). A dialogic understanding of the relationship between CSCL and teaching thinking skills. *International Journal of Computer-Supported Collaborative Learning*, *1*, 143–157. doi:10.1007/s11412-006-6840-8.

Zhang, J., Scardamalia, M., Reeve, R., & Messina, R. (2009). Designs for collective cognitive responsibility in knowledge building communities. *Journal of the Learning Sciences*, *18*(1), 7–44. doi:10.1080/10508400802581676.

Zhu, E. (2006). Interaction and cognitive engagement: An analysis of four asynchronous online discussions. *Instructional Science*, *34*(6), 451–480. doi:10.1007/s11251-006-0004-0.

ADDITIONAL READING

Aviv, R., Erlich, Z., Ravid, G., & Geva, A. (2003). Network analysis of knowledge construction in asynchronous learning networks. [JALN]. *Journal of Asynchronous Learning Networks*, *7*(3), 1–23.

Bereiter, C. (2002). Liberal education in a knowledge society. In Smith, B. (Ed.), *Liberal education in a knowledge society* (pp. 11–33). Chicago, IL: Open Court.

Bereiter, C. (2009). Innovation in the absence of principled knowledge: The case of the Wright brothers. *Creativity and Innovation Management*, *18*(3), 234–241. doi:10.1111/j.1467-8691.2009.00528.x.

Bereiter, C., & Scardamalia, M. (1996). Rethinking learning. In Olson, D. R., & Torrance, N. (Eds.), *The handbook of education and human development: New models of learning, teaching and schooling* (pp. 485–513). Malden, MA: Blackwell Publishers.

Bereiter, C., & Scardamalia, M. (2006). Education for the knowledge age: Design-centered models of teaching and instruction. In Alexander, P. A., & Winne, P. H. (Eds.), *Handbook of educational psychology* (pp. 695–713). Mahwah, NJ: Lawrence Erlbaum Associates.

Berelson, B. (1952). *Content analysis in communication research*. New York: The Free Press.

Bonk, C. J., & Graham, C. R. (2004). *Handbook of blended learning: Global perspectives, local designs*. San Francisco: Pfeiffer Publishing.

Bransford, J. D., Brown, A. L., & Cocking, R. R. (Eds.). (1999). *How people learn: Brain, mind, experience, and school*. Washington, DC: National Research Council/National Academy Press.

Brown, A. L., & Campione, J. C. (1996). Psychological theory and the design of innovative learning environments: On procedures, principles, and systems. In Schauble, L., & Glaser, R. (Eds.), *Innovations in learning: New, environments for education* (pp. 289–325). Nahwah, NJ: Erlbaum.

Chai, C. S., & Tan, S. C. (2009). Professional development of teachers for computer-supported collaborative learning: A knowledge building approach. *Teachers College Record, 111*(5), 1296–1327.

Chan, C. K. K. (2001). Peer collaboration and discourse patterns in learning from incompatible information. *Instructional Science, 29*, 443–479. doi:10.1023/A:1012099909179.

Chan, C. K. K., & van Aalst, J. (2008). Collaborative inquiry and knowledge building in networked multimedia environments. In Voogt, J., & Knezek, G. (Eds.), *International handbook of information technology in primary and secondary education* (pp. 299–316). Dordrecht, the Netherlands: Springer. doi:10.1007/978-0-387-73315-9_18.

Dillenbourg, P. (1999). What do you mean by collaborative learning? In Dillenbourg, P. (Ed.), *Collaborative-learning: Cognitive and computational approaches* (pp. 1–19). Oxford, UK: Elsevier.

Duschl, R. A., & Osborne, J. (2002). Supporting and promoting argumentation discourse in science education. *Studies in Science Education, 38*, 39–72. doi:10.1080/03057260208560187.

Guba, E. G. (1990). The alternative paradigm dialog. In Guba, E. G. (Ed.), *The paradigm dialog* (pp. 17–27). Newbury Park, CA: Sage.

Guba, E. G., & Lincoln, Y. S. (1989). *Fourth generation evaluation*. Newbury Park, CA: Sage.

Hakkarainen, K. (2003). Emergence of progressive inquiry culture in computer-supported collaborative learning. *Learning Environments Research, 6*(2), 199–220. doi:10.1023/A:1024995120180.

Harasim, L. (1990). Online education: An environment for collaboration and intellectual amplification. In Harasim, L. M. (Ed.), *Online education: Perspective on a new environment* (pp. 39–63). New York, NY: Praeger Publishers.

Henri, F. (1992). Computer conferencing and content analysis. In A.R. Kaye (Ed.), Collaborative learning through computer conferencing: The Najaden papers (pp. 115–136). New York: Springer.

Hogan, K., Nastasi, B. K., & Pressley, M. (1999). Discourse patterns and collaborative scientific reasoning in peer and teacher-guided discussions. *Cognition and Instruction, 17*, 379–432. doi:10.1207/S1532690XCI1704_2.

Huisman, M., & Van Duijn, M. A. J. (2005). Software for social network analysis. In Carrington, P. J., Scott, J., & Wasserman, S. (Eds.), *Models and methods in social network analysis* (pp. 270–316). Cambridge, MA: Cambridge University Press. doi:10.1017/CBO9780511811395.013.

Jonassen, D. H. (1994). Thinking technology, toward a constructivistic design model. *Educational Technology, 34*, 34–37.

Mcdonald, J., & Gibson, C. C. (1998). Interpersonal dynamics and group development in computer conferencing. *American Journal of Distance Education, 12*, 7–25. doi:10.1080/08923649809526980.

Muukkonen, H., Hakkarainen, K., & Lakkala, M. (1999). Collaborative technology for facilitating progressive inquiry: The future learning environment tools. In C. Hoadley & J. Roschelle (Eds.), *Proceedings of the CSCL '99 conference* (pp. 406-415). Mahwah, NJ: Lawrence Erlbaum and Associates.

Pozzi, F., Manca, S., Persico, D., & Sarti, L. (2007). A general framework for tracking and analyzing learning processes in CSCL environments. *Innovations in Education and Teaching International, 44*(2), 169–179. doi:10.1080/14703290701240929.

Reffay, C., & Chanier, T. (2003). How social network analysis can help to measure cohesion in collaborative distance-learning. In B. Wasson, S. Ludvigsen, & U. Hoppe (Eds.), *Computer support for collaborative learning: Designing for change in networked environments. Proceedings of CSCL 2003* (pp. 343-352). Dordrecht: Kluwer Academic Publisher.

Shana, Z. (2009). Learning with technology: Using discussion forums to augment a traditional-style class. *Journal of Educational Technology & Society, 12*(3), 214–228.

Woodruff, E., & Meyer, K. (1997). Explanations from intra and inter group discourse: Children building knowledge in the science classroom. *Research in Science Education, 27*(1), 25–39. doi:10.1007/BF02463030.

KEY TERMS AND DEFINITIONS

Assessment: The systematic collection and use of information about educational issues undertaken for the purpose of improving student learning and development.

Blended Course: Courses designed by mixing and integrating online and offline activities.

Community: A group of people having one or more characteristics, or certain attitudes and interests in common.

Content Analysis: A methodology in the social sciences for studying the content of communication.

Interactive Strategies: Ways of interacting in a discussion.

Knowledge Building: A theory arguing that the process of knowledge creation is a work on the improvement of ideas.

Social Network Analysis: Is the methodical analysis of social networks. These networks are depicted in a social network diagram, where nodes are represented as points and ties are represented as lines.

Web-Forum Discussions: Discussions about specific topic carried out in virtual environments.

Chapter 4
Inter–Animation between Utterances in Collaborative Chat Conversations

Traian Rebedea
University Politehnica of Bucharest, Romania

Stefan Trausan-Matu
University Politehnica of Bucharest, Romania

Costin Chiru
University Politehnica of Bucharest, Romania

ABSTRACT

With the wide adoption of instant messaging, online discussion forums, blogs and social networks, online communication has shifted from narration to highly collaborative discussions with multiple authors and discussion threads. However, the theories and methodologies for analyzing this new type of discourse which is different from narration, but also from dialogue, have remained mostly the same. The authors propose a new method for the analysis of this type of discourse, designed especially for multi-party chat conversations where parallel discussion floors and threads exist at the same time. The theoretical underpinning of the inter-animation framework is the detection of links between utterances in order to build a conversation graph that may be used to discover the discussion threads. The framework has been used for analyzing chat conversations of students in Computer Science in order to assess the involvement of each student, the inter-animation of the conversation and the degree of collaborative discourse.

DOI: 10.4018/978-1-4666-4426-7.ch004

INTRODUCTION

The purpose of this chapter is to establish a new theoretical framework, called the *inter-animation framework* for the analysis of collaborative online discourse, that links Natural Language Processing (NLP) and text mining to learning theories where inter-animation is already used such as knowledge building (Rezende & Castells, 2010) and meaning making (Scott & Mortimer, 2005) that are widely adopted as starting points for Computer-Supported Collaborative Learning (CSCL). This framework is designed for the analysis of online discussions, such as chat conversations and discussion forums, where multiple participants are debating given topics, investigating new subjects or collaboratively solving problems in a learning context. Thus, there are two main characteristics of the texts that are suitable for analysis using the inter-animation framework.

- **Structure of the discourse:** They are dialogic by nature, meaning that the unit of analysis is the utterance. For chats and online forums, each utterance is directly bound to the unit of discourse: the discussion turn, which may be a chat reply or a post in a discussion forum.
- **Purpose or of the discourse:** They are encouraging all the participants to express their own opinions for solving a non-trivial task, that might have several correct answers or solving paths, therefore the overall structure of the discourse should be collaborative, with contributions from all (or most) of the participants throughout the whole discussion.

The first characteristic provides a structural constraint for the textual artefact analyzed with the proposed framework by linking each discussion unit directly to the analysis unit: *the utterance*. In this context, an utterance should ideally be seen

as a single and finalized act of speech that holds enough information to be interpreted on its own, such that all the other utterances in the adjacent discourse have the same property. It should be noted that this definition of the utterance is directly related to Bakhtin who considers an utterance to be the "unit of speech communication [...] determined by a change of speaking subjects, that is, a change of speakers" (Bakhtin, 1986, p. 71). Moreover, he also notes:

Any utterance -- from a short (single-word) rejoinder in everyday dialogue to the large novel or scientific treatise -- has, so to speak, an absolute beginning and an absolute end: its beginning is preceded by the utterances of others, and its end is followed by the responsive utterances of others. [...] The speaker ends his utterance in order to relinquish the floor to the other or to make room for the other's active responsive understanding. (Bakhtin, 1986, pp. 71-72)

This definition provided by Bakhtin for an utterance is a very good starting point for a linguistic analysis of discourse that goes beyond the traditionalist theories that are sentence or paragraph-based. However, it also has some loose parts when trying to use it in computational linguistics, as it is mostly philosophical and does not offer any details on how to achieve or derive any practical implementation. This is the most important reason why very few researchers in computational linguistics started from Bakhtin's theory to develop an analysis framework for discourse. However, there have been attempts to use semantic coherence to measure the response between utterances/turns in discussion groups (Dong, 2004), but also more evolved frameworks that aimed to identify a more complex set of links between utterances/turns in chat conversations (Trausan-Matu & Rebedea, 2010).

Although any discourse could be segmented into utterances, in order for the proposed framework to perform well it is important to analyze a discourse that offers a segmentation in utterances of high quality. With this aspect in mind, there are specific types of discourse that have a natural break-down in utterances due to the nature of the environment used for communication. Thus, most of the text-based discussions that take place over the Internet exhibit high quality segmentation into utterances by considering each of the discussion units as an individual utterance. From the wide variety of Internet-based discussions, the most popular ones are: chat conversations (instant messaging), discussion forums, comments on blogs, news, videos, etc., social networking status updates or tweets, and even reviews on products. Although all these types of conversations are suited for analysis, it should be noted that while some have shorter discussion turns that may fragment an individual utterance over several turns (e.g. tweets, social networking status updates and further comments), others are more likely to have longer discussion turns where several distinct utterances are combined into a single turn (e.g. discussion forums, reviews). It may be noted that while synchronous and social platforms are encouraging an over-segmentation of utterances, the asynchronous mediums are usually formed of discussion turns that encompass several distinct utterances in the same turn. Chat conversations are usually at the boundary between these two types of online discourse, with turns usually longer than the first category and with a higher inner cohesion, but still shorter than the turns used in the latter category. To this end, we consider that chat conversations are the most appropriate form of discourse that exhibits high quality segmentation in utterances, when considering the direct mapping of discussion turns to utterances.

The second feature of the discourse that is suited for analysis using the inter-animation framework is related to its purpose, subject and content. Thus, the framework is designed to perform well on discussions where the participants are encouraged

to present their own opinion at any moment of the conversation. Therefore, their contributions should be related to extending the ideas presented up to any given moment and providing more relevant information to the task at hand. Most of this kind of tasks appear in a learning context: collaboratively solving a problem, engaging in a debate on a specific topic, working in teams to plan some work, asking a question where several solutions exist in order to choose the best one. It should be noted that some of these activities arise in any working environment and may be related to informal or lifelong learning. However, the usage of this framework should not be limited to the learning domain, as it could be applied to any discourse.

At the core of the framework is the *inter-animation* that arises in any discourse (Bakhtin, 1981) and that has been previously related to meaning making (Scott & Mortimer, 2005), knowledge building (Rezende & Castells, 2010) and supporting the analysis of collaborative chats (Trausan-Matu et al., 2007). In the following section we shall introduce the theoretical elements for inter-animation as a fundamental theory not only for discourse analysis, but also for collaborative knowledge building. Then we shall focus on adapting this theory for the analysis of online conversations, like chats and forums, constructed in a collaborative learning context by studying the current developments in linguistics for identifying links between turns and discussion threads. The main part of the chapter presents the inter-animation framework for online discussion analysis, by highlighting the ways on how responses (or links, references, interactions) between utterances can be discovered using NLP techniques. A software system that uses the main concepts of the inter-animation framework and that was designed for the analysis of chat conversations and online forums used in CSCL is also presented. The chapter ends with future research directions for improving the inter-animation detection and conclusions.

BACKGROUND

Inter-Animation in Online Discussions

We start from Bakhtin's dialogic theory, which states that language, in general, and any utterance, in particular, is not isolated, but rather "the speaker talks with an expectation of a response, agreement, sympathy, objection, execution, and so forth" (Bakhtin, 1986, p. 69). To this extent, utterances can be seen as speech units that set boundaries in the discourse flow between different *voices*. However, while every utterance has its own specific and individual voice that is dominant, it also contains *echoes* of other voices, thus providing a mechanism for inter-linking of utterances through voices and echoes. As Park-Fuller mentions: "heteroglossia (other-languagedness) and polyphony (many-voicedness) are the base conditions governing the operation of meaning in any utterance" (Park-Fuller, 1986). This constitutes the foundation for assessing that any discourse should have a certain degree of *inter-animation* of voices and ideas. In order to understand what the inter-animation of voices/utterances means in Bakhtin's dialogic theory, we need to start from the following quote: "Within the arena of *almost every utterance an intense interaction and struggle between one's own and another's word* is being waged, a process in which they oppose or dialogically interanimate each other" (Bakhtin, 1981) [emphasis added].

Thus, the term of inter-animation is related to the interaction between different utterances, with other utterances influencing the current one and struggling for being used by future utterances, as echoes or *overtones*. The same relationship between inter-animation and the multitude of links that are bounding the utterances were also noted by Wegerif: "Bakhtin uses the term 'inter-animation' or 'inter-illumination' to indicate *that the meaning of an utterance* is not reducible to the intentions of the speaker or to the response

of the addressee but *emerges between these two*" (Wegerif, 2008) [emphasis added].

The Baktinian notions of polyphony, heteroglossia and inter-animation can be easily applied to spoken language and to online text conversations, but can also be extended to any type of written text. For example, *intertextuality* has been proposed to express the interlinking between any pieces of text: "any text is constructed as a mosaic of quotations; any text is the absorption and transformation of another" (Kristeva, 1980). This definition should not be taken literally, as the author does not simply imply that intertextuality should only be related to "quotations" or other kind of *explicit referencing* that might exist in a text. Kristeva's theory could be seen as the extension of the dialogic theory and inter-animation to texts that says that no text can be completely understood on its own, but only as part of a more complex structure of other texts that might resemble a web structure. This means that any text could be understood differently not only to different readers, but also changing its meaning to the same reader, depending on the relations the reader finds with new texts that reposition the previous one in a different context. It follows that any text is also *implicitly linked* to other ones in a very complex manner, by taking into account a system of codes and interpretations of each of the texts read by any person.

Furthermore, heteroglossia, inter-animation and intertextuality can be seen as one of the starting points of *hypertext* (Landow, 2001), although other philosophers and semioticians have provided their own extensions of Bakhtin's theory and derived the theoretical notion of hypertext. For example, Barthes's "*ideal text*" allows for an open-ended and virtually unfinished textuality that could always extend its meanings by adding paths or links to other elements, thus forming a network or a web: "the networks are many and interact, without any one of them being able to surpass the rest; this text is a galaxy of signifiers, not a structure of signifieds; it has no beginning; it is reversible" (Barthes, 1974). The first time the notion of hypertext was introduced in a paper was in the proposal of the PRIDE (Personalized Retrieval, Indexing, and Documentation Evolutionary) system that worked using an evolutionary file structure (ELF) that was composed of entries, lists and links (Nelson, 1965). If a list is an index, then a link is similar to the hyperlink because it "is a connector, designated by the user, between two particular entries which are in different lists" (Nelson, 1965). In his definition, hypertext means an *extension* or *generalization of text* that can be reached using computers, thus overtaking the barriers and limits imposed by the use of paper for writing. As "such a system could grow indefinitely, gradually including more and more of the world's written knowledge" (Nelson, 1965), it offers the possibility of building a discourse without finality, where different voices can be manually specified by the authors or by the readers. Of course, only with the rise of the World Wide Web (WWW) over 20 years later, hypertext was used to its full potential, but with the technical specifications and limitations imposed by HTML. Later, Nelson viewed hypertext as a form of "non-sequential writing -- text that branches and allows choices to the reader, best read at an interactive screen. As popularly conceived, this is a series of text chunks connected by links which offer the reader different pathways" (Nelson, 1981).

From a practical point of view, it should be noted the concepts of inter-animation, intertextuality and hypertextuality are practically rooted in the existence of *links* or *interactions* between utterances or pieces of texts in general, in speech, written text or any other kind of discourse. Some of these links are *explicit*, due to the nature and medium of communication, like citing a source (in speech, written text or television shows), mentioning a person, using foot-notes to other materials or cross-references in the same text or even by adding hyperlinks in online pages. However, most of the interactions between different utterances or texts are *implicit* due to the difficulties of expressing every explicit interaction even when

the communication medium offers the required functionality to build them (such as hyperlinks). In order to assess the degree of inter-animation in a discourse, discovering implicit links becomes an essential task.

As in all other cases, in online conversations there may be explicit or implicit links between turns. However, besides discussion forums where a post is uttered in reply to another one in the same discussion thread, for chat conversations, social network status updates plus comments and tweets, there usually is not a mechanism for linking a message to a previous one. Of course, there are specific chat environments like Threaded Chat (Smith, Cadiz, & Burkhalter, 2000) or Concert-Chat (Muhlpfordt & Wessner, 2005) that allow referencing previous messages. Though, due to the way the users have learned to use the chat paradigm and also due to the fact that the communication is synchronous, explicit referencing can be perceived as a time-consuming activity in chats. Twitter also has developed an explicit linking mechanism, firstly by adding the "Retweet" option and later by allowing replies to specific tweets. In social networks, such as Facebook, there is no possibility to explicitly reference a previous comment, but you can add a link to another participant in the discussion using the @*Username* notation. Thus, most of the online conversation environments, either synchronous or asynchronous, have defined mechanisms for specifying explicit links between utterances in the same conversation. But what makes online conversations different from other forms of spoken or textual discourse, either offline or online, in order to require these methods for explicit linkage? There are several points to be taken into consideration in order to find a good answer to our question. First, online conversation environments usually allow for a multitude of participants to engage in a specific discussion. Second, online conversations permit the participants to issue turns at the same moment, most times without being able to see what other participants are writing at the same time. And third, most of the participants are not engaged in the whole conversation, but rather answering a specific portion of it, many times just a single utterance without taking into account or even reading all the discussion. Due to these features, the most pertinent answer to the previous question is that most online conversations do not adhere to the standard definition of the *conversational floor* that is used for spoken and written conversation. Thus, explicit links are introduced by the designers of the tools used for online conversations in order to bring more coherence to the discourse, by facilitating the users to add an explicit structure and threading to their discussions.

Both in writing and when speaking only a single speaker and turn can hold the floor at any moment. Moreover, the floor is a social construct, as the floor-holding turn must be accepted by the other participants in the conversation. However, in online conversations the limitations that make for the uniqueness of the floor in spoken or written discourse disappear. Also, the nature of the environment invites multiple participants to engage in a discussion at the same moment in time, thus allowing and encouraging the apparition of different and parallel discussion threads. The limitation of the communication channel used for writing and speaking vanishes, however another "competition for attention or control of the discourse" appears (Cherny, 1999). Thus, the conversational floor shifts from the standard turn-taking definition towards a "shared or collaborative floor" that is more appropriate for the multi-threaded topic discourse that appears in this context (Cherny, 1999). The collaborative floor has also been the starting point for a classification of various types of floors specific to online conversations which has also been proposed by Cherny (1999). The most common such patterns that have been identified in specific conversations are speaker-and-supporter, collaborative and multiple conversational floors (Simpson, 2005). The last one is the most important in our context as it specifies that a main floor and side floors

can exist in parallel during a discussion, as can multiple main floors.

Bakhtin's dialogic theory, that includes heteroglossia, inter-animation and polyphony, has been proposed by some researchers as a new theory of learning to be used for CSCL (Koschmann, 1999). Of course, this learning theory can be applied mostly to text-based collaborative learning situations where utterances can be linked to voices. Thus, studying the "participants' voices (and the voices within their voices)" (Koschmann, 1999) would provide a powerful method for analyzing learning both at an individual level, but also at the group level or the social influence. Furthermore, there have been studies that showed the existence of a link between dialogism used for learning and thinking skills: the quality of individual thinking can be improved by improving the quality of dialogue (online and offline) and that "individual thinking skills originate in conversations, where we learn to reason, to evaluate, to join in creative play and to provide relevant information" (Wegerif, 2006). However, the main difficulty is to determine the quality of a conversation, especially in online multi-party discussions. We propose that the degree of inter-animation can be linked to the quality especially due to the fact that inter-animation assumes that meaning arises from the interaction between utterances, which is an important aspect in collaborative learning. Thus the focus is not on the individual participant or utterance, but on the interplay that appears between different utterances and between different participants. Inter-animation and polyphony have been proposed for assessing the quality of problem solving tasks using chat conversations (Trausan-Matu, Rebedea, Dragan, & Alexandru, 2007; Trausan-Matu & Rebedea, 2009) or for detecting pivotal moments in online discussions by identifying the changes in the degree of inter-animation throughout a discussion (Suthers et al., 2011). It should be noted that although in many collaborative settings, the conversation space is closely inter-linked with the action space, our research is related only to the inter-animation that arises in the former, while ignoring the latter. We acknowledge that a complete treatment of collaboration should also consider the links between utterances and actions, but this goes beyond the purpose of the current framework which uses only the analysis of the conversations by exploiting NLP and text mining technologies. Thus the inter-animation may only be related to the degree of collaborative discourse and not with the collaboration that might arise outside the conversation (e.g. in the action space).

As a conclusion, inter-animation states that in every utterance one may find a multitude of voices from previous utterances that influence the meaning of the current one and the future evolution of the discourse. This is a key assumption in the inter-animation framework for discourse analysis. Furthermore, the true meaning of a text does not only come from its utterances, but also from the links between utterances that inter-animate dialogically. Taking into account that for the types of online conversation used for demonstrating the proposed framework (chats, forums), we used the simplifying assumption that a turn corresponds to an utterance, then one of the most important tasks will be to identify new, implicit links between the utterances in order to build the conversation graph.

Automatic Identification of Implicit Links and Discussion Threads

Because most online conversations encourage the development of multiple conversational floors, they can be viewed as a multi-threaded discourse where each floor accounts for one main thread (and side floors to related smaller threads). New threads usually appear by the division of one of the current ones, but other actions between discussion threads are also important: some threads can rejoin, either by convergence or by divergence of ideas, while other threads can just influence one another although they are not rejoined and thus continue to exist in parallel. During the evolution of a discussion, threads can also become

extinct if no further interest exists in continuing them. Determining the links between utterances in online conversations is a task that is useful for recovering their thread structure, assessing the degree of inter-animation and collaboration in the discourse, but also for segmentation. One of the main problems in assessing these links is the fact that the definition of a link between two utterances is a subjective notion. While some relations that involve repetitions of words or a high degree of lexical and semantic similarity between two utterances (especially when combined with a temporal proximity as well) are obvious, other are much more difficult to agree on due to the low connection between the two utterances. This is also related to Bakhtin's notion of heteroglossia that states not only that in any utterance a multitude of voices may be present, but also that the meaning of any utterance is also governed by the context when it is issued: "The base condition governing the operation of meaning in any utterance. It is that which insures the primacy of context over text [...] All utterances are heteroglot in that they are functions of a matrix of forces practically impossible to recoup, and therefore impossible to resolve" (Bakhtin, 1981, p. 428). In this light, the interactions between utterances are evidence of a coherent discourse structure, therefore their identification is subjective and can be realized automatically only to a certain point and with a given accuracy. Thus, the automatic identification of implicit links between utterances adheres to Bakhtin's opinion that heteroglossia cannot be identified by a purely systematic linguistic approach as these interactions cannot be completely classified and discovered using a closed set of structures.

However, a large set of links can be determined using NLP technologies and the remainder of this chapter shall identify the most effective ones by taking into consideration different elements ranging from conversation analysis (speech acts) and general discourse analysis (transacts, rhetoric structures) to semantics and coherence (semantic similarity) and pragmatics (argumentation acts). Determining the implicit link structure in various types of online conversations has been subject to different studies. For example, Wang, Joshi, Cohen, and Rose (2008) have used cosine similarity and temporal proximity between utterances in order to recover the implicit thread structure within newsgroup discussions. They have experimented with various values for several parameters such as the threshold for the cosine similarity, the number of previous utterances to consider as possible connections or using a dynamic window size and the best F1 score that has been achieved was 0.41. In a slightly different context, Adar, Zhang, Adamic, and Lukose (2004) have tried to identify implicit links between blog posts by making use of the cosine similarity between the text of the post, the similarity of the links present in the blog and in the post and timing information in order to develop a new algorithm for an improved ranking of blogs and blog posts. In their assessment of the correctness of detecting implicit links by making use of a tagged corpora and training a Support Vector Machine (SVM) on the features previously mentioned the accuracy was just 57%. Chat conversations have also been subject to automatic methods for extracting implicit links between utterances. Ogura et al. (2004) have proposed a simple set of rules that exploit the mention of chat users or fragments of the previous utterances, together with other features such as if a participant issued several consecutive replies or if an utterance already has a link attributed to it. They have validated their results on 8 small chats with 2-3 participants, containing a total of 1000 utterances, with an average accuracy of 53%. However, one of the first methods for detecting links between messages in chat-like conversations such as IRC discussions has used only simple rules, such as matching word repetitions and the fact that an user engaged in a discussion thread would be biased to respond to the same thread (Spiegel, 2001). This approach has been enhanced and extended to support users with smarter visualizations of their

interactions not only for IRC conversations, but also for message boards and newsgroups (Donath, 2002). At the end of this discussion, it should be mentioned that there have been other works that considered the automatic identification of discussion thread starts in chats by using a rule-based system together with a combinational approach in order to identify the compound rule that achieved the best score for identifying thread starts (Khan, Fisher, Shuler, Wu, & Pottenger, 2002).

One of the first works that did not employ any automatic analysis to determine links in multi-party online chat-like conversations, but rather a manual encoding of links and threads was done by McDaniel, Olson, and Magee (1996). After an independent analysis of six transcripts containing on average 173 turns done by two researchers, the agreement on thread detection ranged from 15% to 87%. However, most of the disagreements were related to subset-superset of threads, meaning that one of the researchers has divided a thread to a higher level of granularity than the other. This means that the detection of implicit links between turns that could determine such a separation was not very accurate. Although the paper highlights that specific discourse markers such as "coreference, term of address, responses, successive greetings, acknowledgements" (McDaniel et al., 1996) can be used to determine interactions between messages, the team agrees that these are not sufficient and the identification of links and threads require difficult judgements to be made even by human experts. More recent researches in recovering implicit links in multi-party online conversations have extended the feature sets, by adding adjacency pairs between speech acts, coreference resolution and other semantic similarity measures based on WordNet (Trausan-Matu & Rebedea, 2010) and even Latent Semantic Analysis (Trausan-Matu, Rebedea, & Dascalu, 2010). A semantic approach for determining concept formation in online discussion by using the direct relations from WordNet and Latent Semantic Analysis (LSA) was also proposed by (Dong, 2006), although he does not explicitly tried to solve implicit links in discussion but rather the formation of groups of similar concepts. Another interesting approach has devised a probabilistic generative model for the representation of discussion threads in online conversations, based on two simple observations: the probability for a utterance to be replied to is viewed as a linear combination of its recency and its current degree and that participants are biased to respond to utterances that are linked to their earlier posted messages (Kumar, Mahdian, & McGlohon, 2010).

The reconstruction of threads in online discussion forums has also been studied by training classifiers on a subset of forum threads in order to determine the accuracy of these models on new discussions. The features included reply distance between a post and a thread, time difference between posts, quoting a previous message, cosine similarity between messages and the length of the threads. Decision trees proved to have slightly better results than the SVM with an F1 measure of almost 0.93 (Aumayr, Chan, & Hayes, 2011). However, for the dataset used by the authors the baseline algorithm of assigning a link between any utterance and the previous one also had a very good value for the F1 score: 0.80. This result is usually true only in very large discussion forums. However, it should be noted that these results are achieved when considering the task of reconstructing the threads built only with explicit references present in discussion boards, thus ignoring the implicit links that can exist between messages in the same thread or in different ones.

Early work in thread detection in dynamic text message streams (instant messaging, online chat rooms) does not tackle the problem of determining the links between utterances and thus the conversation graph, but rather a simpler task of detecting the messages that are part of the same thread, ignoring the specific links between them. In this case, the problem can be solved using clustering, where the similarity between messages is computed based on the time proximity and on the cosine similarity between different messages (Shen, Yang, Sun, & Chen, 2006). However, the authors show that the best results are obtained when speech acts and adjacency pairs are also taken into consideration. In this case, they solve the thread detection problem with an average F measure of 0.61 on 16 dynamic text streams with the number of distinct threads ranging from 7 to 92.

Later, this specific problem was renamed *conversation disentanglement* and may be considered a special case of the source separation problem that naturally arises in multi-party online conversations (Elsner & Charniak, 2008). Their corpus consisted of 1855 turns from IRC conversations that were manually annotated by 6 different annotators. The average number of parallel discussion floors (or threads) was 2.75 and the results between different annotators were quite sparse: for a conversation with 800 utterances, the annotators have found the average length of discussion threads between 6 and 16 and the total number of threads between 50 and 128. Moreover, the 1-to-1 inter-rater agreement was only 53%, however when considering only the local agreement, this boosts to 81%. While the 1-to-1 accuracy counts only the valid assignments for an utterance to the same thread, the local agreement verifies if each of the previous 3 utterances are either in the same or in another discussion thread than the current message. The automatic determination of the discussion threads combines a classification task with a greedy clustering in threads. The classification task uses a max-entropy classifier that computes on a specific-sized window if two utterances should be in the same thread by using a combination of chat-specific, discourse and content features (Elsner & Charniak, 2010). The chat specific features include time, speaker and mentions of speakers or other names, the discourse features use cue words, detecting questions and long phrases, while the content features use a semantic similarity measure and the existence of domain-specific words in the utterance or not. The 1-to-1 accuracy of the model was 41%, while the local accuracy was 73%. The average score for the F measure reached 0.43. The main difference between the two results is that Shen et al. (2006) use only the explicit links to express a thread, while Elsner and Charniak (2010) manually annotate the new threads, thus using implicit information as well.

Uptake is a notion that is similar to the implicit link defined for online text discussions, but it is used in an extended role for any collaborative activity, not only for textual interactions (Suthers, Dwyer, Medina, & Vatrapu, 2010). The authors consider it "the most fundamental unit of interaction" and it is independent of the interaction medium, appearing whenever "a participant takes aspects of prior events as having relevance for ongoing activity." A simple example of uptake in online text conversations is the use of the explicit link to identify a previous utterance that is linked to the current one. The authors consider this one of the most evident forms of uptake in collaborative activities. In this specific case, the current message uptakes on one it explicitly replies to. In the uptake analysis framework an implicit link is a specific type of *contingency*, which describe a relationship between events in a collaborative activity. This relation highlights the fact that "one event may have enabled or been influenced by other events" (Suthers et al., 2010). However, a textual implicit link is merely a specific subtype of contingency. These are diverse and dependent of each collaborative activity, but have been classified in: media dependency, temporal proximity, spatial organization, inscriptional similarity and semantic relatedness. By adhering to this taxonomy for contingencies, an implicit link in online text discussion is usually an effect of inscriptional similarity and semantic relatedness, but is also affected by temporal proximity.

Table 1 summarizes the diverse landscape of tasks, techniques for solving them, the data used for analysis and the results that were achieved in determining the implicit link structure or just the discussion threads in multi-party online conver- sations. The common denominator of all these tasks is the inherent multi-vocality that exists in these types of conversations which breaks them into several parallel discussion floors or threads. Moreover, all the results presented in the previous pages highlight that these are very difficult tasks (F scores and accuracies are around 50%), demonstrated also by the low inter-rater scores.

CLASSIFICATION OF INTERACTIONS BETWEEN UTTERANCES

Inter-Animation Framework for Multi-Party Online Conversations

By taking into consideration the results presented in the previous sections, it is clear that classical theories for discourse modelling, such as centering (Grosz, Weinstein, & Joshi, 1995) or rhetoric structures (Mann & Thompson, 1987) cannot be successfully used for the analysis of multi-party online conversations. These have been designed primarily for narratives and although there have been studies on adapting them to dialogues and even online conversations, the results were not satisfactory up to this moment. On the other hand, speech acts (Austin, 1962) or dialog acts (Allen & Core, 1997) do not capture all the information needed to model a conversation, especially the transitions and interactions between utterances that represent the most important aspect of the inter-animation framework. Only the adjacency pairs' theory (Schegloff & Sacks, 1973) has been developed for dialogues and may be related to our framework as it considers that some specific types of speech or dialog acts are prone to be followed by other ones that refer them and thus close up an adjacency pair. However, the theory has been mainly developed for a two-interlocutor dialogue model that should be adapted for multi-party on- line conversations that have multiple discussion threads that run in parallel and are inter-mixed.

Table 1. Summary of the different tasks related to determining the implicit links or the discussion threads in multi-party online conversations

Problem	Solution	Data	Results
Retrieving implicit link structure in newsgroups	TF-IDF similarity, time window, penalizing factor proportional to time difference (Wang et al., 2008)	478 messages annotated manually with links (inter-rater 0.87 for 61 messages)	F1 = 0.41
Identifying implicit links between blog posts	SVM with features: cosine similarity between the text of the post, the similarity of the links present in the blog and in each post, timing information (Adar et al., 2004)	Hundreds to thousands of linked posts in blogs (automatically constructed)	Accuracy 57% (on 3 classes)
Identifying implicit links in chats	Rule-based: mentioning chat users or fragments of utterances, consecutive replies by the same participant, whether an utterance already has a link attributed to it (Ogura et al., 2004)	8 small chats with 2-3 participants, containing a total of 1000 utterances	Accuracy 53%
	Rule-based: word repetitions, users engaged in discussion threads are biased to respond to the same thread (Spiegel, 2001)	IRC chats	-
	Adjacency pairs between speech acts, coreference resolution and semantic similarity measures based on WordNet and LSA (Trausan-Matu, Rebedea, & Dascalu, 2010)	Multi party chat conversations with 3-5 students	-
Thread detection in chat and chat-like conversations	Clustering using: proximity between utterances, the cosine similarity between the centroids and the utterances or between different messages, linguistic features (speech acts, adjacency pairs) (Shen et al., 2006)	16 dynamic text streams with the number of distinct threads ranging from 7 to 92 (no manual annotation of implicit links, only explicit links used)	F = 0.61 (average F1 measure defined by authors)
	Max-entropy classifier and clustering using a combination of chat-specific, discourse and content features (Elsner & Charniak, 2010).	IRC conversation logs with 1855 turns manually annotated by 6 different annotators (1-to-1 inter-rater agreement: 53%, local agreement: 81%)	1-to-1 Acc. 41%, Local Acc. 73%, F = 0.43

The inter-animation framework considers that the interactions or links between utterances constitute the backbone for the analysis of online text conversations. Although there are linguistic theories such as the rhetoric structures, that define relations between different elements in a dialogue, they are different from our framework especially because they limit the number of relations to a predefined taxonomy and because they consider that the analyzed discourse is single threaded. Thus, the inter-animation framework considers that the links between utterances are fuzzy or have a certain value that denotes the strength of the link. For any utterance, there may be implicit links to an undetermined number of previous turns and the type of these links may vary a lot. In the remainder of this section the focus will be on defining some of the most important types of linguistic elements that may provide an evidence for interaction between two utterances in a conversation. However, there are many other elements that can be indicators for two interlinked utterances – they have not been presented in this work not only due to limits in the length of the chapter, but also due to the fact that providing an exhaustive taxonomy of implicit links is not possible at this moment. As noted by Suthers et al. (2010), there are also other types of interactions that can arise due to other factors which cannot be captured using our textual analysis approach, such as media-dependent or spatial-proximity contingencies specific to other types of collaborative interactions. Detecting the implicit links in a discussion arises new opportunities for the analysis of online discussions, including the assessment of the degree of inter-animation, by structuring the conversation into a tree or graph-like structure. Thus the main outcome of the framework is the construction of a conversation graph which contains the turns connected by implicit and explicit links of various strengths as shown in Figure 1. The figure is a snapshot from the PolyCAFe system (Rebedea et al., 2010) presented in the further sections. This structure may then be used to compute the discussion threads and to detect the importance of each turn in a thread, mainly based on coherence. More details are offered in the last part of this section, when describing the software implemented based on the inter-animation framework.

Several different methods are needed to detect links between utterances, focusing not only on the properties that are specific to a pair of utterances (e.g. similarity, timing, etc.), but also to discourse properties that are specific to a single utterance (e.g. speech act, argumentation acts, etc.). Thus, in order to be able to capture the various ways that define how interactions between utterances arise, there is a need to address two distinct aspects:

- An analysis of the different classifications that have been proposed for utterances in order to identify how specific links can

arise between different types of utterances, and

- A presentation of possible interaction types between utterances considering other attributes that characterize the textual content of the utterances.

It should be noted that the inter-animation framework is built on several other theories and also makes use of the principles of coherence and cohesion. Therefore, for the classification of utterances dialog acts and argumentation elements are useful for the subsequent analysis. The use of these types of discourse markers in order to identify implicit links between utterances or to detect discussion threads in online conversations has been shown to increase the performance of the developed systems (Shen et al., 2006). It is clear that using even simple heuristics like the following should provide an improvement to methods that do not use the identification of discourse markers for detecting links and threads. However, the focus of the rest of this section shall be to present the primary methods used to detect the most important types of interactions between utterances, assuming that the utterances are already labelled with dialog and/or argumentation acts.

- Greetings in a limited time frame are most likely linked,

Figure 1. Representation of a conversation graph of a chat in PolyCAFe

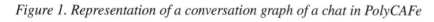

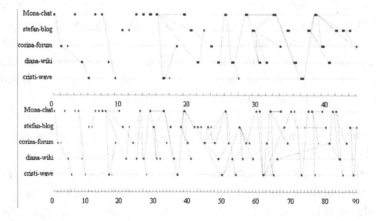

- Answers should be linked to previous questions,
- Acceptance or rebuttals are related to specific statements or arguments,
- Clarifications are likely to follow a request for information and can be followed by thanks or other utterances manifesting their gratitude.

Types of Interactions between Utterances

The classification of utterances plays an important role in order to identify links between utterances by employing heuristics that rely on the pair-wise probabilities for the transition between different types of utterances in a coherent discussion. However, in order to determine all the links between utterances it is clear that the analysis should focus on analyzing several other pairs of utterances to determine whether they are candidates for an implicit link. Several levels of analysis should be employed in order to determine the degree of interaction between any two utterances in a conversation, by focusing on discovering evidence of a coherent discourse on one or more of these levels:

- **Lexical level:** As the basic level of analysis, the lexis provides simple markers that highlight the influence between utterances that are primarily based on repetition of words or phrases. However, this analysis could be extended in order to consider other types of repetitions such as: synonyms, stems and lemmas, lexical chains and paronyms.
- **Discourse/conversation level:** The discourse level analysis can add precious information to the degree of interaction between two utterances. Whether it uses dialog acts, rhetorical structure theory (RST) or argumentation theory, in any conversation the relationships between the acts detected in the two utterances are important to detect a link between them. We

shall only focus on the adjacency pairs' theory, although other theories are useful for our framework, i.e. coherence relations (Sanders, Spooren, & Noordman, 1992).

- **Semantic level:** Even if subsequent utterances may be in different discussion treads, and thus local coherence may be broken at several points, on a higher level the discourse will be coherent. Semantic cohesion is therefore also present in multi-party online conversations and it can manifest in various forms: from the use of related words according to a lexical ontology such as WordNet to using concepts that are similar in latent semantic spaces.
- **Heuristics based on time and on participant:** Utterances issued very fast one after another, especially if they belong to the same participant, may be inter-linked or on the same discussion topic. This point is valid especially for chat conversations (and other online asynchronous discussions) where longer replies are usually broken down into smaller ones in order to hold at least one of the discussion floors of a multi-party chat conversation, for example.

An important aspect of the analysis performed at each layer is that the results are rather independent, although specific stages should combine results from different layers of analysis, as in the case of coreference resolution or detecting links between argumentation acts. The reminder of this section focuses on the most important aspects that influence the detection of interactions between utterances for each layer of analysis taken independently. However, only a combination of all these methods can provide a powerful method for discovering implicit links between utterances in online conversations.

Reiteration

Halliday and Hasan (1976) consider *reiteration* to be the most important form of lexical cohesion. It may vary from the repetition of a lexical item, in its simplest form, to using anaphoric general nouns to refer back to other elements in the discourse, at the other end. In between, are reiterations that use synonyms, near-synonyms and superodinates (hypernyms). Most of the time, reiterations are used for referring back to other nouns or noun phrases and in English are preceded by a reference item, usually *the*, *this* or *that*. Reiterations have similar roles as coreferences and although they can use hypernyms that are far away from the referred term in a lexical ontology – the case of general nouns (such as *person*, *man*, *thing*, *place*, etc.), they still provide more details that just using the personal reference forms specific to coreferences: *she*, *he* or *it*.

In many situations, lexical coherence is established by the reiteration of several lexical items in a given context. However, most times the reiteration can also be expressed using words that have different parts of speech or, more broadly, words that share the same lexical family. Therefore the automatic detection of reiterations should employ not only synonymy, but also stemming or lemmatization. An example where such techniques are useful for identifying implicit links based on reiterations is shown in the following excerpt from a chat conversation:

Wikis are really useful for collaborative projects

I agree, but also blogs can be used to collaborate in small teams

Reiterations can be easily detected in any type of discourse and are useful in recognizing implicit links in online conversations. Table 2 shows a comparison of the most frequent reiterations in three multi-party chat conversations on the same topic. The data considers only the most important 30 repeated lexical items in each conversation, with stemming and synonym expansion using WordNet (shown in the squared brackets). It can be easily noted that several terms are relevant

to only one or two discussions, thus defining implicit links between utterances and spanning discussion threads.

Lexical Chains

Reiteration does not include only lexical repetitions, but also collocations and lexical chains. Collocations might be useful for finding implicit links only if the constituents of an expression known to be a collocation would be in different utterances. However, this situation arises quite infrequently mainly because the meaning of a collocation arises from all its constituents therefore breaking such an expression in two or several utterances might make it more difficult to understand it. On the other hand, Halliday and Hasan (1976) also proposed another type of collocation consisting of words that are usually not adjacent in the text and that span over several lexical items, thus forming "long cohesive chains" or "chains of collocational cohesion" (e.g. *candle… flame… flicker… light*). With regard to this aspect, any lexical item may have a cohesive function with the rest of the discourse although by itself alone there is no explicit indication that it carries a cohesive relation or not. However, these relations are not arbitrary, but actually are a fundamental consequence of the fact that any written or spoken discourse has a certain development of topics and a specific organization. Thus, each lexical item has "its own textual history, a particular collocational environment" that was created by the preceding text and which provides the context for its current occurrence. This is the "instantial meaning" that is specific to each instance of any textual item and that could be easily put in relation with Bakhtin's theory of dialogism, especially voices and inter-animation. Halliday & Hasan consider that the instantial meaning of any occurrence of a lexical item is determined by the related lexical items that define the context. They define the *relatedness* between any two occurrences of lexical items both in terms of proximity in the passage of

Table 2. Frequent reiterations in three chat conversations using stemming and synonym expansion

Repetition	Chat 1	Chat 2	Chat 3
chat: [chat, confabulate, confab, chitchat, chatter, chaffer, natter, gossip, jaw, claver, visit]	56	43	40
forum: [forum, assembly]	33	29	28
wiki: []	31	14	15
employe: [employee]	30	15	18
agre: [agree, hold, concur, concord, match, fit, correspond, check, jibe, gibe, tally, harmonize, harmonise, consort, accord]	29	22	14
custom: [customer, client]	24	21	-
time: [time, clip, meter, metre, sentence]	23	19	16
yes: []	21	28	22
applic: [application, coating, covering, lotion, diligence]	20	-	-
compani: [company, companionship, fellowship, society, troupe, caller, party]	20	17	22
inform: [information, info, data, entropy]	19	-	-
secur: [security, protection, certificate, surety]	18	-	-
technolog: [technology, engineering]	18	-	-
wave: [wave, undulation, waving, wafture]	18	-	19
develop: [develop, evolve, germinate, acquire, grow, produce, get, originate, arise, rise, uprise, explicate, formulate, train, prepare, educate, modernize, modernise, break, recrudesce]	17	-	-
idea: []	17	12	22
OK: [fine, alright]	16	20	14
blog: [blog]	14	21	21
peopl: [people, citizenry, multitude, masses, mass]	14	-	18
document: [document, papers]	13	-	24
product: [productiveness, productivity], [merchandise, ware, product, production, intersection]	13	11	10
answer: [answer, reply, response, solution, result, resolution, solvent]	-	14	9
meet: [meeting, encounter, merging, confluence]	-	13	13
share: [share, partake, apportion, deal]	-	-	20
project: [undertaking, project, task, labor, projection]	-	23	-
support: [support, reinforcement, reenforcement, documentation, keep, livelihood, living, sustenance, supporting, accompaniment, backup, funding, backing]	-	-	32
solut: [solution, answer, result, resolution, solvent, root]	-	29	-

discourse and of proximity in the lexical system: the relative probability that two words tend to co-occur with one another in a language model.

Lexical chains are an extension of cohesive chains and have been defined as "a succession of a number of nearby related words spanning a topical unit of the text" (Morris & Hirst, 1991). There are two important differences from cohesive chains:

- The lexical chains can span over the entire text, therefore there the proximity relatedness defined for cohesive chains is not respected.
- Lexical chains are build using not only lexical relatedness, which can be linked to frequent co-occurring, but also *semantic relatedness* or *similarity*, by making use

of thesauri (Morris & Hirst, 1991), lexical ontologies such as WordNet (Barzilay & Elhadad, 1997; Silber & McCoy, 2002) or even more advanced techniques for computing the semantic relatedness between two words.

The basic measures for computing the (semantic) relatedness of two words (lexical items or even compound words) are using synonyms, antonyms, hypernyms, offsprings and siblings in the hypernym graphs (Barzilay & Elhadad, 1997). However, more complex similarity measures between medium-connected words have also been defined for WordNet (Hirst & St Onge, 1998). This was one of the first works that introduced a weight for the semantic similarity of different words in the context of detecting lexical chains: the length of the path and the number of changes in direction (upwards, horizontal and downwards) in the path connecting two words were considered a penalty for the semantic score. Most of the different methods for computing semantic similarity or relatedness between two words that shall be discussed in the next subsection can be used for determining lexical chains.

One of the most important issues when computing lexical chains is that chains allow only the addition of new words and not deletions of words from the corpora. However, words that do not appear in the corpora may be introduced in the process of building the chains in order to improve the computation efficiency (Hirst & St Onge, 1998). These words are eliminated from the lexical chains in a later phase in order to have only words from the analyzed text in each chain. Furthermore, once a word has been added to a lexical chain (either an existing or a new one) it is not removed and the chain cannot be broken if it loses its global cohesion in time by adding new words to it..

Lexical chains have been used for a wide range of tasks in computational linguistics, such as assessing discourse cohesion (Morris & Hirst, 1991), text segmentation (Manabu & Takeo,

1994), text summarization (Barzilay & Elhadad, 1997) and word sense disambiguation (Manabu & Takeo, 1994). However, they have been also used to determine lexical cohesion and segment multi-party spoken conversations by identifying minimum values of the cohesion (Galley, McKeown, Fosler-Lussier, & Jing, 2003). In a similar manner, lexical chains can be used to identify implicit links between utterances in multi-party online discussions by computing the lexical cohesion and detecting high values as potential candidates for a link. Table 3 shows how two lexical chains consisting of the words *{internet, connection, bandwidth, network, LAN, VPN}* and *{videochat, chat, virtual, meeting}* can be used to determine links between utterances in a chat conversation with 5 participants where the names of the participants are the nicknames they have chosen for the chat, therefore they may have not been pseudonymised.

Adjacency Pairs

One of the most important discourse theories developed especially for dialogues is based on *adjacency pairs* (Schegloff & Sacks, 1973). The authors highlighted that closings or terminal exchanges of messages are a special category of a class of utterance sequences called *adjacency pairs* (or utterance pairs). This sequence of utterances is characterized by five main features:

1. It is composed only by two utterances,
2. These utterances are positioned adjacently,
3. Each of the two utterances was issued by different speakers,
4. The two utterances are related as they are the constituents of a specific pair type and appear in the order specified by it,
5. The first part of any pair type has a discriminative power on all the possible second parts that could follow.

Examples of pair types that appear in most conversations are: greeting-greeting, question-

Table 3. Two lexical chains highlighted in a chat conversation – they can be used to identify implicit links between the utterances that contain words from each chain

64	and if you do not have a good internet connection, clasic **chat** chould also be a solution...	Mona
65	agree...**videochat** requires some bandwidth	Cristi
66	ok...but what about information, what do you think it is the most reliable source of information?	Diana
67	**chat** is fast, simple to use and it does not require such a good internet connection	Mona
68	if it is an inside network i don't think this should be a problem	Stefan
69	well depends on the type of the **meeting**...	Corina
70	what do you mean by inside network?	Mona
71	in the same building?	Mona
72	LAN	Stefan
73	nowadays a fast internet connection is everywhere:)	Cristi
74	or VPN	Stefan
75	true.... internet connection is not really a problem nowadays...	Mona
76	so we all agree that **videochat** is the best solution for a "**virtual**" **meeting**	Mona
77	undoubtedly	Cristi
78	yes!	Corina
79	so.... one activity solved....	Mona
80	ok so for **meetings** we have video **chat**	Stefan

answer, offer-acceptance, etc. The adjacency constraint has been considered not to be valid in many conversational contexts, therefore the modern definition of adjacency pairs accepts the fact that between the first and the second part of an adjacency pair several other utterances may appear (Levinson, 1983). This is especially true in the case of conversations with multiple participants, either spoken or written. In this context, it should be noted that although the adjacency pairs' theory has been developed mainly for a two interlocutor's model, the speaker and the hearer, of spoken discussions, it can also be extended to multi-party online conversations especially when ignoring the adjacency constraint.

Adjacency pairs have been considered very useful in providing organization for conversations. Therefore after the first part of a pair has been identified, it is expected for the second part of the pair to follow. This provides a conversational flow and allows the speakers to determine what types of utterances should follow in order to have a coherent talk (Schegloff & Sacks, 1973). The authors have used adjacency pairs to study the closing of two-party telephone conversations and have reached the conclusion that the closing parts of any conversations are more complex that a simple exchange of *good-byes*. Thus, any conversation may have pre-closing elements (such as asking the interlocutor if everything is clear, if he is not busy at the moment, etc.), but may also initiate a closing sequence and then return to on-topic discussion if agreed by the two interlocutors. Table 4 shows an example of a closing of a chat conversation with 5 participants that has been preceded by a pre-closing and a return to topic and summary of the discussion. In the right column are shown implicit links that can be discovered by making use of adjacency pairs. It can easily be noted that most of the pairs respect the adjacency constraint, but there are several (adjacency) pairs of utterances that have other utterances intermixed between them.

Adjacency pairs can be closely related to dialog acts, because many of the pairs are formed by specific types of dialog acts (e.g. *greeting-greeting, question-answer, proposal-acceptance*). This is one of the main reasons why some corpora that have been manually annotated with dialog acts have also been annotated with adjacency pairs: for example the ICSI meeting recorder dialog act (MRDA) corpus (Shriberg, Dhillon, Bhagat, Ang, & Carvey, 2004). In this context, adjacency pairs have been labelled independently of the type of the pair, therefore only the utterances that define an adjacency pair can be identified without specifying the type of that pair. However, by using the information related to the dialog acts annotations for each utterance involved in the pair, it is possible to determine the type of the underlying adjacency pair as well. As the MRDA corpus contains multi-party discussions, several remarks that are also applicable for chat conversations have been made during the annotation process (Dhillon, Bhagat, Carvey, & Shriberg, 2004):

- Any two utterances involved in an adjacency pair must be produced by different speakers and may not be successive in the conversation.
- Each utterance may be involved in more than a single adjacency pair. The most frequent example is that an utterance that acts as a second part of a given pair may also represent a first part for a subsequent pair.
- Some adjacency pair parts may be continued over several consecutive utterances issued by the same participant.
- Sometimes there may be multiple speakers involved in some adjacency pair part. Usually, this happens for the second part (e.g. several answers for a question), but there are cases where the first part may be composed by several utterances issued by different speakers.

In a similar manner, adjacency pairs can be linked to relationships between specific argumentation acts, especially for linking claims, rebuttals and qualifiers to claims.

Adjacency pairs could be extracted automatically from a large corpus of utterances labelled with dialog acts by computing the frequency of adjacent dialog act bigrams. This approach has been used for a set of tutorial dialogues labelled with only 8 different types of dialog acts and several statistically significant dependent adjacency pairs have been discovered, for example: evaluation question followed by positive feedback, grounding followed by grounding, question followed by statement, etc. (Boyer et al., 2009). This information has been used later to build a hidden Markov model (HMM) together with its transition probabilities for the educational conversations that were analyzed.

Interactions Based on Semantic Similarity

The previous sections demonstrate that the semantic similarity or relatedness between utterances holds an important position in detecting coherence (such as adjacency pairs of arguments) and cohesion (such as lexical chains). On the other hand, semantic relatedness between proximal words is one of the characteristics of the context in most coherent discourses, revealing the meaning of any word. Therefore, semantics in linguistics is related to determining the meaning or interpretation of any occurrence of a lexical item. In any language, genre or discourse a word's true meaning can only be understood in its context, as it may interconnect with other meanings specific to that given language, genre or discourse.

"A meaning only reveals its depths once it has encountered and come into contact with another, foreign meaning: they engage in a kind of dialogue, which surmounts the closedness and one-sidedness of these particular meanings" (Bakhtin, 1986, p. 7) [emphasis added].

Table 4. Example of closing a chat conversation with 5 participants and of implicit links corresponding to adjacency pairs

302	do we covered everything?	Corina	
303	i think so	Diana	LINK TO 302
304	let's see....	Mona	LINK TO 302
305	at leat most of it	Diana	LINK TO 303
306	we talked about meetings	Mona	LINK TO 304
307	advertising our products	Mona	
	... [after pre-closing, a summary follows]		
312	I agree	Cristi	LINK TO 312
313	and communication in the company	Diana	
314	yes..forum and chat in this case	Corina	LINK TO 313
	...		
328	did we miss something?	Corina	
329	i don't think so	Stefan	LINK TO 328
330	it's important to have a real team	Mona	
331	i think most of the activities are covered	Mona	LINK TO 328
332	so... this is it...	Mona	
333	yes, we talked about most of them and even if we did not reach a conclusion every time we did a really good job	Diana	LINK TO 328
334	we must use all the technologies in order to be a succesfull company	Mona	
335	true and we also need to find the perfect balance between them	Diana	
336	and most importnat of all, me must know when to use each of them	Mona	
337	true! So once again we have the same conclusion!	Corina	LINK TO 337
338	yes!	Mona	LINK TO 337
339	So, good job, team! ;) It was really nice talking to you	Mona	
340	okay then! we stop here for tonight! nice chat!:)	Corina	LINK TO 339
341	good night all!	Mona	LINK TO 340
342	good night to everyone	Cristi	LINK TO 341
343	ok...good night then:)	Diana	LINK TO 342
344	good night	Stefan	LINK TO 343

The problem of understanding and assessing the semantic information underlying in any spoken or written discourse has been widely researched from the beginnings of the Artificial Intelligence research. Although various methods have been proposed for solving this problem, there is no consensus about the most suitable one even in our days. In this context, there is a need to employ a diversity of techniques for assessing the semantic relatedness of words and phrases. A first differentiation between the various methods would be to classify them in "*strong*" semantics and "*weak*" semantics. The strong semantics techniques rely on linguistic rules similar to the one available for syntax (Miller & Isard, 1963) or on general, domain and discourse ontologies (Ciccarese et al., 2008). Especially with the expansion of the Semantic Web, several general or upper level ontologies, such as CYC (Matuszek, Cabral, Witbrock, & Deoliveira, 2006), SUMO (Niles & Pease, 2001) or DOLCE (Gangemi, Guarino, Masolo, & Oltramari, 2003) have been developed – they are also used for discourse processing (Noy, 2004). Moreover, discourses specific to a particular theme may benefit from domain ontologies used to improve the semantic information from the upper level ontologies. However, during the last two decades other methods for computing the relatedness of words have been developed starting from exploiting the proximity information available in the large volumes of discourse, especially texts. These methods may be called weak semantics because they do not define any underlying semantic model between the words, but rather exploit the probability distribution and the statistics of two words co-appearing together in a given discourse unit (adjacent words, sentence, paragraph, document, etc.). As the strong AI methods for semantics need a knowledge base or an ontology developed by specialists (e.g. linguists, domain experts, etc.) they are also called *knowledge-based methods*. On the other hand, the statistical "weak AI" semantic models only require a large volume of corpora in order to compute the relatedness of any two words and are therefore known as *corpus-based methods*.

Semantic relatedness between words has been investigated since the early days of AI, when the ideas of semantic memories and spreading activation in networks were initially developed. Semantic similarity is a special case of semantic relatedness that involves the use of a constrained set of relation types in ontologies or taxonomies, such as synonyms and IS-A relationships. Adhering to this definition, *car* and *bicycles* are semantically similar, while *car* and *gasoline* are just semantically related although they appear to be "semantically closer" for a human than the previous example (Resnik, 1995).

Knowledge-based methods primarily use lexical resources built by linguists, such as dictionaries, thesauri and lexical ontologies (Budanitsky &

Hirst, 2006). The use of dictionaries, such as the Longman Dictionary of Contemporary English (LDOCE), or thesauri, as the Roget-structured thesauri, provides the simplest knowledge-based methods for computing similarity between words by turning these resources into simple networks through the use of headwords in LDOCE or categories and indexes in Roget thesauri. A simple method for computing the semantic relatedness of two words based solely on their lexicon definitions is the Lesk measure defined for word sense disambiguation (Lesk, 1986) that is proportional to the number of common words in the two definitions. However, the most used resources for computing the semantic similarity or relatedness are defined for ontologies. Most of them have been especially constructed for the linguistic ontology or lexical database WordNet (Miller, 1995) and make use of the different types of relations defined in it: synonyms, antonyms, related words, hypernyms, hyponyms, meronyms and halonyms. The most used measures for computing the semantic relatedness between two concepts using these methods have been defined by Hirst and St Onge (1998), Jiang and Conrath (1997), Resnik (1995), and Lin (1998). All these measures obtained a good correlation coefficient with human judgements of pair-wise word similarity, ranging between 0.7 and 0.8 (Budanitsky & Hirst, 2006). Nevertheless, none of these measures can be said to surpass the others independent of the test corpus. A similar conclusion has been reached on a larger German corpus; the only difference is that the correlation coefficient had a much lower value, between 0.4 and 0.5 depending on the measure (Cramer & Finthammer, 2008).

On the other hand, corpus-based methods process large amounts of corpora and then make use of the words' distributions and co-appearances in a given unit of analysis (utterance, paragraph, whole document, web page, etc.). One point of particular interest is that these methods return different results depending on the corpora used for training or for computing the statistics. This way semantic relatedness in different domains (or on different topics and even on different genres of discourse) can be computed by choosing the right input documents. On the other hand, using a sufficiently large corpus of general texts one can determine the semantic relatedness regardless of the topic. The simplest measure is the Pointwise Mutual Information (PMI) adapted from Information Retrieval (IR) and from Kullback-Leibler's divergence measure in statistics. When using all the web pages indexed by Google for computing it, PMI has been extended to provide the Normalized Google Distance (NGD) (Cilibrasi & Vitanyi, 2007). LSA (Deerwester, Dumais, Furnas, Landauer, & Harshman, 1990) is a technique that uses singular value decomposition (SVD) and principal component analysis (PCA) in order to reduce the dimensionality of the term-doc matrix. Thus, after performing SVD on the term-doc matrix (X), the dimensionality of the diagonal matrix composed of the singular values is reduced to contain only the most important k elements (largest singular values, with k usually between *200 .. 1000*) thus allowing us to approximate the term-doc matrix in a reduced dimensional space. The reduced dimensionality space is also called the *latent semantic space* and may be used to compute the similarity between words, word sets and texts by applying some transformations and then using the cosine similarity for the newly resulted vectors (Landauer & Dumais, 1997). Other more recent methods for computing semantic relatedness using large corpora are Latent Dirichlet Allocation (LDA), which uses a probabilistic graphical model for representing a mixture of topics (Blei, Ng, & Jordan, 2003), probabilistic LSA (Girolami & An, 2003) and Explicit Semantic Analysis (ESA), which uses Wikipedia articles to build interpretation vectors consisting of the words in each article (Gabrilovich & Markovitch, 2007). ESA has been shown to have a much better correlation with human annotated similarities than other

knowledge and corpus based methods, reaching values above 0.75.

Assessing the semantic relatedness between utterances in multi-party online conversations is a very important factor for determining implicit links between them and for constructing discussion threads. However, in order to have a good evaluation of the degree of semantic relatedness between two utterances, knowledge-based methods for general linguistic ontologies should be combined with corpus-based methods, which can be aimed more at identifying domain specific proximity between concepts. Knowing the pairwise similarity between any two words, one can easily compute the semantic similarity of two utterances or any two portions of text (Mihalcea, Corley, & Strapparava, 2006).

FUTURE RESEARCH DIRECTIONS

At this moment, the inter-animation framework is a novel methodology proposed to analyze online conversations by detecting all different interactions that arise between utterances. While some of them are available explicitly in the discussion, most of them are implicit and need to be detected automatically. This is a very difficult task as it needs to encompass coherence-based methods (such as RST or coherence relations) and cohesion-based methods (e.g. semantic cohesion) from computational linguistics, together with elements specific to conversation analysis (for example, adjacency pairs). Thus, the most important future research direction is to design and implement a system that is built starting from the inter-animation framework. This section describes one of the first such systems and the most complex one existing at this time to our knowledge.

In order to implement a software for discourse analysis based on the inter-animation framework presented in the previous sections, several difficult NLP problems need to be tackled. PolyCAFe

(Rebedea, Dascalu, Trausan-Matu et al., 2010; Rebedea et al., 2011) is a solution that was built on the proposed framework in order to provide a computational perspective of collaboration and of participants' involvement in the chat joint discourse of students involved in CSCL activities. Starting from the explicit and implicit links among utterances, the conversation graph is constructed by connecting utterances and, in some cases, words. In this graph, discussion threads are also identified and by exploiting all these data several measures for evaluating the contribution to the conversation are computed for each participant and for the group as a whole.

Implicit links are automatically identified by means of repetitions, lexical chains, pairs of speech and argumentation acts, semantic similarity and coreferences (Rebedea et al., 2011). In the resulted directed and acyclic graph, each utterance is a node and the weights of edges are given by the interaction strength between the two interconnected utterances mainly based on a semantic similarity score. The orientation of each edge follows the timeline of the chat and the evolution of the discussion in time. Starting from this graph, in a simplistic approach that can be extended, a discussion thread can be identified as a sequence of explicitly or implicitly inter-linked utterances.

The evaluation of the importance of each utterance is centered on a marking process which intertwines 3 perspectives: a *quantitative* one inspired from traditional information retrieval, a *qualitative* dimension based on Latent Semantic Analysis (LSA) and a *social perspective* derived from social network analysis (SNA) applied on the conversation graph. The results for the individual utterances are then used to offer an assessment of each participant in the conversation.

Moreover, starting from the perspective that knowledge advancement can be achieved as a community rather than as individual achievement, the concept of *gain* transposes in our computational approach both personal and collaborative knowledge building. Gain expresses the cognitive

input of each utterance in the overall discourse by taking into consideration its punctual importance (mark) and future impact (echo). The natural way of achieving the split between inner and collaborative knowledge building is by considering the interlocutors within a discussion thread. Therefore, if interlinked (explicitly or implicitly) utterances have the same speaker, we consider that information is derived from self-experience and by continuing internal thoughts. On the other hand, if interlinked utterances have different participants, collaborative gain is identified in the interchange of ideas and knowledge between participants. The degree of collaborative discourse assesses how well these ideas inter-animate each other and how collaborative gain supports the discussion by integrating perspectives from different participants.

A first verification experiment of software was undertaken with 35 senior year students that were enrolled in the Human-Computer Interaction course. The students were grouped into 7 teams of 5 students that had to engage in the following debate using a chat environment: "Which is the best collaboration tool on the Web: wiki, blog, chat, forum or wave?" The resulted chat conversations had between 250-600 utterances and were assessed by 2 or 4 tutors to rank the participants according to the importance they had in the conversation, taking into account both the content of their utterances and their involvement and degree of collaboration with the other participants. Therefore, for each participant of a conversation a rank from 1 to 5 was assigned by each tutor. For experimental and pedagogical reasons, each student was also asked to rank the other participants in his/her conversation using scores from 1 to 4, thus excluding themselves. An example of rankings received from students, tutors and the system is presented in Table 5.

The results of this experiment show that the system achieves a good precision and correlation with the average tutor score: 77% and 94% respectively. In this case the average difference between the tutor score and the system score is of only 0.23 ranks per participant. Table 6 summarizes the correlation and precision between the students, tutors and system.

To conclude, the first results of using Poly-CAFe for the analysis of online chat conversation with multiple participants show that the system is able to assess the level of the participants with a high degree of confidence and its results are highly correlated with the results of the tutors (for a test group of 35 students). We consider that the usage of the inter-animation framework that allows us to build a conversation graph is an important factor for achieving these results. Only after constructing the graph, the system is able to determine the value of an utterance in the context of its own discussion thread. Moreover, the implicit links discovered by the system permit the usage social network analysis techniques on the conversation graph. Thus, we are able to determine participants and utterances that are central to the conversation.

Online conversations with multiple participants are textual artefacts built collaboratively, by linking each utterance to one or more of the previous utterances. An utterance that is not linked in any form to any other utterance would not be considered part of the same discourse. The inter-animation framework has many benefits for processing online textual interactions because it proposes to exploit the links between utterances in order to understand the context of each utterance. The system presented in this section uses state of the art NLP technologies in order to detect as many of the implicit links mentioned in the previous section as possible. Nevertheless, several improvements are still necessary in order to make the analysis more powerful:

1. *Provide a more complex theoretical model*, especially by identifying the best way to compute the interaction strength between each pair of utterances. This way the construction of the conversation graph shall be better specified and the detection of the discussion threads from the graph will be

improved. At this moment, the interaction strength is computed using the semantic cohesion determined using LSA, combined with lexical chains built upon WordNet. All the implicit links discovered using repetitions of relevant concepts from the conversation, adjacency pairs and coreferences are considered to have a maximum strength.

2. *Improve the detection of implicit links* by examining in much more detail how these links arise in online conversations. In order to solve this problem, researchers need to manually annotate chat conversations and discussion forums with implicit links and their types (repetition, cohesion-mainly, coherence-mainly, adjacency pair, etc.) in

Table 5. Example of ranking the participants to a chat conversation by their colleagues, the tutors and the system

Rank	Stud1	Stud2	Stud3	Stud4	Stud5
Stud1	-	2	3	1	4
Stud2	2	-	3	1	4
Stud3	2	3	-	1	4
Stud4	1	2	3	-	4
Stud5	1	2	4	3	-
Stud avg.	2	3	4	1	5
Tutor1	4	1	5	2	3
Tutor2	4	2	5	1	3
Tutor avg.	4	1-2	5	1-2	3
System	4	2	5	1	3

Table 6. Comparison overview of the average rankings provided by tutors, students and the system

Rank	Correlation	Precision	Average distance
Tutors – System	0.94	77%	0.23
Students – System	0.84	66%	0.43
Tutors - Students	0.84	71%	0.40

order to improve the detection process by making use of statistical machine learning. Having these corpora shall also allow the comparison of different methods for detecting implicit links on the same data.

3. *Identify other applications* of the inter-animation theory in other domains beside computer supported education. In our opinion, online discussion forums and other communication technologies should provide better mechanisms to automatically detect the implicit links between a new post and older ones. Moreover, social network analysis, information retrieval and recommender systems would benefit from using the inter-animation framework to improve the number of links between users and pages.

CONCLUSION

Starting from Bakhtin's notions of inter-animation, it can be shown that any discourse holds a high degree of intertextuality. By using these elements in the context of multi-party online conversations, we have suggested that the detection of implicit links in conversations corresponds to detecting interactions between utterances. This task is very important for determining the different discussion threads and for conversation disentanglement. Moreover, interactions between utterances modelled through implicit links are a good starting point for assessing the degree of inter-animation and collaborative discourse in a conversation, the importance of a turn in a specific thread by making use of the conversation graph – the most important element of the inter-animation framework for online conversation analysis presented in this chapter.

However, in order to discover the interactions between utterances, several computational linguistics theories and elements have to be taken into consideration. As a first step it is useful to determine the label of each utterance (such as dialog acts and argumentation acts). Then, the subsequent step involves a pair-wise comparison between utterances in order to assess their cohesion and coherence, using an analysis on several linguistic layers: lexical, semantic, discourse and prosodic. Although not all the elements presented in this chapter can be used in a system for automatic identification of implicit links due to the technical limitations in today's NLP systems, they are theoretically sound and useful for providing a clear and complete view of the proposed framework.

We have also build PolyCAFe – a system that uses the inter-animation framework for analysing multi-party online chat conversations. It identifies implicit links between utterances based on repetitions, lexical chains, adjacency pairs based on dialog and argumentation acts, semantic similarity, and coreferences. Using the conversation graph built with the implicit links, each utterance is analyzed within its own context – the discussion thread that it is part of. The first results of using the system for assessing the participants in the conversations are quite encouraging as it achieves a high correlation with the human annotators.

REFERENCES

Adar, E., Zhang, L., Adamic, L. A., & Lukose, R. M. (2004). *Implicit structure and the dynamics of blogspace.* Paper presented at the Workshop on the Weblogging Ecosystem, 13th World Wide Web Conference (WWW2004), New York, NY.

Allen, J., & Core, M. (1997). *Draft of DAMSL: Dialog act markup in several layers.* Philadelphia, PA: University of Pennsylvania.

Aumayr, E., Chan, J., & Hayes, C. (2011). *Reconstruction of threaded conversations in online discussion forums.* Paper presented at the Fifth International Conference on Weblogs and Social Media - AAAI ICWSM 2011.

Austin, J. L. (1962). *How to do things with words.* Cambridge, MA: Harvard University Press.

Bakhtin, M. M. (1981). *The dialogic imagination: Four essays.* Austin, TX: University of Texas Press.

Bakhtin, M. M. (1986). *Speech genres and other late essays.* Austin, TX: University of Texas Press.

Barthes, R. (1974). *S/Z* (Miller, R., Trans.). Farrar, Straus & Giroux.

Barzilay, R., & Elhadad, M. (1997). *Using lexical chains for text summarization.* In Proceedings of the ACL Workshop on Intelligent Scalable Text Summarization, Madrid, Spain.

Blei, D. M., Ng, A. Y., & Jordan, M. I. (2003). Latent dirichlet allocation. *Journal of Machine Learning Research, 3,* 993–1022.

Boyer, K. E., Phillips, R., Ha, E. Y., Wallis, M. D., Vouk, M. A., & Lester, J. C. (2009). *Modeling dialogue structure with adjacency pair analysis and hidden Markov models.* Paper presented at the Human Language Technologies: The 2009 Annual Conference of the North American Chapter of the Association for Computational Linguistics.

Budanitsky, A., & Hirst, G. (2006). Evaluating WordNet-based measures of lexical semantic relatedness. *Computational Linguistics, 32*(1), 13–47. doi:10.1162/coli.2006.32.1.13.

Cherny, L. (1999). *Conversation and community: Chat in a virtual world.* Stanford, CA: CSLI Publications.

Ciccarese, P., Wu, E., Wong, G., Ocana, M., Kinoshita, J., & Ruttenberg, A. et al. (2008). The SWAN biomedical discourse ontology. *Journal of Biomedical Informatics, 41*(5), 739–751. doi:10.1016/j.jbi.2008.04.010.

Cilibrasi, R. L., & Vitanyi, P. M. B. (2007). The Google similarity distance. *IEEE Transactions on Knowledge and Data Engineering, 19*(3), 370–383. doi:10.1109/TKDE.2007.48.

Cramer, I., & Finthammer, M. (2008). *An evaluation procedure for word net based lexical chaining: Methods and issues.* Paper presented at the Global WordNet Conference 2008, Szeged, Hungary.

Deerwester, S., Dumais, S. T., Furnas, G. W., Landauer, T. K., & Harshman, R. (1990). Indexing by latent semantic analysis. *Journal of the American Society for Information Science American Society for Information Science, 41*(6), 391–407. doi:10.1002/(SICI)1097-4571(199009)41:6<391::AID-ASI1>3.0.CO;2-9.

Dhillon, R., Bhagat, S., Carvey, H., & Shriberg, E. (2004). *Meeting recorder project: Dialog act labeling guide.*

Donath, J. (2002). A semantic approach to visualizing online conversations. *Communications of the ACM, 45*(4), 45–49. doi:10.1145/505248.505271.

Dong, A. (2004). *Quantifying coherent thinking in design: A computational linguistics approach.* Paper presented at the Design Computing and Cognition 2004.

Dong, A. (2006). Concept formation as knowledge accumulation: A computational linguistics study. *Artificial Intelligence for Engineering Design, Analysis and Manufacturing, 20*(1), 35–53. doi:10.1017/S0890060406060033.

Elsner, M., & Charniak, E. (2008). You talking to me? A corpus and algorithm for conversation disentanglement. In *Proceedings of the 2008 Meeting of the Association for Computational Linguistics (ACL 2008)* (pp. 834-842). Columbus, OH.

Elsner, M., & Charniak, E. (2010). Disentangling chat. *Computational Linguistics, 36*(3), 389–409. doi:10.1162/coli_a_00003.

Gabrilovich, E., & Markovitch, S. (2007). *Computing semantic relatedness using Wikipedia-based explicit semantic analysis.* Paper presented at the 20th international joint conference on Artifical intelligence.

Galley, M., McKeown, K., Fosler-Lussier, E., & Jing, H. (2003). *Discourse segmentation of multiparty conversation.* In *Proceedings of the 41st Annual Meeting on Association for Computational Linguistics - Volume 1.*

Gangemi, A., Guarino, N., Masolo, C., & Oltramari, A. (2003). Sweetening WORDNET with DOLCE. *AI Magazine, 24*(3), 13–24.

Girolami, M., & An, A. K. (2003). *On an equivalence between PLSI and LDA.* Paper presented at SIGIR 2003.

Grosz, B. J., Weinstein, S., & Joshi, A. K. (1995). Centering: A framework for modeling the local coherence of discourse. *Computational Linguistics, 21*(2), 203–225.

Halliday, M. A. K., & Hasan, R. (1976). *Cohesion in English.* London, UK: Longman.

Hirst, G., & St Onge, D. (1998). *Lexical chains as representation of context for the detection and correction malapropisms. WordNet: An electronic lexical database (Language, Speech, and Communication).* Cambridge, MA: The MIT Press.

Jiang, J. J., & Conrath, D. W. (1997). Semantic similarity based on corpus statistics and lexical taxonomy. *CoRR.*

Khan, F. M., Fisher, T. A., Shuler, L., Wu, T., & Pottenger, W. M. (2002). *Mining chat-room conversations for social and semantic interactions.*

Koschmann, T. (1999). *Toward a dialogic theory of learning: Bakhtin's contribution to understanding learning in settings of collaboration.* Paper presented at the Computer Support for Collaborative Learning (CSCL'99), Palo Alto.

Kristeva, J. (1980). *Desire in language: A semiotic approach to literature and art.* New York, NY: Columbia University Press.

Kumar, R., Mahdian, M., & McGlohon, M. (2010). *Dynamics of conversations.* Paper presented at the 16th ACM SIGKDD international conference on Knowledge discovery and data mining.

Landauer, T. K., & Dumais, S. T. (1997). A solution to Plato's problem: The Latent Semantic Analysis theory of acquisition, induction and representation of knowledge. *Psychological Review, 104*(2), 211–240. doi:10.1037/0033-295X.104.2.211.

Landow, G. (2001). Hypertext and critical theory. In Trend, D. (Ed.), *Reading digital culture* (pp. 98–108). Oxford, UK: Blackwell Publishers.

Lesk, M. (1986). *Automatic sense disambiguation using machine readable dictionaries: How to tell a pine cone from an ice cream cone.* Paper presented at the 5th annual international conference on Systems documentation.

Levinson, S. C. (1983). *Pragmatics.* Cambridge: Cambridge University Press.

Lin, D. (1998). *An information-theoretic definition of similarity.* Paper presented at the Fifteenth International Conference on Machine Learning.

Manabu, O., & Takeo, H. (1994). *Word sense disambiguation and text segmentation based on lexical cohesion.* Paper presented at the 15th conference on Computational linguistics - Volume 2.

Mann, W. C., & Thompson, S. A. (1987). *Rhetorical structure theory: A theory of text organization.* Los Angeles, CA: University of Southern California, Information Sciences Institute.

Matuszek, C., Cabral, J., Witbrock, M., & Deoliveira, J. (2006). *An introduction to the syntax and content of Cyc.* Paper presented at the 2006 AAAI Spring Symposium on Formalizing and Compiling Background Knowledge and Its Applications to Knowledge Representation and Question Answering.

McDaniel, S. E., Olson, G. M., & Magee, J. C. (1996). *Identifying and analyzing multiple threads in computer-mediated and face-to-face conversations.* Paper presented at the 1996 ACM conference on Computer supported cooperative work.

Mihalcea, R., Corley, C., & Strapparava, C. (2006). *Corpus-based and knowledge-based measures of text semantic similarity.* Paper presented at the 21st national conference on Artificial intelligence - Volume 1.

Miller, G. A. (1995). WordNet: A lexical database for English. *Communications of the ACM, 38*(11), 39–41. doi:10.1145/219717.219748.

Miller, G. A., & Isard, S. (1963). Some perceptual consequences of linguistic rules. *Journal of Verbal Learning and Verbal Behavior, 2*(3), 217–228. doi:10.1016/S0022-5371(63)80087-0.

Morris, J., & Hirst, G. (1991). Lexical cohesion computed by thesaural relations as an indicator of the structure of text. *Computational Linguistics, 17*(1), 21–48.

Muhlpfordt, M., & Wessner, M. (2005). *Explicit referencing in chat supports collaborative learning.* Paper presented at the Proceedings of the 2005 Conference on Computer support for collaborative learning: learning 2005: The next 10 years!

Nelson, T. H. (1965). *Complex information processing: A file structure for the complex, the changing and the indeterminate.* Paper presented at the Proceedings of the 1965 20th national conference.

Nelson, T. H. (1981). *Literary machines: The report on, and of, project xanadu concerning word processing, electronic publishing, hypertext, thinkertoys, tomorrow's intellectual revolution, and certain other topics including knowledge, education and freedom.* Self-published.

Niles, I., & Pease, A. (2001). *Towards a standard upper ontology.* Paper presented at the international conference on Formal Ontology in Information Systems - Volume 2001.

Noy, N. F. (2004). Semantic integration: A survey of ontology-based approaches. *SIGMOD Record, 33*(4), 65–70. doi:10.1145/1041410.1041421.

Ogura, K., Ishizaki, M., Nishimoto, K., Negoita, M., Howlett, R., & Jain, L. (2004). A method of extracting topic threads towards facilitating knowledge creation in chat conversations. Knowledge-based intelligent information and engineering systems (Vol. 3213, pp. 330-336). Springer Berlin/Heidelberg.

Park-Fuller, L. M. (1986). Voices: Bakhtin's heteroglossia and polyphony, and the performance of narrative literature. *Literature and Performance, 7*(1), 1–12. doi:10.1080/10462938609391621.

Rebedea, T., Dascalu, M., Trausan-Matu, S., Armitt, G., & Chiru, C. (2011). Automatic assessment of collaborative chat conversations with PolyCAFe. In EC-TEL 2011 - Towards ubiquitous learning (Vol. Lecture Notes in Computer Science, pp. 299-312). Berlin: Springer Verlag.

Rebedea, T., Dascalu, M., Trausan-Matu, S., Banica, D., Gartner, A., Chiru, C., & Mihaila, D. (2010). Overview and preliminary results of using PolyCAFe for collaboration analysis and feedback generation. In M. Wolpers, P. Kirschner, M. Scheffel, S. Lindstaedt, & V. Dimitrova (Eds.), Sustaining TEL: From innovation to learning and practice (Vol. 6383, pp. 420-425). Springer Berlin/Heidelberg.

Resnik, P. (1995). *Using information content to evaluate semantic similarity in a taxonomy.* Paper presented at the Proceedings of the 14th international joint conference on Artificial intelligence - Volume 1.

Rezende, F., & Castells, M. (2010). Interanimation of voices and argumentative strategies in collaborative knowledge building of physics teachers in an asynchronous discussion group. *Revista Electrónica de Enseñanza de las Ciencias, 9*(2).

Sanders, T. J. M., Spooren, W. P. M., & Noordman, L. G. M. (1992). Toward a taxonomy of coherence relations. *Discourse Processes, 15*(1), 1–35. doi:10.1080/01638539209544800.

Schegloff, E. A., & Sacks, H. (1973). Opening up closings. *Semiotica, VIII*(4), 289–327.

Scott, P., & Mortimer, E. (2005). Meaning making in high school science classrooms: A framework for analysing meaning making interactions. In Boersma, K., Goedhart, M., Jong, O., & Eijkelhof, H. (Eds.), *Research and the quality of science education* (pp. 395–406). Springer. doi:10.1007/1-4020-3673-6_31.

Shen, D., Yang, Q., Sun, J.-T., & Chen, Z. (2006). *Thread detection in dynamic text message streams.* Paper presented at the Proceedings of the 29th annual international ACM SIGIR conference on Research and development in information retrieval.

Shriberg, E., Dhillon, R., Bhagat, S., Ang, J., & Carvey, H. (2004). *The ICSI meeting recorder dialog act (MRDA) corpus.* Paper presented at the Proceedings of the 5th SIGdial Workshop on Discourse and Dialogue.

Silber, H. G., & McCoy, K. F. (2002). Efficiently computed lexical chains as an intermediate representation for automatic text summarization. *Computational Linguistics, 28*(4), 487–496. doi:10.1162/089120102762671954.

Simpson, J. (2005). Conversational floors in synchronous text-based CMC discourse. *Discourse Studies, 7*(3), 337–361. doi:10.1177/1461445605052190.

Smith, M., Cadiz, J. J., & Burkhalter, B. (2000). *Conversation trees and threaded chats.* Paper presented at the Proceedings of the 2000 ACM conference on Computer supported cooperative work.

Spiegel, D. (2001). *Coterie: A visualization of the conversational dynamics within IRC.* Massachusetts Institute of Technology.

Suthers, D., Dwyer, N., Medina, R., & Vatrapu, R. (2010). A framework for conceptualizing, representing, and analyzing distributed interaction. *International Journal of Computer-Supported Collaborative Learning, 5*(1), 5–42. doi:10.1007/s11412-009-9081-9.

Suthers, D. D., Lund, K., Rose, C., Dyke, G., Law, N., Teplovs, C., et al. (2011). *Towards productive multivocality in the analysis of collaborative learning.* Paper presented at the 9th International Conference on Computer-Supported Collaborative Learning (CSCL 2011).

Trausan-Matu, S., & Rebedea, T. (2009). Polyphonic inter-animation of voices in VMT. In Stahl, G. (Ed.), *Studying virtual math teams* (pp. 451–473). New York: Springer. doi:10.1007/978-1-4419-0228-3_24.

Trausan-Matu, S., & Rebedea, T. (2010). A polyphonic model and system for inter-animation analysis in chat conversations with multiple participants. In Gelbukh, A. (Ed.), *Computational linguistics and intelligent text processing* (*Vol. 6008*, pp. 354–363). Springer. doi:10.1007/978-3-642-12116-6_29.

Trausan-Matu, S., Rebedea, T., & Dascalu, M. (2010). Analysis of discourse in collaborative learning chat conversations with multiple participants. In Tufis, D., & Forascu, C. (Eds.), *Multilinguality and interoperability in language processing with emphasis on Romanian* (pp. 313–330). Editura Academiei.

Trausan-Matu, S., Rebedea, T., Dragan, A., & Alexandru, C. (2007). Visualisation of learners' contributions in chat conversations. In Fong, J., & Wang, F. L. (Eds.), *Blended learning*. Addison-Wesley.

Trausan-Matu, S., Stahl, G., & Sarmiento, J. (2007). Supporting polyphonic collaborative learning. *e-Service Journal, 6*(1), 59-74.

Wang, Y.-C., Joshi, M., Cohen, W., & Rose, C. P. (2008). *Recovering implicit thread structure in newsgroup style conversations*. Paper presented at the International Conference on Weblogs and Social Media, Seattle, Washington.

Wegerif, R. (2006). A dialogic understanding of the relationship between CSCL and teaching thinking skills. *International Journal of Computer-Supported Collaborative Learning, 1*(1), 143–157. doi:10.1007/s11412-006-6840-8.

Wegerif, R. (2008). Dialogic or dialectic? The significance of ontological assumptions in research on educational dialogue. *British Educational Research Journal, 34*(3), 347–361. doi:10.1080/01411920701532228.

ADDITIONAL READING

Booth, W. C. (1984). Introduction. In Emerson, C. (Ed.), *Mikhail Bakhtin, problems of Dostoevsky's Poetics* (Emerson, C., Trans.). Minnesota: University of Minnesota Press.

Dascalu, M., Rebedea, T., & Trausan-Matu, S. (2010). A deep insight in chat analysis: Collaboration, evolution and evaluation, summarization and search. In *Proceedings of the 14th International Conference on Artificial intelligence: Methodology, Systems, and Applications* (Vol. LNCS 6304, pp. 191-200). Varna, Bulgaria: Springer-Verlag.

Foucault, M. (1972). *The archaeology of knowledge*. New York: Pantheon Books.

Galley, M., McKeown, K., Hirschberg, J., & Shriberg, E. (2004). *Identifying agreement and disagreement in conversational speech: Use of Bayesian networks to model pragmatic dependencies*. Paper presented at the 42nd Annual Meeting on Association for Computational Linguistics.

Hobbs, J. R. (1990). Topic drift. In Dorval, B. (Ed.), *Conversational organization and its development* (pp. 3–22). Norwood, NJ: Ablex Publishing.

Honeycutt, L. (1994). *What hath Bakhtin wrought? Toward a unified theory of literature and composition*. The University of North Carolina at Charlotte.

Johnstone, B. (1987). An introduction. *Perspectives on Repetition - Text, 7*(3), 205-214.

Joshi, M., & Rose, C. P. (2007). *Using transactivity in conversation summarization in educational dialog*. Paper presented at the SLaTE Workshop on Speech and Language Technology in Education.

Manning, C. D., & Schütze, H. (1999). *Foundations of statistical natural language processing*. Cambridge, MA: MIT Press.

Moser, M., & Moore, J. D. (1996). Toward a synthesis of two accounts of discourse structure. *Computational Linguistics, 22*(3), 409–419.

North, S. (2007). 'The voices, the voices': Creativity in online conversation. *Applied Linguistics, 28*(4), 538–555. doi:10.1093/applin/amm042.

Pedersen, T., Patwardhan, S., & Michelizzi, J. (2004). *WordNet: Similarity: Measuring the relatedness of concepts*. Paper presented at the Demonstration Papers at HLT-NAACL 2004.

Piwek, P., & Stoyanchev, S. (2011). *Data-oriented monologue-to-dialogue generation*. Paper presented at the 49th Annual Meeting of the Association for Computational Linguistics: Human Language Technologies: short papers - Volume 2.

Sanders, T., Spooren, W., & Noordman, L. (2009). Coherence relations in a cognitive theory of discourse representation. *Cognitive Linguistics*, *93*(217).

Searle, J. R. (1969). *Speech acts: An essay in the philosophy of language*. Cambridge: Cambridge University Press. doi:10.1017/CBO9781139173438.

Searle, J. R. (1976). A classification of illocutionary acts. *Language in Society*, *5*(1), 1–23. doi:10.1017/S0047404500006837.

Shrestha, L., & McKeown, K. (2004). *Detection of question-answer pairs in email conversations*. Paper presented at the 20th international conference on Computational Linguistics.

Stavrianou, A. (2010). *Modeling and mining of web discussions*. Université Lumire Lyon 2.

Taboada, M. T. (2004). *Building coherence and cohesion: Task-oriented dialogue in English and Spanish*. John Benjamins Publishing Company.

Tannen, D. (1989). *Talking voices: Repetition, dialogue, and imagery in conversational discourse*. Cambridge, UK: Cambridge University Press.

Toulmin, S. E. (1958). *The uses of argument*. University Press.

van Eemeren, F. H., & Grootendorst, R. (1984). *Speech acts in argumentative discussions: A theoretical model for the analysis of discussions directed towards solving conflicts of opinion*. Foris Publications. doi:10.1515/9783110846089.

Wang, L., & Oard, D. W. (2009). *Context-based message expansion for disentanglement of interleaved text conversations*. Paper presented at the Human Language Technologies: The 2009 Annual Conference of the North American Chapter of the Association for Computational Linguistics.

Wermter, S., & Löchel, M. (1996). *Learning dialog act processing*. Paper presented at the 16th conference on Computational linguistics - Volume 2.

Zitzen, M., & Stein, D. (2004). Chat and conversation: A case of transmedial stability? *Linguistics*, *42*(5), 983–1021. doi:10.1515/ling.2004.035.

KEY TERMS AND DEFINITIONS

Computer-Supported Collaborative Learning: Learning theory that advocates the advantages of social interaction using a computer and its technologies, especially for communication and enhanced interaction.

Conversation Analysis: The multitude of discourse analysis theories and techniques that can be used for analyzing written or spoken conversations. Most of them make use of other elements than just the text or transcript of the discussion.

Conversation Graph: A graph built for any conversation where the utterances are the vertices and the edges are denoted by the implicit links between two utterances. This graph is directed and acyclic and can be thought as a multi-graph as an utterance can respond to any number of previous ones.

Dialogism: Related to inter-animation, dialogism considers that each utterance exists in response to previous ones and exist only for being responded to. Bakhtin considers that dialogism is a fundamental characteristic of human speech, writing and though.

Implicit Links: Any interaction between two utterances in a (online) discussion that has not been pointed out explicitly by its issuer and that can be detecting by analyzing merely the text of the conversation.

Inter-Animation: The complex interactions between different utterances, with other utterances influencing the current one and struggling for being used by future utterances, as echoes or overtones.

Online Conversation Analysis: Conversation analysis adapted for online conversations, especially the ones built by a multitude of participants: instant messaging, chat rooms, online forums, microblogging, article comments and reviews, social network updates and discussions. Although other elements can be used for the analysis (such as timestamps, usernames, etc.), the most important element is the textual artefact that is collaboratively built.

Chapter 5
Using Multimodal Discourse Analysis to Identify Patterns of Problem Solving Processes in a Computer–Supported Collaborative Environment

Shannon Kennedy-Clark
Australian Catholic University, Australia

Kate Thompson
University of Sydney, Australia

ABSTRACT

Recently, there have been calls to undertake deeper analyses of learner interactions in collaborative computer-supported environments, analyses that move beyond code and count, in order to understand collaboration from multiple viewpoints. In this chapter, two analytical approaches are presented, analyzing and interpreting the same conversational data from learners sharing a computer to solve a virtual inquiry. It is proposed that through the combined use of group function analysis and discourse analysis perspectives, a deeper understanding of how learners interacted on both macro and micro levels can be gained. The patterns of successful and non-successful problem solving are established and, from this, factors that may contribute to goal attainment or non-attainment are outlined.

INTRODUCTION

The proliferation of technologies designed to provide learners with an immersive and enriched learning environment presents new challenges for practitioners in understanding the behavior of learners. In parallel, the ability to collect complex datasets (including audio, video and screen capture, for example) means that researchers have the information to answer these complex questions. What is needed is a process of visualizing and analyzing multiple sources of data, from complex

DOI: 10.4018/978-1-4666-4426-7.ch005

instances of learning. Given the progress in the theories of how and what people learn, particularly in fields such as the learning sciences, what is needed is to draw from traditionally opposing perspectives to establish a more systematic approach to understanding these complex learning environments. In order to appropriately answer questions at this level, complex analytical procedures, with multiple coding schemes (Evans, Feenstra, Ryon, & McNeill, 2011) and theoretical frameworks (Suthers et al., 2011) need to be applied. Knowledge of learners' behavior while using innovative tools can inform the design of the tools as well as the tasks.

In research that examines technology-mediated learning, more traditional forms of measurement, such as pre-and post-tests, surveys and interviews, have provided the base data (Barab et al., 2009; Jacobson, Lim, Lee, & Low, 2007; Ketelhut & Dede, 2006). These studies provide minimal information about the *processes* of learning, what learners are doing, saying and responding to in an immersive environment. Reporting on the processes of collaboration and the development of theory and methods of analysis has seen this area develop in the last five years. Reporting on *multiple* measures of process using group decision making and discourse analysis in computer supported collaborative learning (CSCL) is becoming more common (van Aalst, 2009; Evans et al., 2011; Weinberger & Fischer, 2006). One advantage of the use of multiple measures is the ability to report on interaction effects (Weinberger & Fischer, 2006) and relationships between data at different levels, particularly individual contributions to group processes (Ding, 2009). Discussion of how best to analyze and describe the relationship between the individual processes of learning within a collaborative process is ongoing (Friend Wise, Hsiao, Marbouti, Speer, & Perera, 2012; Clara & Mauri, 2010). However, it is generally agreed upon that there is an interaction between the individual, small group, and meso levels of collaboration (Goodyear, Jones & Thompson, forthcoming).

The use of Systemic Functional Linguistics (SFL) has been prominent in computational linguistics as a means of analyzing text-based corpora. In this area, there has been a growing interest in the role of features of language, such as modality, negation and cue words, which complement the already robust body of theoretical studies in this area (Gravano, Hirschberg, & Beňuš, 2012; Moreante & Sporleder, 2012). As Moreante and Sporleder (2012, p. 223) explain, the "emergence of this area is a natural consequence of the consolidation of areas that focus on the computational treatment of propositional aspects of meaning, like semantic role labeling, and a response to the need for processing extra-propositional aspects of meaning as a further step towards text understanding."

In this chapter, the research team's experiences capturing and analyzing patterns of student learning are described, as the data are reinterpreted through the administration of different coding systems and visual representations. The aim is to present an understanding of different levels of the conversations that acknowledges both the macro scale of group goal solving and the micro scale of word choice. By combining data about what students are doing in terms of their interaction with the tool with their discourse, this aspect of the context of their conversation is able to be taken into account. This in turn affects the way the data is visualized, how it is analyzed, and what new research questions are generated.

BACKGROUND

The term *discourse* is applied in a range of different but interrelated ways in social and linguistic research. *Discourse* can be applied to the structure of a particular text; it can be applied to different types of language used in different topic areas, such as political discourse; it can be applied to the style of the speaker, such as native speaker discourse; the gender of a speaker, such as heterosexual discourse; or the purpose of the speaker, such as tourist discourse (Baker, 2006). It should be noted that, for some linguists, the term includes both spoken and written texts, whilst for others spoken language is *discourse* and written language is *text* (Jackson & Stockwell, 2011; Martin & Rose, 2007). In this chapter, discourse will refer to spoken language.

Discourse analysis uses the tools of grammarians to identify the role of words and utterances within a text and the tools of social theorists to explain the meanings (Martin & Rose, 2007). In SFL, there are three general social functions of language use: to enact social relationships, to represent our experiences, and to organize our enactments and representations as a meaningful text (Martin & Rose, 2007). In this sense the discourse is situated within the context of the social activity and the analysis of the grammar is situated within the context of the discourse.

Considerable progress has been made in examining the processes of collaboration, in particular in terms of the importance of time and order. Much of the research on processes of collaboration has examined both synchronous (Ding, 2009) and asynchronous collaboration (Friend Wise & Chiu, 2011), but few address both (Thompson & Kelly, 2012). Theoretical frameworks such as argumentation (Ding, 2009), knowledge building (Schrire, 2006) and decision-making (Reimann, 2009) have been addressed, and measurement of processes by content analysis is common (DeWever, Schellens, Valcke, & van Keer, 2006). In this study, data were collected that allowed the use of content analysis in order to identify decision making and macro- and micro- patterns of discourse, as well as data generated from students' interactions with

the virtual world, in order to incorporate action into the dialogue.

The ability to collect complex datasets, such as audio, video and screen capture, that describe collaborative learning environments provides opportunities to better understand the processes involved in learning. In order to appropriately analyze this data, complex frameworks, with multiple coding schemes (Evans et al., 2011), and theoretical frameworks (Suthers et al., 2011) need to be applied. Tools are being developed to facilitate this process (Dyke et al., 2011), but the field, and the concept, is still nascent. Multiple coding of complex datasets needs to be both focused, using targeted additions of coding, (Weinberger & Fischer, 2006) and broad, beyond one theoretical framework (Suthers et al., 2011).

A number of authors have investigated group decision making in relation to group processes and temporality (Kapur, 2011; Reimann, 2009). The advantages of studying the processes of interaction in CSCL research are regularly discussed and the links with learning outcomes often made (Cox, 2007). Jeong and Chi (2007) studied student self-learning behaviors in asynchronous learning environments for adult learners: their analysis revealed that successful students had more linear learning behaviors that remain consistent across different models. A good deal of research into group decision support systems has shown that groups with a well-designed computer tool have enhanced processing abilities compared to unsupported groups (Poole & Holmes, 1995). It has, however, also been argued that the groups with the additional support and scaffolding may not be able to make use of the resources (Choy, Wong, & Gao, 2008; Markauskaite, 2007).

Less commonly reported is an analysis and discussion of the processes of interaction with the *tool* used for learning (Thompson & Reimann, 2010) and very few studies have examined how collective dyad dynamics can impact upon a learning experience (Sawyer, 2006). Reporting on multiple measures of process is becoming more common (van Aalst, 2009; Evans et al., 2011; Weinberger & Fischer, 2006). One advantage of the use of multiple measures is the ability to report on interaction effects (Weinberger & Fischer, 2006) and on the relationships between data at different levels, particularly individual contributions to group processes (Ding, 2009).

The use of commercial games and virtual worlds in education has garnered ongoing attention due to the number of studies that have demonstrated increased learner engagement and motivation in subjects that are typically difficult to teach. For example, studies in *River City*, a Multi User Virtual Environment (MUVE) developed by Harvard University to help students learn scientific inquiry skills, have consistently shown increased learner motivation (Dede, Clarke, Ketelhut, Nelson, & Bowman, 2005; Ketelhut, 2007; Ketelhut, Clarke, & Nelson, 2010). Other long term studies, such as those conducted using *Quest Atlantis*, have demonstrated that participants are motivated to engage with quests beyond their classroom showing long-term engagement in the world and the development of learner communities (Barab et al., 2009; Barab, Thomas, Dodge, Carteaux, & Tuzun, 2005). The problem of engagement and motivation of learners has been recognized as a factor faced by many institutions (Gee, 2005) and the use of games is viewed as a way to engage and motivate students (Watson, Mong, & Harris, 2011). However, as research on these environments becomes more substantial, new avenues for investigating how students can, potentially, learn in these environments are being articulated.

As the use of educational games becomes more widespread, research is moving beyond engagement and motivation and focusing more on how students learn and how to design activities to support measurable learning in virtual and game based environments. For example, recent studies have shown that games and virtual environments can support and reinforce learning, support higher order thinking, and enable collaboration (de Freitas & Oliver, 2006; de Freitas & Neumann, 2009). Studies by Gill and Dalgarno (2008) and Kennedy-Clark (2011) have focused on educator professional development in the design of learning activities and the use of virtual worlds in the classroom. Moving beyond this, there are examples of studies that have investigated learner processes. Wouters, van Oostendorp, Boonekamp, and van der Spek (2011) analyzed learners' knowledge organization when using a serious game with either verbal or structural assessments. Others have investigated how people collaborate in these environments. Echeverría et al. (2011) found that the social dynamic afforded by collaboration may impact positively on learning outcomes. Keating and Sunakawa (2010) conducted an investigation into how gamers manage two spatial environments for participation, and they proposed the notion of participation cues as useful for explaining how gamers achieve this dual mastery. Research conducted by Thompson, Kennedy-Clark, Markauskaite and Southavilay (2011) analyzed the patterns of collaboration that dyads developed to solve virtual inquiries. These investigations do not present conclusive results from long term studies, but rather show that inroads are being made into how researchers can analyze learners' behavior while they are engaged in these environments in order to understand how the environments, learning activities and assessments might be designed to support student learning.

In this chapter, data from two dyads collaborating in a virtual environment are examined and the results from previously reported studies addressing group and social functions of the dyads are also described for context. The main purpose of doing so is to determine the overlap between these two areas. In making sense of the overlap, the representations of different levels of coded data are presented. Ways to represent and report on data that has been coded and analyzed in multiple ways are still being explored (Ding, 2009); here, representations of periodicity and word arcs are examined as two possibilities. By representing the data in these ways, new avenues of analysis have opened up. The chapter concludes with the results of the combination of the analyses and recommendations for further studies.

METHODOLOGY

This research study was conducted in a scenario-based virtual environment. A scenario or narrative-based virtual world is founded on a story or narrative and information is built into the environment (Barab et al., 2009). The key features of a scenario-based virtual environment include a) an avatar that represents the participant, b) a 3D virtual environment, c) the ability to interact with artifacts and agents, d) opportunities for participants to communicate with other participants synchronously and, in some instances, communicate with intelligent agents and e) a "real world" or a simulated context to provide an authentic experience that a student may not be able to encounter in a classroom environment (Barab et al., 2009; Ketelhut et al., 2010; Squire, Barnett, Grant, & Higginbottom, 2004; Taylor, 2003). This study involves undergraduate and postgraduate students.

Research Design

Multimodal analysis enables researchers to examine many of the areas that could affect student learning, for example, the inquiry process, the learning materials, navigation around the virtual world, and collaboration. By addressing all these separately, and then bringing our knowledge together, researchers have a better understanding of how the elements of students' learning interact, and affect the behavior of learners over time.

When considering the analysis of multimodal discourse around a piece of technology, questions as to what *can* be recorded need to be addressed. Ideally, the interaction between all participants would be recorded in a way that allows easy identification of the speaker, and potentially with the ability to collect information about eye movement (Nüssli, Jermann, Sangin, & Dillenbourg, 2009) or affect (Alzoubi, D'Mello, & Calvo, 2012). Automatic capture of clicks on the screen through data logging within the tool is also essential for efficient analysis, and when collected in combination with data about the context through video screen shots, is ideal.

Coding Schemes

The choice of a coding scheme ties the research question to a particular theoretical stance. In doing so, only one element of learning is addressed, and the reasons for this selection should be articulated. The two coding schemes selected for use in this case study are discussed.

A modified version of the Decision Function Coding System (DFCS) developed by Poole and Holmes (1995) was adopted for the analysis of the collaborative problem solving.

The DFCS allows for problem definition, orientation and solution development (Table 1). Multiple types of data were collected through the use of Camtasia software, which allowed screen capture to be synchronized with interaction data between students and resulted in the modification of the DFCS to include implementation of the decisions made. Previous research has applied the DFCS to longer-term collaborative learning experiences (Reimann, Frerejean, & Thompson, 2009), and subsequent work has found that *implementation* only featured in more complex patterns of interaction (Thompson & Kelly, 2012). In this case study, the decisions were made and implemented immediately; this was felt to be an important addition to the patterns that were ob-

Table 1. Modified coding scheme for collaborative decision making

Category	Code	Definition
Problem definition	1	Statements that define or state the causes behind a problem Statements that evaluate problem analysis
Orientation	2	Statements that attempt to orient or guide the group's processes Statements that evaluate or reflect upon the group's progress or processes
Solution development		
Solution analysis	3a	Statements that concern criteria for the decision making process A direct reference to the solution must be given
Solution suggestions	3b	Suggestion of alternatives
Solution elaboration	3c	Statements that provide detail or elaborate on a previously stated alternative
Solution evaluation	3d	Statements that evaluate alternatives and give reasons, explicit or implicit for the evaluations and therefore include a valuation
Solution Confirmation	3e	Statements that ask for final group confirmation of the decision Statements that concern decisions linked to immediate results
Non task	4	Statements that do not have anything to do with the decision task
Agreement	5	Agreement – response to a question or statement e.g. yeah or yes
Disagreement	6	Disagreement – response to a question or statement e.g. nah or no
Implementation	7	Undertaking agreed upon action

served. It was expected that participants would engage in several decisions in order to come to this conclusion.

The use of discourse analysis has gained prominence as a method of analysis in technology enhanced learning due to the in-depth understanding of the interactions that can be revealed through the analysis of conversations (Gee, 1999; Keating & Sunakawa, 2010; Li & Lim, 2007; Mazur & Lio, 2004; Sawyer, 2006; Steinkuehler, 2006). Collaborative Process Analysis Coding Scheme (CPACS) was developed on the basis of coding systems used by Mazur (2004), Sawyer (2006), Nivre, Allwood, and Ahlsen (1999), and Soter, Wilkinson, Murphy, Rudge, Reninger, and Edwards (2008), and focused on features of speech and macro and micro elements of turn taking. It was hypothesized that rather than focusing on an analysis of the macro levels using a coding system, such as DFCS, as had been done in earlier analyses, a better understanding of what was happening in the conversations could be obtained by combining the macro elements of discourse (Poole & Holmes, 1995) with the micro or grammatical levels that are often the target of discourse analysis (Nivre et al., 1999).

CPACS codes for several systemic functional linguistics phenomena, such as those described by Halliday (1994) and elaborated upon by Martin and Rose (2007). CPACS functions on two levels (Table 2). At the macro level, the action code concerns goal identification and solution, and the content code covers the content of the utterance. At the micro level, the attitudinal code describes the type of attitude each utterance was taking towards the problem solving design; the tense is the marker of temporality; the modality is the degree of certainty; and pronouns relate to personal references.

Visualizations

Traditionally, process diagrams (Reimann, 2009; Kapur, 2011) have been used to represent this group

Table 2. Collaborative process analysis coding scheme (CPACS)

Macro Level		
Category	**Code**	**Definition**
Action	info	Introduce an idea or information
	add	Add information
	sup	Support previous ideas/agreement
	sum	Summarize
	chal	Challenge ideas / disagreement
	uncert	Uncertainty
	quest	Ask a question
	meta	Meta statement about the task or process
	imp	Implementation of agreed action
Content	phat	Social – phatics, salutations, leave taking
	plan	Planning
	topic	Topic
	task	Task
	nav	Navigation/direction
	OT	Off Task
Micro Level		
Category	**Code**	**Definition**
Attitudinal	p	Positive
	n	Negative
	z	Neutral
Tense	pt	Past
	pr	Present
	prc	Present continuous
	ft	Future
	nt	No tense
Modality	sm	Strong modality
	mm	Moderate modality
	wm	Weak/tentative modality
Pronouns	1	First person
	2	Second person
	3	Third person
	4	First person plural
	5	Second person plural
	6	Third person plural

function perspective. In this chapter, diagrams are presented that clarify the order in which events occurred. Two visualizations are provided that demonstrate the variance of sequence between the two dyads.

Markov transition diagrams and others that represent time and order were used. In addition, periodicity is addressed. Periodicity, according to Martin and Rose (2007), organizes discourse in waves of information at the scales of the text, phase, or paragraph, and clause. The wavelength is the spatial period of the wave, which is the distance over which the wave's shape repeats. In the case of our analysis, this wavelength is determined by considering the distance between consecutive corresponding points of the same phase of a problem, which are represented by crests and troughs. Here functions were allocated; a team that achieves true periodicity will display oscillation with the crest or peak of the wave representing the task. If the wave repeats itself, it is a periodic wave and is displaying oscillation (McPherson, 2009). Oscillation is the repetitive deviation, typically in time, of a measure about a central value between two or more different states. In this case it is the state between the identification of a goal and the implementation of a goal. It was predicted that many of a group's functions will result in behavior other than oscillation; these are not discussed in this paper. We have called the behavior of not being able to establish a wave *aperiodic* (McPherson, 2009), that is, a function that is not periodic.

In this respect, conversation arcs were generated. The construction of conversation arcs is related to the identification of similar words within a text. Conversation word arc diagrams exemplify the vocabulary similarities within a text document by drawing arcs connecting segments of a document that share similar vocabulary. This does not consider units such as articles and prepositions, but rather identifies content words, such as nouns.

The value of this is that researchers can identify if learners are returning to or repeating utterances in their problem solving.

CASE STUDY ANALYSIS: INQUIRY LEARNING IN A VIRTUAL WORLD

The MUVE used in this study was *Virtual Singapura*. *Virtual Singapura* was based on Harvard's *River City*. The virtual environment was designed to facilitate the learning of scientific inquiry skills. *Virtual Singapura* is set in 19th century Singapore and is based on historical information about several disease epidemics during that period. In order to create an authentic learning experience, 19th century artifacts from Singapore were included in the environment. These artifacts include historical 3D buildings and agents that represent different ethnic groups in Singapore at the time such as Chinese, Malay, Indian, and Europeans. Participants can also interact with intelligent agents based on actual residents of the city at that time.

Data were gathered through recording the in world actions of eight postgraduate and eight undergraduate education students in their interactions with *Virtual Singapura*. The participants undertook a virtual inquiry that focused on reducing cholera in the city. The participants completed their in world activity in pairs. The task took approximately 40 minutes to complete. The recordings provided three sources of information: audio, video and screen capture. The audio transcriptions were coded according to a modified version of the DFCS (Poole & Holmes, 1995) and CPACS (Kennedy-Clark & Thompson, 2011).

Two of the eight dyads were selected to present in this case study. Dyad 1 was unsuccessful, and did not reach a solution; Dyad 6 did reach a solution. Key elements of the multimodal discourse analysis of the processes involved are discussed. Some of this analysis has been previously reported in other studies, including an examination of the dyads' recall after their experiences (Kennedy-Clark & Thompson, 2011), a discussion of the group functions perspective using the modified decision function coding scheme, (Kennedy-Clark et al., 2011; Thompson et al., 2011), and a SFL perspective at the level of word choice (Kennedy-Clark & Thompson, 2013). These approaches are incorporated into the new framework of macro and micro levels, and the perspectives within each. In this respect, an examination of the crossover between the two levels is presented.

Macro-Level Discourse Analysis

The problem solving phases, or context, were examined with respect to periodicity. Periodicity is temporally constrained and shows the development or non-development of waves of conversation across a temporal axis. After coding the data

using CPACS, a visual pattern of the waves of conversation could be developed.

Figure 1 demonstrates the periodicity of the content code in Dyads 1 and 6. The excerpts presented here were taken between five to ten minutes into the virtual inquiry. Figure 1a is an example of aperiodic behavior. Other analyses showed that Dyad 1 was unable to implement a goal (Thompson et al., 2011). While it appears that their collaboration is forming waves, these oscillate between navigation, planning, phatics and the topic. At this point in their activity, they do not reach the peak of the wave (task). They also display rapid oscillations with numerous phatics. A close examination of their dialogue indicated that they used phatics as a means of reassurance when they reached an impasse (Kennedy-Clark & Thompson, 2011); they were unable to progress beyond these strategies to implement a goal. Figure 1b is an example of periodicity. This

Figure 1. Periodicity of content code

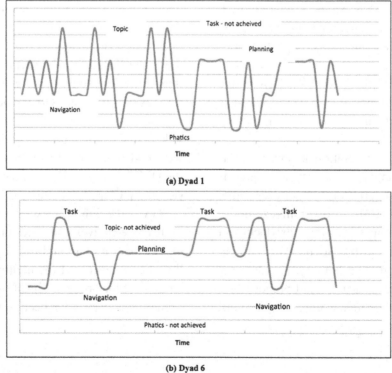

(a) Dyad 1

(b) Dyad 6

Figure 2. Distribution of CPACS content code over time (minutes)

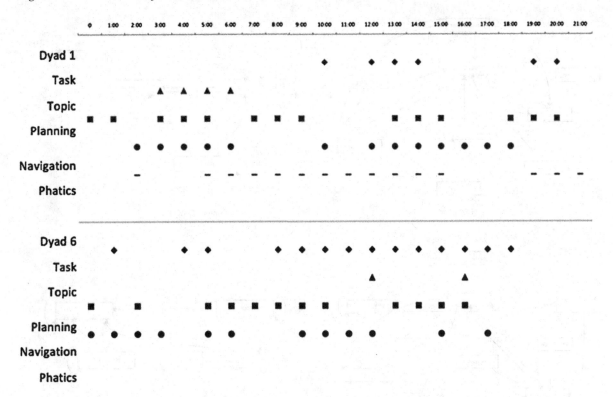

pattern demonstrates the strategies that Dyad 6 implemented in their virtual inquiry. It can be seen that they commenced the cycle with navigation before implementing a task, and then moved into a planning stage which was followed by a discussion on navigation before planning to complete a task. The rapid movement between planning task and navigation is demonstrated here. This example shows the development of periodicity. This was expanded to examine the patterns of the discussion of content through the whole collaboration.

If the content of the discussion throughout the exercise is examined first, different patterns can be seen (Figure 2). The students in Dyad 1 discussed all five areas of content, task, topic, planning, navigation and phatics, throughout the exercise, although topic was only discussed at the beginning and discussion about the task began towards the end of students' activity. Planning and navigation were referred to throughout the exercise. Dyad 1 discussed the topic and the task separately. Given the lack of overlap that can be

seen in Figure 2, it seems unlikely that Dyad 1 achieved periodicity in any part of their collaboration.

Dyad 6 also consistently discussed planning and navigation. Topic was discussed only towards the end of the collaboration, and for a relatively short amount of time. The main difference between the groups in terms of patterns in the content discussed is the discussion of the task itself, and the use of phatics. Dyad 6 began discussing the task very early and continued to address this content throughout the task. This visualization shows that when Dyad 6 discussed the topic, it was in the context of discussing the task. This group did not use phatics, and while phatics are an important part of collaboration, as they show understanding, support, acknowledgment, the lack of phatics does not appear to have had a negative impact upon this dyad's collaboration.

One of the advantages of this multimodal analysis is that it is possible to examine macro-level codes in parallel. A question addressed in previous

Figure 3. First order Markov transitions, DFCS and content (CPACS)

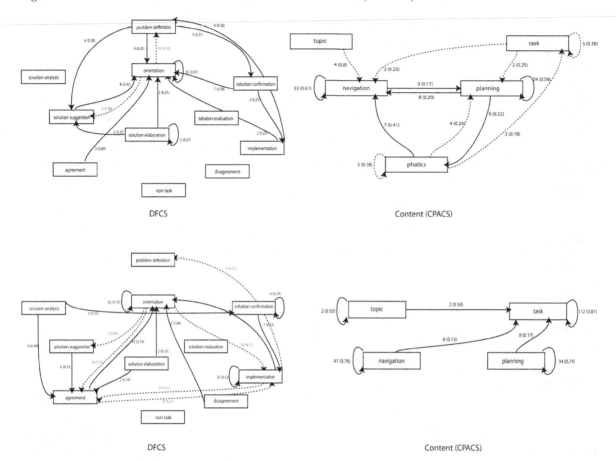

studies was whether a pattern, or multiple patterns, of decision-making indicative of successful collaboration could be identified (Kennedy-Clark et al., 2011; Thompson et al., 2011). To search for such a pattern DFCS was selected. Other coding schemes, such as those concerned with argumentation or negotiation, could also have been used to examine the data at the macro-level from alternate perspectives. First order Markov Models were applied to the coded conversation data for both decision making *and* content, and the following transition diagrams were produced. Figure 3a and Figure 3b were derived using first order Markov Models (Thompson et al., 2011).

Figure 3a shows the content and decision-making transition diagrams for Dyad 1. It is evi-

dent that *solution suggestion* played an important role in their decision-making process. *Solution suggestion* is a phase in decision making similar to brainstorming. Dyad 1 entered this phase after they initially *defined the problem*, as well as after *orienting* themselves, and after *solution elaboration*. *Implementation* was important in this group, with a return to *problem definition* or *orientation* after *implementation*. *Orientation* was also an important phase, with students returning to this after many of the other phases. When the transition diagram of their content is examined, it is evident that the students return to navigation and planning, rather than the task, and appear to transition between planning and other content areas. Dyad 1 was previously described as aperiodic, and this can be seen in the transition diagram, with many paths enacted to the different areas of content.

Figure 3b shows the macro-level transition diagrams for Dyad 6. In terms of decision-making, the importance of *simple agreement* is initially different to that of Dyad 1, as well as the many paths to and from *implementation*. When Dyads 1 and 6 are compared, it can be seen that the successful group also utilized *orientation* often. When the content is examined, the periodicity described earlier can be observed. This is seen in the high probabilities of this group to remain in one area, such as task, once they began. This figure also shows that in Dyad 6 all content areas return to task. What can be seen is that there is no immediate mapping between these two perspectives of the macro-level. The students' decision-making within each of the content codes was examined to see if the patterns were repeated.

Figures 4a and 4b show the presence of key categories of decision making within each area of content. The distribution of decision-making across the different content that the dyads were discussing is evident. In these Figures, x.1 is problem definition, x.2 orientation, x.3 solution development, x.4 non-task, x.5 simple agreement, x.6 simple disagreement, and x.7 implementation. If Dyad 1 is examined, it is evident that they rarely went through all expected steps in the decision-making process, regardless of the content about which they were discussing. In particular, the important agreement and implementation functions are only present when students are discussing the topic. In the transition diagrams (Figure 4a and 4b), only the overall pattern of decision-making could be examined. However, by employing this method of visualization it is evident that Dyad 6 went through the expected steps in their decision making process for planning, navigation, and the task (less so for the topic). The importance of implementation in the task from early on, and of agreement in all categories can be observed.

Micro-Level Discourse Analysis

Previous research examined participants' recall of their experience immediately after, and again after a period of six weeks (Kennedy-Clark & Thompson, 2011). It should be noted that the original scope of the studies was about how to reduce or control disease epidemics in Singapore in the 18th Century. Consequently, historical information was interwoven with the scientific data. During their interactions with the world, all of the groups responded to the visual information in the world. An analysis of the visual and audio recordings taken of the dyads indicated that they discussed characters, locations and tools, such as pictures, while they were in the world. The information that the students recalled immediately after their in-world activities was about the size of buildings, the use of wood as a building material, that there was no machinery, and that the diseases seemed to be more prevalent in different areas of the town as more people were sick in China Town than in European Town. Participants were emailed four to six weeks after their participation in order to ascertain what information they could recall from their use of *Virtual Singapura*. The information was mainly historical in nature, the science inquiry skills were not mentioned nor was the outcome of the problem, but visual information, such as the buildings and residents, was raised. It was concluded that the visual information had more salience to the participants than the scientific information.

It was decided that an examination of the frequency and location of words may identify why there was an emphasis on the physical description of the environment. Conversation word arcs were used to visualize the micro-level discourse because they enabled the identification of the frequency of word use. In this respect, a visual representation of the words that groups were using could be developed. Frequency data can provide an understanding of the dispersion of words through a

Figure 4. Decision-making divided by content area

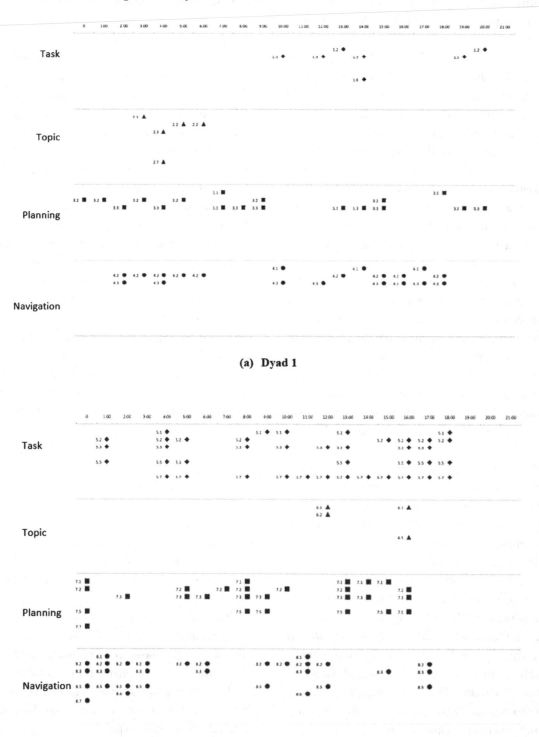

(a) Dyad 1

(b) Dyad 6

text and the social organization from a quantitative paradigm (Baker, 2006). In the following example, an extract has been taken from Dyads 1 and 6 to demonstrate how these two conversations can be visualized. Mid-section pieces of discourse were taken from the conversations (Figure 5).

The progression of the dyads can be demonstrated through these diagrams. Dyad 1 had less repetition of words and took longer to move through a goal. In Figure 5a it can be seen this dyad had two main goals during this excerpt. The first was to talk to an intelligent agent and the second was to get their avatar out of the water. In Figure 5b the speed of Dyad 6's interactions is evident. Repetition of terms included in our coding, such as [reading notes] indicate their continued focus on the task, while their use of 'yep' and 'okay' show the efficient decision-making process. Repetition of affirmations, such as yep and yeah, is consistent with other studies on games corpora. For example, in Gravano et al.'s (2012) study on games corpora they found that the participants made frequent use of affirmative cue words. These affirmative cue words included phrases, such as *alright, gotcha, huh, mm-hm, okay, right, uh-huh, yeah, yep, yes,* and *yup* account for 7.8% of the total words in the corpus. Reasons for using affirmations include agreement, stalling, back channeling and checking (Gravano et al., 2012).

These results show that the groups that were able to implement tasks tended to have clusters of arcs that showed their progression through the world (Kennedy-Clark & Thompson, 2013). For example, they would have clusters of data collection at the hospital or China Town. The simplicity of conversation arcs, both to develop and interpret,

means that they are an effective tool for educators, as group progress can be rapidly established. It was noted that physical locations were used as markers in the conversations to orient the dyads and this use of markers may explain why there was a better recall of the physical elements rather than the scientific details in the follow-up surveys.

The purpose of this is to confirm the patterns noted in the original analysis. Dyad 1 was unable to reach a solution, we have concluded, because of timing issues, even though they were developing effective processes of interaction. Their conversation word arc shows the longer amount of time it was actually taking them to find a solution, and move to the next problem.

Micro- Combined with Macro-Level Discourse Analysis

Previous analysis of this data using CPACS identified patterns for each code in each dyad (Kennedy-Clark & Thompson, 2011). Patterns identified across the groups are presented for the two Dyads in Table 3.

Dyad 1 was unsuccessful in reaching a solution; even though the materials given to this group were a hypothesis and a guided workbook. On analysis of their discourse, it can be seen that, given more time, they most probably would have reached a solution. This dyad produced a high number of utterances, and a relatively even split of utterances between the members of the dyad. On examination of their *action* discourse, it can be seen that they had a process for this category: they generated ideas. Their *content* discourse mainly focused on navigation. Dyad 1's attitude

Table 3. Identified group patterns

	Action	Content	Attitude	Tense	Modality	Pronouns
Dyad 1 (unsuccessful)	Idea generation	Navigation	Learner dependent	Past, present, future	Content dependent	Action dependent
Dyad 6 (successful)	Process – Cyclic	Plan, navigate, collect data	Neutral	Planning and reflecting	Context dependent	Context dependent

Figure 5. Visualization of conversation word arcs

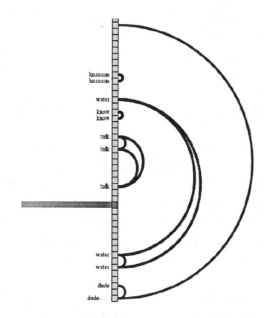

(a) Content arc of Dyad 1's interactions

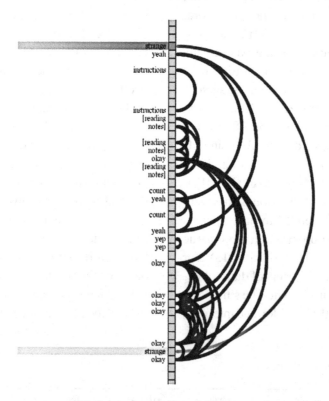

(b) Content arc of Dyad 6's interactions

was learner dependent, the modality was content dependent, and pronoun use was action dependent. The idea generation strategy was not as efficient as other strategies identified in the other dyads (Kennedy-Clark & Thompson, 2011).

Dyad 6 was provided with a workbook that did not contain guidance or a hypothesis: this pair was able to arrive at a problem solution. Dyad 6 had the highest number of recorded utterances of all of the dyads examined. The dyad identified roles, made joint decisions, took turns and negotiated a pathway. Dyad 6 developed a cyclic pattern to their activity, when their *content* was examined it revealed that they planned, navigated, and then collected the data they needed to answer the question. They planned their next activities on the basis of previous successes. Their evident confidence and sense of themselves (*modality*) was dependent on the context. This was a highly complex pattern of interaction, and they produced the highest number of utterances in order to reach a solution under the circumstances, in which they had minimal guidance. The qualitatively observed cyclic pattern was demonstrated in the data. Their conversation arcs were complex, showing rapid movement through the phases of work.

CASE STUDY CONCLUSIONS

The two dyads can generally be described on the basis of the analysis of their discourse and actions. Dyad 1 needed more time to develop and implement effective patterns of interaction. They returned to orient themselves in their decision-making, but did not cycle through agreement or have as many paths to implementing decisions (Figure 3a). When the identified group patterns are examined (Table 3), it is apparent that they focused on navigating through the world, and did not have time to discuss the task effectively (Figure 2), and when they did, their decision making lacked the

necessary elements to ensure that a solution was reached (Figure 4a). They did have ideas, but the micro levels of their discourse were not stable, dependent on the learner, context or action.

Dyad 6, by comparison, was able to achieve a cyclic pattern to their macro levels of collaboration: *action* (Table 3) and *decision-making* (Figure 3a). Decision-making was brought to orientation and agreement was sought often. Implementation played a large role in this process, particularly in the way they discussed the task (Figure 4a), and their micro level patterns were context dependent or stable. This group was successful in terms of their collaboration. Other patterns that separated them from Dyad 1 was the periodicity they achieved in discussing the content, and the thorough nature of their decision making *within* each area of content. This group was effective in making their way through the virtual world, with complex patterns of decision-making and content; supporting by relatively stable micro-level patterns of discourse.

The results suggest that helping students to develop routines for problem solving would be effective. However, this focus on orderly paths to convergence on goals is not consistent with the findings of Poole and Holmes (1995), who found that the orderliness of groups had no clear relationships to consensus to change in group decision making. They found that while a general ordering of activities may prove to be useful, a tight "micromanagement" of the discussion was not necessarily advantageous. This convergence on a goal occurs when students jointly construct understanding of the phenomenon (Kapur & Kinzer, 2009). It does appear that scaffolding of navigation would be particularly useful if it would allow students to concentrate on the task and the topic. However, further analysis to determine whether this was further related to student recall of information is needed. Additional analysis within levels, of individual and combined perspectives, as well as cross level analysis would add even greater depth to our understanding of the enactment of this task.

DISCUSSION

In this chapter, the findings of multimodal coding of discourse data; conversations around the scientific inquiry task that addressed group processes as well as systemic functional linguistics are presented. In doing so, representations of the data to aid in identification of overlap between the two levels of analysis were provided. From the analyses, it is evident that there are certain features of the patterns of decision-making that do appear to be representative of successful collaboration. Here, these features and the successes and challenges of using multiple forms of process analysis will be discussed and the chapter will conclude with a discussion of future research directions in the field.

Discussion of Methodology

The aim of this research was to present initial findings of multimodal coding of discourse data, in order to inform our understanding of group processes; conversations around a scientific inquiry task that addressed group processes as well as systemic functional linguistics. In doing so, representations of the data to aid in identification of overlap between the two levels of analysis were presented. Patterns of decision-making identified using the modified decision function coding scheme do appear to be representative of successful collaboration; however, it is time-consuming to implement, and at this stage, unlikely to be able to be automated. Real-time feedback to either instructors or students seems unlikely.

The representations of SFL were used to identify patterns that repeat at other levels of this data, as a first step in identifying potential indicators of group processes. While tools do exist that support this multimodal coding (Dyke et al.,

2011; Evans et al., 2011), at this initial stage of investigation, it is suggested that they do not offer the same flexibility when searching for patterns. Both representations presented have offered ideas for further research. Aspects of the periodicity figures roughly correlate with the presence of the implementation code in the modified DFCS, an important aspect of the decision-making process. More work needs to be done with regards to identifying other types of behavior, for example exponential, and subsequent correspondence to other group processes.

Conversation word arcs may be useful with regards to identification of repeating patterns. The complex, cyclical nature of Dyad 6's interactions with respect to the micro-level of the words is reflected in the higher level of their decision-making process and periodicity, whereas Dyad 1's word arc shows limited cycling through words, reflecting the limited nature of goal identification. Conversation word arcs may be a good indicator for management of collaborative learning environments. Conversation arcs are relatively easy to generate if transcriptions of conversations, such as online chat data, are on hand. Conversation arcs provide a potential resource for instructors to use in order to quickly ascertain the progression of their students.

By using multiple forms of complementary analysis we have been able to consolidate and confirm the research findings. By developing visualizations of the patterns of problem solving through the use of DFCS and CPACS we have been able to present representations of the conversations that have shown the frequency of behaviors and the changes over time. What this may offer for the design for learning is an understanding of how to scaffold the learning activity to support such changes in collaborative processes; the changes that occur as the groups progress through an activity in a dynamic learning environment, such as a virtual world. Enculturation to the environment and collaboration are both needed symbiotically, learners will need to develop a synergy between the two areas of problem solving and collaboration.

FUTURE RESEARCH DIRECTIONS

Research of this kind, which is used to determine what the discourse can tell us about the progress of students' learning as they interact with a tool, aims to inform further the design of tasks and tools. In particular, the data are examined for patterns to determine whether there are indicators of student progress. The micro-level perspectives of CPACS particularly lend themselves to automated data collection techniques. A framework which acknowledges such measures of progress, and is considered during the design of tasks and tools would be ideal. Correspondingly there is a need to collect real-time data to allow personalized feedback to students. In this sense, macro-level discourse analysis could be used to inform the redesign of the tasks and tools using a design research approach that centered on refining theory and design through ongoing cycles of iteration.

In addition to the impacts on design, the usefulness to instructors of such information on the progress of student work needs to be considered. Real-time feedback to instructors would also be useful. Work has been done around tools other than virtual worlds. Martinez, Yacef, Kay, and Schwendimann (2012) have developed a dashboard for use by instructors when students collaborate around a multi-tabletop learning environment. Tools such as this can help instructors manage the otherwise challenging task of monitoring students' work, troubleshooting, or assessing the input from members of a group. Further work to determine the usefulness of these perspectives, in particular to identify indicators of phases in a process, and the assessment of processes of collaboration around a virtual world is needed. There is also a need to investigate the impact of micro elements of speech, such as pronouns and modality, in combination with the use of tense markers to identify how students plan, organize and execute goals in order to identify patterns that support successful collaboration.

CONCLUSION

Multimodal discourse analysis did allow the research team to more fully understand the processes of learning for the two dyads that were examined in this chapter. Importantly, we were able to note key differences in both macro- and micro-levels of discourse analysis in a successful and unsuccessful group. Further work needs to be done to test and apply those differences in empirical work, and to determine further links. However, examining multiple levels and multiple perspectives did provide the research team with an understanding of the group problem solving processes.

At the conclusion of this chapter, it is acknowledged that one of the main inhibitors of research in this area is finding the nexus between methods of analysis and practical implications for classroom learning. Ultimately, the aim of the research is to be able to develop a set of design patterns to support developers and educators in designing pedagogically sound virtual environments, activities and materials to support collaborative learning in virtual and immersive environments. What our research has found is that by delving beneath the surface of the collaborations, beyond the pre-test post-test and interview data, that there is a complex interplay between the participants and the environment. In this respect, the findings of this study support the premise that for genuine learning to occur, participants need support beyond the task, to include their collaboration as well as in their mastery of the environment.

REFERENCES

Alzoubi, O., D'Mello, S. K., & Calvo, R. A. (2012). Detecting naturalistic expressions of nonbasic affect using physiological signals. *IEEE Transactions on Affective Computing, 3*(3), 298–310. doi:10.1109/T-AFFC.2012.4.

Baker, P. (2006). *Using corpora in discourse analysis.* London: Continuum International Publishing Group.

Barab, S. A., Dodge, T., Ingram-Goble, A., Volk, C., Peppler, K., & Pettyjohn, P. et al. (2009). Pedagogical dramas and transformational play: Narratively-rich games for education. In Lurgel, I. A., Zagalo, N., & Petta, P. (Eds.), *Interactive storytelling* (pp. 332–335). Berlin: Springer. doi:10.1007/978-3-642-10643-9_42.

Barab, S. A., Thomas, M., Dodge, T., Carteaux, R., & Tuzun, H. (2005). Making learning fun: Quest Atlantis, a game without guns. *Educational Technology Research and Development, 53*(1), 86–107. doi:10.1007/BF02504859.

Choy, D., Wong, A., & Gao, P. (2008). *Singapore's pre-service teachers perspectives in integrating information and communication technology (ICT) during practicum.* Paper presented at the AARE 2008. Retrieved from http://www.aare.edu.au/08pap/cho08326.pdf.

Clarà, M., & Mauri, T. (2010). Toward a dialectic relation between the results in CSCL: Three critical methodological aspects of content analysis schemes. *International Journal of Computer-Supported Collaborative Learning, 5*(1), 117–136. doi:10.1007/s11412-009-9078-4.

Cox, R. (2007). Technology-enhanced research: Educational ICT systems as research instruments. *Technology, Pedagogy and Education, 16*(3), 337–356. doi:10.1080/14759390701614470.

de Freitas, S., & Neumann, T. (2009). The use of 'exploratory learning' for supporting immersive learning in virtual environments. *Computers & Education, 52*(2), 343–352. doi:10.1016/j.compedu.2008.09.010.

de Freitas, S., & Oliver, M. (2006). How can exploratory learning with games and simulations within the curriculum be most effectively evaluated? *Computers & Education, 46*(3), 249–264. doi:10.1016/j.compedu.2005.11.007.

de Wever, B., Schellens, T., Valcke, M., & van Keer, H. (2006). Content analysis schemes to analyze transcripts of online asynchronous discussion groups: A review. *Computers & Education, 46*(1), 6–28. doi:10.1016/j.compedu.2005.04.005.

Dede, C., Clarke, J., Ketelhut, D. J., Nelson, B., & Bowman, C. (2005). *Fostering motivation, learning and transfer in multi-user virtual environments.* Paper presented at the American Educational Research Association. Retrieved from http://muve.gse.harvard.edu/rivercityproject/research-publications.htm#2005.

Ding, N. (2009). Visualizing the sequential process of knowledge elaboration in computer-supported collaborative problem solving. *Computers & Education, 52*, 509–519. doi:10.1016/j.compedu.2008.10.009.

Dyke, G., Lund, K., Jeong, H., Medina, R., Suthers, D. D., van Aalst, J., et al. (2011). *Technological affordances for productive multivocality in analysis.* In 9th International Conference on Computer Supported Collaborative Learning. CSCL2011: Connecting computer supported collaborative learning to policy and practice (pp. 454–461). Hong Kong, 4–8 July.

Echeverría, A., García-Campo, C., Nussbaum, M., Gil, F., Villalta, M., & Améstica, M. et al. (2011). A framework for the design and integration of collaborative classroom games. *Computers & Education, 57*(1), 1127–1136. doi:10.1016/j.compedu.2010.12.010.

Evans, M. A., Feenstra, E., Ryon, E., & McNeill, D. (2011). A multimodal approach to coding discourse: Collaboration, distributed cognition, and geometric reasoning. *International Journal of Computer-Supported Collaborative Learning*, *6*(2), 253–278. doi:10.1007/s11412-011-9113-0.

Friend Wise, A., & Chiu, M. M. (2011). *Knowledge construction patterns in online conversation: A statistical discourse analysis of a role-based discussion forum*. In 9th International Conference on Computer Supported Collaborative Learning. CSCL2011: Connecting computer supported collaborative learning to policy and practice (pp. 64-71). Hong Kong, 4–8 July.

Friend Wise, A., Hsiao, Y.-T., Marbouti, F., Speer, J., & Perera, N. (2012). Initial validation of "Listening" behavior typologies for online discussions using mircroanalytic case studies. In J. van Aalst, K. Thompson, M. J. Jacobson, & P. Reimann (Ed.), *The future of learning: Proceedings of the 10th International Conference of the Learning Sciences (ICLS 2012)* (Vol. 1, pp. 56-63). Sydney, Australia: International Conference of the Learning Sciences.

Gee, J. P. (1999). *An introduction to discourse analysis: Theory and method*. New York: Routledge & Kegan Paul.

Gee, J. P. (2005). Good video games and good learning. *Phi Kappa Phi Forum, 85*(2), 33-37.

Gill, L., & Dalgarno, B. (2008). *Influences on pre-service teachers' preparedness to use ICTs in the classroom*. Paper presented at the Hello! Where are you in the landscape of educational technology, ascilite., Melbourne.

Goodyear, P., Jones, C., & Thompson, K. (forthcoming). Computer-supported collaborative learning: Instructional approaches, group processes and educational designs. In Spector, M., Merrill, D., Elan, J., & Bishop, M. J. (Eds.), *Handbook of research on educational communications and technology*. Springer.

Gravano, A., Hirschberg, A., & Beňuš, Š. (2012). Affirmative cue words in task-oriented dialogue. *Computational Linguistics*, *38*(1), 1–39. doi:10.1162/COLI_a_00083.

Halliday, M. A. K. (1994). *Introduction to functional grammar*. London: Arnold.

Jackson, H., & Stockwell, P. (2011). *An introduction to the nature and functions of language* (2nd ed.). London: Continuum International Publishing Group.

Jacobson, M. J., Lim, S. H., Lee, J., & Low, S.-H. (2007). *Virtual Singapura: Design considerations for an intelligent agent augmented multi-user virtual environment for learning science inquiry*. 15th International Conference on Computers in Education.

Jeong, H., & Chi, M. (2007). Knowledge convergence and collaborative learning. *Instructional Science*, *35*(4), 287–315. doi:10.1007/s11251-006-9008-z.

Kapur, M. (2011). Temporality matters: Advancing a method for analyzing problem-solving processes in a computer-supported collaborative environment. *International Journal of Computer-Supported Collaborative Learning*, *6*(1), 39–56. doi:10.1007/s11412-011-9109-9.

Kapur, M., & Kinzer, C. K. (2009). Productive failure in CSCL groups. *International Journal of Computer-Supported Learning*, *4*(1), 21–46. doi:10.1007/s11412-008-9059-z.

Keating, E., & Sunakawa, C. (2010). Participation cues: Coordinating activity and collaboration in complex online gaming worlds. *Language in Society*, *39*(03), 331–356. doi:10.1017/S0047404510000217.

Kennedy-Clark, S. (2011). Pre-service teachers' perspectives on using scenario-based virtual worlds. *Computers & Education*, *57*, 2224–2235. doi:10.1016/j.compedu.2011.05.015.

Kennedy-Clark, S., & Thompson, K. (2011). Using game-based inquiry learning in the study of disease epidemics. *Journal of Virtual Worlds Research. History and Heritage in Virtual Worlds*, *6*(6), 1–25.

Kennedy-Clark, S., & Thompson, K. (2013). Between the lines: The use of discourse analysis in a virtual inquiry to inform learning design. *International Journal of Virtual and Personal Learning Environments*.

Kennedy-Clark, S., Thompson, K., & Richards, D. (2011). *Collaborative problem solving processes in a scenario-based multi-user environment*. In 9th International Conference on Computer Supported Collaborative Learning. CSCL2011: Connecting computer supported collaborative learning to policy and practice (pp. 706–710). Hong Kong, 4–8 July.

Ketelhut, D. J. (2007). The impact of student self-efficacy on scientific inquiry skills: An exploratory investigation in River City, a multi-user virtual environment. *Journal of Science Education and Technology*, *16*(1), 99–111. doi:10.1007/s10956-006-9038-y.

Ketelhut, D. J., Clarke, J., & Nelson, B. (2010). The development of River City, a multi-user virtual environment-based scientific inquiry curriculum: Historical and design evolutions. In M. J. Jacobson & P. Reimann (Eds.), Designs for learning environments of the future (pp. 89-110). New York: Springer Science + Business Media.

Ketelhut, D. J., & Dede, C. (2006). Assessing inquiry learning. Retrieved from *Harvard Graduate School of Education* http://muve.gse.harvard.edu/rivercityproject/documents/lettersnarst2006paper.pdf

Li, D., & Lim, C. P. (2007). Scaffolding online historical inquiry tasks: A case study of two secondary school classrooms. *Computers & Education*, *50*, 1394–1410. doi:10.1016/j.compedu.2006.12.013.

Markauskaite, L. (2007). Exploring the structure of trainee teachers' ICT literacy: The main components of, and relationships between, general cognitive and technical capabilities. *Educational Technology Research and Development*, *55*, 547–572. doi:10.1007/s11423-007-9043-8.

Martin, J. R., & Rose, D. (2007). *Working with discourse: Meaning beyond the clause* (2nd ed.). London: Continuum International.

Martinez, R., Yacef, K., Kay, J., & Schwendimann, B. (2012). *An interactive teacher's dashboard for monitoring multiple groups in a multi-tabletop learning environment. In Proceedings of Intelligent Tutoring Systems* (pp. 482–492). Springer.

Mazur, J. (2004). Conversation analysis for educational technologists: Theoretical and methodological issues for researching the structures, processes and meaning of on-line talk. In Jonassen, D. (Ed.), *Handbook of research for educational communications and technology*. New York: MacMillian.

Mazur, J., & Lio, C. (2004). *Learner articulation in an immersive visualization environment*. Paper presented at the Conference on Human Factors in Computing Systems, Vienna, Austria.

McPherson, A. (2009). *Introduction to macromolecular crystallography* (2nd ed.). New Jersey: Wiley-Blackwell. doi:10.1002/9780470391518.

Moreante, R., & Sporleder, C. (2012). Modality and negation: An introduction to the special issue. *Computational Linguistics*, *38*(2), 223–260. doi:10.1162/COLI_a_00095.

Nivre, J., Allwood, J., & Ahlsen, E. (1999). *Interactive communication management: Coding manual V1.0*. Gotyeborg University.

Nüssli, M., Jermann, P., Sangin, M., & Dillenbourg, P. (2009). Collaboration and abstract representations: Towards predictive models based on raw speech and eye-tracking data. *Proceedings of the 9th international conference on Computer supported collaborative learning* (pp.78-82). Rhodes, Greece, 8 - 13 June.

Poole, M. S., & Holmes, M. E. (1995). Decision development in computer assisted group decision making. *Human Communication Research*, *22*(1), 90–127. doi:10.1111/j.1468-2958.1995.tb00363.x.

Reimann, P. (2009). Time is precious: Variable- and event-centred approaches to process analysis in CSCL research. *International Journal of Computer-Supported Collaborative Learning*, *4*, 239–257. doi:10.1007/s11412-009-9070-z.

Reimann, P., Frerejan, J., & Thompson, K. (2009). Using process mining to identify models of group decision making in chat data. In C. O'Malley, D. Suthers, P. Reimann, & A. Dimitracopoulou (Eds.), *9ᵗʰ International Conference on Computer Supported Collaborative Learning (CSCL2009)* (pp. 98-107). Rhodes, Greece, 8-13 June 2009.

Sawyer, K. (2006). Analyzing collaborative discourse. In Sawyer, K. (Ed.), *The Cambridge handbook of the learning sciences* (pp. 187–204). Cambridge: Cambridge University Press.

Schrire, S. (2006). Knowledge building in asynchronous discussion groups: Going beyond quantitative analysis. *Computers & Education*, *46*, 49–70. doi:10.1016/j.compedu.2005.04.006.

Soter, A. O., Wilkinson, I. A., Murphy, P. K., Rudge, L., Reninger, K., & Edwards, M. (2008). What the discourse tells us: Talk and indicators of high-level comprehension. *International Journal of Educational Research*, *47*(6), 372–391. doi:10.1016/j.ijer.2009.01.001.

Squire, K. D., Barnett, M., Grant, J. M., & Higginbottom, T. (2004). *Electromagentism supercharged! Learning physics with digital simulation games*. Paper presented at the International Conference of the Learning Sciences. Retrieved from http://www.educationarcade.org/files/articles/Supercharged/SuperchargedResearch.pdf

Steinkuehler, C. A. (2006). Massively multiplayer online video gaming as participation in a discourse. *Mind, Culture, and Activity*, *13*(1), 38–52. doi:10.1207/s15327884mca1301_4.

Suthers, D. D., Lund, K., Rose, C., Dyke, G., Law, N., Teplovs, C., et al. (2011). *Towards productive multivocality in the analysis of collaborative learning*. Paper presented at the Connecting computer-supported collaborative learning to policy and practice.

Taylor, T. L. (2003). Multiple pleasures: Women and online gaming. *Convergence: The International Journal of Research into New Technologies*, *9*(1), 21–46. doi:10.1177/135485650300900103.

Thompson, K., & Kelly, N. (2012). *Processes of decision-making with adaptive combinations of wiki and chat tools*. In J. van Aalst, K. Thompson, M. J. Jacobson, & P. Reimann (Ed.), *The future of learning: Proceedings of the 10ᵗʰ International Conference of the Learning Sciences (ICLS 2012)* (Vol. 1, pp. 459-466). Sydney, Australia.

Thompson, K., Kennedy-Clark, S., Markauskaite, L., & Southavilay, V. (2011). Capturing and analysing the processes and patterns of learning in collaborative learning environments. In *9th International Conference on Computer Supported Collaborative Learning. CSCL2011: Connecting computer supported collaborative learning to policy and practice* (pp. 596–600). Hong Kong, 4–8 July.

Thompson, K., & Reimann, P. (2010). Patterns of use of an agent-based model and a system dynamics model: The application of patterns of use and the impacts on learning outcomes. *Computers & Education*, *54*(2), 392–403. doi:10.1016/j.compedu.2009.08.020.

van Aalst, J. (2009). Distinguishing knowledge-sharing, knowledge-construction, and knowledge-creation discourses. *International Journal of Computer-Supported Collaborative Learning, 4,* 259–287. doi:10.1007/s11412-009-9069-5.

Watson, W. R., Mong, C. J., & Harris, C. A. (2011). A case study of the in-class use of a video game for teaching high school history. *Computers & Education, 56,* 466–474. doi:10.1016/j.compedu.2010.09.007.

Weinberger, A., & Fischer, F. (2006). A framework to analyze argumentative knowledge construction in computer-supported collaborative learning. *Computers & Education, 46,* 71–95. doi:10.1016/j.compedu.2005.04.003.

Wouters, P., van Oostendorp, H., Boonekamp, R., & van der Spek, E. (2011). The role of game discourse analysis and curiosity in creating engaging and effective serious games by implementing a back story and foreshadowing. *Interacting with Computers, 23*(4), 329–336. doi:10.1016/j.intcom.2011.05.001.

ADDITIONAL READING

Amiel, T., & Reeves, T. C. (2008). Design-based research and educational technology: Rethinking technology and the research agenda. *Journal of Educational Technology & Society, 11*(4), 29–40.

Attasiriluk, S., Nakasone, A., Hantanong, W., Prada, R., Kanongchaiyos, P., & Prendinger, H. (2009). Co-presence, collaboration, and control in environmental studies. *Virtual Reality (Waltham Cross), 13*(3), 195–204. doi:10.1007/s10055-009-0130-5.

Banerjee, M. B., Capozzoli, M., McSweeney, L., & Sinha, D. (1999). Beyond kappa: A review of inter-rater agreement measures. *The Canadian Journal of Statistics, 27*(1), 3–23. doi:10.2307/3315487.

Barab, S. A., Dodge, T., Thomas, M. K., Jackson, C., & Tuzun, H. (2007). Our designs and the social agendas they carry. *Journal of the Learning Sciences, 16*(2), 263–305. doi:10.1080/10508400701193713.

Brown, A. L. (1992). Design experiments: Theoretical and methodological challenges in creating complex interventions in classroom settings. *Journal of the Learning Sciences, 2*(2), 141–178. doi:10.1207/s15327809jls0202_2.

Cobb, P., Confrey, J., diSessa, A., Lehrer, R., & Schauble, L. (2003). Design experiments in educational research. *Educational Researcher, 32*(1), 9–13. doi:10.3102/0013189X032001009.

Collins, A., Joseph, D., & Bielaczyc, K. (2004). Design research: Theoretical and methodological issues. *Journal of the Learning Sciences, 13*(1), 15–42. doi:10.1207/s15327809jls1301_2.

Confrey, J. (2006). The evolution of design studies as methodology. In Sawyer, R. K. (Ed.), *The Cambridge handbook of the learning sciences* (pp. 135–152). New York: Cambridge University Press.

Dede, C. (2004). Commentaries: If design-based research is the answer, what is the question? A commentary on Collins, Joseph, and Bielaczyc; diSessa and Cobb; and Fishman, Marx, Blumenthal, Krajcik, and Soloway in the JLS Special Issue on Design-Based Research. *Journal of the Learning Sciences, 13*(1), 105–114. doi:10.1207/s15327809jls1301_5.

Demo, D. A. (2001). *Discourse analysis for language teachers.* Online resources: Digests. Retrieved from http://www.cal.org/resources/Digest/0107demo.html

Dick, W., & Carey, L. (1996). *The systematic design of instruction* (4th ed.). New York, NY: Harper Collin.

Dick, W., Carey, L., & Carey, J. O. (2001). *The systematic design of instruction* (5th ed.). New York: Addison-Wesley Educational Publishers.

Edelson, D. C. (2002). Commentary: Design research: What we learn when we engage in design. *Journal of the Learning Sciences, 11*(1), 105–121. doi:10.1207/S15327809JLS1101_4.

Fishman, B., Marx, R. W., Blumenfeld, P., Krajcik, J., & Soloway, E. (2004). Creating a framework for research on systemic technology innovations. *Journal of the Learning Sciences, 13*(1), 43–76. doi:10.1207/s15327809jls1301_3.

Hecht, E. (1987). *Optics* (2nd ed.). Reading, Massachusetts: Addison Wesley.

Johnson, D. W., & Johnson, R. T. (2002). Learning together and alone: Overview and meta-analysis. *Asia Pacific Journal of Education, 22*(1), 95–105. doi:10.1080/0218879020220110.

Kali, Y., & Ronen-Fuhrmann, T. (2011). Teaching to design educational technologies. *The International Journal of Learning Technology, 6*(1), 4–23. doi:10.1504/IJLT.2011.040147.

McKenney, S., Nieveen, N., & van den Akker, J. (2006). Design research from the curriculum perspective. In Van den Akker, J., Gravemeijer, K., McKenney, S., & Nieveen, N. (Eds.), *Educational design research* (pp. 67–90). London: Routledge.

Merrill, M. (2002). First principles of instruction. *Educational Technology Research and Development, 50*(3), 43–59. doi:10.1007/BF02505024.

Mishra, P., & Koehler, M. J. (2006). Technological pedagogical content knowledge: A framwork for integrating technology in teacher knowledge. *Teachers College Record, 108*(6), 1017–1054. doi:10.1111/j.1467-9620.2006.00684.x.

Nevile, M., & Rendle-Short, J. (2009). A conversation analysis view of communication as jointly accomplished social interaction: An unsuccessful proposal for a social visit. *Australian Journal of Linguistics, 29*(1), 75–89. doi:10.1080/07268600802516392.

Plomp, T. (2007). Educational design research: An introduction. In T. Plomp & N. Nieveen (Eds.), *An Introduction to Educational Design Research.* Proceedings of the seminar conducted at the East China Normal University, Shangai (PR China), November 23-26, 2007 (pp. 9-33): SLO Netherlands institute for curriculum development.

Reeves, T. (2006). Design research from a technology perspective. In Akker, J. V. D., Gravemeijer, K., McKenney, S., & Nieveen, N. (Eds.), *Educational design research* (pp. 52–66). New York: Routledge.

Reeves, T. C., Herrington, J., & Oliver, R. (2005). Design research: A socially responsible approach to instructional technology research in higher education. *Journal of Computing in Higher Education, 16*(2), 97–116. doi:10.1007/BF02961476.

Reimann, P. (2010). Design-based research. In Markauskaite, L., Freebody, P., & Irwin, J. (Eds.), *Methodological choices and research designs for educational and social change: Linking scholarship, policy and practice* (pp. 37–50). New York: Springer.

Richards, D. (2006). *Is interactivity actually important?* Paper presented at the 3rd Australasian Conference on Interactive Entertainment (IE'2006). Murdoch University, Perth.

Seedhouse, P. (2005). Conversation analysis as research methodology. In Richards, K., & Seedhouse, P. (Eds.), *Applying conversation analysis.* New York: MacMillan.

Shaffer, D. W., & Gee, J. P. (2011). The right kind of GATE: Computer games and the future of assessment. In Mayrath, M., Robinson, D., & Clarke-Midura, J. (Eds.), *Technology-based assessments for 21st Century Skills: Theoretical and practical implications from modern research.* Information Age Publications.

Shenton, A. K. (2004). Strategies for ensuring trustworthiness in qualitative research projects. *Education for Information*, 22, 63–75.

Shrager, J., & Khlar, D. (1986). Instructionless learning about a complex device: The paradigm and observations. *International Journal of Man-Machine Studies*, 25, 153–189. doi:10.1016/S0020-7373(86)80075-X.

KEY TERMS AND DEFINITIONS

Collaborative Process Analysis Coding Scheme (CPACS): CPACS indexes both task process behavior and grammatical functions. The coding scheme was developed from Poole and Holmes Decision Function Coding System and Halliday's work on systemic functional linguistics. In this coding scheme, the micro level functions, such as tense, modality and pronouns are used to make sense of the macro level utterances.

Computer-Supported Collaborative Learning (CSCL): CSCL is a pedagogical approach wherein learning takes place via social interaction supported by computer or associated technologies. CSCL is characterized by the sharing and construction of knowledge among participants using technology as their primary means of communication or as a common resource.

Decision Function Coding System (DFCS): DFCS indexes task process behavior it is specifically set up to distinguish among statements focused on the problem, on solutions, and on group process, respectively. DFCS developed from nonphasic research which made the point they decisions are not always orderly and that groups go through periods where the group is disorganized. The complexities of decision making are not always captured by a simple, phasic model.

Discourse Analysis (DA): DA is a research method that involves studying the use of language. This may include the analysis of written texts, spoken discursive events, sign language, and any other means through which communication is achieved.

Macro- and Micro-Levels of Discourse: Refers to the two levels at which conversations function. The macro level refers to the function of the conversation while the micro level refers to grammatical items, such as tense, modality, and pronoun use.

Multi-User Virtual Environment (MUVE): MUVE applications incorporate computer graphics, sound simulation, and networks to simulate the experience of real-time interaction between multiple users in a shared three-dimensional virtual world.

Periodicity: Is derived from the noun periodic meaning to occur at a regular interval. Periodicity in physics is associated with waves, for example, waves of light. In problem solving, periodicity refers to the patterns that groups establish to solve a problem as the move through problem identification, planning, execution and evaluation. When groups do not achieve periodicity, their behavior is said to be aperiodic.

Systemic Functional Linguistics (SFL): SFL is a theory of language centered on the notion of language function. Although SFL considers the syntactic structure of language, it the function of language is central i.e. what language does, and how it does it. SFL starts at social context, and looks at how language both acts upon, and is constrained by, this social context.

Chapter 6
Studying the Suitability of Discourse Analysis Methods for Emotion Detection and Interpretation in Computer-Mediated Educational Discourse

Thanasis Daradoumis
Open University of Catalonia, Spain & University of Aegean, Greece

Marta María Arguedas Lafuente
Open University of Catalonia, Spain

ABSTRACT

Conversation analysis (CA) and discourse analysis (DA) methods have been widely used to analyse classroom interaction in conventional educational environments and to some extent in e-learning environments, paying more attention to the 'quality' and purposes the discourse serves to accomplish in its specific context. However, CA and DA methods seem to ignore emotion detection and interpretation when analysing learners' interaction in online environments. Effective regulation of emotion, motivation and cognition in social interaction has been shown to be crucial in achieving problem-solving goals. The aim of this chapter is to provide an in-depth study on the possibility of applying discourse analysis methods in e-learning contexts with implications for emotion detection, interpretation and regulation. The result of this study shows whether a comprehensive approach that includes DA methodological solutions and constructivist strategies (e.g., cognitive dissonance) for emotion detection and interpretation can be elaborated and applied.

DOI: 10.4018/978-1-4666-4426-7.ch006

INTRODUCTION

According to Ortony et al. (1988), emotions are balanced affective states focused on events, agents or objects. Since emotions play such an essential role in human life, they cannot be left aside when modelling systems that interact with human beings. A new branch named "affective computing" appeared in this research line in the late 90s. This branch is divided in turn into two other branches. The first one studies the mechanisms to recognise human emotions or express emotions by means of a computer in a man-machine interaction (Jacques & Vicari, 2007). The second branch investigates the simulation of emotions in machines (synthetic emotions) with the aim of finding out more about human emotions (Laureano-Cruces, 2006).

Many scientific studies have tried to understand what emotions are and how they take place in human beings. For instance, Fehr and Russell (1984, p. 464) state that everyone knows what an emotion is until asked to give a definition. Then it seems that no one knows. Some of the detection methods used has merely classified emotions into categories. The four most common emotions that appear in the lists of many theorists are fear, anger, sadness and happiness (Ekman & Friesen, 1971; Izard, 1977; Plutchik, 1980). The classification of the emotions that are defined as primary, that is to say, that are not composed of other emotions, varies according to the theory that is taken as a reference. The list of models and theories that analyse basic emotions is very long. Feidakis et al. (2011), in a preliminary study in an attempt to classify models and theories of basic emotion, proposed ten basic emotions: anger, happiness, fear, sadness, surprise, disgust and love, anticipation, joy and trust.

According to Ballano (2011), there are also other methods that widen the number of classes with secondary emotions (Abrilian et al., 2005) or mental states such as "concentrated," "interested," and "thoughtful" (Kapoor et al., 2007). However,

all these approaches imply discrete representations, with no relation among each other, and they are not able to reflect the wide range of complex emotions a human being is able to express.

Furthermore, studies about the dimensions of emotions have also been carried out. In the literature, research on learning theories and models revealed the following dimensions according to Hascher (2010): arousal, valence, control, intensity, duration, frequency of occurrence, time dimension, reference point and context.

Starting from the dimensions of emotions, Ballano (2011) argues that certain researchers, such as Whissell (1989) and Plutchik (1980), prefer not to see affective states independently, but rather as interrelated states. These authors consider emotions as a bi-dimensional continuous space, whose axes represent the evaluation and activation of each emotion.

These stimuli and what a person is feeling at all times can be captured by means of techniques such as: facial recognition, recognition of movements and body language, capture of speech patterns and intonation, pupil dilation, heart rate and respiratory rate monitoring, as well as detection of typical smell patterns. For all these purposes, more and more sophisticated devices (sensors) are able to obtain all these data and can be found in the market with no major difficulty. Nonetheless, as regards teaching/learning processes, the least invasive possible techniques should be used.

Another part of the process is to give machines the ability to "understand" human emotions and make them capable of realising what humans are feeling. The aim is to improve people's relationship with them, make the interaction more flexible and offer a pleasant user interface, as well as to allow users to focus their attention on a specific element or situation and improve their decision-making, by adapting to the context of each moment.

In order to do so, and following the objective of this chapter, we carried out an in-depth study about the possibility of applying discourse analysis methods in e-learning contexts with implications in the detection, interpretation and regulation of emotions.

In section 2 we set the base of our work, while in section 3 we review the state of the art of the discourse analysis methods used for educational purposes, such as *sentiment analysis* or *opinion mining,* and *rhetorical structure theory.* In section 4, we carry out a study of the different teaching models and strategies that can be implemented in the virtual classroom and used by teachers, in order to analyse the interaction of the different participants in the classroom and give students an appropriate affective feedback to guide them, advise them and help them according to their needs and states of mind. In section 5, we focus on technologies and how both synchronous and asynchronous computer-mediated communication technologies as well as new media and web 2.0 technologies (e.g. social networks and wikis) apply to educational discourse. Finally, we end this chapter with a section in which we discuss the existing issues and the solutions that have been proposed, as well as our main perspectives. The result of this study shows whether a comprehensive approach that includes DA methodological solutions and constructivist strategies (e.g. cognitive dissonance) for emotion detection and interpretation can be elaborated and applied.

BACKGROUND

One of the main concerns in the educational field is that of making knowledge more meaningful and long-lasting. The teaching-learning process has to be an active process where technologies must serve as tools to support knowledge building and skill development in students by taking into account the students' specific cognitive characteristics that can facilitate and complement this process (Silva et al., 2006).

The topic we want to develop in this chapter is in line with the latest research carried out in virtual environments dedicated to teaching-learning processes. These studies do not only take into account the skills and/or cognitive abilities that students must have or acquire in this process, but also their affective abilities and/or skills, which cannot be separated from the previous ones.

Our research focuses on the development of models of the teaching-learning process that go deeper into new forms of interaction that emulate and improve human communication skills and promote critical thinking with the objective of improving learning. This is done by showing that the quality of the relationships, whether it is those taking place in pairs (student-student) or among the different users of the classroom (student-teacher), is the key to an effective learning.

To this end, it is important to analyse and evaluate the emotional state of the participants in the discourse in the virtual classroom, so that we can achieve a better and more thorough understanding of their learning process. In turn, we must be able to give them an appropriate affective feedback that will guide them, advise them and help them according to their needs and states of mind.

Gross and Silva (2005) propose that the appropriate incorporation of communication tools into education and teaching processes can favour the collaboration between learners. In this sense, Computer-Mediated Communication (CMC) can support an interactive and collective process of knowledge construction where students produce knowledge by actively formulating ideas and which are constructed and shared as a consequence of the reactions and responses of others (Harasim et al., 2000). To this end, emotional learning should take advantage of it in order to improve the whole potential of motivation, affective and social consciousness in the cognitive, affective and emotional relationships that take place in a virtual environment.

One of the raised challenges originates from the fact that the communication of emotions among people is carried out in a natural way through various channels such as the tone of voice, facial expression, words, etc. Therefore, a multimodal system, that uses information from several sources to perform an analysis of emotional communication among people, will achieve a better understanding of the user's emotional state.

Another limitation is the availability of resources. The search for resources should consider those that are the least invasive in the learners' environment so that their attention is not distracted from their learning process. Furthermore, resources must be accessible both socially and economically to the largest possible number of students. For example, most of the computers in a laboratory as well as almost all the portable devices are equipped with a camera that can be used for facial expression recognition.

In this respect, text is an important modality for emotion detection, because most computer user interfaces nowadays include text tools (Valitutti et al., 2004). Once the information we want to use is obtained from different means, a new challenge consists in merging the different information types to obtain a global and consistent result. Once again, this gives rise to a new field of study in which new works are constantly appearing (Gunes et al., 2008). Finally, it is necessary to add the lack of annotated multimodal databases and the complexity of evaluating the results obtained to all the elements that have previously been explained (Ballano, 2011).

EXPLORING DISCOURSE ANALYSIS METHODS USED FOR EDUCATIONAL PURPOSES

The main question we face in this work is how we can measure emotions by applying discourse analysis methods. Emotion is never objective or systematically measurable. It is a subjective "com-

motion," a response to an external stimulus with physical and organic manifestations. The brain receives sensory information which it decodes and to which it gives a meaning. This generates manifestations and phenomena in our body.

We therefore need to model a personalised learning system that will allow not only the analysis of the learners' expressions, but also let them express both their knowledge and their emotions, making them improve not only their knowledge and cognitive abilities but also their social abilities and self-understanding.

In addition, we need to bear in mind that an emotion is not only expressed through words (written text or dialogue in the virtual classroom) but also implies connotations in both their oral expression (intonation, emphasis, pauses, silences, etc.) and their expression through gesture (body language, eye movement, face colour, etc.).

The analysis of feelings and opinions towards an entity are classified on a scale that is similar to the valence scale used in emotion models (Calvo, 2009). The text is classified by its general feeling, in order to determine for example whether it is a positive or negative critique. This new trend in emotion research consists in the lexical analysis of texts with the aim of identifying the words that can predict the affective states of the authors (Calvo & D'Mello, 2010).

Carrillo de Albornoz (2011), in his doctoral thesis, describes a new approach to the classification of texts according to emotional polarity and intensity, based on the semantic analysis of the text and on the use of advanced linguistic rules. The objective is to determine when a sentence or document expresses a positive, negative or neutral feeling, as well as its intensity. The method uses an algorithm of semantic disambiguation to work at a conceptual rather than term level, and uses the *SentiSense* affective lexicon, developed to extract emotional knowledge and represent each text entry as a group of emotional categories.

Asher et al. (2009) distinguish three main approaches: the discrete approach where emotions are a small set of basic, innate and universal concepts (Ekman, 1970; Izard, 1971), the dimensional approach that proposes dimensions underlying emotional concepts (Osgood et al., 1957; Russell, 1983) and finally, the appraisal approach where emotions are defined as the evaluation of the interaction between someone's goals, beliefs, etc., and his environment (Ortony et al., 1988; Martin & White, 2005).

In the field of sentiment analysis, in order to achieve a precise evaluation of opinion in texts, Natural Languages Processing (NLP) systems must go beyond the expressions of positive and negative feelings and identify a wide range of expressions of opinion, including motivations, recommendations and speculations, as well as how they are discursively related in the text.

According to Carrillo de Albornoz (2011), the main problem of these systems is the lack of importance given to the semantic and linguistic aspect. On the one hand, most of the approaches do not take into account the emotional meaning of words, and are simply based on the appearance and frequency of terms; and the few approaches that use polar expressions usually work with terms instead of concepts, without taking into consideration the multiple meanings a word can have and which can considerably affect the correct identification of subjectivity. On the other hand, this type of systems do not usually take into account the linguistic constructions that can affect subjectivity detection, such as negation, quantifiers or modals, and the few works that have addressed this issue usually merely identify their presence, without studying or treating their effect. Finally, these works depend too much on the domain; that is to say, once the system has been trained with documents on a certain domain, its application on texts in a different domain, especially if the vocabulary is very different, produces very deficient results.

In one of the most recent research works, Maks and Vossen (2012) proposed the development of the Lexicon model that opens new lines in the development of systems in this field. Their model combines the insights from a rather complex model like Framenet (Ruppenhofer et al., 2010) with operational models like SentiWordNet (Esuli & Sebastiani, 2006), where simple polarity values (positive, negative, neutral) are applied to the entire lexicon, in addition to accounting for the fact that words may express multiple attitudes.

Furthermore, the study carried out by Balahur et al. (2012) for the development of EmotiNet, although it is limited by the domain and the small amount of knowledge it currently contains, represents an appropriate semantic resource to capture and store the structure and semantics of real facts and the prediction of emotional responses caused by chains of actions.

In the field of Natural Languages Processing (NLP) and Intelligent Tutoring Systems (ITS), discourse analysis methods have been applied in recent research to interpret user language inputs. For instance, the "AutoTutor" project developed by Graesser et al. (2012) presents components that include an animated conversational agent, dialogue management, speech act classification, a curriculum script, semantic evaluation of student contributions, and electronic documents (e.g., textbook and glossary).

In this line, Lintean et al. (2012) have presented "Meta Tutor," a project that describes the architecture of an intelligent tutoring system that puts emphasis on two components that rely on natural language processing (NLP) techniques: (1) detection of students' mental models during prior knowledge activation (PKA), a meta-cognitive strategy based on student-generated PKA paragraphs, and (2) a micro-dialogue component that handles sub-goal assessment and feedback generation during sub-goal generation (SG).

Finally, another theory widely used as a discourse analysis method is Rhetorical Structure Theory (RST). RST is a text organisation theory which has led to areas of application that are beyond its original objectives: discourse analysis and text generation. Its application has been important in several areas: discourse analysis, theoretical linguistics, psycholinguistic and computational linguistics. Its applications in computational linguistics are multiple: generation of translations, analysis, synthesis, evaluation of arguments, performance test, etc. (Taboada & Mann, 2006). Some of these areas in which RST has been applied include, in addition to the work carried out in other languages, the studies conducted in other media, such as dialogue and multimedia (Daradoumis, 1995; Hovy & Arens, 1991; Matthiessen et al., 1998; Bateman et al., 2000). In addition, RST has been used not only to generate coherent texts with the appropriate discourse markers (Grote et al., 1997b; Scott & de Souza, 1990), but also to generate the appropriate intonation in speech synthesis (Grote et al., 1997a.).

RST was developed through the analysis of texts from written monologues, but it does not exclude the analysis of dialogues in their original phrasing. A few studies have tried to apply the original or modified RST to dialogues. Fawcett and Davies (1992) propose the RST analysis of conversations.

Later on, Daradoumis (1995) developed a new application of RST in its extended version (Dialogic, RST), with new relations to capture the exchange structure of conversation (tutorial dialogue in this case). The analysis of the data he carried out was based on an approach that integrated several models and methods in order to model educational interactions, including rhetorical structure theory. He analysed how knowledge distribution can be seen in the context of the student-student interaction and how it can be studied in a virtual learning environment. This involves the definition of the appropriate situations of collaborative learning and the distinction of two levels of student interaction, discourse and action level. At discourse level, the essential element is the interaction between pairs (the participants must interact with one another to plan an activity, distribute the tasks, explain, clarify, give information and opinions, obtain information, evaluate and contribute to

the resolution of problematic issues, and so on). At the level of action, the working objects (e.g. documents, graphs), which are created and used by the actors who participate in the interaction, have been considered.

One of the principles that have characterised Rhetoric since antiquity is its statement that human emotions are an essential component of action and individual and collective thinking (Tapia, 2007). Though emotion is not an obstacle to cognition, there are widely spread theories on the emotional difficulties that can occur during learning. Although RST has never been applied to the study/analysis of emotions, we consider its inclusion in a comprehensive model and face it as an important challenge in our research. Given the dynamics of RST in discourse analysis, we propose its extension on the basis of new relations, called emotional relations, by means of which we are able to analyse not only the cognitive aspect of discourse but also its emotional aspect. The objective of this work is the construction of the emotional structure of discourse (text or dialogue), expressed by means of emotional relations.

TEACHING MODELS AND STRATEGIES

The educational task of training students in a comprehensive way has found its place and an answer in several environments that show their advances both in the understanding of socio-affective and ethical skills and the way to train them, and in the studies that reflect the benefits and great impact of respective research programmes. This type of social and emotional learning experiences (SEL - Social and Emotional Learning) constitutes a process to help the members of the educational community in which students are taught to develop the skills that we all need to manage our relationships and work in a an effective and ethical manner.

These skills include recognising and managing our emotions, developing affection and concern for the others, establishing positive relationships, responsible decision-making and managing difficult situations constructively and ethically. A large body of scientific research has determined that students' academic performance and their attitudes towards school can be improved significantly thanks to SEL. SEAL in the United Kingdom (Department for education and skills, UK, 2005a; 2005b) or CASEL in the United Stated (Collaborative for Academic, Social and Emotional Learning, 2006) are examples of that.

In addition to achieving great progresses in the development of educational policies that make up these dimensions, several studies and international research give relevant results that show how socio-affective and ethical education integrated in the school curriculum, in addition to promoting mental health, benefiting the ethical development of students and their development as citizens, and preventing risk behaviours, leads to improvements in academic learning (Romagnoli & Valdés, 2007).

Moreover, knowing the student's learning style allows the teacher to plan a personalised learning strategy that is appropriate to the student's learning style, which includes managing an effective communication with the student and among students, which will in turn favour effective learning. For instance, identification of a personalised learning style can take place in the analysis of a conversation carried out in the virtual classroom among all its participants. At the same time, identifying the emotional state of each participant during the conversation and combining it with their learning style will let the teacher apply the necessary strategies to give the emotional support that is suitable for each student. Finally, teachers will also need to have the necessary means to follow up the students' cognitive and emotional states during the learning process.

There are different projects that have analysed the role played by emotions in communication among people. Emotalk is one of these projects and shows the need to get rid of this false dichotomy between rational communication and emotional communication. This way, every emotional process is built from a cognitive perception. That is to say, every feeling is built from what is known, thought and elaborated, but, in order to be operative, every rational decision implies emotions or concerns. No decision can be totally objective and free from emotional or sentimental implications. Therefore, beyond the "dichotomous" discourse, it is interesting to know how we can develop "skills" to give emotional importance to our structures of persuasion.

As a consequence, our analysis of conversation must lead us to the building of a model in which students can grow cognitively, favouring attitudes in an emotional environment that is affective, effective and stable, as well as attitudinally, that is to say, allowing them to develop their skills and offering them the possibility to acquire new ones.

Student Learning Styles

The analysis of learning styles offers indicators that help to guide a person's interactions with existential realities. One of the clearest and most precise definitions is the one proposed by Keefe (1988): "Learning styles are characteristic, cognitive, affective and physiological behaviours that serve as relatively stable indicators of how learners perceive, interact with, and respond to the learning environment."

This way, students can become aware of their own learning resources, review the most needed aspects of optimisation, reflect on their own learning process, in function of the requirements of their academic and social environment, thus achieving not only a better academic performance in terms of qualification, but also a wider range of learning resources. According to constructivist theories, the educational process consists in teaching students to learn by means of active and participative teaching models that are focused on teaching-learning processes and individual differences. In fact, based on this paradigm learning is a process of processes

(Beltrán, 1993) whose identification and diagnosis will allow the implementation of programmes of educational intervention aimed at improving the quality of learning from a global perspective. In addition, from this perspective, the concept of autonomous self-regulated students, who know their own cognitive process and are responsible for the control of their learning, prevails.

The student style can be induced and generated at the beginning of a course. Different authors have shown diagnostic tools whose validity and reliability has been proved in different studies over the years through widely used and scientifically proven methods that include surveys and questionnaires. Some of them are shown in Table 1.

Teaching Strategies

Once the student's learning style has been determined, we need to capture and process all the emotional information obtained as a result of the student interaction with the e-learning environment in an intelligent manner; besides, the generated feedback must adapt to the student style in the most effective and least intrusive way.

People learn to behave in a coherent manner at several levels (in particular, when they think, feel, do and say). As such, we should consider any element of cognition, especially any previous knowledge or perceptions one may have, as well as any attitudes, beliefs or feelings about their physical environment or other groups of people.

In line with the constructivist theory, *cognitive dissonance* emerges as an important strategy in the student's learning. Most of the research on this strategy focuses on one of the four great paradigms: the false-belief paradigm (discrepancy), the induced-compliance paradigm, the free-choice paradigm and the effort-justification paradigm. In educational discourse analysis, creating and solving cognitive dissonance can have a powerful impact on the learning motivation of students (Aronson, 1995). Psychologists have incorporated cognitive dissonance in the styles of basic learning processes, in particular in constructivist models. Meta-analytical methods suggest that interventions, which cause cognitive dissonance to achieve directed conceptual change, have been demonstrated through numerous studies to significantly improve science learning and reading (Guzzetti et al., 1993).

However, studies have only been carried out at a cognitive level, without taking into account the emotions experienced by the students to whom

Table 1. Diagnostic tools

AUTHORS	INSTRUMENT
Jerome Kagan (1966)	*Matching Familiar Figures Test*
Herman Witkin (1971)	*Group Embedded Figures Test*
A. Grasha & S. Riechmann (1974)	*Student Learning Styles Questionnaire*
David Kold (1976)	*Learning Style Inventory*
Ronald Schmeck, Fred Ribich & Nerella Ramanaiah (1977)	*Inventory of Learning Processes*
Rita Dunn & Kennel Dunn (1978)	*Learning Style Inventory*
James Keefe (1979)	*Learning Style Profile*
Bert Juch (1987)	*Learning Profile Exercise*
Bernice McCarthy (1987)	*4MAT System*
Richard M. Felder & Linda K. Silverman (1988)	*Index of Learning Styles*
Honey & Mumford (1988)	*Learning Styles Questionnaire*
Alonso, Gallego & Honney (1992, 1994)	*Learning Styles Honey-Alonso Questionnaire (CHAEA)*
Robert Sternberg (1997)	*Thinking Styles Inventory*
Catherine Jester (1999)	*Learning Style Survey for College*
S. Whiteley & K. Whiteley (2003)	*The Memletics Learning Styles Inventory*

Sources: Alonso (1992) & García Cué (2006)

dissonance is induced. Our interest focuses on detecting which emotions students feel as well as the degree to which they experience these emotions and the moment at which they occur. In particular, it is important to analyse the causes that trigger these emotions and how we can transform them into an effective learning, taking into account that their transformation can depend on individual factors, such as resistance to change, socio-cultural factors, support from other fellow students to perform the change of cognition, or acquisition of new necessary skills to overcome dissonance.

NEW GENERATION AND WEB 2.0 COMMUNICATION TECHNOLOGIES APPLIED TO EDUCATIONAL DISCOURSE

Constructivism "proposes that learning environments should support multiple perspectives or interpretations of reality, knowledge construction, and context-rich, experience-based activities" (Jonassen, 1991). New technologies now have a great impact on students' learning styles, and this should lead to changes in the teaching methods.

According to Piaget's constructivist theory, there are two principles in the teaching and learning process: learning can be seen as an active process; it should be complete, genuine and real learning (Piaget, 1978). In this respect, emotional aspects play a fundamental role in the user's interaction, not only from a hedonic perspective of the use of interactive products (Jordan, 1998), but also because emotional states affect cognitive processes (Norman, 2002). In other words, the user's affective states have an influence on how well this person solves rational problems. More specifically, according to Brave and Nass (2002), emotions affect attention and memorisation, as well as the user's performance and their evaluation.

As regards technology, it is necessary to incorporate specific tools in the virtual classroom that will facilitate communication of both intentions and feelings that can be easily recognised both by the teacher and the students. The incorporation of these tools is based on the design of man-machine interaction systems in which communication is carried out as naturally as possible.

To do so, Web 2.0 has numerous synchronous (chats, videoconferences, etc.) or asynchronous tools (debate areas, forums, etc.) that allow the development of communication among the different members of the classroom and help the teacher analyse the conversation in order to determine when and how he or she should intervene (with the help of an audio file, a video, an image, a virtual reality, music, etc.) (Feidakis et al., 2010).

With the upcoming of new technologies (such as wikis, social networks, blogs...), students not only have instantaneous access to a world of unlimited information, but they are also offered the ability to control the direction of their own learning.

Traditionally, research in the field of Human-Computer interaction has focused on the user's abilities and cognitive processes, and only studied their rational behaviour, thus leaving aside their emotional behavior (Djajadiningrat et al., 2000; Dillon, 2001; Brave & Nass, 2002; Picard & Klein, 2002).

In the search for more integrative and inclusive design solutions, references to "User Experience" (UX), as a new approach for the development of interactive products, have become popular in the last few years, mainly in the professional field of web development. According to D'Hertefelt (2000), the User Experience represents an emerging change of the usability concept, where the objective is not to merely improve the user's performance in the interaction -effectiveness, efficiency and easiness to learn- but also to try to solve the strategic problem of the product's utility and the psychological problem of the pleasure and entertainment derived from its use.

Furthermore, Dillon (2001) proposes a simple model that defines the User Experience as the sum of three levels: Action, what the user does; Result, what the user obtains; and Emotion, what the user feels. The difference from other definitions is that the author decomposes the triggering phenomenon (interaction) into two levels, Action and Result, and then emphasises the emotional aspect of the resulting experience.

According to Feidakis et al. (2010), there are two predominant trends as regards emotion when we talk about the design of learning systems and environments. The first trend is based on recognising, decoding and exporting emotion/affection patterns in the user-computer interaction. What the user/student really wants and how he or she is feeling at a certain time and in a specific place is considered valuable information that can really lead to personalised computer systems. The possibility of monitoring students' emotions is an attractive concept (Arroyo et al., 2009). The second approach questions not only the way of educating through the use of emotion/affection, but also the way of educating emotions/affection. Substantial theories have been established, that recognise the existence of emotions related to learning (Kort & Reilly, 2002; Goleman, 1995; Csikszentmihalyi, 1990; Gardner, 2006).

According to Fitzgerald (1998), the new generation of technological software applied to education will have a great power as it will include characteristics of Artificial Intelligence (AI), 3D interactive elements in an immersion environment, animated intelligent agents and support animations (Laureano-Cruces, 2004; Laureano-Cruces et al., 2005). Animated pedagogical agents are the state of the art in the design of Human-Computer interfaces. The credibility of these agents generates trust, a trust that will be based on the personalisation and capacity of adaptation of the agents to the student's learning style, to the attitudes and preferences as regards the agent's visual quality and its aptitudes regarding the behaviours that emulate those of humans during its intervention (Lester & Stone, 1997, Jaques & Vicari, 2007).

The new technological advances and the development of new tools for virtual teaching environments must take into consideration the fact that cognition and emotion are inseparable in the teaching-learning processes. The emotions that are detected in the virtual environment during cognitive processes can be positive or negative. However, our research focuses on detecting and interpreting the emotions that students experience through their learning processes, which the teacher can subsequently use to make students aware of what they are going through and thus improve learning. The ultimate aim of our research is to develop a human-computer interaction system that will facilitate the expression and evaluation of those emotions in the communication carried out in the virtual classroom by means of specific discourse analysis methods. This evaluation will be further completed by examining both the students' and the teacher's degree of knowledge of the system, the difficulty to use it, the scaffolding tools that are available to solve the problems that may arise, as well as the alternative media which, although they may seem redundant, may allow the actors in the classroom to consider alternative ways when faced with different difficulties that are not easy to predict. This should be done in a way that allows students to have access to all necessary resources and alternative means in the classroom so they are not forced to look for technological tools outside it.

OUR SOLUTION AND ITS APPLICATION IN A CASE STUDY

In today's constructivist learning environments centred on the student, where students develop their learning processes overtime, teachers' work is highly demanding. From a theoretical perspective, we need to construct a solid conceptual framework that integrates and expands on existing ideas and methods to build a new integrated approach. From a technological point of view, we need to translate this framework into a robust system that captures and integrates all the theoretical ideas and serves as an important means to test and evaluate the entire process in real virtual learning situations.

At a theoretical level, our approach is partially based on the Activity Theory (AT) (Engeström et al., 1999), a theory that has been particularly useful in methodologies of qualitative research (e.g., in etnography case studies). It provides a method to understand and analyse a phenomenon, find patterns and make inferences through interactions that describe those phenomena. A particular activity is a goal-oriented or intentional interaction of an individual with an object through the use of tools. These tools externalise the shapes mental processes take as they manifest in constructions, whether they are physical or psychological. AT recognises the internalisation and externalisation of cognitive processes implied in the use of tools, as well as the transformation or development that results from the interaction (Fjeld et al., 2002). In our case, the application of AT consists in making several participants (students) collaborate and interact with specific objects (such as text and dialogue) through the use of specific tools (a wiki and a chat respectively) to carry out goal-oriented activities. These activities presented through language can incorporate a non-intrusive approach for the detection of emotion through exploring different possibilities that aim at the automatic extraction of emotions in student-created texts. In addition, this approach can provide dynamic recommendations for activities as well as adaptation of content according to the emotions, at each given moment, thus offering affective and effective feedback to students (Rodríguez et al., 2012).

To achieve this, we used questionnaires at the beginning of the learning activity to extract students' learning style profile, which provides initial information about the cognitive level, skills, emotional status, attitudes and expectations of each student for the learning process. This also func-

tions as a reference to the teacher when it comes to determining the prerequisites, the format of the learning content and the development of activities using methods such as Project-based Learning, Problem-based Learning or Case-based Learning, within the paradigm of Computer Supported Collaborative Learning (CSCL).

To complete the theoretical framework of our approach we also used, on the one hand, constructivist strategies such as *cognitive dissonance* to detect which emotions were produced in the interactions between the different individuals within the environment (teacher-student or student-student) during the phases of knowledge exchange. The use of this strategy allows us to identify possible activating or inhibiting emotional causes and consequences of the dissonance, as well as its influence both on students' emotional situations and behaviours and on habit and behaviour modification. It also allows us to anticipate possible situations that may generate dissonance to try to avoid them minimise their impact or use their presence as an advantage for a more effective learning. Lastly, the emotional impact of dissonance on the experience can be significant (in a positive or a negative way), when contrasting opinions in a group, whereas member participation could be conditioned by the intensity of the dissonance which is present among its members. The reduction of dissonance or a part of it may improve the participation of the less favoured members.

On the other hand, the analysis of the emotions is completed by applying an extension of the RST (Rhetorical Structure Theory) that is based on the use of *coherent relationships* between two adjacent text units to conduct discourse analysis (texts and dialogues) in the areas of Processing of Natural Language (Mann & Thompson, 1988). The extension of the theory centres on finding *emotional relationships* between two text or dialogue units, with the objective of constructing the emotional structure of the discourse (text or dialogue). The application of the integrated approach helps the system (and as a consequence, the teacher, too) to induce the dissonant elements and their emotional relationship in a controlled manner, both in collaborative tasks that the students are asked to carry out and in the conversations that students participate. Thus, we know when specific emotions arise and what causes them, and we are able to provide the appropriate feedback.

Finally, our approach also includes elements from the analysis of feelings (Pang & Lee, 2008; Liu, 2012) to detect emotions both in students' individual tasks and groupwork (i.e. wiki elaboration). The objective is to detect problems/weak points (or strong points) in different aspects of the teaching-learning process that may require immediate formative action. We can also discover positive or negative opinions that may allow us,

for example, to prevent student abandonment, to measure their satisfaction, to analyse their opinions and to predict the evolution of an action. The spontaneity and immediacy of social media, combined with the permanent access to them that latest technologies offer, allow us to eliminate the delay between the generation and the publication of an opinion. Our model is represented in Figure 1.

To summarise, discourse analysis and evaluation of the cognitive process not only confirm that the new knowledge has been assimilated and new skills have been acquired but also achieve the detection, interpretation and transformation of the emotions that arose during the learning process, thus helping their development. In this sense we need to act timely. In each step of the learning process we need to evaluate not only the

Figure 1. Graphical representation of the emotion analysis model (including affective feedback)

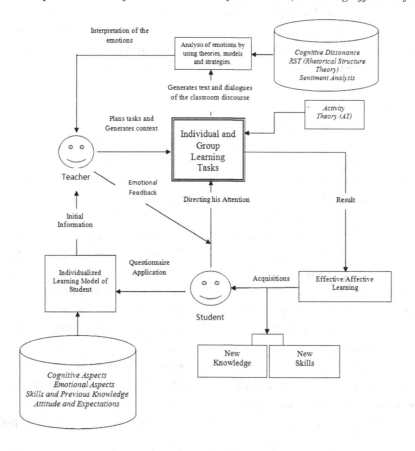

level of the knowledge acquired but also the obtained emotional level as well as the attitude towards the learning process itself.

It is important at this point that the teacher's feedback takes time into account. Without being obsessive or abusive, the teacher will consider the duration of the student's learning process in two ways: the time needed to carry out an activity and the time the student has available. In this context, emotions can be used to initiate actions that direct the student's attention to the cognitive goal that needs to be completed. The ultimate aim is to provide an environment where students feel safe, comfortable, valued and confident that they will receive the necessary help to achieve their goals.

To demonstrate the appropriateness of our model for the analysis of emotions in an educational discourse setting, we designed the following case study which we applied to a real situation.

Application of Our Model in a Real Case Study

We designed a case study with an experimental group of twenty 3rd-year college students of Technical Engineering in Computing Systems, taking Operative Systems II in the Moodle Platform. We divided students in 5 groups of 4 members. Given this scenario and based on the Activity Theory (AT), each group worked in a collaborative way to create a Wiki page that explains how to install a content delivery platform (Moodle, Blackboard, etc) through an Apache server (Wamp, Xamp, etc). In parallel, students were expected to express their opinions, criticisms and arguments in a free way on the Wiki (in this sense they also implicitly expressed their feelings both in the text that they produced themselves and in the text their group members produced). Also, in order to take part in decision-taking processes, they had to use a chat at specific moments. To facilitate dialogue and promote an interesting and focused interaction, the teacher asked 4 questions, purposely centred to

provoke an effect of *cognitive dissonance* between the group members. The effect of this strategy was to create a very active dialogue between the 4 members of each group, with diverse opinions, in several cases opposed to one another, and with a very pronounced emotional expression.

We applied our model to analyse the emotions produced among the contributions that students made during the Wiki construction, which lasted 2 weeks, and during the conversation that lasted 1 hour. Applying our extension of RST to the text/Wiki (combined with sentiment analysis) and to the dialogue (combined with the *cognitive dissonance* strategy) we achieved the construction of the emotional structure of the produced discourse, as it is shown in Figures 2 and 3.

As seen in Figure 2a, the Wiki text was split in segments (denoted by numbers in parentheses) that clearly convey a specific goal, following the paradigm of Grosz and Sidner (1986). According to their theory, discourse structure is composed of three separate but interrelated components: the structure of the sequence of utterances (called the linguistic structure), a structure of purposes (called the intentional structure), and the state of focus of attention (called the attentional state). The linguistic structure consists of segments of the discourse into which the utterances naturally aggregate. The intentional structure captures the discourse-relevant purposes, expressed in each of the linguistic segments as well as relationships among them. The attentional state is an abstraction of the focus of attention of the participants as the discourse unfolds. Upon this resulting structure we proceeded to apply our extension of RST model to obtain the emotional structure of the text, as shown in Figure 2b.

Furthermore, the conversation among group members that was carried out in the chat was split in several segments – again denoted by numbers in parentheses– which represent the linguistic structure of the conversation (i.e., the different exchange types and moves issued by each par-

Figure 2. a) Text of wiki, b) emotional structure of the text (wiki)

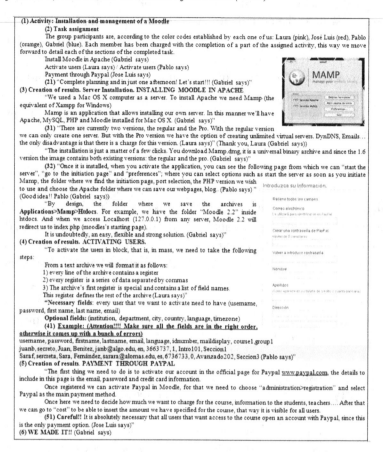

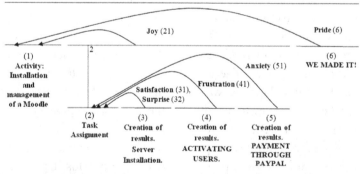

ticipant in the conversation), as shown in Figure 3a. According to Clark and Schaefer (1989), each move is seen as a contribution to discourse and carries a specific goal. The combination of different moves forms the so-called Exchange Structure (Martin, 1992). Again, upon this structure we first applied the dialogic RST model of Daradoumis (2005) to annotate the role (nucleus or satellite) that each move plays in the exchange structure

(Figure 3a). Then we applied a further extension of RST to obtain the emotional structure of the conversation, as shown in Figure 3b.

To carry out the analysis of discourse we based our work on the latest implementation of the RST tool (O'Donnell, 2000) which we extended in order to cover and supply additional relations of emotional type. Due to space restrictions we cannot provide the details of the tool application,

Figure 3. a) Chat conversation with linguistic structure and RST analysis, b) emotional structure of the conversation (b1, b2 and b3)

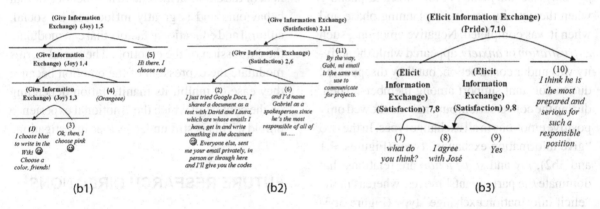

(b1)   (b2)   (b3)

but only some application guidelines on both the text and the dialogue as well as the interpretation of the analysis results.

Application Guidelines and Interpretation of the Analysis Results

Our discourse analysis method was applied in several phases:

First phase: Both the text and the conversation were divided into segments in order to discover and show one or more emotions in them. With regard to the Wiki text, division was carried out according to the intentional structure of the text (Grosz & Sidner, 1986), that is, of the contribution goals as issued by each group member. With regard to

the chat dialogue, division was carried out at two levels, first at the exchange level and then at the move level inside each exchange (Martin, 1992). Doing so, we create a clear association between the intentional and the emotional structure of discourse in both modes (text and dialogue).

Second phase: All segments were numbered sequentially and we refer to them as units of analysis.

Third phase: Both the Wiki text and the conversation were analysed segment by segment by the extended RST Tool and all emotions detected in each segment were tagged.

Fourth phase: Deployment of the RST Tool results in constructing the emotional structure of both the text and the conversation as shown in

Figures 2b and 3b. The emotional structure of discourse provides a nice graphical representation of how and which emotions appear as the discourse expands during an interaction as well as the way these emotions evolve and affect the intentional structure of discourse.

Fifth phase: In this phase it is important to associate the emotional to the intentional structure of discourse to explore how participants' emotions affect their goals and vice-versa. This phase is currently under research and more work is needed to find and describe solid results.

We now turn to provide a brief discussion and interpretation of the results of our analysis. First, during the construction of the wiki, our analysis showed that positive emotions such as *satisfaction, joy, surprise* and *pride* predominated, especially when the activity was in its planning phase and when it was completed. Negative emotions, such as *frustration* or *anxiety*, appeared while the activity was under construction, but they disappeared due to constant support among members. Then, during the conversation, our analysis showed only positive emotions in all exchange types. In the two "give information exchange" types (Figures 3b1 and 3b2), *joy* and *satisfaction* are relations that dominate the participants' moves, whereas in the "elicit information exchange" type (Figure 3b3) *satisfaction* and *pride* relations appear.

Both discourse types (and especially the conversation one) convey a good harmony among group members, and thus a smooth and effective collaboration among them, which facilitated the expression of their emotions and contributed to carry out the activity successfully. In the general case, this approach could show the teacher how the virtual class is behaving and evolving as an on-line community, how tasks are shared and progress, whether problems or conflicts appear across time and how affect the individuals and the group as a whole. Having a graphical representation of the emotional structure of discourse gives both the teacher and the students a means to have a clear image of the individual and group affective state which, combined with the individual intentions (as we expect to investigate), will allow the teacher to critically revise the learning situation, intervene and monitor students' performance.

In addition, group members can become aware of their partners' emotional state, which allows them to become supportive when needed. Positive feelings can also liven up the group's mood, which increases self-esteem and effort, reduces abandonment and pushes the group towards the successful completion of its tasks. Finally, difficult situations such as anxiety or fear can be detected easily and supported accordingly either by the teacher or by the group partners.

Finally, the behavioural or expressive component of the emotion includes a number of external behaviours and is greatly influenced by social, cultural and educational factors that can modulate the expression of the emotion. The social norms modulate the expression of the emotion because they ease or inhibit its manifestation depending on the context in which the emotional experience unfolds. This is still under further investigation.

FUTURE RESEARCH DIRECTIONS

At this stage of our research we have built an initial prototype that we applied for experimentation in an exploratory case study (that included a wiki creation and discussion in the form of a chat) with an experimental group. We did not have the possibility of leading a parallel experiment with a control group. We are planning to do it in the near future. Our purpose at this stage was to test our model in a real situation and gain experience as well as get feedback so as to improve our model and build a more solid one so as to apply it in a more complex situation (involving both an experimental and a control group).

As we mentioned above, another important issue is to associate the emotional with the intentional structure of discourse in order to see how participants' emotions affect their goals and vice-versa. Moreover, to strengthen and consolidate our integrated approach of emotion detection, we would like to combine our RST approach with sentiment analysis methods, which will also verify the reliability of our current results.

Once we have completed our analysis, we need to develop the means of reaction to mediate and regulate students' e-learning processes. Affective pedagogical agents or tutors have been widely used in e-learning environments in a variety of ways (Beale & Creed, 2009; Frasson & Chalfoun, 2010). This work will lay the foundations for the design of an affective virtual agent/tutor that is able to intervene and mediate in the e-learning processes of students, providing them with an appropriate affective feedback that will guide, advise and help them according to their needs and feelings. For this purpose, we will first study how the virtual tutor should manage time with the aim of providing feedback at the right time. Therefore, we need to have clear evidence of when the tutor should appear: only when feelings are detected in the student or should the tutor wait to see the student's subsequent reactions? Knowing the moment at which the tutor should appear is the result of our analysis phase, which indicates the appropriate period of time during which the tutor should intervene to control and support the student's learning process emotionally and in an appropriate manner.

In addition to the emotional characteristics that the intelligent virtual tutor should have, thanks to which it will be able to answer students as educationally, communicatively, empathetically as possible and at the appropriate time, our future work will deal with other important aspects, characteristics and problems. Among these problems we can highlight design issues, such as the tutor's aspect, which may be as human as possible or simply take the form of an animated character. Its aspect may even change with time and it may

take different forms at different times, depending on each specific situation. Even though interesting advances have been made in user interface design, there are situations that require a tutor with a particular image in order to prevent any negative effects on the students' emotional state.

In long-term virtual learning practices, it is interesting to determine the factors that lead students to remain in the same negative affective state through a certain period of time that is considered detrimental and dangerous, since this can lead to a significant reduction of the quality of learning, failure and even withdrawal from studies. In this case, it requires making students react in time, guide them and help them in an appropriate manner so that they can come out of this negative affective state and get into a more positive one. In order to do this, we need to be able to gather all the data related to the activity that is being carried out by the students (since students can participate in various learning tasks, such as debates, discussion forums sending questions and problems, class workspaces working on a task, etc.). In this line, it requires the study of how students manage time in their learning processes. It is necessary to know if they feel that they have enough time to carry out a learning activity or whether they feel stressed and frustrated by the lack of time as well as what kind of emotions they express and how these emotions evolve over this period of time.

CONCLUSION

In this work, the focus of interest of our research is the discourse analysis of the educational process, in which our concern is the appropriate detection and interpretation of students' behaviours and moods and how they influence their learning. As we have seen, there are as many ways of learning as there are human beings, and in the same way we believe that there are as many ways of feeling as there are individuals, and our concern focuses on the combination of both to favour an affective-effective learning process. As a consequence, as we have already explained, emotion and cognition cannot be separated when designing teaching-learning processes in a virtual environment.

In short, our proposal is giving an important added value to the field of distance learning by trying to provide solutions to a problem (the management of students' emotions) that has not been well addressed and valued until now and that has an enormous influence on the students' participation and performance in their learning. Furthermore, it will help teachers to better understand the role and influences of emotions in teaching processes and will guide them so they can plan these processes in a better and more effective way.

REFERENCES

Abrilian, S., Devillers, L., Buisine, S., & Martin, J. C. (2005). EmoTV1: Annotation of real-life emotions for the specification of multimodal affective interfaces. In *Proceedings of the 11th International Conference on Human-Computer Interaction (HCII'2005)* (pp. 1-11). Las Vegas, Nevada, USA, 22–27 July 2005.

Alonso, C. (1992). *Análisis y diagnóstico de los estilos de aprendizaje en estudiantes universitarios.* (Unpublished doctoral dissertation). Tomo I. Madrid: Colección Tesis Doctorales. Editorial de la Universidad Complutense.

Aronson, E. (1995). *The social animal.* New York, NY: W.H. Freeman and Co..

Arroyo, I., Cooper, D. G., Burleson, W., Woolf, B. P., Muldner, K., & Christopherson, R. (2009). Emotion sensors go to school. In Dimitrova, V., Mizoguchi, R., du Boulay, B., & Grasser, A. (Eds.), *Artificial intelligence in education. Building learning systems that care: From knowledge representation to affective modeling. Vol. Frontiers in Artificial Intelligence and Applications* (pp. 17–24). Amsterdam: IOS Press.

Asher, N., Benamara, F., & Mathieu, Y. Y. (2009). Appraisal of opinion expressions in discourse. *Lingvisticae Investigationes, 32*(2), 279–292. doi:10.1075/li.32.2.10ash.

Balahur, A., Hermida, J. M., & Montoyo, A. (2012). Building and exploiting emotinet, a knowledge base for emotion detection based on the appraisal theory model. *IEEE Transactions on Affective Computing, 3*(1), 88–101. doi:10.1109/T-AFFC.2011.33.

Ballano, S. (2011). *Evaluación de un sistema multimodal de reconocimiento de emociones.* (Unpublished master's thesis). Universidad de Zaragoza, Zaragoza.

Bateman, J., Delin, J., & Allen, P. (2000). Constraints on layout in multimodal document generation. In *Proceedings of the First International Natural Language Generation Conference. Workshop on Coherence in Generated Multimedia* (pp. 7-14). Mitzpe Ramon, Israel.

Beale, R., & Creed, C. (2009). Affective interaction: How emotional agents affect users. *International Journal of Human-Computer Studies, 67*(9), 755–776. doi:10.1016/j.ijhcs.2009.05.001.

Beltrán Llera, J. (1993). *Procesos, estrategias y técnicas de aprendizaje.* Madrid. Editorial Síntesis, S.A.

Brave, S., & Nass, C. (2002). Emotion in human-computer interaction. In Jacko, J., & Sears, A. (Eds.), *The human-computer interaction handbook: Fundamentals, evolving technologies and emerging applications* (pp. 91–96). Hillsdale, NJ: Lawrence Erlbaum Associates.

Calvo, R. (2009). Incorporating affect into educational design patterns and technologies. In *Proceedings of the 9th IEEE international conference on advanced learning technologies* (pp. 1-5). Riga, Latvia. Retrieved February 5, 2013, from http://sydney.edu.au/engineering/latte/docs/Calvo09-Icalt.pdf

Calvo, R. A., & D'Mello, S. K. (2010). Affect detection: An interdisciplinary review of models, methods, and their applications. *IEEE Transactions on Affective Computing*, *1*(1), 18–37. doi:10.1109/T-AFFC.2010.1.

Carrillo de Albornoz, J. (2011). *Un Modelo Lingüístico-Semántico Basado en Emociones para la Clasificación de Textos según su Polaridad e Intensidad*. (Doctoral Thesis). Universidad Complutense de Madrid, Spain.

Clark, H., & Schaefer, E. (1989). Contributing to discourse. *Cognitive Science*, *13*, 259–294. doi:10.1207/s15516709cog1302_7.

Collaborative for Academic. Social and Emotional Learning. (2006). *About CASEL*. Retrieved May 28, 2012, from http://www.casel.org/about/index.php

Csikszentmihalyi, M. (1990). *Flow: The psychology of optimal experience*. New York: Harper and Row Publishers Inc..

D'Hertefelt, S. (2000). *Emerging and future usability challenges: Designing user experiences and user communities*. Netherlands: InteractiveArchtecture.com. Retrieved May 3, 2012, from http://users.skynet.be/fa250900/future/vision20000202shd.htm

Daradoumis, T. (1995). Using rhetorical relations in building a coherent conversational teaching session. In Beun, R. J., Baker, M. J., & Reiner, M. (Eds.), *Dialogue and instruction* (pp. 56–71). Heidelberg, Berlin: Springer-Verlag. doi:10.1007/978-3-642-57827-4_5.

Department for education and skills, UK. (2005a). *Social and emotional aspects of learning... improving behaviour... improving learning*. Retrieved May 3, 2012, from http://webarchive.nationalarchives.gov.uk/20110809101133/nsonline.org.uk/node/87009

Department for education and skills, UK. (2005b). *Excellence and enjoyment: Social and emotional aspects of learning guidance*. Retrieved May 3, 2007, from http://public.merlin.swgfl.org.uk/establishments/803/QandS/Wellbeing/SealResourcesCD/data_folder/docs.html

Dillon, A. (2002). Beyond usability: Process, outcome and affect in human-computer interactions. *Canadian Journal of Library and Information Science*, *26*(4), 57–69.

Djajadiningrat, J. P., Overbeeke, C. J., & Wensveen, S. A. G. (2000). Augmenting fun and beauty: A pamphlet. In *Proceedings of DARE 2000 on Designing Augmented Reality Environments* (pp. 131-134). Elsinore, Denmark.

Ekman, P. (1970). Universal facial expressions of emotion. *California Mental Health Research Digest*, *8(4)*, 151-158. Retrieved April 24, 2012, from http://www.paulekman.com/wp-content/uploads/2009/02/Universal-Facial-Expressions-of-Emotions1.pdf

Ekman, P., & Friesen, W. V. (1971). Constants across culture in the face and emotion. *Journal of Personality and Social Psychology*, *17*(2), 124–129. doi:10.1037/h0030377.

Engeström, Y., Miettinen, R., & Punamäki, R. L. (1999). *Perspectives on activity theory*. Cambridge University Press. doi:10.1017/CBO9780511812774.

Esuli, A., & Sebastiani, F. (2006). SentiWordNet: A publicly available lexical resource for opinion mining. In *Proceedings of the 5th Conference on Language Resources and Evaluation (LREC-2006)* (pp. 417-422). Genova, Italy.

Fawcett, R. P., & Davies, B. L. (1992). Monologue as a turn in dialogue: Towards an integration of exchange structure and rhetorical structure theory. In Dale, R., Hovy, E., Rösner, D., & Stock, O. (Eds.), *Aspects of automated language generation* (pp. 151–166). Berlin: Springer. doi:10.1007/3-540-55399-1_11.

Fehr, B., & Russell, J. A. (1984). Concept of emotion viewed from a prototype perspective. *Journal of Experimental Psychology. General, 113*, 464–486. doi:10.1037/0096-3445.113.3.464.

Feidakis, M., & Daradoumis, T. (2010). A five-layer approach in collaborative learning systems design with respect to emotion. In F. Xhafa et al. (Eds.), *2nd International Conference on Intelligent Networking and Collaborative Systems (INCOS 2010)* (pp. 290-296). Washington, DC: IEEE Computer Society.

Feidakis, M., Daradoumis, T., & Caballé, S. (2011). Endowing e-learning systems with emotion awareness. In L. Barolli et al. (Eds.), *3rd International Conference on Networking and Collaborative Systems (INCOS 2011)* (pp. 68-75). Washington, DC: IEEE Computer Society.

Fitzgerald, P. (1998). The EyeCue system: A prototype for the next generation of educational technology. *Meridian Computer Technologies Journal, 1*(2). Retrieved June 13, 2012 from http://www.ncsu.edu/meridian/jun98/june98.pdf

Fjeld, M., Lauche, K., Bichsel, M., Voorhorst, F., Krueger, H., & Rauterberg, M. (2002). Physical and virtual tools: Activity theory applied to the design of groupware. *The Journal of Collaborative Computing – Special Issue of CSCW on Activity Theory and the Practice of Design, 11*(1-2), 153-180.

Frasson, C., & Chalfoun, P. (2010). Managing learner's affective states in intelligent tutoring systems. In Nkambou, R., Mizoguchi, R., & Bourdeau, J. (Eds.), *Advances in intelligent tutoring systems* (pp. 339–358). Springer-Verlag. doi:10.1007/978-3-642-14363-2_17.

García Cué, J. L. (2006). *Los estilos de aprendizaje y las tecnologías de la información y la comunicación en la formación del profesorado*. UNED, España. Dirigida por: Catalina M. Alonso García. Disponible en: http://www.estilosdeaprendizaje.es/JLGCue.pdf

Gardner, H. (2006). *Multiple intelligences: New horizons*. New York: Basic Books.

Goleman, D. (1995). *Emotional intelligence*. New York: Bantam Books.

Graesser, A. C., D'Mello, S., Hu, X., Cai, Z., Olney, A., & Morgan, B. (2012). AutoTutor. In McCarthy, P., & Boonthum-Denecke, C. (Eds.), *Applied natural language processing: Identification, investigation and resolution* (pp. 169–187). Hershey, PA: Information Science Reference.

Gros, B., & Silva, J. (2005). La formación del profesorado para su labor docente en espacios virtuales de aprendizaje. *Revista Iberoamericana de Educación, 36*(1). Retrieved May 24, 2012, from http://www.campus-oei.org/revista/tec_edu32.htm

Grosz, B., & Sidner, C. (1986). Attention, intentions, and the structure of discourse. *Computational Linguistics, 12*(3), 175–204.

Grote, B., Hagen, E., Stein, A., & Teich, E. (1997a). Speech production in human-machine dialogue: A natural language generation perspective. In Maier, E., Mast, M., & Luperfoy, S. (Eds.), *Dialogue processing in spoken language systems* (pp. 70–85). Berlin: Springer. doi:10.1007/3-540-63175-5_38.

Grote, B., Lenke, N., & Stede, M. (1997b). Ma(r)king concessions in English and German. *Discourse Processes*, *24*, 87–117. doi:10.1080/01638539709545008.

Gunes, A., Inal, A., Adak, M. S., Bagci, E. G., Cicek, N., & Eraslan, F. (2008). Effect of drought stress implemented at pre–or post–anthesis stage on some physiological parameters as screening criteria in chickpea cultivars. *Russian Journal of Plant Physiology: a Comprehensive Russian Journal on Modern Phytophysiology*, *55*(1), 59–67. doi:10.1134/S102144370801007X.

Guzzetti, B. J., Snyder, T. E., Glass, G. V., & Gamas, W. S. (1993). Promoting conceptual change in science: A comparative meta-analysis of instructional interventions from reading and science education. *Reading Research Quarterly*, *28*(2), 117–155. doi:10.2307/747886.

Harasim, L., Hiltz, S. R., Teles, L., & Turoff, M. (1995). Network learning: A paradigm for the twenty-first century. In *Learning networks: A field guide to teaching and learning online* (pp. 271–278). Cambridge, MA: MIT Press.

Hascher, T. (2010). Learning and emotion: Perspectives for theory and research. *European Educational Research Journal*, *9*, 13–28. doi:10.2304/eerj.2010.9.1.13.

Hovy, E. H., & Arens, Y. (1991). Automatic generation of formatted text. In *Proceedings of the 9th AAAI National Conference on Artificial Intelligence* (pp. 92-96). Anaheim, California.

Izard, C. E. (1971). *The face of emotions*. New York: Appleton-Century-Crofts.

Izard, C. E. (1977). *Human emotions*. New York: Plenum Press.

Jaques, P., & Vicari, R. M. (2007). A BDI approach to infer student's emotions in an intelligent learning environment. *Computers & Education*, *49*(2), 360–384. doi:10.1016/j.compedu.2005.09.002.

Jonassen, D. H. (1991). Evaluating constructivist learning. *Educational Technology*, *31*(9), 28–33.

Jordan, P. W. (1998). Human factors for pleasure in product use. *Applied Ergonomics*, *29*(1), 25–33. doi:10.1016/S0003-6870(97)00022-7.

Kapoor, A., Burleson, W., & Picard, R. W. (2007). Automatic prediction of frustration. *International Journal of Human-Computer Studies*, *65*(8), 724–736. doi:10.1016/j.ijhcs.2007.02.003.

Keefe, J. W. (1988). *Profiling and utilizing learning style*. Reston, VA: National Association of Secondary School Principals.

Kort, B., & Reilly, R. (2002). Analytical models of emotions, learning and relationships: Towards an affect sensitive cognitive machine. In *Proceedings of the International Conference on Virtual Worlds and Simulation (VWSim 2002)* (pp. 1-15). San Antonio, Texas. Retrieved February 15, 2013, from http://affect.media.mit.edu/projectpages/lc/vworlds.pdf

Laureano-Cruces, A. (2004). Agentes Pedagógicos. In *En el XVII Congreso Nacional y III Congreso Internacional de Informática y Computación de la ANIEI* (pp. 1-10). Tepic, Nayarit.

Laureano-Cruces, A. (2006). Emociones Sintéticas y Avatars. División de Ciencias y Artes para el Diseño (Ed.), *Reflexión a la Acción* (pp. 251-255). Retrieved April 24, 2012, from http://ce.azc.uam.mx/profesores/clc/04_proyecto_de_inv/comp_suave/EmocionesSint.pdf

Laureano-Cruces, A., Terán-Gilmore, A., & Rodríguez-Aguilar, R. M. (2005). Cognitive and affective interaction in a pedagogical agent. In *XVIII Congreso Nacional y IV Congreso Internacional de Informática y Computación de la ANIEI* (pp. 1-7).Torreón, Coah.

Lester, J., & Stone, B. (1997). Increasing believability in animated pedagogical agents. In Memories Autonomous Agents '97 (pp. 16-21). Marina del Rey, California.

Lintean, M., Rus, V., Cai, Z., Witherspoon-Johnson, A., Graesser, A. C., & Azevedo, R. (2012). Computational aspects of the intelligent tutoring system MetaTutor. In McCarthy, P., & Boonthum-Denecke, C. (Eds.), *Applied natural language processing: Identification, investigation and resolution* (pp. 247–260). Hershey, PA: Information Science Reference.

Liu, B. (2012). *Sentiment analysis & opinion mining. Synthesis Lectures on Human Language Technologies*. Morgan & Claypool Publishers.

Maks, I., & Vossen, P. (2012). A lexicon model for deep sentiment analysis and opinion mining applications. *Decision Support Systems, 53*(4), 680–688. doi:10.1016/j.dss.2012.05.025.

Mann, W. C., & Thompson, S. A. (1988). Rhetorical structure theory: Toward a functional theory of text organization. [from http://www.sfu.ca/rst/index.html]. *Text, 8*(3), 243–281. Retrieved February 4, 2013 doi:10.1515/text.1.1988.8.3.243.

Martin, J. R. (1992). *English text: Systems and structure*. Amsterdam: Benjamin Press.

Martin, J. R., & White, P. R. (2005). *The language of evaluation: Appraisal in English*. Basingstoke, New York: Palgrave Macmillan.

Matthiessen, C., Zeng, L., Cross, M., Kobayashi, I., Teruya, K., & Wu, C. (1998). The Multex generator and its environment: Application and development. In *Proceedings of ACL Workshop on Natural Language Generation* (pp. 228–37). Montréal, Canada.

Norman, D. A. (2002). Emotion and design: Attractive things work better. *Interactions Magazine, ix*(4), 36-42. Retrieved February 4, 2013, from http://www.jnd.org/dn.mss/emotion_design_at.html

O'Donnell, M. (2000). RSTTool 2.4 - A markup tool for rhetorical structure theory. In *Proceedings of the International Natural Language Generation Conference (INLG'2000* (pp. 253-256). Mitzpe Ramon, Israel.

Ortony, A., Clore, G., & Collins, A. (1988). *The cognitive structure of emotions*. Cambridge: Cambridge University Press. doi:10.1017/CBO9780511571299.

Osgood, C. E., Suci, G., & Tannenbaum, P. (1957). *The measurement of meaning*. University of Illinois Press.

Pang, B., & Lee, L. (2008). Opinion mining and sentiment analysis. *Foundations and Trends in Information Retrieval, 2*(1–2), 1–135. Retrieved July 10, 2012, from http://www.cs.cornell.edu/home/llee/omsa/omsa-published.pdf

Piaget, J. (1997). *La representación del mundo en el niño*. Madrid: Morata.

Picard, R. W., & Klein, J. (2002). Computers that recognise and respond to user emotion: Theoretical and practical implications. *Interacting with Computers, 14*(2), 141–169. doi:10.1016/S0953-5438(01)00055-8.

Plutchik, R. (1980). *Emotion: A psychoevolutionary synthesis*. New York: Harper & Row.

Rodriguez, P., Ortigosa, A., & Carro, R. M. (2012). Extracting emotions from texts in e-learning environments. In *Proceedings of the 6th International Conference on Complex, Intelligent & Software Intensive Systems* (pp. 887-893). Palermo, Italy: IEEE Computer Society.

Romagnoli, C., & Valdés, A. M. (2007). *Relevancia y beneficios del desarrollo de habilidades emocionales, sociales y éticas en la escuela*. Documento Valoras UC.

Ruppenhofer, J., Ellsworth, M., Petruck, M., Johnson, C., & Scheffzcyk, J. (2010). *Framenet II: Theory and practice* (e-book). Retrieved May 25, 2012, from http://framenet2.icsi.berkeley.edu/docs/r1.5/book.pdf

Russell, J. A. (1983). Pancultural aspects of human conceptual organization of emotion. *Journal of Personality and Social Psychology, 45,* 1281–1288. doi:10.1037/0022-3514.45.6.1281.

Scott, D., & de Souza, C. S. (1990). Getting the message across in RST-based text generation. In Dale, R., Mellish, C., & Zock, M. (Eds.), *Current research in natural language generation* (pp. 47–73). London: Academic Press.

Silva, B., Cruz, E., & Laureano-Cruces, A. (2006). Análisis para identificar los Estilos de Aprendizaje para el modelado del Dominio del Conocimiento. Paper presented at the XIX *Congreso Nacional y V Congreso Internacional de Informática y Computación de la ANIEI.* Tuxtla Gutiérrez, Chiapas.

Strapparava, C., & Valitutti, A. (2004). WordNet-affect: An affective extension of WordNet. In *Proceedings of the 4th International Conference on Language Resources and Evaluation (LREC 2004)* (pp. 1083-1086). Lisbon, Portugal.

Taboada, M., & Mann, W. C. (2006). Rhetorical structure theory: Looking back and moving ahead. *Discourse Studies, 8*(3), 423–459. doi:10.1177/1461445606061881.

Tapia, A. (2007). *El arbol de la retorica.* Retrieved May 24, 2012, from http://elarboldelaretorica.blogspot.com.es/2007/05/emocin-y-cognicin.html

Valitutti, C., Strapparava, C., & Stock, O. (2004). Developing affective lexical resources. *PsychNology Journal, 2*(1), 61–83.

Whissell, C. M. (1989). The dictionary of affect in language. In R. Pultchik & H. Kellerman (Eds.), Emotion-theory, research and experience, Vol. 4, The measurement of emotions (pp. 113-131). New York, NY: Academic Press, Inc.

ADDITIONAL READING

Ahern, T. C., Peck, K., & Laycock, M. (1992). The effects of teacher discourse in computer-mediated discussion. *Journal of Educational Computing Research, 8*(3), 291–309. doi:10.2190/HFPW-JYR3-YMBE-0J7D.

Angeli, C., Valanides, N., & Bonk, C. J. (2003). Communication in a web-based conferencing system: The quality of computer-mediated interactions. *British Journal of Educational Technology, 34*(1), 31–43. doi:10.1111/1467-8535.00302.

Bannan-Ritland, B. (2002). Computer-mediated communication, elearning, and interactivity: A review of the research. *Quarterly Review of Distance Education, 3*(2), 161–180.

Buissink-Smith, N., Mann, S., & Shephard, K. (2011). How do we measure affective learning in higher education? *Journal of Education for Sustainable Development, 5*(1), 101–114. doi:10.1177/097340821000500113.

Byrnes, H. (2002). Methods of text and discourse analysis. *Modern Language Journal, 86*(1), 136–137.

Cano, F. (2005). Consonance and dissonance in students' learning experience. *Learning and Instruction, 15*(3), 201–223. doi:10.1016/j.learninstruc.2005.04.003.

Conati, C. (2002). Probabilistic assessment of user's emotions in educational games. *Journal of Applied Artificial Intelligence, 16,* 555–575. doi:10.1080/08839510290030390.

Craig, S. D., Graesser, A. C., Sullins, J., & Gholson, B. (2004). Affect and learning: An exploratory look into the role of affect in learning with AutoTutor. *Journal of Educational Media, 29,* 241–250. doi:10.1080/1358165042000283101.

Cukier, W., Ngwenyama, O., Bauer, R., & Middleton, C. (2009). A critical analysis of media discourse on information technology: Preliminary results of a proposed method for critical discourse analysis. *Information Systems Journal, 19*(2), 175–196. doi:10.1111/j.1365-2575.2008.00296.x.

Falout, J., Elwood, J., & Hood, M. (2009). Demotivation: Affective states and learning outcomes. *System, 37*(3), 403–417. doi:10.1016/j.system.2009.03.004.

Georgakopoulou, A. (2002). Methods of text and discourse analysis. *Journal of Pragmatics, 34*(9), 1305–1308. doi:10.1016/S0378-2166(02)00039-5.

Gibbs, W., & Bernas, R. (2007). Computer-mediated-communications, learning style, and visualizing online educational conversations. *Journal of Computing in Higher Education, 18*(2), 25–50. doi:10.1007/BF03033412.

Hammersley, M. (2003). Conversation analysis and discourse analysis: Methods or paradigms? *Discourse & Society, 14*(6), 751–781. doi:10.1177/09579265030146004.

Herring, S. C. (2004). Computer-mediated discourse analysis: An approach to researching online behavior. In Barab, S. A., Kling, R., & Gray, J. H. (Eds.), *Designing for virtual communities in the service of learning* (pp. 338–376). New York: Cambridge University Press. doi:10.1017/CBO9780511805080.016.

Holt, B. J., & Hannon, J. C. (2006). Teaching-learning in the affective domain. *Strategies, 20*(1), 11–13. doi:10.1080/08924562.2006.10590695.

Kalender, D. (2007). Applying the subject "cell" through constructivist approach during science lessons and the teacher's view. *Journal of Environmental & Science Education, 2*(1), 3–13.

Litman, D. J., & Forbes-Riley, K. (2004). Predicting student emotions in computer-human tutoring dialogues. In *Proceedings of the 42nd annual meeting of the association for computational linguistics* (pp. 352-359). East Stroudsburg, PA: Association for Computational Linguistics.

Meyer, D. L. (2009). The poverty of constructivism. *Educational Philosophy and Theory, 41*(3), 332–341. doi:10.1111/j.1469-5812.2008.00457.x.

Nola, R. (1997). Constructivism in science and in science education: A philosophical critique. *Science & Education, 6*(1-2), 55–83. doi:10.1023/A:1008670030605.

Prabowo, R., & Thelwall, M. (2009). Sentiment analysis: A combined approach. *Journal of Informetrics, 3*(2), 143–157. doi:10.1016/j.joi.2009.01.003.

Richardson, V. (2003). Constructivist pedagogy. *Teachers College Record, 105*(9), 1623–1640. doi:10.1046/j.1467-9620.2003.00303.x.

Sidnell, J. (2010). *Conversation analysis: An introduction.* London: Wiley-Blackwell.

Ten Have, P. (1999). *Doing conversation analysis. A practical guide.* Thousand Oaks: Sage.

Tolmie, A., & Boyle, J. (2000). Factors influencing the success of computer mediated communication (CMC) environments in university teaching: A review and case study. *Computers & Education, 34*(2), 119–140. doi:10.1016/S0360-1315(00)00008-7.

Van Overwalle, F., & Jordens, K. (2002). An adaptive connectionist model of cognitive dissonance. *Personality and Social Psychology Review, 6*(3), 204–231. doi:10.1207/S15327957PSPR0603_6.

Wittmann, S. (2011). Learning strategies and learning-related emotions among teacher trainees. *Teaching and Teacher Education*, 27(3), 524–532. doi:10.1016/j.tate.2010.10.006.

Wodak, R., & Meyer, M. (2001). *Methods of critical discourse analysis*. London: SAGE.

KEY TERMS AND DEFINITIONS

Cognitive Dissonance: A discomfort caused by holding conflicting cognitions (e.g. ideas, beliefs, values, emotional reactions) simultaneously.

Computer-Mediated Educational Discourse: A sociopsychological approach to CMC by examining how humans use "computers" (or digital media) to manage interpersonal interaction and to study of teacher response and to support to pupils' learning.

Constructivist Theory: Learning theory focuses on how students build their knowledge and skills.

Conversation Analysis: An approach to the study of social interaction, embracing both verbal -and non-verbal conduct, in situations of everyday life.

Discourse Analysis Methods: A general term for a number of approaches to analysing written, vocal, or sign language use or any significant semiotic event.

Effective Learning: Effective learning taking into account the student's emotional state.

Emotions: The various bodily feelings associated with mood, temperament, personality, disposition, and motivation and also with hormones and neurotransmitters.

Sentiment Analysis: The application of natural language processing, computational linguistics, and text analytics to identify and extract subjective information in source materials.

Chapter 7
Social Networks and Creative Writing in EFL

Reima Al-Jarf
King Saud University, Riyadh, Saudi Arabia

ABSTRACT

A sample of Facebook creative writing club pages created by Arab Facebook users and a sample of Facebook creative wall posts from each creative writing club page were collected and examined. The study aimed to find out the types of creative text forms (genres), themes and discoursal features of the Facebook English creative texts posted by non-native writers. In addition, a sample of Facebook Arab creative writers who are non-native speakers of English was surveyed to find out the personal, social, and cultural factors that impact their creativity in English as a foreign language. The chapter describes the data collection and analysis procedures and the challenges that a researcher faces in collecting, sorting out and analyzing creative texts posted on the Facebook wall. It reports results quantitatively and qualitatively. Implications for developing creative writing skills in foreign/second language learners using Facebook are given.

INTRODUCTION

Social networks such as Facebook and Twitter have been used by Arab users for many purposes such as reporting breaking news, posting special events, launching political campaigns and special causes, announcing family gatherings and sending seasons' greetings. Another emerging type of wall posts is creative writing in English which is their foreign and/or second language. Some EFL/ESL Arab Facebook users post lines of verse, short

anecdotes or points of view, express emotions, personal experiences, interpersonal relations, sarcastic comments and/or inspirational stories or sayings written in literary style. A sample of Facebook creative writing pages created by Arab Facebook users was selected. Then a sample of creative Facebook wall posts from each creative writing page was collected and examined. A sample of Facebook Arab creative writers who are non-native speakers of English was surveyed to find out the reasons for their creative writing

DOI: 10.4018/978-1-4666-4426-7.ch007

activities in English as a foreign language. This chapter aims to find out the types of creative genres, types of creative writing themes posted and features of the Facebook creative discourse in English by Arab non-native writers and the characteristics of the Facebook environment that nurtured their creativity.

BACKGROUND

In foreign language classrooms, some students and instructors feel that writing is a chore. Some students are hesitant to write because they might be inhibited, might be afraid of making mistakes or because they are incapable of generating ideas. To enhance students' writing skills, in general, and creative writing, in particular, researchers have utilized several instructional strategies and practices, such as collaborative creative writing activities and projects (Feuer, 2011; Vass, 2002), the integration of cooperative learning, journalizing, and creative writing (Bartscher, Lawler, Ramirez, & Schinault, 2001), using wordless picture books (Henry, 2003), plot scaffolding (O'Day, 2006), the cluster method (Sahbaz & Duran, 2011), the integration of creative and critical written responses to literary texts in different genres (Wilson, 2011) and others.

In addition to the above classroom techniques, several technologies have been utilized in the past two decades to develop L1 and L2 students' writing abilities. For example, early studies by Casella (1989) found the word processor to be an effective tool in helping students compose poetry, because of its formatting features and ease of revision (Casella, 1989). Similarly, the integration of electronic mail and word-processing in an intermediate pre-academic ESL course improved the academic writing abilities of nonnative students who responded to writing prompts using electronic mail and word processing. Improvement

was noted in the use of cohesive features, length of text produced in each medium and text-initial contextualization (Biesenbach-Lucas & Weasenforth, 2001). Another effective technology was presentation software, such as PowerPoint, which were used by elementary school students to create electronic books that integrate text, audio, and graphics. The presentation software was used to introduce the concept, plan the story on paper with the help of a worksheet, create the story on the computer, and share it with others (Hodges, 1999).

Apart from word-processing, e-mail, and Powerpoint presentations, many earlier studies used specially designed systems and programs to develop students' writing skills. For example, *Systeme-D*, a word processing program for creative writing in French, helped students exploit more of the linguistic features as well as the system's dictionary (Scott, 1990). Another computer program called *The Bald Headed Chicken* assisted primary-level and limited-English-speaking students used to manipulate graphics and text, to create their own stories, and to save them on disk or print them (Gammon, 1989). A computer network available to schools, called the *Writers in Electronic Residence (WIER)*, enabled students to post their creative writings which were then discussed by professional writers, students and teachers (Owen, 1995). Furthermore, *KidPub*, a World Wide Web site, was designed to accept stories submitted by or on behalf of children and young people under the age of 16 and publishes them, giving each story its own Web page. With the help of a mentor, a child published a story via this Website. The system allowed her to track the number of times her story was read, as well as reading and responding to reader comments and reactions (Keiner, 1996).

At a later stage, online journal writing, computer labs, and online courses were used to enhance students' writing ability. In their case study, Guzzetti and Gamboa (2005) described how adolescents used online journal writing as a literacy practice, how and why they choose to read and compose online journals as electronic texts, how they respond to post-typographical texts and design their own texts. They use online journal writing for social connection, identity formation and representation, and as a link to school literacy assignments.

Not only were technologies used to enhance children and adolescents' writing skills, but they were also used to help ESL college writers to develop their writing skills. For example, a course in computer-aided writing was implemented at South Seattle Community College (SSCC) to teach writing to college transfer and ESL students at SSCC. Instructors reported several advantages of the use of English computer labs such as speed and ease of revisions, providing drills and practice of skills and a professional look to students' papers. They also reported several disadvantages such as the increased demand on students' time, students' over-reliance on spelling and thesaurus programs, and computers' inability to store previous drafts (Bentley & Bourret, 1991). In Al-Jarf's (2007) study, *Nicenet*, an Online course Management System, encouraged Saudi freshman students of different proficiency levels to write poems and short stories in English as a foreign language.

Since 2005, social networking platforms, such as Facebook and Twitter, have been popular in online communication among adult Internet users. They have been used for many purposes such as reporting breaking news, posting special events, launching political campaigns and special causes, announcing family gatherings, sending seasons' greetings, posting photos and videos of interest to them and posting comments and viewpoints on social, political, economic, educational issues and world events. They have also been used by students and instructors as a communication and instructional medium. A review of the literature has shown a rising interest in the academic applications of social networking sites and studies

have investigated several issues such as: The educational use of social networking technology in higher education (Hung & Yuen, 2010), their influence on high school students' social and academic development (Ahn, 2010), their impact on academic relations at the university (Rambe, 2011), using them for experiential learning (Arnold & Paulus, 2010), for situated learning (Mills, 2011), in intensive English program classroom from a language socialization perspective (Reinhardt & Zander, 2011), for online role-plays to develop students' argumentative strategies (Beach & Doerr-Stevens, 2011), to recruit undergraduate students (Ferguson, 2010), to foster interdisciplinary and cross-cohort student communication during workforce training (Levine, Winkler, & Petersen, 2010), appropriate professional behavior for faculty and college students on social networks (Malesky & Peters, 2012), and others.

In the area of foreign/second language learning, in particular, a multitude of Facebook pages are available, and learners can join those to develop their listening, speaking, reading, general writing skills, and knowledge of grammar and vocabulary. Facebook also has a multitude of creative writing pages for students, amateurs as well as professional creative writers. Even on non-academic Facebook pages, many English and Arabic posts are characterized by their creative expression and artistic style.

Despite the importance of social networks as a medium for creative writing, studies that investigate the effects of using social networks such as Facebook and Twitter on the production of creative texts and that explore the forms, themes, discoursal features of creative texts posted on adult social networks are lacking. In this respect, Hesse (2010) notes:

… as digital tools and media expand the nature and circulation of texts, composition studies should pay more attention to craft and composition of texts not created in response to rhetorical situations.

To fill the gap in this area of research, the present study aims to examine a sample of Facebook creative writing by a sample of non-native English-speaking Arab adults. It aims to find out the types of forms, themes and discoursal features of the Facebook creative texts written by non-native writers of English, describe the Facebook creative writing environment and Facebook activities that initiated creative writing, report the personal and social factors that affect creativity in L2, and provide guidelines for nurturing creativity in EFL/ESL students based on the findings. Specifically, the study aims to answer the following questions: (i) What kind of creative writing forms and themes are posted on Facebook by non-native speakers of English? (ii) What are the characteristics of the Facebook English creative discourse by non-native speakers of English? (iii) What are the characteristics of the Facebook creative writing environment in English as a foreign/second language? (iv) What Facebook activities initiated creative writing by non-native speakers of English? (v) What personal and social factors impact the Facebook creative texts by non-native speakers of English?

To answer those questions, the study will describe how the samples of Facebook creative writing pages, of creative texts and of creative writers were selected, how the sample of creative texts was analyzed according to theme and types and how discourse features were identified. It will also describe the questionnaire survey and how the sample of Facebook creative writers was surveyed to find out the personal and social factors that affect their creative endeavors. It is noteworthy to say that the aim of this study is not to conduct an extensive literary critical analysis of the creative texts. Rather the text analysis aims to explore the characteristics of the Facebook environment that was conducive to creative writing by non-native speakers of English.

The study of the effects of social networks on the production of creative discourse by non-native English-speakers is especially interesting

and results of the analysis will contribute to our understanding (especially writing instructors) of their creativity on Facebook. The study will describe ways in which peer collaboration can resource, stimulate and enhance the production of creative texts. The benefits of teaching writing through social networks, especially to non-mainstream students who are usually inhibited by traditional writing instruction in the classroom will be demonstrated as well. Insights can be gained from the results and used to improve the general teaching of creative writing to EFL students; thus expanding the pedagogical repertoire available to writing instructors.

METHODOLOGY

To answer the questions of the present study, a sample of Facebook creative writing club pages, a sample of creative texts selected from the Facebook clubs and a sample of creative writers who are members of those clubs were selected. Each of which is described in detail below.

Sample of Creative Writing Facebook Pages

Facebook was searched for English creative writing clubs/pages. Several search terms were used: "Writing club," "creative writing club," "creative writing group," "creative writers' club," "inspirational writing" and "English clubs." A total of 313 creative writing and creative writers' Facebook pages were found. However, About 70% of those received fewer than 50 likes. Those creative writing Facebook pages belong to universities, colleges, schools, non-profit and community organizations, centers for creativity, and individuals. Most of them were created by US users. and are for creative writers who are native speakers of English. About 10 Facebook creative writing pages created and used by non-native speakers of English in India, Pakistan, Nigeria, the Czech Republic,

147

Egypt, Algeria and Saudi Arabia were found. For purposes of the present study, only creative writing Facebook pages created by writers who are non-native speakers of English in Saudi Arabia and Egypt were found. The sample selected had to meet several criteria: The club page should not be part of a professional English language teaching and learning club/page and should not be part of formal writing courses. Creative writing clubs with fewer than 10 likes or members, those created two months ago and those with members who are native speakers of English were excluded. Thus, the final sample consisted of three Facebook creative writing club pages that met the above criteria. The following is a brief description of each:

1. **Riyadh Writing Club (RWC) (http://www. facebook.com/RiyadhWritingClub):** It was created by two Saudi female creative writers; it joined Facebook on April 6, 2011, has received 267 likes, and has 16 contributing creative Saudi female writers. The RWC page is complementary to the creators' *Wordpress* blog (http://riyadhwritingclub. wordpress.com/). The aims of the page are: *to bring together the talented female writers in Riyadh, Saudi Arabia. Its intention is to activate imagination and enable receiving constructive criticism from like-minded, talented, and creative people.*

2. **Riyadh' Creative Writers and Designers on Facebook (RCWD) (http://www.facebook.com/riyadhcreativewriters):** It was created by a single male creative writer. It joined Facebook on March 15, 2010 and has received 472 likes. The aim of the page is to *"express thought in words."*

3. **English Inspiration Club in Egypt (EIC) (http://www.facebook.com/ pages/English-Inspiration-Club-in-Egypt/116333485136837):** It was created by a group of Egyptians; it joined Facebook on September 13, 2011, and has received 162

likes. The aims of the page are: *to spread the quality of Education for English in Egypt… learn English to get more knowledge and better communication with other cultures… (and learn) from each other.*

EIC is not limited to creative or inspirational writing; grammar rules, usage tips, quizzes and vocabulary enrichment exercises are also posted.

Sample of Creative Texts

To have a sufficient sample of creative texts, all posts (entries) and related comments (sub-entr*ies) in the three Facebook clubs were collected. The author browsed through all of the posts in each club and only posts that are creative were selected. Posts with an*nouncements, advertisements, links to articles, videos, compliments, news stories, texts written in a foreign language other than English, and texts with academic or journalistic style were excluded. Creative texts copied or cited from other authors, sources or websites were also excluded. The sample of creative texts included only original texts written by members of the club themselves. The final corpus of Facebook discourse included a total of 385 creative texts: 104 creative texts from RWC, 236 creative texts from RCWD, and 45 creative texts from EIC in Egypt. Poems constituted 22% of the creative posts and 78% were reflections and short narratives (short stories). The creative texts varied in length: From one line to about a page. However, most consisted of few lines, due to limitations of space on Facebook. The unit of creative discourse analysis chosen was the single post (entry) regardless of its length and excluding the comments (sub-entries) it received.

The author faced several challenges in selecting the sample of creative texts. First, Facebook posts are not permanent in nature. Some authors choose to delete some of their posts for no obvious reason. Some creative texts that were located by the author disappeared although they were present a month or even a week earlier. What helped keep track of those was that she saved all of the club posts in PDF format. A second challenge was locating creative texts and sorting out stories by author or topic. Although Facebook has a timeline that displays all of the stories posted each month by all members of a particular club, it does not have an analytics tool or App for sorting out stories by author or topic and does not give statistics nor lists all posts by a single author as it is the case in online forums. In addition, posts are not archived under tags, as it is the case in blogs, to facilitate the browsing and searching process. To locate and sort out creative and non-creative posts, the author had to print all of the club pages, browse through the posts one by one, read each post and count those that are creative. Locating, browsing through all posts, sorting out creative and non-creative texts and calculating the number of creative texts posted by each writer manually was time-consuming.

Sample of Creative Writers

Only members of the creative writing clubs who have creative contributions were selected. The sample consisted of total of 60 (48 females and 12 males) Facebook creative writers selected from the three clubs: 41 creative writers (35 females and 6 males) from RWC; 15 creative writers (10 females and five males) from RCWD and 4 creative writers (one male and three female) from EIC. Creative writers from RWC are all Saudis and are native speakers of Arabic; most members of RCWD are Arab and few are Indians and Pakistanis who live in Saudi Arabic and speak both Arabic and English as a second language; and those of the EIC are Egyptian and are native-speakers of Arabic. Most of the subjects are in their twenties. Some are students studying English literature; others are studying journalism, business, information technology or social work. Some are professionals: English teachers, journalists, businessmen,

information technology specialists, and lawyers. Five subjects are in high school and three are as young as 15 years old. Most went to an English-medium school at least half of their school years and studied in English in college.

Other than posting in the creative writing club, members of the RWC have a group Wordpress blog where they publish their creative work; half of the members of the RCWD have their own blog; Ali, the founder, has 4 blogs and few post their poems on poetry.com.

Some of the challenges that the author faced while collecting personal data about the subjects are that many do not post information about themselves such as age, major, education or nationality on Facebook; and others make their own Facebook page private and thus their personal data could not be accessed. Some do not provide contact details and do not respond to Facebook messages.

Questionnaire Surveys

The sample of Facebook creative writers selected was surveyed and each was asked open-ended questions about their creative writing activities on Facebook. The questions requested information about their age, major area of study, type of work, where they went to school; whether they went to an English-medium school; how they develop and polish their writing skill in English; why they chose Facebook to post their creative work; in what ways Facebook helped them to write creatively; whether they knew other members prior to joining the Facebook creative writing club; the role that Facebook club members play in their creative writing process and productivity.

The questions were sent to each member through his/her Facebook account and answers were received through my Facebook message service. 65% of the subjects responded to the author's questions probably because they do not know her or because of inappropriate timing as questionnaire were sent out in the fasting month of Ramadan which coincided with the summer holiday.

There were more female than male respondents and all of the respondents agreed to participate in the study and answer the survey questions, to have excerpts of their work cited in this chapter and to have their first names referred to herein. Respondents were assured that their identities and associated responses will remain confidential and will be used for research purposes only. As a matter of fact some were happy to be part of a research study and did not mind the citation of their work as it is publicly published on Facebook.

Data Analysis

Identifying Creative Texts, Their Forms, Themes and Features

To help identify creative texts, an operational definition of creative texts was used. Features given by the following definitions were taken into consideration in sorting out creative and non-creative posts.

According to Fraser (2006):

Creativity concerns novelty and originality... Creative writers surface original ideas through constructing their own creative texts. They generate novel responses and multiple interpretations. Creative texts reveal unique voices that range from the playful to the dramatic in their creative exploration of what it means to be human.

Your Dictionary (2012) defines creative writing as:

Writing that expresses ideas and thoughts in an imaginative way. The writer gets to express feelings and emotions instead of just presenting the facts." The dictionary adds that *"the best way to define creative writing is to give a list of things that are and that are not considered creative writing."*

Witty and LaBrant (1946) define creative writing as:

...a composition of any type of writing at any time primarily in the service of such needs as: (1) the need for keeping records of significant experience, (2) the need for sharing experience with an interested group, and (3) the need for free individual expression which contributes to mental and physical health.

In a study by Cheung, Tse, & Tsang (2003), in which they asked 449 Chinese language teachers to define creativity in writing, the teachers identified imagination, inspiration and original ideas as components of effective writing.

Based on the above definitions, creative texts that focus on a writer's free self-expression, i.e., those in which the writers express feelings and emotions and reveal unique voices and those characterized by novelty, imagination, inspiration and originality were considered creative and were selected. Creative texts could be poems, novels, novella, short stories, epics, autobiography/ memoir, creative personal and journalistic essays, flash fiction, playwriting/dramatic writing television scripts, screenplays, songs, lyrics, wise sayings, reflections...etc. Academic, technical and journalistic writing were not considered creative.

To be considered narrative (novels and fiction), a text should have characters, point of view, plot, setting, dialogue (fiction), style (fiction), theme and motif no matter how short it is. To be considered a poem, a text should be characterized by rhyme schemes, sound elements figurative language and/or images. Sophistication level was determined on the bases of types of sentence structures, sentence length and complexity, word choice, style, use of innovative expressions, figurative language and rhythm. Correctness of grammar, spelling, punctuation and capitalization and appropriateness of the text layout to a particular genre were noted.

For validation purposes, two raters who are professors of English literature were asked to sort out a sample of texts into creative and non-creative, identify the forms, themes, and discoursal features of those creative texts. To help the raters identify the types of creative texts, i.e. their genre, it was necessary to give them some background about the aims of the study, the authors of the excerpts and the Facebook creative writing clubs. Providing the raters with the page links where the excerpts are located helped them comprehend and identify their types more accurately than giving them the excerpts in isolation, i.e. out of context. For example, when a rater was given the excerpt below from RWC in isolation, i.e. without providing any information about the author and where it was taken from, she thought it was a "diary," not a "poem."

I will write my way home tonight; I will write my way to you. Love, you may ask: But where do you find me? I find you in music. Every sweet song, and every strum of the guitar that comes through my headphones brings you out. I find you in literature. In every word...

The type of genre was mis-identified, because of the word *"write."* But when she saw it on Facebook, and she browsed through the RCW page, she was able to identify the genre more accurately. Results of the analyses by the author and the two raters were compared and disagreements were resolved by discussion.

Identifying the Factors Affecting Facebook Creativity

Creative writers' responses to the open-ended questions were sorted out and personal and social reasons that affect their creative writing activities were identified; in addition to conclusions based on a content analysis of the subjects' posts and comments received.

Quantitative and Qualitative Data Analyses

The total number of creative texts and percentages of creative texts belonging to each category (poem, reflections or short narrative) were calculated. The themes and discoursal features of the creative texts collected are reported and described qualitatively. Responses to the questionnaire results are also reported qualitatively. Where excerpts are cited, the authors' real first names are also cited.

RESULTS AND DISCUSSION

Type of Creative Writing Forms and Themes Posted

Analysis of the creative texts collected from the three Facebook creative writing clubs has shown that creative writers in the present study post poems, short narratives (stories), reflections (spiritual and otherwise), religious supplications, points of view, words of wisdom, inspirational sayings and motivational thoughts and advice written in literary style. They express emotions (love, nostalgia, disappointment, misery, cruelty, abandonment, alienation ... etc), write about personal experiences, observations, philosophy, interpersonal relations, social issues, and/or Islamic beliefs (See examples 1, 4 and 9, 10, 12, 15 in the Appendix). The same author may write several types of genres: Poems, reflections and short narratives as in the case of Ali and Sameera (See Examples 1 to 4 and 6 to 8).

Being Muslim, the influence of Islamic culture and Islamic beliefs is very evident in the themes creative writers in the present study write about and in how they view the world, other humans, relationships and other life issues expressed especially in their reflections, advice and motivational sayings as in Examples 3, 4, 7 and 16. Ali from

RCWD even states his Islamic faith/stance very clearly in one of his posts:

The post below is written to MYSELF alone...I write ALL things with ME or God as the subjects or advise in general to people...Either I am addressing Him or finding fault in Me or Sharing wisdom I know, heard or experienced and find it to be reality...My life is about me and my Creator ...

Activities that Triggered Creative Writing

The RWC founders post "projects" that constitute themes for club members to write voluntarily about and post. A total of 12 projects have been posted: "Being human, coffee, conspiracy, Eve, glass, John, letter, new beginnings, nostalgia, the paranormal, the world, turning point" and a total of 104 creative texts were written under those 12 projects, most of which are poems. Examples 10-14 show texts (all poems) posted under the theme "Coffee." The content in many of the posts has nothing to do with the 'project' theme. Examples 10-12 are unrelated whereas Examples 13 and 14 mention "coffee" in the content. Some of the posts are poems with verses laid out next to each other, rather than under each other as it customary in poem layout (See examples 11-14).

In the other two clubs (RCWD and EIC); members are free to post anything. However, some members of EIC begin a story and ask other members to complete it. Some request other club members to design creative logos and comment on them as in Figure 1. The creator of *RCWD* is also an artist and his creative posts are reflections on some paintings or scenes posted as Figure 2 shows.

Characteristics of Creative Discourse

Creative texts written by members of RWC and RCWD are more sophisticated than those written by EIC members. Members of the two former clubs are of a higher proficiency level in English. They exhibit more verbal originality and verbal flexibility as in Examples 1 to 14 even when very simple language is used as in Examples 1, 4, 5, 6, 12. They used more sophisticated themes and details, innovative expressions *(strappy heals, flung across, perched, haunting),* innovative im-

Figure 1. Logo and creative comment from EIC

Figure 2. Poem describing a painting from RCWD

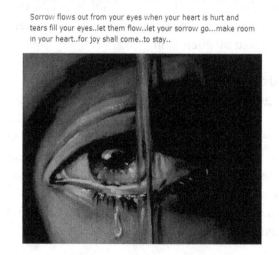

ages and figures of speech *(the crushing weight of disappointment; fire-eyed; desert of your mind; well of wisdom; you wore nothing but your skin; Victoria-Beckham-like sunglasses)* and almost made no grammatical, spelling and punctuation mistakes. As mentioned earlier, the lines of the poems in RWC are laid out next to each other like prose as in Examples 11 to 14, may be because of the Facebook formatting limitations. However, this does not affect comprehensibility, vividness, and effectiveness of language and style.

On the other hand, members of the EIC are mainly students learning the basics of the English language. Therefore their creative texts were written at their own ability level and they are less imaginative and innovative in their theme and style. They made more grammatical and spelling errors as in Zoha, Emi and Mamadou's poems in Examples 15, 16 and 17. Although Zoha's poem is sophisticated in theme, expressions, vocabulary and style, she made mistakes in verb tenses, has many misplaced commas, and spelled the first person singular pronoun "I" in lower case (See underlined errors in Example 15). Emi capitalized every single word for no reason, did not know the English equivalents to the Arabic and Islamic words "hijab" and "Gheebah" and sometimes uses meaningless expression such as "Please Winder And More Moddest Cloths." Mamadou misspelled "harry," used non-standard forms such as "gonna," "ur" and "FRV" *and* capitalized the last line which makes is difficult to tell whether it is a note or part of the poem. Writers like Zoha, Emi and Mamadou do not seem to worry about grammatical, spelling and punctuation mistakes as they write for communication and their aim, as expressed in their other posts, is to practice their English.

Another feature is that informal and conversational English is more evident in the creative writing of the three clubs under study than formal English. This is evident through the use of contracted verb forms, imperative verbs and the second person pronoun "you." The reader feels that those writers are talking to him//her. Use of spoken English makes ideas, images and expressions more vivid.

Findings about the sophistication level of the language used by creative writers in the present study are contradictory with the assumptions and results of Tin's study (2011) in which he investigated opportunities for creative language use and the emergence of complex language in creative writing tasks with high formal constraints (acrostics) and those with looser formal constraints (similes). Formal constraints lead to complex and creative language use, transforming familiar utterances into unfamiliar ones, shaping and reshaping learners' language syntactically and lexically, paradigmatically, and syntagmatically. Tin concluded that for learners' language to develop in complexity, conditions that require them to access L2 directly to construct new ideas are needed for both L2 forms and meaning to co-evolve. In the present study, the sophistication level of the creative texts is not due to any formal constraints as the three Facebook creative writing clubs are for amateur creative writers and not part of a formal creative writing course. No constraints on style, length, theme, content or deadlines for posting their work are imposed on the writers. No constraints are imposed on linguistic accuracy and correctness as even less proficient writers have the courage to post their poems without being inhibited by their linguistic inadequacies. Talent, wide reading, self-motivation and desire for self-expression, the subjects reported, seem to affect creativity.

Factors Affecting Creativity in L2 Writers

In her analysis of the processes of creative writing, Morgan (2006) argued that intuition and analysis, the conscious and unconscious, working together, and the social and personal are all involved in these processes. She concluded that personal as well as social, cultural and disciplinary factors are at play in the development of creative work. In another study, Jonesa and Issroffb (2005) investigated the role of affective factors in three main areas of collaboration: In settings where learners are co-located, in on-line communities and to support and develop socio-emotional skills. Their results stressed affective issues in learning technologies in a collaborative context. Learner attitude, motivation, and emotional state were found to be very important.

As in Morgan and Jonesa and Issroffb's studies, results of the questionnaire-survey in the present study revealed that both personal and social factors play a role in the subjects' creativity. Creative writers in the present study tended to be intrinsically motivated and enthusiastic. Area of specialty, educational level, and proficiency level in English do not seem to be factors leading to creative writing. All creative writers reported that they are avid readers, write a lot and have an urge for expressing themselves. All of the members of the RWC share a Wordpress blog where they post their creative work, and several members of RCWD have their own Wordpress blog; Ali has four blogs. Other members, such as Eman, reported that they post poem on the Poetry.com website. Creative writers of lower proficiency level reported that they are always motivated by creative writers of a higher proficiency level. They learn from them and see examples of good writing. Some members also indicated that the Facebook writing club is a fast way of publishing their creative work. That is why each blog is connected to a Facebook page containing samples of their work and links referring to their blog posts.

Another important personal factor is the centrality of emotions in the observed creative text and expression. All creative writers produce poems, reflections and short stories that are meaningful and original. They tend to express their feelings and emotional involvement with a personal expe-

rience that they had or their views of an issue or philosophy about something (See Examples 1, 6, 7, 10 to 14). Ali says:

Emotions need education. They need pacification and guidance. Emotions are so powerful that they can take the heart to extremes of despair and to the greatest heights of joy. Both resulting in destruction of the soul or even the body sometimes. These same emotions can be the source of good health and a good life if nurtured by wisdom. Wisdom, which is acquired from reflections and realizations of existence...

Ali also wrote:

What is expressed reveals what one may seek to discover. I have ventured into my own soul and mind to discover my real self. My inner self. Is any knowledge in this world sufficient to define to me myself? And, is there anything that deserves to be defined more?

No. It is only my own expression of my thoughts and Realities that will reveal to me what I am and in acquiring this knowledge I shall know mankind...and you...

These findings are also consistent with findings of studies by Vass (2007) and Vass, Littleton, Miell, and Jones (2008) in which they conducted longitudinal observations of ongoing classroom-based collaborative writing activities conducted with 24 British children in grades 3 and 4, aged 7-9. A functional model was developed to analyze the cognitive processes associated with creative text composition (engagement and reflection) via an in-depth study of collaborative discourse. A key finding was the centrality of emotions in the observed creative writing sessions. Their results also highlighted the role of emotion-driven thinking in phases of shared engagement and creative-thinking.

As for social factors affecting creativity, results of the questionnaire-survey showed that most of the creative writers in the present study like to share their feelings and thoughts with readers and other members of the Facebook club. They also reported that the Facebook creative writing club, as a social network, has a positive effect on their creativity and on their attitude towards writing as it creates an open and supportive environment, where creative writing is appreciated, and authors are encouraged to trust their own linguistic ability. The Facebook writing club nurtures their creativity in every way possible. It makes writing an enjoyable task. They dive into the writing task because it is exciting, challenging and fun. They feel comfortable and unthreatened to reach maximal creativity. As a result, a positive personal relationship with other members of the Facebook writing club is fostered, although the members reported that they did not know each other before joining the Facebook club. Here is what Hassan says about the club:

I enjoy collaborating; it is what we do in EIC; different ideas make me pause; i practice English while decorating my mind; i enjoy UNDERSTANDING.

Peer support, interaction and feedback among members of the Facebook club were also important. Creative writers in the present study receive *"likes,"* positive comments, encouraging remarks, and words of admiration from other club members such as *"Mashallah," "Go," "well said,"* as shown in Figures 3 and 4. Such positive comments and remarks make them feel good about themselves and enhance their motivation. Analysis of the members' comments has shown that more proficient members do not correct grammatical, spelling or punctuation mistakes of less proficient writers. No matter how poor the writing is, no negative comments are given. Comments are usually given on the content, not the form of what is posted.

Example of the comments that Emi received on her poem are:

EIC: *great massage Emi...and nice advice..keep it up.*
Aya: *like this.*
Deepak: *Osome!*

Other members show their admiration and appreciation of a post by requesting to share the post with others as in Figure 3.

This way, the Facebook club provides a non-threatening environment for trying out new ways of expressing themselves in English. Environmental friendliness prevails in the Facebook club. Writers of lower proficiency level, such as Emi, feel free to make mistakes without being afraid of losing marks or receiving negative comments regarding their mistakes as in a formal classroom setting.

Furthermore, analysis of the members' comments has shown that more proficient members in RCWD give more sophisticated comments; some respond creatively on the theme and look view it from a different angle. For example they reflect upon the ideas of the post as in Figure 4. Such comments help expand the theme of the original post and enrich the writer's outlook and creative

Figure 3. Post and comments, i.e., interaction from RCWD

Figure 4. Post and comments, i.e., interaction from RCWD

thinking. Here again, as Vass (2007) indicated, peer interaction and collaboration can resource, stimulate and enhance creative writing. Also, it shows writers' reliance on the collaborative floor which was indicative of joint focus and intense sharing, thus facilitating mutual inspiration in the content generation phases of the writers' writing activities (Vass, 2007). Members of the Facebook creative writing clubs in this study, as Bruno (2002) indicated, seem to serve as a source of constant evolving inspiration and a place where there is trust, no matter of what the students write and whether they are native speakers, as in Bruno's study, or L2 learners, as in the present study. The Facebook club fosters participants' creative freedom in producing a well-formed piece of writing showing appropriate control of tone, style, and register (Howarth, 2007). Findings of the presents study are also consistent with findings of Al-Jarf's (2007) study who found that the collaborative, supportive and motivating environment of the Online Course Management System contributed

to the development of freshman students' creative writing ability.

As in the present study, several researchers emphasized the effect of a supportive learning environment and of peer feedback provided to student creative writers using other forms of technology or receiving traditional classroom instruction. For example, Hyland (1993) indicated that use of word processors for developing writing skills of foreign language students created unrealistically high expectations regarding learning gains and indicated that only teachers could improve the situation through a supportive learning environment. Essex (1996) noted that most children enter school with a natural interest in writing, and teachers can become actively involved in teaching creative writing to their students, and highlighted the effectiveness of peer feedback in the creative writing process. In addition, Kaufman, Gentile, and Baer's (2005) study supported the use of peer feedback among gifted novice creative writers. They also recommended the use of collaborative feedback in gifted classrooms.

FUTURE RESEARCH DIRECTIONS

The present study starts a new line of research in the study of Facebook discourse and in using social networking websites such as in language learning in general and creative writing, in particular. Future research may investigate the forms, themes and discoursal features of creative texts posted on Facebook writing clubs by writers who are native speakers of English compared to non-native speakers and factors that affect their productivity can be investigated and compared. Since Twitter does not allow the posting of tweets longer than 140 characters, the forms, themes and discoursal features of English creative tweets by native and non-native speakers of English may be subject of further investigation by future research. The discoursal features of Arabic creative writing on social networks such as Facebook and Twitter and comparisons of creative writing skills on social networks in both English (L2) and Arabic (L1) by the same authors are still open for further investigation. In addition, future research may investigate the effects of using a writing class Facebook club by EFL students as a supplement to in-class college instruction on writing achievement, the effects of integrating creative texts from the Facebook creative writing clubs in classroom reading and writing instruction and may compare traditional writing teaching techniques with those that integrate Facebook or Twitter in writing instruction in second language classrooms.

To encourage and produce more research in the area of discourse and social networks, Facebook and Twitter need to add an analytics tool or App whereby researchers can get statistics about posts and tweets according to subject and author. Tags can be added to the Facebook timeline. These would also facilitate browsing and sorting out of posts and tweets and make the processes less tedious and less time-consuming.

CONCLUSION

The present study examined a sample of Facebook creative writing texts created by Arab Facebook users to find out the kinds of creative writing forms and themes posted; the characteristics of the Facebook English creative discourse and creative writing environment in English as a foreign/second language; the Facebook activities that initiated creative writing by non-native speakers of English and the personal and social factors that impacted the Facebook creative texts by non-native speakers of English. It was found that creative writers in the present study, even those who are 15 years old and are still high school students, like to share their feelings and thoughts about themes of their choice with the other Facebook creative writing club members. They find the Facebook

environment supportive as they receive positive feedback and "likes" from them. Thus the Facebook nurtures their creativity and makes writing an enjoyable task.

Findings of the present study show, as James (2008) indicated, that all people have a creative potential, and that the right environment with prompts and encouragement can elicit creative work to a degree. Although talent, motivation and desire play an important role in creative writing, creative writing also involves tools, techniques and concepts. Since creative writing is subjective and personal, novice writers need to acquire those tools and techniques in order to experiment, practice, and master them.

Based on the findings of the present study, writing instructors can do much to nurture creative writing skills in their students. They can encourage them to get involved in writing-based extracurricular activities that take place outside the formal college or classroom setting, such as arranging writing contests to develop students' writing skills, spending more time on interactive writing rather than independent and solitary writing and creating a Facebook writing club/page as a supplement to in-class instruction. To encourage students to write freely, enjoy writing and share thoughts and experiences, a Facebook environment that is supportive and safe for trial and error is necessary. All an instructor needs to do is to convince the students to get in touch with their inner voices and encourage them to write for communication rather than focusing on grammatical and spelling correctness as it is usually the case in the classroom. "Likes" and positive feedback are essential. Students need to feel free to express themselves and need to feel good about themselves and what they can do and achieve. A writing group, such as a Facebook writing class page can be a source of constant evolving inspiration and a place where there is trust (Bruno, 2002).

Developing creative writing skills via a Facebook writing class page can go through graded steps depending on the students' proficiency level and writing ability: (i) posting a picture, painting or logo and asking the students to describe it; (ii) posting an inspirational quote and having the students comment on it; (iii) posting story starters such as "once upon a time ..., why do you think that ..., have you ever wondered ..., imagine that…, pretend that ..., what if ..., a funny/sad thing happened..." and asking the students to finish the story. Such an activity will help them use their imagination and express their feelings; (iv) Working on a collaborative project or theme of their choice; and (v) free writing and journaling. Students' poems and short stories can be published on the Facebook wall and the number of "likes" on each poem or story can be tracked and comments responded to.

Simple poetry selected from the three Facebook writing clubs described in the present study may be posted on the writing class Facebook page and/or in-class instruction. It can be used with all learners, even those with limited literacy and proficiency in English (Peyton & Rigg, 1999). Teaching great poetry to students can enhance their perceptions, improve their writing, challenge their minds, and enrich their lives as well (Certo, 2004). It provides rich learning opportunities in language, content, and community building. Repetition of words and structures encourages language play with rhythmic and rhyming devices. Poetic themes are often universal. When teachers and students write and read poetry together, they connect with texts and with one another in powerful ways as well. Such activities are believed to help develop L2 students writing skills, in particular, and creative writing skills, in particular.

REFERENCES

Ahn, J. (2010). *The influence of social networking sites on high school students' social and academic development.* (Unpublished doctoral dissertation). University of Southern California, Los Angeles. Retrieved July 30, 2012, from http://gateway.proquest.com/openurl?url_ver=Z39.88-2004&rft_val_fmt=info:ofi/fmt:kev:mtx:dissertation&res_dat= xri:pqdiss&rft _dat=xri:pqdiss:3417985

Al-Jarf, R. (2007). Online instruction and creative writing by Saudi EFL freshman students. *The Asian EFL Journal Professional Teaching Articles, 22*(August). Retrieved July 30, 2012, from http://www.asian-efl-journal.com/pta_Aug_07_rajl.php

Arnold, N., & Paulus, T. (2010). Using a social networking site for experiential learning: Appropriating, lurking, modeling and community building. *The Internet and Higher Education, 13*(4), 188–196. doi:10.1016/j.iheduc.2010.04.002.

Bartscher, M., Lawler, K., Ramirez, A., & Schinault, K. (2001). *Improving student's writing ability through journals and creative writing exercises.* ERIC Document Reproduction Service No. ED455525.

Beach, R., & Doerr-Stevens, C. (2011). Using social networking for online role-plays to develop students' argumentative strategies. *Journal of Educational Computing Research, 45*(2), 165–181. doi:10.2190/EC.45.2.c.

Bentley, J., & Bourret, R. (1991). *Using emerging technology to improve instruction in college transfer.* ERIC Document Reproduction Service No. ED405011.

Biesenbach-Lucas, S., & Weasenforth, D. (2001). E-Mail and word processing in the ESL classroom: How the medium affects the message. *Language Learning & Technology, 5*(1), 135–165.

Bruno, M. (2002). *Creative writing: The warm-up.* ERIC Document Reproduction Service No. ED464335.

Casella, V. (1989). Poetry and word processing inspire good writing. *Instructor, 98*(9), 28.

Cheung, W., Tse, S., & Tsang, H. (2003). Teaching creative writing skills to primary school children in Hong Kong: Discordance between the views and practices of language teachers. *The Journal of Creative Behavior, 37*(2), 77–98. doi:10.1002/j.2162-6057.2003.tb00827.x.

Creto, J. (2004). Cold plums and the old men in the water: Let children read and write great poetry. *The Reading Teacher, 58*(3), 266–271. doi:10.1598/RT.58.3.4.

Essex, C. (1996). *Teaching creative writing in the elementary school.* ERIC Document Reproduction Service No. ED391182.

Ferguson, C. (2010). *Online social networking goes to college: Two case studies of higher education institutions that implemented college-created social networking sites for recruiting undergraduate students.* ERIC Document Reproduction Service No. ED516904.

Feuer, A. (2011). Developing foreign language skills, competence and identity through a collaborative creative writing project. *Language, Culture and Curriculum, 24*(2), 125–139. doi:10.1080/07908318.2011.582873.

Fraser, D. (2006). The creative potential of metaphorical writing in the literacy classroom. *English Teaching: Practice and Critique, 5*(2), 93–108.

Gammon, G. (1989). You won't lay an egg with the bald headed chicken. *B. C. The Journal of Special Education, 13*(2), 183–187.

Guzzetti, B., & Gamboa, M. (2005). Online journaling: The informal writings of two adolescent girls. *Research in the Teaching of English, 40*(2), 168–206.

Henry, L. (2003). *Creative writing through wordless picture books.* ERIC Document Reproduction Service No. ED477997.

Hesse, D. (2010). The place of creative writing in composition studies. *College Composition and Communication, 62*(1), 31–52.

Hodges, B. (1999). Electronic books: Presentation software makes writing more fun. *Learning and Leading with Technology, 27*(1), 18–21.

Howarth, P. (2007). Creative writing and Schiller's aesthetic education. *Journal of Aesthetic Education, 41*(3), 41–58. doi:10.1353/jae.2007.0025.

Hung, H., & Yuen, S. (2010). Educational use of social networking technology in higher education. *Teaching in Higher Education, 15*(6), 703–714. doi:10.1080/13562517.2010.507307.

Hyland, K. (1993). ESL computer writers: What can we do to help? *System, 2*(1), 21–30. doi:10.1016/0346-251X(93)90004-Z.

James, D. (2008). A short take on evaluation and creative writing. *Community College Enterprise, 14*(1), 79–82.

Jonesa, A., & Issroffb, K. (2005). Learning technologies: Affective and social issues in computer-supported collaborative learning. *Computers & Education, 44*(4), 395–408. doi:10.1016/j.compedu.2004.04.004.

Kaufman, J., Gentile, C., & Baer, J. (2005). Do gifted student writers and creative writing experts rate creativity the same way? *Gifted Child Quarterly, 49*(3), 260. doi:10.1177/001698620504900307.

Keiner, J. (1996). *Real audiences-worldwide: A case study of the impact of WWW publication on a child writer's development.* ERIC Document Reproduction Service No. ED427664.

Levine, A., Winkler, C., & Petersen, S. (2010). The CUNY young adult program--utilizing social networking to foster interdisciplinary and cross-cohort student communication during workforce training. *Journal of Asynchronous Learning Networks, 14*(3), 74–80.

Malesky, L., & Peters, C. (2012). Defining appropriate professional behavior for faculty and university students on social networking websites. *Higher Education: The International Journal of Higher Education and Educational Planning, 63*(1), 135–151.

Mills, N. (2011). Situated learning through social networking communities: The development of joint enterprise, mutual engagement, and a shared repertoire. *CALICO Journal, 28*(2), 345–368.

Morgan, W. (2006). Poetry makes nothing happen: Creative writing and the English classroom. *English Teaching: Practice and Critique, 5*(2), 17–33.

O'Day, S. (2006). *Setting the stage for creative writing: Plot scaffolds for beginning and intermediate writers.* ERIC Document Reproduction Service No. ED493378.

Owen, T. (1995). Poems that change the world: Canada's wired writers. *English Journal, 84*(6), 48–52. doi:10.2307/820891.

Peyton, J., & Rigg, P. (1999). *Poetry in the adult ESL classroom.* ERIC Document Reproduction Service No. ED439626.

Rambe, P. (2011). Exploring the impacts of social networking sites on academic relations in the university. *Journal of Information Technology Education, 10*, 271–293.

Reinhardt, J., & Zander, V. (2011). Social networking in an intensive English program classroom: A language socialization perspective. *CALICO Journal, 28*(2), 326–344.

Sahbaz, N., & Duran, G. (2011). The efficiency of cluster method in improving the creative writing skill of 6th grade students of primary school. *Educational Research Review, 6*(11), 702–709.

Scott, V. (1990). Task-oriented creative writing with systeme-D. *CALICO Journal, 7*(3), 58–67.

Tin, T. (2011). Language creativity and co-emergence of form and meaning in creative writing tasks. *Applied Linguistics, 32*(2), 215–235. doi:10.1093/applin/amq050.

Vass, E. (2002). Friendship and collaborative creative writing in the primary classroom. *Journal of Computer Assisted Learning, 18*(1), 102–110. doi:10.1046/j.0266-4909.2001.00216.x.

Vass, E. (2007). Exploring processes of collaborative creativity--The role of emotions in children's joint creative writing. *Thinking Skills and Creativity, 2*(2), 107–117. doi:10.1016/j.tsc.2007.06.001.

Vass, E., Littleton, K., Miell, D., & Jones, A. (2008). The discourse of collaborative creative writing: Peer collaboration as a context for mutual inspiration. *Thinking Skills and Creativity, 3*(3), 192–202. doi:10.1016/j.tsc.2008.09.001.

Wilson, P. (2011). Creative writing and critical response in the university literature class. *Innovations in Education and Teaching International, 48*(4), 439–446. doi:10.1080/14703297.2011.617091.

Witty, P., & Labrant, L. (1946). *Teaching the people's language.* New York: Hinds, Hayden & Eldredge. Retrieved July 30, from http://archive.org/stream/teachingpeoplesl00witt#page/n3/mode/2up

Your Dictionary. (2012). Retrieved July 30, 2012, from http://reference.yourdictionary.com/word-definitions/definition-of-creativewriting.html

ADDITIONAL READING

Allmann, K. (2009). Arabic language use online: Social, political, and technological dimensions of multilingual internet communication. *The Monitor, (Winter)*. Retrieved July 30, 2012, from http://web.wm.edu/so/monitor/issues/15-1/5-allmann.pdf

Aviram, A., & Talmi, D. (2005). The impact of information and communication technology on education: The missing discourse between three different paradigms. *E-learning, 2*(2), 169–191. doi:10.2304/elea.2005.2.2.5.

Bahr, C., Nelson, N., & Van Meter, A. (1996). The effects of text-based and graphics-based software tools on planning and organizing of stories. *Journal of Learning Disabilities, 29*(4), 355–370. doi:10.1177/002221949602900404 PMID:8763551.

Barker, V. (2012). A generational comparison of social networking site use: The influence of age and social identity. *International Journal of Aging & Human Development, 74*(2), 163–187. doi:10.2190/AG.74.2.d PMID:22808625.

Barron, M. (2007). Creative writing class as crucible. *Academe, 93*(6), 40–43.

Bartesaghi, M., & Hanson, A. (2011). Understanding social networking: The benefit of discourse analysis. In D. Cook & L. Farmer's (Eds.), Serve, reflect, act: A primer on applied qualitative research by librarians. Chicago, IL: ACRL.

Baya'a, N., & Daher, W. (2012). From social communication to mathematical discourse in social networking: The case of Facebook. [IJCEE]. *International Journal of Cyber Ethics in Education, 2*(1).

Bizarro, P. (2004). Research and reflection in English studies: The special case of creative writing. *College English, 66*(3), 294. doi:10.2307/4140750.

Blythe, H., & Sweet, C. (2001). Both sides now II: Some practical suggestions for creative writing exercises in the literature classroom. *Eureka Studies in Teaching Short Fiction, 1*(2), 30–34.

Boyd, D., & Ellison, N. (2007). Social network sites: Definition, history, and scholarship. *Journal of Computer-Mediated Communication, 13*(1), 210–230. doi:10.1111/j.1083-6101.2007.00393.x.

Chigona, A., & Chigona, W. (2008). Mix it up in the media: Media discourse analysis on a mobile instant messaging system. *The Southern African Journal of Information and Communication, 9*, 42–57.

Conroy, T. (2001). Writing possibilities: Email and the creative writing classroom. *Journal of Cooperation & Collaboration in College Teaching, 10*(2), 61–67.

Crews, T., & Stitt-Gohdes, W. (2012). Incorporating Facebook and Twitter in a service-learning project in a business communication course. *Business Communication Quarterly, 75*(1), 76–79. doi:10.1177/1080569911431881.

Davies, J. (2012). Facework on Facebook as a new literacy practice. *Computers & Education, 59*(1), 19–29. doi:10.1016/j.compedu.2011.11.007.

Everett, N. (2005). Creative writing and English. *The Cambridge Quarterly, 34*(3), 231–242. doi:10.1093/camqtly/bfi026.

Firek, H. (2006). Creative writing in the social studies classroom: Promoting literacy and content learning. *Social Education, 70*(4), 183–186.

Garcia, E., Annansingh, F., & Elbeltagi, I. (2011). Management perception of introducing social networking sites as a knowledge management tool in higher education: A case study. *Multicultural Education & Technology Journal, 5*(4), 258–273. doi:10.1108/17504971111185090.

Hartill, G. (1994). *Creative writing: Towards a framework for evaluation.* ERIC Document Reproduction Service No. ED379408.

Helson, R. (1996). In search of the creative personality. Arnheim award address to division 10 of the American psychological association. *Creativity Research Journal, 9*(4), 295–306. doi:10.1207/s15326934crj0904_1.

Jansen, B. (2011). Classifying ecommerce information sharing behaviour by youths on social networking sites. *Journal of Information Science, 37*(2), 120–136. doi:10.1177/0165551510396975.

Julier, L. (2003). *Re-theorizing the role of creative writing in composition studies: Cautionary notes towards re-thinking the essay in the teaching of writing.* ERIC Document Reproduction Service No. ED479202).

Junco, R. (2012). The relationship between frequency of Facebook use, participation in Facebook activities, and student engagement. *Computers & Education, 58*(1), 162–171. doi:10.1016/j.compedu.2011.08.004.

Kayode, B., Zamzami, I., & Olowolayemo, A. (2012). Students' orientation towards interpersonal communication in online social networking sites. *Multicultural Education & Technology Journal, 6*(1), 36–44. doi:10.1108/17504971211216300.

Kelen, C. (2002). Why we should teach creative writing. *English Teacher: An International Journal, 5*(3), 265–276.

Kelly, B. (2007). *Linguistics and the development of community in computer mediated conversation.* Macquarie University Press Release. Retrieved July 30, 2012, from http://www.ict.csiro.au/hail/Abstracts/2007/BarbaraKelly.htm

Lee, C. (2002). Literacy practices in computer-mediated communication in Hong Kong. *The Reading Matrix, 2(June).* Retrieved July 30, 2012, from http://www.mediensprache.net/archiv/pubs/2925.pdf

Marksberry, M. (1963). *Foundation of creativity.* London: Harper & Row.

Miller, R., Parsons, K., & Lifer, D. (2010). Students and social networking sites: The posting paradox. *Behaviour & Information Technology, 29*(4), 377–382. doi:10.1080/01449290903042491.

Mukherjee, D., & Clark, J. (2012). Students' participation in social networking sites: Implications for social work education. *Journal of Teaching in Social Work, 32*(2), 161–173. doi:10.1080/08841233.2012.669329.

Nguyen, T. (2011) Twitter: A platform for political discourse or social networking. *Global Tides, 5.* Retrieved July 30, 2012, from http://digitalcommons.pepperdine.edu/globaltides/vol5/iss1/11

Nishimura, Y. (2003). Linguistic innovations and interactional features of casual online communication in Japanese. *Journal of Computer-Mediated Communication, 1.* Retrieved July 30, 2012, from http://jcmc. indiana.edu/vol9/issue1/nishimura.html

Pardlow, D. (2003). *Finding new voices: Notes from a descriptive study of why and how I learned to use creative-writing pedagogy to empower my composition students--and myself.* ERIC Document Reproduction Service No. ED474934.

Parker, C., Saundage, D., & Lee, C. (2011). Can qualitative content analysis be adapted for use by social informaticians to study social media discourse? A position paper, *in ACIS 2011: Proceedings of the 22nd Australasian Conference on Information Systems: Identifying the Information Systems Discipline* (pp. 1-7). Sydney: Association of Information Systems (AIS).

Piazza, C. L., & Wallat, C. (2008). Exploring multicultural discourse in information technology documents. *Multicultural Education & Technology Journal, 2*(4), 184–199. doi:10.1108/17504970810911025.

Rambe, P. (2012). Critical discourse analysis of collaborative engagement in facebook postings. *Australasian Journal of Educational Technology, 28*(2), 295–314.

Richardson, T., & Jensen, O. (2003). Linking discourse and space: Towards a cultural sociology of space in analyzing spatial policy discourses. *Urban Studies (Edinburgh, Scotland), 40*(1), 7–22. doi:10.1080/00420980220080131.

Shaughnessy, M. (1991). *The supportive educational environment for creativity.* ERIC No. ED360080.

Su, H. (2003). The multilingual and multi-orthographic Taiwan-based internet: Creative uses of writing systems on college-affiliated BBSs. *Journal of Computer-Mediated Communication, 9*(1). Retrieved July 30, 2012, from http://jcmc.indiana.edu/vol9/issue1/su.html

Subrahmanyam, K., Reich, S. M., Waechter, N., & Espinoza, G. (2008). Online and offline social networks: Use of social networking sites by emerging adults. *Journal of Applied Developmental Psychology, 29*(6), 420–433. doi:10.1016/j.appdev.2008.07.003.

Taiwo, R. (2010). *Handbook of research on discourse behavior and digital communication: Language structures and social interaction.* IGI Global. doi:10.4018/978-1-61520-773-2.

Taranto, G., Dalbon, M., & Gaetano, J. (2011). Academic social networking brings web 2.0 technologies to the middle grades. *Middle School Journal, 42*(5), 12–19.

Temizkan, M. (2011). The effect of creative writing activities on the story writing skill. *Educational Sciences: Theory and Practice, 11*(2), 933–939.

Thompson, M. (2005). ICT, power and developmental discourse: A critical analysis. *The Electronic Journal of Information Systems in Developing Countries, 20*(4), 1-26. Retrieved July 30, 2012, from http://www.ejisdc.org/ojs2/index.php/ejisdc/article/viewFile/122/122

Toth, L., & Baker, S. (1990). The relationship of creativity and instructional style preferences to overachievement and underachievement in a sample of public school children. *The Journal of Creative Behavior, 24*(3), 190–198. doi:10.1002/j.2162-6057.1990.tb00540.x.

Urlaub, P. (2011). Developing literary reading skills through creative writing in German as a second language. *Unterrichtspraxis/Teaching German, 44*(2), 98-105.

Wallace, P., & Howard, B. (2010). Social networking tools to facilitate cross-program collaboration. *EDUCAUSE Quarterly, 33*(4).

Wang, C. (2012). Using Facebook for cross-cultural collaboration: The experience of students from Taiwan. *Educational Media International, 49*(1), 63–76. doi:10.1080/09523987.2012.662625.

Warschauer, M., El Said, G., & Zohry, A. (2002). Language choice online: Globalization and identity in Egypt. *Journal of Computer-Mediated Communication, 7(4).* Retrieved July 30, 2012, from http://onlinelibrary.wiley.com/doi/10.1111/j.1083-6101.2002.tb00157.x/full

Wodzicki, K., Schwammlein, E., & Moskaliuk, J. (2012). Actually, I wanted to learn: Study-related knowledge exchange on social networking sites. *The Internet and Higher Education, 15*(1), 9–14. doi:10.1016/j.iheduc.2011.05.008.

Zappavigna, M., & Martin, J. (2012). *Discourse of twitter and social: How we use language to create affiliation on the web.* India, Chinnai. *Continuum.*

KEY TERMS AND DEFINITIONS

Affective Factors: Affective factors in creative writing include learner attitude, motivation, and emotional state.

Creative Discourse: A formal way of thinking expressed through language. It is characterized by novelty, imagination, inspiration and originality.

Creative Writing: It is writing in which the writer expresses feelings and emotions and reveal unique voices. It is characterized by novelty, imagination, inspiration and originality.

Creative Writing Forms: These include poems, novels, novella, short stories, epics, autobiography/memoir, creative personal and journalistic essays, flash fiction, playwriting/dramatic writing television scripts, screenplays, songs, lyrics, wise sayings, reflections…etc. Academic, technical and journalistic writing were not considered creative.

Creative Writing Themes: They express emotions (such as love, nostalgia, disappointment, misery, cruelty, abandonment, alienation …etc.), personal experiences, observations, philosophy, interpersonal relations, social issues, and/or beliefs.

Discourse: It is often described as "language-in-use" or "socially situated text and talk," i.e., how written, oral and visual texts are used in specific contexts to make meanings, as opposed to analysing language-as-an-abstract-system (Discourse Analysis: http://www.discourse-analysis.de/).

Facebook Wall: It is the original profile space where Facebook users' content is shown. It allows the posting of messages for the user to see while displaying the time and date the message was written (Wikipedia: http://en.wikipedia.org/wiki/Facebook_features).

Personal Factors: Those include learner attitude, motivation, and emotional state.

Social Factors: Social factors in creative writing include desire to share feelings and thoughts with readers and members of an online community.

Social Networking Services: It is an online service, platform, or site that focuses on facilitating the building of social networks or social relations among people who share interests, activities, backgrounds, or real-life connections. Examples of social networking services are Facebook, Twitter, Google+, Myspace and LinkedIn. Social networking sites allow users to share ideas, activities, events, and interests within their individual networks (Wikipedia: http://en.wikipedia.org/wiki/Social_ networking_service).

APPENDIX

Examples of Creative Texts

Example 1: Ali wrote in the RCWD:

Sorrow flows out from your eyes when your heart is hurt and tears fill your eyes..let them flow..let your sorrow go...make room in your heart..for joy shall come..to stay..

Example 2: Ali wrote in the RCWD:

I find you wandering in the desert of your mind looking for an oasis. Seeking that drop of water that would make the desert a garden of beauty. I see you looking and I see that you are tired. In your search, you forgot to look somewhere... in the well of wisdom - your heart. Look there, you will find your beloved ready to make your mind a place of peace and security...

Example 3: Ali wrote in RCWD:

Come forth, rise from out of thy body..said the angel to him..it is time. He stood outside his body..light so bright and fragrance everywhere. It was time to return to His One Allah..the One that loved him more than his own mother could. The One that cherished his existence like only the Creator could..he knew then..that he was returning home..finally..

Example 4: Ali wrote in RCWD:

When you see a beautiful person..praise the creator..not the person..

Example 5: A poem written by Sameera in RCWD:

If I feel
If I know
If I see
A Wrong...
YET...
I turn away
I ignore
I cover up
WHAT AM I ?
A coward
A hypocrite
A liar
SORRY...
Must Stop
Must Speak

Must Resist
OR I'll BE JUST AS...
Evil
Dishonest
Mischievous
AS
I feel
I know
I see
THE OTHER PERSON TO BE!!!

Example 6: A reflection written by Sameera in RCWD:

People are to be loved and things are to be used. The problem arises when things are loved and people are used.....

Example 7: A reflection written by Sameera in RCWD:

God created Human Beings as the most superior of his creations but they insist on acting like the lowest of creatures - deceiving, lying and cheating & God lets them be till all limits have been crossed and then reckoning.....

Example 8: Abdulaziz from RCW reflects on the project "Conspiracy":

I, one of the many citizens of the current world, have asked questions that were too uninspiring to be asked; why has the world lost its sweet flavor? And the bitter taste never left? Why are the sweat drops that we suffer to make fall into other men's pockets?

The thoughts we proudly claim are only meant to be thought, the tears that we shed fall into the never ending river of sadness, every time I look into a pure soul I find the same black dots that tarnish their beauty.

Yes, we have been alienated; we are now the property of the strongest, we have lost every single characteristic that define us as human beings. We might as well strongly oppose to the idea but let's face it, we are now pieces of a puzzle, and when our roles end, we get nuclear bombs flying towards us.

I, one of the many citizens of the current world, am full of laughter for our sad misfortune.

Example 9: "The Unforgettable Past" by Eman Saif from RCWD

The ghost of memories is haunting my mind
I'm trying to escape but its pulling me behind
my body is aching peace I want to find
my soul is bleeding, for life it has declined...

The ocean of the past is filled with sin
the waves are crashing and I'm drowning in
my thoughts are chasing me, away far away i want to swim
I'm breaking up, i wish i couldn't remember how my life has been...
I'm pouring out my heart its filled with regret
its color is black another memory is a threat
a threat to spill the black blood on my last sunset
then my life will come to an end, is this the only way to forget?

Example 10: "Coffee" by Mimi from RCWC

I remember when we laid in bed You wore nothing but your skin, And the blanket I slid on you. You said you'd rather wear nothing but me, all day Feel nothing but the tips of my fingers On every inch of your body. I said I'd always love you, you said you would too...

Example 11: "Coffee" by Hala

I want you fire-eyed, helpless, and passion-driven. I want you irrational and guilt-stricken. I want you spiteful, conflicted, loving, I want you going, coming, and running. I want you heaving, shoving, scream-ing, sighing, pulling, pushing, laughing, lying. I want you holding my face in the palms of your hands and crying I don't want...

Example 12: "Coffee" by Meshael

I will write my way home tonight; I will write my way to you. Love, you may ask: But where do you find me? I find you in music. Every sweet song, and every strum of the guitar that comes through my headphones brings you out. I find you in literature. In every word...

Example 13: "Coffee" by Nouf

The elevator door opened as she strutted out in all her glory and shame. The strappy heals that were flung across the room the night before were barely clinging on to her feet. Huge Victoria Beckham-like sunglasses were perched on her perfectly altered nose, hiding the puffy eyes and the smudged mascara. Click-clack. She walked...

Example 14: "Coffee" by Albutol

"One more," he says. Over steaming mugs, in musty (misty) rooms, amongst nicotine-clouded heads, - one more. Stay, he pleads without words, the hanging promise of mahogany tinted liquid of wood roasted beans. Stay. "One more," he tells the waiter. The empty chair a shade of the drink, a shade of his skin, a...

Example 15: "Blood" by Zoha Khalid

False,

False dreams, false people, false world
Each hand is dirty with the blood
My utmost desire to again reveal
The wonders that die long ago
The treasures about thy, regale
Fluttered in mind, in heart grow
But the desires are ^ never ending flood
Each hand is dirty with the blood
My corniest, attributes, prevails
The boat on ^ sea, with ^ wave it sails
Mysteries thy, told, stories thy tell
To make me determined, they always fails
No one is pure as a beautiful bud
Each hand is dirty with the blood
Growing in the massive, disastrous way
Even no time to settle and pray
Walk or run, but be the best
No one cares, they always say
After every thunder rain, I am covered with mud
Each hand is dirty with the blood

Example 16: "wake Up !!!" by Emi Zen wrote from EICE:

Please Wake Up Before It's Too Late
If You Aren't Praying, Please Pray.
If You Aren't Lowering Your Gaze, Please Do.
If You Are Mistreating Your Parents, Please Stop.
If You Are Listening To Music, Please Replace It With Qur'an.
If You Are Swearing A Lot, Talking Behind People's Back, Please Fix This And Stop.
If You Aren't Wearing Hijab, Please Do.
If Your Cloths Are Tight, Rrevealing, Non-Islamic, Please Winder And More Moddest Cloths.
If You Are Making "Gheebah" And Talk Behind Your Sisters Back, Please Stop.
What Are You Waiting For ?? Sudden Death ??
Where's NO WAY TO REPENT ?!!!
Fear ALLAH !
Wake UP ... REPENT !

Example 17: By Mamadou

It's good to dream....but better to be realistic
It's good to harry..... but better to go safe and slow
It's easy to start.......but hard to keep it up
*It's better not to start something that you * not gonna End in a good way...*
WITH YU GUYS.....JUST SOME WORDS ...UP FRV

Chapter 8
Second Language Learners' Spoken Discourse:
Practice and Corrective Feedback through Automatic Speech Recognition

Catia Cucchiarini
Radboud University, The Netherlands

Helmer Strik
Radboud University, The Netherlands

ABSTRACT

This chapter examines the use of Automatic Speech Recognition (ASR) technology in the context of Computer Assisted Language Learning (CALL) and language learning and teaching research. A brief introduction to ASR is first provided, to make it clear why and how this technology can be used to the benefit of learning and development in second language (L2) spoken discourse. This is followed by an overview of the state of the art in research on ASR-based CALL. Subsequently, a number of relevant projects on ASR-based CALL conducted at the Centre for Language and Speech Technology of the Radboud University in Nijmegen (the Netherlands) are presented. Possible solutions and recommendations are discussed given the current state of the technology with an explanation of how such systems can be used to the benefit of Discourse Analysis research. The chapter concludes with a discussion of possible perspectives for future research and development.

INTRODUCTION

Research on L2 learning has indicated that although exposure to the target language and usage-based learning are essential elements in the learning process, these are not always sufficient to guarantee target-like proficiency (Ellis, 2008;

Ellis & Bogart, 2007). Focus on linguistic form provided through corrective feedback may help improve form accuracy in L2 spoken discourse. Unfortunately, in traditional teacher-fronted lessons there is generally not enough time for sufficient practice and feedback on speaking performance.

DOI: 10.4018/978-1-4666-4426-7.ch008

In this setting, the interest in applying ASR technology to L2 learning has been growing considerably in recent years (Eskenazi, 2009). ASR-based CALL systems would make it possible to offer sufficient amounts of practice in L2 speaking and to provide automatic feedback on different aspects of L2 spoken discourse. In this sense, ASR-based CALL systems would constitute an interesting supplement to traditional L2 classes. In addition, such systems can provide speaking practice in a private environment, which is a considerable advantage as speaking tasks are known to cause anxiety in L2 learners (Young, 1990). Moreover, L2 learners can practice at their own pace whenever they want.

In light of these advantages, research and development in this field have increased in recent years, and many systems have been developed that provide different forms of feedback on a variety of aspects of L2 spoken discourse. The majority of systems with a speech interactive nature address L2 pronunciation, which is considered a particularly challenging skill in L2 learning. A comprehensive overview of ASR-based commercial systems for L2 pronunciation is provided by Witt (2012). Many of these systems, however, do not contain important and desirable features of feedback on L2 pronunciation, such as immediate, detailed feedback on individual segments in the context of meaningful communicative tasks involving connected speech. In addition, CALL systems that are intended for practicing grammar skills and for improving accuracy in general do not support spoken interaction, but tend to resort to drag-and-drop exercises and typing (Bodnar, Cucchiarini, & Strik, 2011).

Against this background a number of projects were started at our lab which were aimed at conducting research and developing technology that would be conducive to the realization of ASR-based CALL systems that support practice and automatic feedback on L2 spoken discourse in line with insights from L2 learning research and L2 learners' requirements.

The aim of this chapter is to inform the reader about recent developments in the field of ASR-based CALL research and to indicate how these can lead to new methods and paradigms for the acquisition of spoken discourse in a second language. We first provide a brief introduction to ASR, to make it clear for the reader why and how this technology can be used to the benefit of learning and development in L2 spoken discourse. We then go on to provide an overview of the state of the art in research on ASR-based CALL. Subsequently, we present a number of relevant projects conducted at our lab and discuss possible solutions and recommendations for the development of ASR-based CALL systems and for the use of such systems to the benefit of Discourse Analysis. We then conclude with a discussion of possible perspectives for future research and development.

BACKGROUND: AUTOMATIC SPEECH RECOGNITION (ASR)

Standard ASR systems are generally employed to recognize words. The ASR system consists of a decoder (the search algorithm) and three 'knowledge sources': the language model, the lexicon, and the acoustic models. The language model (LM) contains probabilities of words and sequences of words. Acoustic models are models of how the sounds of a language are pronounced; in most cases so-called hidden Markov models (HMMs) are used, but it is also possible to use artificial neural networks (ANNs). The lexicon is the connection between the language model and the acoustic models. It contains information on how the words are pronounced, in terms of sequences of speech sounds. Therefore, the lexicon contains two representations for every entry: an orthographic transcription representing how a word is written and a phonological transcription representing how a word is pronounced. Since words can be pronounced in different ways, lexicons often contain more than one entry for some words, i.e. the pronunciation variants, which indicate possible pronunciations of one and the same word.

ASR is a probabilistic procedure. In a nutshell, ASR (with HMMs) works as follows. The LM defines which sequences of words are possible, for each word the possible pronunciation variants and their transcriptions (sequences of speech sounds) are retrieved from the lexicon, and for each speech sound in these transcriptions the appropriate acoustic model (HMM) is retrieved. Everything is represented by means of a huge probabilistic network: an LM is a network of words, each word is a network of pronunciation variants and their transcriptions (sequences of speech sounds), and for each of the speech sounds in these transcriptions the corresponding HMM is a network of its own. In this huge complex network paths have probabilities attached to them. For a given (incoming, unknown) speech signal the task of the decoder is to find the optimal global path in this network, using all the probabilistic information. In standard word recognition the output then consists of the labels of the words on this optimal path: the recognized words. However, the optimal path can contain more information than just that concerning the word labels, such as information on pronunciation variants, the phone symbols in these pronunciation variants, and even the segmentation at phone level.

STATE-OF-THE-ART IN ASR-BASED COMPUTER ASSISTED LANGUAGE LEARNING (CALL) RESEARCH AND APPLICATIONS

Research on L2 acquisition underlines the importance of usage-based learning and skill-specific practice (Ellis, 2008; DeKeyser & Sokalski, 1996; DeKeyser, 2007) when it comes to learning to speak and write a second language: if learners want to speak a second language fluently and accurately, it is necessary for them to practice speaking it. Relevant in this respect are Swain's output hypothesis

(Swain, 1985) which emphasizes the role of output in L2 learning and Schmidt's (1990) 'noticing hypothesis' which underlines that awareness of discrepancies between the learner's output and the L2 is necessary for the acquisition of a specific linguistic item. To achieve this kind of awareness exposure to the L2 and L2 output are not always sufficient (Ellis & Bogart, 2007) and corrective feedback is often required to help learners focus on formal aspects of their L2 speech production and stimulate them to attempt self-improvement (Havranek, 2002).

However, various studies on the use of corrective feedback in the classroom have indicated that the feedback provided by L2 teachers is often inconsistent, ambiguous, arbitrary, and idiosyncratic (Carroll & Swain, 1993; Iwashita, 2003; Sheen, 2004). Many of the studies on corrective feedback have produced mixed results (Norris & Ortega, 2000; Lyster & Saito, 2010), but there are indications that explicit feedback is more effective than implicit, potentially ambiguous feedback (Lyster, 1998; Bigelow, delMas, Hansen, & Tarone, 2006), that feedback does not work when it is erratic and inconsistent (Chaudron, 1988), that feedback should be intensive (Han, 2002), that it should be appropriate to learners' readiness (Mackey & Philp, 1998), and that it should provide opportunities for self-repair and modified output because these induce learners to revise their hypotheses about the target language (Lyster & Ranta, 1997; Panova & Lyster, 2002; Havranek, 2002).

For L2 spoken discourse achieving a sufficient amount of practice and feedback in the classroom can be difficult, mainly owing to lack of time. The emergence of CALL systems that make use of ASR has opened up possibilities of developing language learning environments that offer sufficient practice and corrective feedback that is intensive, consistent, personalized and that offers opportunities for self-repair and modified output. This has spawned a considerable amount of research and development in this field.

One of the issues to be addressed in this line of research is the automatic recognition of L2 speech. In the section on ASR we tried to explain the complexity of this procedure, assuming that it is native speech that has to be recognized. When it comes to recognizing the speech of people who are no native speakers of the language in question, the problem to be solved becomes much more complex, especially if these non-native speakers are still in the process of learning the target language. This is because L2 speech can deviate from native speech at the level of the individual sounds, the prosody, the word forms and the word order. Deviations in individual sounds, word forms and word order may thus affect the main components of a speech recognizer mentioned in the previous section: the acoustic models, the lexicon and the language model. Furthermore, L2 speech tends to contain more disfluencies and hesitation phenomena than native speech, which also pose problems to ASR.

Many of the first studies that considered employing ASR technology in the context of L2 learning focused primarily on the automatic assessment of different aspects of L2 oral proficiency, in particular L2 pronunciation (Coniam, 1999; Bernstein, Cohen, Murveit, Rtischev, & Weintraub, 1990; Neumeyer, Franco, Weintraub, & Price, 1996; Eskenazi, 1996; Cucchiarini, Strik, & Boves, 1997; Witt & Young, 1997). The results showed that automatic testing of certain aspects of oral proficiency was feasible: the scores obtained by means of ASR technology were strongly correlated with human judgments of oral proficiency (Franco, Neumeyer, Digalakis, & Ronen, 2000; Neumeyer, Franco, Digalakis, & Weintraub, 2000; Cucchiarini, Strik, & Boves, 2000a; 2000b; 2002).

This technology was also adapted and employed to realize systems and products for L2 language instruction and practice such as EduSpeak (Franco et al., 2000), Tell me More (www.tellmemore.com/), the Tactical Language Training System (Johnson et al., 2004), Carnegie Speech NativeAccent (Eskenazi, Kennedy, Ket-

chum, Olszewski, & Pelton, 2007), SpeakESL (http://www.speakesl.com/), Saybot (Chevalier & Cao, 2008; www.saybot.com), and Rosetta Stone (www.rosettastone.com). A comprehensive overview of ASR-based commercial systems for L2 pronunciation is provided by Witt (2012). Most of these products have the advantage that they stimulate L2 spoken output and in this sense they comply with Swain's view on language learning (Swain, 1985). Some of them, however, appear to be less satisfactory when it comes to pinpointing discrepancies between the learner's output and the target utterance, as is emphasized in Schmidt's requirements concerning noticing (Schmidt, 1990). The limitations of these systems in detecting and diagnosing errors in L2 spoken discourse may lead to corrective feedback that is unsatisfactory in various respects: not detailed enough, not always comprehensible, not personalized (Menzel, Herron, Bonaventura, & Morton, 2000; Neri, Cucchiarini, Strik, & Boves, 2002).

In addition, most of the systems that employ ASR to support spoken interaction and provide corrective feedback address L2 pronunciation, while CALL systems that are aimed at practicing grammar skills in general offer training through typing or drag and drop and do not employ ASR to support spoken interaction, to detect grammatical inaccuracies in the learners' spoken discourse and eventually provide specific feedback on grammatical discrepancies between the learners' spoken discourse and the target language (Bodnar et al., 2011).

Possible alternatives to practice a second or foreign language are provided by communities which offer the opportunity of interacting with other learners or native speakers through Computer Mediated Communication. (CMC). CMC has been shown to contribute to a comfortable interactional context that favors language learning (Payne & Whitney, 2002; Payne & Ross, 2005; Dickinson, Eom, Kang, Lee, & Sachs, 2008), but has received criticism with respect to the provision of corrective feedback. One of the shortcomings of CMC seems indeed to be that the interlocutors are not always capable of providing feedback that is relevant and accurate (Dickinson et al., 2008).

PRACTICE AND CORRECTIVE FEEDBACK IN L2 SPOKEN DISCOURSE: THE CONTRIBUTION OF ASR TECHNOLOGY

After the first studies that addressed automatic assessment of oral proficiency (Cucchiarini et al., 2000a; 2000b; 2002), research at our lab subsequently focused mainly on automatic error detection in L2 oral proficiency, with a view to developing and improving systems that could be used for independent practice and corrective feedback in L2 spoken discourse and for conducting research on different aspects of language learning.

An ASR-based CALL system that has to provide corrective feedback on speech utterances will first of all have to determine what the learner is trying to say (speech recognition) before proceeding to an analysis of the form of the utterance (error detection). As mentioned above, this first step of speech recognition may be very difficult in the case of non-native speakers, in particular those that are still in the process of learning a second or foreign language. Once an incoming utterance has been recognized as being an acceptable attempt at producing the response required, additional analyses may be required depending on the types of errors that have to be detected. For this purpose we employed a two-step procedure in which (1) first the content of the utterance is determined (what was said, speech recognition), and (2) subsequently the form of the utterance is analyzed (how it was said, error detection).

A common approach to limit the difficulties in speech recognition consists in applying techniques that restrict the search space and make the task easier. In line with this approach, we combined strategies aimed at constraining the output of the learner so that the speech becomes more predict-

able with techniques aimed at improving the decoding of non-native speech. The former is done by using elicitation techniques that direct the learners to certain responses. In the case of pronunciation this can be easily realized by asking students to read sentences out loud from the screen. In the case of grammar, it is more challenging to design tasks that allow the students enough freedom to be able to show whether they master a given construction, and that, at the same time, produce constrained, predictable output (see below). For the latter, i.e. improving decoding, we resorted to the use of predefined lists of possible (correct and incorrect) responses for each exercise.

Since learners thus have some freedom in formulating their responses, it first has to be determined which utterance (of the predefined list) was spoken, which is done by means of utterance selection. There is always the possibility that the learner's response is not present in the predefined list or that utterance selection does not select the correct utterance from the list. To check this, utterance verification is carried out. In the first step of the two-step procedure, two phases can thus be distinguished, (1a) utterance selection, and (1b) utterance verification (UV). Experiments conducted so far indicated that reasonable levels of accuracy could be obtained at the stage of (1a) utterance selection (about 8-10%) and (1b) utterance verification (10%) (van Doremalen, Strik, & Cucchiarini, 2009).

ASR TECHNOLOGY AND ERROR DETECTION IN L2 PRONUNCIATION

The algorithms used for automatic assessment of oral proficiency were generally aimed at calculating automatic scores that were maximally correlated with human scores of oral proficiency and could thus be considered to reflect how human raters valued L2 speech (Franco et al., 2000; Neumeyer et al., 2000; Cucchiarini et al., 2000a; 2000b; 2002). In general, such automatic scores were calculated at a rather global level, for instance for several utterances by the same speaker, because in this way more reliable measures could be obtained (Kim, Franco, & Neumeyer, 1997). Such measures might be suitable, and in certain cases even preferable, for testing purposes, for assessing the problems of individual speakers, for providing overviews of words or phonemes that appear to be difficult and suggesting remedial exercises for the problematic cases. However, such overall measures are generally not specific enough for practice and feedback purposes.

Research on corrective feedback in L2 learning has indicated that one of the drawbacks of feedback by L2 teachers is that it is often ambiguous, while L2 learners could profit from more explicit and informative feedback (Lyster, 1998; Bigelow et al., 2006). For these reasons research on the use of ASR in the context of L2 learning was directed at error detection by developing suitable techniques for calculating scores at a more local level such as the word or the phoneme, which could be used as a basis for providing feedback on an individual basis, for instance in the context of remedial exercises. For pronunciation error detection we studied different approaches.

As explained above, once the learner's utterance has been recognized as being an acceptable attempt at producing the response required, additional analyses may be required. In the case of pronunciation error detection, the speech recognizer has to go through the same utterance and carry out a stricter analysis to determine whether the sounds have been pronounced correctly. For this purpose, we applied different methods.

ASR-based metrics such as posterior probabilities and (log) likelihood ratios (Franco et al., 2000; ISLE 1.4, 1999; Menzel et al., 2000) are often employed. Research has shown that these confidence measures can be used for detecting pronunciation errors (Franco et al., 2000; ISLE 1.4, 1999; Menzel et al., 2000; Witt, 1999). One of these measures is the so-called goodness of

pronunciation (GOP) metric (Witt, 1999). Detailed studies conducted on the GOP algorithm (van Doremalen, Cucchiarini, & Strik, 2010; Kanters, Cucchiarini, & Strik, 2009; Strik, Truong, de Wet, & Cucchiarini, 2007; 2009) have revealed that, if properly trained, GOP works satisfactorily; e.g. in the Dutch-CAPT system (see Figure 1) 80-95% of the sounds were classified correctly. However, there are large variations between individuals and sounds. If specific settings (thresholds) could be used for each person-sound combination, better results could be achieved (Kanters et al., 2009), but in practice this is not possible. And since the GOP algorithm has some other limitations, we studied possible alternative measures (e.g. van Doremalen et al., 2010).

Another approach we experimented with is based on acoustic phonetic features. Using these features classifiers were trained to carry out pronunciation error detection. For certain problematic sounds acoustic phonetic classifiers produced better performance than the GOP algorithm (Strik et al., 2007; 2009).

In a third approach we used phonetic information in a different way. Since sounds are often not distributed uniformly in the acoustic space (e.g. the Dutch vowels), it is better to use a variant of the GOP in which different weights are employed for the different sounds. The resulting measure, called wGOP, yielded better results than the standard GOP (van Doremalen et al., 2010).

Finally, in another approach it is also possible to generate pronunciation networks for the different sounds. For instance, learners of Dutch often realize the /x/ as /k/, or the /a/ as /A/ (Neri, Cucchiarini, & Strik, 2006). Such known, frequent errors can then be included in the pronunciation network of that sound. The ASR then has to find the best path in these pronunciation networks. In this way, it is not only possible to detect whether a sound was pronounced correctly or not, but also which error was made. However, a disadvantage of this method is that only errors that have been included

Figure 1. Screenshot of the Dutch-CAPT system. The user first watches a video, then plays a role in a dialogue and gets feedback on pronunciation errors.

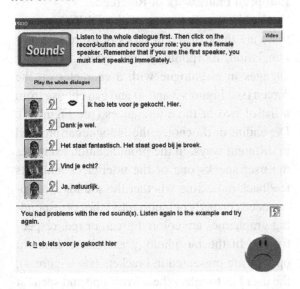

in the pronunciation networks can eventually be detected.

The different approaches described above can also be combined. The challenge then is to find the proper combination of approaches and settings that yields the best results. Most approaches, such as the often applied (supervised) machine learning approach, require large amounts of annotated data in order to train the classifiers. Since obtaining annotated data is laborious, we have been studying other ways to carry out pronunciation detection. The acoustic-phonetic approach mentioned above is already a first step in that direction. Another approach we studied consists in introducing plausible, artificial errors (Kanters et al., 2009) in already existing corpora. In this method, we first obtained overviews of errors that L2 learners frequently make. We then artificially introduced these errors in native speech corpora that were then employed as training material to develop error detectors we eventually implemented in the Dutch-CAPT system. Language learners then used the Dutch-CAPT system; their interactions were

recorded and annotated afterwards. Analyses of these annotations showed that the performance of the error detectors trained on artificially introduced pronunciation errors in real use was comparable to the performance during development. This is remarkable given that speech technology performance in real use is often lower than performance during development. This particularly applies when there is a training-testing mismatch, which was the case here as training was based on errors artificially introduced in native speech, while testing was based on actually made errors in non-native speech. A possible explanation for this finding is that we carefully introduced artificial errors according to substitution patterns we had derived from analyses of actually occurring errors (Kanters et al., 2009).

In the 'Dutch Computer-Assisted Pronunciation Training' (Dutch-CAPT) project (http://hstrik. ruhosting.nl/Dutch-CAPT/) a pronunciation training program was developed to provide automatic feedback on segmental (phoneme) errors (see Figure 1). We evaluated this system by comparing production data by an experimental group of adult Dutch L2 learners with different L1s and proficiency levels who used the Dutch-CAPT system, with those of a control group that did similar exercises, but did not get feedback on pronunciation errors. The learners in the two groups had been living in the Netherlands and had followed DL2 lessons. Already after two short sessions of about 30-60 minutes, we could observe that the decrease in the number of pronunciation errors was significantly larger for the experimental group compared to the control group that did not receive feedback (Cucchiarini, Neri, & Strik, 2009; Neri, Cucchiarini, & Strik, 2008).

Before developing a CALL system, we generally try to obtain an overview of frequent errors made by language learners by combining information found in the literature, expertise of language teachers, and analysis of data. Even if the artificial error procedure described above is used, such an overview is essential to carefully introduce plausible errors in the right context. We have already derived overviews of frequent segmental errors for different combinations of first (L1) and target (L2) languages: many L1s - Dutch (Neri et al., 2006), Spanish - Dutch (Burgos, Cucchiarini, van Hout, & Strik, 2013), and Dutch - English (Cucchiarini, van den Heuvel, Sanders, & Strik, 2011).

ASR TECHNOLOGY AND ERROR DETECTION IN L2 SYNTAX AND MORPHOLOGY

Based on the promising results we obtained with the Dutch-CAPT system on pronunciation, we decided to extend our approach to other aspects of L2 spoken discourse such as morphology and syntax.

This work was carried out within the framework of the DISCO project ('Development and Integration of Speech technology into Courseware for language learning,' see Figures 2-4), which was aimed at developing the prototype of an ASR-based CALL system for practice and feedback in Dutch L2 speaking performance (Strik, Cornillie, Colpaert, van Doremalen, & Cucchiarini, 2009; Strik, Colpaert, van Doremalen, & Cucchiarini,

2012; http://hstrik.ruhosting.nl/DISCO/). The system is intended for adult learners with different L1s at the A2 proficiency level of the Common European Framework of Reference.

Within the dialogues of the DISCO system there are three different types of exercises: pronunciation, morphology, and syntax. The user engages in a dialogue with a character on the screen (see Figures 3 and 4) and can choose from a list of two or three utterances (see Figure 4). Depending on the choice, the dialogue can proceed in different ways. In the pronunciation exercises the user speaks one of the utterances and gets feedback indicating whether the sounds are pronounced correctly or incorrectly (the corresponding graphemes are colored green or red, respectively). In the morphology exercises, different options are presented in brackets (see Figure 4), the user has to select the correct one and speak it up. If it is not correct, the word chosen is colored red. Finally, in the syntax exercises, words are presented in groups which the user has to put in the right order when speaking up the utterance. If the order is not correct, the groups of words are colored red (see Figure 3).

For each grammar exercise a language model is built based on the prompts shown on the screen. The language model contains the possible re-

Figure 2. A screenshot of the DISCO system. The user can choose an interlocutor ('spraakmakker' – 'speech buddy') to speak to. The topics vary: a train journey, choosing a course, and going to the shop with a broken DVD player, respectively.

Figure 3. A screenshot of the DISCO system. It concerns a syntax exercise: words were presented in groups, and the user had to put them in the right order. In this example the spoken utterance was incorrect, and this is why the last three word groups (in 'blocks') are colored red. In the bottom-right corner (below the waveform of the recorded utterance) three options are provided: 1. listen to utterance spoken by the learner again, 2. listen to a pre-recorded correct (native) example, 3. proceed to the next exercise. In addition, there is a 4th option: the user can click on the microphone on the left, and try again.

sponses by the user. For a spoken utterance, the ASR system then tries to determine what was said by finding the most likely path in the language model. In this way it is possible to determine whether the spoken utterance was correct or not, and what kind of feedback should be provided.

However, to be able to perform automatic error detection at the level of morphology and syntax, it was necessary to have overviews of such grammatical errors in L2 spoken discourse. For this purpose, we developed novel procedures to obtain information on L2 grammatical errors from L2 speech data (Strik, van de Loo, van Doremalen, & Cucchiarini, 2010; Strik, van Doremalen, van de Loo, & Cucchiarini, 2011).

Several evaluation tests have been carried out to assess different aspects of the system. The results show satisfactory performance in detecting morphology and syntax errors, while user tests indicate that students are very positive about the system and consider it useful for improving their oral skills in Dutch L2 (Cucchiarini, van Doremalen, & Strik, 2012).

ASR TECHNOLOGY AND CORRECTIVE FEEDBACK ON L2 SPOKEN DISCOURSE

In addition to developing appropriate techniques for error detection, realizing suitable ASR-based systems for L2 speaking practice requires knowledge of how corrective feedback can best be provided. Many of the studies on the effect of corrective feedback on L2 development do not agree on which feedback forms best contribute to increasing linguistic competence in which learners (Lyster & Saito, 2010). Implicit feedback forms like recasts are particularly preferred in communicative contexts because they are discrete and do not interrupt the communication flow, but, for the same reason they are not always perceived as corrective feedback and often go unnoticed (Nicholas, Lightbown, & Spada, 2001; Lyster, 2004; Ellis & Sheen, 2006; Ellis, Loewen, & Erlam, 2006; Loewen & Philp, 2006). The effectiveness of recasts also appears to be related to the learner's degree of schooling, with more educated learners

Figure 4. A screenshot of the DISCO system. It concerns a morphology exercise: the user can select one of the three utterances, and has to speak the words in the correct way.

profiting more from recasts than less educated learners (Bigelow et al., 2006). Prompts are so-called negotiation of form techniques which are considered to be effective because they induce learners to reprocess their output (Lyster, 1998; 2004) and to produce "pushed output" (Swain, 1985; de Bot, 1996), but which have been criticized because they would contribute to linguistic knowledge and not to competence (Ellis & Sheen, 2006). Moreover, in so far as prompts appeal to metalinguistic skills, they are also likely to have a differential effect on learners with differing educational levels.

The evidence accumulated so far seems to suggest that the uncertainty that still exists as to how corrective feedback on L2 spoken discourse can best be provided is mainly due to the impossibility so far to create appropriate research conditions to offer feedback that is systematic, consistent, intensive, and clear enough to be perceived as such, and that provides opportunity for self-repair and modified output (El Tatawi, 2002). The use of ASR technology in the context of CALL offers the opportunity of providing corrective feedback on L2 spoken discourse under near-optimal conditions (Penning de Vries, Cucchiarini, Strik, & Van Hout, 2011). Within the framework of the project

'Feedback and the Acquisition of Syntax in Oral Proficiency' (FASOP) (http://hstrik.ruhosting.nl/FASOP/), an ASR-based CALL system is used to conduct experiments on the effect of different forms of corrective feedback on oral syntax practice and acquisition (see Figure 5). Dutch L2 learners are pre-tested before undergoing specific training in L2 syntax through different versions of the CALL system that provide different forms of feedback. The ASR-based CALL system also logs all interactions between the learner and the system. Post-tests are then administered to determine the effects of the feedback (see Figure 6). In addition, detailed analyses of the logs also provide useful information which can be employed to get a more complete picture of the learning process. The first results are encouraging (Bodnar, Penning de Vries, Cucchiarini, Strik, & van Hout, 2011).

SOLUTIONS AND RECOMMENDATIONS

In the previous sections we have presented some of the issues that have to be addressed in developing systems for L2 learning that employ ASR for providing practice and feedback in L2 spoken

Figure 5. A screenshot of the FASOP system. Learners first watch a video clip and then answer questions. In this example, the tutor is asking 'What does it say on the box that Melvin has packed his things in ?' To answer, learners compose an utterance using the prompt and word groups presented on the screen. All (='Allemaal') the word groups in the blue box have to be used, and only one ('Eentje') word group from the box in green.

Figure 6. Overview of the FASOP experiment: 'QNAIRE' – questionnaire, GJT – grammatical judgment test, DCT – discourse completion test.

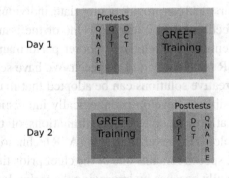

discourse. This overview has made it clear that these issues are not trivial and that research is still required to optimize the technology. On the other hand, the research presented already indicates that the technology is mature enough to be employed in innovative learning methods for L2 spoken discourse and innovative research in Discourse Analysis. In this section we pay attention to what can already be realized with the current technology (solutions and recommendations). In the following section, we consider what kind of research should be conducted not only to improve the technology, but also to obtain better ASR-based CALL systems and to allow more innovative research in the field of Discourse Analysis.

First, the issue of L2 speech recognition still constitutes a challenge and research on how to achieve better performance is still a priority for many applications. However, there are strategies for circumventing the existing problems and still develop useful applications with acceptable performance (van Doremalen, Cucchiarini, & Strik, 2010). One of these strategies consists in reducing the search space by having the learners perform highly constrained tasks. We have seen above that this approach works satisfactorily even for morphology and syntax exercises, in which learners need to be given a certain amount of freedom in speech performance to be able to show whether they master certain grammatical constructions or not.

Second, with respect to error detection various approaches have been proposed which achieve varying levels of performance. Also in this respect further research is required to improve the algorithms and obtain higher levels of detection accuracy for different components of L2 spoken discourse. In the meantime, it is also important to consider what can already be realized with the present levels of accuracy, which, for certain aspects of L2 spoken discourse, may be already satisfactory. As we have seen in the Dutch-CAPT and DISCO projects, even systems that do not achieve 100% accuracy can still be useful for language learners.

Third, it is well-known that the traditional classroom is limited in its ability to stimulate the development of communicative competences in language learners (e.g. Demo, 2001). By using ASR-based CALL systems learners can participate in (simulated) dialogues, providing many opportunities for (practicing and studying) interaction. Since such CALL systems can be available 24/7, they allow for many contact hours and considerable amounts of exposure.

Fourth, in addition to the advantages ASR-based CALL systems can offer for L2 learning, there are also important research benefits for Discourse Analysis. For instance, an ASR-based CALL system can be used for acquiring data on L2 learning. These data are in the form of speech recordings collected in realistic situations that can subsequently be employed for different types of Discourse Analysis research such as phonetic and phonological research (McCarthy, 1992), for research on individual differences in second language learning and for "research" by the learners' themselves (Demo, 2001; Celce-Murcia & Olshtain, 2000; McCarthy & Carter, 1994; Riggenbach, 1999) to make them aware of possibly problematic features. The special advantage of these data is that they come with the relevant information for further automatic processing such as alignments between the speech signals and the orthographic and phonemic representations, and confidence measures.

Furthermore, ASR-based CALL systems can be designed and developed in such a way that it is possible to log details regarding the interactions with the users, as was the case in the DISCO project. By way of illustration, this logbook can contain the following information: what appeared on the screen, how the user responded, how long the user waited, what was done (speak an utterance, move the mouse and click on an item, use the keyboard, etc.), the feedback provided by the system, how the user reacted on this feedback (listen to example (or not), try again, ask for ad-

ditional, e.g. meta-linguistic, feedback, etc.). So when language learners use an ASR-based CALL system to practice oral skills all their utterances can be recorded in such a way that it is possible to know exactly in which context the utterance was spoken, i.e. it can be related to all the information in the logbook mentioned above.

Such a corpus and the corresponding log-files can be useful for various types of Discourse Analysis: for research on language acquisition and second language learning, for studying the effect of various types of feedback on individual learners, for research on various aspects of man-machine interaction.

ASR-based CALL systems also open up new avenues of research, because they allow research conditions that were hitherto impossible to create. As mentioned above, in the FASOP project the impact of corrective feedback on the acquisition of syntax in oral proficiency (http://hstrik.ruhosting.nl/FASOP/) is studied through an ASR-based CALL system that makes it possible to investigate how individual learners process corrective feedback on oral skills on-line.

FUTURE RESEARCH DIRECTIONS

In the previous sections we have presented research aimed at developing and improving ASR-based CALL systems that can offer practice in L2 spoken discourse and can provide appropriate, individualized feedback to L2 learners. One of the issues we mentioned is relatively poorer performance of ASR technology on L2 speech. We have seen that creative solutions can be adopted that make it possible to develop pedagogically interesting applications, in spite of the limitations of the technology. However, improving ASR technology for L2 speech remains one of the chief priorities. Especially because by improving the technology it would be possible to realize applications that allow less constrained interactions between the learner and the system. In turn this would make these applications more realistic and pedagogically more interesting

Similarly, error detection algorithms also need to be improved to allow for more reliable applications that provide learners with the feedback they need to improve their L2 spoken discourse. Research should address the improvement of algorithms and metrics for both pronunciation error detection and grammar error detection in L2 spoken discourse. With respect to pronunciation error detection, one of the problems in studies addressing error detection accuracy concerns the need for appropriate corpora and test materials for benchmarking. In general, the accuracy of automatic error detection is determined through comparisons with human performance on the same tasks (Cucchiarini et al., 2009). However, the enormous effort required in obtaining the human annotations that are necessary for this purpose constitutes a serious problem in this type of research. This calls for new research paradigms that rely less on manually annotated corpora while still making it possible to gauge the accuracy of error detection algorithms in a reliable and valid manner. In our research we resorted to artificially created annotations of L2 speech errors that plausibly reflect the errors that are actually made by L2 learners. Along similar lines new approaches need to be proposed.

In addition to these more technological priorities for further research are of course research agendas that address pedagogical and usability issues. While it is important that the ASR technology employed in ASR-based CALL systems works properly, it is equally important to pay attention to how learners experience and perceive such systems, to how ASR-based CALL systems contribute to boosting motivation and enhancing learner autonomy. Such data can be easily collected through questionnaires, as is usually done in research on motivation in L2 learning, and can subsequently be employed in learner modeling to develop CALL systems that are tailored to individual learners in terms of communication, feedback, learning strategies and preferences.

In the previous section, we mentioned a number of examples of how ASR-based CALL systems could provide new data and paradigms for research in Discourse Analysis. However, there are also other directions that could be pursued and that could provide new insights in Discourse Analysis. For instance, the fact that ASR-based CALL systems provide easy access to realistic speech data could be exploited by studying these speech data from different perspectives. Recent developments in language and speech technology make it possible, for example, to investigate emotions and affective state in language learners through language and speech. In turn, such information could be employed to get a better understanding of the language learning process and of how learners experience it, which could eventually lead to more advanced and more dynamic approaches to motivation and learner modeling. With respect to systems that employ questionnaires to collect data on motivation and individual preferences, systems that rely on automatic analyses of emotions and affective state through language and speech have the advantage that they can automatically adapt to their users and their mood, status, and changing preferences.

In relation to the topics addressed in the present volume, it is also relevant to find out how ASR-based CALL systems can be employed in connection with computer-mediated discourse and synchronous computer-mediated communication (CMC) technologies and how they can be used to the benefit of Discourse Analysis. We saw above that with respect to L2 learning and feedback CMC technologies do not always provide the appropriate solutions (Dickinson et al., 2008), which makes it interesting to investigate whether combining these different technologies might lead to more flexible, reliable, and adequate learning environments.

Finally, it seems that different lines of research could address the issue of adaptivity, which has not been explicitly addressed in the present chapter, but which looms large in ASR-based research (van Doremalen, Cucchiarini, & Strik, 2011). Adaptivity should not be limited to the different components of ASR, but should also extend to other aspects of the CALL systems, such as adapting exercises to the proficiency level of the learner, or adapting the type of feedback provided to the preferences of individual learners. These different forms of adaptation can be realized through student modeling and are likely to improve user satisfaction and motivation.

CONCLUSION

Research has shown that if learners want to speak a language fluently and accurately, it is necessary for them to practice speaking. However, currently there are generally not enough possibilities to do so. ASR-based CALL systems do offer these possibilities, and this explains the recent interest in deploying ASR technology in the context of language learning.

Developing CALL systems for practice and feedback in L2 spoken discourse is complex and challenging because L2 speech is highly variable and substantially differs from standard speech. Still, with current state-of-the-art technology it is possible to develop useful CALL systems, but this clearly requires a combination of expertise. So far the focus has been on pronunciation. Our research has shown that it is also possible to develop systems for practicing grammar in spoken discourse and providing useful feedback.

Although it is already possible to build useful CALL systems, there is much room for improvement. With improved speech technology it will be possible to relax the constraints, improve the performance, and use the technology for different goals, in more natural, intuitive, and pedagogically sound ways. Furthermore, besides pronunciation and grammar, ASR-based CALL systems could also be developed for other aspects such as prosody, vocabulary, and formulaic language. Finally, more insights and expertise are required on how to optimally design, develop, and use these

systems. ASR-based CALL systems can be combined with other types of learning, e.g. classical teacher-fronted classrooms, CMC, collaborative learning, and we need to study how these different approaches can be optimally combined. Different combinations of methods should be tested in practice for different types of learners, to study aspects such as user satisfaction, motivation, and effectiveness.

In any case, ASR-based CALL systems offer new and exciting possibilities; they will be used more and more, and will gradually improve. It is also likely that they will develop in new directions, e.g. CALL systems for mobile devices, which will really make it possible to learn everywhere 24/7, game like elements might be added, teachers and learners might have more possibilities to influence the content, and systems will become increasingly adaptive.

REFERENCES

Bernstein, J., Cohen, M., Murveit, H., Rtischev, D., & Weintraub, M. (1990). Automatic evaluation and training in English pronunciation. [Kobe, Japan.]. *Proceedings ICSLP*, *90*, 1185–1188.

Bigelow, M., delMas, R., Hansen, K., & Tarone, E. (2006). Literacy and the processing of oral recasts in SLA. *TESOL Quarterly*, *40*(4), 665–685. doi:10.2307/40264303.

Bodnar, S., Cucchiarini, C., & Strik, H. (2011). Computer-assisted grammar practice for oral communication. *Proceedings of the 3rd International Conference on Computer Supported Education (CSEDU)* (pp. 355-361). Noordwijkerhout, The Netherlands.

Bodnar, S., Penning de Vries, B., Cucchiarini, C., Strik, H., & van Hout, R. (2011). Feedback in an ASR-based CALL system for L2 syntax: A feasibility study. *Proceedings of the SLaTE-2011 workshop* (pp. 1-4). Venice, Italy.

Burgos, P., Cucchiarini, C., van Hout, R., Strik, H. (in press). *Phonology acquisition in Spanish learners of Dutch: Error patterns in pronunciation.*

Carroll, S., & Swain, M. (1993). Explicit and implicit negative feedback: An empirical study of the learning of linguistic generalizations. *Studies in Second Language Acquisition, 15,* 357–386. doi:10.1017/S0272263100012158.

Celce-Murcia, M., & Olshtain, E. (2000). *Discourse and context in language teaching.* New York: Cambridge University Press.

Chaudron, C. (1988). *Second language classrooms.* New York: Cambridge University Press. doi:10.1017/CBO9781139524469.

Chevalier, S., & Cao, Z. (2008). Application and evaluation of speech technologies in language learning: Experiments with the Saybot Player. [Brisbane, Australia.]. *Proceedings of Interspeech, 2008,* 2811–2814.

Coniam, D. (1999). Voice recognition software accuracy with second language speakers of English. *System, 27,* 49–64. doi:10.1016/S0346-251X(98)00049-9.

Cucchiarini, C., Neri, A., & Strik, H. (2009). Oral proficiency training in Dutch L2: The contribution of ASR-based corrective feedback. *Speech Communication, 51*(10), 853–863. doi:10.1016/j.specom.2009.03.003.

Cucchiarini, C., Strik, H., & Boves, L. (1997). Automatic assessment of foreign speakers' pronunciation of Dutch. [Rhodes, Greece.]. *Proceedings Eurospeech, 1997,* 713–716.

Cucchiarini, C., Strik, H., & Boves, L. (2000a). Different aspects of expert pronunciation quality ratings and their relation to scores produced by speech recognition algorithm. *Speech Communication, 30*(2-3), 109–119. doi:10.1016/S0167-6393(99)00040-0.

Cucchiarini, C., Strik, H., & Boves, L. (2000b). Quantitative assessment of second language learners' fluency. *The Journal of the Acoustical Society of America, 107*(2), 989–999. doi:10.1121/1.428279 PMID:10687708.

Cucchiarini, C., Strik, H., & Boves, L. (2002). Quantitative assessment of second language learners' fluency: Comparisons between read and spontaneous speech. *The Journal of the Acoustical Society of America, 111*(6), 2862–2873. doi:10.1121/1.1471894 PMID:12083220.

Cucchiarini, C., van den Heuvel, H., Sanders, E., & Strik, H. (2011). Error selection for ASR-based English pronunciation training in 'My Pronunciation Coach.' [Florence, Italy.]. *Proceedings Interspeech, 2011,* 1165–1168.

Cucchiarini, C., van Doremalen, J., & Strik, H. (2012). *Practice and feedback in L2 speaking: An evaluation of the DISCO CALL system.* Paper presented at Interspeech 2012. Portland, Oregon.

Day, E. M., & Shapson, M. (2001). Integrating formal and functional approaches to language teaching in French immersion: An experimental study. *Language Learning, 51,* 47–80. doi:10.1111/j.1467-1770.2001.tb00014.x.

De Bot, K. (1996). The psycholinguistics of the output hypothesis. *Language Learning, 46,* 529–555. doi:10.1111/j.1467-1770.1996.tb01246.x.

DeKeyser, R. (2007). *Practice in a second language. Perspectives from applied linguistics and cognitive psychology.* UK: Cambridge University Press.

DeKeyser, R. M., & Sokalski, K. J. (1996). The differential role of comprehension and production practice. *Language Learning, 46*(4), 613–642. doi:10.1111/j.1467-1770.1996.tb01354.x.

Demo, D. (2001). *Discourse analysis for language teachers. ERIC Digest. ERIC Clearinghouse on Languages and linguistics.* Washington, DC: Center for Applied Linguistics.

Derwing, T. M., Munro, M. J., & Carbonaro, M. (2000). Does popular speech recognition software work with ESL speech? *TESOL Quarterly, 34,* 592–603. doi:10.2307/3587748.

Dickinson, M., Eom, S., Kang, Y., Lee, C. M., & Sachs, R. (2008). A balancing act: How can intelligent computer-generated feedback be provided in learner-to-learner interactions? *Computer Assisted Language Learning, 21*(4), 369–382. doi:10.1080/09588220802343702.

Dlaska, A., & Krekeler, C. (2008). Self-assessment of pronunciation. *System, 36,* 506–516. doi:10.1016/j.system.2008.03.003.

Doughty, C. J., & Long, M. H. (2003). Optimal psycholinguistic environments for distance foreign language learning. *Language Learning & Technology, 7*(3), 50–80.

El Tatawi, M. (2002). Corrective feedback in second language acquisition. *Working papers in TESOL and Applied Linguistics, 2,* 1-19.

Ellis, N., & Larsen-Freeman, D. (2006). Language emergence: Implications for applied Linguistics. *Applied Linguistics, 27*(4), 558–589. doi:10.1093/applin/aml028.

Ellis, N. C. (2008). Optimizing the input: Frequency and sampling in usage-based and form-focused learning. In Long, M. H., & Doughty, C. (Eds.), *Handbook of language teaching* (pp. 139–158). Oxford: Blackwell.

Ellis, N. C., & Bogart, P. S. H. (2007). Speech and language technology in education: The perspective from SLA research and practice. *Proceedings SLaTE* (pp. 1-8). Farmington, PA.

Ellis, R., Loewen, S., & Erlam, R. (2006). Implicit and explicit corrective feedback and the acquisition of L2 grammar. *Studies in Second Language Acquisition, 28,* 339–368. doi:10.1017/S0272263106060141.

Ellis, R., & Sheen, Y. (2006). Reexamining the role of recasts in second language acquisition. *Studies in Second Language Acquisition, 28,* 575–601. doi:10.1017/S027226310606027X.

Eskenazi, M. (1996). Detection of foreign speakers' pronunciation errors for second language training – preliminary results. [Philadelphia, Pennsylvania.]. *Proceedings ICSLP, 96,* 1465–1468.

Eskenazi, M. (2009). An overview of spoken language technology for education. *Speech Communication, 51,* 832–844. doi:10.1016/j.specom.2009.04.005.

Eskenazi, M., Kennedy, A., Ketchum, C., Olszewski, R., & Pelton, G. (2007). The NativeaccentTM pronunciation tutor: Measuring success in the real world. *Proceedings of the SLaTE-2007 workshop,* Farmington (pp. 124-127). PA, USA.

Franco, H., Abrash, V., Precoda, K., Bratt, H., Rao, R., & Butzberger, J. et al. (2000). The SRI Eduspeak system: Recognition and pronunciation scoring for language learning. [Dundee Scotland.]. *Proceedings ESCA ETRW INSTi, L2000,* 123–128.

Franco, H., Neumeyer, L., Digalakis, V., & Ronen, O. (2000). Combination of machine scores for automatic grading of pronunciation quality. *Speech Communication, 30,* 121–130. doi:10.1016/S0167-6393(99)00045-X.

Han, Z. (2002). A study of the impact of recasts on tense consistency in L2 output. *TESOL Quarterly, 36,* 542–572. doi:10.2307/3588240.

Havranek, G. (2002). When is corrective feedback most likely to succeed? *International Journal of Educational Research, 37,* 255–270. doi:10.1016/S0883-0355(03)00004-1.

Heift, T., & Schulze, M. (2007). *Errors and intelligence in computer-assisted language learning: Parsers and pedagogues.* New York: Routledge.

Hulstijn, J. (2002). Towards a unified account of the representation, processing and acquisition of second language knowledge. *Second Language Research*, *18*(3), 193–223. doi:10.1191/0267658302sr207oa.

ISLE 1.4. (1999). Pronunciation training: Requirements and solutions. ISLE Deliverable 1.4. Retrieved February 27, 2002, from http://nats-www.informatik.uni-hamburg.de/~isle/public/D14/D14.html

Iwashita, N. (2003). Negative feedback and positive evidence in task-based interaction: Differential, effects on L2 development. *Studies in Second Language Acquisition*, *25*, 1–36. doi:10.1017/S0272263103000019.

Johnson, W. L., Beal, C. R., Fowles-Winkler, A., Lauper, U., Marsella, S., Narayanan, S., & Papachristou, D. (2004). Tactical language training system: An interim report. *Intelligent Tutoring Systems*, 336-345.

Kanters, S., Cucchiarini, C., & Strik, H. (2009). The goodness of pronunciation algorithm: A detailed performance study. *Proceedings SLaTE-2009 workshop* (pp. 1-4). Warwickshire, England.

Kim, Y., Franco, H., & Neumeyer, L. (1997). *Automatic pronunciation scoring of specific phone segments for language instruction. Proceedings of Eurospeech* (pp. 645–648). Greece: Rhodes.

Larsen-Freeman, D., & Cameron, L. (2008). Research methodology on language development from a complex systems perspective. *Modern Language Journal*, *92*, 200–213. doi:10.1111/j.1540-4781.2008.00714.x.

Loewen, S., & Philp, J. (2006). Recasts in the adult English L2 classroom: Characteristics, explicitness, and effectiveness. *Modern Language Journal*, *90*, 536–556. doi:10.1111/j.1540-4781.2006.00465.x.

Lyster, R. (1998). Negotiation of form, recasts, and explicit correction in relation to error types and learner repair in immersion classrooms. *Language Learning*, *48*, 183–218. doi:10.1111/1467-9922.00039.

Lyster, R., & Ranta, L. (1997). Corrective feedback and learner uptake. *Studies in Second Language Acquisition*, *19*, 37–66. doi:10.1017/S0272263197001034.

Lyster, R., & Saito, K. (2010). Oral feedback in classroom SLA: A meta-analysis. *Studies in Second Language Acquisition*, *32*, 265–302. doi:10.1017/S0272263109990520.

Mackey, A., & Philp, J. (1998). Conversational interaction and second language development: Recasts, responses, and red herrings. *Modern Language Journal*, *82*, 338–356. doi:10.1111/j.1540-4781.1998.tb01211.x.

Mak, B., Siu, M., Ng, M., Tam, Y.-C., Chan, Y.-C., & Chan, K.-W. (2003). PLASER: Pronunciation learning via automatic speech recognition. *Proceedings of the HLT-NAACL 2003 Workshop on Building Educational Applications using Natural Language Processing* (pp. 23-29). Edmonton, Canada.

McCarthy, M. (1992). *Discourse analysis for language teachers*. New York: Cambridge University Press.

McCarthy, M., & Carter, R. (1994). *Language as discourse: Perspectives for language teachers*. New York: Longman.

Menzel, W., Herron, D., Bonaventura, P., & Morton, R. (2000). Automatic detection and correction of non-native English pronunciations. [Dundee, Scotland.]. *Proceedings of InSTIL, L2000*, 49–56.

Neri, A., Cucchiarini, C., & Strik, H. (2006). Selecting segmental errors in L2 Dutch for optimal pronunciation training. *IRAL -. International Review of Applied Linguistics in Language Teaching*, *44*, 357–404. doi:10.1515/IRAL.2006.016.

Neri, A., Cucchiarini, C., & Strik, H. (2008). The effectiveness of computer-based speech corrective feedback for improving segmental quality in L2 Dutch. *ReCALL*, *20*(2), 225–243. doi:10.1017/S0958344008000724.

Neri, A., Cucchiarini, C., Strik, H., & Boves, L. (2002). The pedagogy technology interface in computer assisted pronunciation training. *Computer Assisted Language Learning*, *15*, 441–467. doi:10.1076/call.15.5.441.13473.

Neumeyer, L., Franco, H., Digalakis, V., & Weintraub, M. (2000). Automatic scoring of pronunciation quality. *Speech Communication*, *30*(2), 83–93. doi:10.1016/S0167-6393(99)00046-1.

Neumeyer, L., Franco, H., Weintraub, M., & Price, P. (1996). Automatic text independent pronunciation scoring of foreign language student speech. [Philadelphia, Pennsylvania.]. *Proceedings ICSLP*, *96*, 1457–1460.

Nicholas, H., Lightbown, P. M., & Spada, N. (2001). Recasts as feedback to language learners. *Language Learning*, *51*, 719–758. doi:10.1111/0023-8333.00172.

Norris, J. M., & Ortega, L. (2000). Effectiveness of L2 instruction: A research synthesis and quantitative meta-analysis. *Language Learning*, *50*, 417–528. doi:10.1111/0023-8333.00136.

Panova, I., & Lyster, R. (2002). Patterns of corrective feedback and uptake in an adult ESL classroom. *TESOL Quarterly*, *36*, 573–595. doi:10.2307/3588241.

Payne, J. S., & Ross, B. M. (2005). Synchronous CMC, working memory, and L2 oral proficiency development. *Language Learning & Technology*, *9*(3), 35–54.

Payne, J. S., & Whitney, P. J. (2002). Developing L2 oral proficiency through synchronous CMC: Output, working memory, and interlanguage development. *CALICO Journal*, *20*(1), 7–32.

Penning de Vries, B., Cucchiarini, C., Strik, H., & Van Hout, R. (2011). Adaptive corrective feedback in second language learning. In De Wannemacker, S., Clarebout, G., & De Causmaecker, P. (Eds.), *Interdisciplinary approaches to adaptive learning. A look at the neighbors, Communications in Computer and Information Science series* (pp. 1–14). Heidelberg: Springer Verlag. doi:10.1007/978-3-642-20074-8_1.

Riggenbach, H. (1999). Discourse analysis in the language classroom: *Vol. 1. The spoken language*. Ann Arbor, MI: University of Michigan Press.

Rohde, D., & Plaut, D. (1999). Language acquisition in the absence of explicit negative evidence: How important is starting small? *Cognition*, *72*, 67–109. doi:10.1016/S0010-0277(99)00031-1 PMID:10520565.

Russel, J., & Spada, N. (2006). The effectiveness of corrective feedback for second language acquisition: A meta-analysis of the research. In Norris, J., & Ortega, L. (Eds.), *Synthesizing research on language learning and teaching* (pp. 131–164). Amsterdam: John Benjamins Publishing Company.

Schmidt, R. W. (1990). The role of consciousness in second language learning. *Applied Linguistics*, *11*, 129–158. doi:10.1093/applin/11.2.129.

Sheen, Y. (2004). Corrective feedback and learner uptake in communicative classrooms across instructional settings. *Language Teaching Research*, *8*, 263–300. doi:10.1191/1362168804lr146oa.

Strik, H., Colpaert, J., van Doremalen, J., & Cucchiarini, C. (2012). The DISCO ASR-based CALL system: Practicing L2 oral skills and beyond. *Proceedings of the Conference on International Language Resources and Evaluation (LREC 2012)* (pp. 2702-2707). Istanbul, Turkey.

Strik, H., Cornillie, F., Colpaert, J., van Doremalen, J., & Cucchiarini, C. (2009). Developing a CALL system for practicing oral proficiency: How to design for speech technology, pedagogy and learners. *Proceedings of the SLaTE-2009 workshop* (pp.1-4). Warwickshire, England.

Strik, H., Truong, K., de Wet, F., & Cucchiarini, C. (2007). Comparing classifiers for pronunciation error detection. [Antwerp, Belgium.]. *Proceedings of Interspeech, 2007,* 1837–1840.

Strik, H., Truong, K., de Wet, F., & Cucchiarini, C. (2009). Comparing different approaches for automatic pronunciation error detection. *Speech Communication, 51*(10), 845–852. doi:10.1016/j.specom.2009.05.007.

Strik, H., van de Loo, J., van Doremalen, J., & Cucchiarini, C. (2010). Practicing syntax in spoken interaction: Automatic detection of syntactic errors in non-native utterances. *Proceedings of the SLaTE-2010 workshop* (pp.1-4). Tokyo, Japan.

Strik, H., van Doremalen, J., van de Loo, J., & Cucchiarini, C. (2011). Improving ASR processing of ungrammatical utterances through grammatical error modeling. *Proceedings of the SLaTE-2011 workshop* (pp.1-4). Venice, Italy.

Swain, M. (1985). Communicative competence: Some roles of comprehensible input and comprehensible output in its development. In Gass, M. A., & Madden, C. G. (Eds.), *Input in second language acquisition* (pp. 235–253). Rowley, MA: Newbury House.

van Doremalen, J., Cucchiarini, C., & Strik, H. (2010). Using non-native error patterns to improve pronunciation verification. [Tokyo, Japan.]. *Proceedings of Interspeech, 2010,* 1–4.

van Doremalen, J., Cucchiarini, C., & Strik, H. (2010). Optimizing automatic speech recognition for low-proficient non-native speakers. *EURASIP Journal on Audio, Speech, and Music Processing, 2010,* 1–13. doi:10.1155/2010/973954.

van Doremalen, J., Cucchiarini, C., & Strik, H. (2011). Speech technology in CALL: The essential role of adaptation. In De Wannemacker, S., Clarebout, G., & De Causmaecker, P. (Eds.), *Interdisciplinary approaches to adaptive learning. A look at the neighbors, Communications in Computer and Information Science series, 26* (pp. 56–69). Heidelberg: Springer Verlag. doi:10.1007/978-3-642-20074-8_5.

van Doremalen, J., Strik, H., & Cucchiarini, C. (2009). Utterance verification in language learning applications. *Proceedings of the SLaTE-2009 workshop* (pp.1-4). Warwickshire, England.

Witt, S. (1999). *Use of speech recognition in computer assisted language learning.* (Unpublished doctoral dissertation). University of Cambridge, UK.

Witt, S. (2012). Automatic error detection in pronunciation training: Where we are and where we need to go. *Proceedings IS ADEPT* (pp. 1-8). Stockholm, Sweden.

Witt, S., & Young, S. (1997). Language learning based on non-native speech recognition. [Rhodes, Greece.]. *Proceedings Eurospeech, 1997,* 633–636.

Young, D. J. (1990). An investigation of students' perspectives on anxiety and speaking. *Foreign Language Annals, 23,* 539–553. doi:10.1111/j.1944-9720.1990.tb00424.x.

ADDITIONAL READING

Benzeghiba, M., Mori, R. D., Deroo, O., Dupont, S., Erbes, T., & Jouvet, D. et al. (2007). Automatic speech recognition and speech variability: A review. *Speech Communication, 49*(10-11), 763–786. doi:10.1016/j.specom.2007.02.006.

Chapelle, C. A. (2007). Technology and second language acquisition. *Annual Review of Applied Linguistics, 27,* 98–114. doi:10.1017/S0267190508070050.

D'Mello, S., & Graesser, A. (2006). Affect detection from human-computer dialogue with an intelligent tutoring system. In J. Gratch, M. Young, R. Aylett, D. Ballin, & P. Olivier (Eds.), *Proceedings of the 6th International Conference on Intelligent Virtual Agents (IVA 2006)* (pp. 54-67). Marina del Rey, California, USA.

DeKeyser, R. (2005). What makes learning second-language grammar difficult? A review of issues. *Language Learning, 55,* 1–25. doi:10.1111/j.0023-8333.2005.00294.x.

Delmonte, R. (2011). Exploring speech technologies for language learning. Retrieved February 6, 2013, from http://www.intechopen.com/books/speech-and-language-technologies

Dörnyei, Z., & Ushioda, E. (2009). *Motivation, language identity and the L2 self.* Bristol: Multilingual Matters.

Doughty, C. J., & Long, M. H. (2003). Optimal psycholinguistic environments for distance foreign language learning. *Language Learning & Technology, 7*(3), 50–80.

Egan, K. (1999). Speaking: A critical skill and challenge. *CALICO Journal, 16,* 277–293.

Ehsani, F., & Knodt, E. (1998). Speech technology in computer-aided learning: Strengths and limitations of a new CALL paradigm. *Language Learning & Technology, 2,* 45–60.

Ellis, R., & Barkhuizen, G. (2005). *Analyzing learner language.* Oxford: Oxford University Press.

Engwall, O., & Balter, O. (2007). Pronunciation feedback from real and virtual language teachers. *Computer Assisted Language Learning, 20,* 235–262. doi:10.1080/09588220701489507.

Flege, J. (1995). Second-language speech learning: Theory, findings and problems. In Strange, W. (Ed.), *Speech perception and linguistic experience* (pp. 229–273). Timonium, MD: York Press Inc..

Gass, S. M., & Selinker, L. (2008). *Second language acquisition.* New York: Routledge.

Hincks, R. (2005). Measures and perceptions of liveliness in student oral presentation speech: A proposal for an automatic feedback mechanism. *System, 33,* 575–591. doi:10.1016/j.system.2005.04.002.

Housen, A., & Kuiken, F. (2009). Complexity, accuracy, and fluency in second language acquisition. *Applied Linguistics, 30,* 461–473. doi:10.1093/applin/amp048.

Kapoor, A., & Picard, R. W. (2005). Multimodal affect recognition in learning environments. *Proceedings of the 13th Annual ACM International Conference on Multimedia MULTIMEDIA '05* (pp. 677-682). New York: ACM Press.

Levis, J. (2007). Computer technology in teaching and researching pronunciation. *Annual Review of Applied Linguistics, 27,* 184–202. doi:10.1017/S0267190508070098.

Long, M. (1990). Maturational constraints on language development. *Studies in Second Language Acquisition, 12,* 251–285. doi:10.1017/S0272263100009165.

Markowitz, J. (1996). *Using speech recognition.* NJ: Prentice Hall.

Neri, A. (2007). *The pedagogical effectiveness of ASR-based computer assisted pronunciation training.* (Unpublished doctoral dissertation). Radboud University Nijmegen.

Price, P. (1998). How can speech technology replicate and complement good language teachers to help people learn language? [Marholmen, Sweden.]. *Proceedings STiLL, 98,* 103–106.

Strange, W. (1995). Cross-language studies of speech perception and production in second-language learning. In Strange, W. (Ed.), *Speech perception and linguistic experience* (pp. 3–45). Timonium, MD: York Press Inc..

Tomokiyo, L. (2001). *Recognizing non-native speech: Characterizing and adapting to non-native usage in speech recognition*. (Unpublished doctoral dissertation). Carnegie Mellon University.

Witt, S., & Young, S. (2000). Phone-level pronunciation scoring and assessment for interactive language learning. *Speech Communication, 30*, 95–108. doi:10.1016/S0167-6393(99)00044-8.

Zechner, K., Higgins, D., Xi, X., & Williamson, D. (2009). Automatic scoring of non-native spontaneous speech in tests of spoken English. *Speech Communication, 51*(10), 883–895. doi:10.1016/j.specom.2009.04.009.

KEY TERMS AND DEFINITIONS

ASR: Automatic speech recognition.

CALL: Computer Assisted Language Learning.

Corrective Feedback: Any indication to the learners that their use of the target language is incorrect (Lightbown, P.M., & Spada, N. (1999). *How languages are learned* (pp. 171-172). Oxford, UK: Oxford University Press.).

Error Detection: The process by which errors are found (detected) in an utterance.

Grammatical: Pertaining to the grammar of a language and its rules.

L2: Second language.

Morphology: The science and study of forms and formation of words.

Output: Language produced by an L2 learner, either oral or written.

Syntax: The study and rules of the relation of words to one another as parts of the structures of sentences.

Section 2
Electronic Discourse Analysis:
Innovations in Theory, Methods, and Applications in Research on Society and Culture

Chapter 9
Critical Electronic Discourse Analysis:
Social and Cultural Research in the Electronic Age

Bob Hodge
University of Western Sydney, Australia

ABSTRACT

This chapter investigates and endorses the integration of two existing research traditions, electronic discourse analysis (EDA) and critical discourse analysis (CDA), into a more powerful and comprehensive form of analysis of electronic discourses, Critical Electronic Discourse Analysis (CEDA). It sets this analytic project against the massive, unpredictable changes in culture and society which are associated with the electronic media revolution. It argues for innovative forms of analysis, in which 'electronic discourse analysis' acquires two over-lapping interpretations: electronically enabled analysis of discourses in all media; and all forms of analysis of electronic discourses and the social forms they express. It uses McLuhan and multi-modality theory to argue for major continuities and significant breaks in semiotic modes over long periods. It argues that powerful innovations in analysis and technology need to recognize and incorporate the two fundamental semiotic modes, digital and analogue, and not seek to replace one with the other.

INTRODUCTION

Critical discourse analysis (CDA) has become a leading tradition for analysing issues of language and society as they are expressed in and act through discourse (Wetherell, Taylor, & Yates, 2001). In some respects, this tradition sets the benchmark for the critical analysis of discourse as a social, political and cultural force. Yet most current forms of CDA do not engage closely with electronic forms and processes of discourse, Electronic Discourse Analysis (EDA). In this chapter I will

DOI: 10.4018/978-1-4666-4426-7.ch009

argue that a strong union and dialogue between these two strands has exciting possibilities for both, as Critical Electronic Discourse Analysis (CEDA). CEDA can produce more powerful and comprehensive analyses that would illuminate both fields in their current forms. It can feed innovation across all areas affected by electronic discourse, adding a critical dimension that is often lost in more technologically oriented forms of research.

CDA emerged in the 1970s in a context where the force and effects of specific media of communication were treated as largely irrelevant for analyses of what mattered, messages and effects of power, in the medium that mattered, verbal language, mostly in its written form. That productive but simplifying assumption is no longer plausible. Electronic media technologies using digital coding systems have exploded in the past 50 years. They have transformed the communications landscape, drastically altering the available strategies for exercising or resisting power which were the major theme for critical discourse analysis. Many have claimed there has been a communication revolution that has changed the rules of the game. It is necessary to undertake a fundamental review of what critical discourse analysis now is and what it can and should do, in and for the new agendas of the electronic age.

Conversely, as the present book illustrates, the technological dimensions of electronically mediated forms of discourse are so new and ill-understood that the task of criticism of these processes and products has tended to be deferred or relegated to a subsidiary place, and electronic discourse analysis has only recently emerged. This chapter will look at these developments, CDA and EDA, from both sides. It will look at EDA in two complementary senses: as the analysis of electronic discourse and the social forms it rests on, and as the use of electronic forms or aids to analysis, deployed on objects in old or new media or both. In both these senses, EDA generates new objects for critical analysis, while offering new resources for general critical discourse analysis.

The chapter will argue that this new scope and the new concepts that underpin it turn out to strengthen the enterprise of CDA, bringing back into it some dimensions of language and social processes which it should never have ignored. At the same time, this form of analysis, CDA plus EDA in tandem (or CEDA, as I have called it), can together establish a general perspective on what kind of world is being created by electronic texts and practices, as the context for analysis of subtle but potent meanings and effects of electronic forms. In this way it can shift electronic discourses from a specialist and marginalized place in the spectrum of social and discursive activities to a central and more widely valued (and widely studied) position.

BACKGROUND

The claimed media 'revolution' – if there is one – has to be analysed in the forms in which it manifests itself, but many of the claims themselves are made in verbal language, and analysing them draws on the classic resources of CDA. To illustrate the practices of CDA and show their value for understanding how electronic forms are currently constructed in powerful discourses, I quote the title of a recent electronic publication, published under the auspices of the MIT Sloan School of Management: *Race Against the Machine: How the Digital Revolution Is Accelerating Innovation, Driving Productivity, and Irreversibly Transforming Employment and the Economy* (Brynjolfsson & McAfee, 2012).

Traditional CDA is good at taking pieces of text apart to reveal complex ideological forms and processes. The analysis of discourse about electronic discourses and practices may seem esoteric and remote from EDA practitioners' interest in the construction and analysis of the electronic discourses themselves, but I will argue that these surrounding discourses play a crucial role in legitimating and shaping electronic practices. In this case, these influential authors promote a 'digital revolution' which ought to give high value to everyone who works with electronic media. However, a critical perspective warns practitioners to be aware that this is not a blank cheque. There is always fine print, meanings to be picked up by CDA, affecting which aspects of electronic forms are central and which are not.

The meaning of the title and the text it accompanies appears straightforward. It seems to take for granted the assumption that there is a digital revolution, and that it is having massive and irreversible effects on economic life. CDA does not immediately address the issue of whether this is true or not. I personally would more or less agree with this statement, but the first question to ask from a CDA perspective is: who is saying this, to whom, on behalf of what interests, for what possible effects?

In beginning to answer this question I note the very different effects and presumed audiences of the title and the subtitle. The main title may allude to the *Terminator* films, which project a future in which a vast computer system, Skynet, has taken over the planet and wages war on humanity. The films dramatize human resistance, feeble but effective in each film. Through the allusion the authors imply that computers are scary things, and humans ought to fight them.

Yet the subtitle seems to proclaim the opposite ideology. Do not "race against the machine," the authors say, but go for the ride. This contradiction is a typical example of an ideological complex (Hodge & Kress, 1988), a functional set of contradictions, which critical analysis can use to uncover symptomatic tensions in an apparently united position. In this case, we can ask why these authors have such a contradictory position on digital technology and the digital revolution.

This question comes into better focus if we set it into a social and discursive framework. I note that this title and article emanate from a managerial source and discourse, designed for managerial readers. The allusion to the blockbuster films, then,

is a reference to popular knowledge these readers can be supposed to have, embedded in and subordinated to the managerial discourse. The subtitle then addresses the core concerns these managerial readers can be supposed to have, relating to innovation, productivity and employment. It arouses and exploits an ambivalence these readers can be supposed to have about this revolution.

One kind of reader, who is not invoked, however, is someone who actually knows about electronic technologies. These authors published their text online and probably composed it using a word-processor, but it is basically a conventional print work. They draw on their expertise as consumers of popular culture to proclaim that the digital revolution has already happened. They already know all about it, and they do not need any producer or analyst of electronic discourse to tell them anything.

This identifies a deeper contradiction in this powerful discourse about electronic discourse that practitioners need to be aware of. The new rulers of the brave new world are the same old rulers of the old one: the literate managerial class. The expertise of experts in this technology is so deeply devalued in their discourse that the act of devaluing it is itself displaced from view. The celebration of the 'digital' or 'electronic' revolution by these influential prophets is designed to aggrandize themselves, not those working with and developing the technologies.

A problematic term in this discourse is 'revolution.' 'Revolution' makes a big but ambiguous claim, which shifts in different contexts. These writers use a business discourse in which changes can be called 'revolutions,' but the capitalist system itself is left intact. Critical discourse analysis comes from a Marxist tradition in which a 'revolution' could be expected to be more far-reaching to count as such.

However, this difference cannot be reduced to a rhetorical difference of emphasis. Marx and Engels (1975) in the classic text *Manifesto of the Communist Party* used the term in different senses with a different and opposite effect. They called the bourgeoisie a 'revolutionary' class, able to revolutionise the means of production in fact to put off the final political transformation Marxists envisaged, to a new political and social order. That is, one level of revolution can hold back or reverse a revolution at a higher level.

Brynjolfsson and McAfee describe the "digital revolution" in terms that can be understood in the Marxist scheme. They see a revolution in technology, specifically in the development of digital technologies, as producing major knock-on transformations in economics, labour and productivity. Yet in some important ways their critique is superficial. They portray technological development as if it operated in a social vacuum, producing social effects – massive unemployment, for instance – which are seen as undesirable for those affected, but they see no reason to moderate the system. They describe the new winning strategies for businesses in the new world, without seeing disastrous consequences as any reason to change or moderate the electronically driven new forces.

Their analysis of the transformations in digital technologies illustrates what I am calling a superficial approach. According to them these transformations obey Moore's law, a proposition developed from an observation by Intel founder Gordon Moore in the 1960s, based on developments in computer engineering (Castells, 2000, p. 39). Moore observed that over the previous decade, computers had doubled in power every two years. This 'law' projects an exponential growth along these lines, with no limit.

There are many problems with such laws, from a critical perspective. One is that they rapidly lead to impossible and unsustainable sizes and inevitable collapse. If such claims are taken seriously, they need to be carefully scrutinized. For instance, Moore was an entrepreneur, not an academic, and he changed his prediction to fit changing facts. Yet Moore's law is confidently

recycled in managerial discourse as though it has the same status as Newton's famous laws.

Brynjolfsson and McAfee do not mention counter evidence. Digital analyst Kennedy (2008) analysed Microsoft programs between 2000 and 2007, and found that the latest systems had half the speed of the early ones. He called this "The Great Moore's Law Compensator," a development that cancelled out the improvements following from Moore's law by what he called "bloat," added features which slowed down processing speed while increasing profit (Kennedy, 2008, p. 1).

Brynjolfsson and McAfee's use of Moore and non-use of Kennedy illustrate the practical need for a critical approach by everyone working with electronic forms of discursive production and interpretation. They use an unexamined claim about computer technologies to extrapolate to an equally unexamined mega-claim about this total set of technologies. Kennedy, who they probably do not know about, illustrates a critical approach which combines informal CDA and informal EDA, based on a practitioner perspective. The new software for Microsoft Office, including the digital and conventional signs in its coding, can be understood as a kind of discourse, which he sees as full of redundancies, expressing the single social meaning of maximization of profit. That is a core message Brynjolfsson and McAfee would understand well.

CEDA can alert all buyers and users of this kind of electronic discourse to the way management discourses penetrate both the creation and marketing of this major piece of software. Although it mainly uses CDA about claims about things electronic and digital, it provides a critical framework for understanding the contexts in which those who produce and analyse electronic discourses must work. This insight would not come from EDA alone, but it is vital for electronic workers. That is why they need CEDA, as context and complement to EDA.

FOUNDATIONS FOR A NEW CRITICAL ELECTRONIC DISCOURSE ANALYSIS

The Semiotic Basis

The multiplicity of codes deployed in modern communication systems has forced CDA out of its comfortable reliance on purely verbal, mainly print media, and EDA needs to follow. This more ample conceptual space has been called semiotics. Here I will argue that social semiotics (see e.g. Hodge & Kress, 1988; Van Leeuwen, 2005) is the main source for the core concepts needed to understand the digital revolution, and the electronic forms and practices of discourse within it.

Of the three terms in common use to describe this technological revolution, 'electronic' comes from physics, the material basis for these technologies; 'information' comes from communication technologies; and 'digital' refers to coding systems. In this sense digital comes from semiotics, but has been appropriated by engineering. It is useful to take it back to semiotics again, to make some important distinctions that have been lost in its translation.

In computer engineering, input and output are in digital codes. 'Digital' derives from the Latin word *digitus*, a finger, as used in counting. Its importance comes from its value in computational systems, which use codes which are discrete and binary. Technologies based on this code are expanding rapidly, replacing technologies based on analogue codes; that is, codes which are not discrete or binary. This gives rise to the impression that digital codes are opposed to analogue codes and will soon replace them.

However, codes are different to technologies. In semiotics, Charles Peirce (1958), a founding father of the field, proposed a three-member classification of kinds of sign which is still seen as basic. 'Analogue' signs are similar to what he called 'iconic' signs. Iconic signs communicate by being like what they represent, as pictures do. Peirce opposed these to two other kinds of sign. 'Indexical' signs are linked by causal chains. Digital signs are an important kind of indexical sign, where the link is formed by a process of computation that may be very long. 'Symbolic' signs are linked only by convention, as with the sounds and meanings of verbal languages.

All three kinds of sign in Peirce's model are essential for understanding electronic discourse and the digital revolution. Conventional signs have not disappeared or diminished in electronic discourse. More words are circulated, not less. Specifically, computer languages are also made up of conventional signs which are arbitrary, as are menus and other conventions in electronic pages. What geeks understand better than their non-electronic fellows is a larger set of conventional meanings of many of these signs, in a language framework.

Likewise, digital technologies reproduce and circulate analogue signs, such as images of all kinds, on a larger scale than has ever been possible before. What Brynjolfsson and McAfee call a 'digital' revolution is equally a revolution in the other two codes. Yet there is a significant change: not the elimination of other codes by the digital, but a systemic effect of this technology on the three kinds of sign. Reality is often an analogue signal, which human perception and thought turns into both digital and analogue forms, which are then communicated to others via digital, analogue, or conventional forms. These are then interpreted by receivers into their own versions of the world, constituted by a play of analogue and digital.

In this process, which long pre-dates electronic technologies, digital codes have always been present, and analogue codes are so fundamental that they are in no danger of becoming obsolete. What digital technologies do is to link perception, thought and communication via translation into

195

digital code, which is then re-translated back into the constituent codes. Industrial formats tend to take analogue signals, turn these into digital forms for storage, manipulation and circulation, and then reprocess them back into the familiar analogue and conventional forms that are still preferred and used better by human users. Digital codes in digital technologies play a key role in circuits of signs, in processes which often transform analogue to digital and back again.

Visual images illustrate the case. The visual field is a complex form, full of different patterns and shades. Digital technologies break this down into computable discrete components, which are stored and manipulated and then presented to viewers who recreate something that corresponds to the original analogue complexity. But this is not a simple and effortless triumph of digital over analogue. Vast amounts of computing power are sometimes needed to only seem to match analogue forms, as in the expensive process of creating virtual realities. These products will then be judged largely by analogue standards, not digital. To some extent this pattern is shifting, as consumers of electronic product are learning to be tolerant of the inadequacies of digital forms. This change is only just beginning, and it is hard to say how it will unfold, or what its consequences will be. This indeed is an area of current uncertainty, requiring predictions to be cautious. However, there is no reason to suppose that analogue signs are facing extinction. They will be crucial in any foreseeable future.

Brynjolfsson and McAfee (2012) implicitly recognize this point, in other terms. They make a distinction between what they call computation and 'pattern recognition,' and note that machines are overwhelmingly superior at computation (digital codes), but far less skilled in 'pattern recognition.' This is the race, they say, that humans can still compete in and maybe win. Their interest is primarily strategic, to point out where humans may still seek employment in a world of digital

processes, but it can also be the basis for a critical approach to electronic discourse, and to the discourse of those who seek to control it.

A Framework for Understanding the Electronic Revolution

Writing two decades before CDA was born, Marshall McLuhan (1964) offered a powerful and influential picture of media systems in the electronic age, but without reference to semiotics or critical theory. Perhaps for this reason, CDA did not incorporate his insights. EDA now lives in the age he projected, so perhaps for that reason its practitioners commonly do not turn to his work. However, both traditions need a theory of his scope to help understand and operate in the new media environment.

McLuhan described the coming media revolution and tried to think about it before the internet; before the full explosion of digital technologies; before the word 'cyberspace' was invented. He ought to be irrelevant now. But he was like Janus, the Roman god who looked both ways, to the past and the future. In order to explain the future he went far back into the history of communications. To do so, he found he needed to develop a far broader idea of what communication is. He established a broad basis for the study of media revolutions as social phenomena that has not been superseded.

McLuhan identified two major trends, both of which are even more evident today in the electronic landscape. One was the impact of media technologies in making possible new forms of social organization and new forms of thought. The other was to connect globalisation with these developments. Both propositions are important for analysing electronic and non-electronic forms of discourse and the social practices that feed into and are sustained by them.

One key premise was contained in his slogan "The medium is the message" (McLuhan, 1964). One ancestor of this proposition is aesthetics, where the problem of how art has meaning was resolved through the proposition that 'form is content.' McLuhan (1964) extended "medium" to cover all semiotic modes. In a sweeping statement he talked of media as "extensions of man (*sic*)." They extend all senses, producing a multi-semiotic regime of extended senses. For him, media also extend other human capacities. So 'communication systems' for McLuhan include transport systems and movements of bodies and goods, all of which are now deeply permeated by electronic technologies on small and large scales.

McLuhan also incorporated social relations as part of his idea of the message of media. This connects with the concept of ideology in CDA, which includes a concern with the way media institutions and practices construct and maintain versions of society. To this McLuhan added a useful distinction between two kinds of code, one with high definition and low participation, the other with the opposite. These correspond to digital and analogue codes.

In these terms, digital codes tend to produce segmentation in texts and in society. Analogue codes counter those tendencies. As with all binaries, these oppositions are too simplistic. Analogic and digital, continuous and discrete codes can combine in different ways in both representations and social forms. But however simplistic they may be, his two categories are valuable for analysis of all electronic forms and practices of discourse, because they constantly ask three basic questions: how are the meanings of this text affected by its form? How are the social relations constructed through this practice affected by its form? How are meanings and social relations mediated by this form?

As a useful tool for a kind of critical analysis McLuhan introduced the idea of media as 'prosthetics.' Extensions of the senses gave them new capacities but also, he insisted, carried limitations. There was always some loss, hidden by what was gained, or minimized by those who gained from

it. This insight is heuristically useful. It makes us always look for the downsides of any medium system. Electronic practices and discourses are not exempt from this rule. Brynjolfsson and McAfee's analysis is superficial because they did not ask what is lost as well as what is gained by the electronic revolution, nor what can be done about recovering the losses.

In what follows I hope to show the practical as well as theoretical value of McLuhan's framework for the study of discourse, electronic and non-electronic, against a background of massive changes – a 'revolution' – and equally profound continuities. The complex relationship of CDA and EDA to each other and to their social contexts only makes sense in terms of a theory on this scale, dealing with the deep effects, social and cognitive, of different media regimes.

From CDA to Multi-Modality in the New Electronic Landscape

My aim in this chapter is to weave together the distinct strands of CDA and EDA. To do so I need to outline where CDA comes from, and where it might or ought to go in the future to intersect with developments in electronic media. The following account is designed for readers of this book, who cannot be assumed to know this specialized field. It is brief, schematic, partial and critical, a personal perspective from a participant in an ethnographic framework, designed only to contribute to the particular argument of this chapter, not to offer anything more comprehensive.

My history of CDA in the English language tradition begins with the publication in 1974 of an article "Transformations, Models and Processes" (Hodge & Kress, 1974), designed to be a manifesto for critical linguistics. The immediate context for this work was the impetus from the student movements of 1968, with their critique of the operations of power and domination in governments and business in western democracies, supported as they believed by the mainstream curriculum. Critical linguistics was a response to this critique. It married a critical form of the discipline of linguistics to critical social theory, to forge a tool for the analysis of power and ideology exercised through language.

As I reflect on my own thinking as someone involved in this development, it now seems to me that the 1968 student movements shaped CDA more than I had realized. The most urgent problematic, as it seemed from the perspective of the 1968 movements, were the subtle strategies of dominance exercised by a ruling elite, exercised through dominant modes of language and media: language carried in the most prestigious form (formal, written English) through mainstream media (mainly print but also television). Other forms and media were not entirely ignored, but it seemed viable to mount the major critique using mainly mono-semiotic media and texts.

Critical linguistics was developed in two books: *Language as Ideology* (Kress & Hodge, 1979) and *Language and Control* (Fowler, Hodge, Kress, & Trew, 1979). This tradition was criticized by Thompson (1984) because it lacked a sufficiently solid social theory. Norman Fairclough (1989) met this need in part by developing the project (which would be later named Critical Discourse Analysis) by drawing on Michel Foucault's theories of discourse.

Foucault is a giant figure in modern social theory, but his work carried some inadvertent limitations in CDA as a potential basis for CEDA. He began his career as an intellectual historian, analysing mainly written archives. He was not initially a discourse theorist or analyst, and he had no need to grapple with contemporary media. His turn to discourse, signalled by a major statement in 1971 (translated into English in Foucault, 1972) has been attributed (MacDonnell, 1986) to his response to the French authorities' reactions to the 1968 student movements. But although he supported the student protests and agreed with many of their ideas, he did not see any new forms of communication emerging from this source. It is only recently, with the massive use of social media in protest movements, such as the Arab Spring, that critical thinkers see the need to look at the potential role of electronic forms in social movements. Such preoccupations and limitations of critical theorists contributed to blind spots in what critical analysts of discourse saw as the major issues of the time.

At the same time as Fairclough was developing CDA, Bob Hodge and Gunther Kress (1988) brought out the semiotics implicit in critical linguistics in what they called social semiotics. 'Semiotics' reflected a recognition that power and other social forces operate through many semiotic modes, and the aims of critical analysis could not be adequately met by analysing only verbal language. Semiotics as a broad field was relevant to this form of analysis, but especially inspiring was the work of French writer Roland Barthes (1971). His *Mythologies* was published in English in 1971 but incorporated articles written in the pre-electronic 1950s. This can be seen as the foundational work for critical forms of semiotics.

In spite of their common origins, for two decades the two branches of CDA, social semiotics and mono-semiotic CDA, functioned largely independently, with mono-semiotic CDA dominant. The two have now begun to converge, mainly through the work of Gunther Kress and Theo Van Leeuwen (2001) on what they called multi-modality: texts composed or transmitted in more than one major semiotic mode. In this chapter I argue that a semiotic base is indispensable for electronic discourse analysis in its two forms, as electronically enhanced analysis and as analysis of discourse operating through different media or modes. A mono-semiotic form of CDA is intrinsically inadequate for both tasks. Multi-modal analysis is not just a supplement to mono-semiotic CDA; it provides an essential framework for CEDA today.

Multi-modal analysis in the hands of Kress and Van Leeuwen makes some subtle but important contributions to discourse analysis. They start from the challenge of new forms of media organization, the proliferation of multi-media forms seen as radically new. Where previous semiotic orders, in their view, consisted of different relatively self-contained modes, each with its own semiotic system, its own 'grammar,' multi-media systems involve many modes with patterns of exchange between them. In previous dispensations, social semiotics could study distinct systems and grammars. In the electronic age multi-modal concepts are needed to track these movements.

Like McLuhan, Kress and Van Leeuwen had a Janus perspective. This can be seen in their analysis of the role of lay-out in print forms and web pages (Kress & Van Leeuwen, 1996). They showed that words and images or even words alone are organized and given meaning by lay-out as a coding system. Left versus right encoded given and new. Top and bottom encoded ideal and real/everyday. Centre and periphery encoded degrees of importance.

The first two of these codes are digital systems, though they do not use digital technology. On the contrary, they have a long history in pre-electronic technologies. The third code is analogue, again with a long history. All, however, are also conventional to some degree. All three can co-exist in a single page, which is thus multi-modal irrespective of the technological stage of development.

In this analysis, a page of writing, in print or electronic media, with or without images, is already multi-modal, superimposing spatial elements of the text with its words. I will call this "embedded multi-modality," to distinguish it from parallel multi-modality, as in multi-media texts which combine words and pictures. This is different again from the multi-modality produced by transformations between different modalities, e.g. from speech to writing or analogue to digital, which I call "serial multi-modality." The Janus paradox in this picture is that Kress and Van Leeuwen came to see something that was always there in writing but was invisible, until it was seen

from the perspective of electronic discourses and their multi-modality.

Kress and Van Leeuwen see the 'revolution' or transition to electronic media in different terms to McLuhan. For them there is not a decisive move from the dominance of one mode (writing) to another (electronic), but from one form of multiple modalities where the modes are relatively fixed to one where they form a more fluid, dynamic system. Using the semiotic terms digital and analogue reveals a paradox: the multi-media system driven by digital technologies is the more analogue system, with less discrete boundaries, and the ability to create and circulate more analogue meanings. This is the same paradox we have seen before: digital technologies enable analogue codes. CEDA methods of analysis, then, need stronger not weaker capacities for analogue analysis.

Yet digital analysis still remains an essential component of any analysis. The play of digital and analogue is fundamental to human perception and thought, as well as communication and language. The CDA tradition, in the various English and French strands that make it up, is biased towards analogue forms, detecting, analysing and critiquing patterns of meaning and relationship at the small scale in pieces of language, and at the larger scale of social bodies and institutions.

Methods in the social sciences have traditionally been divided into two categories, quantitative and qualitative, which have sometimes organized hostile paradigms of research. Behind these two research methods lies the fundamental semiotic distinction between analogue and digital: complex patterns versus methods of counting. One effect of the explosion of digital technologies is that huge numbers of instances are thrown up; many patterns whose scale goes beyond human capacities for seeing patterns, which then draw on the human capacity for reading analogue signs.

These quantitative forms of analysis remain important, but they are not enough. Many social scientists now advocate "mixed methods" (O'Leary, 2004), combinations of quantitative and qualitative methods ('qual' and 'quant' as they are sometimes called). Given the combinations of different codes and scales in the new electronic environment, CEDA cannot afford to remain mono-modal in its approach. Mechanistic forms of mixed methods are still likely to be inadequate, to track and critique the movements that constitute social processes in the present age. Both analogue and digital are needed, in dialogue with each other, in research methods as they are in the electronically permeated social world.

Electronic Analysis of the New Media World

In this section I illustrate the issues raised in the previous discussion as they bear on electronic methods of analysis, and a political world now shaped by digital media and attitudes, and practices arising from them (Busby, 2009). Political life in democratic forms of government is an important area for research for EDA allied with CDA as CEDA. Modern politicians now use new media, but it is an open question how far this has transformed political processes. On the surface it may seem that little has changed. The same political parties and coalitions dominate parliaments. But a McLuhan-scale framework raises questions whether the scale of the difference may be underestimated because it affects the whole system, not just one part of it.

The material I analyse in this section has been published in an article investigating an aspect of this theme (Hodge & Matthews, 2011), which readers may wish to consult for a fuller description of the background. The research assembled data around a key recent dramatic event in Australian political life, a coup exercised by Australian Labor Party (ALP) factional bosses against then Prime Minister Kevin Rudd in favour of his then deputy, Julia Gillard, in 2010. The speed of the coup took everyone by surprise, including Rudd.

There were of course many factors at play, but one interpretation emphasized the role of new media technology:

The specific sequence of events leading to Kevin Rudd's destruction began with the results of an opinion poll.

Specifically, it was a 'word cloud,' a cluster of the words that voters offered when asked to describe their prime minister.

Each word is printed in a type size to reflect how commonly it came up. The dominant word glaring from the 'cloud' was 'arrogant,' followed by 'weak.' Never mind that these seem to convey wildly different conceptions of the man. The Labor powerbrokers who commissioned the poll were only concerned that both are bad qualities for a prime minister.

But asked the word that best described Julia Gillard, the dominant word in her cloud was 'strong,' followed by 'capable.' This was the poll on which factional bosses based their case for replacing Rudd with Gillard. (Hartcher, 2010, "Dark Clouds," para. 1-4)

In what follows I will illustrate some aspects of a CEDA approach in practice, attending specifically to the different balances of CDA and EDA in this broad approach.

CDA and the Manipulations of Electronic Discourse

I will begin with a similar point as was illustrated in the case of Brynjolfsson and McAfee. One use of electronic expertise (EDA) is to use it to see through manipulative and misleading claims made about electronic processes. In this case, the digital technology invoked, word-clouds, does not do what is claimed for it. That initial observation is the way into a more comprehensive critical analysis of wider political processes, some of which do not involve electronic media.

Word-clouds are part of a rapidly-growing set of digital tools through which political operators and market researchers use ephemeral data to seek to manage attitudes and beliefs among an amorphous populace. 'Wordle' (Feinberg, 2009) is the founding brand name for word-clouds, which are non-interactive, unlike some tag-clouds. According to the Many Eyes website, which hosts a suite of freeware tools, Wordle

was designed to give pleasure, and not to provide reliable analytic insight. That said, many people have found unexpected uses for it, from presenting the gist of a text to displaying personal identity.

The layout algorithm differs from most other word-clouds (including the Many Eyes tag-cloud) in its efficient use of typographical space. An entire tiny word may appear inside the letter O of a big word, for example. (Many Eyes, n.d., "Expert Notes," para. 1-2)

This and similar technologies seem to offer a more complex picture of changing realities, yet they are simpler and less powerful than they are made to seem. This software was driven by algorithms with two different functions. One kind was a word frequency counter, a basic component in most word data mining programs. This operation produces an output in digital form, a rank order of frequency of terms. However simple it seems, it can do this for much more data than humans can. This is something computers do extremely well.

The second kind of algorithm modifies this digital output to make it look like an analogue output. Frequency is realized as size, and these words of different sizes are then packaged in a display that looks as if it is an analogue sign, in which meaning is contributed by patterns and configurations. Human interpreters feel that the page has more meaning than it has, because they interpret it as an analogue sign, with meanings that are more familiar. This is an illusion, but it is part of a trick which deceived these faction bosses, or which they used to deceive their party members.

This trick is part of a widespread phenomenon in electronic discourse, an example of serial multi-modality where an analogue text is produced out of digital processes, then interpreted as if it is more analogue than it is, even when (as happens in this case) the analogue rests on an underlying digital code. One reason this effect works as well as it does in political life is because of the role of another analogue sign, the ideological complex we have already looked at, whose persuasive picture of media realities says that digital truths have greater status than analogue truths, even when (as here) their digital basis is disguised. These politicians are persuaded by pretty analogue pictures from digital technologies they do not really understand.

McLuhan's point about the unaccounted costs of new technologies applies in this case, where these politicians think they do not have to do the work to find out what people really think, because they trust the technology: in this case, to their detriment. To the point here is McLuhan's emphasis on the social message of the media; specifically, the social and cognitive effects of analogue and digital signs. In this case, this technology allowed these politicians to think they were in direct touch with the elusive 'mind of the Australian community,' which they could package and control as a weapon against their colleagues in their coup. In practice, the illusion that they were in touch with the community allowed them to replace a real but difficult knowledge of what people were wanting with a fantasy that distanced them.

CEDA has a complex role in this analysis. CDA shows how and why they thought they could pull off the trick. EDA shows what was fundamentally wrong with the trick. The two approaches combined show how CEDA affords a deeper understanding of the role of all these technologies, new and old, in contemporary political processes.

Using the Technology

I do not want to imply that these technologies are always ineffectual, but the contrary. In this section I argue that digital resources framed by a critical CEDA perspective can throw new light on complex situations. Two things are needed. One is a careful EDA approach that is clear about the strengths and limitations of the digital technology. The second is a strengthening of the chains of analogue and digital signs in processes of action and research.

As a first step towards investigating this situation, I decided to generate my own word-cloud, to explore different uses and interpretations of this technology. Digital technologies offer some valuable and accessible resources. They can collect and store large amounts of data in digital formats, and allow them to be manipulated by word-clouds and other, more powerful technologies. In this chapter I want to emphasize some of these potentialities.

The faction bosses used text from focus groups: oral performances recorded electronically and then downloaded into their system. I did not have access to this material, but in any case, from a CEDA perspective, I doubt whether this form of oral discourse deserves to be so privileged. Rogers (2010, p.441) has argued that data from the

internet is now the fastest and most reliable way of getting news 'from the ground' in contemporary media-rich societies. Much of the politicians' effort in collecting this kind of oral discourse data may have been wasted.

Instead of ALP focus groups, I used web resources, and the various everyday search engines that now make searches manageable. I used a readily accessible national news archive, ProQuest ANZ Newsstand, a compilation of news media for Australian and New Zealand, and searched for 'climate change' and 'polls,' refined by 'Rudd,' between April 27, 2010 and July 16, 2010, a 3-month period. I then fed this material into Wordle, and generated the image which appears as Figure 1. I did the same for Gillard, the coup victor, but that image is not included here.

In this picture, cloud structures provide no information. Only size matters. But it matters richly, as an analogue sign. 'Gillard' and 'Rudd' dominate their pages, a consequence of using them as terms to divide the corpus. 'Gillard' is less important in the Rudd map than 'Rudd' is in the Gillard map. From this we could infer, using only size as an indicator, that the meaning of Gillard is less separable from Rudd than the other way around. In the Rudd map, 'climate' and 'change' loom slightly larger than in the Gillard map, but it is not a game-changer. 'Per cent,' the sign of a discourse of calculation, is massive, even more so in the Gillard map than the Rudd map, but again the difference is not a game-changer.

Figure 1. Word-cloud for search on 'climate change' and 'polls,' refined by 'Rudd.' Data sourced from ProQuest ANZ Newsstand, 27 April 2010 to 16 July 2010.

If these maps based on news media data had been fed into the ALP political process, the message would have been very different to the lessons drawn from the word-clouds of focus group results. The news media word-clouds say the two politicians are barely distinguishable; that Gillard was more interrelated to Rudd than vice versa; and that climate change is a big issue, for either leader, for the party, and the government. This data suggests policy advocacy, not leadership change.

A careful EDA analysis does not come up with the spectacular results the coup leaders wanted, but it does come up with some solid indicators, presented in analogue forms that make them more accessible without being misleading. EDA analysis within a CEDA framework has a potential contribution to political analysis and action.

Creative Use of Digital Software

As I have pointed out, Wordle is not a fair candidate to show how politicians could use simple, readily available data mining software to address political problems. I now show the outcomes of our use of Leximancer, a more powerful analytic program (Smith & Humphreys, 2006). Leximancer algorithms use a word frequency count to build what the programmers call 'concepts,' formed from words that travel together. In the same way, 'concepts' build up to 'themes.' This software is easy to use, and large amounts of material can be input from the net, with only a small amount of preparation. That is what I did with the materials I had collected, which would have been well within the scope of a political party, manageable even for a concerned citizen.

Leximancer adds some visualization tools to this mix. Visualization makes the outputs user-friendly. It also produces analogue signs that can be incorporated into a CEDA analysis to produce a richer set of potential meanings. In the program, 'themes' are represented as circles of greater or less size, corresponding to the frequencies of the component concepts. A simple analogue tool

can change the size of theme-circles, and hence their number. These present as images of the scale and relationship between major meanings. The program also allows 'pathways' to be shown which link component concepts, representing the closeness of the respective terms to each other in the corpus. Figure 2 shows one Leximancer image.

In analysing this image I will show how it can be safely treated as an analogue sign within a CEDA framework. This may seem like the same fault I criticized the ALP faction bosses for. The crucial difference is that this reading is heuristic, a discovery process, looking for patterns. It is not treated as a proof. It uses the suggestive power of analogue signs without being used by them, interpreting them as serial multi-modal chains, not as proofs of what a public thinks.

To show how these signs can be interpreted, I used a pathway tool to highlight the route from 'climate change' to 'Mr. Rudd' in Figure 2. Leximancer shows a circuitous route for Rudd. The direct link goes to 'government.' The diagram is a picture that suggests that in this corpus Rudd is not directly connected with the issue of climate change, in spite of its status as a problem for the government.

This may seem counter-intuitive. However, that is one of the most useful properties of this software as a heuristic (discovery) device. Leximancer's digital algorithms work blindly with exact words, and sometimes come up with what seem like absurd pictures. In this case, 'Rudd' is the same person as 'Mr. Rudd' and 'Prime Minister,' but he is dispersed across the semantic map, into many themes. Instead of asserting common sense, that Rudd is the same person under all these names, we ask what the different terms may mean. Symptomatically, Rudd as 'Prime Minister' is not in the *climate change* theme, not even in the *Rudd* theme. The 'Prime Minister' is defined purely by his place in the leadership struggle and his standing in the polls. Only as 'Mr. Rudd' does he appear in the *climate change* theme, diagnosing a potentially dangerous set of cleavage lines in his

Figure 2. Leximancer concept map with climate change–Mr. Rudd pathway. Data sourced from ProQuest ANZ Newsstand, 27 April 2010 to 16 July 2010.

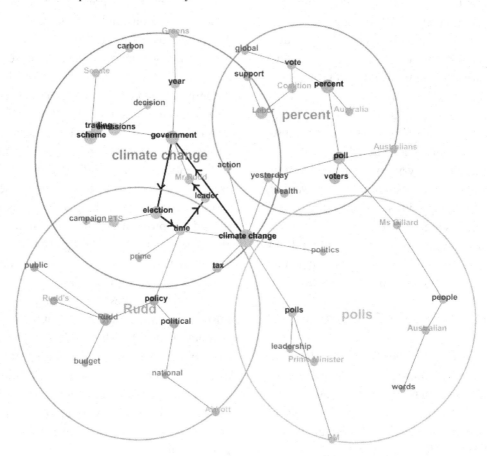

image. Such semantic disunity is death, and so it proved for Rudd's political fate.

As in the Wordle word-clouds I looked at, the *percent* theme is prominent. It overlaps with *polls*, and more so with *climate change*. This result illustrates some important points about different uses of this technology. The prominence of *percent* may seem like noise, an irrelevant product of the technology that should be ignored. In fact Leximancer has a 'kill' function, which eliminates any result users deem irrelevant. However, this is also an avenue where creative analogue interpretation can see important meanings, ones produced by the digital technology but which make no sense in those terms.

In this case it captures two different strands of meaning, the first about linearly measured

political popularity, the second a policy issue relating to the percent reduction of carbon emissions. The prominence of *percent* in a map like this one, configured to only four theme circles, suggests the dominance of a linear, computational way of thinking about both climate change and Rudd's fate.

This is an analogue reading of an analogue sign produced by digital processes, working with digital redactions of materials ultimately derived from analogue forms. At every point of this multimodal chain there are human agents in social relationships who play a role in what is transmitted and to what effect. Yet in this framework, digital analysis of digital technology – that is, EDA - remains vital. CDA and EDA need to be managed as two complementary moments within a single overall analytic strategy and approach, as CEDA, so that humanity can work with computers and not against them, to address problems in society and culture in the electronic age.

RECOMMENDATIONS

The main aim of this chapter is to show how CDA and EDA can and should be complementary forms of analysis, their innovations arising as much from new integrated uses of old technologies as from unexpected uses for new technologies. Within this framework it has also suggested how complementary the two activities within EDA – analysis of digitally produced forms of discourse and digitally enhanced forms of analysis – are when directed to problems of contemporary society. The simple basic recommendation of the chapter, then, is that researchers and practitioners in the two communities, CDA social researchers with a main base in analogue disciplines and EDA researchers with a base in digital disciplines, should learn from each other in a single CEDA learning community. I break this recommendation down into component parts, to recognize and overcome the barriers that currently exist between the two.

1. Researchers from the two communities need to recognize the unprecedented scale and scope of the electronic revolution under way, as it affects both the forms of discourse and society and the methods of analysing these forms. This is the challenge that makes it so necessary for CEDA to exist.
2. Technological innovations have causes and effects well beyond the conscious intentions of those who develop or use them. Developers and users need to cultivate a greater awareness of these social dimensions, and take some responsibility for them. These innovations are changing everyone's world, so everyone must develop some level of critical consciousness. That critical consciousness

cannot be achieved even within an expanded CEDA framework. Some kind of Total Discourse Analysis (TDA), not discussed in this chapter, is a desirable broader framework for CEDA.
3. Those committed to social and cultural action and change cannot take media for granted, trusting in mono-media action or analysis. CEDA is not an optional extra now, but the only way to understand the main games in contemporary society and culture.
4. The pervasive quality of contemporary media is a dynamic form of multi-modality, in old and new media. Technological innovations are continually throwing up new forms of multi-modality, so multi-modal analysis has to be built into all forms of CEDA.
5. A key reason for the gulf between social science/humanities and technological/scientific disciplines has been the central role that has historically developed in each around the two fundamental codes, digital and analogue. Yet the continual interplay between digital and analogue codes in life, perception, language and thought is so fundamental that each discipline needs the concepts and analytic techniques to track both kinds of code, and their patterns of interaction. EDA and CDA need to converge around the incorporation of this duality of codes in their analytic models and practices.

FUTURE RESEARCH DIRECTIONS

Both EDA and CDA will develop more powerful and innovative methods of analysis if they pool their resources, as recommended in this chapter. For CEDA as an integrated field of research, the explosion of new media will provide a continual source of new objects for critical social science research, as the social implications and consequences of each is slowly revealed by detailed empirical research.

The larger framework for research on electronic media and their social and cultural consequences will come from globalization studies. Researchers in this rapidly growing field already have strong hypotheses about the consequences of new information technologies (e.g. Castells, 2000), but these hypotheses need to be tested out against emerging developments in electronic technologies and the discourses they produce. Conversely, this broader framework should provide suggestive hypotheses to guide close research on particular developments in new media, either individually or cumulatively.

CONCLUSION

This chapter has attempted to sketch out the big picture of the massive and unpredictable changes in culture and society associated with the electronic media revolution. It argues that, paradoxically, changes on this scale cannot be understood if continuities are ignored in the process of determining what changes are real and important. The concerns of traditional forms of critical inquiry for basic human values like justice and well-being are not rendered obsolete by new technologies, but the contrary. Human beings are social animals formed by millions of years of evolution, still vital components of the interface between reality and computers. Yet these concerns can guide CEDA to better understand and describe these technologies; what has already developed and what is still to come. Whether CDA officially expands to become CEDA, or EDA develops its critical dimension as CEDA or under some other name, this is only a matter of words. Each of these traditions needs the other, in order to be adequate to deal with the huge and exciting challenges confronting us all today.

ACKNOWLEDGMENT

The author would like to thank the Australian Research Council for funding the collection of data: Ingrid Matthews, for collecting and helping interpret the data: and Dr Michelle Kelly for crucial commentary at a critical stage of the chapter.

REFERENCES

Barthes, R. (1971). *Mythologies*. London, England: Jonathan Cape.

Brynjolfsson, E., & McAfee, A. (2012). *Race against the machine: How the digital revolution is accelerating innovation, driving productivity, and irreversibly transforming employment and the economy*. Lexington, MA: Digital Frontier Press.

Busby, R. (2009). *Marketing the populist politician: The demotic democrat*. London, England: Palgrave Macmillan. doi:10.1057/9780230244283.

Castells, M. (2000). *The rise of the network society*. London, England: Blackwell.

Fairclough, N. (1989). *Language and power*. London, England: Longmans.

Feinberg, J. (2009). *Wordle*. Retrieved September 23, 2010, from http://www.wordle.net

Foucault, M. (1972). Orders of discourse. *Social Sciences Information. Information Sur les Sciences Sociales, 10*(2), 7–30. doi:10.1177/053901847101000201.

Fowler, R., Hodge, B., Kress, G., & Trew, T. (1979). *Language and control*. London, England: Routledge.

Hartcher, P. (2010, June 26). Dark clouds that spelt doom for a prime minister. *The Sydney Morning Herald*. Retrieved from http://www.smh.com.au

Hodge, B., & Kress, G. (1974). Transformations, models and processes: Towards a usable linguistics. *Journal of Literary Semantics, 4*(1), 4–18.

Hodge, B., & Kress, G. (1988). *Social semiotics*. Oxford, England: Polity Press.

Hodge, B., & Matthews, I. (2011). New media for old bottles: Linear thinking and the 2012 Australian election. *Communication, Politics and Culture, 44*(2), 95–111.

Kennedy, R. C. (2008). *Fat, fatter, fattest: Microsoft's kings of bloat*. Retrieved August 23, 2012, from http://www.infoworld.com/t/applications/fat-fatter-fattest-microsofts-kings-bloat-278

Kress, G., & Hodge, B. (1979). *Language as ideology*. London, England: Routledge.

Kress, G., & Van Leeuwen, T. (1996). *Reading images: The grammar of visual design*. London, England: Routledge.

Kress, G., & Van Leeuwen, T. (Eds.). (2001). *Multimodal discourse: The modes and media of contemporary communication*. London, England: Bloomsbury Academic.

Macdonell, D. (1986). *Theories of discourse: An introduction*. Oxford, England: Blackwell.

Many Eyes. (*n.d.*). Word cloud generator guide. Retrieved December 22, 2012, from http://www-958.ibm.com/software/data/cognos/manyeyes/page/Word_Cloud_Generator.html

Marx, K., & Engels, F. (1975). Manifesto of the Communist party. In *Collected works* (*Vol. 6*, pp. 1845–1848). London: Lawrence and Wishart.

McLuhan, M. (1964). *Understanding media: The extensions of man*. London, England: Routledge.

O'Leary, Z. (2004). *The essential guide to doing research*. London, England: Sage.

Peirce, C. (1958). *Values in a universe of chance: Selected writings of Charles S. Peirce (1839-1914)*. Garden City, NY: Doubleday.

Rogers, R. (2010). Internet research: The question of method. *Journal of Information Technology & Politics, 7*(2–3), 241–260. doi:10.1080/19331681003753438.

Smith, A., & Humphreys, M. (2006). Evaluation of unsupervised mapping of natural language with Leximancer concept mapping. *Behavior Research Methods, 38*(2), 26–79. doi:10.3758/BF03192778 PMID:16956103.

Thompson, J. B. (1984). *Studies in the theory of ideology*. Cambridge, England: Polity Press.

Van Leeuwen, T. (2005). *Introducing social semiotics*. London, England: Oxford University Press.

Wetherell, M., Taylor, S., & Yates, S. (Eds.). (2001). *Discourse theory and practice: A reader*. London, England: Sage.

ADDITIONAL READING

Barthes, R. (1977). *Elements of semiology*. New York, NY: Hill and Wang.

Berger, J. (1972). *Ways of seeing*. Harmondsworth, England: Penguin.

Corner, J., & Pels, D. (Eds.). (2003). *Media and the restyling of politics: Consumerism, celebrity and cynicism*. London, England: Sage.

Fairclough, N. (1992). *Discourse and social change*. Cambridge, England: Polity Press.

Foucault, M. (1979). *Discipline and punish: The birth of the prison*. Harmondsworth, England: Penguin.

Foucault, M. (1981). The history of sexuality: Volume 1, an introduction. Harmondsworth, England: Penguin.

Gee, J. P. (2005). *Situated language and learning: A critique of traditional schooling*. New York, NY: Routledge.

Gee, J. P. (2011). *An introduction to discourse analysis: Theory and method* (3rd ed.). New York, NY: Routledge.

Harvey, D. (1990). *The condition of postmodernity: An enquiry into the origins of cultural change*. Oxford, England: Blackwell.

Jenkins, H. (2006). *Convergence culture: Where old and new media collide*. New York, NY: New York University Press.

Kress, G. (2003). *Literacy in the new media age*. London, England: Routledge. doi:10.4324/9780203164754.

Kress, G. (2010). *Multimodality: A social semiotic approach to contemporary communication*. London, England: Routledge.

Kress, G., & Van Leeuwen, T. (Eds.). (2001). *Multimodal discourse: The modes and media of contemporary communication*. London, England: Bloomsbury Academic.

Kress, G., & Van Leeuwen, T. (2006). *Reading images: The grammar of visual design* (2nd ed.). London, England: Routledge.

Lenhart, A., Purcell, K., Smith, A., & Zickuhr, K. (2010). *Social media and mobile internet use among teens and young adults*. Washington, DC: Pew Research Centre.

Lévy, P. (1997). *Collective intelligence: Mankind's emerging world in cyberspace*. Cambridge, MA: Perseus Books.

Louw, P. E. (2010). *The media and political process* (2nd ed.). London, England: Sage.

Monaghan, R. (2008). *Social media: The business case and beyond*. London, England: Ark Group.

Mumford, L. (1934). *Technics and civilisation*. New York, NY: Harcourt Brace.

Negroponte, N. (1995). *Being digital*. New York, NY: Knopf.

O'Halloran, K. (2005). *Mathematical discourse: Language, symbolism and visual images*. London, England: Continuum.

Thorburn, D., & Jenkins, H. (2003). *Rethinking media change: The aesthetics of transition*. Cambridge, MA: MIT Press.

Toffler, A. (1970). *Future shock*. London, England: Bodley Head.

Van Leeuwen, T. (2005). *Introducing social semiotics*. London, England: Routledge.

Van Leeuwen, T. (2008). *Discourse and practice: New tools for critical discourse analysis*. Oxford, England: Oxford University Press.

KEY TERMS AND DEFINITIONS

Analogue Codes and Technologies: Forms of code whose units are not discrete and consist of patterns, which remain crucial in the new electronic environment.

Critical Discourse Analysis (CDA): Any form of analysis which is critical to some degree, as well as the specific tradition known as CDA.

Digital Codes and Technologies: Forms of code, with units that are discrete and binary, which pre-exist electronic technologies, but which have gained new forms and been radically shaped by their role in electronic technologies.

Electronic Discourse Analysis (EDA): Electronically enhanced analysis of any form of discourse, and/or the analysis of discourses arising in and out of the operations of electronic media.

Media Revolution: A change in the configuration of structures of mode and media so fundamental that it produces basic, far-reaching systemic changes across a society and culture.

Multi-Modality: The union of more than one semiotic mode in the production of meaning, whether in parallel, as in multi-media; serial, as in the processes of flow constituting media messages; or embedded, where a single form of text operates with more than one mode constituting it. Multi-modality can include different channels (visual, verbal etc.) or different fundamental modes (e.g. analogue, digital).

Semiotics: The study of the construction, circulation and effects of all kinds of signs in all channels: the essential base for analyzing radically new and rapidly changing media landscapes.

Chapter 10
Writing to Meet Your Match:
Rhetoric and Self-Presentation for Four Online Daters

Christyne Berzsenyi
Pennsylvania State University (Wilkes-Barre), USA

ABSTRACT

After ten years, Internet dating has become mainstreamed with members producing and consuming a great deal of written text before meeting face-to-face. Through a twenty-one-prompt questionnaire and follow up interviews, four case study participants describe their efforts at self-reflection, self-representation, and interaction with other members. The following chapter analyzes email questionnaire responses and interview excerpts that discuss each participant's perceptions of the rhetorical process of writing profiles, interpreting others' profiles, and exchanging emails to facilitate courtship. In addition, this chapter analyzes the discourse of participants' self-presentations in comparison with their reported self-perceptions and impression management strategies. Findings suggest that more effective members composed their e-texts after a methodical process of understanding the communication genre, the expectations and behaviors of their target audiences, and their own relationship objectives. Further, participants with greater experience with cyber dating have more positive experiences, which led to positive attitudes and greater satisfaction with e-dating.

INTRODUCTION

More than ten years have passed since AOL instant messengers used chat rooms to meet others from remote locations and Internet dating has been added to singles' repertoire of ways to meet new people and make romantic connections. As evidenced by television commercials, Internet dating has become mainstream, with 15 million profiles on Match.com, 5 million users on eHarmony.com, 3 million on Perfectmatch.com, and with 225,000 members on Plenty-of-Fish.com. In addition, there are services that target narrower markets such as USMilitarysingles.com, Christiansingles.com, PlanetOut.com for gay members, Furries.meetup.com for fantasy fans who enjoy

DOI: 10.4018/978-1-4666-4426-7.ch010

role-playing as animals, and JDate.com for Jewish users, to name a few (ConsumerSearch, 2012). Further, CraigsList.com, Twitter.com, Facebook. com, and even LinkedIn's 2012 "Hitch.me" are just a few examples of electronic social networks not designed specifically for dating but have been used by users for meeting people for friendship, family reunion, romance, partnership, and sex. Clearly, there has been a revival and re-imagining of the age old service of match making, mediated by Internet dating service providers (Lawson, 2012, pp. 189-90).

Unlike other forms of match making, Internet dating involves producing and consuming a great deal of written text before meeting face-to-face. In fact, techno-rhetorician Michael Day notes a resurgence of written correspondence as an "electronic epistolary renaissance:"

And just in the last year, some of my students have begun to confide in me that they were finding partners online. Could this reliance on text as a vehicle for feeling be a resurgence of the art of the love letter, through which, in days of yore, suitors had to prove their intelligence and wits in writing? Might it also in some ways echo the letters of those caught by cultural tradition in arranged or mail-order marriages, making a stab in the dark at relaying the essence of self in text? (M. Day, personal communication. February 17, 2007)

Facilitating courtship, online dating services gather members, who are looking for an attractive picture and package while there are others who are not just interested in a good picture. The latter, initiates relationship-building, which depends in part on clear and vigorous writing via the Internet. While less communicative individuals may rely primarily on pictures, phone conversations, and face-to-face meetings early on, more serious members develop relationships through writing before moving on to more immediate forms of communication. In both cases, members are part of a rhetorical and social process as they navigate through the ever-fluid communications of information exchange, self-representation and impression management, compatibility assessment, and relationship building—however brief or lengthy these processes may be per individual.

This project has been an invaluable opportunity to get "behind the screens" with four independent and adventurous individuals as they pursue love, sex, and/or companionship with the help of dating services. The following represents case study research that combines a questionnaire, discourse analysis of various e-dating documents, and interviews about individuals' perceptions of their rhetorical processes while Internet dating--how they adapt their written identity constructions and interactive messages to their sense of audience and relationship goals.

BACKGROUND: PROJECTING IDENTITY, IMPRESSION MANAGEMENT, AND MEETING OTHERS ONLINE

Internet dating relationships are made possible by the personal profile, are initiated by the first email, and are sustained by the subsequent emails and instant messages between corresponding profile authors. Importantly, relationships evolve toward face-to-face meeting with each act of reading and writing, or they end from incompatibility, or lack of availability. In addition to digital photos, verbal textual features portray a persona through general content and stylistics that signify emotions and attitudes. Effective interlocutors develop strategies for projecting and interpreting expression, emotional content, and subtle nuances of meaning in order to interpret personality and compatibility for responsive communicative action or decision not to respond. According to Herring and Zelen-kauskaite (2009), computer-mediated communication (CMC) language, including nonstandard typography and orthography, is a "consciously employed register shaped by properties of the technological medium and by situational factors such as topic, purpose, and participant characteristics" (p.6). Furthermore, individuals using the "symbolic currency" of language appropriate to the communication venue accrue social capital (e.g., social acceptability) (Herring & Zelenkauskaite, 2009, p.6).

In addition to these socializations to discursive membership, successful Internet daters become sensitive to issues of appropriate humor, style, and response times, which convey the author's personality and attentiveness (Orr, 2004, pp. 37-38). Such decisions about "self-identification," as R. Schlenker (1998) explains, involves individuals engaging in a process of showing oneself to be a particular type of person with continuity over time and within context "through definition, description, evidence, inference, interpretation, analogy, or treatment" (p. 65). The purpose of self-identification ranges between "the attempt to gain or convey useful information about the self to the attempt to control the reactions of other people" (p. 65). Put another way, individuals' self-presentations of "who I am" are both an expression of one's concept of self and a projection of a rhetorical process of impression management, which "consists of behaviors by a person that has the purpose of controlling or manipulating the attributions and impressions formed of that person by others" (Tedeschi, 1981, p. 3). Importantly, Internet daters, just as individuals in most communicative situations, operate under a "working consensus" that the self or impression of the projected-self is reliable, meaning that the individual possesses the attributes performed in the profile and subsequent emails (Goffman, 1959, p. 17).

As daters "get to know" one another to a subjectively satisfactory extent and mutually perceive attraction, compatibility and/or developing intimacy, they move closer to meeting face-to-face, which can happen in a matter of hours, days, weeks, months, or years. This timeframe depends on the individual's availability, sense of security, cyber dating experience, and relationship goals for real spaces. In fact, for some e-daters, conventionally gendered romance develops through the exchange of email messages or love letters. Over time, e-daters are "e-swept up" in the mutual disclosure of life stories, identity factors, and desired qualities in a partner and relationship, replete of the physical realities of their daily lives, often resulting in disappointment during their real space "interviews" or "auditions" (Vitzthum, 2007). While Goffman (1959) argues for the importance of individuals' first impressions in everyday life, he emphasizes consistency of identity projections for developing relationships:

The initial projection commits him to what he is proposing to be and requires him to drop all pretenses of being other things. As the interaction among the participants progresses, additions and modifications in this initial informational state will of course occur, but it is essential that these later developments be related without contradiction to, and even build up from, the initial positions taken by the participants. (pp. 10-11)

Discrepancies between online selves and real space selves typically culminate in phrases such as "I liked him/her better online" or "I preferred being on the phone than in person." Such an evaluative conclusion would most likely result in the termination of the relationship building process.

While online, authors can more strategically control the presentation of their identities than in real space meetings. Authors' identity construction need not be based on overt plans for unethical, manipulative self-presentation; self-identification can emerge from truths and facts mixed with self-deception, insecurity, strong desire to become other than they are, optimistic and creative re-imagining, or lack of introspection and self-awareness. Professional journalist and independent e-dating scholar V. Vitzthum (2007) explains a function of writing profiles and e-correspondences: "Writing is where we make sense of things, build arguments and theories, confess, declare, confront—where we take risks. By starting on the electronic page, online dating plunges us into intimacy while we try on new ways of being" (p. 21). The romantic e-daters, especially, can write themselves as the hero/heroine of a love story, "rebirthing themselves" online as "avatars" with presentations of their idealized or "better" selves (Vitzthum, p. 46). Moreover, competitive consumption in the dating marketplace involves participants in cutting through the sales clutter: "branding their identities" with statements of interest, favorite things, and personal narratives; "pitching themselves" as a desirable and unique product for consideration by others, and scanning the catalogue of profiles to discriminately shop for their mates (Heino et al., 2010; Vitzthum, 2007). Collaboratively, they construct their relationship. Once internet daters confront each other's full selves in offline meetings, the impressions of online identity and relationship compare and contrast with their real life identities and expectations of relationships. When successful, e-daters further develop their relationship in real spaces. When less successful, one or both e-daters "fell in love with written constructs," that were just shy of the whole picture of "who I am" and "what I want," resulting in disappointment, a sense of betrayal, a perceived waste of time, and/or simply another first date that will not lead to a second (Vitzthum, 2007, p. 11). In other words, the process and relationship would end there.

Though writing a profile is an opportunity for self-introspection, assessment, discovery, and expression, honesty is a slippery concept (Berzsenyi, 1999; Porter, 1998; Gurak, 1997; Rubin, 1996; Turkle, 1995; Howard, 1997). Within the context of internet dating, honesty is a sincere attempt to represent personal information, experiences, priorities, feelings, intentions, and the actual circumstances of their offline or "real" lives and bodies. In fact, some Internet daters feel committed to what scholars are calling hyperhonesty: "the proclivity to reveal as much as possible in writing about the self, including weaknesses as well as strengths" (Baker, 2005, pp. 21-22). The rationale for total honesty is avoidance of wasting time with misleading self-presentations that lead to disappointment when face-to-face, a self-defeating action if real life relationships are the goal. However, disclosing unflattering information immediately can deter others from meeting face-to-face (Gibbs, Ellison, & Heino, 2006). Applied to the context of online dating, sincere or honesty-motivated participants deploy self-identification to serve individual purposes of projected self and corresponding relationship initiation.

On the contrary, deceptive daters provide false information as they pretend to be truthful and intimate in order to disingenuously elicit trust in others (Gwinnell, 1998, p. 94). With catchy headlines and usernames, profiles operate as personal advertisements with deceivers using "white lies" or "harmless lies" about current relationship and parenthood status, weight, age, income, location, personal history of accomplishments and missed opportunities, flexibility for relocation or lifestyle changes, openness to and acceptance of others' differences, and the like. Through dishonest manipulation, some members try to control how others will view them—positive or negative valence—and achieve relationship goals (Gibbs, Ellison, & Heino, 2006, p. 151) or manage their readers' impressions of them so that their self-presentations are perceived in positive ways (Leary, 1995).

However, there is a danger in creating even the most appealing profile: "People who are discovered to be unlike what they claim to be are regarded as incompetent (e.g., uninsightful, ignorant), weak (e.g., insecure), egotistical (e.g., braggarts), or deceptive (e.g., liars), depending on the type and extent of the perceived inaccuracy" (Schlenker, 1998, p. 83). Even some individuals who are committed to honesty can and do misrepresent themselves unintentionally because of an inaccurate self-concept, omissions about demographics or current photographs, or projections of idealized selves that are deeply ingrained and confused with current selves (Gibbs et al., 2006). According to their 2006 survey, 94% of respondents disagreed that they intentionally misrepresented themselves in their profiles or online communications (pp. 169-70). Clearly, there are discrepancies between how individuals view themselves and present themselves, compared with how others' view them, relegating honest self-projection a complicated discursive act. Further, the process of self-presentation is dependent on a high degree of self-awareness, clear sense of online dating relationship goals, adeptness with analyzing dating profiles and the online dating audience, and facility with rhetorical tactics for creating a desirable impression with appropriate discursive and nonverbal interactions with the target audiences: "attractiveness, similarity [in values], likability, competence [and potency], effort [and exertion], and virtue" (Leary, 1995, p. 105). However, online dating takes on substantial additional challenges to self-presentation addressed by Leary (1995): The "self-promoter's paradox," "the ingratiator's dilemma," and "the multiple audience problem" (pp. 101, 107, 109). More specifically, daters need to self-promote in order to write a descriptive profile about their values and interests, provide exemplification in narratives that show their personalities, and include concise personal histories for a mass audience of individuals in a dating service who are likely to be skeptical of the truth in self-promoting identities. Just like in resumes, positive impressions are achieved when positive attributes are highlighted. However, negative impressions are also created and managed from numerous verbal and nonverbal projections of identity, whether offline or online. When too much self-aggrandizing occurs, writers risk audience's disaffection from their self-presentations of unappealing and narcissistic bravado, self-promoting complacency, and personal inauthenticity (Leary, 1995).

Notably, the challenges are many and have been integrated into this multi-approach study of electronic discourse among those writing to meet their match. The following breaks down specific examples of the topics of this chapter's features for analysis:

- Types of Interlocutor Relationships,
- Subjective discourses,
- Varying degrees of rhetorical savvy within this emotionally-risky/adventurous,
- Public communicative context,
- Hidden agendas,
- Strategic omissions, understatements, and amplifications,
- Blatant but human shortcomings in the face of media pressures,
- Mistrusting but wishful romanticizing,
- Acts of self-sabotage,
- The desire to love and to be loved, social, physical, communicative, expressive, and connected with others.

Given the challenges of negotiating so many communicative and contextual factors, it is a bit of a wonder that people meet online or offline. By performing the analytical processing and production of discourse as rhetorical action, individuals maneuver within cyber communities of dating hopefuls, skeptics, and players in the search for their personal matches.

METHOD: DISCOURSE ANALYSIS AND ETHNOGRAPHY

Researchers who study human behavior must take into account potential biases in the subjects' self-reporting, as the research participants may desire to make a positive impression on the researcher—desire to appear likeable, competent, emotionally stable, intelligent, cooperative, helpful, behaving as they "should" in terms of the project aims, etc. (Gibbs, Ellison, & Heino,

2006, p. 161). Heeding this cautionary note, the four subjects were reassured that their responses are fully anonymous, with their names and other obvious identifiers removed or changed. Second, the projects' objectives were partially shrouded, with observational and behavioral description goals expressed while evaluative functions in the analytical reporting and findings omitted. Doing so enabled some prevention of adaptive responding in which respondents skew their remarks to the project objectives so as to make the impression of an effective dater or ineffective dater, an effort that would neither be useful nor conclusive. Third, the research subjects read instructions and completed the questionnaire electronically, without a researcher being physically present, to ease their concerns about being negatively judged. As Leary (1995) concludes, "Despite all of these precautions, researchers often worry that their results are contaminated by subjects' self-presentations" (p. 111), particularly the performative and rhetorical purposes of impression management.

Imbued with these concerns, this project aims to understand how individuals perceive their experiences, self-identifiers, and intentions of impression management, which makes prompting participants to self-report and self-assess their writing and reading process and perspectives a logical method of research. However, relying purely on participants' testimonies would limit assessment of the rhetorical process and its assessment of e-dating competence to their subjective, emotionally involved positions. Discourse analysis of participants' e-dating profiles enabled a public perspective of their rhetorical activities within a context-specific relationship-building process in cyber spaces via the computer. With all of these layers and facets of writing—rhetoric, form, convention, culture, context, technology, physical bodies, emotions, and human behavior—the endeavor to study e-dating is complicated and full of opportunities to disserve participants by abstracting their process out of its reality (Warnock, 1984, p. 21). Nevertheless, the quest to

realize more about interlocutors in this dynamic communication process compels this project forward with caution.

In 2002, in the early stages of full-service online dating companies, when this project was in its inception, participants were commonly considered with suspicion and fear, embarrassingly indicative of either loneliness and desperation or carelessly daring behavior with cyber predators in hiding. Assumptions of the dignity and self-respect of waiting for love to arrive at one's life space without effort still prevailed, combined with a superstitious dependence of fate to make it happen when "it's meant to be." Clearly, looking for love in an active way, such as online dating, threatened contextual social conventions held and practiced by so many. Therefore, relatively few individuals participated in the beginning, and those that did often maintained secrecy about doing so, which posed an obstacle to this study. Stated interests in online dating with friends, family, colleagues, community co-activists, etc. were met with mixed reactions of worry, surprise, curiosity, dismissal, and the occasional admission of personal experience with it. The fascinating opportunities to hear others' stories and inquire about their sense of satisfaction with the services progressed to requests to view their profiles. After inquiries and personal conversations with individuals in my academic and personal acquaintanceships, ten were serious candidates for this study because of their honesty and experience. Among them, a few seemed reluctant to share that part of themselves beyond the narratives they provided, expressing unavailability for further discussion. A few others could not articulate their desires and intentions, seeming to lack enough self-awareness, purposeful self-presentation and impression management, and a clear sense of what is successful or unsuccessful about their profile or approach to communication.

As the group got smaller, a qualitative study of the four participants combined with the electronic discourse analysis method of their e-dating materials made most sense. The selected four individuals were both willing to share their online self-presentations and impression management texts with me and had the self-awareness and communicative literacy to describe and evaluate their rhetorical, discursive experiences in response to questions being developed in the course of the project. Qualitative, context-based ethnographic description provides rich, specific, personal, and detailed data to examine. Analyzing the process, background histories, and relationship intentions of individual e-daters offers specific, context-informed rhetorical and cultural information, not generalized statistical data of trends in behavior. Electronic discourse analysis of identity profiles, questionnaire responses, and subsequent, further-focused e-interviews provide a rich body of subjective material from which to better understand how individuals report pursuing online dating.

The participants include four e-daters of varying degrees of self-awareness, relationship goals, and rhetorical sophistication in self-presentation and impression management, though each met the challenge of expressing personal feelings and experiences: emotional vulnerability, romantic dreams, dating hopes turned disappointments, mistakes made, and lessons learned. Though not meant to be taken as representative of a particular demographic segment, participants had variations in socio-economic status and income, sex, gender, age, nationality, race, regional residence, computer literacy, and educational background. While a diverse group, all four participants have at least a college bachelor's degree, enabling their basic to advanced competent cyber literacy, rhetorical sophistication, and ability to articulate choices, which has facilitated my learning from their stories of their successes, best e-dating context-based discursive practices, as well as their sense of satisfaction and dissatisfaction with the process and their own involvement.

To generate targeted information, a 21-prompt questionnaire was devised and revised and disseminated electronically for electronic receipt of participants' qualitative data. The first questions address personal status and demographics, and the second group of questions target perceptions of computer literacy and technological experience. The remainder of the questions invites participants to self-report and self-assess their Internet dating experiences in terms of their relationship goals, rhetorical objectives to attain these goals, learning curve with the services and their subgenres of self-presentation for impression management, and self-discoveries. While participants took a few weeks to complete and send back the questionnaire with their responses, their online profiles were analyzed for verbal discourse and the nonverbal messages and graphical elements to derive a sense of their e-dating identities, first impressions, and invitational cues for interaction with others. Next, for three to five hours, each participant was interviewed via email to follow up on revealing or vague questionnaire responses to identify ways that individuals balance self-identification and disclosure with writing strategies for producing profiles and correspondences designed for targeted members. Impressions of their online identities were compared with their intentions at self-presentation and impression management. Further, exchanges about best practices and missed opportunities elicited narratives of dating successes and disappointments. Finally, participants assessed their perceptions of satisfaction or dissatisfaction with the process. Six years later, each participant was contacted for follow up on their dating experiences, relationships, discoveries, and self-assessments, incorporating these ongoing reflections and stories into this current chapter's discussion of their best and worst practices and lasting attitudes.

It has been important to keep in mind that perceptions of success and failure are subjective. For example, Luke, who dates casually, considers one date per week to be a "slow week," while Juliet, who is cautious and selective, would define that as a successful week. With another example, Juan directly expresses desires for "hooking up" while Kate finds such offers to be offensive and superficial. Finally, Luke generally initiates meeting face-to-face by the third email exchange, while Juliet delays offline meetings until she feels comfortable with the person, which could take weeks. Their distinct goals, styles of interaction, generational dispositions, gender roles, cultural values and perspectives, and comfort zones with strangers reflect the rich diversity that exists across Internet dating services. In order to learn from this spectrum of daters, conscious self-reminders helped to focus on analysis and refrain from judging participant's motivations, values, attitudes, and practices, regardless of how they differed from my own, to represent their stories fairly. The next section presents some of their stories, self-reflections, and an analyses of key features in their self-presentational discourse: interlocutor relationship cues (sentence mode, use of humor, conversation dynamics), relationship goals, rhetorical strategies (degree and type of self-disclosure, attentiveness, projected interest in mutual self-information exchange and relationship building, etc.), and level of active involvement in both receiving and sending of correspondences.

DISCUSSION: RESPONSES TO QUESTIONNAIRE AND FOLLOW-UP INTERVIEWS

Kate: Over the years, my profile has changed in response to how others have communicated with me or interpreted my ads. In an earlier version of my profile, I stated that I was a 'liberal person' and that I was looking for the same. Apparently, to some, liberal means sexually liberated or indiscriminate or "anything goes." One time, a man who stated, "no homophobes" on his profile, which I thought was great, wrote to me and said, "I am bisexual but prefer relationships with women." In response, I wrote, "Why do you prefer dating women? Is it because you like sex with men but prefer the social

legitimacy of a heterosexual relationship?" Well, he never wrote back to me after that. Maybe he didn't like being called on the truth or hear my direct questioning. In any case, I don't want to waste my time with playboys.

The first participant named "Kate" is a 30 year old recent divorcee with national and ethnic roots in the former Soviet Union but has earned her Ph. D in English in the United States. With extensive education in visual and information rhetorics, Kate has gone into a related occupation in e-library database design and operation at a private Liberal Arts college on the West Coast. Noticeably, Kate has very high computer literacy with regard to graphics design and editing and web page construction, which is why she began her memberships with Internet dating services: "I loved that I could do research, which is something I'm good at, to find the right kind of man to date--without alcohol or physical lust." Kate's response reflects her desire to use her education in rhetoric and composition to achieve her social goals, taking advantage of the reading and writing components for constructing her "me page" with photos of her with a dance group and passionate comments about her pastime in Latin ballroom dancing: "I love to dance! I want a dancing partner to tango and salsa with. You should know how to dance or be willing to learn." Her strong convictions also come through her profile when expressing her priorities on "educated, professional man, not a party boy," criteria with which she assesses men's suitability for "marriage."

Kate is a goal-oriented individual who seeks a committed relationship for marriage, in part for the emotional and financial partnership she seeks but also for the Green Card U.S. citizenship she pursues. Approaching Internet dating with "hyperhonesty" (Baker, 2005), or complete self-revelation, Kate tries to carefully, ethically, and specifically present her positive as well as negative traits in order to find highly compatible individuals. Refusing to waste her time and emotion online or offline with incompatible individuals, Kate constructs "dialectical interlocutor relationships" as she asks direct questions with straightforward communication on controversial topics to determine conflicts and agreements (Berzsenyi, 1999). Also, she uses witty humor, challenging repartee, and provocative personal anecdotes (testing for incompatible conservatively-oriented and discriminatory viewpoints) as part of a screening process before proceeding to meet offline. She believes that "honesty is the best way to project my real self and hopefully attract someone who thinks I'm appealing. In other words, I want my profile to be a 'what you see is what you get' version of myself." She is convinced that a full disclosure approach will scare away unsuitable men while more compatible men will appreciate it and want to meet her and find out more.

While she enjoys the process, Kate describes a methodical and serious approach:

I have mixed feelings. I like it, and I think it is as successful as other forms of meeting people and dating. However, I find it to be time-consuming as it involves a lot of reading and writing of profiles and emails and instant messages to narrow choices and choose good possibilities to meet in person.

Per week, Kate estimates receiving fifteen email inquiries, replying to some of them, and sending five initial email inquiries of interest in members. When receiving email inquiries, Kate reads the email message and the member's profile to determine whether a respondent is compatible and if she wants to respond or not. Then, if she decides to respond, she spends about an hour planning and revising her message, carefully considering what to include and exclude in her "information-giving" and "information-seeking" reply. She acknowledges that her approach and process may be slower than many members': "I have some friends who have sort of stock paragraphs that they send as first contact emails or first response emails, but I tailor each email

to each member's profiles and email messages, which takes time to think through and play out carefully." With long-term relationship goals in mind, Kate carefully scrutinizes candidates' written communications and employs highly conscious and deliberate rhetorical actions.

In order to participate most effectively, Kate devotes time weekly to updating her posted profile so that her ad appears at the top of members' search lists and has the "recently updated" tag. This regular maintenance writing supports her efforts to find a compatible man:

Over the year and a half, I trimmed the profile to be more concise and less overwhelming to readers. I got some feedback from more experienced male members and friends that my profile was too wordy, like over explaining, formal, and all over the place in content and that it didn't show my personality enough. . . though I think that does show my sometimes scattered personality. So, I made revisions and edited the profile. Also, I tried to show more humor so that it sounds like my own sense of humor and less serious. I hoped to be appealing to the kind of guy I like.

Here, Kate suggests how her academic training and high level of literacy were both an advantage and a disadvantage to her success with the dating service. Through informal research and feedback from more experienced members, Kate was adapted to the conventions of this online forum and developed a stronger sense of how her target audience might view and respond to her online identity. Also, she reports having read over "countless" women's profiles to see what others were doing in order to model her own revisions on what she determined were the "best practices." For example, she added to her profile self-deprecating humor about her clumsiness and over-analytical nature to present her "down-to-earth disposition" and "willingness to acknowledge flaws," which she thought constructs a more likeable identity. With these composing behaviors, Kate admits that her profile is still longer than average, more descriptive, which she explains is her "strategy for testing to see if a man wants conversation or just somebody to shake her head and agree with whatever he says—definitely not me." For Kate, this "weeding out" function is necessary for finding a compatible person with whom she can construct the "dialectical relationship" among strong equals that would enable her to stay in a long term relationship with someone.

Other changes Kate made include the search results information that provides a brief introduction to the profiled individual with their screen name, headline (like an email subject line), and thumbnail photograph (if they have one posted). These quick first impression bits of information are crucial components of the self-representation and relationship initiation process (Schwartz, p. 39). Aware of this rhetorical issue, Kate describes the revision process of changing her headline:

Originally my headline was "scintillating" but then wondered if men thought that I was boasting about being scintillating when I was just using what I think is a fun, powerful word. I changed the headline to "Ready?" to show that I am an upbeat, open, and positive person with a sense of adventure and challenge, which is true about me.

Unlike some e-daters, Kate is not embarrassed about using an online dating service or afraid of meeting at safe, public places "with our own cars." While Kate wants to present her identity in a positive light, she is adamant about being as honest as possible with regard to her "excessively analytical" side, "difficulty with stress," "athletic but with a few extra pounds," and "activism." Doing so provides readers with representative information on which to make a decision about meeting her face-to-face. Projecting confidence and good self-esteem, she's careful to avoid understatements or exaggerations in her self-presentation because she wants men viewing her profile to feel familiar with whom she is and not to experience surprise

or disappointment should they meet in real space dates. To illustrate her point, she describes her disappointment when going on a first date:

I agreed to meet a 27 year old guy at a restaurant-bar for a drink. I arrived for our happy hour date, looked around the room, and didn't recognize him until he called out my name. He was not as well groomed, twenty pounds heavier and not as counter-culture stylishly dressed as his picture. He got so drunk, inhaled 8 drinks in a couple of hours, and was suspiciously no longer in computer programming, working as a baker's helper.

In her questionnaire response, Kate explains the reasons she didn't go out with him for a second date: "He's a liar, insecure, doesn't have his life together, and disappointing." Faced with the discrepancies between his compatible self-presentation online and his less compatible real life identity, Kate went on a first date with him but with no interest in any further intimacy or relationship. While Kate recognizes that such misinformation is a part of the Internet dating process, she is also convinced that it's just as much a part of offline dating. She narrates stories of lies she's been told face-to-face at bars such as "I'm not married or anything" when the man was engaged and a month away from getting married; "I work in construction and live with my brother," when he didn't have a job and slept on the couch where his brother, wife, and baby live and tolerate him; and "I don't do drugs," when he was a cocaine addict recently released from jail for possession. Kate remarks, "I wish lying were exclusive to online dating so that I could avoid it." She remains cautious, but active online as an interlocutor: both an interactive initiator and a responder of communication, which works within and outside of traditional gender roles that mostly relegate women to passive respondents rather than active originators of relationships.

Since beginning Internet dating a year and a half prior to our interview, Kate has changed her profile 13 times, posted various pictures to show her as she is in different aspects of her life ("dressed up, casual, sweats and a ponytail with my dog, in work clothes"), experimenting with approaches to first impressions but maintaining what she sees as her "real self." While she is now more successful at interacting with suitable matches online, she doesn't meet many face-to-face:

I ask for several pictures taken on different days so that you can see him in different moods/contexts/ time periods to get a sense of their sense of style, attitude, demeanor, and lifestyle, which help me make decisions about compatibility. I'm getting good at ruling them out before getting to the dates. However, I hardly ever go on dates now.

Jokingly, Kate expresses doubt about whether she is a highly successful "personality investigator" or a "self-defeating paranoid." While still deciding how to interpret her more recent strategies for screening members, Kate expresses general satisfaction and continues to experiment with this rhetorical process of mate finding.

Luke: I had swapped a few emails with this Corporate Comm. teacher at one of the local colleges, and I suggested that we meet for drinks on a late Saturday afternoon, leaving my options open for later that night. She picked this cool, small import beer bar, which showed good taste. We met up at 4 in the afternoon and had a couple of beers. It was going well, good conversation. So, we leave for a restaurant and get a bite to eat, nothing serious or formal, just casual. Again, good conversation, more attractive than her picture, which is unusual. This girl sells herself short, but, that's cool, too... At about 10:30, we make-out in the parking lot and go our separate ways. It's still early, so I go to this neighborhood bar where I live and hook up with this exotic dancer. The next day, I get this email that reads like a technical

report—my pros and cons. Amazing—with tables, bullets. I couldn't believe how much thought she had put into a barely-existent relationship. I was impressed that she called me on my shit, like my photograph, which was of my brother and my ex-girl friend, and a bunch of other stuff. Really smart, direct like a canon, hot ass. . . just wanted too much from me.

In this narrative, "Luke" shows his sharp sarcasm, appreciation of written communication, and desire for casual dating. A white male, 33-years of age during the questionnaire and interview, he's a technical writer and correspondent journalist from Northeastern Pennsylvania with eight years experience online, socializing in chat rooms and through early inceptions of dating services to the present --Match.Com, Yahoo Personals, and Nerve Personals. With casual sexual encounters and short-term relationships in mind, Luke admits to using strategic, selective self-presentational profile writing to attract particular types of women to ensure a positive impression and desired response. Since he is "not in it for the long haul," Luke is not concerned about being dishonest, deceptive, or manipulative to get what he wants, as evidenced by the photograph of his brother that he used in his ad. Further, his story demonstrates his rhetorically effective use of self-presentation to play a dominant and calculating role in e-dating, a cyberforum he treats like a game of textual exchange replete of emotional connections to his target audience, even when he likes them. Strategizing ways to increase his response rate with women, Luke admits, "It's a numbers game." Therefore, he writes to several women daily.

Luke describes having extensive experience and a high degree of confidence in using his communication abilities to assert power over others: "I have fun getting people off guard and uncomfortable and seeing how they respond without a script of what to do." In the "About my life and what I'm looking for" section of his profile, Luke almost taunts viewers: "Well too bad for all you girls who failed to respond. You missed out." This excerpt illustrates how Luke self-presents as an arrogant, cavalier individual who initiates interaction with women through teasing provocation, direct confrontation, and self-possessed enticement, establishing "hierarchical interlocutor relationships" (Berzsenyi, 1999). Luke is generally controlling the conversation, expressing criticisms, challenging their authority and comfort levels, and pushing social boundaries of appropriate behavior and interaction. He verbally spars to create a desired competitive communication dynamic (Berzsenyi, 1999, p. 233) and immediately ends contact with those who get "too emotionally dependent." As a communicative tool for verbal banter, sarcasm is evident throughout his profile, which is part of Luke's strategy for scaring off those who cannot keep up with him or don't "get him." A bit caustic at times in his snap statements or retorts, Luke is brazen in his insensitivity toward others and his primary focus on his own interests and needs to be "entertained by," "stimulated intellectually by," or surprised by members. Through directness, Luke lures as well as frightens off members in order to socialize with compatible partners of repartee. As described, he prefers to maintain an emotional distance when e-dating.

Of the four case studies, Luke violates the greatest number of netiquette guidelines such as inflammatory discourse, disregard, and harsh criticism to accomplish his dating goals, which are qualities of "agonistic interlocutor relationships" (Berzsenyi, 1999). Interestingly, he is the most active e-dater and expresses the most satisfaction with dating services. Often, Luke confidently reports having "three or four dates in one week with different women from different cities." Luke is interested in meeting "casual sex and activity partners, nothing serious, nothing long term." While he insists that his actions with dates are always consensual, he admits to deliberately deceiving women into dating him by establishing a broad relationship preference of "any" [activity partner,

short-term relationship, long-term relationship]: "because I want the whole list of them to come up to attract attention and increase my chances of a response." Without shame, Luke describes his discursively manipulative tactics with women to serve his needs. Other misrepresentations revolve around his residence, income, and education. Luke is interested in educated, professional women who seek educated, professional men. Having experience with less educated women, Luke comments that they typically were "vulgar" and "didn't have much to say or offer but sex;" he "got bored quickly." Instead, to solicit responses from professional women, especially in urban areas, Luke targets members from large cities within a few hours driving distance. He claims in his profile, which he changes frequently, to reside in the city where the women he targets identify as their residence. When asked whether women get angry with him for lying about his residence, he said, "Well, when they ask, and some don't ask for a while, but the smart ones do—I let them know that I'm there on weekends two times a month on business or visiting friends, and that seems to take care of things." So, once again, dishonesty pays off because he gets what he wants, one or two dates.

When asked about exaggerating his income to $75,000-99,000 a year (actually $35,000) and his education level as "graduate degree" (He's a few credits from a bachelor's degree.), Luke said, "Well, I'm trying to attract professional women, especially from these big cities, and you have to have these kinds of incomes and educations to be a professional living in these areas. Otherwise, they don't bother." Clearly, Luke's reasoning is rhetorically sound, and his self-presentation and impression management methods are highly successful. However, ethically, his discursive practices are strategically dishonest, manipulative, flippant, arrogant, competitive, and emotionally detached—qualities that construct hierarchical and agonistic interlocutor relationships along a continuum of conflict and cooperation among interlocutors. Maintaining these relationship types, Luke has a current profile picture with a challenging smirk and confident, knowing eyes with changing headlines such as "If you dare!" and "Whatever, Ladies" to tempt women drawn to boyish, cavalier, self-aware first-impressions.

As a result of his highly conscious rhetorical explorations, Luke has discovered he is more successful in some geographical regions than others, a lesson he's used to revise his profile. Luke denies having any regrets about falsely advertising his interests and stats. For Luke, initial misrepresentations support his goals of casual dating, providing him with the impetus to continue. Overall, Luke expresses great satisfaction with Internet dating services, constantly changing his strategies, playing with the process, and enjoying the challenges of meeting new people.

Juan: The biggest surprise I've ever had with Internet dating was with this guy named "Tony" who described himself like a really butch Italian type, which I like. When I was traveling for a training workshop in the city, I looked for a date there, found his ad, and arranged in an email to meet up with him in Chelsea at this biker bar after work. So, I was in my business clothes and feeling a little overdressed, but it was a last minute date. I got there a little early and ordered myself a drink to relax. Then, this woman came up to me and asked me if I was Juan. I said, "Yes." Then, with this soft voice and these big hands, she reached out and shook my hand saying, "Nice to meet you. I'm Tony or Antonia." He must have noticed my surprise because he quickly said, "You did read the whole ad didn't you? I said that I like to dress up." He does a little twirl, and I was speechless. It's not that I have a problem with cross dressing. I've been to many drag shows, even won a couple of them. But it's really not what turns me on. So, we had a drink together, talked about the area, and I headed back to my friend's house. Since

then, I am careful about reading the ads thoroughly to avoid misunderstanding before meeting anyone.

During the interview, "Juan" was a 24-year old native Central American gay man who identifies fully with his Latino heritage and citizenship, speaking English as a second language since he immigrated to the United States when he was 6 years old. Raised in New York City, Juan left his abusive home at the age of 15 and struggled to earn a living, working full-time as he completed his high school education with an honors diploma and a college scholarship. While critical of American capitalism, exploitation overseas, and civil rights, Juan values the benefits of his education at a private, liberal arts college in the Midwest, having studied performing arts and the humanities. After graduation, he's been working for a year and a half for a nonprofit organization. As his story suggests, Juan is intelligent, resilient, knows what he wants, learns from his experiences, and quickly adapts his behavior for success.

With a sense of adventure, he has a high degree of competence and comfort, moving quickly from new acquaintanceship online to face-to-face date offline. As Juan's job requires him to travel 50% of his time, traditional dating strategies such as visiting bars challenges his schedule. Therefore, his laptop becomes a vital tool for keeping in touch with friends as well as for meeting new ones from remote locations across the country. Juan's recent college education and daily use of computers for work has prepared him for truncated online dating, facilitated by high proficiency with profile composition, email correspondence, frequent web accessibility, and real-time chat exchange. In fact, Juan uses three different Internet dating services: Planet Out, Gay.com, and Bgay.com. When striving for casual sex, Juan is confident that, if he wants a date even as soon as that same day, he can answer an ad or respond to an email he's gotten and meet a man that night with the explicit shared goal of "hooking up." However, his relationship goals with Internet dating are varied from "just being able to find a sexually compatible and appealing person, to the potential of finding a partner or at least a good friend." When I asked him if he would prefer to be in a long term relationship, he said, "I am looking for fun, but open to whatever may develop. If it's the right guy, I'm all in."

Accordingly, he has different profiles to serve his various goals and needs. For the casual dating profile, Juan keeps it "short and simple" with the headline "Tango anyone?" with his profile focusing on sexual innuendoes such as "up for it" and sexual attraction, and erotic desires and fantasies of "multiple limber, contorted, and intertwined positions." He complements the vivid verbal depictions with photographs to show his young, lean body in tight, dance clothing. When questioned further about how he indicates the desire for casual sex on the profile, he explained, "It comes across in the language I use in my ad and messages: 'Straightforward fun, play,' you know, 'not serious, out to have a good time'-- natural play stuff." He continues by explaining how he identifies other potential casual sexual partners' ads: "Profiles that don't go on and on about themselves or wanting a relationship." With explicit verbal cues, Juan explains that gay men looking to "hook up" can find one another: "The service I use provides a forum for gay men to initiate casual sexual encounters; it's not unusual or embarrassing. People just say what they're looking for." For example, Juan says in his casual profile's "About Me" section, "easy going and all kinds of fun...." and is interested in "action/sex" and "intense talk and action" with "older men." In the casual sex profiles, Juan avoids giving many personal details or preferences so that the connection remains on the physical and not relationship.

For the serious relationship profile with a different dating site, he elaborates on his personal background and interests and explains the kind of partner and partnership he would like: "Personality, sense of humor, and intelligence are big pluses to me. Looks are more of a bonus---like icing on a cake. Beauty fades but dumb is forever. Looking for romance but will settle for friendship or just good ol' conversation. Enjoy chatting and making new friends." These personal and emotional elaborations enable readers to determine compatibility while the photos present physical appearance. Juan chooses modest photographs that focus more on his face than body to support his relationship goals, not just sexual objectives, and to present his attentiveness, warmth, and smile.

With an honest and intellectually daring communicative style, Juan constructs "dialectical interlocutor relationships," which maintain peer-level relationship dynamics with direct and challenging but respectful dialogue. His profile descriptions and emails are blunt but inviting to interaction rather than the silencing that can result from more dominant banter. Through his descriptive as opposed to confrontational or judgmental discourse, Juan shows and speaks his desire to engage in a real space relationship and interaction with other consenting adults (Berzsenyi, 1999). With his varied rhetorical approaches, Juan generally considers himself good at attracting someone who is interested in the same things as he is. However, he does receive messages from men who really don't match his posted interests: "I guess they think that it's worth a try, and there have been times when it was." Internet dating continues to engage Juan in the dynamic challenges of understanding himself better and meeting new people.

While many dating sites enable members to say "drug and disease free," homosexual services specifically address HIV status. After asking Juan about this in terms of how he felt about it and how it affected his participation in Internet dating, he responded:

Since HIV/AIDS is unfortunately definitely a part of dating among gay men, all three sites I use have a check box for indicating status and that helps to put it out on the table right away so that it's not an issue when you meet. It's already dealt with, and, if a guy responds to an ad for someone who is positive, then, he accepts that status and whatever risks he believes are there during sexual contact. Also, he knows that sex would have to be protected sex.

Juan further explains that members avoid having an emotionally uncomfortable conversation about HIV status, which is equally hard for the positive person, who has an ethical obligation to communicate his status. In turn, the HIV negative person should ask a date's status for his or her own protection. Unfortunately, Juan understands that not everyone who is HIV positive is aware of his health status or is honest about it in the ads. Given the varying degrees of accuracy, disclosure, and consideration projected in profiles, Juan insists on being careful.

Juan summarizes his success with Internet dating: "No long-term romantic relationships have come from it, but I have made quite a few good friends and have had episodes of fun sex." As Juan has connected with casual or short-term partners, he's clearly successful at meeting his relationship goals and states feeling very satisfied with the processes, services, and memberships at this stage of his life and his new, mobile career.

Juliet: I agreed to go out with this man who says he's 53, which is the age I claim on my ad, and his picture is reasonably handsome. I mean. Let's face it. Nobody looks that good at this age. But he looked nice enough . . . a credit card company manager or something like that. I arrive there a couple of minutes early and sat down at a table near the window so that I could see him coming. I'm waiting for another fifteen minutes, a bad sign, already late on the first date. Then, this man comes over to my table with a bouquet of flowers, and I don't know who he is. He introduces himself as "Dan." I barely recognized him from the photograph. He said that the picture was a "few years old," but that was one of

the few pictures he has of himself. And his friends think he hasn't changed at all in fourteen years. Well, I didn't want to tell him the truth. Anyway, we continue through the evening. We ate dinner at this lovely bistro with traditional music that was too loud, but the food is good. After he drank four glasses of wine, being a good Catholic, he confesses to having impotence. Oh, Lord. That's not something I want to deal with in a relationship. I didn't see him again.

The witty, critical, and vivid story of a disappointing first date is told by "Juliet," a spirited, attractive, and intelligent retired 62 year old white female, who was born and raised in Eastern Europe, moved to Southern California when she was in her early twenties, earned a bachelor's degree in the US, and completed 30 years of graphic design experience in the field. A mother, divorcee, and continually self-educating and highly cultured woman, Juliet volunteers as a docent at a museum and has a moderate degree of computer literacy. As the story reveals, Juliet constructs her identity as younger than she is because she is attracted to youthful men, a self-presentational strategy she sees as common and ethically acceptable among women of her generation. Clearly, dating for her involves sexual activity eventually with a professional, social, and physical peer. However, her participation in online dating is constructed by traditional European gender roles in which women are pursued, demure, modest, and the passive recipients of inquiring messages and other invitations for dating, while men are the pursuers, bold, and dominant actors to initiate dating. Therefore, Juliet's role in e-dating is limited to her waiting to be approached online by men and deciding if and how to interact with them.

When asked about her socializing with friends, Juliet explains that they are mostly married or unwilling to go out to singles arenas designed for people her own age. Like most women, particularly from her generation and traditional upbringing, she doesn't like to go out on her own. Therefore, she sees Internet dating as her best opportunity to meet men for long-term relationships. Because of her embarrassment about online dating, she has not shared her profile with friends and reports uncertainty about how well presented her profile is. When describing her perception of how her audience does or may react to her profile, Juliet writes, "No idea. Wish someone would tell me." However, she has not sought feedback about her profile. When asked to critique the strengths and weaknesses of her self-presentation, she writes, "I don't really think it's about me; it's the other person who decides about my profile." Underlying her comments is the unquestioning confidence in the veracity of her self-presentation and the certitude that she has no means of managing impressions to better attract desirable males. In her "About Me" section in her profile, Juliet explicitly acknowledges having doubts about her viewers wanting to get to know her through the profile: "Nobody has the attention span to read it all the way." This statement seems counter-effective to her goal of ingratiating herself to a man who is interested in conversation, getting to know someone well, and developing closer relationships. Powerless while waiting for any response from evaluating viewers, Juliet is convinced that it's futile to imagine her audience's viewpoint or to affect their impressions; therefore she undermines or even sabotages her endeavors.

In labeling herself, Juliet says, "I'm a mature but young-at-heart and body woman with culture and intelligence." What Juliet projects, perhaps inadvertently, is a kind of social class superiority and negative attitude about members and the e-dating process, which may result in intimidating, repelling, or attracting male members. From her self-reporting of limited responses, it seems that the more likely reactions are among the former possibilities. Though her self-presentation and impression management strategies are not successful, she defends her word choices and identity construction as being honest and true. Juliet resists

developing a rhetorical perspective beyond her description of her ideal date and relationship: "educated, professional man who likes to travel with a long-term partner." Besides understating her age, Juliet has few rhetorical strategies and, thus, lacks direction in revising her profile for the target audience.

While Juliet's approach is largely a-rhetorical, she feels confident about her general literacy skills, giving her the poise to participate in Internet dating: "My most recent experience was honky dory until we actually met face to face. To me that means that the written part of it is really not a problem for me." Despite believing in her writing competence, she isn't able to detect incompatibility, whether related to poor physical appearance or sexual dysfunction. As she feels it's inappropriate to explicitly state her expectations of sexual health or other physical appearance preferences (with no guarantee she would get an accurate answer), she isn't determining compatibility online. Her intimacy-building process is defined by a nonconfrontational approach, communicating to maintain harmony with individuals in empathic interlocutor relationships. Her communication style comprises of encouraging others to expound on their life stories, praising others' attributes or actions, asking nonthreatening questions of clarification, and inviting general information exchange (Berzsenyi, 1999, p. 234). Building empathic relationships with men online, Juliet maintains conventionally polite interaction with strangers but does not get at those sensitive issues that concern her most. She doesn't want to give the impression of being sex-obsessed or superficial, but she emphasizes the essential nature of "attraction" and "being well suited to one another." With initial screening of incompatible daters done online, and secondary screenings in person to weed out mismatched dates, Juliet feels frustrated.

Despite evaluating Internet dating as ineffectual, Juliet keeps trying. She expresses being skeptical but hopeful: "I came to the conclusion that meeting someone in an unplanned social setting and going slowly has a better chance for a relationship than the Internet way. . . . However, I also understand that our lifestyles are changing with technology and maybe we can perfect the new ways of finding potential partners." A modern woman mixed with traditional values, Juliet continued dating online with some fun dates and new acquaintance-friends, but no long term relationships.

FINDINGS: SIX YEARS LATER: LESSONS LEARNED ABOUT RHETORIC AND INTERNET DATING

All four of the participants had distinct relationship goals, communication styles, strategies for self-disclosure and intimacy formation, and unique personal backgrounds and demographic make-ups. Therefore, to generalize about what strategies always work in net environments or for given relationship goals would be erroneous. The value of studying these participants' online dating as case studies is providing how honesty, quantity of experience with e-dating, intent, and valence affect participants' sense of strategic and self-presentation competence and confidence (Gibbs et al., 2006). However, three of the four participants express being strategically successful, meaning they found the kinds of dating relationships they were striving for online. For three of them, their strategies were, rhetorically speaking, reasonable choices for their relationship purposes and target audiences within the context of their specific online dating sites. While Juliet expresses being unsuccessful rhetorically, not having found long term relationship partners online, she is self-assured of her self-presentational success in conveying who she is and what she desires in a relationship (Gibbs et al., 2006).

Since this case study research began, 6 years have passed. For Juan, Internet dating enabled him to meet casual sexual partners, friends, and even a long-term relationship for the last two years.

Since they agreed to construct an "open relationship," each is free to have casual sex with others on agreed upon occasions. After they moved to a new large city, Juan had to make new friends, become familiar with the city and its resources, and discover social opportunities. In order to meet casual partners, Juan explains how Internet dating is useful:

You have the potential of partner sorting in a much faster rate than by old conventional means. Right away, you can classify what you are looking for, what you expect and what you won't compromise on. Whether this be looks, profession, interest, sexual fetishes, political leaning and culture, with a click of a mouse you can eliminate what would be countless hours of dating and casual conversation in order to get to the right match.

As he explains, Internet dating has been instrumental for creating a more efficient and focused search process for meeting his social goals. Juan still feels positive about "the potential for many happy matches to be made over the Internet, be it just a one-night stand or a relationship. Juan's long-term experiences of Internet dating have taught him that "I can get what I want by tweaking my ads to the dating service and type of guys." Highly literate in these social forums, Juan has taken the time to understand the conventions and cultural norms of the individual cyberspaces he inhabits, adjusting and strategizing the discourse and graphical elements of his self-presentations to achieve intended impressions and relationship aims.

For Luke, Internet dating has enabled him to meet partners for casual encounters and short-term relationships. Since the project started, Luke has changed jobs, moved to a major city in another state, makes the "six figures" he had once lied about, and continues to date casually, using Internet dating services. After about 10 years of Internet dating, Luke reports having met 287 women. His writing style has evolved to a greater sophistication with more responses to his profile than he can follow up on. In response to reading that his profile narrative is humorous but with subtle, difficult-to-detect sarcasm, he writes:

Which is perfect since it's a fantastic filter. I only get people who Get It--advanced critical thinking skills. With a sincere narrative, I get so much silly crap. But now I get people who are belly-chucklers.

With the increase in membership and women's willingness to initiate contact, Luke no longer strives for the greatest number of responses, which is overwhelming to manage. Clearly, he no longer tries to attract a broad range of women anymore. Instead, he is successfully targeting his profile to women who share his sharp wit and emotional reserve, though he reports having to "cut them off" when they do get too serious.

For Kate, Internet dating was a forum for meeting a life partner. Two years after joining three Internet dating services, Kate met a man online and has since married him. When asked what she felt were her secrets to success, Kate explained in an email:

I think it's a few things. Perseverance helps--the fact that I was willing to 'get back on the horse' after many dates with different people that ended in some disappointment or anger or rejection. Plus, my attitude was that each date was an adventure. I read communications carefully, between the lines, to get a sense of the person, and watched for inconsistencies. And I wrote specifically and attentively for each person.

Kate recommends Internet dating because it gave her access to members outside of her professional, social, and geographical circles. She no longer uses dating services but uses social networks, blogs, and other cyberspaces for connecting to others with similar interests.

After a couple of years, Juliet decided that Internet dating was not working for her. Why was Juliet unsuccessful? Although the goals and strategies vary, Juan, Luke, and Kate have had successful experiences with Internet dating, meaning that they've accomplished what they set out to do. Since the number of older members had been much lower than those of younger members, Juliet has a disadvantage. In contrast with Luke, Juliet's relationship goals have been much more challenging to achieve than her own, and Juan's have had greater flexibility with a broader target audience than her own. Related to the age issue, older members tend to hold attitudes of suspicion regarding computer-mediated communication than younger users, attitudes which seem to have been prohibitive to her success at times. Furthermore, Juliet felt stigmatized as an Internet dating service member while younger Kate, for example, was more comfortable with it and vocal about her participation, enabling the exchange of ideas that strengthened the focus of her purposeful writing. In addition, Juliet has a strong cultural identification with her heritage, having come to the U.S. after her formative years. How her upbringing and cultural make-up might have produced an outsider identity is unclear and beyond the scope of this study. However, her especially formal English language training does distinguish her word choice and articulation of feelings, insights, and past experiences from the more casual average American's or immigrant's more limited vocabulary in English.

While men's specific reactions to Juliet's persona are beyond my knowledge, certainly, nationality impacts identity constructions and relationship formations. For example, Juliet did not initiate contact with men, only responded to those who contacted her profile, which related to her social role as a woman needing to wait for men to approach her. In contrast, Kate initiated contact with men routinely—in fact, with the man she ended up marrying. She reinforces a key factor, which is that she "researched and selected carefully the men I talked with more or met in person. I didn't wait for men to just find me. I looked, too." Logically, the more one interacts online, the greater the chances of success. Accordingly, Juliet is not comfortable initiating contact, which means she will have fewer opportunities to meet men online and, later, in person. Finally, Juliet is reserved about asking personal questions as well as disclosing personal information with others, which can negatively affect intimacy formation online. She sums up her Internet dating experiences:

I find that women of my age, including myself, get a number of responses from much younger men, twenties and thirties, who are perhaps either perverted with mother-obsessions or want to be supported financially by mother-substitutes. The ones who are my age often are living in mobile homes, in other states, or have no common interest with me. The ones I am interested in are not interested in me, maybe because of my looks, age and who knows what else. I seem to have been doing better meeting people face to face.

After some attempts at finding suitable dates, Juliet has given up on Internet dating to continue with "being in the right place at the right time" chance encounters that are "meant to be."

FUTURE RESEARCH DIRECTIONS

As findings from this case study of questionnaire and interview response and electronic discourse analysis of the participants' texts, a natural extension of this research would be the development of a rhetorical heuristic. Such an exploratory and productive tool would provide e-daters with a means for raising self-awareness and a discursive action plan for projecting desired identities and relationship goals. With the objectives of facilitating cyber communicators' rhetorical perspective and actions, a heuristic designed to guide writers in creating public self-presentations as well as private message exchanges would serve well. Based on some of the questions in the survey and more generalized versions of the follow up questions from the internet interviews, such a heuristic could direct interlocutors to engage with greater self-awareness, genre-based efficacy,

context-informed deliberation, and rhetorical sophistication. Even with these potential benefits, some interpersonal communication elements cannot be aided with a heuristic. For example, negative attitudes about the cyber dating process, inhibiting fears of interacting with strangers, low self-esteem, unreasonable expectations of others and the process, rigid notions about participating online, or the like, cannot be modified with the use of a composition tool. However, with practice, e-daters can increase their personal comfort with the process that would be designed to aid in the processes of self-discovery, vivid and potent self-identification, and effective interlocutor relationship building. Notwithstanding, a heuristic for interlocutor e-dating would be a theoretical and practical contribution to cyber communication.

CONCLUSION

Mainstream American society is increasingly technologically-mediated, with e-dating being a clear example of conventionalized context for millions of people's social lives. Certainly, degrees of availability, perceived attractiveness, and idiosyncratic preferences cannot be denied as strong forces that affect the mate selection and communication process to face-to-face meeting. For user support, there are resources available to assist individuals with dating interaction, as even the popular author and television "life strategist" Dr. Phil McGraw has worked with Match.com to help members develop new strategies for pursuing relationship goals. However, this study shows that having the resources available is not solving the problem. Members must have the desire to learn where to locate and effectively use resources and then to be willing to apply the strategies in writing. Accordingly, the participants who experienced greater dating success and satisfaction with the process also projected:

- A disposition of openness to the process of communicating with other members without being stymied by over generalized skepticism or anxiety.

- Realistic and discernible self-presentations.
- Clear, consistent, and specific relationship goals with the suitable descriptions and identifiers for careful impression management.
- Enjoyment and confidence in their e-dating participation and tended to update their profiles more frequently in response to feedback received or not, which also improved their profile's visibility to others.
- Greater activity within the online dating services, which increased opportunities for dates with compatible members.

While greater numbers increase one's odds of meeting one's match, they are not necessarily affecting higher rates of compatible dates to less compatible dates overall. More specifically, these high volume interlocutors write both invitational emails as well as response emails.

To some extent, the "numbers game" has proven true with these daters; however, rhetorical quality of interaction also factored in the ratio of online relationships to offline dates, though the exact rates could not be determined. Because participants deleted dating history documentation prior to this project, they could not accurately report rates of compatible dates. Through subjective self-reporting, Kate epitomizes the participants' consensual sentiment: "The more you do it, the more you are likely to find what you want." Further, as Gibbs et al. (2006) have shown, positive experiences lead to positive attitudes and to greater satisfaction with Internet dating in general as well as with personal success. In this case study, the participants had varying levels of activity and, accordingly, varying levels of satisfaction and perceived success.

In addition, these e-dating members became more effective when they strategically composed their e-texts after a methodical process of rhetorically analyzing the communication media and its conventions, the specific expectations and behaviors of their target audiences, and their own specific relationship objectives in connection with appropriate literacy skills to make them a reality. More explicitly, effective rhetorical process includes the following:

- Self-awareness of one's own fears, hopes, relationship history, computer literacies, physical realities, and social values fundamental to the whole process;
- Knowledge of the rhetorical genre features (Swales, 1990) used in Internet dating along with its contextually-based conventions of discursive behaviors and communal participation;
- Understanding of target or desired audience members;
- Clarity of relationship goals; and
- Consciousness in deliberately applying the strategies learned to other rhetorical factors.

Among my participants, the most sophisticated rhetoricians have the greatest satisfaction and perceived success with the process. Conversely, the less rhetorically sophisticated daters feel less successful and satisfied with less discursive control over their profiles and interactions with others.

RECOMMENDATIONS

Hence, students are online in public self-presentational and interactive forums without adequate literacy training for the unique rhetorical challenges of communicating in cyberspaces. Especially, adolescents are ill-equipped to recognize and protect themselves against predators that appear online as nonthreatening, fun, and interested in getting to know their emotionally vulnerable selves. Situated in anonymous and disembodied communication, cyber predation must be addressed with awareness, education, and pedagogical research to discover the best ways to identify passive aggressive, manipulative, overly friendly, exceedingly accommodating and complimentary messaging, and so forth—qualities of predatory or disingenuous messaging. Developing theoretical heuristics can help Internet users recognize what is written, the style in which it is written, the implication of the message, the information that is left out or contradicted from previous messages, and the like. After all, it is through discourse that dangers as well as friendships are constructed online. On the one hand, the rhetorical education needs to be delivered for students to recognize rhetorical trouble signs of manipulation through false flattery and idealized self-presentations, persistent coaxing, eventual insistence, and emotional bartering. On the other hand, a contextually applied rhetorical education can be used to build healthy, lasting relationships in most cyber communities of social networking from online to offline.

Hopefully, academics, interpersonal relationship professionals, and education administrators are discussing how the university's curriculum may need adjustment to accommodate the new writing and social interaction challenges emerging with the Internet, impacting all aspects of people's lives and relationships.

REFERENCES

Baker, A. J. (2005). *Double click: Romance and commitment among online couples.* Cresskill, NJ: Hampton Press.

Berzsenyi, C. (1999). Teaching interlocutor relationships in electronic classrooms. *Computers and Composition, 16*(2), 229–246. doi:10.1016/S8755-4615(99)00004-3.

ConsumerSearch. (2012, February). Online dating: Comparing the top sites. Retrieved June 10, 2012, from http://www.consumersearch.com/online-dating/review

Ellison, N. B., Heino, R. D., & Gibbs, J. L. (2006). Managing impressions online: Self-presentation processes in the online dating environment. *Journal of Computer-Mediated Communication, 11*(2), 152–177. doi:10.1111/j.1083-6101.2006.00020.x.

Faust, E. (2012, April 16). *Definition of online dating.* In eHow. Retrieved November 04, 2012, from http://www.ehow.com/about_6679610_definition-online-dating.html

Gibbs, J. L., Ellison, N. B., & Heino, R. D. (2006). Self-presentation in online personals: The role of anticipated future interaction, self-disclosure, and perceived success in Internet dating. *Communication Research, 33*(2), 152–177. doi:10.1177/0093650205285368.

Goffman, E. (1959). *The presentation of self in everyday life.* NY: Double Day Anchor Books.

Gurak, L. J. (1997). *Persuasion and privacy in cyberspace: the online protests over lotus marketplace and the clipper chip.* New Haven, CT: Yale University Press.

Gwinnell, E. (1998). *Online seductions: Falling in love with strangers on the Internet.* New York, NY: Kodansha America, Inc..

Heino, R. D., Ellison, N. B., & Gibbs, J. L. (2010). Relationshopping: Investigating the market metaphor in online dating. *Journal of Social and Personal Relationships, 27*(4), 427–447. doi:10.1177/0265407510361614.

Herring, S., & Zelenkauskaite, A. (2009). Symbolic capital in a virtual heterosexual market: Abbreviation and insertion in Italian iTV SMS. *Written Communication, 26*(1), 5–31. doi:10.1177/0741088308327911.

Howard, T. (1997). *The rhetoric of electronic communities. New Directions in Computers and Composition Studies Series.* Greenwich, CT: Ablex Publishing Corporation.

Lawson, H. M., & Leck, K. (2012). Dynamics of Internet dating. *Social Science Computer Review, 24*(2), 189–208. doi:10.1177/0894439305283402.

Leary, M. R. (1995). *Impression management and interpersonal behavior*. Madison, WI: Brown and Benchmark Publishers.

McQuail, D. (2005). *Mcquail's mass communication theory* (5th ed.). London: Sage Publications.

Orr, A. (2004). *Meeting, mating, and cheating: Sex, love, and the new world of online dating*. Upper Saddle River, NJ: Reuters Prentice Hall.

Porter, J. (1998). *Rhetorical ethics and internetworked writing*. Greenwich, CT: Albex.

Rubin, R. (1996). Moral distancing and the use of information technologies: The seven temptations. In Kizza, J. M. (Ed.), *Social and ethical effects of the computer revolution* (pp. 124–135). Jefferson, NC: McFarland & Company, Inc. Publishers.

Schlenker, B. R. (1998). Identification and self-identification. In Schlenker, B. R. (Ed.), *The self and social life* (pp. 65–99). NY: McGraw-Hill Book Company.

Schwartz, J. (2000). *The complete idiot's guide to online dating and relating*. Indianapolis, IN: Que Corporation.

Selfe, C. L. (1999). *Technology and literacy in the twenty-first century: The importance of paying attention*. Urbana, IL: National Council of Teachers of English.

Swales, J. M. (1990). *Genre analysis: English in academic and research settings*. Great Britain: Cambridge University Press.

Tedeschi, J. T., & Riess, M. (1981). Identities, the phenomenal self, and laboratory research. In Tedeschi, J. T. (Ed.), *Impression management theory and social psychological research* (pp. 3–22). NY: Academic Press, Inc..

Turkle, S. (1995). *Life on the screen: Identity in the age of the Internet*. New York, NY: Simon and Schuster.

Vitzthum, V. (2007). *I love you, let's meet: Adventures in online dating*. New York, NY: Little Brown and Company.

Warnock, J. (1984). The writing process. In Moran, M. G., & Lunsford, R. F. (Eds.), *Research in composition and rhetoric* (pp. 3–26). Westport, CT: Greenwood Press.

ADDITIONAL READING

Anderson, D., Atkins, A., Ball, C. E., Millar, K. H., Selfe, C., & Selfe, R. (2006). Integrating multimodality into composition curricula: Survey methodology and results from a CCCC research grant. *Composition Studies, 34*(2), 59–84.

Anonymous. (2009, April 30). Online dating: Case study—Dating direct affinity. *New Media Age*. Proquest.

Ball, C. (2004). Show, not tell: The value of new media scholarship. *Computers and Composition, 21*(4), 403–425.

Barton, E., Stygall, G., & Gundlach, R. (Eds.). (2002). *Discourse studies in composition*. Cresskill, NJ: Hampton Press.

Bernd, M., Machilek, F., & Schütz, A. (2006, June). Personality in cyberspace: Personal websites as media for personality expressions and impressions. *Journal of Personality and Social Psychology, 90*(6), 1014–1031. doi:10.1037/0022-3514.90.6.1014 PMID:16784349.

Ding, H. (2007). Confucius's virtue-centered rhetoric: A case study of mixed research methods in comparative rhetoric. *Rhetoric Review, 26*(2), 142–159. doi:10.1080/07350190709336706.

Doveling, K., von Scheve, C., & Konijn, E. A. (Eds.). (2011). *The Routledge handbook of emotions and mass media*. NY: Routledge.

Fisman, R., Iyengar, S. S., Kamenica, E., & Simonson, I. (2008). Racial preferences in dating. *The Review of Economic Studies*, *75*, 117–132. doi:10.1111/j.1467-937X.2007.00465.x.

Frazzetto, G. (2010). The science of online dating. Science and society feature. *EMBO Reports*, *11*(1), 25–27. doi:10.1038/embor.2009.264 PMID:20033090.

Goralnick, J. (2009, January 27). 6 concrete lessons-learned in online relationship-building, as presented to the GBTC. In *Technotheory*. Retrieved August 20, 2012, from http://www.technotheory.com/2009/01/6-concrete-lessons-learned-in-online-relationship-building-as-presented-to-the-gbtc/

Gunter, B. (2007). Internet dating: A British survey. *New Information Perspectives*, *60*(2), 88–98.

Jones, S. E., & LeBaron, C. D. (2002). Research on the relationship between verbal and nonverbal communication: Emerging integrations. *The Journal of Communication*, *52*, 499–521. doi:10.1111/j.1460-2466.2002.tb02559.x.

Karpf, D. (2012). Social science research methods in internet time. *Information Communication and Society*, *15*(5), 639–661. doi:10.1080/1369 118X.2012.665468.

Krisanic, K. (2008). *Motivations and impression management: Predictors of social networking site use and user behavior. University of Missouri - Columbia*. ProQuest Dissertations and Theses.

Lauer, C. (2009). Contending with terms: Multimedia and multimodal in the academic and public spheres. *Computers and Composition*, *26*(4), 225–239. doi:10.1016/j.compcom.2009.09.001.

Leinonen, P., Jarvela, S., & Lipponen, L. (2003). Individual students' interpretations of their contribution to the computer-mediated discussions. *Journal of Interactive Learning Research*, *14*(1), 99–122.

Lemke, J. (1995). *Textual politics: Discourse and social dynamics*. London: Taylor & Francis.

Moran, M. G., & Lunsford, R. (Eds.). (1984). *Research in composition and rhetoric*. Westport, CT: Greenwood Press.

Rhetorical analysis of Match.com. (2009, December 2). *Claire's E-portfolio* [Wordpress Weblog]. Retrieved November 10, 2012, from http://www.mengebcd.wordpress.com/rhetorical-analysis/

Selfe, C. L. (2009). The movement of air, the breath of meaning: Aurality and multimodal composing. *College Composition and Communication*, *60*(4), 616–663.

Smiljana, A. (2008). From text to gesture online: A microethnographic analysis of nonverbal communication in the Second Life virtual environment. *Information Communication and Society*, *11*(2), 221–238. doi:10.1080/13691180801937290.

Thurlow, C., Lengel, L., & Tomic, A. (2004). *Computer-mediated communications: Social interaction and the internet*. London: Sage Publications.

Walther, J. B. (2006). Nonverbal dynamics in computer-mediated communication, or:(and the net:('s with you:) and you:) alone. In Patterson, M. L., & Manusov, V. (Eds.), *The SAGE handbook of nonverbal communication* (pp. 461–479). Beverly Hills, CA: Sage. doi:10.4135/9781412976152.n24.

Wysocki, A. F. (2004). Opening new media to writing: Openings and justifications. In F. Wysocki, J. Johnson-Eilola, C. Selfe, & G. Sirc (Eds.), Writing new media: Theory and applications for expanding the teaching of composition (pp. 1–41). Logan: Utah State University Press.

Yee, N., Bailenson, J. N., Urbanek, M., Chang, F., & Merget, D. (2007). The unbearable likeness of being digital: The persistence of nonverbal social norms in online virtual environments. *Cyberpsychology & Behavior, 10*(1), 115–121. doi:10.1089/cpb.2006.9984 PMID:17305457.

KEY TERMS AND DEFINITIONS

Computer-Mediated Communication: "(CMC) is defined as any communicative transaction that occurs through the use of two or more networked computers (Mcquail, 2005). While the term has traditionally referred to those communications that occur via computer-mediated formats (e.g., instant messages, e-mails, chat rooms), it has also been applied to other forms of text-based interaction such as text messaging" (Thurlow, Lengel, & Tomic, 2004).

Impression Management: "Consists of behaviors by a person that has the purpose of controlling or manipulating the attributions and impressions formed of that person by others" (Leary, 1995, p. 105).

Interlocutor Relationships: Describes individuals participating in a dialogue or conversation, and, in this case, in a technologically-mediated interaction that initiate and construct patterns of discourse attributable to categories of relationships (Berzsenyi, 1999).

Online Dating (OD), E-Dating, or Internet Dating: A dating system which allows individuals, couples and groups to make contact and communicate with each other over the Internet, usually with the objective of developing a personal, romantic, or sexual relationship (Faust, 2012).

Online Dating Services: Usually provide unmoderated matchmaking over the Internet, through the use of personal computers or cell phones.

Self-Identification: Involves individuals engaging in a process of showing oneself to be a particular type of person with continuity over time and within context "through definition, description, evidence, inference, interpretation, analogy, or treatment." The purpose of self-identification ranges between "the attempt to gain or convey useful information about the self to the attempt to control the reactions of other people" (Schlenker, 1998, p. 65).

Self-Presentation: Individuals' projections of personality and character are both an expression of one's concept of self and a projection of a rhetorical process of impression management (Tedeschi, 1981, p. 3).

Techno-Rhetoric: "A complex set of socially and culturally situated values, practices, and skills involved in operating linguistically within the context of electronic environments, including reading, writing, and communicating" (Selfe, 1999, p. 11).

APPENDIX

Online Dating Goals and Writing

Name:

Age:

Sex: M/F

Education: HS equiv/A/B/M/Ph.D.

1. What made you decide to start using an online dating service?
2. How long have you been using an online dating service?
3. How many and which online dating services are you using?
4. What have been your goals for using an online dating service?
5. What are your feelings and attitudes about the process of online dating?
6. What features of your profile did you want to emphasize or complete with the greatest care and why? (pre-selected personality trait choices, photo, stats, narrative, handle and headline)
7. How was your profile designed to help you get a response from your ideal match?
8. What reasoning made you decide to include or exclude a photo of yourself in your profile?
9. How would you describe your online dating persona—the personality you project in your profile and emails? What shows this?
10. How do you think your online dating persona is being interpreted by users in general? What makes you say so?
11. What do you think your profile illustrates to others about who you are? How?
12. Critique your profile. What are its strengths and weaknesses? What makes you seem attractive or unattractive to others?
13. When responding to a profile, what are your goals?
14. When responding to a profile, what strategies do you use?
15. Describe a comfortable and successful online dating process.
16. Describe what would be an uncomfortable and unsuccessful online dating process.
17. What aspects of writing did you feel you needed to develop to be more effective and more comfortable with online dating?
18. What aspects of computer literacy did you feel you needed to develop to be more effective and more comfortable with online dating?
19. How successful do you feel you have been with online dating?
20. How effective do you think online dating services are at helping you meet your ideal matches?
21. Are you still dating online? If not, why? If yes, what are your future plans with online dating?

Chapter 11
Engaging in Scientific Controversies in Science Blogs:
The Expression of Allegiance and Ideological Commitment

María-José Luzón
University of Zaragoza, Spain

ABSTRACT

The weblog incorporates technical capabilities which facilitate interaction and make it easy to exchange information and engage in discussion about controversial issues. This chapter presents a methodological framework to study how both allegiance and conflict are expressed and constructed in scientific controversies in science blogs. The study is based on the exploration of three controversies, related with global warming, the effects of vaccination and the role of women in science. A corpus of weblog comments to six posts which triggered off a dispute over these controversial issues was searched for indicators both of social behaviour and of rude or verbally offensive behaviour. The study shows how blog comments are used by participants to signal their allegiance to a particular group within the disciplinary community, their ideological commitments, and their rejection of opposing standpoints and competing claims.

INTRODUCTION

Academic weblogs are becoming increasingly popular as tools to share information and opinions about science-related topics and as online discussion forums. The weblog incorporates technical capabilities (e.g. links, comment software, trackbacks) which facilitate interaction within and across weblogs and make it easier for scholars and the interested public to engage in discussion about discipline-specific topics. The attributes of weblogs (open forum, asynchronous communication exchanges, linking, highly social nature) enable a type of interaction different from face-to-face interaction and from the communication in other conventional academic genres (Boyd, 2003; Mortensen & Walker, 2002; Walker, 2006). Weblogs are usually open forums, meaning that

DOI: 10.4018/978-1-4666-4426-7.ch011

entries and comments can be read and answered by a large readership, thus offering scholars an open digital arena to interact with members of a discipline but also with academics in other research areas and non-academic interested public. Communication is asynchronous and messages are saved, so that the whole discussion can be accessed, and any comment can be selected to be answered back. Linking makes it possible to expand the conversation by joining two discussion threads on the same issue in different blogs. Finally, blogs are a good example of "social software," i.e. software supportive of conversational interaction, social networks and social feedback (Boyd, 2003). They support the desire of individuals to affiliate in order to achieve their personal goals and allow for the creation of new social groupings, not necessarily overlapping with in-person communities, and for the emergence of new social conventions. These features explain why posts on socially controversial issues in science blogs trigger a large number of comments, giving rise to arguments in which collective opponents are involved.

This chapter will examine these socio-scientific controversies in science blogs written in English, focusing on discursive features used by participants (bloggers and commenters) to express their relational behaviour towards other participants in the blog and to construct and reaffirm their identity as members of an online group, that is, features used to signal participants' allegiance to a particular group, their ideological commitments, and their rejection of opposing views and ideas. For this purpose, we will analyze the interaction that takes place through posts and comments, focusing on those features that act as markers of social and antisocial behaviour. Previous research on CMC has shown that both indicators of social behavior and of rude behaviour can be used to express allegiance to a group (Dennen & Pashnyak, 2008; Luzón, 2011; Upadhyay, 2010). Therefore, the specific questions that will be addressed are: (i) which are the indicators of social and rude or

verbally offensive behaviour in weblog scientific controversies? (ii) how do these indicators contribute to the construction of group identity?

BACKGROUND

Science Blogs as Platforms for Scientific Controversies

Researchers on the sociology of science distinguish between controversies over knowledge claims which take place mainly within the scientific community and scientific controversies with a social dimension because of their social, ethical, political or economic implications, e.g. controversies over climate change or abortion (Martin, 2011; Stewart, 2009). Stewart (2009) defines this last type of controversies as "extended argumentative engagements over socially significant issues" which comprise "communicative events and practices in and from both scientific and nonscientific spheres" (p. 125). Drawing on Fairclough (1992; 1995), Stewart underscores two important and related aspects to take into account in the discursive analysis of controversies. The first is that controversies are not single communicative events but chains of communicative events (Fairclough, 1995), and therefore their analysis requires attending to the links between these communicative events. The second is the importance of intertextuality and interdiscursivity in the context of controversies. Intertextuality refers to the "property texts have of being full of snatches of other texts, which may be explicitly demarcated or merged in, and which the text may assimilate, contradict, ironically echo, and so forth" (Fairclough, 1992, p. 84). Thus the texts that constitute controversies frequently incorporate references to and quotations from other texts. In addition, controversies are complex in terms of interdiscursivity, incorporating elements and discourse practices from different genres or types of discourse.

Scientific controversies are concomitant with the development of science and occur in many diverse forums. Although authors of research papers aim at showing objectivity in the expression of ideas, and avoid emotional language and explicit disagreement, argumentation and debate are the basis of science progress and the expression of strong opinions and highly subjective views is common in other academic communicative events, such as private conversations, discussion sessions in conferences, peer reviews or editorials (Salager-Meyer, 2001). Weblogs provide a new social space for scholars to engage in overt and personal argument, since, as some researchers (Hodsdon-Champeon, 2010; Mabry, 1997; Moshtagh, 2009) have pointed out, online discussion forums offer special advantages for carrying out debates and controversies. One of these advantages, of which participants are highly aware, is that their contributions and thus their views may be read by a potentially worldwide readership (Crystal, 2006, p. 214). The fact that people with different background (from experts to interested public) and different experiences may participate in the discussion and express their different attitudes and position also contributes to the creation of controversies (Moshtagh, 2009). In addition, the persistence of the text and the "cut-and-paste" feature facilitate quoting, contextualizing the response and presenting an antagonistic exchange in a single message. As Mabry (1997) remarks, an arguer can strategically frame his/her argument by inserting segments of a previously distributed message along with counterclaims refuting the position advanced in that message.

One online discussion forum especially suitable for scientific controversies is the science weblog. Research on academic and science blogs (e.g. Davies & Merchant, 2007; Efimova & de Moor, 2005; Mortensen & Walker, 2002; Walker, 2006) has revealed that bloggers use them, among other purposes, to increase their visibility and develop respect and reputation as knowledge-able members of a disciplinary community and to collaborate and interact with others, and thus identify themselves as members of a group and strengthen the links within the group. Although interaction with others may take the form of cross-blog conversations through citation in blog entries or links in blogrolls (Efimova & de Moor, 2005), the most useful tool to contribute to a weblog conversation is the comment. Comments are used by blog readers to provide feedback and evaluate the blog entry and to share views and discuss any point related to the post both with other readers and with the blogger (bloggers themselves very frequently answer back and provide further information through comments, thus taking part in the interaction). The possibility to comment can give rise to long communicative exchanges where anybody interested in the topic may take part. In blogs with commenting-capabilities, comments offer connectivity after the post publication and thus play a key role in the creation and support of communities (Dennen & Pashnyak, 2008).

Individuals who interact through a specific weblog form a "community of blogging practice": a group of people "who share certain routines and expectations about the use of blogs as a tool for information, identity, and relationship management" (Schmidt, 2007, Abstract). Bloggers sharing similar interests tend to be connected through links and comments in each other's blogs. Although some bloggers may blog infrequently, include few hyperlink connections to other blogs, and get few or no comments, there are also "active and engaged bloggers who post, comment, and link frequently, creating a kernel of conversational community based on personal networks facilitated by blogging tools and associated technologies" (Lampa, 2004, para. 2). In some cases the same participants contribute messages (posts or comments) to several related blogs, and the discussion of the same issue may take place throughout these blogs. This is the case of the controversial discussions analyzed in this paper, where some of the participants are frequently contributing members in a blogging community.

A crucial attribute of most of these blogging communities is their lack of clear boundaries and unrestricted membership. The science we-blogs analyzed here are open to the public, not restricted to peers working in the same field. Due to the sense of anonymity and to the equalization process that tends to take place in CMC, relations of social power among the members of a blogging community are defined in a different way from face-to-face communication. Baym (2006, p. 69) discusses three consistent findings in studies of online groups, which may throw some light on the relational behaviour among participants in science blogs: online groups are "normatively regulated, hierarchical and often very supportive." Group members share a set of social meanings which include identities, relationships, group-specific forms of expression and norms for interaction. Social hierarchies emerge online and are based on patterns of prior interaction and participation, with light users and heavy users, who generate the largest volume of posts and use a variety of ways (e.g. sharing knowledge, showing excellence in some skills) to present themselves in a socially favourable light and gain status within the group. As for the supportive nature of online groups, Baym (2006) reports on research that shows that most groups provide social, expert or informational support and a sense of belonging to a group of people.

The formation of online (individual and group) identities through self-representation and social interaction is one of the main affordances of social media (Boyd, Golder, & Lotan, 2010; Turkle, 1995). Drawing on previous literature on the concept of identity, Delahunty (2012, p. 409) discusses three aspects that help to define identity formation in asynchronous discussions: (i) identity is complex: it is dynamic, negotiable, multi-faceted, continuously redefined over time and space, and situational; (ii) identity is socially constructed through interaction with others "and is shaped by self-perception, the perceptions of others, and the interpersonal power relations at play" (Delahunty, 2012, p. 409); (iii) identity is constructed, negotiated and interpreted through language. This claim is in line with Ivanic's (1998) notion of the "discoursal self," i.e. the way writers use discourse to convey an impression of who they are. Interaction in weblog controversies can therefore be viewed as social practice through which the identity of the participants is constructed.

The notion of identity can include both personal (individual) and social (collective or group) aspects of the self (Simon, 2004; Tajfel & Turner, 1986). As blogs are social media, they offer new possibilities for the formation of individual and collective identities. Social theories of identity (see Simon, 2004; Tajfel & Turner, 1986) hold that social identity is derived from the sense of belonging to a social category or group. When social identity is prominent, it influences social behaviour, since a shared sense of identity has an emotional significance (members of a group tend to have a favourable bias towards other members of their own group and promote respect for them) and individuals which are strongly identified with a social cause may become "diehards who support their group in word and deed against all odds" (Simon, 2004, p. 184).

The Expression of Social and Antisocial Behaviour in CMC

CMC research has shown that argumentative exchanges and hostility are frequent in the discourse of some computer mediated groups (Angouri & Tselinga, 2010; Kiesler, Siegel, & McGuire, 1984; Kleinke, 2008; Lorenzo-Dus, Garcés-Conejos, & Bou-Franch, 2011; Mabry, 1997; Moor, Heuvelman, & Verleur, 2010; Upadhyay, 2010). These studies of impoliteness and hostility in CMC have examined different online contexts, ranging from discussion lists and online fora to responses to articles and editorials in online media and comments in YouTube. Early research in CMC (Kiesler et al., 1984) attributed this high frequency of hostile language to the medium. Kiesler et al. (1984) argued that CMC is less personal than face-to-face communication, since it provides fewer "social context cues" and exhibits fewer indicators of "social presence." "Social presence," a concept introduced by Short, Williams, and Christie (1976), is the feeling of the other participants' immediacy and involvement in the communicative interaction. According to Sproull and Keisler (1986), the effects of the lack of social context cues include uninhibited communication, with more hostile and intense language (i.e., flaming) and a reduction in the perceived status differences between participants. The technological determinism implicit is these theories has been challenged by more recent theories (see Walther, 2011) and it is now widely accepted that the linguistic and discursive features of CMC (including the expression of social and antisocial behaviour) should be accounted for taking into consideration both technological and social/ situational/ contextual factors and focusing on language use as social practice (Herring, 2007; Walther, 2010).

Some researchers have long argued that CMC allows users to engage in social messages, since the lack of social context cues and other medium features can be strategically used by communicators to manipulate their identity and present themselves selectively, thus making their best impression (Tong & Walther, 2011; Walther, 1996). Several studies have demonstrated that, despite the lack of non-verbal cues, CMC has specific social and affective affordances (e.g. anonymity that enables intimate disclosures, easy contact with like-minded people, possibility to edit messages), which stimulate social interaction, identity performance and explicit emotion communication (e.g. Jones, 2009; Kreijns, Kirschner, & Jochems, 2002; Walther, 2007) and have shown that online discourse displays a high number of indicators of social behaviour (Derks, Fischer, & Bos, 2008; Luzón, 2011; Swan & Shih, 2005).

A factor that has been claimed to play an important role in the way people interact online is deindividuation and the salience of a social identity. The theory of *Social Identity model of Deindividuation Effects* (SIDE) (Reicher, Spears, & Postmes, 1995; Spears & Lea, 1994), based on the social identity theory of Tajfel and Turner (1986), holds that the anonymity of CMC facilitates a shift from a personal to a group or social identity ("depersonalization"). If an online user experiences this social identification, the user will relate to others on the basis of in-group/ outgroup dynamics, will focus on shared communalities and group concerns, and will conform to perceived group norms. Recent research on impoliteness in CMC suggests that this sense of group identity can help to account for some features of CMC, including what is considered uninhibited behaviour. Applying Simon's (2004) social psychological theory of identity, Upadhyay (2010) analyzed reader's responses to views expressed by journalists in online media and found that impoliteness is used by respondents to identify themselves as social agents committed to supporting a position collectively held by the members of the group, as opposed to the views of outgroup members. Similarly, in their analysis of postings responding to the "Obama Reggaeton" YouTube video, Lorenzo-Dus et al. (2011) found that impoliteness was related to the formation of group identity. The patterns of impoliteness realization corresponded to those expected within the SIDE model for online contexts in which social identity is salient. Antagonistic groups defined themselves "in us versus them terms" (p. 2591): the ingroup members explicitly associate the members of antagonistic groups with negative aspects and disassociate from them.

CORPUS AND METHOD

Corpus

The study is based on the examination of three controversies developing in six posts (two for each controversy) written in 2009, 2010 and 2011, and their comments (100 comments for each controversy). The six posts were published in popular science blogs written in English and all of them generated a heated discussion in the comments. In one of the controversies the complete threads of comments to the posts were analyzed (100 comments). In the other controversies posts got a higher number of comments (125 in one of them, and 399 in the other), so the first fifty comments to each post were selected. The first controversial discussion (controversy 1), consisting of posts and comments in the blogs *The Intersection* and *Aetiology*, was triggered by the publication of the book *The Oxford Book of Modern Science Writing*, edited by Richard Dawkins (2008), and revolves around the consideration of women as scientists. The fact that Professor Dawkins only selected 3 texts written by women of 83 texts in the book triggered critical weblog posts from female science bloggers, who considered that female scientists were unfairly underrepresented. The post in *Aetiology* links to that in *The Intersection* and to Dawkins' reply in the comments. Interestingly, the blogger posting at *The Intersection* ends her entry with the following sentence "Dr. Isis, Rebecca, Sci, Sciencewomen, Janet, Zuska, Tara… we have work to do," calling other female science bloggers into action and using vocatives and inclusive "we" to signal solidarity and group self-awareness. The second controversy (controversy 2) is over the blog entry "Should Boys Be Given the HPV Vaccine? The Science Is Weaker than the Marketing," where Jeanne Lenzer, a medical investigative journalist, claims to provide evidence against the administration of the HPV vaccine to boys. The entry was posted to the blog *The Crux,* hosted by *Discover*

magazine. The second post in this controversy ("Is the HPV vaccine 'weak science?' (Hint: no)" in *Aetiology*) is intended to refute Lenzer's claim. The third controversy (controversy 3) is related to the issue of global warming, and was triggered by a study on the impact that the changes in clouds may have on climate. This paper contradicted a previous publication by a skeptic climate scientist and the authors of both papers, and their supporters, defended their own views and attacked the other's claims in the blogosphere, in the blogs *Real Climate* and *Roy Spencer's blog.*

As we can see, the six posts selected either triggered a dispute over these controversial issues or contributed to a dispute already initiated in another blogpost. These posts and comments are part of more widespread disputes between supporters and critics of opposing views regarding these three issues. The three controversies were initiated by critics to the three publications mentioned above and developed not only in these blogs but also in other online forums, especially in other blogs. In some cases bloggers or commenters make reference to a comment in another blog or link to a thread in another forum. The fact that online controversies may spread across different sites and reach a large public reflects that the participation framework for these interactions is different from that of face-to-face interaction. Commenters may respond to a specific blog entry or comment, but their responses are probably intended for a larger readership, including people contributing to the thread in the blog and other readers that may get to this blog from other online forums.

Analytical Framework

In order to examine how participants in science blog discussions express allegiance to a group, I analyzed the corpus looking for indicators both of social presence and of rude or verbally offensive behaviour. Most studies of social presence in CMC have used content analysis and have adopted, with some minor changes, the analytical template developed by Rourke, Anderson, Garrison, and Archer (1999) to assess social presence in online discussions. Rourke et al. (1999) identified twelve indicators of social presence belonging to three categories: affective indicators, interactive indicators, and indicators of cohesiveness and group commitment. Since indicators of social presence provide evidence of affectivity, engagement and solidarity, it is a useful concept to consider when analyzing positive relational behaviour in any type of CMC. However, in order to analyze antisocial behaviour we need an analytical template which also includes indicators of impoliteness and hostile/ flaming behaviour. The notion of impoliteness, proposed by Culpeper (1996) to account for the cases in which the speaker does not attempt to support the other's face but to be explicitly impolite, has been fruitfully used in recent research to explore rudeness and hostility in CMC contexts (Angouri & Tselinga, 2010; Lorenzo-Dus et al., 2011; Upadhyay, 2010).

The data in this study were analyzed on a coding scheme developed by the author for the analysis of entries and comments in academic blogs (Luzón, 2011). This coding scheme was in turn based on Rourke et al.'s (1999) categories and further research on social presence in CMC (e.g. Swan & Shih, 2005), but also on research on interpersonal interaction, especially in casual conversation (Eggins & Slade, 1997) and academic written and spoken discourse (e.g. Hyland, 2000; 2008), uninhibited behaviour and impoliteness (e.g. Culpeper, 1996; Wang, 1996), and on indicators emerging from the data.

The coding scheme includes three categories of indicators of social presence: *affective indicators* (i.e. personal expressions of emotion, feelings and mood), *cohesive indicators* (i.e. verbal behaviours that convey a sense of group commitment, such as inclusive pronouns) and *interactive indicators* (i.e. indicators providing evidence that the other is attending to the interaction and willing

to contribute). It also includes three categories of indicators of rude/ antisocial behaviour: *indicators of negative socioemotional behaviour* (i.e. personal expressions of negative emotions or feelings which project conflict), *indicators of group exclusion* (i.e. expressions of relational dominance and refusal to consider the other as a valid member of the community), and *indicators of confrontational interaction* (i.e. interaction intended to seek confrontation). The different types of indicators of social and antisocial behaviour that were coded for, with their definition, are presented respectively in Tables 1 and 2. As can be seen, indicators include micro-linguistic features (e.g. pronouns) and discourse-pragmatic features (e.g. humour, disagreement, irony). For a list of research sources that justify the inclusion of these indicators in the coding scheme see Luzón (2011). Two coders (the author and a second trained coder) independently identified and coded indicators of social and antisocial behaviour in the corpus, with an intercoder reliability rate of 0.85 (Holsti, 1969). Disagreements were resolved through discussion and consensus.

The quantitative analysis involved in coding and quantifying indicators provides interesting results on the incidence of the different types of indicators in science blog argumentative discussions and helps to reveal patterns of relational behaviour. However, as Herring (2010) rightly points out, this approach is not suitable to analyze interaction through blog entries and comments. In the first place, several elements may function as indicators of either social or antisocial behaviour depending on the context (e.g. emoticons, vocatives, second person pronoun). In addition, the analysis of discourse-pragmatic features requires taking into account one or several previous messages, that is, previous turns in the conversation. Finally, as we will see later on, the social or antisocial behaviour of participants is not signalled by a single indicator but by several, which work together to reinforce and stress the writer's posi-

Table 1. Indicators of social behaviour

Indicator	Definition
AFFECTIVE	
Paralanguage	Non verbal expressions of emotion (e.g. acronyms, emoticons, repetitious punctuation)
Informal expressions of oral discourse	----
Verbal expressions of emotion	Use of words that indicate positive emotion
Humour	Affective use of humour (teasing, understatements, jokes). Forms of jocularity that seem to be intended to elicit amusement.
Self-disclosure	Sharing personal information
COHESIVE	
Vocatives	Addressing or referring to participants by name
Inclusive pronouns	Using inclusive pronouns to refer to the group
Appeal to shared knowledge	Expressions that reflect the sharing of knowledge
INTERACTIVE	
Acknowledgement	Quoting from and referring directly to the contents of others' messages
Approval	Positive evaluation expressing approval or interest; complimenting; thanking
Agreement/ Polite disagreement	Expressions of agreement or mild/hedged disagreement with others' messages
Collaboratively following the thread	Answering questions; giving further information
Request/ invitation to respond	Asking questions or otherwise inviting response

Table 2. Indicators of antisocial behaviour

Indicator	Definition
NEGATIVE SOCIEMOTIONAL BEHAVIOUR	
Paralanguage	Non verbal expressions of negative emotion (e.g. emoticons, capitalization)
Verbal expressions of emotion	Conventional expressions of negative emotion
Irony, sarcasm	Antisocial use of humour- sarcasm, irony
GROUP EXCLUSION	
Vocatives	Addressing or referring to participants by name (to identify the target of the attack)
Excluding you	Using "you" contrasting it with an explicit or implicit "we"
Personal attacks	Insults, calling names, use of derogatory nominations
Disassociate from the other	Denying common ground with the other
CONFRONTATIONAL INTERACTION	
Argument criticism	Negative evaluation of the other's argument (e.g. adjectives); rebuking or criticizing the other's argument
Quoting and referring to for confrontation	Cut-and-paste editing for mocking or for strong disagreement
Strong disagreement/ correction	Expressions used to disagree or correct the other without redressing
Imperatives/ directives	Using imperatives and directives for confrontation

tion. Therefore, a careful analysis of the indicators in their context was necessary in order to determine how they are used by participants to express consensus with the members of the ingroup and conflict with members of the group holding opposing views.

RESULTS

Tables 3 and 4 present the frequencies of indicators of social and antisocial behaviour. In the postings analyzed the incidence of indicators of antisocial behaviour (1.84 indicators per message) was considerably higher than that of indicators of social behaviour (1.26 indicators per posting). In the remainder of the paper I will focus my attention on the analysis of the different indicators.

Indicators of Social Behaviour

Affective Indicators

Previous research has shown that social indicators of affectivity are relatively frequent in academic blogs (both in entries and comments) (Luzón, 2011). However, these markers are scarce in messages contributing to scientific controversies: there are only two occurrences of humour (see example 1, where the humourous effect is constructed by linking to content outside the blog), six of verbal expressions of emotion (e.g. "it puzzled the hell out of me") and five of self-disclosure. Four of these five examples occur in the threads over vaccination, where participants talk about personal experiences which help to provide evidence for their position (example 2).

1. *Women tend to be driven by culture to non-scientific careers, and as a result simple statistics mean that men will dominate. At least until all the gender bending chemicals in our food and environment feminize a lot more men [link to an article in The Telegraph,*

with the title "Why are boys turning into girls"] (Aetiology)

2. *My 11-year old daughter is vaccinated for HPV. My 9-year-old son will be vaccinated. I wish they'd had the vaccine when I was younger, so I didn't have first-hand knowledge of the Smoke Shark, who still haunts my dreams (Aetiology)*

The most frequent affective markers are informal expressions of oral discourse (e.g. "Gotcha," "I dunno") which help to convey the sense of immediacy, and paralanguage, i.e. acronyms, emoticons, manipulation of grammatical markers (e.g. "Faaantastic"), and parenthetical metalinguistic cues (e.g. 'Argh', 'Ohhhhh'). Examples (3) and (4) illustrate different functions of emoticons:

3. **Abel @ #10:** *Difficult to figure out as there are a) multiple submissions from many blogs, b) multi-author blogs, c) people who write on multiple blogs, d) blogs whose title does not tell me immediately "Oh, I know this blog and the author is M or F," e) blogs whose authors hide their gender and I don't know, and f) so many hundreds of entries to check....:-S (The Intersection)*

4. *Apologies to Dr Dawkins if I've maligned his editorial decisions based on a faulty understanding of the book's remit. I look forward to seeing the writing of this generation of female science writers (or scientists who write) represented in the sequel tome, when it comes out in 2108 ;) (The Intersection)*

Example (3) is an answer to another comment by Abel. The frowning face expresses the writer's sadness for not being able to answer Abel's question and thus satisfy the needs of a member of the blogging community. Example (4) is an answer to a comment by Dr Dawkins, where he says that the anthology does not include recent contributions. The smiley in (4) is a case of sarcastic or ironical emoticon (Dresner & Herring, 2012), whose function is to emphasize the irony of the comment and

Table 3. Frequencies of indicators of social behaviour

	Controversy 1	Controversy 2	Controversy 3	Total
Paralanguage	4	5	4	13
Expressions of oral discourse	3	14	1	18
Verbal expression of emotion	3	3	0	6
Humour	1	0	1	2
Self-disclosure	0	5	0	5
Total affective	**11**	**27**	**6**	**44**
Vocatives	9	8	18	35
Inclusive pronouns	25	69	43	137
Appeal to shared knowledge	5	3	6	14
Total cohesive	**39**	**80**	**67**	**186**
Acknowledgement	1	3	2	6
Approval	7	9	6	22
Agree/ disagree	8	5	2	15
Collaboration	35	14	28	77
Request/ invitation	7	7	14	28
Total interactive	**58**	**38**	**52**	**148**
Total social events	**108**	**145**	**125**	**378**

Table 4. Frequencies of indicators of antisocial behaviour

	Controversy 1	Controversy 2	Controversy 3	Total
Paralanguage	9	2	3	14
Verbal expression of emotion	5	11	0	16
Irony, sarcasm	12	8	9	29
Total socioemotional	**26**	**21**	**12**	**59**
Vocatives	15	24	9	48
Excluding you	11	45	15	71
Personal attacks, insults	27	30	24	81
Disassociation	4	9	10	23
Total group exclusion	**57**	**108**	**58**	**223**
Argument criticism	11	26	25	62
Quoting and referring	16	19	20	55
Disagreeing/ correcting	53	44	41	138
Imperatives/ directives	9	4	3	16
Total confrontational	**89**	**93**	**89**	**271**
Total antisocial events	**172**	**222**	**159**	**553**

to indicate that the message's propositional content is not to be taken seriously. Emoticons like the one in (4) have been considered social indicators because they are intended for the ingroup members. Irony has two audiences, "one who is essentially the 'butt' of the irony and another audience who is 'in' to the ironical intent and appreciates the irony" (Attardo, 2001, pp. 117). Ironic comments strengthen the in-group links with that audience who shares the negative evaluation and appreciates the humour in the comment. The emoticon in (4) is clearly a wink to the readers who are "in" to the ironical comment.

Cohesive Indicators

The number of indicators of cohesive behaviour was higher, the most frequent being inclusive pronouns (45.6 per 100 messages) and vocatives (11.6 per 100 messages). Inclusive pronouns are frequently used by participants in weblog controversies to refer to the whole readership of the blog (e.g. 5) with the purpose of bringing the readers to the writer's interpretation and opinion or reminding them of shared knowledge. They may also refer to a narrower group, such as participants sharing the writer's opinion or other members of the writer's discipline. In example (6) the context of the claim suggests that "we" refers to those climate scientists researching "cloud feedback" who share the writer's views on this topic.

5. *But we owe it to a generation of our kids to offer that protection now, and not in 10 years time when it's too late and they have already been infected (The Crux).*
6. *Dessler's paper claims to show that cloud feedback is indeed positive (...). This would in turn support the IPCC's claim that anthropogenic global warming will become an increasingly serious problem in the future. Unfortunately, the central evidence*

contained in the paper is weak at best, and seriously misleading at worst. It uses flawed logic to ignore recent advancements we have made in identifying cloud feedback (Roy Spencer's blog).

As in other types of online discussions forums (see Moshtagh, 2009), in weblog discussions vocatives are used to identify the addressee when there are a high number of comments to a blog entry (or to identify the different addressees when the writer replies to several previous comments), and to establish and maintain social relationships. In some cases the writer uses the number of the comment to identify the addressee, alone or in combination with the vocative (see example 3). Finally, although jargon and the use of specialized terminology is frequent in the corpus, there were only 14 examples of explicit references to shared understanding, in some cases in combination with first person pronoun (e.g. "we know this happens with other vaccines").

Interactive Indicators

The most frequent interactive indicator was collaboration: participants express their engagement by contributing further to the issue introduced in the post in a collaborative mode, i.e. adding further information, providing references and links that could be useful for the discussion, answering questions. Some participants in controversial threads contribute to the discussion without taking any sides or provide information to support one side of the argument without making this support explicit. In those cases, it is usually clear for anyone following the discussion thread which side the writer is taking. In example (7), the author clearly supports the view that female science writers are underrepresented in Dawkins book:

7. *Just did a quick eye-scan of Open Laboratory anthologies, which are community collected, judged and edited.*
   2006: 10 women out of 51 entries included in the book.
   2007: 18 out of 53
   2008: 17 out of 52
   Not yet 50% but better than Dawkins.... (The Intersection)

In many cases collaboration takes the form of linking to sites where readers (or a specific reader) may find information that helps to support one position in the controversy or information the addressee is interested to get. Hyperlinks are very useful in online argumentation since they provide support by using external sources of data. The commenter in example (8) provides information for a previous commenter who has shown his/her interest in that information:

8. *"If Lindzen has written a follow-up to his debunked 2009 paper, I have not seen it in press yet."* [quotation from previous comment]
   http://www.eike-klima-energie.eu/uploads/media/Lindzen_Choi_ERBE_JGR_v4.pdf Submitted to JGR apparently, although I am unsure if it has finally been published (Roy Spencer's blog)

Other cohesive indicators are scarce in the corpus. Although acknowledgement and approval are frequent moves in science blog comments (Luzón, 2011), this is not the case in the comments contributing to controversial threads (see (9) for an example of approval). Surprisingly, there are also few comments with explicit expressions of agreement (5 occurrences per 100 messages) (see examples (10) and (11)). The expressions of agreement are frequently combined with markers of opposition to the views of the other group, as illustrated in example (12) where "I agree with dyson" is used to support criticism targeted at another

participant. Similarly, in (13d) the writer aligns himself with previous commenters (13b/13c) who share his disagreement on the "innocent" nature of some cellular abnormalities expressed in the blog entry "Should Boys Be Given the HPV Vaccine?" (13a):

9. *Dr. Dessler, thanks for the direction to the e-mails. Really enjoyed reading them and experiencing two scientists bouncing their theoroms off of each other. Really nice to see science evolving before my eyes. Keep it up! (Real Climate)*

10. *ARJ has hit the nail on the head perfectly (Aetiology)*

11. *There are, as Ms Lenzer points out, many reasons to worry about the push to have this vaccine given widely (The Crux)*

12. *I'll second dyson's comments.(..) I agree with dyson that many of your arguments are cherry picked and ideological (The Crux)*

13. a. *...most of the cervical changes (...) were innocent cellular abnormalities (The Crux)*
    b. *I do again disagree strongly with the "innocent" comment. This description is incredibly minimizing to every woman who's ever had to deal with treatment/removal of a lesion.*
    c. *'Innocent cellular abnormalities', my ass.*
    d. *Yeah, something which has a 1 in 20 chance of becoming cancer doesn't seem "innocent" to me (Aetiology)*

A few messages are used to ask questions or otherwise invite/ request response. There are various types of social questions and requests in a controversy. Commenters may ask for information that others may have or for another participant's opinion, or they may ask for clarification when there is a problem of misunderstanding or vagueness. In all cases the question reflects the questioner's assumption of an intimate relation and of the others' willingness to answer or give support.

14. *Just for comparisons sake, does any one have information about clinical trials for men that is not funded by Merck? (Aetiology)*

Indicators of Antisocial Behaviour

See Table 4 for the frequencies of indicators of antisocial behaviour.

Socioemotional Indicators

Paralanguage and verbal expressions of emotion can act not only as markers of positive socioemotional behaviour, but also of negative behaviour, as the following examples illustrate:

15. *wtf. pointless to the point of frustration (The Intersection)*
16. *— this vaccine has NOT been shown to prevent actual CANCER (as opposed to cellular neoplasia) in any meaningful way (Aetiology)*
17. *BAAAAAAAAAHAHAHAHAHA…. obscurity, you crack me up… now go back to that page where you got all the ENSO related terms from and start reading… but don't try to understand MJO just yet, that's way too advanced for you (Roy Spencer's blog)*

Example (15) is the end of a comment on the blogger's post, where the acronym "wtf" (what the fuck) is used to reinforce the criticism and disagreement with the post. In (16) capitals emphasize disagreement with the view expressed in a previous comment and in (17) the parenthetical metalinguistic cue "BAAAAAAAAAAHAHAHA-HAHA" is combined with verbal expression of emotion, used ironically ("You crack me up"), and with a personal attack questioning the intelligence of the addressee. In these controversial threads the number of verbal expressions of emotion to convey rude behaviour is higher than the number of these expressions as markers of social behaviour. Other examples are "I am getting so terribly tired

of hearing these empty words," "It's a shame," "Very disappointed," "Knock me down with a feather," or "My ass," used to express disbelief.

A very frequent marker of antisocial behaviour in weblog comments is irony and sarcasm. Since, in addition to the target of the irony, ironical comments have another audience who shares the ironical intent and appreciates the irony (Attardo, 2001), irony helps both to construct conflict and refute others' arguments by ridiculing them and to construe consensus with those that are "in" to the ironical comment. For instance, in the thread about the low number of women in the *The Oxford Book of Modern Science Writing* there are several ironical comments alluding to the fact that it is nonsense to expect a quota for any group (e.g. 18). The fake intimacy conveyed by discursive markers ("mind you," "right?") in these examples emphasizes the irony, the condescending tone and the playful hostility.

18. *In addition to being a misogynist, the list of authors also reflects Dawkins is a racist: mind you, 1/4 of the authors should have been Chinese, 1/5 Indians, etc. in order to reflect the world's population. Also, he's a homophobe for not including at least 3 gay authors. And he seems to be oblivious to the fact that the world isn't limited to Europe and North America. Right? (Aetiology)*

Indicators of Group Exclusion

There is a high number of messages (74.3 per 100 messages) where the participants want to make it clear that they and the addressee(s), or other people referred to, belong to two opposing collectives. Two markers of group exclusion frequent in weblog controversies are vocatives and second person pronouns. While vocatives may be a marker of intimacy and solidarity in weblog controversies, they may also be used to identify the target of an attack. For instance in the entry "The science boy's club strikes again" in *Aetiology*, the blogger quotes a fragment of a comment in another blog and then she uses the vocative to introduce a condescending remark (e.g. 19). The author implies an intimacy with the addressee that does not exist, and this way construes the vocative as negatively marked. The fact that commenters consciously use vocatives to boost the hostility of the comment is shown by the comment in example (20). This comment was not taken from the analyzed corpus but belongs to another discussion thread on the paper on cloud positive feedback by Andrew Dessler.

19. *Other comments in the thread are also depressing. Dave24 notes:*
    The author of the material doesn't matter. The substance does. Dawkins created a collection of works that he personally found relevant and important. (...)
    Yes Dave, I'm sure we're all well aware these are Dawkins' personal preferences. The question is *why* are those choices so "weiner-centric" (Aetiology)

20. *Andrew, first, please don't take offense to the familiar term of address, it's simply that I don't know the appropriate formal term, such as Dr. or Prof, or Mr...(Watts up with that)*

The second person pronoun is very frequently used to attack the opponent, establishing an opposition between two collectives of arguers, "we" and "you." "You" may refer to an individual addressee or to a whole group of people holding a view. The pronoun "you" is often combined with imperatives or aggressive questions intended to attack the opponent.

21. *Could you please stop entertaining conspiracy theories and mixing your belief system and politics with science. (Roy Spencer's blog)*

In the corpus, there are also instances of personal attacks, derogatory nominations, put-downs, and blatant insults towards people who hold different views on an issue. Since the controversies in the corpus are carried out in science blogs, opponents are sometimes accused of not having enough expert knowledge to contribute to debate in this environment or of not complying with the norms and methodology of scientific research or the moral values of science, e.g. objectivity, disinterestedness. That way, the credibility of those on the other side is undermined. The commenters in examples (22-23) question the intelligence and the knowledge of the addressees (or of the target of the attack), as a way to belittle their statements. The commenters in examples (24-26) characterize other participants as not proceeding scientifically in the research of this issue, thus suggesting that their claims are not valid.

22. *Unlike you, I am sane and have some degree of intelligence (Aetiology)*

23. *Obscurity, I can't believe I'm reading this... you're debating a subject which requires a working knowledge of ENSO, yet you do not possess that knowledge (Roy Spencer's blog)*

24. *As-is, you've "framed" your point very well. Accuracy be damned, of course, as it always is on The Intersection. Sheesh (The Intersection)*

25. *Your smug, ad hominem and holiler-than-thou blog is full of all sorts of anti-scientific claims that should make an epidemiologist blush (Aetiology)*

26. *You conveniently ignore all this by adopting a stance that violates the fundamental tenets of scientific reasoning, by ASSUMING, uncritically and without evidence, that vaccinating 7 year olds will solve any or all of these problems (Aetiology)*

There are also expressions to deny common ground with the other and show that the people that are the target of the criticism belong to a different group:

27. *But if this is the best they can do, the scientists aligning themselves with the IPCC really are running out of ideas to help shore up their climate models (Roy Spencer's blog)*

Indicators of Confrontational Interaction

This is the category of indicators of antisocial behaviour with the highest number of occurrences (90.3 per 100 messages). Although explicit quoting is the least frequent of these indicators, there is a high number of references to others' comments. Many of the occurrences of disagreement or argument criticism are combined either with explicit quoting or with different types of intertextual references (e.g. summaries, paraphrases, interpretations) to previous comments, as can be seen in the examples illustrating disagreement and argument criticism below.

In the controversy corpus participants often quote parts of other messages in order to answer and refute them. This citation-and-reply strategy contributes to the structural coherence of conversation developed in comments by providing a link between separate messages, and helps to contextualize the response and select which parts of the previous message the participant is responding to (Severinson, 2010). In her analysis of intertextuality within a newsgroup discussion on racial discrimination, Hodsdon-Champeon (2010) found that quotations were often used to express a negative stance towards the statements in the quoted text. Similarly, in our corpus quoting is very frequently combined with disagreeing: participants quote fragments from other texts to challenge others' views and strengthen their own argument (e.g. 28). In many cases participants fo-

cus on an evaluative word used by an opponent to show their disagreement with that evaluation, e.g. "solid" in example (28) and "pointless" in example (29). Participants in the controversial threads also use another strategy typical of online discussions (e.g. Hodsdon-Champeon, 2010; Severinson, 2010): interspersing quotations and responses to create the illusion of "multiple conversational turns" in a single message. Commenters enhance the force of their arguments by shifting between statements that disagree with their stance and their own statements supporting this stance.

28. *@Amos Zeeberg, who said about Jeannes latest comment:*
   While this is her personal take, it's a scientifically solid and interesting one, so we're happy to help get it out.
   Jeanne has tackled none of the science, and her response is hardly scientifically "solid." It consists of sleight of hand evasions of the issue of vaccine efficacy, cherry-picked quotes to support her confirmation bias, and multiple strawmen. (The Crux)

29. *This isn't just "pointless." It's yet one more example of women being overlooked and dismissed. (This comment is an answer to a previous comment: "Taking into account the sex of each author is completely pointless.") (Aetiology)*

Disagreeing and correcting always involve some (implicit or explicit) reference to the content of one or several previous messages. For instance, the comments in (30b/c) are a response to that in (30a), which in turn is used by the author (the editor of *Discover*, the magazine in whose blog the post which is the object of the controversy was published) to disagree with objections to Lenzen's claims in previous comments, labelling them "philosophical." These three turns in the controversial exchange reflect how participants use disagreement and intertextuality to align themselves with other participants and against the other collective of arguers. Example (31b) is an answer to a statement in Lenzen's blog entry (31a), but what the author does is to provide his own interpretation of Lenzen's words and disagree with it. Attribution involving interpretation and judgement (e.g. interpreting someone' words, attributing a belief to somebody, accusing someone of something) seems to be frequent in conflict articles (Hunston, 2005) to criticize previous researchers. In the controversy corpus commenters also very frequently offer their own (sometimes biased) summaries and interpretations of others' words, but, unlike in conflict articles, the other has the possibility to respond. Therefore, correction sometimes implies defending oneself from an accusation made by a member of the opposing group and accusing the other of misrepresenting one's words and of trying to undermine one's credibility (e.g. 32):

30. *a. Hi. I think some of these points are subjective, nearly philosophical questions.*
    b. Hi Amos, I disagree strongly that much of it is philosophical, but will wait to see the response.
    c. Amos, Misrepresenting the study endpoints, misrepresenting the diseases that can be prevented and their seriousness, misrepresenting the relative frequency of side effects is NOT "philosophical" in the slightest. (The Crux)

31. *We already have a pretty terrific way to prevent most cervical cancer deaths, and it's called the Pap smear.*
    The pap smear is a screen and it's disingenuous to suggest that it's a good alternative to an effective vaccine. (The Crux)

32. *You also make accusations not in evidence. I've never suggested an either/or approach for cancer control. I think the vaccine should be yet another tool in the arsenal. (Aetiology)*

Participants also attack others' position by evaluating negatively their claims, arguments, ideas or theories (e.g. "false arguments," "flawed analysis," "weak evidence," "incorrect conclusions," "unsupported hypothesis"). These criticisms are related to the values of the scientific community and to the criteria by which members of this community are judged, e.g. competence in research and argument. Opponents are often criticized for using logical fallacies in their arguments, e.g. making a naked assertion (i.e. an assertion without any evidence, proof, or other support), resorting to strawman arguments (i.e. arguments based on the deliberate misrepresentation of the opponent's position) or ignoring/ missing important facts and thus deriving false conclusions.

33. *The reductio ad absurdum 'arguments' that various other minorities were also not represented seems disingenuous, given that women are half the human race, not 10-20% (Aetiology)*

34. *First, your attempt to compare the abortive attempts to do carotid artery bypasses to the HPV vaccine trials is comparing chalk and cheese (The Crux)*

35. *You are ignoring the fact that to determine the effect of clouds on SST you can't take just the downward shortwave effect and ignore the cloud greenhouse effect (Real Climate)*

36. *What does she base this conclusion on? (...) She uses the 4-year-old NEJM study demonstrating the efficacy of the then-new vaccine as the main basis of her claim, and it's a house of cards from there. (Aetiology)*

As many of the examples in this chapter have shown, markers of relational behaviour do not occur in isolation but combine with other markers to achieve the desired effect. This can be clearly seen is in the following longer fragment of a comment in the blog *The Crux*:

37. @raz:

I take it you are accusing the scientists who conducted these studies of having financial reasons to dismiss research findings unacceptable to the funders of their research. That's quite a claim. Let's break it down. By the phrase "dismissing research findings unacceptable to their sponsors" you imply that they will not only dismiss their "true" findings, but of course they will have to substitute alternative "favorable" data, in other words deliberately falsify what their own research has found. (..).

I don't think you comprehend who is doing this research either – their careers are not dependent upon one pharma sponsor. Look at the dozens of institutions mentioned in the Appendix, would you, and the clinical and research centers they come from and positions they hold. (...)

All quite implausible, I think any rational person would agree. I am sorry your arguments here seem to have degenerated to the level of whining: "Pharma shill!." I'd far rather discuss the science. But then most antivaccine campaigners prefer the easy option. (The Crux)

The writer uses different types of antisocial indicators to oppose and attack another commenter and by doing so express his allegiance to an ideological position: vocatives to identify the target of the attack ("@raz"), second person pronouns with report verbs which interpret and evaluate ("you are accusing," "you imply"), combined with imperatives and impolite requests ("Look," "would you"), point-by-point quoting and disagreeing, personal attacks involving claiming incomprehension on the part of the target and insults ("I don't think you comprehend" "Any rational person would agree"), argument criticism ("your arguments here seem to have degenerated to the level of whining"), disassociation between "I" and "you"- "most

antivaccine campaigners" (you whine/ I discuss the science). All these devices help the writer to discredit the previous commenter and refute his claim, and at the same time disassociate himself from the people defending this view and show his allegiance to the group standing for the opposite view, which is presented as supported by science.

DISCUSSION OF RESULTS

The analysis of relational communication in academic or science-related online forums can profit from a combination of methods used for the analysis of online discourse, academic discourse, and conversational discourse. The coding scheme used here for content analysis included indicators used in previous research of social presence in online discussions. However, as the purpose of the research was to study social and antisocial behaviour in science blog controversial exchanges, I also considered features that discourse analysts, especially those studying academic discourse and conversational discourse, have identified as markers of affectivity, engagement, solidarity or conflict (e.g. vocatives, humour, indicators of shared knowledge, irony). Some of these markers (e.g. argument criticism) are closely tied to the values of the academic community and to what is considered as acceptable behaviour in this community.

The quantitative content analysis has revealed patterns in the discourse of controversial exchanges in science blogs. Participants in these interactions use discursive strategies aimed at creating and maintaining affective and solidarity relations in the community but also strategies intended to construe confrontation and conflict. The analysis has shown that indicators of antisocial behaviour are remarkably more frequent than indicators of social behaviour. This finding contrasts with results of previous research on comments in science/ academic blogs (Luzón, 2011) which revealed a much higher incidence of indicators of social behaviour, suggesting that commenters in science blogs tend to favor a supportive and collaborative attitude rather than an antagonistic one. This study therefore shows that controversial discussions in science weblogs have distinctive features and that participants in these controversies signal their allegiance to a particular group by construing conflict with those who support rival theories/ideas, rather than by using indicators of solidarity. This is in agreement with previous findings that the expression of disagreement and conflict is used by writers in argumentative discourse to identify themselves with a group (Hunston, 2005; Upadhyay, 2010). For instance, Hunston (2005) suggests that some distinctive features of conflict articles (i.e. articles where a writer explicitly expresses his/her opposition to another writer or paper) are intended to construct and strengthen consensus with members of a disciplinary subgroup. In the same line, Upadhyay (2010) found that respondents in online forums use linguistic impoliteness to refute a group's ideological views and thus identify themselves with another collective holding opposing views.

In each of the controversies analyzed here members of the blogging community take part in the interaction to align themselves with others who share their ideological point of view and against others advocating for the opposite viewpoint. However, a qualitative analysis of the data reveals that some indicators of social behaviour are not used to express affiliation to one of the two antagonistic collectives involved in the controversy, but to express solidarity and engagement with the whole blogging community interacting through a specific blog (or through several related blogs). This is the case, for instance, of contributions to the thread where the commenter does not want to take sides but only to share information and express reciprocity and sociability with anybody sharing their interest in the topic, or of comments with affective indicators intended to attenuate the polarized antagonistic tone of the discussion.

As pointed above, although a quantitative analysis uncovers patterns in science weblog controversies and reveals that these interactions have distinctive features, indicators of relational behaviour are context-dependent and determining their function in the interaction requires a qualitative analysis. The detailed examination of long threads of comments has made it possible to analyze the intertextual relations between messages and to discover how participants react to previous messages in order to align themselves with a previous writer's stance or oppose it. This qualitative analysis also shows that interpersonal relations and group allegiance are not usually signaled by isolated indicators, but by several indicators combined in a single message to strengthen the writer's stance.

FUTURE RESEARCH DIRECTIONS

The coding scheme used to analyze social and rude or verbally offensive behaviour in this research could be applied to the analysis of relations in any type of online interaction. While other pieces of research focus either on social behaviour, e.g. studies of politeness or social presence (Rourke et al., 1999; Swan & Shih, 2002), or rude/ hostile behaviour (Upadhyay, 2010), I propose here a more encompassing framework which allows to examine both aspects of relational interaction. This seems to be a suitable framework if we take into account that various indicators are usually combined to convey the writer's intended meaning.

This paper is part of a larger research agenda on the features of academic/ science weblogs and their place within the system of academic genres. Academic blogs may fill a gap in scholarly communication as spaces which facilitate new social practices and new ways to interact. The technological affordances of weblogs provide an extension of the social contexts in which scholars can interact not only with peers but also with the interested public. The analytical framework proposed here could be used to study how discourse in online academic forums (and more specifically in academic blogs) differs from or compares to discourse in other scientific forums, i.e. academic interactions in formal and informal contexts, such as discussion sessions in conferences or academic seminars, coffee talks, hallway interactions. It can also be used to compare academic weblog discourse to the discourse of academic genres where criticism and conflict are allowed, both those where positive and negative evaluation may be provided (e.g. reviews, referee reports) and those where negative evaluation and criticism is more frequent (e.g. editorials, conflict papers).

In addition, since science blogs are open forums where anybody can contribute, future studies could examine whether the offline identity of participants, in the cases where this identity is made public (e.g. their status as researchers working in a research institution; their gender), influences the way they use the strategies analyzed here to construct their online identity.

CONCLUSION

This study has shown that participants in science blog controversies use a wide range of discourse strategies to identify themselves with one of two antagonistic groups and to defend the ideological view of this group. Relationship forming and maintaining in online forums is a dynamic and ongoing process and the identities of the commenters as members of a group sharing an ideological position is constructed interactionally, through their responses to previous writers.

In order to maintain the position of the group and to show allegiance to that group, contenders usually adopt strategies that attack and refute the opponents' stance rather than strategies that express affectivity and solidarity with their ingroup. Although this blatant attack of others is not common in other types of academic discourse, the features and technological affordances of weblogs facilitate the development of an individual's social

identity and support the desire of individuals to affiliate to defend their (and their social groups') positions. Weblogs are social spaces which offer scholars and interested public the possibility to engage in controversial discussion, without having to adhere to the strict politeness constraints of other academic genres.

The discourse of science weblog controversies is a hybrid discourse, which combines elements and practices deriving from academic culture with others inspired in other formats of CMC, and should therefore be analyzed considering the values of academic discourse, the dialogic nature of online discussion forums, and the technological affordances of weblogs. Therefore, the integration of concepts used for the analysis of interpersonality/ social presence and conflict/ hostility in academic discourse and online discourse facilitates the identification of indicators of relational behaviour and their function. The analytical model used in this research, where quantitative and qualitative analysis complement each other, offers a comprehensive means of investigating the resources used by participants in science blog controversies to express their allegiance to a group and ideological commitment. The close qualitative analysis of the indicators in the corpus reveals how opponents defend their ideological stance and the ways in which they negotiate their relationship both with their in-group and with the out-group.

REFERENCES

Angouri, J., & Tseliga, T. (2010). "You have no idea what you are talking about!" From e-disagreement to e-impoliteness in two online fora. *Journal of Politeness Research, Language, Behaviour, Culture*, 6(1), 57–82.

Attardo, S. (2001). *Humorous texts: A semantic and pragmatic analysis*. Berlin, Germany: Mouton de Gruyter. doi:10.1515/9783110887969.

Baym, N. (2006). Interpersonal life online. In Livingstone, S., & Lievrouw, L. (Eds.), *The handbook of new media* (pp. 62–76). London, UK: Sage Publications.

Boyd, D., Golder, S., & Lotan, G. (2010, January). *Tweet, tweet, retweet: Conversational aspects of retweeting on Twitter*. Paper presented at the Hawaii International Conference on System Sciences (HICSS-43), Kauai, HI.

Boyd, S. (2003). Are you ready for social software? *Darwin Magazine (IDG)*. Retrieved June 11, 2012, from http://stoweboyd.com/post/2325281845/are-you-ready-for-social-software

Crystal, D. (2006). *Language and the Internet.* Cambridge, UK: Cambridge University Press. doi:10.1017/CBO9780511487002.

Culpeper, J. (1996). Towards an anatomy of impoliteness. *Journal of Pragmatics, 25,* 349–367. doi:10.1016/0378-2166(95)00014-3.

Davies, J., & Merchant, G. (2007). Looking from the inside out: Academic blogging as new literacy. In Lankshear, C., & Knobel, M. (Eds.), *A new literacies sampler* (pp. 167–198). New York, NY: Peter Lang.

Dawkins, R. (2008). *The Oxford book of modern science writing*. Oxford, UK: Oxford University Press.

Delahunty, J. (2012). "Who am I?:" Exploring identity in online discussion forums. *International Journal of Educational Research, 53,* 407–420. doi:10.1016/j.ijer.2012.05.005.

Dennen, V., & Pashnyak, T. (2008). Finding community in the comments: The role of reader and blogger responses in a weblog community of practice. *International Journal of Web Based Communities, 4*(3), 272–283. doi:10.1504/IJWBC.2008.019189.

Derks, D., Fischer, A. H., & Bos, A. E. R. (2008). The role of emotion in computer-mediated communication: A review. *Computers in Human Behavior, 24,* 766–785. doi:10.1016/j.chb.2007.04.004.

Dresner, E., & Herring, S. C. (2012). Emoticons and illocutionary force. In Riesenfel, D., & Scarafile, G. (Eds.), *Philosophical dialogue: Writings in honor of Marcelo Dascal* (pp. 59–70). London, UK: College Publication.

Efimova, L., & de Moor, A. (2005). Beyond personal web publishing: An exploratory study of conversational blogging practices. In *Proceedings of the 38th Annual Hawaii International Conference on System Sciences (HICSS'05)*. Retrieved May 5, 2012, from http://origin-www.computer.org/csdl/proceedings/hicss/2005/2268/04/22680107a.pdf

Eggins, S., & Slade, S. D. (1997). *Analysing casual conversation*. London, UK: Cassell.

Fairclough, N. (1992). *Discourse and social change*. Malden, MA: Blackwell.

Fairclough, N. (1995). *Media discourse*. London, UK: Arnold.

Herring, S. C. (2007). A faceted classification scheme for computer-mediated discourse. *Language@Internet, 4,* article 1. Retrieved October 21, 2012, from http://www.languageatinternet.org/articles/2007/761

Herring, S. C. (2010). Web content analysis: Expanding the paradigm. In Hunsinger, J., Allen, M., & Klastrup, L. (Eds.), *The International handbook of Internet research* (pp. 233–249). Berlin, Germany: Springer Verlag.

Hodsdon-Champeon, C. (2010). Conversations within conversations: Intertextuality in racially antagonistic online discourse. *Language@Internet, 7,* article 10. Retrieved May 11, 2012, from http://www.languageatinternet.org/articles/2010/2820.

Holsti, O. R. (1969). *Content analysis for the social sciences and humanities*. Reading, MA: Addison Wesley.

Hunston, S. (2005). Conflict and consensus. Constructing opposition in Applied Linguistics. In Tognini-Bonelli, E., & Lungo Camiciotti, G. (Eds.), *Strategies in academic discourse* (pp. 1–16). Amsterdam: John Benjamins.

Hyland, K. (2000). *Disciplinary discourses: Social interactions in academic writing*. Harlow, UK: Pearson Education Limited.

Hyland, K. (2008). Persuasion, interaction and the construction of knowledge: Representing self and others in research writing. *International Journal of English Studies*, 8(2), 8–18.

Ivanič, R. (1998). *Writing and identity: The discoursal construction of identity in academic writing*. Amsterdam: John Benjamins.

Jones, R. H. (2009). "Inter-activity:" How new media can help us to understand old media. In Rowe, C., & Wyss, E. L. (Eds.), *Language and new media: Linguistic, cultural and technological evolutions* (pp. 13–31). Cresskill, NJ: Hampton Press.

Kiesler, S., Siegel, J., & McGuire, T. W. (1984). Social psychological aspects of computer-mediated communication. *The American Psychologist*, 39, 1123–1134. doi:10.1037/0003-066X.39.10.1123.

Kleinke, S. (2008). Emotional commitment in public political Internet message boards. *Journal of Language and Social Psychology*, 27(4), 409–421. doi:10.1177/0261927X08322483.

Kreijns, K., Kirschner, P. J., & Jochems, W. (2002). The sociability of computer-supported collaborative learning environments. *Journal of Educational Technology & Society*, 5(1), 8–22.

Lampa, G. (2004). Imagining the blogosphere: An introduction to the imagined community of instant publishing. In L. J. Gurak, S. Antonijevic, L. Johnson, C. Ratliff, & J. Reyman (Eds.), *Into the blogosphere: Rhetoric, community, and culture of weblogs*. Retrieved May 5, 2012, from http://blog.lib.umn.edu/blogosphere/imagining_the_blogosphere.html

Lorenzo-Dus, N., Garcés-Conejos, P., & Bou-Franch, P. (2011). On-line polylogues and impoliteness: The case of postings sent in response to the Obama Reggaeton YouTube video. *Journal of Pragmatics*, 43, 2578–2593. doi:10.1016/j.pragma.2011.03.005.

Luzón, M. J. (2011). "Interesting post, but I disagree:" Social presence and antisocial behaviour in academic weblogs. *Applied Linguistics*, 32(5), 517–540. doi:10.1093/applin/amr021.

Mabry, E. A. (1997). Framing flames: The structure of argumentative messages on the net. *Journal of Computer Mediated Communication*, 2(4). Retrieved February 29, 2012 from http://jcmc.indiana.edu/vol2/issue4/mabry.html

Martin, B. (2011). Debating vaccination: Understanding the attack on the Australian Vaccination Network. *Living Wisdom*, 8, 14–40.

Moor, P. J., Heuvelman, A., & Verleur, R. (2010). Flaming on YouTube. *Computers in Human Behavior*, 26(6), 1536–1546. doi:10.1016/j.chb.2010.05.023.

Mortensen, T., & Walker, J. (2002). Blogging thoughts: Personal publication as an online research tool. In A. Morrison (Ed.), Researching ICTs in context (pp. 249-279). Oslo, Norway: InterMedia Report.

Moshtagh, M. (2009). *The development of controversies: From the Early Modern Period to online discussion forums*. Bern, Switzerland: Peter Lang.

Reicher, S., Spears, R., & Postmes, T. (1995). A social identity model of deindividuation phenomena. In Stroebe, W., & Hewstone, M. (Eds.), *European Review of Social Psychology (Vol. 6)*. Chichester, UK: Wiley. doi:10.1080/14792779443000049.

Rourke, L., Anderson, T., Garrison, D. R., & Archer, W. (1999). Assessing social presence in asynchronous, text-based computer conferencing. *Journal of Distance Education*, 14(3), 51–70.

Salager-Meyer, F. (2001). From self-highlightedness to self-effacement: A genre based study of the socio-pragmatic function of criticism in medical discourse. *LSP and Professional Communication, 1*(2), 63–84.

Schmidt, J. (2007). Blogging practices: An analytical framework. *Journal of Computer-Mediated Communication 12*(4), article 13. Retrieved March 15, 2012, from http://jcmc.indiana.edu/vol12/issue4/schmidt.html

Severinson, E. K. (2010). To quote or not to quote: Setting the context for computer-mediated dialogues. *Language@Internet, 7*, article 5. Retrieved May 11, 2012, from http://www.languageatinternet.org/articles/2010/2820

Short, J., Williams, E., & Christie, B. (1976). *The psychology of telecommunication*. London, UK: Wiley.

Simon, B. (2004). *Identity in modern society: A social psychological perspective*. Oxford, UK: Blackwell. doi:10.1002/9780470773437.

Spears, R., & Lea, M. (1994). Panacea or panopticon? The hidden power in computer-mediated communication. *Communication Research, 21*(4), 427–459. doi:10.1177/009365094021004001.

Sproull, L., & Kiesler, S. (1986). Reducing social context cues: Electronic mail in organizational communication. *Management Science, 32*, 1492–1512. doi:10.1287/mnsc.32.11.1492.

Stewart, C. (2009). Socio-scientific controversies: A theoretical and methodological framework. *Communication Theory, 19*, 124–145. doi:10.1111/j.1468-2885.2009.01338.x.

Swan, K., & Shih, L. F. (2005). On the nature and development of social presence in online course discussions. *Journal of Asynchronous Learning Networks, 9*(3), 115–136.

Tajfel, H., & Turner, J. (1986). An integrative theory of intergroup conflict. In Worchel, S., & Austin, G. W. (Eds.), *The social psychology of intergroup relations* (pp. 33–47). Monterey, CA: Brooks/Cole.

Tong, S. T., & Walther, J. B. (2011). Relational maintenance and computer-mediated communication. In Wright, K. B., & Webb, L. M. (Eds.), *Computer-mediated communication in personal relationships* (pp. 98–118). New York, NY: Peter Lang Publishing.

Turkle, S. (1995). *Life on the screen: Identity in the age of the Internet*. New York, NY: Simon and Schuster.

Upadhyay, S. (2010). Identity and impoliteness in computer-mediated reader responses. *Journal of Politeness Research, Language, Behaviour, Culture, 6*(1), 105–127.

Walker, J. (2006). Blogging from inside the ivory tower. In Bruns, A., & Jacobs, J. (Eds.), *Uses of blogs* (pp. 127–138). New York, NY: Peter Lang Publishing.

Walther, J. B. (1996). Computer-mediated communication: Impersonal, interpersonal, and hyperpersonal interaction. *Communication Research, 23*(1), 3–43. doi:10.1177/009365096023001001.

Walther, J. B. (2007). Selective self-presentation in computer-mediated communication: Hyperpersonal dimensions of technology, language, and cognition. *Computers in Human Behavior, 23*, 2538–2557. doi:10.1016/j.chb.2006.05.002.

Walther, J. B. (2010). Computer-mediated communication. In Berger, C. R., Roloff, M. E., & Roskos-Ewoldsen, D. R. (Eds.), *Handbook of communication science* (2nd ed., pp. 489–505). Thousand Oaks, CA: Sage. doi:10.4135/9781412982818.n28.

Walther, J. B. (2011). Theories of computer-mediated communication and interpersonal relations. In Knapp, M. L., & Daly, J. A. (Eds.), *The handbook of interpersonal communication* (4th ed., pp. 443–479). Thousand Oaks, CA: Sage.

Wang, H. (1996). Flaming: More than a necessary evil for academic mailing lists. *The Electronic Journal of Communication, 6*. Retrieved May 11, 2012, from http://www.cios.org/EJCPUB-LIC/006/1/00612.HTML

ADDITIONAL READING

Abrams, Z. (2003). Flaming in CMC: Prometheus' fire or Inferno's? *CALICO Journal, 20*(2), 245–260.

Baym, N. (2010). *Personal connections in the digital age*. Malden, MA: Polity Press.

Baym, N. K., & Zhang, Y. B. (2004). Social interactions across media: Interpersonal communication on the Internet, telephone and face-to-face. *New Media & Society, 6*(3), 299–318. doi:10.1177/1461444804041438.

Blood, R. (2004). How blogging software reshapes the online community. *Communications of the ACM, 47*(12), 53–55. doi:10.1145/1035134.1035165.

Bruns, A. (2008). *Blogs, Wikipedia, Second Life, and beyond: From production to produsage*. New York, NY: Peter Lang.

Culpeper, J. (2008). Reflections on impoliteness, relational work and power. In Bousfield, D., & Locher, M. A. (Eds.), *Impoliteness in language* (pp. 17–44). Berlin, New York: Mouton de Gruyter.

Dennen, V. (2009). Constructing academic alter-egos: Identity issues in a blog-based community. *Identity in the Information Society, 2*(1), 23–38. doi:10.1007/s12394-009-0020-8.

Ewins, R. (2005). Who are you? Weblogs and academic identity. *E-Learning, 2*(4), 368-377. Retrieved May 11, 2012, from http://dx.doi.org/10.2304/elea.2005.2.4.368

Graham, S. L. (2007). Disagreeing to agree: Conflict, (im)politeness and identity in a computer-mediated community. *Journal of Pragmatics, 39*, 742–759. doi:10.1016/j.pragma.2006.11.017.

Herring, S. C. (2001). Computer-mediated discourse. In Schiffrin, D., Tannen, D., & Hamilton, H. E. (Eds.), *Handbook of discourse analysis* (pp. 612–634). Oxford, UK: Blackwell.

Herring, S. C. (2004). Computer-mediated discourse analysis: An approach to researching online behavior. In Barab, S. A., Kling, R., & Gray, J. (Eds.), *Designing for virtual communities in the service of learning* (pp. 338–376). Cambridge, New York: Cambridge University Press. doi:10.1017/CBO9780511805080.016.

Herring, S. C., Scheidt, L. A., Wright, E., & Bonus, S. (2005). Weblogs as a bridging genre. *Information Technology & People, 18*(2), 142–171. doi:10.1108/09593840510601513.

Hyland, K. (2005). Stance and engagement: A model of interaction in academic discourse. *Discourse Studies, 7*(2), 173–192. doi:10.1177/1461445605050365.

Hyland, K., & Diani, G. (Eds.). (2009). *Academic evaluation: Review genres in university settings*. Basingstoke, UK: Palgrave MacMillan. doi:10.1057/9780230244290.

Kirkup, G. (2010). Academic blogging: Academic practice and academic identity. *London Review of Education, 8*(1), 75–84. doi:10.1080/14748460903557803.

Kjellberg, S. (2010). I am a blogging researcher: Motivations for blogging in a scholarly context. *First Monday, 15*(8). Retrieved May 15, 2012, from http://firstmonday.org/htbin/cgiwrap/bin/ojs/index.php/fm/article/view/2962

Lea, M., O'Shea, T., Fung, P., & Spears, R. (1992). "Flaming" in computer-mediated communication: Observations, explanations and implications. In Lea, M. (Ed.), *Contexts of computer-mediated communication* (pp. 89–112). London, UK: Harvester-Wheatsheaf.

Lewin, B. A. (2005). Contentiousness in science: The discourse of critique in two sociology journals. *Text, 25*, 723–744. doi:10.1515/text.2005.25.6.723.

Locher, M. A., & Watts, R. J. (2005). Politeness theory and relational work. *Journal of Politeness Research, 1*(1), 9–33.

Makri, K., & Kynigos, C. (2007). The role of blogs in studying the discourse and social practices of mathematics teachers. *Journal of Educational Technology & Society, 10*(1), 73–84.

Matsuda, P. K. (2002). Negotiation of identity and power in a Japanese online discourse community. *Computers and Composition, 19*(1), 39–55. doi:10.1016/S8755-4615(02)00079-8.

Qian, H., & Scott, C. (2007). Anonymity and self-disclosure on weblogs. *Journal of Computer-Mediated Communication, 12*(4), article 14. Retrieved March 15, 2012, from http://jcmc.indiana.edu/vol12/issue4/qian.html

Rees-Miller, J. (2000). Power, severity, and context in disagreement. *Journal of Pragmatics, 32*(8), 1087–1111. doi:10.1016/S0378-2166(99)00088-0.

Rice, R. L., & Love, G. (1987). Electronic emotion: Socio-emotional content in a computer-mediated communication network. *Communication Research, 14*(1), 85–105. doi:10.1177/009365087014001005.

Stuart, K. (2006). Towards an analysis of academic weblogs. *Revista Alicantina de Estudios Ingleses, 19*, 387–404.

Swan, K. (2002). Immediacy, social presence, and asynchronous discussion. In Bourne, J., & Moore, J. C. (Eds.), *Elements of quality online education* (*Vol. 3*, pp. 157–172). Needham, MA: Sloan Center for Online Education.

Thurlow, C., Lengel, L., & Tomic, A. (2004). *Computer-mediated communication: Social interaction and the Internet*. London, UK: Sage Publications.

Wolf, A. (2000). Emotional expression online: Gender differences in emotion use. *Cyberpsychology & Behavior, 3*(5), 827–833. doi:10.1089/10949310050191809.

KEY TERMS AND DEFINITIONS

Blogging Community: A conversational community formed by people who share similar interests and are connected through blogging tools, i.e. comments, links in the body of the blog entries or in blogrolls.

Group Identity: The sense of one's self as a member of a social group. It is based on a single attribute (e.g. roles, behaviours, attitudes) "that one shares with other, but not all other, people in the relevant social context" (Simon, 2004, p. 50). Identity is dynamic and negotiable, developed through social interactions by means of language.

Indicators of Antisocial Behaviour: Linguistic and discourse-pragmatic features used by writers to construe conflict and disagreement with other participants in the interaction.

Indicators of Social Behaviour: Linguistic and discourse-pragmatic features used by writers to construct interpersonal relations with other participants in the interaction.

Science Blog (or Academic Blog): A blog about academic and discipline related topics written by a person with some expertise in a scientific field.

Social Presence: The perception of the others' engagement and immediacy in a mediated communication. It involves constructing relationships with others through social and emotional interactions in a shared space.

Socio-Scientific Controversies: Extended argumentative engagements over scientific issues with social, ethical, political or economic implications, which usually involve scientific experts disagreeing publicly to defend their standpoint.

Weblog: A frequently updated Web page, consisting of many relatively short postings, organized in reverse chronological order, which tend to include the date and a comment button so that readers can answer.

Weblog Comment: Contribution by a blog reader used to share views and discuss any point related to the post both with other readers and with the blogger.

ENDNOTES

1. This research has been carried out within the framework of the project FFI2012-37346 (Spanish Ministry of Economy and Competitiveness).

Chapter 12

Interactive Advertising:
Displays of Identity and Stance on YouTube

Patricia Mayes
University of Wisconsin – Milwaukee, USA

ABSTRACT

Recent attempts to theorize identity using sociolinguistic, discourse analytic, and conversation analytic frameworks have focused on discursive constructions of speakers' identities, especially emphasizing the point that identities are constructed moment by moment through social interaction. Although such frameworks arguably are designed with face-to-face, synchronous interaction in mind, it is well known that other types of discourse, traditionally thought of as distant, asynchronous, and solitary (or non-interactive), are being used in new ways, due to rapid developments in technology. These developments suggest that all language use is inherently interactive, if not interactional (i.e., synchronous). In this chapter, the author uses insights from social semiotics and frameworks grounded in the analysis of spoken interaction to analyze a commercial in conjunction with unelicited comments from people who viewed the commercial on YouTube. The author's analysis focuses on the multimodal expression of meaning potentials as well as their uptake and the stances displayed in response.

INTRODUCTION

It is by now well established that consumption plays an important role in social positioning, a trend that has become increasingly apparent over the past few decades, with the rise of post-Fordist "flexibility" and the associated changes in labor markets. In addition, scholars in many areas have noted that discourse is playing an increasingly important role in such positioning. For example, a common feature of advertising is the use of linguistic or other semiotic means such as imagery to position recipients in desirable identities, associated with consumption (Fairclough, 1995). Furthermore, over the past few decades, the communicative function of *promotion* has been generalized and effectively "colonized" other genres, to the extent that everything – "goods, services,

DOI: 10.4018/978-1-4666-4426-7.ch012

ideas or people" – are now viewed as objects of sales transactions (Fairclough, 1995, p. 138). As Bucholtz (2007) argues, "neoliberalism's guiding metaphor for the organization of institutions also invites people to reimagine themselves as consumers first and foremost" (p. 371).

Not only has there been a generalization of promotion as a communicative function, there has also been a broadening of the kinds of appeals used in promotional discourse. For example, corporate advertising, the prototypical promotional discourse, makes use of what Klein (2000) refers to as "lifestyle branding" (p. 16), which promotes the selling of "a philosophy of life" (Boggio, 2010, p. 146) rather than just a product. This type of advertising, also called *high-concept advertising*, has a goal of "transcend[ing] the prosaic function of the product and bring[ing] it to a higher spiritual ... level in order to make those who wear or use these products feel as part of an experience, a lifestyle" (Boggio, 2010, p. 149). Clearly, in order to be effective, these ads must create not only lifestyles, but also identities, both of which potential consumers evaluate positively.

In the second decade of the 21st century, the changes described above might seem ubiquitous, unremarkable, and therefore not warranting further study. However, the fact that promotion has become such a naturalized communicative function in a relatively short period of time is what makes it significant. In addition, much of the existing research on this topic has used a non-interactive, "one-sided" approach, examining the discourse produced by advertisers and excluding people's reactions to it. Indeed, the goal of these studies is to examine how language and other semiotic resources are used in ads to create meaning potentials, or possible interpretations. There are few studies of whether and/or how people who view ads actually take up these meaning potentials and respond. Bucholtz' (2007) study is an

exception. She critiques some of the recent work on advertising and consumer culture as strongly deterministic, arguing that people's responses to advertising and brands are projected rather than actually investigated. Focusing on how adolescents make sense of and interact with global market forces at a local level, she argues that "youth do not simply fall into a predetermined economic script written by corporate marketers, but take up much more complex and ambivalent relationships toward consumption" (p. 372).

It is true that how children and adults respond to and interact with advertisements in their everyday lives has not drawn much attention from researchers. Although marketing firms do surveys, focus groups, and now even track *hits* and *likes* on the internet, this information does not explain how people respond to ads as they are viewing them. Even in my own previous work, involving Starbucks Corporation, I took a one-sided approach, examining only the discourse produced by Starbucks. (See Mayes, 2010.) In this chapter, I intend to add to these findings, by incorporating another side of the story – the unelicited responses of people who view advertisements on the internet and post their comments on YouTube.com. Analyzing an advertisement, in conjunction with these responses, will enable further investigation of how semiotic resources are used in identity work. One of my goals is to further our understanding of the discursive construction of identity and stance in relation to an advertisement, but I also have a second, methodological goal of furthering our understanding of how people interact with the semiotic resources of promotional discourse in a new way. Indeed, the possibility of responding to ads, as well as to other people who view the same material, is a relatively recent development. As these new, interactive ways to disseminate and respond to semiotic resources are developed, linguistic and discourse analytic theories that focus on dialogicality and moment-by-moment interaction will be particularly useful.

In the next section, I give a brief overview of the area of social semiotics, which focuses on how possible meanings, including those expressing identity (or positioning), are conveyed through multiple modes in discourse. Then, I review current theories that emphasize the dynamic and intersubjective nature of identity and stance, as constructed through social interaction. Next, I outline the framework used to analyze a commercial and the responses posted by people who viewed the commercial on YouTube. In essence, I combine elements of social semiotics and discourse analytic frameworks that focus on identity and stance as interactive (if not, interactional) accomplishments. Before concluding, I discuss some of the limitations of this study, focusing in particular on future directions.

BACKGROUND

Much of the research concerning advertising comes from a media/cultural studies perspective or from Critical Discourse Analysis (CDA). This research often focuses on semiotic systems in addition to language, and has pioneered and developed the incorporation of image analysis that is used in some discourse analytic work. For example, van Leeuwen and Jewitt's (2001) *Handbook of Visual Analysis* uses a variety of approaches, focusing in particular on images, but also on multimodality to a certain extent.

For this study, the framework known as *social semiotics* is most applicable because it places some focus on *positioning*, essentially describing systematic means for expressing identities. Social semiotics can be considered a spin-off of systemic functional grammar (SFG), an approach developed by Halliday (1978) to describe language as part of a social semiotic system, grounded in meaning, or communicative function. Social semiotics is similar to SFG, but focused on how semiotic resources other than language are used systematically to convey meaning, and thus multimodality might be considered its primary focus (van Leeuwen, 2005). With respect to advertising, this includes, for example, the text and images in print media and billboards, the images, language, and sound tracks in commercials, as well as web sites and other formats that use multiple modes to promote a product, service, idea, etc.

Iedema's (2001) analysis of a documentary film is an illustrative example because it focuses on the images, sounds, and language in each scene, as well as on how these elements work together. He uses the three-way distinction between the metafunctions associated with semiotic systems developed by Lemke (1989) and based in Halliday's (1978) original model of SFG. The first metafunction, referred to as *representation,* examines how meanings are represented through multiple modes such as "visually, verbally, musically or sound-wise" (Iedema, 2001, p. 191).

The second metafunction *orientation* concerns "how meanings position characters and readers-viewers" (Iedema, 2001, p. 192). Iedema discusses a variety of ways that such identity work can be accomplished, including the angle of the camera, whether the shot is a close up or shot at a distance, and whether the camera moves with the subject, in order to convey dynamism. In addition, he examines how the soundtrack contributes to positioning, by creating either intimacy or social distance between the sound and the recipient. For example, in analyzing the documentary film, he argues that "[t]he busy noises [of physicians and nurses at work] are more likely to inter-personally appeal to us than the controlled sounds" (p. 192) associated with the meetings of hospital administrators.

The third metafunction *organization* concerns how the different levels of meaning are linked together as a whole. Following van Leeuwen (1985), Iedema argues for the importance of rhythm in film: He suggests that rhythm is not only important in "interweav[ing] speech, sound, movement, image editing and macro-textual structuring" (p.192), it is also important in how texts are interpreted. (See also van Leeuwen, 2005.)

Social semiotics can be considered ground-breaking because it has provided a systematic way to analyze non-linguistic aspects of meaning in conjunction with language. However, one drawback to this approach, touched on in the introduction to this chapter, is the tendency to focus on analysts' interpretations, or *possible* recipient interpretations, as seen through the eyes of the analyst. For example, although Fairclough (2001) has argued in favor of "interactional analysis" (p. 239) of face-to-face discourse, television programs, and even written discourse, this approach still seems focused on analysts' interpretations: "Texts are written with particular readerships in mind and are oriented to (and anticipate) particular sorts of reception and responses, and are therefore also interactive" (pp. 239-40). Although this statement is undoubtedly true, it implies relying on one's own interpretation (as an analyst) of possible recipient responses, rather than relying on *actual* responses. Iedema (2001) explains this point with respect to the analysis of film,

Social semiotics centres on the issue of how I, as the viewer, am positioned by the tele-film in question, and how I see certain social allegiances and values as being promoted over others. In that sense, social semiotics denies there is a gap between text or product and audience. (p. 187)

Jewitt and Oyama (2001) also mention this point with regard to image analysis, saying that a social semiotic analysis "attempt[s] to describe a *meaning potential*, a field of possible meanings, which need to be activated by the producers and viewers of images" (p. 135; my emphasis).

The focus on analysts' interpretations described above is in direct contrast with discourse analytic approaches designed to analyze interaction as it occurs moment by moment. These interactional approaches examine both utterance and response

as they are occurring, thus using participants' responses to analyze the meanings of a particular utterance rather than only relying on the analyst's interpretation. In particular, from its inception, conversation analysis has focused on the sequential nature of interaction, grounding analysis in participant uptake and response. For example, in the very early work of Schegloff and Sacks (1973), they argued that the way an utterance is designed makes particular types of responses conditionally relevant (e.g., adjacency pairs such as question – answer, invitation – acceptance/rejection, etc.), and they used recorded conversational data to show how this occurs in the moment of speaking. Other discourse analytic approaches, in sociolinguistics and linguistic anthropology, have also recognized the importance of this participant orientation. Before moving on to my data and analysis, I will discuss this kind of approach in more detail, focusing on how interactional approaches are used in the analysis of identity and stance.

IDENTITY AND STANCE IN INTERACTION

Once considered a fixed and stable part of the individual psyche, *identity* has been redefined in recent years and in many disciplines is now understood as dynamic, intersubjective, and (at least partially) constructed in the moment of interaction between participants. A number of studies have analyzed identity as an interactional accomplishment, but here I focus on those that make a connection between identity and stance. Johnstone (2007) defines *stancetaking* as "the moment-by-moment choices speakers make that index their relationship to what they say" (p. 51), and Du Bois (2007) points to various terms have been used to refer to this kind of action, including *evaluation*, *assessment*, and *appraisal* (p. 142). Both Johnstone and Du Bois suggest that actions that align or disalign social actors are key components in stancetaking, and Johnstone also links alignment/disalignment with identity, as do Bucholtz and Hall (2005). In addition, Bucholtz (2007) suggests that "the habitual taking of stances, and interactional dynamics may sediment into social relations" (p. 379), including identities.

In the area of conversation analysis, there have been a number of studies, suggesting how identities are accomplished interactionally (e.g., Antaki & Widdicombe, 1998; Benwell & Stokoe, 2010; Widdicombe, 1998; Widdicombe & Wooffitt, 1995). Perhaps most relevant here is the work of John Heritage and his colleagues who link stancetaking actions (or "assessments") and the moment-by-moment construction of interpersonal relationships (Heritage, 1997; Heritage & Clayman, 2010; Heritage & Raymond, 2005; Raymond & Heritage, 2006). As Raymond and Heritage (2006) put it, "We suggest that the management of rights of knowledge and, relatedly, rights to evaluate states of affairs can be a resource for invoking identity in interaction" (p. 680).

Bucholtz and Hall's (2005) framework is also useful for analyzing identity in interaction because, after defining the concept quite broadly as "the social positioning of self and other" (p. 586), they go on to break down this definition into a set of overlapping principles, which can be applied straightforwardly. Most relevant for this analysis is the principle of *relationality*, actually a set of three subprinciples that focus on intersubjectivity, and capture the different ways participants affiliate or disaffiliate with the stances displayed in the moment of speaking. They include adequation/distinction (or similarity/difference), authentication/denaturalization (or genuineness/artifice), and authorization/illegitimation (or authority/delegitimacy).

Although framed as "a preliminary sketch" (p. 139), Du Bois' (2007) framework for analyzing stance is undoubtedly groundbreaking, and is the one that I will use most in this analysis. He notes that there are different types of stance acts (e.g., evaluative, positioning, aligning, and epistemic), but argues that it would be too simplistic to merely come up with a list that would continue

to proliferate. In order to capture the complexity of stancetaking, stance must be understood as "emerg[ing] across successive utterances through processes of dialogic action" (p. 145). He goes on to explicate three components that allow us to see how stance emerges: 1) the stancetaker – the person conveying a stance; 2) the object of stance – an entity about which a stance is expressed; 3) the stance that the stancetaker is responding to – this requires us to "look back" in the prior discourse, thereby focusing on emergence and dialogicality as well as the forging of intersubjective relations of alignment/disalignment (p. 146).

Du Bois' (2007) definition of stance highlights the important relationship between stancetaking and identity work, referred to as "position[ing]" and "calibrat[ing] alignment between stancetakers" (p. 139). What is a new and useful contribution to other theories of identity or social positioning is the idea that stance is a triangle, rather than just a dialogic relation between two participants. In other words, in addition to arguing that stancetaking *is* dialogic action, this framework emphasizes the fact that stances are assumed in relation to something else – something "out there" in the world, or what Du Bois refers to as "objects of interest" (p. 139). Thus the importance of material objects in identity work is made explicit in this framework, and this is useful in analyzing the comments people make about the commercial I focus on here, and more generally, it is also useful in making the link between consumption, identity, and stance explicit.

APPROACH USED IN THIS ANALYSIS

My purpose here is to use the frameworks discussed above to analyze a commercial, first from the perspective of what social semiotics can tell us about how meanings (especially those related to identities or positioning) are represented through the different modes used in the commercial, and second from the perspective of how viewers create identities through stance displays in their comments on YouTube. Thus this study is designed to find out more about what Iedema (2001) refers to as the "gap between text or product and audience" (p. 187) rather than assuming from the outset that such a gap does not exist.

I should note that I am not claiming that my analysis is "interactional" in the sense of the studies reviewed earlier in the previous section, which focus on identity or stance as they are created moment by moment, in real time interaction (e.g., in face-to-face talk, phone calls, etc.). Rather, I use the term "interactive analysis," to capture the fact that I am focusing on *both* utterances and responses, even though they produced at a temporal (and perhaps spatial) distance (e.g., letters, discussion boards, email, etc.). Although interactive analysis does not focus on immediate and spontaneous aspects, as interactional analysis of face-to-face interaction would do, our understanding of the role of advertising in creating consumer identities in online contexts will benefit from considering advertising to be inherently interactive and examining both the ads themselves as well as people's responses.

It has been widely noted that there is a complex relationship between identity, social class, and consumption, but space limitations preclude a thorough treatment of this issue. Although I use terms such as *elite* and *upper class* to discuss both meaning potentials and people's comments, I assume that these are local, discursively constructed aspects of social identity, rather than indexes of actual, socioeconomic status in a broader sense, outside of this context.

THE SIGNATUREHOME COMMERCIAL

The 30-second commercial analyzed here was produced by Time Warner Cable (TWC) and uploaded to YouTube on September 26, 2011 (http://www.youtube.com/watch?v=UkDVQev8nZc). It advertises a service called *SignatureHome*. According to the voiceover in the commercial, the service

provides access to a technician who connects and maintains in-home technology, "with a level of personal attention and professional expertise that is unmatched." The commercial conveys through multiple modes that those who purchase the service are elite consumers, and one of the primary means of conveying this message is through the positioning of the characters in the video. Because it is my purpose to look at multimodal aspects of this commercial, I will present some general information about it and then describe each scene.

Description of the Commercial

All of the scenes in the SignatureHome commercial are shot with movement of the camera, as it pans from one scene to the next across space and time, as the characters appear to go about their daily activities. The actors in the video do not speak, but there is a voiceover and also one- or two-word messages appearing on the screen concerning the features of the service and the kinds of electronic devices that are covered. The only other sound is a soothing, romantic music track, which plays throughout the commercial. The entire video is shot in black and white, but all of the display screens for the electronic devices are brightly colored. Most of the video takes place in what is supposed to be a large penthouse that is sparsely furnished and appears very spacious, features that also works to highlight the electronic devices that are visible in various scenes. I should also note that it is likely that the viewer is supposed to assume that the four actors in the commercial are a family: a husband, wife, son, and daughter. However, in the description below, I refer to them simply as *man*, *woman*, *boy*, and *girl*. Figures 1-6 in the Appendix show some of the scenes described.

Scene 1: The first scene is a cityscape, viewed from slightly above, and showing a high-rise apartment building. The viewer has the illusion of flying over and looking at the lit-up penthouse from a distance. The voiceover (beginning in Scene 1 and continuing through

Scene 2) says, "Introducing Signature-Home."

Scene 2: The camera pans through a living room where a man with a book in his hand is strolling around the room, gazing at an electronic screen on the mantel that shows a vivid, orange, fire-like image (see Appendix Figure 1). Momentarily, the screen changes to a blue-green, ocean-like image. The living room is modern and spacious, but the most noticeable point is the images on the screen.

Scene 3: The camera switches to the bedroom, showing the back of a woman, dropping her bathrobe to the floor. In the next shot, a man becomes visible in the bed and the woman has (apparently) just joined him. He is holding a handheld electronic device. The woman is wearing a short black negligee that becomes more visible in the next shot, which is taken from a distance and shows the woman from her side, looking toward the man so that the viewer sees the back of her head. As the camera transitions to this shot the words *enhanced TV* appear at the bottom left side of the screen. The most noticeable feature of this shot is the only object in color, a large wide-screen TV, which displays some (purple-tinged) images from an ongoing program. The man gradually becomes more visible, as the camera pans in for a close-up of the couple, who are leaning toward one another. The man pulls the woman toward him (Appendix Figure 2) and kisses her on the forehead. The viewer can also see the handheld device on the man's lap more clearly. The voiceover says, "Experience the ultimate selection of products from Time Warner Cable."

Scene 4: The viewer sees the back of a boy who is walking down a hallway, holding an electronic tablet, as the word *wireless* appears at the bottom right side of the screen. Because this device is smaller, the color of its screen is less noticeable. In the distance, there is a girl, running out of a doorway toward what appears to be a dining room with light streaming in from large windows at the end of the room (see Appendix Figure 3). The voiceover (spanning Scenes 4 and 5) says, "with a level of personal attention and professional expertise that is unmatched."

Scene 5: It is apparently morning, and from a distance, all four characters are shown in the kitchen. The girl is seated at the table, and the other three are milling about. The boy is holding some type of drink, and the man and woman are holding large, white, ceramic mugs. The camera pans in for a close-up of the man, who is leaning on the counter holding the large mug, and the woman, who is closer to the viewer but standing at an angle. Although her face is initially toward the viewer, she is looking down, giving the impression that she is involved in some activity (see Appendix Figure 4). As the camera pans toward a more complete frontal view of the man, the woman turns toward him. Beginning at the end of this scene and continuing through Scene 6, the voiceover says, "You'll have a dedicated specialist, who'll tailor everything just right for you."

Scene 6: The woman, shown facing the viewer but looking down, is leaning toward the bathtub drawing a bath, as the words *personal concierge* appear at the bottom right side of the screen (see Appendix Figure 5). She is positioned in the middle of the viewing screen, and her mirror image is visible on the left side of the screen. There is no wall behind her, just a large window that displays part of the cityscape, and a blind is coming down over the window. As the woman leans over, placing her hand on the edge of the tub, the camera pans in for a close-up of an expensive looking ring on her left hand.

Scene 7: The living room is shown from above, and the word *wideband* appears on the bottom right side of the screen. As the woman sits down on the couch and opens a laptop, the viewer can see the bright blue screen. The voiceover says, "and who is on call."

Scene 8: This scene starts by showing the back of the woman's head, which is out of focus, as she turns to the side. The focal point is the man who is at the other end of the hall looking toward her and the viewer, while he puts on his suit jacket. In the next shot, the woman has turned and is walking toward the man. As the words *advanced DVR* appear on the bottom left side of the screen, a large widescreen TV with the image of a bright, red rose becomes visible. The woman is wearing a dress and carrying a light jacket, suggesting that the couple is going out for the evening. The voiceover (spanning Scenes 8 and 9) says, "day or night should you ever need assistance. It's a class of service you might have thought had disappeared from the world."

Scene 9: The woman is carrying two large glasses of red wine across the room toward the man who is seated on a couch, facing the camera. Only the woman's right hand and shoulder are visible, as the camera focuses on the wine. The man is looking at an electronic tablet, and a balcony and the city lights are visible in the background. The next shot shows the woman sitting next to the man, and each has a glass of red wine. She leans back as he puts his arm around her shoulder, and they gaze at each other. She seems to be smiling, although it is a bit hard to tell because her profile is only barely visible (see Appendix Figure 6).

Scene 10: The commercial ends, and the city lights fade out as the SignatureHome trademark (*SignatureHome™*) becomes visible in the middle of the screen, with a phone number underneath. The next shot shows the TWC logo, and the words "Time Warner Cable" are displayed vertically to the right of the logo. The phone number still appears beneath the

logo, and the web site address has appeared under the phone number. At the bottom of the screen, the copyright information for the logo and trademark are displayed. The voiceover says, "SignatureHome. Exclusively for you, exclusively from Time Warner Cable." The musical track also ends at this point.

Meaning Potentials

In this section, I explore how semiotic resources are used in the SignatureHome commercial to express meaning potentials, focusing primarily on identities and positioning of the characters as well as potential consumers.

Images and Camera Work: According to Iedema (2001), in film movement from shot to shot within a scene conveys "dynamism, urgency and immediacy" (p. 192). This technique is used throughout the SignatureHome commercial, as the camera pans through the different rooms, suggesting a sense of dynamism and activity. In addition, switches from one scene to the next occur very abruptly, which not only conveys temporal distinctions, but also seems to increase the sense of dynamism, as each scene shows the characters actively engaged in different activities during what is taken to be a typical day in their lives. This dynamism, along with the other features below suggest an elite, or as the voiceover puts it, "exclusive" lifestyle and identities that match.

The SignatureHome commercial also uses some techniques that Machin and van Leeuwen (2007) have associated with generic photographs such as those collected in large image banks like Getty Images. Rather than conveying information about specific subject matter, these photographs are designed to convey general categories of people, places, and objects, which are useful in current advertising and branding practices because they allow as many people as possible to identify with the lifestyles portrayed in the images (Machin & van Leeuwen, 2007). One technique used for indexing settings and identities is the inclusion of "props" (p.154) in images. For example, Machin and van Leeuwen found that computers were typically used to connote offices or work. In contrast, in the SignatureHome commercial, electronic devices are only associated with leisure time and home. This contrast may be seen as indexing the exclusivity of the SignatureHome service because it suggests that people who use the service can afford to have the latest technology in every room of their home, not just at work. It also suggests that they have a lot of leisure time to use the technology and would not need to spend that time adjusting it because they have the service.

There are also other props that index identities associated with exclusivity and upper-class tastes. For example, the ring on the woman's finger (Scene 6) is used to suggest that she is the man's wife, but also that she is from a privileged class that can afford such items. It also seems likely that some of the less expensive props such as the large red wine glasses and large, white, ceramic mugs are used to index elite tastes. Indeed, these items are found in more expensive restaurants and stores that cater to the upper-middle class. Of course, the setting itself – the penthouse – which is portrayed as being located in a large city like New York, also suggests that the characters' identities are consistent with being able to afford the lifestyle portrayed in the commercial. The rooms of the penthouse have some of the features Machin and van Leeuwen (2007) found to be associated with "generic interiors" (p. 152) in image bank photographs. For example, there are many windows, and the space is uncluttered and open, with a feeling of "brightness and airiness" (p.152). They mention that photographers they interviewed said that these settings create a sense of "optimism, delicacy, and beauty" (p. 152), and Machin and van Leeuwen argue that "the world of the image bank image is the bright and happy world of 'positive thinking' favoured by contemporary corporate ideology" (p. 152). Another aspect of such "positive thinking" is the idea that upward mobility is possible and attainable through desirable lifestyles such as the

one portrayed in the SignatureHome commercial. The setting works in conjunction with smaller props and other features to send one coherent, consistent message, backing up the explicit mentions of "exclusiv[ity]" and "class[y] service" in the voiceover.

Machin and van Leeuwen also discuss the models that are used in generic images, describing them as "clearly attractive, but not remarkable" (p. 155). They explain that image bank photos must be reusable by different clients, so they cannot be recognizable. In the case of commercials, this may be less of a concern, since the goal is not to create a video that is reusable in this sense. The reason may be that viewers (or "consumers") will more easily identify with actors who are attractive but not especially striking in appearance. The SignatureHome commercial focuses mostly on the man and woman, who are both slim, attractive, and appear to be in their mid to late thirties, but they are not known, recognizable actors. The woman is made to seem attractive because she has long dark hair that swishes around in several of the scenes, but her face is never shown clearly, for example, from a full, in-focus, frontal angle.

The above point about the physical positioning of the characters can be further analyzed in terms of what Jewitt and Oyama (2001) refer to as "point of view" (p. 135). They argue that the physical placement of people, places, and objects in images creates symbolic meanings that are accessible to viewers. They explain that these are potential meanings that are conveyed through the vertical and horizontal angles between the viewer and the people or objects in an image. For example, if the image of a person is at eye-level, there is a relation of symbolic equality. On the other hand, with respect to looking up, the viewer is positioned in a symbolically less powerful position; likewise, looking down positions the viewer as symbolically more powerful. They also argue that with respect to the horizontal angle, there is a symbolic relation of involvement/detachment. A direct frontal view can create involvement, whereas a profile view may create a relation of detachment. In the SignatureHome commercial, six of the scenes are shot at eye-level, and four are shot from above or slightly above. For example, in Scene 1, the viewer sees the high-rise apartment from a distance and slightly above; in Scene 4, the viewer seems to be looking at the tablet over the boy's shoulder; in Scene 6, the ring is shot from slightly above; and Scene 7 is shot at a very high angle, as if the viewer is on the ceiling, looking down over the woman, as she opens the laptop. Jewitt and Oyama's (2001) contention that eye-level shots can index an equal relation between viewer and character, in the context of advertising, could suggest that the viewer can have the same lifestyle as the characters. In addition, although it is possible that the scenes shot from above suggest that the viewer has symbolic power (e.g., they can choose the lifestyle portrayed), I believe that these scenes also suggest detachment in that the viewer is looking at the lives of this "family" in an almost voyeuristic way, as a distant observer. This message of detachment is also conveyed through the horizontal angle in that very few of the scenes show an in-focus, frontal view of the characters. Many of the shots are taken at a distance and the viewer sees the profile or sometimes the back of the character. In the few cases where there is a frontal view of a character's face, it is shot at a distance and appears somewhat out of focus. The use of profile views, distance, and out of focus shots reinforces the message that the viewer is a detached observer that has been afforded a rare glimpse into the intimacies of the lives of others. All of this taken together could suggest that the observer is in a position of power with respect to those being observed. It is also true that profiles and distant, out-of-focus shots reinforce the message that these generic actors are unremarkable and ordinary, thus facilitating viewer identification.

Another point that can be made about the horizontal angle is that when a frontal (or nearly frontal) view of one of the characters is shown, four of the six are the man. The other two are the woman. These differences in how the man and woman are presented in the commercial could suggest that the woman is treated more like one of the props, and the man is the main character. As will be shown below, a few of the comments by viewers do seem to suggest that the woman is viewed as one of the props (at least by those particular viewers).

Language: As noted, the only language used in the commercial is the voiceover and the words that appear on the screen in some of the scenes. These techniques work together not just to explain the services customers would receive if they purchase the product, but more importantly, to reinforce the message in the images that this service is part of an elite lifestyle. The first utterance of the voiceover, repeated as example (1), explicitly introduces the SignatureHome service, which is of course the topic of the commercial:

(1)   Introducing: SignatureHome.

This is followed by example (2), which uses the adjectives *ultimate* and *unmatched* to claim that SignatureHome is the best, while also claiming that it provides *personal attention* and *professional expertise*, two features associated with elite tastes.

(2)   Experience the ultimate selection of products from Time Warner Cable with a level of personal attention and professional expertise that is unmatched.

The imperative functions to suggest that the viewer do the specified action. However, the verb *experience* does not express an agentive action, but rather a psychological state. Indeed the subject of a clause with *experience* as the predicate is an *experiencer* rather than an agent. Using this kind of non-agentive predicate has the effect of making the directive seem less direct, a suggestion rather than a command. Substituting a verb like *watch* in which the subject *is* the agent has the effect of making the sentence sound more like a command.

The subtle directive achieved with *experience* is more likely to persuade potential customers than a direct order would be. In addition, this sentence begins as the couple is shown in the bedroom (Scene 3), an image that also indexes sexual desire, and the verb choice aligns with this meaning.

The next sentence is presented in (3), and perhaps the most obvious point to be made is the explicit mention of the addressee as the second person pronoun *you*.

(3)　You'll have a dedicated specialist, who'll tailor everything just right for you, and who is on call day or night should you ever need assistance.

Once again, these mentions of *you* position the addressee not in the semantic role of an agent, but as a possessor, benefactive, and experiencer respectively, thus suggesting an identity that is served by others. The sentence itself is a declarative statement of a hypothetical future, conveyed through the modality: The modal *will* expresses both the future (hypothetical) nature of the claim and also relative certainty on an epistemic scale. This suggests that the statement will become fact if *you* act to purchase the SignatureHome service. Of course, the specific wording such as *dedicated specialist, tailor everything just right for you,* and *on call day or night* further index the high social status of potential recipients of this service. This point is repeated in the next sentence, which explicitly mentions *class*:

(4)　It's a class of service you might have thought had disappeared from the world.

In addition, *world* is mentioned, which together with *class*, may be understood as suggesting that recipients of the SignatureHome service are members of an elite global social class. The embedded clause *you might have thought had disappeared from the world* may also be taken as suggesting that the service providers are able to read the minds of these *new* global elites and predict their needs in advance.

Finally, the last statement, presented in (5), indexes the elite status of recipients of the SignatureHome service and the service provider (TWC) by linking the word *exclusively* to each of these referents via the service itself.

(5)　SignatureHome: Exclusively for you, exclusively from Time Warner Cable.

(1) and (5) mirror each other, in both content and form. Both mention the SignatureHome service, and (5) sums up the point that has been the focus of the commercial. (1) and (5) are phrases rather than complete sentences, and they seem to function as boundaries between the real world and the claims in (2)-(4). These claims constitute another "reality" – the one created by the commercial, which *is* presented in complete sentences. This parallel structure adds rhythm, which van Leeuwen (2005) defines as an "alternation between two states: an up and a down, a tense and a lax, a loud and a soft, a night and day" (p. 182), thus broadening the idea to include more than just the rhythmic pulses of speech and music. Quoting van Leeuwen (1985), Iedema (2001) also contends that "rhythmic grouping" (p. 193) helps create semantic coherence within a text.

Rhythm also plays a role in the words that appear on the screen, as they are matched either to what the viewer is seeing or, in one case, to what is heard through the voiceover. For example, in Scene 3, as a large widescreen TV is shown in the bedroom, the words *enhanced TV* appear on the screen; in Scene 4, as the boy appears with a tablet, presumably accessing the internet as he is walking down the hall, the word *wireless* appears on the screen; in Scene 7, as the woman sits on the couch, opening the laptop, the word *wideband* appears; finally, as the second large widescreen monitor appears in the living room in Scene 8, the words *advanced DVR* also appear. In Scene 6, rhythmic coherence is established between the words *personal concierge* that appear on the screen and the voiceover, which at that moment says the words *a dedicated specialist*.

Most of the words that appear on the screen in this fashion are designed to solve a problem that Boggio (2010) noticed for high-concept car ads. As discussed in the introduction, high-concept advertising has been characterized in various ways as focused on positive experiences and lifestyles rather than products. Machin and van Leeuwen (2007) connect it to "the bright and happy world of 'positive thinking'" (p. 152), and Boggio characterizes it as focused on "a higher spiritual level" (p. 149). She goes on to argue, however, that in the case of high-tech products such as cars, "there seems to be a predicament to unveil the human-made technology" (p. 149), presumably because a focus on such details would disturb the fantasy and refocus attention on the realities of everyday life.

In the SignatureHome commercial, the problem of revealing the technical features of the service is resolved through the one- and two-word displays at the bottom of the screen. This allows the main point of the ad to be the desirable, elite lifestyle, and the corresponding elite social positioning, indexed by the images, voiceover, and music. This way of organizing the information in the commercial is consistent with Kress and van Leeuwen's (1996) analysis of multimodal texts, in which images near the top of a frame express the "ideal," whereas written text placed in the lower part of a frame expresses the "real" (p. 193).

Other Aspects of the Soundtrack: Another aspect of the voiceover that helps convey the desirability of the lifestyle and associated identities is the voice quality – a soft, female voice that sounds calm and relaxed, but also sensual. There is also a musical soundtrack of the genre sometimes referred to as "mellow jazz" or "smooth jazz." Interestingly, the musical score is not just subtle, background music, but is rather loud. However, the voiceover is also at a relatively high volume, so both can easily be heard.

Rhythm is apparent in how the two components of the soundtrack (the music and the voiceover) work with the images. For example, there is a similarity between the woman's soft, sexy voice and the soft jazz score. In terms of timing, the song begins with a soft piano playing at the beginning of the commercial. Other instruments begin playing at important points in the scenes. Indeed, the horn is only heard at certain points, and these coincide with prominent shots. For example, in Scene 5, just as a (more or less) frontal view of the couple becomes visible, the horn is heard for the first time. It plays again in Scene 6, as the close-up shot of the ring is shown, in Scene 8 as a frontal view of the man is shown, in Scene 9 as another (more or less) frontal shot of the couple appears, and finally in Scene 10, as the words *Time Warner Cable* appear along with the logo. The only other scene with a frontal shot is the one in the bedroom (Scene 3). It is also treated as prominent with regard to the musical score, as that is the point at which most of the other instruments (except the horn) begin to play.

All of the elements, visual, language, and sound work together in various ways to convey the concept of an elite, desirable lifestyle with a lot of leisure time and the suggestion that a service like SignatureHome would increase a person's leisure time. In effect, this suggests that the elite identities associated with this desirable lifestyle are relatively easy to acquire.

VIEWERS' DISPLAYS OF IDENTITY AND STANCE IN RESPONSE TO THE COMMERCIAL

In this section, I analyze the responses made by people who viewed the commercial and posted their comments on the YouTube site, using insights from the frameworks designed to analyze identity in interaction and described earlier in the chapter. In particular, I focus on stance displays.

Overview of the Comments

The YouTube site where the commercial is housed contained 38 posts on June 15, 2012. I analyzed all of these posts, many of which contain more than one comment. I have broken the posts down into 47 comments that display stances toward stance objects such as the props, the SignatureHome service, and the commercial as a whole. Table 1 summarizes the stances displayed in the comments, as positive, negative, or neutral, as well as the entity being evaluated (the stance object). I should note that the purpose of Table 1 is neither to create a set of discrete categories for coding stance displays, nor to quantify the results. The categories *positive*, *negative*, and *neutral* are oversimplified, and the numbers are quite small. My only purpose is to give an overview of the kinds of comments people posted.

Table 1 shows that 33 of the 47 comments are positive, and most of these concern the musical soundtrack, followed by the penthouse apartment. Other aspects of the commercial that are evaluated positively include props such as the ring (referred to by the posters as a *wedding band* or *wedding ring*), the image of the rose on the video screen, and the woman, referred to as *the wife*.

Table 1. Stance displays in YouTube posts

Stance Object	Positive	Negative	Neutral	Total
TWC		1	1	2
Commercial	1	5[1]		6
SignatureHome		1		1
Music[2]	18[3]	1	1	20
Penthouse	6			6
Voiceover	2			2
Ring	3[4]			3
"Wife"	1	1		2
Image of Rose	1			1
Poster/Comment[5]	1	2		3
Cityscape			1	1

Interestingly, only one of the posts contains a positive comment about the commercial as a whole; on the other hand, there are five negative comments, and one poster made a negative comment about TWC and about the service itself. In the next section, I give examples of some of the comments made in individual posts, followed by examples of comments in which one poster responded to another. I have not altered any of the wording, spelling (including the use of upper-case letters), or punctuation in the original posts. The only change is the addition of pseudonyms, P (Poster) 1-33 to refer to the posts of different writers, where relevant. Because this is a public site that does not require a user name, password, or login in order to see the comments, pseudonyms are a convenience rather than a necessity.

Individual Comments Responding to the Commercial

In analyzing the meaning potentials of the commercial earlier, I suggested that the visual elements, language, and musical soundtrack all work together to suggest a desirable lifestyle, and indeed, that is the point of high-concept advertising (Boggio, 2010; Machin & van Leeuwen, 2007). That the viewers of the commercial who posted on YouTube have also interpreted the meaning of the commercial in this way is apparent in the posts: Indeed, as shown in Table 1, many of the posts display stances evaluating the desirability of the specific props in the commercial, and a few display stances in which the commercial as a whole is the stance object. Example (6) is an example of the former type, in which the stance object is *that penthouse*.

(6)   OMG!!!! I want that penthouse !!!!

The exclamation *OMG* displays a positive evaluation of the stance object and conveys the writer's affective response, as do the exclamation points. The predicate *want* then serves to position

Table 2. Diagraphic representation of stance displays in example (6)

Poster	Stance Subject	Positions/Evaluates	Stance Object
2		OMG	
2	I	want	that penthouse

the writer with respect to the stance object. Du Bois (2007) used "stance diagrams" to provide an iconic representation of stance displays. Example (6) is represented in this way in Table 2.

Other stance displays found in these posts were less explicit, as is shown in (7) and (8).

(7)   I keep playing this!! who's song is it!!? HELP!!?

(8)   Seriously.. Where can I find the wedding band? Anyone know?

In (7), the poster makes a statement and asks a question, indirectly suggesting that the stance object *this [song]* is desirable. The aspect marker *keep* in *keep playing* and the punctuation index affect and urgency. In (8), *seriously* also adds urgency to the question *where can I find the wedding band*, indexing the desirability of the stance object *the wedding band*, and positioning the viewer as needing the object.

As mentioned, in addition to evaluating the props in the commercial, some posters evaluated the commercial as a whole in terms of its overall message. However, only one of these posts was positive; it is shown in (9).

(9)   It's a gorgeous song; and I play it over and over just because it's beautiful. But more than anything, I believe part of the commercial's allure is the idea that this service is being marketed to us; common folk- as well as those who live their life in affluence; and you can be in the moment through the lingering last chords of the song, feeling what it's like to live a life of luxury, wealth and care free beauty....

This post not only evaluates the stance object *a song* as *gorgeous* and then *beautiful*, it also adds much more specific information about how the writer interprets the commercial as a whole, and the role the song plays in conveying this meaning. For example, the writer evaluates the commercial as *allur[ing]* and takes the position of *believ[ing]* its appeal, going on to explain how the song is used to *market[ ] to us common folk*, while implying that the images in the video also have that effect. Indeed, the use of the pronoun *you* in its generic sense in the last sentence may be understood as positioning the poster and other viewers as able to access *a life of luxury*. These comments also suggest how the different modes in the commercial work together to show this lifestyle and connote that it is something that is available to all. For this poster at least, many of the meaning potentials discussed above seem to have been realized.

The rest of the comments that evaluate the commercial as a whole, or in one case, TWC, display various negative stances. (10) is an example. It makes the point that the commercial suggests that in order to have an affluent lifestyle, all a person needs to do is buy the SignatureHome service.

(10) Sign up for Signature Home, and you will instantly have a hot wife in your bed, two beautiful children, and will live in a $20 million penthouse...NOT.

This example critiques the commercial by pointing out the social positioning of potential viewers who identify with the male actor. It explicitly evaluates the stance object *the penthouse*, as expensive (*$20 million*), and perhaps more importantly, the characters, as *hot* and *beautiful*, adjectives linked to the *wife* and *children*, respectively. The post also explicitly links the portrayed lifestyle to the purchase of the SignatureHome service, saying that this is the overall message of the commercial. Finally, this claim is denied by the single capitalized word *NOT*, indexing the poster's disalignment with this message. More specifically, *NOT* functions to "denaturalize," or subvert "claims to the inevitability or inherent rightness of identities" (Bucholtz & Hall, 2005, p. 602), and to index the falseness of the monolithic identities portrayed in the commercial. The post in (11) has a similar message, beginning with an implicit critique, expressed as a rhetorical question, and followed by an explicit statement of the commercial's main point – *that anyone can afford to have a Signature Home.* The final sentence indexes the writer's stance of skepticism, suggesting that the identities of the characters are elite, affluent people, who *would laugh at the idea of having to scrimp and save.* This statement disaligns the writer with the commercial's message, by denaturalizing the identities of the characters and suggesting that they are not as they seem.

(11) This penthouse scene is supposed to represent the average family? The idea of the ad is that anyone can afford to have a Signature Home and save some money. These folks would laugh at the idea of having to scrimp and save.

So far, I have discussed posts that responded to the commercial rather than to other posters. The writers of these posts take stances concerning various aspects of the lifestyle portrayed by TWC. In some cases, they evaluate specific props that index an elite lifestyle, such as the penthouse, the ring, or the "wife" (who was treated like a prop in some of the posts); other posts (such as (9) through (11)) not only evaluate the props, but also the commercial as a whole.

One of the goals of Du Bois' (2007) framework for analyzing stance was to articulate "a well-defined program for substantive research on observed instances of dialogic interaction" (p. 140), thus advancing the notion of dialogicality beyond mere theory. It is at this point that I turn to a discussion of dialogicality. The dialogic nature of social interaction is more readily obvious in the face-to-face interaction discussed by Du Bois than in the data discussed here. Indeed, his analysis highlighted the importance of the prior discourse, suggesting that the value of a particular stance utterance may change as participants respond, producing new stance acts or incrementally changing the previous stance act. Although the stance acts analyzed here are not displayed in real time, moment by moment, these data are still inherently dialogic. For example, examining the posters' comments in (6) through (11) allows us to understand the meaning potentials of the prior discourse (the commercial), as those meanings are realized and/or changed. Of course not everyone who views a commercial posts a comment, but when they do, they enact a dialogic interaction. Whether these posters identify with or critique the identities indexed in the commercial, their comments provide evidence that those meaning potentials are not just the analyst's interpretation. In addition, they also help further our understanding of "why stance should come to wield both subtlety and power in the dynamics of social life" (Du Bois, 2007, p.141). Indeed, dialogicality is revealed by examining how the posted comments relate back to the commercial, yet this is not the only way it is apparent. In the stance displays directed at others' posts, and discussed below, dialogicality is perhaps even more apparent.

Comments in Response to another Poster

The comments discussed in the last section contain examples in which posters take stances that converge or diverge with the meaning potentials displayed in the commercial, but these are not the only actions involving stance in the posts. Some posters responded to others' posts, displaying alignment or disalignment in relation to the stance of the other, much as Du Bois (2007) found in face-to-face interaction. He contends that alignment is "continuously variable in principle" (p. 162) and can be adjusted incrementally with each utterance. As Du Bois uses the term, alignment can be "convergent, divergent, or … ambiguous between the two" (p. 162). Example (12) is an example in which the stances of two posters converge.

(12) **P4:** HOLY SHIT IDC ['I don't care']
        ABOUT TIME WARNER I WANT
        THAT HOUSE!!!
      P5: I'M WITH YOU MAN!
      P4: lol right!! and i also wouldnt mind the
        wife either ;)

In this example, P4 first displays ambivalence toward the stance object *Time Warner* through the expression *IDC*, and continues on to evaluate the stance object *that house* as desirable, using the

predicate *want*. P5's *I'm with you man* displays a convergent stance, to which P4 responds with an affective expression of alignment *lol right* and an evaluative statement about another stance object *the wife*. Du Bois (2007) used "diagraphs" (p. 160), similar to the stance diagram in Table 2, to represent the dialogic relations between stances iconically. Example (12) is displayed in this way in Table 3.

Table 3 suggests how stance is discursively constructed: A stance subject evaluates an object (and/or takes a position with respect to that object); a second stance subject then also evaluates that object, responding to the previously expressed stance, and in the process, taking a position on the alignment scale. Du Bois refers to this sequence of stance displays as a "stance lead" (lines 1-3 in example (12)) and a "stance follow" (line 4 in (12)) (p. 161).

Example (13), also represented in Table 4, is another example of stance displays in response to the post of another.

Table 3. Diagraphic representation of stance displays in example (12)

Poster	Stance Subject	Positions/Evaluates	Stance Object	Aligns
4	I	Holy shit … DC	Time Warner	
4	I	want	that house	
5	I	{want}	{that house}	'm with you man
4				lol right
4	I	wouldn't mind…either	the wife	

Table 4. Diagraphic representation of stance displays in example (13)

Poster	Stance Subject	Positions/Evaluates	Stance Object	Aligns
17		by the mindless drivelers	{musicians}	
18		no	it (song)	it isn't
19		ignorant	bla8ant (P17)	-ly
17		perhaps just rightfully opinionated	{P17}	or

(13) **P17 (bl8ant[6]):** the song is "ain't got no talent" by the mindless drivelers

    P18: no it isnt

    P19: "bla8ant"ly ignorant.

    P17: or perhaps just rightfully opinionated?

Clearly, evaluating, positioning, and aligning are not three separate stance acts or types of stance act, but rather three aspects of one action, in which "the stancetaker 1 evaluates an object, 2 positions a subject (usually the self), and 3 aligns with other subjects" (Du Bois, 2007, p. 163). The diagraph makes it clear which linguistic constructions are expressing the three aspects of stance. However, unlike the examples of face-to-face interaction examined by Du Bois, some stance acts in these posts do not explicitly mention the stance subject (the poster). For example, as shown in (13) and Table 4, the posters do not say *I think* or anything else that explicitly connects them to the evaluations, yet clearly the position or evaluation displayed is that of the poster. Instead, P17's negative evaluation of the song is delivered implicitly through sarcasm: *"ain't got no talent" by the mindless drivelers*. This stance may be considered disaligning with many of the previous posts (or posters) through the principle of *distinction* (Bucholtz & Hall, 2005). Indeed, P17's evaluation contrasts with the stances expressed in 18 of the 20 posts in which the song is the stance object. P18 takes a position opposing that of P17, also demonstrating disalignment or distinction from P17 with respect to the song. P19 then makes a comment about a different stance object, evaluating the poster (P17) as *bla8antly ignorant*, obviously disaligning with P17, through the adjective *ignorant*. In Table 4, I have also suggested that the primary function of *–ly* is to display and reinforce that disalignment due to what Du Bois (2007) refers to as "resonance" (p. 160). The comment as a whole resonates, or displays a parallel structure, with P17's user name *bl8ant*, and *–ly*, in conjunction with *ignorant*, indexes disaffiliation. Likewise,

P17 indexes disalignment with P19, using *or* and a predicate that signals a different evaluation *rightfully opinionated*, while maintaining the resonance of the parallel structure.

Although I have been pointing to many similarities between stance acts in face-to-face contexts and in this very different context, I do not want to discount the obvious differences between the two contexts. Indeed, the main point I have been arguing in favor of is a more nuanced understanding of the ways in which written language and indeed other semiotic resources such as images and music are inherently interactive, if not interactional. To put it more simply, all of these ways of expressing meaning are done with a recipient in mind and with the assumption that some reaction or response will be forthcoming, even if the exact recipient(s) are not known and the response is not immediate. Still, as conversation analysts and other interactionists, working to describe sequential organization in many different contexts, have convincingly demonstrated, it cannot be denied that spoken interaction is unique for a number of reasons, but most importantly, because it unfolds at the moment of speaking. Displays of identity and stance acts are no different: Stance acts in face-to-face contexts can be modified at the moment of speaking, as for example, when two participants co-construct a stance. Nevertheless, the identity displays and stance acts found in discussion boards, blogs, or YouTube posts, can be altered incrementally (if not at that moment) through the grammatical resource of resonance, as was shown in example (13).

Another difference between the stance displays in the YouTube posts and examples from face-to-face interaction is that many of the posts are more complex. In Du Bois' (2007) study, most of the stance leads and follows were performed with single clauses (although sometimes there was also a dependent clause), whereas the posts often involved multiple sentences and/or complex sentences with several dependent clauses. This difference is related to well-documented differences between spoken and written language. (See, for example, Biber, 1988; Chafe, 1982; 1985; Ochs, 1979; Olson, 1977; Ong, 1982; Tannen, 1982a; 1982b.) Indeed, intonation units, the primary unit of spoken language, are typically quite short – one to seven words (Chafe, 1994; Chafe & Danielewicz, 1987), and mostly do not involve complex syntactic embedding (Chafe, 1994; Pawley & Syder, 1983). Not only are many of the comments in the posts more grammatically complex, they are also more complex in terms of what is being evaluated, often including evaluations of more than one stance object. For example in 10-12, several props are evaluated, and those evaluations are used in turn to evaluate the commercial as a whole. A final example of one poster responding to another displays this kind of complexity.

(14) **P9:** So these people have kids, but their house is so clean that you could eat off the toilet? Really?

P10: its a fucking commercial what does it matter?

P9's stance lead evaluates the object *their house* as *so clean you could eat off the toilet*. At the same time, the rhetorical question juxtaposes two ideas, that *these people have kids* and that *their house is so clean ...*, indexing P9's position of skepticism and disalignment with regard to the stance object *the commercial*. *Really?* makes P9's position questioning the commercial's representation of reality a little more explicit. Interestingly, P10's response first evaluates the stance object the *commercial* as *fucking*, but this comment is then followed by an act of disalignment with P9, not with respect to whether or not the commercial is credible, but rather with respect to the idea of commenting on a commercial at all. The stance display as a whole *it's a fucking commercial what does it matter?* indexes P10's position that no commercial represents reality. Of course, this kind of complex stance display with more than one stance object probably also occurs in face-to-face

interaction, but because Du Bois' (2007) analysis was a first attempt to theorize stance and suggest a framework for further research, this issue was not discussed.

FUTURE RESEARCH DIRECTIONS

This chapter is a first attempt to bring together social semiotics and the analysis of moment-by-moment social interaction, and it is, therefore, not surprising that it brought up many additional questions that I did not have space to address, or in some cases, even mention. Here, I summarize a few of these issues in the hope that they will spur further research. The first issue is that, although we know that multimodal discourse is a context-dependent composite of semiotic resources that convey meanings in multiple ways, teasing apart how each resource is used at a particular moment is extremely complex. Furthermore, examining how all of these resources work together adds another level of complexity, and I was only able to suggest some of the directions this kind of analysis might take. The commercial I chose was a particularly good example of how meaning potentials may be used to display not only desirable lifestyles but also social positioning associated with such lifestyles, and many of the meaning potentials were realized in posters' comments. Thus the analysis provided evidence that ordinary people, who are not analysts, link consumption and identity. Additional research examining the relationship between meaning potentials and viewers' comments with regard to other commercials or even other types of promotional discourse is warranted.

Another issue that is not well understood and which I mentioned only briefly is the relationship between identity, social class, and consumption. Since the publication of Bourdieu's (1984) *Distinction: A Social Critique of the Judgment of Taste*, social theorists have believed that social class is, at least partially, defined according to a person's ability to make fine distinctions about goods and services, or what is commonly referred to as *taste*. Although there is obviously a link between making such distinctions and identity, as displayed through stancetaking, the relationship between this kind of identity work and social class is not well understood. Bourdieu focuses only on the relationship between distinction and social class, without considering the interaction between class and other kinds of social groupings such as age, gender, or ethnicity (Lury, 1996). Indeed, Bucholtz (2007) says that *distinction* is relevant to identity work along "any dimension of differentiation between social groups" (p. 378). More work is needed to define social class and to tease apart its relation to these dimensions.

Another interesting point that I only discussed briefly is the use of rhythm to organize semiotic resources and convey meaning. Although I found that the voiceover and the music, or the images and the words appearing on the screen, used rhythm to create a coherent message, much more could be said about this. Indeed, Du Bois' (2007) idea of *resonance*, which he relates to "dialogic syntax" (p. 160), may be similar to van Leeuwen's (1985; 2005) concept of rhythm. Resonance and dialogic syntax have only been applied to language; rhythm has been used to refer to similarities and dissimilarities within and across semiotic resources, but these two ideas could be used together in order to develop a more comprehensive theory of indexical meaning that incorporates social semiotics.

Of course, an obvious question that could be fleshed out in much more detail is related to what have been described in the past as differences between spoken and written language (Chafe, 1982; Tannen, 1982b) or planned and unplanned discourse (Ochs, 1979). These questions obviously relate to context, and there have been significant changes in the way language is used due to technological developments. In some cases, our ability to communicate across space and time mimics face-to-face language use to a certain extent, as for example, when using a program like Skype. On the other hand, some types of written communication (e.g., text messaging or chatting) now allow writing to be more interactive than was previously the case. Each of these new ways of using language is somewhat different, a point I mentioned only briefly in discussing the stance displays on YouTube in comparison to the face-to-face stance displays studied by Du Bois (2007). This issue could be studied in more depth, increasing our understanding of language use in the wide variety of new contexts that are now commonplace. Of particular interest, is the question of how being able to respond in the moment of speaking versus not being able to do so affects the way language is used, both in terms of the kinds of meanings people express as well as the kinds of semiotic resources they use to express those meanings.

CONCLUSION

This study had two primary goals: 1) to contribute to our understanding of discursive constructions of identity in an online context centered around advertising and consumption; 2) to expand on existing frameworks designed to analyze different modes of conveying meaning in advertising using social semiotics, by incorporating insights from theories designed to analyze talk from an interactional perspective. Clearly, these two goals are linked because I needed to use the insights from interactional theories in order to expand beyond what social semiotics reveals about advertising and social positioning. In order to accomplish these goals, I divided the analysis into two parts: First, I analyzed a commercial from a social semiotic perspective, showing how the images, language, and soundtrack worked together to create a set of meaning potentials that index a desirable lifestyle and social identities. Then, using insights from frameworks that see displays of identity and stance as interactional accomplishments that are realized and modified incrementally, I showed how people who viewed the commercial and posted comments on YouTube displayed various stances concerning the commercial. Whether theses stances were positive, negative, or somewhere in between with regard to the commercial, they provided evidence that the posters had interpreted the meaning potentials of the commercial much as was suggested in the social semiotic analysis. The second part of the analysis thus provided support for the first part, the possible meanings of the semiotic resources. What the analysis of the stance displays added, however, was information about how the posters evaluated the commercial, and how they positioned themselves with respect to the commercial's message and/or other posters.

The essence of dialogicality, which Bakhtin (1986) captured when he referred to the *utterance* (whether spoken or written) as "a real unit of speech communion," (p. 67) is the idea that any utterance is part of a system of utterance/response, not just an individual unit. Although dialogicality as described this way might seem to see language as a sort of static artifact, the underlying principle suggests that language is representative of the subjective actions of individual participants. Examining both utterance and response is thus a way of looking at intersubjectivity (Du Bois, 2007). This insight accords with longstanding practices in disciplines focused on interaction: In conversation analysis, *participants'* reactions to and displays of understanding form the basis of analysis, and there is a focus on how each action creates and maintains the relation between self and other. As Raymond and Heritage (2006) suggest, the resources that conversational participants routinely use are *general* linguistic devices and sequential order, which "nevertheless can be used in the fabrication of identities of exquisite *specificity and particularity*" (p. 701; my emphasis).

In the past, it has rarely been possible to examine how people respond to discourse that is disseminated at a distance to multiple, unknown audience members (such as the commercial analyzed here) because there was no way to gather and analyze people's natural responses. New technology has changed that by creating the possibility of response even at a distance, and new methods that treat all language use as interactive will provide more insight. An analysis solely based on meaning potentials is partial because the possibilities are only realized through the actions of others, as they make known their interpretation and stance. I hope to encourage other discourse analysts to take a more interaction-based approach. As has long been understood by conversation analysts and other interactionists, this is a way to strengthen an analysis, and the most persuasive way to support it.

REFERENCES

Antaki, C., & Widdicombe, S. (Eds.). (1998). *Identities in talk*. London: Sage Publications.

Bakhtin, M. M. (1986). The problem of speech genres. In Emerson, C., & Holquist, M. (Eds.), *Speech genres and other late essays* (pp. 60–102). (McGee, V. W., Trans.). Austin: University of Texas Press.

Benwell, B., & Stokoe, E. (2010). Analysing identity in interaction: Contrasting discourse, genealogical, narrative, and conversation analysis. In Wetherell, M., & Mohanty, C. T. (Eds.), *The Sage handbook of identities* (pp. 82–103). Los Angeles: Sage Publications. doi:10.4135/9781446200889. n6.

Biber, D. (1988). *Variation across speech and writing*. Cambridge: Cambridge University Press. doi:10.1017/CBO9780511621024.

Boggio, C. (2010). Automobile advertising for cultural elites: A multimodal analysis. In Evangelisti Allori, P., & Garzoni, G. (Eds.), *Discourse, identities and genres in corporate communication* (pp. 145–161). Bern: Peter Lang.

Bourdieu, P. (1984). *Distinction: A social critique of the judgment of taste*. Cambridge, MA: Harvard University Press.

Bucholtz, M. (2007). Shop talk: Branding, consumption, and gender in American middle-class youth interaction. In McElhinny, B. S. (Ed.), *Words, worlds, and material girls: Language, gender, globalization* (pp. 371–402). Berlin: Mouton de Gruyter. doi:10.1515/9783110198805.4.371.

Bucholtz, M., & Hall, K. (2005). Identity and interaction: A sociocultural linguistic approach. *Discourse Studies*, *7*(4-5), 585–614. doi:10.1177/1461445605054407.

Chafe, W. (1982). Integration and involvement in speaking, writing, and oral literature. In Tannen, D. (Ed.), *Spoken and written language: Exploring orality and literacy* (pp. 35–54). Norwood, NJ: Ablex.

Chafe, W. (1985). Linguistic differences produced by differences between speaking and writing. In Olson, D. R., Hildyard, A., & Torrance, N. (Eds.), *Literacy, language, and learning: The nature and consequences of reading and writing* (pp. 105–123). Cambridge: Cambridge University Press.

Chafe, W. (1994). *Discourse, consciousness, and time: The flow and displacement of conscious experience in speaking and writing*. Chicago: University of Chicago Press.

Chafe, W., & Danielewicz, J. (1987). Properties of spoken and written language. In Horowitz, R., & Samuels, F. J. (Eds.), *Comprehending oral and written language*. New York: Academic Press.

Du Bois, J. W. (2007). The stance triangle. In Englebretson, R. (Ed.), *Stancetaking in discourse: Subjectivity, evaluation, and interaction* (pp. 139–182). Amsterdam: John Benjamins.

Fairclough, N. (1995). *Critical discourse analysis: The critical study of language*. London: Longman.

Fairclough, N. (2001). The discourse of New Labour: Critical discourse analysis. In Wetherell, M., Taylor, S., & Yates, S. J. (Eds.), *Discourse as data: A guide for analysis* (pp. 229–266). London: The Open University/Sage.

Halliday, M. A. K. (1978). *Language as a social semiotic*. London: Edward Arnold.

Heritage, J. (1997). Conversation analysis and institutional talk: Analysing data. In Silverman, D. (Ed.), *Qualitative research: Theory, method and practice* (pp. 161–182). London: Sage Publications.

Heritage, J., & Clayman, S. (2010). *Talk in action: Interactions, identities, and institutions*. West Sussex, UK: Wiley-Blackwell.

Heritage, J., & Raymond, G. (2005). The terms of agreement: Indexing epistemic authority and subordination in talk-in-interaction. *Social Psychology Quarterly*, *68*(1), 15–38. doi:10.1177/019027250506800103.

Iedema, R. (2001). Analysing film and television: A social semiotic account of hospital: An unhealthy business. In van Leeuwen, T., & Jewitt, C. (Eds.), *Handbook of visual analysis* (pp. 183–204). London: Sage Publications.

Jewitt, C., & Oyama, R. (2001). Visual meaning: A social semiotic approach. In van Leeuwen, T., & Jewitt, C. (Eds.), *Handbook of visual analysis* (pp. 134–156). London: Sage Publications.

Johnstone, B. (2007). Linking identity and dialect through stancetaking. In Englebretson, R. (Ed.), *Stancetaking in discourse: Subjectivity, evaluation, and interaction* (pp. 49–68). Amsterdam: John Benjamins.

Klein, N. (2000). *No logo*. New York: Picador.

Kress, G., & van Leeuwen, T. (1996). *Reading images: The grammar of visual design*. London: Routledge.

Lemke, J. (1989). Semantics and social values. *Word*, *40*(1-2), 37–50.

Lury, C. (1996). *Consumer culture*. New Brunswick, NJ: Rutgers University Press.

Machin, D., & van Leeuwen, T. (2007). *Global media discourse: A critical introduction*. London: Routledge.

Mayes, P. (2010). Corporate culture in a global age: Starbucks' "social responsibility" and the merging of corporate and personal interests. In Trosborg, A. (Ed.), *Pragmatics across cultures* (pp. 597–628). Berlin: De Gruyter Mouton.

Ochs, E. (1979). Planned and unplanned discourse. In T. Givón (Ed.), Discourse and syntax (Syntax and semantics, Vol. 12). New York: Academic Press.

Olson, D. R. (1977). From utterance to text: The bias of language in speech and writing. *Harvard Educational Review*, *47*, 257–281.

Ong, W. (1982). *Orality and literacy: The technologizing of the word*. London: Methuen. doi:10.4324/9780203328064.

Pawley, A., & Syder, F. (1983). Natural selection in syntax: Notes on adaptive variation and change in vernacular and literary grammar. *Journal of Pragmatics*, *7*, 551–579. doi:10.1016/0378-2166(83)90081-4.

Raymond, G., & Heritage, J. (2006). The epistemics of social relations: Owning grandchildren. *Language in Society*, *35*, 677–705. doi:10.1017/S0047404506060325.

Schegloff, E. A., & Sacks, H. (1973). Opening up closings. *Semiotica*, *8*, 289–327. doi:10.1515/semi.1973.8.4.289.

Tannen, D. (Ed.). (1982a). *Spoken and written language: Exploring orality and literacy*. Norwood, NJ: Ablex.

Tannen, D. (1982b). Oral and literate strategies in spoken and written language. *Language*, *58*, 1–21. doi:10.2307/413530.

van Leeuwen, T. (1985). Rhythmic structure of the film text. In T. A. van Dijk (Ed.), Discourse and communication – New approaches to the analysis of mass media discourse and communication (pp. 216-232). Berlin: de Gruyter.

van Leeuwen, T. (2005). *Introducing social semiotics*. London: Routledge.

van Leeuwen, T., & Jewitt, C. (Eds.). (2001). *Handbook of visual analysis*. London: Sage Publications.

Widdicombe, S. (1998). Identity as an analysts' and a participants' resource. In Antaki, C., & Widdicombe, S. (Eds.), *Identities in talk* (pp. 191–206). London: Sage Publications.

Widdicombe, S., & Wooffitt, R. (1995). *The language of youth subcultures: Social identity in action*. New York: Harvester Wheatsheaf.

ADDITIONAL READING

Bucholtz, M. (1999). Purchasing power: Gender and class imaginary on the shopping channel. In Bucholtz, M., Liang, A. C., & Sutton, L. A. (Eds.), *Reinventing identities: The gendered self in discourse* (pp. 348–368). London: Oxford University Press.

Chafe, W. (1979). The flow of thought and the flow of language. In Givón, T. (Ed.), *Discourse and syntax*. New York: Academic Press.

Chafe, W. (1987). Cognitive constraints on information flow. In Tomlin, R. (Ed.), *Coherence and grounding in discourse*. Amsterdam: John Benjamins.

Chouliaraki, L., & Fairclough, N. (1999). *Discourse in late modernity: Rethinking critical discourse analysis*. Edinburgh: Edinburgh University Press.

Couper-Kuhlen, E., & Selting, M. (2001). Introducing interactional linguistics. In Selting, M., & Couper-Kuhlen, E. (Eds.), *Studies in interactional linguistics* (pp. 1–22). Amsterdam: John Benjamins.

Davies, B., & Harré, R. (1990). Positioning: The discursive production of selves. *Journal for the Theory of Social Behaviour, 20,* 43–63. doi:10.1111/j.1468-5914.1990.tb00174.x.

Duranti, A. (2009). The force of language and its temporal unfolding. In Turner, K., & Fraser, B. (Eds.), *Language in life, and a life in language: Jacob Mey – A festschrift* (pp. 63–71). Bingley, UK: Emerald Group Publishing.

Fairclough, N. (2003). *Analysing discourse: Textual analysis for social science research*. London: Routledge.

Ford, C. E., & Thompson, S. A. (1996). Interactional units in conversation: Syntactic, intonational, and pragmatic resources for the management of turns. In Ochs, E., Schegloff, E. A., & Thompson, S. A. (Eds.), *Interaction and grammar* (pp. 134–184). New York: Cambridge University Press. doi:10.1017/CBO9780511620874.003.

Gee, J. P., Hull, G., & Lankshear, C. (1997). *The new work order: Behind the language of the new capitalism*. New York: Westview Press.

Goodwin, C. (1979). The interactive construction of a sentence in natural conversation. In Psathas, G. (Ed.), *Everyday language: Studies in ethnomethodology* (pp. 97–121). New York: Irvington.

Halliday, M. A. K. (1994). *An introduction to functional grammar* (2nd ed.). London: Edward Arnold.

Harris, R., & Rampton, B. (2009). Ethnicities without guarantees: An empirical approach. In Wetherell, M. (Ed.), *Identity in the 21st century: New trends in changing times* (pp. 95–119). London: Palgrave Macmillan.

Heritage, J. (1984). *Garfinkel and ethnomethodology*. Cambridge: Polity Press.

Heritage, J. (2011). A Galilean moment in social theory? Language, culture and their emergent properties. *Qualitative Sociology, 34,* 263–270. doi:10.1007/s11133-010-9180-y.

Heritage, J. (2012). Epistemics in action: Action formation and territories of knowledge. *Research on Language and Social Interaction, 45,* 1–29. doi:10.1080/08351813.2012.646684.

Heritage, J., & Stivers, T. (2012). Conversation analysis in sociology. In Sidnell, J., & Stivers, T. (Eds.), *Handbook of conversation analysis* (pp. 659–673). Boston: Wiley-Blackwell.

Hodge, B., & Kress, G. (1988). *Social semiotics*. Cambridge: Polity Press.

Hutchby, I., & Wooffitt, R. (2008). *Conversation analysis* (2nd ed.). Cambridge: Polity Press.

Jaworski, A., & Thurlow, C. (2009). Taking an elitist stance: Ideology and the discursive production of social distinction. In Jaffee, A. (Ed.), *Perspectives on Stance: Sociolinguistic Perspectives* (pp. 195–226). New York: Oxford University Press. doi:10.1093/acprof:oso/9780195331646.003.0009.

Jewitt, C. (1997). Images of men. *Sociological Research Online, 2*(2). Retrieved October 5, 2012, from http://www.socresonline.org.uk/2/2/6.html

Jewitt, C. (Ed.). (2009). *The Routledge handbook of multimodal analysis*. London: Routledge.

Jewitt, C., & Kress, G. (Eds.). (2003). *Multimodal literacy*. New York: Peter Lang.

Mendoza-Denton, N. (2002). Language and identity. In Chambers, J. K., Trudgill, P., & Schilling-Estes, N. (Eds.), *The handbook of language variation and change* (pp. 475–499). Oxford: Blackwell.

Rampton, B. (2010). Social class and sociolinguistics. *Applied Linguistics Review*, *1*, 1–22. doi:10.1515/9783110222654.1.

Thurlow, C. (2007). Fabricating youth: New-media discourse and the technologization of young people. In Johnson, S., & Ensslin, A. (Eds.), *Language in the media: Representations, identities, ideologies* (pp. 213–233). London: Continuum.

van Leeuwen, T. (1991). Conjunctive structure in documentary film and television. *Continuum*, *5*(1), 76–114. doi:10.1080/10304319109388216.

van Leeuwen, T. (1999). *Speech, sound, music*. London: Macmillan.

van Leeuwen, T. (2008). *Discourse and practice: New tools for critical discourse analysis*. Oxford: Oxford University Press.

Wetherell, M. (1998). Positioning and interpretative repertoires: Conversation analysis and post-structuralism in dialogue. *Discourse & Society*, *9*, 387–412. doi:10.1177/0957926598009003005.

Wooffitt, R. (2005). *Conversation analysis and discourse analysis*. London: Sage.

KEY TERMS AND DEFINITIONS

Dialogicality: The idea that when people express meaning, they engage with ideas already expressed by another and may use the same or similar semiotic resources to do so.

High-Concept Advertising: A type of advertising that focuses on emotions, experiences, and/or desirable lifestyles rather than the products or services being marketed.

Identity: The social positioning of self and other (Bucholtz & Hall, 2005, p. 586).

Index: A linguistic form or other semiotic resource that (indirectly) signals social meaning.

Interactional Approach: A set of frameworks originally designed to analyze face-to-face interaction in that they examine utterances and responses as they occur in the moment.

Intersubjectivity: The relation between two subjectivities that emerges in dialogic interaction.

Meaning Potential: The field of possible meanings in relation to a particular semiotic resource.

Semiotic Resource: The actions and/or objects used to communicate.

Social Semiotics: A subdiscipline related to systemic functional grammar, but focused on how semiotic resources other than language are used systematically to convey meaning.

Stance: The positioning of self and other with respect to some object.

ENDNOTES

1. One comment is repeated verbatim but attributed to two different posters.
2. Includes one comment about the musicians rather than the music.
3. Three of these posters made two positive comments.
4. One poster made two of these comments.
5. Includes comments about another poster or about the comment of another poster.
6. This is the actual name used by this poster on the YouTube site. I have included it in order to demonstrate the resonance in this example.

APPENDIX

Figure 1. SignatureHome commercial, scene 2 (© 2011 Time Warner Cable Enterprises LLC. Used with permission.)

Figure 2. SignatureHome commercial, scene 3 (© 2011 Time Warner Cable Enterprises LLC. Used with permission.)

Figure 3. SignatureHome commercial, scene 4 (© 2011 Time Warner Cable Enterprises LLC. Used with permission.)

Figure 4. SignatureHome commercial, scene 5 (© 2011 Time Warner Cable Enterprises LLC. Used with permission.)

Figure 5. SignatureHome commercial, scene 6 (© 2011 Time Warner Cable Enterprises LLC. Used with permission.)

Figure 6. SignatureHome commercial, scene 9 (© 2011 Time Warner Cable Enterprises LLC. Used with permission.)

Chapter 13

Statistical Discourse Analysis:
Testing Educational Hypotheses with Large Datasets of Electronic Discourse

Ming Ming Chiu
University at Buffalo, State University of New York, USA

Gaowei Chen
University of Pittsburgh, USA

ABSTRACT

Educators are increasingly using electronic discourse for student learning and problem solving, partially due to its time and space flexibility and greater opportunities for information processing and higher order thinking. When researchers try to statistically analyze the relationships among electronic discourse messages however, they often face difficulties regarding the data (missing data, many codes, non-linear trees of messages), dependent variables (topic differences, time differences, discrete, infrequent, multiple dependent variables) and explanatory variables (sequences of messages, cross-level moderation, indirect effects, false positives). Statistical discourse analysis (SDA) addresses all of these difficulties as shown in analyses of social cues in 894 messages posted by 183 students during 60 online asynchronous discussions. The results showed that disagreements increased negative social cues, supporting the hypothesis that these participants did not save face during disagreements, but attacked face. Using these types of analyses and results, researchers can inform designs and uses of electronic discourse.

INTRODUCTION

Educators are increasingly using electronic discussions (e.g., discussion boards, knowledge building environments, blogs) to have students solve problems and to help them learn. These electronic discussions offer students greater flexibility to communicate at different times and in different locations. Furthermore, the explicit and permanent displays of writing (and drawing) and longer time for reflection offer students greater opportunities for information processing and higher order thinking (Hara, Bonk, & Angeli, 2000; Tallent-Runnels, Thomas, Lan, Cooper, Ahern, & Shaw et al., 2006). As a result, students are not only creating voluminous amounts of electronic discourse data, but they are doing so at a faster rate.

DOI: 10.4018/978-1-4666-4426-7.ch013

While many studies have counted attributes of separate electronic discourse messages (e.g., Garrison, Anderson, & Archer, 2001; Gress, Fior, Hadwin, & Winne, 2008; Hara et al., 2000; Rafaeli & Sudweeks, 1998; Tallent-Runnels et al., 2006), they have not examined the relationships within sequences of messages. Within threads of messages, participants can respond to earlier actions and/or invite future actions. By analyzing these relationships across messages, researchers can improve their understanding of the social and cognitive dynamics of electronic discourses and help educators improve students' learning and discussions.

Suitable statistics methods can help researchers test hypotheses about these relationships on large data sets to build an empirically-supported knowledge base. However, statistically analyzing online interaction processes often requires addressing difficulties regarding the data set, outcome variables, and explanatory variables. Data issues include missing data, content analysis/coding, and non-linear trees of messages.

Difficulties involving dependent variables include differences across online discussion topics, similarities in adjacent messages, discrete (not continuous) variables, infrequent occurrences of focal events, and multiple dependent variables. Explanatory variable issues include sequences of messages, context-dependent effects, indirect effects across levels, and false positives.

In this chapter, we introduce how statistical discourse analysis (SDA; Chiu, 2008a, Chiu & Khoo, 2005) addresses the above analytic difficulties. To contextualize the methodological issues, we test whether earlier messages affect the likelihood of specific attributes in each message. For example, people often express personal affect or attitudes towards others during a discussion, a *social cue* ("Oh, I get it now"; "☺"). Hence, we can test which attributes of earlier messages affect the likelihood of a positive cue in the current message. In this study, we do so by applying SDA to 894 messages by 183 participants on 60

high school mathematics topics on a mathematics problem solving website. The analyses and results can help us build empirically-supported understanding to inform and improve educators' designs and uses of electronic discourse.

BACKGROUND

During an electronic discussion, a group of participants exchange ideas by sending and receiving messages. Like face-to-face discourse, electronic discourse involves individuals responding to others' recent messages and inviting others' future messages. When participants agree or disagree with the content of the previous message, they refer back into the past; in contrast, asking questions or issuing commands projects forward into future messages. These links connect series of sequential events (or time-series data). Moreover, if there are multiple discussion topics/groups, the electronic discourse also has multilevel structure (messages nested within topics).

Unlike face-to-face discourse, electronic discourse can have messages along many threads. Due to a weaker turn-taking mechanism, electronic discussants can respond to any previous message, especially during asynchronous discussions. As such, electronic discussions often proceed along multiple threads and generate non-linear trees of messages. While some of the messages receive many responses, others receive none (which would end the specific discussion branch; Hewitt, 2005; Thomas, 2002). See Figure 1 for an example of the tree relationships between a topic and its 13 responses. The number "0" denotes the initial problem; "1" through "13" indicates 13 chronological reply messages, where "1" refers to the earliest reply and "13" refers to the last reply. In this tree of messages, the topic and its replies were linked to one another by multiple threads and single connections. Messages in each thread were ordered by time, but they were not necessarily consecutive. For example, message #5 followed message #2 (not #4) and message #13 followed message #5 (not #12).

Despite the multilevel, time series, and non-linear features of electronic discourse, most previous studies of electronic discussion have focused on the aggregate properties of individual messages during a discussion (e.g., Garrison et al., 2001; Gress et al., 2008; Hara et al., 2000; Tallent-Runnels et al., 2006). These results showed that many participants processed information at high cognitive levels during electronic discussions, in contrast to many face-to-face discussions, supporting the claim that electronic discussions can promote participants' knowledge contributions. Furthermore, participants tended to add social cues (e.g., "Hi"; "☺") in their messages to maintain social presence and build social relationships in online environments.

Few studies have systematically examined the relationships among messages to characterize electronic discussion processes (e.g., Chen & Chiu, 2008; Wise & Chiu, 2011). Research questions regarding the social and cognitive processes during a discussion can include 1) Which characteristics of a group of students, an individual, or sequences of recent messages (micro-time context) influence the likelihood of others responding to a message? 2) Which of the above characteristics influence the likelihood of a desirable (or undesirable) message attribute (e.g., new idea, positive social cue)? 3)

Figure 1. Mapping the tree of relationships between a problem and its reply messages

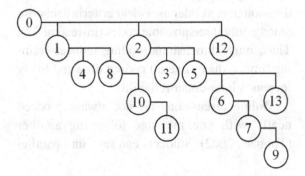

How do the attributes of a teacher's messages influence subsequent student messages? SDA can capture the richness of electronic discourse by addressing such questions. By understanding how students post messages to interact with one another during electronic discussions, researchers can help educators improve their students' learning and problem solving over the internet.

STATISTICAL DISCOURSE ANALYSIS

Statistically analyzing relationships among electronic messages requires addressing analytic difficulties regarding the entire data set, dependent variables and explanatory variables. See Table 1. Data issues include missing data, content analysis/coding and non-linear trees of online messages. Difficulties involving outcomes include nested data, differences across time, discrete outcomes, infrequent outcomes and multiple outcomes. Explanatory variable issues include sequences, context-dependent effects, indirect effects and false positives. While past studies have tried to address these questions by analyzing data across time with conditional probabilities (e.g., Parks & Fals-Stewart, 2004), sequential analysis (Lehmann-Willenbrock & Kauffeld, 2010), Logit regressions (Pevalin & Ermisch, 2004), non-linear dynamic models (Gorman, Amazeen, & Cooke, 2010) or pattern analysis (Stachowski, Kaplan, & Waller, 2009), these methods do not adequately address differences across groups, differences across individuals, attributes of sequences of messages or differences across time (Mercer, 2008; Reimann, 2009). Statistical discourse analysis (SDA) addresses all of these issues as follows (Chiu, 2008a; Chiu & Khoo, 2005).

Overall Data Set

SDA addresses the overall data set issues (missing data, content analysis/coding, parallel talk, mes-

Table 1. Addressing each analytic difficulty with statistical discourse analysis

Analytic difficulty	Statistical Discourse Analysis strategy
Data Set	
• Missing data (0110??10)	• Markov Chain Monte Carlo multiple imputation (Peugh & Enders, 2004)
• Content analysis (A, B, … Z)	• Multi-dimensional coding (Chiu & Khoo, 2005)
• Non-linear trees of messages (Λ)	• Record previous message to map tree structure of messages (Chen & Chiu, 2008)
Dependent variables	
• Differences across discussion topics ($D_5 \neq D_7$)	• Multilevel analysis (aka Hierarchical linear modeling; Bryk & Raudenbush, 1992; Goldstein, 1995)
• Similarities in adjacent messages ($t_7 \sim t_8$)	• I^2 index of Q statistics (Huedo-Medina, Sanchez-Meca, Marin-Martinez, & Botella, 2006)
• Discrete variable (yes/no)	• Logit (Kennedy, 2008)
• Infrequent dependent variables (e.g., $P[Y] = 12\%$)	• Logit bias estimator (King & Zeng, 2001)
• Multiple dependent variables (Y_1, Y_2, …)	• Multivariate outcome models (Goldstein, 1995)
Explanatory variables	
• Sequences of messages (X_{t-2} or $X_{t-1} \rightarrow Y_0$)	• Vector Auto-Regression (VAR, Kennedy, 2008)
• Moderation across levels (e.g., Message x Discussion)	• Random effects cross-level moderation (Goldstein, 1995)
• Indirect, multi-level mediation effects ($X \rightarrow M \rightarrow Y$)	• Multilevel M-tests (MacKinnon, Lockwood, & Williams, 2004)
• False positives (Type I errors)	• Two-stage linear step-up procedure (Benjamini, Krieger, & Yekutieli, 2006)

sage trees) with Markov Chain Monte Carlo multiple imputation (MCMC-MI), multi-dimensional coding and storage of the previous message to enable reconstruction of the entire message tree. Missing data can (a) bias the results, (b) raise the complexity of the data analyses and (c) reduce estimation efficiency (Peugh & Enders, 2004). We use MCMC-MI to estimate the values of the missing data, which addresses this issue more effectively than deletion, mean substitution, or simple imputation, according to computer simulations (Peugh & Enders, 2004).

Ideally, the content analysis uses a unit of analysis with clear boundaries (e.g., an online message) and categories that are mutually exclusive, exhaustive and sufficiently comprehensive to test one's hypotheses. As the number and complexity of categories rise however, (a) the training time for coders and the overall coding time rise, (b) coding conflicts rise, (c) internal consistency and inter-coder reliability fall, (d) degrees of freedom

in the explanatory model fall and (e) precision falls (Chiu & Khoo, 2005).

By using a multi-dimensional coding scheme with corresponding decision trees, SDA can capture the data's complexity, reduce the number of needed variables, increase inter-coder reliability and thereby model complex phenomena. For example, Chiu's (2000) individual action framework has three dimensions (evaluation, knowledge content, invitation to participate). Because each dimension has three categories, this framework can capture 27 different types of action (27 = 3 x 3 x 3). By coding one dimension at a time with a decision tree, a coder uses clear criteria to choose among only three possible codes (instead of 27). Thus, multi-dimensional coding reduces training time, reduces overall coding time and likely increases inter-coder reliability.

Online discussions do not always proceed neatly with one message following another (Thomas, 2002). Students can split into parallel discussions, and multiple messages can respond to one message (see Figure 1). To address this issue, the database includes a variable that identifies and stores the message to which a message responds (Chen & Chiu, 2008). By tracing the predecessor of each message, we can reconstruct the entire tree of messages in a discussion.

Dependent Variables

SDA addresses the dependent variables issues (nested data, time, discrete, infrequent or multiple dependent variables) with multilevel analysis, an I^2 index of Q statistics, multilevel cross-classification, Logit, Logit bias estimation and multivariate outcomes models. Electronic discourse can involve nested data (messages within discussions; individuals within groups within classrooms, etc.). Failure to account for similarities in messages within the same discussion (vs. different discussions), by the same person (vs. different people), within the same group (vs. different groups) or within the same classroom (vs. different classrooms) can underestimate the standard errors (Goldstein, 1995). SDA addresses these issues by modeling nested data with a multilevel analysis (Goldstein, 1995; cf. hierarchical linear modeling, Bryk & Raudenbush, 1992).

As adjacent messages are often more similar than messages that are far apart from one another, failure to model this similarity (serial correlation of errors) can bias the results (Kennedy, 2008). To address this issue, an I^2 index of Q statistics tested all groups simultaneously for serial correlation of residuals in adjacent messages (Huedo-Medina et al., 2006). If the I^2 index shows significant serial correlation, adding the outcome variable value of the previous message often eliminates the serial correlation (e.g., when modeling the outcome variable *positive social cue*, add whether a *positive social cue* occurs in the previous message [*positive social cue* (–1)] as an *explanatory* variable;

Chiu & Khoo, 2005). Then, SDA models these differences across time with a multilevel cross-classification (Goldstein, 1995).

The outcomes are often discrete (a *positive social cue* occurs in a conversation or it does not) rather than continuous (e.g., test scores), so standard regressions such as ordinary least squares can bias the standard errors. To model discrete outcome variables, we use a Logit regression (Kennedy, 2008). As infrequent outcomes can bias the results of a Logit regression (King & Zeng, 2001), we compute the Logit bias with a Logit bias estimator (King & Zeng, 2001) and remove it.

Multiple outcomes can have correlated residuals that can underestimate standard errors (Goldstein, 1995). If the outcomes are from different levels, analyzing them in the same model over-counts the sample size of the higher level outcome(s) and results in biased standard errors. If multiple outcomes are from different levels of analysis, separate analyses must be done at each level. To model multiple outcomes at the same level of analysis, we use a multivariate outcome, multilevel cross-classification (Goldstein, 1995).

Explanatory Variables

SDA addresses the explanatory variable issues (sequences, context-dependent effects, indirect effects and false positives) with a vector auto-regression (VAR, Kennedy, 2008), multilevel random effects, multilevel M-tests and the two-stage step-up procedure. A VAR combines characteristics of sequences of recent messages into a local time context (*micro-time context*) to model how they influence a subsequent message. For example, the likelihood of a positive social cue in a message might be influenced by characteristics of earlier messages (e.g., disagreement in the previous message) or earlier writers (e.g., past mathematics achievement of the writer of the previous message). To identify interaction effects across levels, SDA uses multilevel random effects (Goldstein, 1995).

Single-level mediation tests can detect indirect effects (rather than direct effects), but applying these tests to nested (multilevel) data can bias results downward. To test whether explanatory variables show indirect effects through intermediate variables properly, SDA uses multilevel M-tests (MacKinnon et al., 2004).

Lastly, testing many hypotheses also increases the risk of false positives (Type I errors; Benjamini et al., 2006). The two-stage linear step-up procedure reduces false positives more effectively than 13 other methods, according to computer simulations (Benjamini et al., 2006).

SHOWCASING STATISTICAL DISCOURSE ANALYSIS

In this section, we showcase SDA by testing hypotheses regarding social cues on 60 online asynchronous discussions in which 183 students posted 894 messages. We first define social cues (positive, negative) in this study, followed by a specific set of hypotheses and a data set drawn from Chen, Chiu, and Wang (2012b). Then, we show how we used the strategies in SDA to address them.

Definition of Social Cues

In this case, we define a social cue as a group member's expressed personal affect or attitude toward others during a discussion. Hence, social cues here refer to the cues expressed in a face-to-face conversation turn or an online discussion message. Specifically, positive social cues refer to group members' expressions of positive affective states (e.g., "Oh, I get it now"; "☺") or show positive attitudes toward others when giving greetings (e.g., *"Welcome, John"*), emphasizing agreements (e.g., "I *totally* agree with you!"), inviting elaborations politely (e.g., *"Could you*

please explain your steps further?"), or showing appreciation (e.g., *"Thanks* for your explanation"; Brown & Levinson, 1987; Hara et al., 2000; Rourke, Anderson, Garrison, & Archer, 2001). In contrast, negative social cues express negative affective states (e.g., "I'm so stupid"; "☹") or negative attitudes toward others, such as rude disagreements ("You are wrong!!!"), flaming ("No, I'm not, YOU are wrong!!!"), and insults/face attacks ("Who do you think you are?"; Herring, 1994; Kim & Raja, 1991; McKee, 2002).

Hypotheses

We examine how evaluations (agreements, disagreements) in recent messages affect the likelihood of a current message's positive or negative social cues. An evaluation of another person's action can affect the previous participant's public self-image (*face*; Brown & Levinson, 1987; Chiu, 2008b), thereby influencing their social relationship during the subsequent discussion. When agreeing with an idea for example, an online discussion participant can add positive social cues to support the previous participant, promote his or her face, and enhance their positive social relationship (Brown & Levinson, 1987). Participants who feel strongly about an idea might add extra affective words (e.g., "Aha, I agree with you") or emoticons (e.g., "Right ☺"), which parallel smiling agreements in face-to-face discussions. In contrast, participants who agree but do not feel strongly are less likely to post a message. As agreements often support positive social relationships (Brown & Levinson, 1987; Chiu, 2008b), a participant can respond to an agreement (e.g., "I agree with your answer") by adding positive social cues in the response (e.g., "Thanks ☺") to further promote their positive social relationships (Vinagre, 2008; Walther, 1992).

In contrast, when online discussion participants disagree with a previous idea, they might be less likely to use positive social cues. During online discussions, the anonymity and reduced face concerns allow participants to disagree with one another more freely (Reinig & Mejias, 2004). Thus, participants might be less likely to use positive social cues to soften or redress disagreements (e.g., "I don't agree with how you solved it"); or they might even add negative social cues to disagree rudely due to the reduced normative constraints of online discussions (e.g., adding exclamation marks, "You made it too complicated!!!!!"). In responding to disagreements, participants might also be less likely to use positive social cues. Like face-to-face disagreements, online disagreements (e.g., "Nope, you're wrong") can also threaten face by lowering public perception of the previous participant's competence (Brown & Levinson, 1987). Hence, a previous participant is less likely to respond to a disagreement with positive social cues. If the previous participant perceives the disagreement as a personal attack, he or she might retaliate with negative social cues to protect his or her own face while attacking the previous speaker's face ("No, I'm not, you are wrong!"; Gottman & Krokoff, 1989; Tracy & Tracy, 1998, *face attack*).

In sum, we have the following hypotheses regarding evaluations' effects on social cues during online discussions.

H-1: After an agreement, positive social cues are more likely.

H-2: After a disagreement, positive social cues are less likely, while negative social cues are more likely.

In addition to evaluations, knowledge content and social cues in recent messages might also influence the likelihood of positive and negative social cues during asynchronous, online discussions. Furthermore, we controlled for several recent message attributes, such as knowledge content (new ideas, justifications), social cues, message number (a greater number indicates a later post), message length (number of words in a message), and time interval between adjacent

messages. Note that these message-level variables differ from higher-level individual characteristics that might influence the conversation –such as displayed online gender (masculine, feminine, or no gender-identifying characteristics), past post experience (e.g., number of past posts), and topic initiator (initiator vs. replier) (Collins, 1992; Sproull & Kiesler, 1986).

Data

A computer random number generator selected 60 topics from the High School Basics (HSB) community on the Art of Problem Solving website (AoPS, artofproblemsolving.com) over nine months, excluding problems with less than four reply messages. The data set included 183 participants' 894 reply messages on the 60 topics, which consisted of 35 algebra, 11 geometry, and 14 number theory and counting problems. All 60 topics had both masculine and feminine participants. The website statistics showed that most of these participants were high school students aged 12 to 16 years. About 80% of them were from the US and the rest were from other countries such as Argentina, Japan, and UK. The participants did not necessarily know each other outside this community. They communicated with one another voluntarily, without teacher moderation or course evaluation.

Analysis Procedure

We applied the strategies in SDA to address the above difficulties during the analysis. We first mapped the tree structures of the online discussion messages and used a multi-dimensional coding scheme to code the data. Then, we analyzed the data by using multivariate outcome, multilevel logit to model the dependent variables. We also used I^2 index of Q statistics (Huedo-Medina et al., 2006) to test for serial correlation of residuals of the regressions. To address explanatory variable issues, we used vector auto-regression (VAR,

Kennedy, 2008), multilevel M-tests (MacKinnon et al., 2004), and two-stage linear step-up procedure. The analysis proceeded in the order described below.

Mapping Tree Structure

In this electronic discourse, each of the 60 topics received 6 to 26 ($M = 15$) reply messages in each thread, but they were often not consecutive (nonlinear). Moreover, the multi-threaded discussion mode had many unresponsive messages, which made it difficult to track a message's parent messages (Thomas, 2002). To identify the relationships between a topic and its responses, we mapped its tree structure (see example in Figure 1; Chen & Chiu, 2008). The forum's interface design constrained each message to respond to the topic or a previous reply message, which helped form clear connections and avoid ambiguous relationships among messages.

Mapping the tree structure of the messages in a topic enabled us to generate two sets of variables: current message variables and earlier message variables. *Current message* (0) variables captured characteristics of the current message. *Earlier message* ($-n$, where $n = 1, 2, 3, 4, ...$) variables captured characteristics of messages posted before the current message in the same thread. Respectively, variables at lag 1 or (-1) measured characteristics of the previous message to which the current message responded; lag 2 variables (-2) measured the characteristics of the message to which the previous message (-1) responded; and so on. Consider message #11 in Figure 1. Positive social cue (0) measured if #11 included a positive social cue. Meanwhile, positive social cue (-1) measured if its previous message, message #10, included a positive social cue. Positive social cue (-2) measured if the message two connections prior, message #8, included a positive social cue, and so on.

Multi-Dimensional Coding

Our coding framework consists of mutually exclusive and exhaustive categories. Moreover, the multi-dimensional simplicity increases the tractability of coding for large sample statistical analyses (Chiu, 2000). The unit of coding was a complete message that a participant posted on the online discussion forum. Specifically, each message was coded along five dimensions: social cue, evaluation, new idea, justification, and individual characteristics. See Table 2 for the coding categories and examples.

Two students, working separately, coded each of the 894 messages. Then, they compared their results and resolved all coding disagreements by discussion and consensus. Inter-rater reliability was computed with Krippendorff's α (2004), which can be applied to incomplete data, any sample size, any measurement level, any number of coders or categories, and scale values. Ranging from -1 to 1, an α exceeding 0.66 shows satisfactory agreement (Krippendorff, 2004). The web server automatically recorded each participant's number of past posts, message number, message length, and the time interval between two consecutive messages in a thread. To track the variables in earlier messages ($-1, -2, ...$) along the multi-threaded structure of the online discussions, a computer program identified the relationships of messages and aided the coding of earlier message variables ($-n$).

Multilevel Logit Analysis

A two-level Logit model properly models the binary outcome variable positive social cue (or negative social cue). First, we added topic-level variables as control variables: *algebra* topic, *geometry* topic, and *number theory or counting* topic (a **Topic**$_t$ vector).

$$\pi_{ij} = p(positive\_social\_cue_{ij} = 1 \mid \textbf{Topic}_{0j}, \beta_{0r}) = F(\beta_0 + \beta_{0t}\textbf{Topic}_{0j} + f_{0j}) \quad (1)$$

Table 2. Coding of an online discussion segment on the topic: "How do you find x in x2 + 3x = 40?"

#[a]	Individual[b]	Message	SC[c]	EPM[d]	NI[e]	JU[f]	R[g]
1.	*Sue*; F; 1103	I got −8, 5. Try to factor with this formula: $ax^2 + bx + c =$ $a(x- (-b+)/2a) (x- (-b-)/2a)$	N	*	√	J	T[h]
2.	*Jim*; M; 107	I checked with the formula, −8 and 5 are correct:-)	☺	+	R	~	1
3.	*Sue*; F; 1103	Thanks, Jim.	☺	+	N	N	2
4.	*Leo*; M; 1279	You made it tooooooo complicated!!!	☹	–	N	N	1
5	*Sue*; F; 1103	What is your way of solving the problem?	N	*	N	N	4

[a.]Message number in time order.

[b.]Individual characteristics:*nickname*, displayed gender (masculine [M], feminine [F], or no gender-identifying characteristics [N]), and the number of past posts.

[c.]Social cue (SC): positive SC [☺], negative SC [☹], no SC [N].

[d.]Evaluation of the previous message (EPM): Agreement [+], disagreement [–], ignore/neutral [*].

[e.]New ideas (NI): correct, new idea [√]; wrong, new idea [X]; new idea with unknown validity [U]; repetition [R]; no mathematics content [N].

[f.]Justification (JU): justification [J], no justification [~], no mathematics content [N].

[g.]Responding to which message.

[h.]Topic message.

The probability (π_{ij}) that a positive social cue$_{ij}$ occurs at message i in topic j is determined by the expected value of a positive social cue$_{ij}$ and the Logit link function F in which f_{0j} is the deviation of topic j from the overall mean β_0 (see Kennedy, 2008). As the likelihood ratio test is not reliable for this estimation method, Wald tests were used to test for the significance of additional explanatory variables (Goldstein, 1995). Non-significant variables were removed.

A vector auto-regression (VAR, Kennedy, 2008) combined characteristics of sequences of recent messages into a local time context (micro-time context) to model how they influence the subsequent messages. We added current message variables (0) as control variables: message number, message length, and time interval between messages (**MessageControl**$_m$).

$$\pi_{ij} = F(\beta_0 + \beta_{0t}\mathbf{Topic}_{0j} + \beta_{mj}\mathbf{MessageControl}_{ij} + \beta_{ah}\mathbf{Participant}_{ij} + \beta_{cj}\mathbf{CurrentMessage}_{ij} + \beta_{ej}\mathbf{EarlierMessage}_{(i-1)j} + \phi_{ej}\mathbf{EarlierMessage}_{(i-2)j} + \gamma_{ej}\mathbf{EarlierMessage}_{(i-3)j} + \eta_{ej}\mathbf{EarlierMessage}_{(i-4)j} + f_{0j})$$
(2)

Next, we added current participant variables (0): masculine, feminine, number of past posts, and initiator (**Participant**).

We then entered the predictors sequentially in order of temporal occurrence and theoretical importance. First, we tested the hypotheses by entering current message variables (0): agreement; disagreement; correct, new idea; wrong, new idea; new idea with unknown validity; repetition; justification; and no justification (**CurrentMessage**).

Then, we tested for interaction effects among pairs of significant variables in **CurrentMessage**. Non-significant variables and interactions were removed from the specification. Next, we tested if the c regression coefficients ($\beta_{cj} = \beta_{c0} + f_{cj}$) differed significantly at the topic level ($f_{cj} \neq 0$?; Goldstein, 1995). If yes, we kept these additional parameters in the model.

Next, we entered lag variables measuring the properties of earlier messages ($-n$), first at -1, then at -2, then -3, and lastly, -4. First, we added -1 variables at the message level: positive social cue (-1); negative social cue (-1); agreement (-1); disagreement (-1); correct, new idea (-1); wrong, new idea (-1); new idea with unknown validity (–1); repetition (–1); justification (–1); no justification (–1); masculine (–1); feminine (–1); number of past posts (–1); initiator (–1); and message length (–1) (**EarlierMessage**).

Likewise, we applied the procedure for **CurrentMessage** to **EarlierMessage**. Then, we repeated the procedure for lags –2, –3, and –4 of the variables in **EarlierMessage**. Like β_{cj}, the following symbols ϕ_{ej}, γ_{ej}, and η_{ej} denote the regression coefficient matrices for the variables in **EarlierMessage** but at lags –2, –3, and –4 respectively. We used an alpha level of .05 for all statistical tests. We controlled for the false discovery rate (FDR) with Benjamini et al.'s (2006) two-stage linear step-up procedure.

Serial Correlation

We used Higgins and Thompson's (2002) I^2 index to modify the Ljung-Box Q statistics (Ljung & Box, 1979) for testing serial correlation in the residuals of the regressions for all topics (Huedo-Medina et al., 2006). While the Q statistic is suitable for analyzing one conversation topic, its statistical power varies as a function of the number of topics. Moreover, the Q statistic only tests the existence of heterogeneity, but not the extent of it (Huedo-Medina et al., 2006).

To solve these problems, we quantified the extent of heterogeneity from the n topics by creating an I^2 index that compares the Q value with its expected value assuming homogeneity (Huedo-Medina et al., 2006). The I^2 index does not depend on the degrees of freedom, and simultaneously assesses the statistical significance and the extent of heterogeneity (Huedo-Medina et al., 2006). See Chen, Chiu, and Wang (2012a) for the underlying mathematics equations.

If the residuals are serially correlated, the parameter estimates are inefficient and standard error estimates are likely biased (Kennedy, 2008). If so, we add lagged outcome variables (lags of positive or negative social cue [–1, –2, …]) as explanatory variables. If needed, the serial correlation can be modeled directly (see Goldstein, Healy, & Rasbash, 1994, for details).

Total Effects of Each Explanatory Variable

Based on the multilevel analysis results, the path analysis estimated the direct and indirect effects of the significant explanatory variables separately to compute their total effects (Kennedy, 2008; MacKinnon et al., 2004). We first computed the direct effect of an explanatory variable (e.g., x_1) on an outcome variable (e.g., positive social cue; i.e., $[x_1 \rightarrow$ positive social cue]). Then, we computed the indirect effect of x_1 on positive social cue, if any. If x_1 also affected the likelihood of a positive social cue through another explanatory variable x_2, we combined the effect of x_1 on x_2 and the effect of x_2 on positive social cue to obtain the indirect effect of x_1 on positive social cue ($[x_1 \rightarrow x_2] * [x_2 \rightarrow$ positive social cue]). Lastly, we added the direct and indirect effects to get the total effects of x_1 on positive social cue ($[x_1 \rightarrow$ positive social cue] $+ [x_1 \rightarrow x_2] * [x_2 \rightarrow$ positive social cue]).

As time constrains the direction of causality, the explanatory variables were entered in temporal order into the path analysis. To facilitate the interpretation of these results, we converted the total effects (E) of each explanatory variable to odds ratios, indicated by the percentage increase or decrease (+ E% or – E%) in the likelihood of an outcome variable (Judge, Griffiths, Hill, Lutkepohl, & Lee, 1985). See Chen et al. (2012a) for the computational details.

We repeated the above analyses with multilevel Probit to test if the results depended on the Logit distribution. The predictive accuracy of the final model was estimated by comparing the final model's prediction of whether a positive or negative social cue occurred at each message in each topic (positive social cue $*_{ij}$; negative social cue $*_{ij}$) with the social cue's actual pres-

Results

The multilevel variance components model showed that neither positive nor negative social cues differed significantly across topics, so single level analyses at the message level were adequate. Krippendorff's α for social cues, evaluations, new ideas, and justifications showed high inter-rater reliabilities (0.93, 0.89, 0.85, and 0.81 respectively; agreement percentages: 96%, 90%, 93%, and 89%).

The Logit models had a 77% and 83% accuracy rate for predicting positive and negative social cues, respectively, in any given message (y^*_{ij} vs. y_{ij}). The corresponding Probit models produced similar parameter estimates. Furthermore, for both positive and negative social cues, the final model's Q statistics and I^2 index showed no significant serial correlation of residuals for the 60 topics up to lag 3 (lag 1, 2, and 3: $p > .05$ and I^2 index = 0 for all lags; $Q_{positive\ social\ cues}$ = 36, 66, 92, $Q_{negative\ social\ cues}$ = 56, 89, 111, and df = 60, 119, 177, respectively). So, the time-series models were likely appropriate.

The results showed that participants' agreements yielded more positive social cues, whereas their disagreements yielded fewer positive social cues and more negative social cues, supporting H-1 and H-2. Agreement in the current message (0) increased the likelihood of a positive social cue in the same message (+18%: 19% → 37%; when an agreement occurred, a positive social cue in the same message occurred 37% of the time; when an agreement did not occur, a positive social cue in the same message occurred 19% of the time; see Figure 2). An agreement in the previous message (−1) also increased a positive social cue (0)'s likelihood (+10%: 19% → 29%). Note that agreement (0) and agreements (−1) both increased a positive social cue (0)'s likelihood slightly through indirect effects (Agree [0] → Justify [0] → Positive social cue [0] = −13% × −7% = +1%; Agree [−1] → Disagree [0] → Positive social cue [0] = −18% × −8% = +1%).

Both current and previous agreements were linked to more positive social cues in the current messages, showing that participants were likely to add positive social cues both in their own agreements and in responding to others' agreements. These results suggest that the online discussion participants were likely to use positive social cues together with agreements, thereby reinforcing their social relationships during the discussion.

In contrast, disagreements (0) reduced the likelihood of a positive social cue (−8%: 19% → 11%) and increased the likelihood of a negative social cue (+16%: 20% → 36%), supporting the disagreement hypothesis. When disagreeing with previous ideas, participants were less likely to use positive social cues and more likely to add negative social cues. These results suggest that these participants tended not to help others save face by disagreeing politely; on the contrary, they often used negative social cues to disagree rudely and attack face (Tracy & Tracy, 1998).

Unlike agreements, disagreements in the previous messages did not affect a participant's social cue in the current message. Although online discussion participants might often use negative social cues to disagree rudely with others, these disagreements were not more likely to elicit negative social cues. Unlike face-to-face discussants, online discussants did not behave rudely after a rude disagreement (cf. Chiu & Khoo, 2003), supporting the view that the face threat of a disagreement is likely smaller in online discussions (Reinig & Mejias, 2004).

In sum, the above analysis of 894 messages by 183 participants on 60 high school mathematics problems showed that the evaluations during online discussions can influence a participant's use of social cues. As participants often used negative social cues when disagreeing, teachers can discourage face attacks via negative social cues and

Figure 2. Path analysis of significant explanatory variables of positive social cue (0) and negative social cue (0) using two-level Logit. Values are standardized parameter coefficients. Solid boxes and arrows (→) indicate positive effects, dashed boxes and arrows (---) indicate negative effects, and thicker lines indicate larger effect sizes (The +4% relationship between message number (0) and positive social cue corresponds to a 50% increase above the mean message number.).

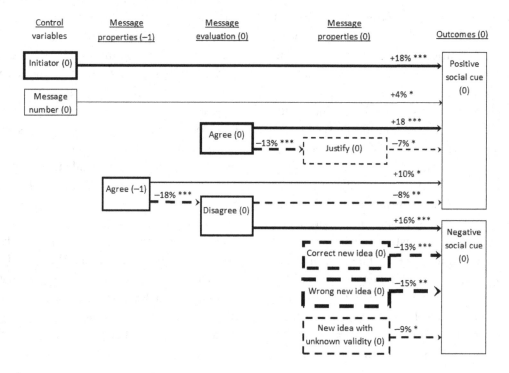

instead foster disagreements that help save face with more positive social cues. Online academic forum designers can also consider creating online environments that hinder the use of negative social cues. By doing so, teachers and forum designers can support both the social relationships among students and their online collaborative learning.

DISCUSSION

In this chapter, we explicated how researchers can move beyond aggregate counts of separate messages to analyze relationships among sequences of electronic discourse messages with SDA. By considering sequences, we can address research questions about how students (and teachers) influence one another during electronic discourse.

While many difficulties encumber analyses of such sequences, SDA addresses each of them. Lastly, we discuss some practical implications.

Complementing summary aggregates of individual message attributes during electronic discourse, SDA examines the dynamic social and cognitive relationships among students' messages that affect the likelihoods of these message attributes. The SDA results of the above study tested models of desirable and undesirable attributes of messages using explanatory variables at multiple levels (message, individual) and sequences of prior actions (micro-time context). For example, SDA reveals the asymmetries in the relationships between evaluations (agree, disagree) and social cues (positive, negative), showing that neither agree vs. disagree nor positive vs. negative social cues are simple opposites. The SDA also examined whether these relationships among explanatory variables and dependent variables differed across topics and whether indirect effects occur. In short, SDA tests systematic, explanatory models of multiple attributes of messages, while accounting for differences across topics.

The use of SDA in this study suggests how it can be applied to address questions regarding (a) responsiveness to messages during electronic discourse, (b) factors that influence the likelihood of a message attribute and (c) the impact of teacher messages on student messages. Just as positive social cue is a dichotomous yes/no variable, we can create a responsiveness variable to test which message attributes, individual characteristics, group properties, etc. will attract (or discourage) others to respond to a message. Likewise, the dependent variables (types of social cues) can be replaced with any desirable (or undesirable) message attributes to create explanatory models of them. Lastly, teacher messages can be captured as one of many possible explanatory variables (teacher message vs. student message) that might possibly account for differences in likelihoods of message attributes of students. For example, researchers examining teacher-led electronic discussion can use SDA to test how different types of teacher questions (yes/no, open, etc.) might affect subsequent students' subsequent messages.

Answering such questions require dealing with many analytic difficulties involving the entire data set, dependent variables and explanatory variables. To address the data set difficulties (missing data, many codes, non-linear trees of messages), SDA uses Markov Chain Monte Carlo multiple imputation, multi-dimensional coding, and mapping of the tree structure of the messages. SDA addresses the dependent variable issues (differences across discussion topics, similarities in adjacent messages, discrete, infrequent, multiple dependent variables) with multilevel analysis, an I^2 index of Q statistics, Logit, Logit bias estimator, and multivariate outcome models. To address the explanatory variable issues (sequences of messages, moderation effects across levels, indirect effects, false positives), SDA includes vector auto-regression, random effects cross-level moderation, multilevel M-tests and two-stage linear step-up procedure.

Like traditional regressions, SDA has several limitations. SDA assumes a linear combination of explanatory variables (Non-linear aspects can be modeled as non-linear functions of variables [e.g., log (time)].) SDA also requires independent and identically, distributed residuals and minimum sample sizes that depend on the number of levels. The following can serve as rules of thumb (Goldstein, 1995). To do a multilevel analysis, the sample size at the highest level (in this case, the topic) should be as large as possible, at least 20. Moreover, each lower level should have at least 5 times more data points than the level above it. At the lowest level of a multilevel analysis however, the number of data points for a specific topic can be very small, even just one (Braun, Jones, Rubin, & Thayer, 1983; Chiu & Khoo, 2005).

The results have several practical implications for teachers regarding social cues. First, justifications reduce the likelihood of a positive social cue, suggesting that when students are reasoning about the content, they can devote less effort to positive social cues. Hence, during students' justifications, teachers need not be concerned about the absence of positive social cues.

However, the negative social cues during disagreements can be a concern for teachers. In un-moderated forums, disagreements were often accompanied by negative social cues. To address this issue, teachers can encourage students to evaluate one another's ideas slowly and carefully, thereby reducing impulsive, false disagreements that might yield negative social cues and face attacks. Furthermore, this suggests an important role for a teacher during online discussions: fostering disagreements that help save face with more positive social cues and discouraging face attacks via negative social cues. By doing so, teachers can support both students' social relationships and online collaborative learning.

To reduce negative social cues during disagreements, teachers can also encourage students to focus on providing new information rather than simply disagreeing. The result that new ideas were less likely to be accompanied by negative social cues suggests that expressing new ideas focuses students on providing content rather than on negative social cues, which can hinder the latter's use.

FUTURE RESEARCH DIRECTIONS

Future research areas for electronic discourse analysis include modeling changes in social networks and computer coding for large data sets. Integration of SDA with social network analysis can help model (a) how the social network of participants influences the likelihood of participant actions and conversely, (b) how sequences of messages or posts modify the participants' social network.

As codes are needed for SDA, automatic computer coding would allow analyses of large data sets with SDA. (Sampling portions of the data omits substantial data, which can bias the results as noted earlier in the discussion of missing data.) Computer coding can be based on either a set of fixed decision rules or human codes for similar data (Erkens & Janssen, 2008; Rosé, Wang, Arguello, Stegmann, Weinberger, & Fischer, 2008). Whether computer coding is comparable to external human coding remains an open research area.

CONCLUSION

As researchers can move beyond aggregate counts of separate messages, they can begin considering research questions that require analyzing relationships among sequences of electronic discourse messages. However, addressing such questions require dealing with many analytic difficulties involving the entire data set (missing data, many codes, non-linear trees of messages), dependent variables (differences across discussion topics, similarities in adjacent messages, discrete, infrequent, multiple dependent variables) and explanatory variables (sequences of messages, moderation effects across levels, indirect effects, false positives). By addressing all of these difficulties, statistical discourse analysis enables researchers to model how electronic discussion messages are related to one another.

This study of 894 messages by 183 students on 60 high school mathematics problems showed that characteristics of recent messages influenced the likelihood of a social cue during asynchronous, online discussions. Specifically, students' evaluations of one another's messages were linked to more social cues (agreements increased positive social cues, while disagreements increased negative social cues). In contrast, their knowledge content was linked to fewer social cues, showing the relationships between cognition and socio-emotional expressions (new ideas reduced negative social cues, while justifications reduced positive social cues). Meanwhile, social cues did not affect the likelihood of a subsequent social cue. These results show how messages in online discussions create a local context that influences students' uses of social cues.

REFERENCES

Benjamini, Y., Krieger, A. M., & Yekutieli, D. (2006). Adaptive linear step-up procedures that control the false discovery rate. *Biometrika*, *93*, 491–507. doi:10.1093/biomet/93.3.491.

Braun, H. I., Jones, D. H., Rubin, D. B., & Thayer, D. T. (1983). Empirical Bayes estimation of coefficients in the general linear model from data of deficient rank. *Psychometrika*, *489*(2), 171–181. doi:10.1007/BF02294013.

Brown, P., & Levinson, S. C. (1987). *Politeness*. New York: Cambridge University Press.

Bryk, A. S., & Raudenbush, S. W. (1992). *Hierarchical linear models*. London: Sage.

Chen, G., & Chiu, M. M. (2008). Online discussion processes: Effects of earlier messages' evaluations, knowledge content, social cues and personal information on later messages. *Computers & Education, 50*(3), 678–692. doi:10.1016/j.compedu.2006.07.007.

Chen, G., Chiu, M. M., & Wang, Z. (2012a). Social metacognition and the creation of correct, new ideas: A statistical discourse analysis. *Computers in Human Behavior, 28*(3), 868–880. doi:10.1016/j.chb.2011.12.006.

Chen, G., Chiu, M. M., & Wang, Z. (2012b). Predicting social cues during online discussions: Effects of evaluations and knowledge content. *Computers in Human Behavior, 28*(4), 1497–1509. doi:10.1016/j.chb.2012.03.017.

Chiu, M. M. (2000). Group problem solving processes: Social interactions and individual actions. *Journal for the Theory of Social Behaviour, 30*(1), 27–50. doi:10.1111/1468-5914.00118.

Chiu, M. M. (2008a). Flowing toward correct contributions during group problem solving. *Journal of the Learning Sciences, 17*(3), 415–463. doi:10.1080/10508400802224830.

Chiu, M. M. (2008b). Effects of argumentation on group micro-creativity. *Contemporary Educational Psychology, 33*, 383–402. doi:10.1016/j.cedpsych.2008.05.001.

Chiu, M. M., & Khoo, L. (2003). Rudeness and status effects during group problem solving: Do they bias evaluations and reduce the likelihood of correct solutions? *Journal of Educational Psychology, 95*, 506–523. doi:10.1037/0022-0663.95.3.506.

Chiu, M. M., & Khoo, L. (2005). A new method for analyzing sequential processes: Dynamic multi-level analysis. *Small Group Research, 36*, 1–32. doi:10.1177/1046496405279309.

Collins, M. (1992). *Flaming: The relationship between social context cues and uninhibited verbal behavior in computer-mediated communication.* Retrieved December 15, 2010, from http://www.mediensprache.net/archiv/pubs/2842.htm

Erkens, G., & Janssen, J. J. H. M. (2008). Automatic coding of dialogue acts in collaboration protocols. *International Journal of Computer-Supported Collaborative Learning, 3*(4), 447–470. doi:10.1007/s11412-008-9052-6.

Garrison, D. R., Anderson, T., & Archer, W. (2001). Critical thinking, cognitive presence, and computer conferencing in distance education. *American Journal of Distance Education, 15*(1), 7–23. doi:10.1080/08923640109527071.

Goldstein, H. (1995). *Multi-level statistical models*. Sydney: Edward Arnold.

Goldstein, H., Healy, M., & Rasbash, J. (1994). Multilevel models with applications to repeated measures data. *Statistics in Medicine, 13*, 1643–1655. doi:10.1002/sim.4780131605 PMID:7973240.

Gorman, J. C., Amazeen, P. G., & Cooke, N. J. (2010). Team coordination dynamics. *Nonlinear Dynamics Psychology and Life Sciences, 14*, 265–289. PMID:20587302.

Gottman, J. M., & Krokoff, L. J. (1989). The relationship between marital interaction and marital satisfaction: A longitudinal view. *Journal of Consulting and Clinical Psychology, 57*, 47–52. doi:10.1037/0022-006X.57.1.47 PMID:2487031.

Gress, C. L. Z., Fior, M., Hadwin, A. F., & Winne, P. H. (2008). Measurement and assessment in computer-supported collaborative learning. *Computers in Human Behavior, 26*, 806–814. doi:10.1016/j.chb.2007.05.012.

Hara, N., Bonk, C. J., & Angeli, C. (2000). Content analysis of online discussion in an applied educational psychology course. *Instructional Science, 28*, 115–152. doi:10.1023/A:1003764722829.

Herring, S. C. (1994). Politeness in computer culture: Why women thank and men flame. In *Cultural performances: Proceedings of the third Berkeley women and language conference* (pp. 278-294). Berkeley, CA: Berkeley Women and Language Group.

Hewitt, J. (2005). Toward an understanding of how threads die in asynchronous computer conferences. *Journal of the Learning Sciences, 14*(4), 567–589. doi:10.1207/s15327809jls1404_4.

Higgins, J. P. T., & Thompson, S. G. (2002). Quantifying heterogeneity in a meta-analysis. *Statistics in Medicine, 21*, 1539–1558. doi:10.1002/sim.1186 PMID:12111919.

Huedo-Medina, T. B., Sanchez-Meca, J., Marin-Martinez, F., & Botella, J. (2006). Assessing heterogeneity in meta-analysis. *Psychological Methods, 11*, 193–206. doi:10.1037/1082-989X.11.2.193 PMID:16784338.

Judge, G. G., Griffiths, W. E., Hill, R. C., Lutkepohl, H., & Lee, T. C. (1985). *The theory and practice of econometrics* (2nd ed.). New York: Wiley.

Kennedy, P. (2008). *A guide to econometrics.* Cambridge, MA: MIT Press.

Kim, M. S., & Raja, N. S. (1991). *Verbal aggression and self-disclosure on computer bulletin boards.* Paper presented at the Annual Meeting of the International Communication Association, Chicago, IL, May.

King, G., & Zeng, L. (2001). Logistic regression in rare events data. *Political Analysis, 9*, 137–163. doi:10.1093/oxfordjournals.pan.a004868.

Krippendorff, K. (2004). *Content analysis.* Thousand Oaks, CA: Sage.

Lehmann-Willenbrock, N., & Kauffeld, S. (2010). The downside of communication: Complaining cycles in group discussions. In Schuman, S. (Ed.), *The handbook for working with difficult groups* (pp. 33–54). San Francisco: Jossey-Bass/Wiley.

Ljung, G., & Box, G. (1979). On a measure of lack of fit in time series models. *Biometrika, 66*, 265–270. doi:10.1093/biomet/66.2.265.

MacKinnon, D. P., Lockwood, C. M., & Williams, J. (2004). Confidence limits for the indirect effect: Distribution of the product and resampling methods. *Multivariate Behavioral Research, 39*, 99–128. doi:10.1207/s15327906mbr3901_4 PMID:20157642.

McKee, H. (2002). "YOUR VIEWS SHOWED TRUE IGNORANCE!!!": (Mis)Communication in an online interracial discussion forum. *Computers and Composition, 19*, 411–434. doi:10.1016/S8755-4615(02)00143-3.

Mercer, N. (2008). The seeds of time: Why classroom dialogue needs a temporal analysis. *Journal of the Learning Sciences, 17*, 33–59. doi:10.1080/10508400701793182.

Parks, K. A., & Fals-Stewart, W. (2004). The temporal relationship between college women's alcohol consumption and victimization experiences. *Alcoholism, Clinical and Experimental Research, 28*(4), 625–629. doi:10.1097/01.ALC.0000122105.56109.70 PMID:15100614.

Peugh, J. L., & Enders, C. K. (2004). Missing data in educational research. *Review of Educational Research, 74*, 525–556. doi:10.3102/00346543074004525.

Pevalin, D. J., & Ermisch, J. (2004). Cohabitating unions, repartnering and mental health. *Psychological Medicine, 34*, 1553–1559. doi:10.1017/S0033291704002570 PMID:15724885.

Rafaeli, S., & Sudweeks, F. (1998). Interactivity on the nets. In Sudweeks, F., McLaughlin, M., & Rafaeli, S. (Eds.), *Network and netplay: Virtual groups on the Internet* (pp. 173–189). Cambridge, MA: MIT Press.

Reimann, P. (2009). Time is precious. *International Journal of Computer-Supported Collaborative Learning*, *4*(3), 239–257. doi:10.1007/s11412-009-9070-z.

Reinig, B., & Mejias, R. (2004). The effects of national culture and anonymity on flaming and criticalness in GSS-supported discussions. *Small Group Research*, *21*(6), 698–723. doi:10.1177/1046496404266773.

Rosé, C. P., Wang, Y. C., Arguello, J., Stegmann, K., Weinberger, A., & Fischer, F. (2008). Analyzing collaborative learning processes automatically. *International Journal of Computer-Supported Collaborative Learning*, *3*(3), 237–271. doi:10.1007/s11412-007-9034-0.

Rourke, L., Anderson, T., Garrison, D. R., & Archer, W. (2001). Methodological issues in the content analysis of computer conference transcripts. *International Journal of Artificial Intelligence in Education*, *12*, 8–22.

Sproull, L., & Kiesler, S. (1986). Reducing social context cues: Electronic mail in organizational communication. *Management Science*, *32*, 1492–1512. doi:10.1287/mnsc.32.11.1492.

Stachowski, A. A., Kaplan, S. A., & Waller, M. J. (2009). The benefits of flexible team interaction during crises. *The Journal of Applied Psychology*, *94*, 1536–1543. doi:10.1037/a0016903 PMID:19916660.

Tallent-Runnels, M. K., Thomas, J. A., Lan, W. Y., Cooper, S., Ahern, T. C., Shaw, S. M., & Liu, X. (2006). Teaching courses online. *Review of Educational Research*, *76*(1), 93–135. doi:10.3102/00346543076001093.

Thomas, M. J. W. (2002). Learning within incoherent structures: The space of online discussion forums. *Journal of Computer Assisted Learning*, *18*, 351–366. doi:10.1046/j.0266-4909.2002.03800.x.

Tracy, K., & Tracy, S. J. (1998). Rudeness at 911: Reconceptualizing face and face attack. *Human Communication Research*, *25*, 225–251. doi:10.1111/j.1468-2958.1998.tb00444.x.

Vinagre, M. (2008). Politeness strategies in collaborative e-mail exchanges. *Computers & Education*, *50*, 1022–1036. doi:10.1016/j.compedu.2006.10.002.

Walther, J. B. (1992). Interpersonal effects in computer-mediated interaction: A relational perspective. *Communication Research*, *19*(1), 52–91. doi:10.1177/009365092019001003.

Wise, A. F., & Chiu, M. M. (2011). Analyzing temporal patterns of knowledge construction in a role-based online discussion. *International Journal of Computer-Supported Collaborative Learning*, *6*(3), 445–470. doi:10.1007/s11412-011-9120-1.

ADDITIONAL READING

Allison, P. D., & Liker, J. K. (1982). Analyzing sequential categorical data on dyadic interaction: A comment on Gottman. *Psychological Bulletin*, *91*, 393–403. doi:10.1037/0033-2909.91.2.393.

Anderson, T. W., & Goodman, L. A. (1957). Statistical inference about Markov chains. *Annals of Mathematical Statistics*, *28*, 89–110. doi:10.1214/aoms/1177707039.

Bakeman, R., & Gottman, J. M. (1986). Observing interaction: An introduction to sequential analysis. Cambridge: Cambridge.

Bakeman, R., & Quera, V. (1995). Analyzing interaction. New York: Cambridge.

Chiu, M. M. (2001). Analyzing group work processes: Towards a conceptual framework and systematic statistical analyses. In Columbus, F. (Ed.), *Advances in psychology research* (*Vol. 4*, pp. 193–222). Huntington, NY: Nova Science Publishers.

Chiu, M. M. (2004). Adapting teacher interventions to student needs during cooperative learning. *American Educational Research Journal*, *41*, 365–399. doi:10.3102/00028312041002365.

Christ, T., Arya, P., & Chiu, M. M. (2012). Collaborative peer video analysis: Insights about literacy assessment & instruction. *Journal of Literacy Research*, *44*, 171–199. doi:10.1177/1086296X12440429.

Cohen, J. (1960). A coefficient of agreement for nominal scales. *Educational and Psychological Measurement*, *20*, 37–46. doi:10.1177/001316446002000104.

Dabbs, J. M. Jr, & Ruback, R. B. (1987). In Berkowitz, L. (Ed.), *Dimensions of group process: Amount and structure of vocal interaction* (*Vol. 20*, pp. 123–169). Advances in experimental social psychology San Diego: Academic Press. doi:10.1016/S0065-2601(08)60413-X.

Davidson, R., & MacKinnon, J. G. (1993). *Estimation and inference in econometrics*. Oxford: Oxford University Press.

Enders, W. (1995). *Applied econometric time series*. New York: Wiley.

Goldstein, H., & Rasbash, J. (1996). Improved approximations for multi-level models with binary responses. *Journal of the Royal Statistical Society. Series A, (Statistics in Society)*, *159*, 505–513. doi:10.2307/2983328.

Gottman, J. M., & Roy, A. K. (1990). *Sequential analysis: A guide for behavioral researchers*. New York: Cambridge University Press. doi:10.1017/CBO9780511529696.

Grasa, A. A. (1989). *Econometric model selection: A new approach*. Dordrecht: Kluwer. doi:10.1007/978-94-017-1358-0.

Green, S. B. (1991). How many subjects does it take to do a regression analysis? *Multivariate Behavioral Research*, *26*, 499–510. doi:10.1207/s15327906mbr2603_7.

Greene, W. H. (1997). *Econometric analysis* (3rd ed.). New York: Prentice-Hall.

Hamilton, J. D. (1994). *Time series analysis*. Princeton: Princeton University Press.

Lu, J., Chiu, M. M., & Law, N. (2011). Collaborative argumentation and justifications: A statistical discourse analysis of online discussions. *Computers in Human Behavior*, *27*, 946–955. doi:10.1016/j.chb.2010.11.021.

Lütkepohl, H. (1985). Comparison of criteria for estimating the order of a vector autoregressive process. *Journal of Time Series Analysis*, *6*, 35–52. doi:10.1111/j.1467-9892.1985.tb00396.x.

Maddala, G. S., & Kim, I. M. (1998). *Unit roots, cointegration and structural change*. New York: Cambridge University Press.

Molenaar, I., Chiu, M. M., Sleegers, P., & van Boxtel, C. (2011). Scaffolding of small groups' metacognitive activities with an avatar. *International Journal of Computer-Supported Collaborative Learning*, *6*, 601–624. doi:10.1007/s11412-011-9130-z.

Papoulis, A. (1984). Brownian movement and Markov processes. In Papoulis, A. (Ed.), *Probability, random variables, and stochastic processes* (2nd ed., pp. 515–553). New York: McGraw-Hill.

Rasbash, J., & Woodhouse, G. (1995). *MLn command reference*. London: Multilevel Models Project, Institute of Education.

Robinson, P. M. (1982). On the asymptotic properties of estimators with limited dependent variables. *Econometrica*, *50*, 27–42. doi:10.2307/1912527.

Tabachnick, B. G., & Fidell, L. S. (1989). *Using multivariate statistics* (2nd ed.). New York: Harper & Row.

KEY TERMS AND DEFINITIONS

Electronic Discussion (Online Discussion): A discussion in which online participants exchange ideas by posting messages on an electronic medium that is visible to each other.

Multi-Dimensional Coding Scheme: A means of classifying each datum using sets of categories that are mutually exhaustive and mutually exclusive within each set.

Multi-Threaded Discussion: A discussion in which messages occur along multiple threads.

Online Discussion Message: The content that an online discussion participant posts at one time.

Online Discussion Topic: A topic that initiates an online discussion and visually groups the reply messages.

Social Cue: A participant's expressed personal affect or attitude toward others during a discussion.

Statistical Discourse Analysis: A statistical method to test hypotheses about whether explanatory variables at multiple levels are associated with significantly higher or lower likelihoods of the dependent variables and whether these associations differ across contexts or across time.

Time Series: Data ordered along the dimension of time.

Chapter 14
Analyzing Blending Social and Mass Media Audiences through the Lens of Computer-Mediated Discourse

Asta Zelenkauskaite[1]
Drexel University, USA

ABSTRACT

In recent years, mass media content has undergone a blending process with social media. Large amounts of text-based social media content have not only shaped mass media products, but also provided new opportunities to access audience behaviors through these large-scale datasets. Yet, evaluating a plethora of audience contents strikes one as methodologically challenging endeavor.

This study illustrates advantages and applications of a mixed-method approach that includes quantitative computer-mediated discourse analysis (CMDA) and automated analysis of content frequency. To evaluate these methodologies, audience comments consisting of Facebook comments and SMS mobile texting to Italian radio-TV station RTL 102.5 were analyzed. Blended media contents through computer-mediated discourse analysis expand horizons for theoretical and methodological audience analysis research in parallel to established audience analysis metrics.

INTRODUCTION

Social media have transformed not only media consumption and production, but also the audiences (Livingstone, 2004). Increased non-professional audience content integration in mass media settings thus is an observed trend, rather than an exception (Karlsen, Sundet, Syvertsen, & Ytreberg, 2009). User contributions through social media in the past years constitute a large variety of online content exchanges (Doyle, 2010). In addition to call-in participation, mass media companies have expanded audience contributions through text-based communication, known as "backchannels" (Herring, 2004). Audiences contribute to the mass media programs – ranging from entertainment to political debates, and news – with tweets, Facebook messages,

DOI: 10.4018/978-1-4666-4426-7.ch014

and mobile texting. Currently, text-based participation expanded through social networking sites. Increased user contributions, particularly in online environments, have been ascribed to "prosumer culture" (Jenkins, 2006). Bruns (2010) discussed professional and amateur content blurring in terms of "produsage" where users not only read contents but also share, rate, and exchange comments on social media outlets. In light of increased social media, audience research is presented with new challenges to meaningfully analyzing audiences' contents.

While challenging, text-based contributions opened opportunities to study audience behaviors where user-based programming has been particularly popular, especially in European, Latin American contexts with growing popularity in Asia. Audience contribution through text messaging formats was analyzed in Norwegian contexts (Beyer, Enli, Maasø, & Ytreberg, 2007; Enli, 2007). User interactions through text were studied in Italian settings (Zelenkauskaite & Herring, 2008a). Texting as a form of personal ads were analyzed in a Lithuanian (Zelenkauskaite & Herring, 2008b), Spanish and Colombian cases were compared by Mafé, Blas, and Tavera-Mesías (2010), to name a few. In these text-based, mediated environments, user interaction with the program was predominantly based via text-based technologies such as mobile phone texting. Subsequently, audience contributions were extended to social networking sites such as Facebook (Beyer et al., 2007; Enli, 2007; Enli & Syvertsen, 2007; Mafé et al., 2010; Zelenkauskaite & Herring, 2008a; Zelenkauskaite & Herring, 2008b).

With growing popularity of social media and increasing amount of user-based contents, methodological challenges are still lingering. Challenges include the large-scale dataset management, time sensitivity of user-generated content (UGC), the dynamic nature of the con-

tent, and no predefined consistency in content flows. These challenges, related to audience contributions, highlight the need to re-evaluated audiences' analysis methodologically. The need to re-configure methodological trajectories in studying audiences becomes especially pronounced in the recent decade when media are becoming more multiplatform (Blythe & Cairns, 2009; Livingstone, 1999; 2004) in the context of "convergence culture" (Jenkins, 2006). Despite new opportunities that social media and interpersonal media bring to the study of mass media audiences, little research has been devoted to the analysis of text-based audience interactions through social media.

To address methodological issues, computer-mediated discourse analysis has proven to be a useful tool to analyze user communicative practices and behaviors in online settings (Herring, 2001; 2004; 2007). CMDA has been further extended to account for convergent media settings that combine mass media and social media (Herring, 2009; 2013). The goal here is to examine advantages and shortcomings of automated tools comparing them with manually coded CMDA and to evaluate the utility of CMDA as an approach to large-scale datasets.

The article is structured as follows. The article first explicates the CMDA. Next, it discusses the intertwined nature of audience research is presented in light of social media and mass media paradigms. Computer-mediated discourse analysis is illustrated as a bridging tool that analyses audience in the era of multimodal mass communication. Then, CMDA approach is applied to a case study analysis of Italian multimodal Radio-TV-Web station RTL 102.5. Finally, it provides theoretical, methodological, and practical implications of this approach and looks at various pitfalls that can plague audience analysis by using quantitative discourse analysis approach.

BACKGROUND

Computer-Mediated Discourse Analysis Explicated

To analyze audiences' behaviors in blended media environments, computer-mediated discourse analysis was applied in this study. Herring (2004) defines computer-mediated discourse in the following way:

CMDA as an approach to researching online behavior provides a methodological toolkit and a set of theoretical lenses through which to make observations and interpret the results of empirical analysis. (p. 4)

The CMDA approach resides in a linguistic discourse analysis tradition and involves the micro-linguistic, context-independent level of structure, and the macro hierarchical level, as well as, the participation level of a given social phenomenon (Herring, 2011). Micro-linguistic and structure-based analyses have been extensively applied in various online media contexts that range from interpersonal media to social media. Micro-linguistic and structure-based computer-mediated discourse analysis is predominantly based on manual coding and frequency of the categories. It is a useful framework for various units of analyses that range from structure, meaning, interaction, and social behavior (Herring, 2004).

Computer-mediated discourse analysis was proven to be a valuable tool to analyze online linguistic behaviors not only on a micro-level but also on a content-independent structural level. Examples of the latter include a comprehensive analysis of instant message exchanges in a dyadic setting that was performed on around 2,000 utterances (Baron, 2010). Structure and discourse strategies such as sequential organization of messages in dyadic exchanges were analyzed through CMDA. Individual communicative

styles were compared in two different contexts: short text messages communication and IM communication (Ling & Baron, 2007). The analysis provided insights about the differences between communicative practices in these two modes. Text messages were found to be longer, contained more contractions compared to IM messages. Short-message service exchanges have presented rich data revealing turn-taking and interactional coherence strategies as ways to assess social presence (Spagnolli & Gamberini, 2007). The meaning of small talk on users' online wall posts on social networking site Orkut revealed politeness strategies among its participants (Das, 2010). Micro-level computer-mediated language analysis of mobile texting in Swedish contexts revealed disambiguation communicative strategies in mediated environments (Hård af Segerstad, 2005). Text-based comments left to Spanish Youtube videos were used to analyze users' linguistic expression (Bou-Franch, Lorenzo-Dus, & Blitvich, 2012). Twitter tweet posts were analyzed to study emergent practices of user interaction by using the @ sign (Honeycutt & Herring, 2009).

CMDA approach has been thus further theorized to account for communication in multimodal environments (Androutsopoulos & Beißwenger, 2008; Herring, 2009). Herring (2009) defines multimodal interactive environments as convergent media computer-mediated communication or CMCMC as environments, distinct due to interactive component which is often secondary by design and accompanies the main information or entertainment-related activities such as television. Examples of CMCMC include interactive television where mass media content is primary by design, while user social interaction broadcast concurrently is secondary. CMDA has been thus a valuable approach to study micro-level meanings that underlie audience exchanges in CMCMC. A fine-grained manual coding of text message exchanges in interactive television revealed the lack of coherence in television-mediated interactions (Zelenkauskaite & Herring, 2008a).

Analyzing Changing Audiences

Active audience participation has been studied since the inception of mass media. Talk radio programs in particular provided a solid ground to research active audiences. Audience call-in participation and the manner in which host interacts with audiences was analyzed by employing qualitative discourse analysis (Hutchby, 1996). In digital contexts, MacGregor (2007) proposed to study feedback traffic as an instant quantitative measurement of audience behavior, given that online environments provide the possibilities to attend to such behaviors. Similarly, mass media outlets started to devote attention to audience behaviors through social media. Audiences' comments are increasingly brought for the editorial considerations in newsroom meetings (Lowrey & Woo, 2010). In light of increasing readers' comments, blogger comments were also taken into account as a source in the newsrooms (Howe, 2007; Klein, 2009; Lowrey & Mackay, 2008; Lowrey & Woo, 2010). Thus, in previous mass media contexts, according to contribution level, audiences' voices have been placed along a continuum from passive viewers to fan cultures (Abercrombie & Longhurst, 1998; Jenkins, 2006).

As a result, audience participation challenges classical perception of audience analysis not only theoretically, but also methodologically (Carpentier, 2007; Doyle, 2010). Livingstone (1999) underlines the need to reconceptualize mass audiences:

Mediated communication is no longer simply or even mainly mass communication (from one to many) but rather the media now facilitate communication among peers (one to one and many to many). (p. 4)

Livingstone (1999), thus, emphasizes the changing nature of the audiences, where audiences' communicative needs go beyond interaction with mass media outlets. The need to study audiences in a context of social media is related to the shift from a media-centric view to an audience-centric view. Audience-centric view entails that audiences' needs are regarded as a key aspect. Digital media use and increased ways of audience feedback have drawn attention to media companies. In the news contexts, feedback monitoring has emerged as an increasingly popular phenomenon due to an audience's comment availability (McKenzie, Lowrey, Hays, Chung, & Woo, 2012).

Audience analysis in the digital era reconfigures the notions of audience analysis in various ways, thus providing new challenges and opportunities to audience analysis. The first challenge of audience analysis is based on the premise audience fragmentation. In a cross-platform realm, audiences are more mobile, thus they tune-in the programming whenever they are on thus questioning the concept of a solidified mass audience (Livingstone, 2004). Fragmentation also provides new opportunities to get multifaceted insights about audiences.

The second challenge reflects the spatial dimension. Conceptualized as audience spatial dispersion, it was proposed as a contributing factor to audiences' invisibility (McQuail, 1997). Mass audiences do not belong to any given space. Social media concentrate mass audiences around a given mass media outlet. Through contributions or engagement with audience text-based contributions, mass audiences are physically present through their texts in a social media stream.

Finally, audiences' invisibility (McQuail, 1997) is considered as another challenge of audience analysis. Mass media audiences have been categorized as "outside of the range of direct observation and record" (McQuail, 1997, p. 6). Yet, this study shows that audiences become visible through social media and mobile phone contributions to the programming. Thus, by studying audiences through the lens of social media it is possible to account for two challenges that were pointed out by McQuail (1997) in mass media contexts – the visibility of audiences or the direct access to the audiences and the juxtaposition of the audiences in a given space.

Blended Audience in Multiplatform Settings

The changing aspect of audiences is based on the blending nature between mass audience and online users. Blended audiences are particularly pronounced in multiplatform settings. Through the process of contributions to online and mass media, audiences blend with no clear distinction between mass media audiences and online users. Through the blending process, media platforms no longer compartmentalize audiences – the same audiences are present in multiple platforms. Blending audiences is operationalized as audiences that extend the notion of mass media audiences to social media. Specifically, blending mass media audiences comprise mass media audiences as well as social media users who engage with mass media products through social media. Thus, audiences' contributions are becoming increasingly integral part of mass media contexts (Bolin, 2010; Livingstone, 1999).

The blending process of the audiences intersects social and mass media, once the Internet was attributed to function as a mass medium (Moris & Ogan, 1996). The active side of user contribution constitutes a shared component between the Internet and mass media. Users' experiences in online environments have been theorized as early as 1990, when the interactive nature of online environments had been first observed (Rafaeli, 1988) and compared to mass media contexts (Rafaeli, 1989). Interactive applications in the last decade became ubiquitous in the social media scene, and then moved to the mass media realm. Thus, with the increased social media feedback, users become

co-producers of the content and become visible not only to the broadcasters, but also to the other audience members (Bruns, 2010).

In the social media paradigm, users' behaviors started to be explored based on their contribution frequency, as well as linguistic expression. User contributions have been analyzed not only to study the contents but as a proxy to classify online users and their behaviors. For example, in Wikipedia contexts, users have been analyzed through their contribution quantity and nature of contributions (Ortega, Gonzalez-Barahona, & Robles, 2008; Viégas, Wattenberg, Kriss, & Ham, 2007); users were classified by the longevity – the time spent and contribution frequency in various Wikipedia namespaces (Zelenkauskaite & Massa, 2011); user-editor interrelation with text-based article contents were analyzed through content contributions (Iba, Nemoto, Peters, & Gloor, 2010). Linguistic expression was used to classify Youtube users through interaction types through content tagging (Paolillo, 2008).

The present study is based on an overarching question which asks: How to account for the blended audiences that involve social media mass media? In particular, this study aims to answer the following questions: What are recurrent content topics discussed through social media and to whom are the contents addressed in an automatically extracted large-scale corpus compared to manually-coded corpus? How does the nature of contents evolve over time?

METHOD

To analyze the nature of audiences' interactions and addressees to whom contents are directed through social media outlets, a leading interactive Italian radiovision[2] RTL 102.5 was studied. RTL 102.5 started out as radio and expanded to TV, and the Web radio. With the rise of social media, the station started integrating text-based audience contributions. In addition to listening to the radio and call-ins, audience members can send a text message (SMS) from their phone or comment on the station's Facebook wall whenever, just as they do in their interpersonal networks. RTL 102.5 case serves as an example of the technologically forward-looking radio station. It pioneered integrating social media outlets starting with mobile texting in 2001 and audience contribution via Facebook in 2009.

RTL 102.5 uses a radio talk show format for part of its programming, which is heavily dependent on the audience. Viewers and listeners therefore may function as co-producers of the programming content (Enli & Syvertsen, 2007). There are no specific guidelines given to the audiences with regards to the acceptable content types. Audiences are simply given a phone number to which they can send a message which is advertised during the program on the bottom of the screen, as well as announced by the speakers in a given program. In addition, once messages from Facebook are integrated, RTL 102.5's Facebook wall URL is provided as well on the bottom of the screen of the televised version of the program. SMS messages were first integrated by RTL 102.5 in 2003 as a result of an agreement between the Acotel group and the station. Even now, RTL 102.5 listener calls are only broadcast twice during a two-hour program on average, while the incorporation of SMS and Facebook messages is much higher, especially in the radiovision part of the program where messages are displayed on TV screens.

RTL 102.5 station is available on at least three types of platforms: radio, television (satellite and digital terrestrial television, channel 750), and internet with live streaming of both radio and television. It is also possible to download applications that allow for connections to radio via cell phones (smartphones). The station broadcasts on all the platforms simultaneously. Programming runs 7 days a week, 24 hours a day. Most of the programs are divided into two-hour time slots. During all these programs, audience members can

send messages to the programs, either via SMS or by posting on the program's Facebook wall. The station decides which messages to include in the program to be broadcast. This radio-TV station has on average five million listeners a day and is one of the top radio stations' in Italy according to average listeners per day (Audiradio, 2009).

Figure 1 displays a screen shot how messages appear on televised version of the radio which can be accessed via tradition television and also digital terrestrial TV on channel 750. The same screen can also be viewed on RTL's website by choosing online streaming via audiovision.

The bottom of the screen is graphically divided by a horizontal line. In Figure 1 the space below the line contains an SMS message with text in Italian: *Sorellina ti voglio tanto bene! Daniela* ['My little sister, I love you so much! Daniela']. This is one of the messages sent by the spectators and listeners of RTL that was selected to be broadcast during the program. At the top-left corner of the screen is RTL 102.5 's logo and the clock indicating time. The top-right corner contains the name of the singer in the music video being played and the title of the song that is being sung at the moment.

Audience contribution via mobile texting (SMS) is stored on the RTL 102.5 website, "com-

Figure 1. RTL 102.5 television screenshot: televised version with SMS message (March 22, 2011) (© 2012, RTL 102.5. Used with permission.)

munity" section. It contains a complete list of the 200 most recent SMS messages that were sent to the program by their audiences. Messages are displayed as they are posted in real time in reverse chronological order, with the newest messages replacing the oldest ones. Archived messages includes the date, the time (hour, minute, second), and the text of the message (that contains up to 160 characters with spaces – the regular length of a typical SMS message).

RTL 102.5 also encourages audience contributions via the RTL 102.5 Facebook group profile. Audience members who are Facebook subscribers are encouraged to leave comments on the group's wall. Comments left on a subsection of the group's wall titled *youONair* are sometimes selected for broadcasting. Anyone willing to post on or read the RTL 102.5 Facebook wall's *youONair* section must first confirm it by clicking the "like" button. A list of Facebook users who "liked" this section's Facebook group can be seen in the left corner below the RTL logo. By December 12, 2010, 300,745 people had "liked" it. Messages for potential broadcast have to be placed in the *youONair* section, which states the following at the top: *Scrivi il tuo messaggio che potrebbe essere visualizzato in "Radiovisione" sul canale 750 di Sky e tv digitale* ['Write your message; it could be shown in *Radiovision* on the Sky 750 channel or digital terrestrial.'] There were 15,794 "likes" below this post, indicating that many audience members are eager to have their messages aired. The "like" button is followed by a button for "Audiovision" which links directly to the RTL website's live streaming of the program. Messages posted by audience members are displayed in reverse chronological order. Similar to other Facebook pages, each message is accompanied by the user's profile picture, first name, last name, the text of the message, and the time when the message was posted (date, hour, minutes). Messages do not bear additional costs from RTL 102.5, except for the mobile provider fees for SMS.

Data

Data for RTL 102.5 case study were collected from 1st January 2011 to 30th April 2011: sample comprised a total of 370,491 messages that combine SMS (N=308,339); and Facebook messages (N=62,152). All these messages were sent by the audience members, reflecting a high audience contribution level to this station. From the total sample, the following stratified samples were used to perform further analyses. To contextualize the frequency of the messages over time, a composite week was constructed. Composite week sampling comprises a random sample of seven days of the week randomly selected from the entire sample. It accounts for variability of the contents, thus giving a representative dataset that can be generalizible for the entire sample.

To identify the most salient keywords, a ten-day stratified sample was analyzed (January 18th-28th, 2011). It included 27,064 messages equal to 411,062 words. While subsamples for one-day analysis, January 18th comprised 2.146 messages or 33,081 words. For this analysis a word-frequency was performed and visualized through frequency graphs. To illustrate semantic relatedness of the words in a given message, a cluster-based dendrogram was performed using automated software (Provalis, 2012).

A randomly selected subsample of 2,000 messages was coded manually to account for addressee analysis by using a composite day sampling procedure which includes randomly selected hour-based time slots. To analyze the addressee of messages, computer-mediated discourse analysis techniques were used that take account of medium-based and situational factors (Herring, 2004; 2007). Messages were coded based on a coding scheme established by Zelenkauskaite & Herring (2008a) to study the addressees to whom messages were directed. Analyses were applied to SMS and Facebook messages.

Coding

To employ a macro-level computer-mediated discourse analysis, word frequency, and dendrogram were used as techniques that quantitatively identifies the range of content themes. A dendrogram was used as a technique that subsequently organized data through hierarchical content structure (Provalis, 2012).

To validate the data analysis, randomly selected sample was manually coded for the addressee. Based on the assumptions that underlie CMCMC, this study applied the CMDA approach to study audience addressee to analyze messages that are sent by the audience members through SMS and Facebook to RTL 102.5 programming and broadcast on its televised version. Unit of analysis was an utterance of a message. A single message could have more than one utterance and addressee. The following example shows two-utterance message with two addressees:

[1] Vi ascolto tutte le mattine un saluto dal bar me exita... Barbara ti amo

[I listen to you all the mornings and send you greetings from bar me exita... Barbara, I love you]

The example [1] was coded for addressee as program for the first part of the message, while the second part of the message was coded as directed to one person. A complete addressee codebook with examples is presented in Table 1.

Table 1. Addressee codebook

Code	Description	Example (original)	Example (translation)
To program	Coded as present when the utterances were addressed to RTL 102.5 or to specific announcers.	RTL siete grandi!	RTL you are great!
To one person	Coded as present when the utterances were addressed to a specific audience member.	mi manchi da morire fragolina. TI AMO	I miss you to death, little strawberry. I LOVE YOU
To all public	Coded as present when the utterances were addressed to audience members as a whole (referring as to "all of you").	Ciao a tt da teresa da Cerignola. 1 bacione....	Hello to everyone from Teresa from Cerignola. A kiss...
No addressee	Coded as present when the utterances did not contain an explicit addressee.	Aiuto...mi sto innamorando...anna	Help...I am falling in love...anna

Interrater Reliability

An additional 100 SMS messages and 100 Facebook wall "youONair" section wall messages were randomly collected to conduct interrater reliability tests. Two coders coded 10% of the messages to test the reliability of the established coding categories. The code values assigned were compared using Krippendorff's alpha (2004) as a reliability measurement. Krippendorff's alpha is considered one of the most rigorous and conservative interrater reliability tests for content analysis; it controls for the types of content as well as the number of coders (Krippendorff, 2004). A level of .60-.70 agreement between the coders was considered the threshold of reliability (Lombard, Snyder-Duch, & Bracken, 2002).

RESULTS

Message Flows

To provide contextual background about the frequency of message posting, messages were plotted over the period of a composite week to assess the intensity of message flow over the weekdays compared to weekends. In addition, messages flows were analyzed over a course of a given day. Thus, in addition to message content, and structure such as length, large-scale datasets from social media can provide access to content flows over time.

Table 2. Message distribution over a composite week

Month	Day	Weekday	Messages (total N)
March	14	Mo	2,712
April	26	Tue	3,072
January	26	We	1,987
February	3	Thur	2,537
February	25	Fri	3,569
March	19	Sat	3,890
April	10	Sun	2,897
Average			2,952

Figure 2. Grand average of message distribution by hour over a composite week

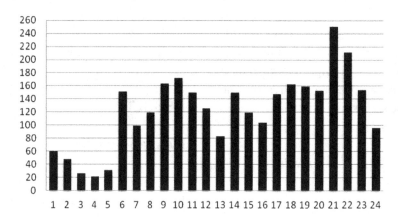

Table 2 shows that on average, messages flows differ. As expected, Friday and Saturday are the most active days in relation to audience contributions, while Wednesday is the least active day. To account for generalizability for this sample, a grand-average of audience participation was calculated by averaging out messages by hour in a composite-week sample.

Figure 2 displays that messages' flows differed based on a given hour with peaks at 6am, 10-11am, increases around 6pm-7pm and the highest peak at 9pm-10pm.

Word Frequency

To answer the first research question *What are recurrent content topics discussed through social media by their users in an automatically extracted large-scale corpus compared to manually-coded corpus?* The following steps were taken: First, automated message analysis was performed to assess the salience of the contents. Word frequency was counted for a 10-day week period of time and compared with the subsample of a single day. A single-day data was further divided into three phases of the day–morning, afternoon, and evening–to identify the most salient content changes over the course of a day.

Figure 3. Word frequency distribution for a ten-day sample

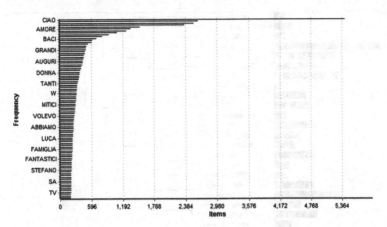

A ten-day sample comprised messages with the average of 15 words or 86 characters. A one-day sample from January 18th presents with similar results where messages were equal to 15 words and message length by characters equaled 89 characters including spaces.

Word distribution of the 10-day worth of sample comprising 411,062 words showed the following word-frequency lists.

Word frequency distribution in Figure 3 shows the top list consisted of the following words: hi, love, kisses, great, greetings, woman, many, long live, awesome, I wanted, we have, luca, family, fantastic, Stefano, knows, TV.

Word Frequency over Time

To test if content differs within a given time-frame. Contents were divided through the arch of one day (January 18th, 2011) into three arbitrarily assigned groups: morning (ranging from 3am-9am); afternoon (ranging from 9am-7pm); and night (ranging from 7pm-3am).

Morning (3am-9am) programming comprised the word frequency list featured the greeting word *ciao* as the most frequent item, followed by this sequence: women, for, RTL, no, Alberto, children, it is necessary, bruno, fulvio, good, people, mother, I would like, family, work, equality, radio, kisses,

make, wives, Bisi, good morning, things, Marco. These keywords refect the essence of the two programs that are displayed at night directed by Alberto Bisi and Fulvio Giuliani as well as they transition into the subsequent program called *The Family*.

Afternoon programming included the word frequency list such as hello, RTL, you, all, I am, you are, with, my, greet, my, I love, always, kiss, thank you, love, kisses, no, great, I want, good morning, women, a lot, years, to do, all, when, life, good, hour, song, day, Proce, friends, work, heart, fantastic, great, today, I would like, Angelo, company, marco, man, thing, love, then, radio, only, berlusconi, family, greetings. This word-cloud speaks to the fan-based positive audience feedback that is based on greetings, kisses, love, appreciation of the radio's company. It addresses messages to the program announcers Proce and Angelo, mentions a program *The Family*. It also covers place such as work, issues such as Berlusconi.

In the evening, the most prominent keyword was found to be hello ('*ciao*') followed by I love, RTL, for, love, that, no, greeting, I want, kiss, night, antonio, anna, greetings, guys, I love you, I would like, good, greetings, kisses, company, woman, laura, mother, sara, waste, miss you, I think, money, you make, good, friends, listening, beautiful, father, also, fog, I can, soon, awesome,

Figure 4. Dendrogram the most prominent cluster in a 9am-7pm similarity cluster

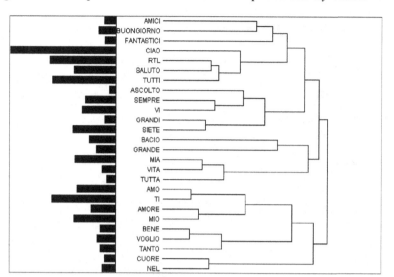

Figure 5. Dendrogram the most prominent cluster in a 7pm-3am (the cluster above) and 3am-9am (the cluster below) similarity cluster

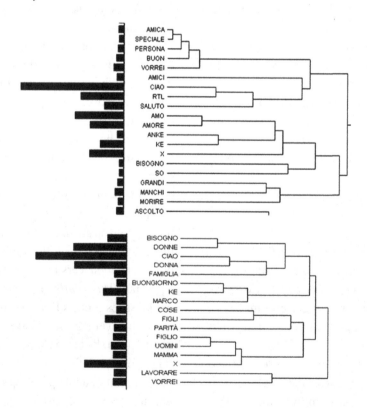

music, person, night, I hope, stefano, a lot, and wants.

These keywords comprise the positive fandom messages that express love, greetings and descriptives such as awesome and great. However, it reflects that messages are directed to individuals through references such as 'I love you', 'mother', and 'I miss you.' It also refers to community mentioning the word 'friends.' It emphasised weather condition descriptives of the day such as 'fog', referred to issues 'money', made temporal refernece 'night.'

Content Clusters over Time

A more detailed analysis was obtained through word similarity dendogram that clusters keywords into themes based on similarity and proximity on a message level.

From 9am to 7pm the most prominent cluster in dendrogram comprised the segment displayed in Figure 4. It centers around three big themes: appraisals to RTL; greetings to friends of RTL; love sentiments expressed to the loved one through this radio station.

Dendrogram of the most prominent cluster of the 7pm-3am and 3am-9am segments (with highest peaks of used content) comprises the thematic segments illustrated in Figure 5.

Dendrogram's cluster from 7pm-3am (the above cluster of Figure 5) was surrounded by the words ciao ['hello'], RTL, and saluto ['greeting'] constitutes one nucleo of communication referring to the radio program itself. While the other correlary contains words such as I love ['amo'], a friend ['amica'], and special ['speciale'] referring to a single user. The presence of word clusters referring to the fact that audience members talk

with the program as well as they express emotions to a single person throughI miss you ['manchi'] or love ['amore']. The most prominent cluster was composed by two main co-occuring items produced by dendrogram. Dendrogram analysis infers that users actualy engage into conversations that go beyond conversation to the radio station.

The dendrogram's segment for 3am-9am (corresponding to the lower cluster of Figure 5) is centered on words such as: need, women which is further related to hi, woman, family. The other larger cluster comprises the following words: hello, that Marco, things, children, parity, child, man, mother, to work, I would like.

Message Addressee

Given that quantitative word similarity dendrogram shows that contents refer to single person as well as to the radio station, messages were further analyzed to assess the addressee. This analysis was performed to answer the second part of the research question that aimed to compare automated and manually-assessed findings. Utterance analysis per message shows that majority of messages contained only one addressee comprising $n=1,471$ messages (73.6%) followed by two addressees comprising $n=478$ messages (23.9%). Three addressees were found in $n=50$ cases (2.5% of the sample); 4 addressees were found 1 time (.1%).

Addressee analysis is summarized in the Table 3.

Relative to addressee, Table 3 shows that majority of the contents were addressed to a single person or to audience members as a whole (user-to-user and user-to-all audience members combined) resulting in $n=1,090$ utterances. User-to-program comprised $n=912$ cases. Mes-

Table 3. Addressee analysis for 2,000 messages

Addressee	To program	To one person	To all public	No addressee	Total
Total	912	563	527	582	2,584

sages directed to unspecified addressee resulted in n=582 utterances (user-to-no addressee category).

DISCUSSION

This study analyzed audiences through the lens of text-based audience contributions via a unified broadcast stream of Facebook and mobile texting to the radio-TV program. Automated analysis tools were proven to be useful to identify most salient themes that were found to cluster around greetings, interaction with the program and centered on specific themes that were related to the specific topics discussed in the program. Moreover, topics pertinent to interpersonal communication were also present. Word frequency reflected the most salient content discussed in the program. However, for a ten-day subsample, the multiplicity of identified theme-clusters made it challenging to identify clear-cut themes. Word-cluster data representation was more manageable with message counts at approximately 3,000 messages per day, providing the binary nature of radio-centered interaction and interpersonal interaction. Data segmented into three periods of a given day revealed specific topics and addressees of a given interaction.

Period-based analyses' results led to manually-coded CMDA, showing that overall, messages were addressed not only to the program, but also messages between the users. In fact, addressee analysis showed that indeed messages contained multiple addressees that included not only radio station and its personnel but also to other users. Moreover, there were slightly fewer messages directed to the program (n=912) compared to the combined number of user-to-user and user-to-audience messages that comprised 1,090 messages. Moreover, there were quite a large number of messages with no clear addressee. This finding indicates that audiences contribute contents to the audience overall, emulating traditional broadcaster's role. As for contents, while the majority

of messages consisted of one utterance, yet about 23% messages contained two utterances showing that audience members engaged into messages that were directed to several addressees which can comprise more than one audience member, or the radio-tv station itself.

Quantitative computer-mediated discourse analysis based on frequency counts aims mostly towards the most salient content and leaves out less prominent content themes. Methodologically, this can be considered as a limiting factor. To account for such limitations, advancements on quantitative automated tools based on word frequency open new research opportunities for discourse analysis (Pennebaker & Graybeal, 2001). In particular, frequency-based word count provides insights about discourses that have conversational topics, while are less informative about interpersonal topics that are aimed towards small talk rather than topic discussion. Dendrogram-based content hierarchies provide a more fine-grained analysis of conversation. These automated tools thus can be successfully applied as diagnostic tools that identify a terrain of conversations. More fine-grained analyses could be performed in a micro-scale based on specific research questions.

One caveat of automated analysis is that word frequency analysis and cluster-based data can be meaningful only if the researcher is familiar with the context of a given dataset. Otherwise, the valence of the emerged themes can be mis-interpreted. For example, words can be used in positive or negative contexts. In contexts, where there are multiple addressees, content keywords can be attributed to any given addressee. In addition, only the most salient contents emerge in dominant positions, while less prominent topics get lower hierarchical prominence in the analysis. Also, automated coding can not reveal the absence of certain categories. For example, no addressee was found relatively frequent in manual coding, while in automated coding would not be able to reveal this aspect. However, the shortcoming related to not capturing the absent categories is related to content analysis overall, yet not specific to automated word frequency analysis (Krippendorff, 2004).

Solutions and Recommendations

Audience analysis through CMDA bears practical implications. In addition to social science research that advances the understanding of audiences' behaviors, audience analysis through CMDA can serve as tools for media organizations, being especially relevant for media organizations that incorporate UGC into their programming through backchannels such as social media. Audience analysis can be applied to access contribution flows and contextualization of the contents to overcome design-based challenges.

Large-scale datasets of audience contributions can serve as tools to study incoming audience's content and its development over time. Message flows can provide insights about audience engagement levels during specific time-frames ranging from monthly analysis to week analysis, days of the week analysis, and hour-by-hour analysis. Such analyses can provide insights about audience behaviors during a given time-frame, as well as focus on particular issues. Such content flow analysis can be used as a proxy to understand audience activity for a given time-frame or a program. It could be used as a diagnostic tool to assess the level of audience involvement levels. By knowing when audiences are mostly involved, editorial logics of content integration could be matched accordingly.

Specific recommendations in light of the findings of this study include the need to evaluate the interpersonal nature of audience members' communication, given that results of this study indicate that audiences actively engaged in interpersonal communication, in addition to communicating with the program. Media organizations could highlight the most prominent content by providing a constantly-changing word cloud. This prominent content could be displayed and updated to their

audience members to enhance levels of audience contributions thus further engage audience members. Media producers could provide audiences a summary of communicative contents by constantly changing word cloud on their website or Facebook wall. Content synthesis through automated CMDA of audiences' contributions and constant update on content change reflect inclusivity of diverse topics of interests by the radio station.

The other practical recommendation to the radio stations would be to diversify the contents that audiences send to the program, based on content and addressee types. Specifically, if content is dedicated to the audience members, they can be broadcast during specific time slots, dedicated to a specific addressee. For example, "audience time" could be defined as time specifically dedicated to audience interaction, in a one-hour programming; while reactive content could be aired during the time when the speakers pose their questions or trigger prompts to them.

Finally, audience contents that are unified in a single stream and simultaneously broadcast on at least four platforms – radio programming, televised radiovision, web-based programming, and portable devices such as iPad or smarphone – could be diversified and streamed in more prominent ways. There could be possible to access the aggregator of all contents with each platform; as well as subscribe to the aggregated messages, as well as subscribe only for a certain number of filtered contents based on identified criteria such as program time, addressee or another. Such content aggregator approach would provide users with a perception of increased agency of content selection control that would be tailored to their personal needs rather than ongoing stream of content that loses its relevance to the generic audience.

FUTURE RESEARCH DIRECTIONS

This study analyzed audience exchanges through computer-mediated discourse analysis through social media backchannels such as Facebook and SMS of traditional media to extend ways to analyze mass media audiences. However, this approach can be subject to several limitations. The approach treating audiences through their textual expression poses some limitations. Given that not all the audience members actively engage into content contribution, the active audience is limited in numbers. However, active audiences define the core audience behaviors on a given channel, station, or program. In other words, audiences' messages through Facebook and mobile texting provide ways to assess what really matters to the audiences, the way they want to exchange if they are given such a possibility. However, the results obtained in CMDA have to be interpreted contextually – taking into a close consideration the extent to which contents are moderated.

The case of a national radio-TV station represents a small fraction of audience members' contributions compared to the total number of listeners per day (which was estimated to be five million). Thus a 3,000 of active users compared to five million listeners is a small proportion of the audience. However, compared to a number of aired call-ins by audience members, that comprises about two calls from a listener per a given hour, or 48 per 24 hours, 3,000 messages per day is a much higher number. Also, this finding is compliant with the research in mass media context, showing that the expectation for all audience members to be active is overrated (Abercrombie & Longhurst, 1998). In fact, active participation expectation has been dismissed as well as in online contexts, where the presence of passive users – the lurkers – was argued to constitute a great part, sometimes a majority of online forums' users (Rafaeli, Ravid, & Soroka, 2004). However, these active audience members are given much prominence with the programming. Despite the limited percentage of activity, these audience members are given an exceptional prominence compared to the passive listeners because their contents get actually broadcast on TV, web, and

also shape the program's content. Finally, a case study methodology, as other methodologies suffer from its limitations, yet provide benefits such as rich data analysis that other methodologies cannot offer (Flyvbjerg, 2006).

Future studies could employ computer-mediated discourse analysis to study content selection process and associated implications in addition to studying the types of addresses and exchanged contents. Future studies could address the analysis of reciprocal exchanges that would allow the frequency of such exchanges, despite the fact that the number of responses was not very low, consistent with the previous research on audience exchanges in *Allmusic* channel *Inbox* program (Zelenkauskaite & Herring, 2008a). Future studies could provide a better understanding of audience contributions types in other contexts – such as moderated interactive programming where specific criteria are established for the content inclusion. Also, other contextual variables that influence audiences could be considered such as guidelines of best practices. However, in the case of RTL 102.5 given that there are no restrictions, this analysis shows how it is important for the audiences to incorporate interpersonal messages while maintaining radio-based communication.

Despite the fact that the studied contents are publicly available on the television screen as well as audience members are aware that their content will be publicly posted, audience research is subject to ethical considerations. Addressee analysis coding provides only information regarding overall data while leaving out the specifics of it. Similarly, the contents have been coded as larger categories "personal content" without defining specifics of that content. Such messages might include greetings. The others provide quite specific information about audience members' location. From this perspective CMDA as a method to study any type of contents should ensure audience members' privacy while still expanding scholarly and practical knowledge that is associated with the content exchange in which audiences engage.

In this study, CMDA was contextualized with content traffic analysis. Future studies would couple CMDA with content traffic analysis or with other methodological approaches, such as focus groups, questionnaires, in-depth interviews to provide a richer understanding of blending mass media and social media audiences. More cases studies should be conducted to account for various culture-specific aspects of mass audience and social media blending. Future studies could provide a better understanding of these audience contribution patterns by comparing controlled contexts with the ones what are pre-defined. Also, audience gratifications could be studied to understand the underlying forces for such participation, as well as content selection process could be studied, how messages are handled, selected, and integrated into the programming to provide a more complete understanding of this blending audience phenomenon.

CONCLUSION

CMDA has been employed to study user behaviors through their linguistic expression as ways to analyze user behaviors exemplified by Italian convergent Radio-TV-Web station RTL 102.5. This case study exemplified how computer-mediated discourse analysis provides new opportunities to analyze audiences in complex multimedia environments.

The study found that automated word-frequency was a useful diagnostic tool to identify the most salient terms that emerge from the large dataset. Word cluster analysis was found to be useful for a more context-sensitive analytical tool for salient theme and its context such as addressee extraction. Addressee analysis was cross-validated through manually-coded computer-discourse analysis on a randomly selected dataset and found support for the automated data cluster extraction. The findings of RTL 102.5 audience analysis behavior through text suggest that audience members in addition to the radio-based content, triggers, and responses to the programming also send messages to each other. The conclusion of this study is that CMDA revealed audience-based contents that were sent to the program. This result shows that communication occurred not only with the radio station, but audiences were involved in interpersonal communication. This study presents CMDA as methodological approach established in computer-mediated communication paradigm to study online users who are also mass audiences aiming at contributing to audience analysis studies and studies of changing media landscapes.

Broader implications of automated computer-mediated discourse are that existing modes of audience inquiry can be coupled with the text-based audience discourse. The availability of the plethora of audiences' online user data gives access to audiences' through their contents thus increasing mass media audiences' visibility through their text-based contents, as well as address issues regarding the difficulty of studying fragmented audiences. Thus, audiences are studied through the backchannels such as social media building on previous research proposing the idea that active audiences serve as a proxy to understanding to audience behaviors (Abercrombie & Longhurst, 1998).

The benefit of computer-mediated discourse analysis resides in its power to study user interaction, which occurs through the text through social media outlets. User contributions through the texts become a valuable source to understand language-based interaction of the users in online environments (see Herring, 2001) which could potentially be coupled with other audience methodologies. This study proposes computer-mediated discourse analysis as a methodological tool that serves to capture fragmented audiences' behaviors on various platforms through their contributions.

CMDA thus is proposed as an integral framework that was applied to a micro-level, combined with more macro-levels quantitative analyses such as audience participation patterns to account for changing media landscapes. Analysis of interactive audiences through CMDA provides an additional perspective to account for increasing complexity of audience studies that in interactive contexts that blend audiences. Facebook users, SMS users and radio and TV audiences blend traditional mass media audiences with online users. RTL 102.5 suggests that CMDA as methodological approach can provide an additional lens to audience analysis to account for audience as the most salient exchanged content types as ways to deal to what McQuail identifies as "alternative models" as audience-sender relationship that emerges in a mass media contexts (McQuail, 1997). Given that CMDA and audience analysis share overlapping areas of inquiry, an integrative approach could enrich the changing concept of audiences. Based on RTL 102.5 analysis this study suggests an integrative approach to study blended audiences that combines automated and manual coding categories extracting macro and micro levels of quantitative computer-mediated discourse coupled with another metrics established in audience analysis paradigm.

There are several implications to study audiences' participation and interaction through social media within mass media contexts. First, theoretically, such analysis contributes to audience analysis research by providing insights about the most active, core members of their audiences as well as an extension to general understanding of audiences (Abercrombie & Longhurst, 1998). Practical implications include contributions to multiplatform mass media design that would fulfill communicative needs of the audiences. In addition, mixed methodological approaches to study online data are proposed considering not only publicly available data points increase in quantity, but also in light of emergent trends in data aggregation through such paradigms as Internet of Things and Big Data (Amer-Yahia, Doan, Kleinberg, Koudas, & Franklin, 2010) where data have to be meaningfully analyzed and interpreted.

Finally, despite the fact that media contexts are changing, audience participation and contribution via social media and mobile texting serve as a powerful tool to reveal audience participation patterns, structure, and nature of these conversations. Given this increasing number of text-based UGC expressed through social media and interpersonal media in mass media contexts, audiences behaviors enacted through texts, provide new opportunities to study audiences.

REFERENCES

Abercrombie, N., & Longhurst, B. (1998). *Audiences: A sociological theory of performance and imagination*. London: Sage.

Amer-Yahia, S., Doan, A., Kleinberg, J., Koudas, N., & Franklin, M. (2010). Crowds, clouds, and algorithms: Exploring the human side of "big data" applications. In A. K. Elmagarmid & D. Agrawal (Eds.), *Proceedings of SIGMOD International Conference on Management of data* (pp. 1259-1260). Indianapolis, IN, USA.

Androutsopoulos, A., & Beißwenger, M. (2008). Introduction: Data and methods in computer-mediated discourse analysis. *Language@Internet, 5*. Retrieved December 10, 2012, from http://www.languageatinternet.org/articles/2008/1609

Audiradio. (2009). *Dati Audiradio annuale 2009*. Retrieved October 10, 2010, from http://www.audiradio.it/upload/File/Dati%20Audiradio%20annuale%202009.pdf

Baron, N. S. (2010). Discourse structures in Instant Messaging: The case of utterance breaks *Language@Internet, 7*. Retrieved October 11, 2012, from http://www.languageatinternet.org/articles/2010/2651

Beyer, Y., Enli, G. S., Maasø, A. J., & Ytreberg, E. (2007). Small talk makes a big difference: Recent developments in interactive, SMS-based television. *Television & New Media*, *8*(3), 213–234. doi:10.1177/1527476407301642.

Blythe, M., & Cairns, P. (2009). Critical methods and user generated content: The iPhone on YouTube. In *Proceedings of the 27th international conference on Human factors in computing systems*. Boston, MA, USA.

Bolin, G. (2010). Digitalization, multiplatform texts, and audience reception. *Popular Communication*, *8*(1), 72–83. doi:10.1080/15405700903502353.

Bou-Franch, P., Lorenzo-Dus, N., & Blitvich, P. G.-C. (2012). Social interaction in YouTube text-based polylogues: A study of coherence. *Journal of Computer-Mediated Communication*, *17*(4), 501–521. doi:10.1111/j.1083-6101.2012.01579.x.

Bruns, A. (2010). *Blogs, Wikipedia, Second life, and beyond: From production to produsage*. New York: Peter Lang Publishing.

Carpentier, N. (2007). Participation, access, and interaction: Changing perspectives. In V. Nightingale & T. Dwyer (Eds.), New media worlds: Challenges for convergence (pp. 214-231). New York: Oxford.

Das, A. (2010). Social interaction process analysis of Bengalis' on Orkut. In Taiwo, R. (Ed.), *Handbook of research on discourse behavior and digital communication: Language structures and social interaction* (pp. 66–87). Hershey, PA: Information Science Reference. doi:10.4018/978-1-61520-773-2.ch004.

Doyle, G. (2010). From television to multi-platform. *Convergence: The International Journal of Research into New Media Technologies*, *16*(4), 431–449. doi:10.1177/1354856510375145.

Enli, G. S. (2007). Gate-keeping in the new media age: A case study of the selection of text-messages in a current affairs programme. *Javnost - The public*, *14*(2), 47-62.

Enli, G. S., & Syvertsen, T. (2007). Participation, play and socializing in new media environments. In Dwyer, T., & Nightingale, V. (Eds.), *New media worlds: Challenges for convergence* (pp. 147–162). South Melbourne: Oxford University Press.

Flyvbjerg, B. (2006). Five misunderstandings about case-study research. *Qualitative Inquiry*, *12*, 219–245. doi:10.1177/1077800405284363.

Hård af Segerstad, Y. (2005). Language use in Swedish mobile text messaging. *Mobile Communications* (Vol. 31, pp. 313-333). Springer: London.

Herring, S. C. (2001). Computer-mediated discourse. In Schiffrin, D., Tannen, D., & Hamilton, H. (Eds.), *The Handbook of discourse analysis* (pp. 612–634). Oxford: Blackwell Publishers.

Herring, S. C. (2004). Computer-mediated discourse analysis: An approach to researching online behavior. In Barab, S. A., Kling, R., & Gray, J. H. (Eds.), *Designing for virtual communities in the service of learning* (pp. 338–376). New York: Cambridge University Press. doi:10.1017/CBO9780511805080.016.

Herring, S. C. (2007). A faceted classification scheme for computer-mediated discourse. *Language@Internet*, *4*. Retrieved December 24, 2012, from http://www.languageatinternet.org/articles/2007/761

Herring, S. C. (2009). *Convergent media computer-mediated communication: Introduction and theory. Panel on Convergent Media Computer-Mediated Communication*. Paper presented at the Internet Research 10.0, Milwaukee, WI.

Herring, S. C. (2011). Computer-mediated conversation, Part II. Special issue. *Language@ Internet, 8*. Retrieved December 24, 2012, from http://www.languageatinternet.org/articles/2011

Herring, S. C. (2013). Discourse in Web 2.0: Familiar, reconfigured, and emergent. In Tannen, D., & Tester, A. M. (Eds.), *Georgetown University round table on languages and linguistics 2011: Discourse 2.0: Language and new media* (pp. 1–25). Washington, DC: Georgetown University Press.

Honeycutt, C., & Herring, S. C. (2009). Beyond microblogging: Convesation and collaboration via Twitter. In *Proceedings of the Forty-Second Hawai'I International Conference on System Sciences* (pp. 1-10). Los Alamitos, CA: IEEE Press.

Howe, J. (2007). *To save themselves, US newspapers put readers to work*. Retrieved August 17, 2012, from http://www.wired.com/techbiz/media/magazine/15-08/ff_gannett?currentPage=all

Hutchby, I. (1996). Power in discourse: The case of arguments on a British talk radio show. *Discourse & Society, 7*(4), 481–497. doi:10.1177/0957926 596007004003.

Iba, T., Nemoto, K., Peters, B., & Gloor, P. A. (2010). Analyzing the creative editing behavior of Wikipedia editors: Through dynamic social network analysis. Social and Behavioral Sciences, 2(4), 6441-6456.

Jenkins, H. (2006). *Convergence culture: Where old and new media collide*. New York: University Press.

Karlsen, F., Sundet, V. S., Syvertsen, T., & Ytreberg, E. (2009). Non-professional activity on television in a time of digitalization: More fun for elite or new opportunities for ordinary people. *Nordicom Review, 30*(1), 19–36.

Klein, B. (2009). Contrasting interactivities: BBC radio message boards and listener participation. *The Radio Journal: International Studies in Broadcast and Audio Media, 7*(1), 11–26. doi:10.1386/rajo.7.1.11/1.

Krippendorff, K. (2004). *Content analysis: An introduction to its methodology*. Thousand Oaks: Sage.

Ling, R., & Baron, N. S. (2007). Text messaging and IM: Linguistic comparison of American college data. *Journal of Language and Social Psychology, 26*(3), 291–298. doi:10.1177/0261927X06303480.

Livingstone, S. (1999). New media, new audiences? *New Media & Society, 1*(1), 59–66. doi:10.1177/1461444899001001010.

Livingstone, S. (2004). The challenge of changing audiences: Or, what is the audience researcher to do in the age of the internet? *European Journal of Communication, 19*(1), 75–86. doi:10.1177/0267323104040695.

Lombard, M., Snyder-Duch, J., & Bracken, C. C. (2002). Content analysis in mass communication: Assessment and reporting of intercoder reliability. *Human Communication Research, 28*(4), 587–604. doi:10.1111/j.1468-2958.2002.tb00826.x.

Lowrey, W., & Mackay, J. (2008). Journalism and blogging: A test of a model of occupational competition. *Journalism Practice, 2*, 64–81. doi:10.1080/17512780701768527.

Lowrey, W., & Woo, C. W. (2010). The news organization in uncertain times: Business or institution? *Journalism & Mass Communication Quarterly, 87*(1), 41–61. doi:10.1177/107769901008700103.

MacGregor, P. (2007). Tracking the online audience: Metric data start a subtle revolution. *Journalism Studies, 8*, 280–298. doi:10.1080/14616700601148879.

Mafé, C. R., Blas, S. S., & Tavera-Mesías, J. F. (2010). A comparative study of mobile messaging services acceptance to participate in television programmes. *Journal of Service Management, 21*(1), 69–102. doi:10.1108/09564231011025128.

McKenzie, C. T., Lowrey, W., Hays, H., Chung, J. Y., & Woo, C. W. (2012). Listening to news audiences: The impact of community structure and economic factors. *Mass Communication & Society, 14*(3), 375–395. doi:10.1080/15205436.2010.491934.

McQuail, D. (1997). *Audience analysis*. Thousand Oaks, London, New Delhi: Sage Publications.

Morris, M., & Ogan, C. (1996). The Internet as mass medium. *Journal of Computer-Mediated Communication, 1*(4). Retrieved May 10, 2012, from http://jcmc.indiana.edu/vol1/issue4/morris.html

Ortega, F., Gonzalez-Barahona, J. M., & Robles, G. (2008). On the inequality of contributions to Wikipedia. In *Proceedings of the 41st Annual Hawaii International Conference on System Sciences*. Waikoloa, HI, USA.

Paolillo, J. C. (2008). Structure and network in the YouTube core. In *Proceedings of the 41st Annual Hawaii International Conference on System Sciences*. Waikoloa, HI, USA.

Pennebaker, J. W., & Graybeal, A. (2001). Patterns of natural language use: Disclosure, personality, and social integration. *Current Directions in Psychological Science, 10*(3), 90–93. doi:10.1111/1467-8721.00123.

Provalis. (2012). *Provalis research*. Retrieved November 5, 2012, from http://provalisresearch.com/products/content-analysis-software/

Rafaeli, S. (1988). Interactivity: From new media to communication. In Hawkins, R. P., Wiemann, J. M., & Pingree, S. (Eds.), *Sage annual review of communication research: Advancing communication science* (*Vol. 16*, pp. 110–134). Beverly Hills, CA: Sage.

Rafaeli, S. (1989). Interacting with media: Parasocial interaction and real interaction. In Ruben, B. D., & Lievrouw, L. A. (Eds.), *Mediation, information, and communication* (*Vol. 3*, pp. 125–184). New Brunswick, NJ: Transaction Publishers.

Rafaeli, S., Ravid, G., & Soroka, V. (2004). Delurking in virtual communities: A social communication network approach to measuring the effects of social and cultural capital. In *Proceedings of the 37th Hawaii International Conference on System Sciences*. Los Alamitos, CA: IEEE Press. Retrieved December 24, 2012, from http://www.languageatinternet.org/articles/2011

Spagnolli, A., & Gamberini, L. (2007). Interacting via SMS: Practices of social closeness and reciprocation. *The British Journal of Social Psychology, 46*(2), 343–364. doi:10.1348/014466606X120482 PMID:17565786.

Viégas, F., Wattenberg, M., Kriss, J., & Ham, F. V. (2007). Talk before you type: Coordination in Wikipedia. In *Proceeedings of the 40th Annual Hawaii International Conference on System Sciences*. Los Alamitos, CA: IEEE Press.

Zelenkauskaite, A., & Herring, S. C. (2008a). Television-mediated conversation: Coherence in Italian iTV SMS chat. In *Proceedings of the Forty-First Hawai'i International Conference on System Sciences*. Los Alamitos, CA: IEEE Press.

Zelenkauskaite, A., & Herring, S. C. (2008b). Gender differences in personal advertisements in Lithuanian iTV SMS. In Sudweeks, F., Hrachovec, H., & Ess, C. (Eds.), *Proceedings of Cultural Attitudes Towards Technology and Communication 2008* (pp. 462–476). Murdoch, Australia: School of Information Technology, Murdoch University.

Zelenkauskaite, A., & Massa, P. (2011). Digital libraries and social web: Insights from Wikipedia users' activities. In *IADIS Multiconference on Computer Science and Information Systems* (pp. 39-47). Rome, Italy.

ADDITIONAL READING

Androutsopoulos, J. (2006). Introduction: Sociolinguistics and computer-mediated communication. *Journal of Sociolinguistics*, *10*(4), 419–438. doi:10.1111/j.1467-9841.2006.00286.x.

Armstrong, C. B., & Rubin, A. M. (1989). Talk radio as interpersonal communication. *The Journal of Communication*, *39*(2), 84–94. doi:10.1111/j.1460-2466.1989.tb01031.x.

Avery, R. K., Ellis, D. G., & Glover, T. W. (1978). Patterns of communication on talk radio. *Journal of Broadcasting*, *22*(1), 5–17. doi:10.1080/08838157809363862.

Colombo, F. (2004). Interactivity and digitalization of the television system: An introduction. In F. Colombo (Ed.), *TV and interactivity in Europe: Mythologies, theoretical perspectives, real experiences* (pp. 7-14). Milano: V&P Strumenti.

Dahlgren, P. (1995). *Televisoin and the public sphere*. London: Sage.

Enli, G. S. (2009). Mass communication tapping into participatory culture: Exploring strictly come dancing and Britain's Got Talent. *European Journal of Communication*, *24*(4), 481–493. doi:10.1177/0267323109345609.

Erjavec, K., & Kovačič, M. P. (2009). A discursive approach to genre: Mobi news. *European Journal of Communication*, *24*(2), 147–164. doi:10.1177/0267323108101829.

Georgakopoulou, A., & Goutsos, D. (2004). *Discourse analysis: An introduction* (2nd ed.). Edinburgh: Edinburgh University Press. doi:10.3366/edinburgh/9780748620456.001.0001.

Herring, S. C. (2010). Web content analysis: Expanding the paradigm. In Hunsinger, J., Allen, M., & Klastrup, L. (Eds.), *The International Handbook of Internet Research* (pp. 233–249). Berlin: Springer Verlag.

Kensing, F., Simonse, J., & Bødker, K. (1998). Participatory design at a radio station. *Computer Supported Cooperative Work*, *7*(3-4), 243–271. doi:10.1023/A:1008683004336.

Kjus, Y. (2009). Impact of prestige programs on production practices: The case of crossmedia and audience participation in public service organization. *Journal of Media Practice*, *10*(2&3), 167–184. doi:10.1386/jmpr.10.2-3.167_1.

Ling, R. (2005). *The sociolinguistics of SMS: An analysis of SMS use by a random sample of Norwegians. Mobile Communications* (*Vol. 31*, pp. 335–349). London: Springer.

Nastri, J., Peña, J., & Hancock, J. T. (2006). The construction of away messages: A speech act analysis. *Journal of Computer-Mediated Communication*, *11*(4), 1025–1045. doi:10.1111/j.1083-6101.2006.00306.x.

Page, B. I., & Tannenbaum, J. (1996). Populistic deliberation and talk radio. *The Journal of Communication*, *46*(2), 33–54. doi:10.1111/j.1460-2466.1996.tb01473.x.

Rafaeli, S., & Sudweeks, F. (1997). Networked interactivity. *Journal of Computer-Mediated Communication, 2*(4). Retrieved December 21, 2012, from http://jcmc.indiana.edu/vol2/issue4/rafaeli.sudweeks.html

Rettie, R. (2009). SMS: Exploiting the interactional characteristics of near-synchrony. *Information Communication and Society, 12*(8), 1131–1148. doi:10.1080/13691180902786943.

Roscoe, J. (2004). Multi-plaform event television: Reconceptualising our relationship with television. *Communication Review, 7*, 363–369. doi:10.1080/10714420490886961.

Rubin, A. M., & Step, M. M. (2000). Impact of motivation, attraction, and parasocial interaction on talk radio listening. *Journal of Broadcasting & Electronic Media, 44*(4), 635–654. doi:10.1207/s15506878jobem4404_7.

Ruddock, A. (2007). *Investigating audiences.* London: Sage.

Sanger, C., Taylor, A., & Vincent, J. (2005). An SMS history. In Hamill, L., Lasen, A., & Diaper, D. (Eds.), *Mobile world* (pp. 75–91). London: Springer.

Sihvonen, T. (2003). TV chat communities. In Tarkka, M. (Ed.), *Digital television and the consumer perspective: National Consumer Research Centre discussion papers* (pp. 30–33). Torshavn, Faroe Islands.

Skjerdal, T. S. (2008). New media and new editorial challenges: Lessons from Norway. *Informacijos Mokslai, 47*, 66–77.

Squires, L. (2011). Voicing "sexy text": Heteroglossia and erasure in TV news broadcast representations of Detroit's text message scandal. In Thurlow, C., & Mozcrek, K. (Eds.), *Digital discourse: Language in the new media* (pp. 3–26). New York, London: Oxford University Press. doi:10.1093/acprof:oso/9780199795437.003.0001.

Svoen, B. (2007). Consumers, participants, and creators: Young people's diverse use of television and new media. *ACM Computer in Entertainment, 5*(2). Retrieved December 20, 2012, from http://cie.acm.org/articles/consumers-participants-and-creators/

Tuomi, P., & Bachmayer, S. (2011). The convergence of TV and Web (2.0) in Austria and Finland. [Lisbon, Portugal.]. *Proceedings of EuroITV, 11*, 55–64. doi:10.1145/2000119.2000131.

Turow, J. (1973). Talk show radio as interpersonal communication. *Journal of Broadcasting & Electronic Media, 18*(2), 171–179.

Van Dijck, J. (2009). User like you? Theorizing agency in user-generated content. *Media Culture & Society, 31*(1), 41–58. doi:10.1177/0163443708098245.

Van Dijk, J. (2004). Digital media. In Downing, J. D. H., McQuail, D., Schlesinger, P., & Wartella, E. (Eds.), *The Sage handbook of media studies* (pp. 145–164). Thousand Oaks, CA: Sage Publications. doi:10.4135/9781412976077.n8.

Vorderer, P. (2000). Interactive entertainment and beyond. In Vorderer, D. Z. P. (Ed.), *Media entertainment: The psychology of its appeal* (pp. 21–36). Mahwah: Lawrence Erlbaum Associates.

Walther, J. B., Carr, C. T., Choi, S. S. W., Deandrea, D. C., Kim, J., Tom Tong, S., & Van der Heide, B. (2010). Interaction of interpersonal, peer, and media influence sources online: A research agenda for technology convergence. In Papacharissi, Z. (Ed.), *Networked self: Identity, community, and culture on social network sites* (pp. 17–38). New York, London: Routlege.

Ytreberg, E. (2004). Formatting participation within broadcast media production. *Media Culture & Society, 26*(5), 677–692. doi:10.1177/0163443704045506.

Ytreberg, E. (2009). Extended liveness and eventfulness in multi-platform reality formats. *New Media & Society, 11*, 467–485. doi:10.1177/1461444809102955.

KEY TERMS AND DEFINITIONS

Audiences: Refers to mass media audiences.

Blending Audiences: Audiences that comprise or constitute a part of social media users and mass media audiences.

Computer-Mediated Communication: When humans interact with each other via computer networks.

Computer-Mediated Discourse Analysis (CMDA): Herring (2004) defines CMDA as "an approach to the analysis of computer-mediated communication (CMC) focused on language and language use; it is also a set of methods (a "toolkit") grounded in linguistic discourse analysis for mining networked communication for patterns of structure and meaning, broadly construed."

Interpersonal Media: Applications that allow for interpersonal user exchange.

Mass Media: Refers to traditional media outlets, traditionally viewed by mass media audiences, examples of which comprise but are not limited to television, radio, newspapers.

Short Message Service (SMS): Mobile texting that occurs through mobile devices or mobile device supported platforms. It comprises users-to-user interaction through message exchange, as well as text-message services that are established through tertiary parties, including commercial services such as text-based messages to banks, as well as entertainment services such as SMS messages to the TV and radio programming.

Social Media: Comprise web applications that allow user interaction and content distribution and exchange. Examples of which include but are not limited to social networking sites such as Facebook, microblogging such as Twitter, as well as online chat.

Users: Refers to web users, online users, social media users.

ENDNOTES

1. The author thanks Ernest Hakanen for revisions of this manuscript and thanks anonymous reviewers for suggestions that improved this manuscript.

2. Radiovision refers to the term used by RTL 102.5 that refers to the radio and the visual component of the radio programming broadcast via TV.

Chapter 15
Reflections of Professional Practice:
Using Electronic Discourse Analysis Networks (EDANs) to Examine Embedded Business Emails

Julio Gimenez
The University of Nottingham, UK

ABSTRACT

Emails have become a central genre in business communication, reflecting both how people communicate and how they go about their professional practices. This chapter examines embedded business emails as reflections of the professional practices of the regulatory and policy department of a multinational based in London, UK. It argues that the nature of online communication in international organisations, with its high levels of intertextuality and interdiscursivity, requires multidimensional analytical approaches that are capable of capturing its complexity and dynamics. To this end, the chapter introduces electronic discourse analysis networks (EDANs) as one example of such approaches. It begins with a brief review of the literature that has informed the study reported on here before it discusses EDANs as its analytical framework. Using a group of embedded emails and a number of networked data sets, the chapter shows how EDANs can be used to further our understanding of professional online communication.

INTRODUCTION

The last two decades have witnessed an increasing interest in email communication, with a particular focus on business contexts (Akar, 2002; Gains, 1999; Nickerson, 2000; Orlikowski & Yates, 1994; Turner, Grube, Tinsley, Lee, & O'Pell, 2006; among many others). Approaches to investigating

email in business communication have ranged from analysing emails as electronic media, through isolating their textual features, to examining the relationship between emails and their context of production and consumption (e.g. Akar, 2002; Daft & Lengel, 1986; Gains, 1999; Gimenez, 2000; Nickerson, 2000). Early studies showed a marked interest in determining the capability

DOI: 10.4018/978-1-4666-4426-7.ch015

of emails as a means of communication (Daft & Lengel, 1986; Lengel & Daft, 1988), concluding, inter alia, that they were less rich than other media (e.g. face to face) in terms of the possibilities they offered users. Important as these first studies were, they focused too narrowly on the richness of the medium, failing to examine emails in their context of use.

Later studies (e.g. Markus, 1994) brought context of use into consideration and managed to identify contextual factors that influence people's choice of media. The focus of attention thus shifted to the examination of factors such as corporate policies about the use of electronic media for communication (Markus, 1994), organizational practices (Nickerson, 2000), and interpersonal and power relationships (Hinds & Kiesler, 1995; Markus, 1994) that could influence media choice. Other studies have produced more linguistic analyses of emails by looking at their internal features in an attempt to discern whether they represented a new means of communication (e.g. Gains, 1999) or an emerging new genre (e.g. Gimenez, 2000). More recently, studies have taken a more socio-linguistic approach and have focused on the dialectical relationship between email, users, context and corporate culture, highlighting the interplay between email and communication purposes (e.g. Nickerson, 2000); email and corporate reality (Akar, 2002; Louhiala-Salminen, 2002); email, task demand, technology availability and organisational culture (Ho, 2011; van den Hoof, Groot, & de Jonge, 2005); and email, user proficiency and media packaging (Turner & Reinsch, 2007; 2011); among others.

Despite the plethora of studies that have been conducted since the late 1980s, there is still certain paucity in analytical methods that would allow us to understand the full complexity of email communication from a discursive perspective. For example, embedded emails, a frequent genre in contemporary international communication with their chain of messages that includes the message initiator, the middle messages and the message terminator (Gimenez, 2006), constitute complex communicative practices that require rather sophisticated analytical methods to unpack their textual and communicative nature. In embedded emails intertextual and interdiscursive elements are central to message composition and message understanding as discursive realities in today's electronic corporate communication.

This chapter thus argues that the nature of online communication in international organisations requires multidimensional analytical approaches that can both cope with its complexity and capture its dynamics. In support of this argument, it reports on a study that followed a practice-oriented approach and used electronic discourse analysis networks (EDANs), a multidimensional analytical framework, in order to examine business emails as discursive representations of the professional practices and the procedures of a regulatory and policy department at a multinational corporation based in London, UK.

The chapter first presents a brief review of the research that has informed the study reported on here. Against this background, it presents and discusses EDANs as its analytical framework and analyses a number of embedded business emails. Next, the chapter describes the results of such an analysis, followed by an examination of the significance of the results. Finally, it concludes by drawing attention to the need for more discourse-oriented analytical methods such as EDANs which would allow us to gain a fuller understanding of the reality of professional online communication.

BACKGROUND

Since the late 1980s the interest in email communication has grown considerably. Although early research isolated emails from their context of use in order to study them as a means of communication and determine their richness in comparison with other media (e.g. face-to-face) (e.g. Daft & Lengel, 1986; Lengel & Daft, 1988), it did not take long for researchers in the field to realise that examining emails in their organisational setting would produce more interesting understandings of their role in business communication. Thus, a plethora of studies was conducted in an attempt to discover, inter alia, the influences that context of use could have on users' choices (Markus, 1994), the interaction between email and communication practices in organisations (Nickerson, 2000), the role of emails in the discourse activities of managers (Louhiala-Salminen, 2002), and in the construction of corporate reality between multinationals and their subsidiaries at local and global levels (Gimenez, 2002). One of the most influential of these studies was Markus's (1994) that demonstrated that if context was considered then variables such as message purpose, technology availability and professional practices became more significant factors in users' decisions than media richness, as early studies had argued.

The shift in research attention from email as a medium to email as communication practice has helped to advance our understanding of on-line communication in general and email communication in particular as part and parcel of the communication practices of international organisations.

A group of studies representing this shift has shown a marked tendency to focus on aspects such as the register, syntax and language of business emails (e.g. Gains, 1999; Gimenez, 2000; Mallon & Oppenheim, 2002), which has led some researchers in the field to question the capability of business emails for qualifying as a new electronic genre (e.g. Gains, 1999). However, a number of studies have managed to identify structural features (e.g. 'To', or 'Cc', or 'Bcc'), as well as recurring obligatory and optional generic features or moves (e.g. establishing email communication and defining message features), thus demonstrating that business emails are in fact an emerging new genre with its own recurring generic features and text types (such as criticizing, informing, apologizing) that contribute to easing its production and interpretation[1] (Baron, 1998; Crystal, 2001;

Gimenez, 2005; Mulholland, 1999; Nickerson, 2000; Wollman-Bonilla, 2003).

Recent research on business email communication has moved away from the debate on whether emails represent a genre on their own right. Instead, it has taken a more interactive perspective, looking at how the elements identified in earlier studies interrelate with one another, showing a more rounded, even if also more complicated, picture. van den Hoof, Groot, and de Jonge (2005), for example, have reiterated that the choices of media that users make respond not only to personal preferences but also to situational demands of the task at hand, the organisational culture as well as the availability of communication technologies. In a similar vein, Turner and Reinsch (2007; 2011) have observed that business communicators have become more proficient users of new technologies and online genres, and thus are now able to package a variety of media (e.g. emails, text and IM) in order to meet the communication needs of the workplace.

These studies illustrate the increasing and diverse research interest in business email communication in international organisations. By the same token, they showcase emails as a central genre in business communication that both records and reflects the professional practices of business people. However, despite the in-depth understanding of the nature and dynamics of email communication in corporate settings that studies in the field have produced over the last 25 years or so, there is still a need for more complex analytical tools that can help us to capture and understand the full complexity of electronic communication in corporate settings. This is illustrated in the study reported on here as described in the next section.

Context of the Study

As stated above, the study reported on in this chapter looked at email communication to examine how it recorded and reflected the practices and procedures of a group of professionals at the regulatory and policy department of a multinational corporation based in London, UK. Before looking at how emails discursively represented the professional practices of this group of professionals, this section briefly describes the culture, practices and procedures of the department in an attempt to provide relevant information about the context of the study.

The multinational where the study took place is a telecommunications conglomerate with a wide portfolio of services on land, at sea and in the air, headquartered in London, UK. Its regulatory and policy department is a central component in the business of the corporation. The department is in charge of applying for licences prior to the commercialisation of their products in countries other than the UK. The licences they need to obtain from the government of the countries where they intend to expand their business are normally highly regulated by local laws and thus the department has always found it more convenient to work with a local partner company, as will be shown later in the chapter.

As is the case with most regulatory and policy departments, the culture of the department in this study can be described as highly regulated by established procedures and clearly defined roles, both of which materialise in strongly authority-driven practices. Thus its contextual structure is seen to exert a strong influence on the activity of the department. Due to the nature of its business, procedures are central to most of its activities and the people working in it are expected to adhere to them as closely as possible and in accordance to their roles.

This is manifested in the professional practices of the department and its members. There are procedures that determine what is discussed by means of what genres (e.g. conference calls to discuss terms of a contract), and by whom, both the participants that need to take an active part in the practice (e.g. the Board of Directors) as well as those who need to be summoned upon to act as witnesses (e.g. legal advisers).

As will be illustrated later in the chapter, embedded emails are one of the communication genres that discursively represent these professional practices, showing the text-internal (constituting intertextuality) and text-external (constituting interdiscursivity) elements (Bhatia, 2004; 2008; 2010) that intervene and support such practices. This points to the complexity of the practices of the department which are a reflection of its highly regulated activities. To be able to analyse these practices, the study adopted a multidimensional approach that became a highly flexible analytical tool, capable of rendering ways in which complexity can be understood and analysed and able to produce more relevant research outcomes to inform our understanding of online communication. This is further explored in the next section.

Analytical Framework

As mentioned earlier, this chapter argues that in order to capture the complexity of online communication, which has become more increasingly dependent on intertextuality (e.g. meanings being shaped by connections between texts) and interdiscursivity (e.g. relationships between discursive practices), multidimensional analytical approaches are needed. Against this background, the study reported here adopted a practice-oriented approach and used electronic discourse analysis networks (EDANs) as its analytical framework. As a multidimensional analytical approach, EDANs consist of a variety of networked data sets (e.g. emails, narratives, documents and artefacts) collected from the same context of interaction in order to provide multifaceted explorations of professional practice (Gimenez, 2010). By the same token, EDANs are presented as a methodological advance which has been designed to make up for the paucity of multidimensional techniques to cope with the complexity of online communication in international organisations. As a way of illustration, the chapter reports on the way the study examined professional practices as represented in the embedded emails produced by the members of the regulatory and policy department of a multinational corporation.

One clear advantage of multidimensional approaches like EDANs is that they move away from reducing complexity to a one-dimension entity and offer instead triangulated ways of looking at complex issues from a variety of analytical perspectives afforded by multiple data sets all generated in the same context of interaction. Exploring interaction data from the same context provides a more in-depth and, at the same time, more multifaceted view of how professional communication practices come to be realised. By the same token, it offers the opportunity to ground understanding and the products of professional practice in people's everyday professional and/or discursive performances such as email communication.

Although contextualised in a different field of knowledge, a number of studies have argued for multidimensional analytical approaches to examine the complexity of human relationship and interaction (e.g. Fidel, Pejtersen, Cleal, & Bruce, 2004; Lamb & Kling, 2003; Sonnenwald, Wildemuth, & Harmon, 2001). Lamb and Kling's (2003) study in the field of human-information interaction offered an example of a multidimensional approach based on a variety of data sets. They used a context-based institutionalist approach to examine the elaborate use of intranets in American firms and the role of information and communication technologies (ICTs) among academic and industry scientists. To this end, they developed a framework that consisted of four dimensions of data: Affiliation (relationships that connect members to different networks), Environment (regulated practices circumscribing organisational activity), Interactions (resources mobilised by members to interact with others), and Identity (formulations of self as individual and collective entities). Following this multidimensional approach, Lamb and Kling managed to provide more rounded and critical descriptions of

the complexities involved in the use of intranets and the role of ICTs. In a similar vein, Sonnenwald, Wildemuth, and Harmon (2001) designed a multidimensional conceptual framework to study the complexity involved in human-information interaction. This time, however, the framework emerged from field studies and observations of different groups and the bringing together of theories and research traditions form disciplines such as communication, sociology, and psychology. A third option for developing multidimensional approaches involves collecting multiple data and networking them thematically. This is how EDANs have been developed.

Figure 1 shows how the data for the study were collected and thematically organised in networks for analytical purposes. As can be seen, embedded emails constitute the central element of the networks, and were the first to be collected and thematically analysed (1). Based on the preliminary analysis of the emails, related documents that the participants had written or were writing at the time of the study were selected and examined (2). Next, participants were interviewed and the narratives about professional practice that resulted from the interview data were thematically related to the emails and documents selected (3). The analysis of the data collected in 1-3 was later complemented by the research notes the researcher had made during various observation periods (4), followed by a collection of thematically related artefacts (5). Although this description of the framework seems to suggest a rather linear model, the actual gathering and analysis of the data was more cyclical in nature.

As shown in Figure 1, the sets of complementary data (2-5) were organised around the embedded emails-the core data in this network (1). Different members of the department were interviewed using loosely organised questions after the initial analyses of the emails and the documents. These interviews produced narratives about departmental professional practices. These narratives provided personal views that comple-

Figure 1. Organisation and analysis of data for EDANs

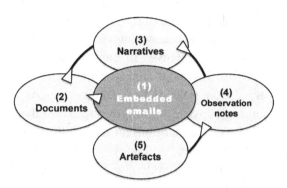

mented the analyses of emails and documents. The observation notes had a similar purpose. Although they were loosely structured, the notes aimed at complementing issues that were already emerging from the analysis of other data sets. Further information about the professional activity of the department was provided by documents and artefacts. These are very important ethnographic elements in EDANs as they document activities in which participants get involved for purposes other than the study. Documents and artefacts like organisational charts, flyers advertising their activities, as well as documents and pictures showing their history can provide invaluable insight into understanding a group's activities and existence. They are similarly important as they have experienced no or very little researcher

intervention- only that of being selected for research purposes- and can offer essential supporting or contradicting evidence, thus presenting a more nuanced description of the issues being investigated.

Table 1 shows a network that was built for the study and that is the focus of analysis in this chapter. As can be observed, the embedded emails record a typical activity by the department, that is, a negotiation over the documents needed for a licence application; the narratives and the artefacts show further aspects of the department's practices; and the documents illustrate the procedures that the department normally follows in negotiating a new licence application. The observation notes provide further insight into the culture and practices of the department when involved in such an activity, which may not have been captured by the other types of data.

Networking Data to Design EDANs

Networking data is central to the design of EDANs. Based on previous work on building data networks (Gimenez, 2010), Tables 2, 3, and 4 show detailed step-by-step descriptions of the analytical procedures needed for networking data in order to build an electronic discourse analysis network. The procedures are divided into three stages: core data collection, complementary data selection and analysis and network building, and intertextual

Table 1. An example of an electronic discourse analysis network (EDAN)

Emails (Core data)	Narratives (complementary data)	Documents (complementary data)	Artefacts (complementary data)
Embedded emails: "*Legal info for [name of local partner]*": Negotiating documents for a licence application	(1) "*Necessary documents to proceed with the licence application*" (James[2]) (2) "*Why we need to do it this way*" (Ann) (3) "*These are our witnesses*" (Frank)	(1) Linked documents (2) The procedures laid out by the department	(1) The department organisational diagram (2) The department website
Observation notes (complementary data) (notes about connected genres, procedures & roles, and confidentiality issues)			

and interdiscursive analyses. Each stage, which is described in a separate table, starts with a brief theoretical comment before introducing the actual analytical steps. After each stage, and before the researcher moves on to the next stage in the analytical process, the procedures include a 'check' that reminds him/her of important considerations at that specific stage and intends to minimise analyst biases.

EMAILS AS DISCURSIVE REPRESENTATIONS OF PROFESSIONAL PRACTICE

This section of the chapter is divided into two parts. In the first, material elements (documents and procedures) that are part of the negotiation and the agents (the people involved in it) together with their responsibilities are described. The second part discusses the representational value of emails.

Documents, Procedures, Agents and Responsibilities

The three central messages in the embedded email that have been analysed as core data for the purpose of this chapter are shown in Figure 2[3]. The messages show a negotiation over a request from the multinational's local partner company for a document certifying that the signing member of the department has Power of Attorney, and for documents to be notarized and apostilled[4] as required by the government of the country where the local partner is located.

It is interesting to note at this point that the messages in this embedded email not only record a particular business negotiation but also illustrate what is normally involved in such negotiations: material elements, i.e. documents and procedures that are part of the negotiation, and agents, i.e. the people involved in it together with the power and responsibilities conferred by their roles. Thus emails like the one examined in this chapter provide references to both intertextual (mainly text-internal) and interdiscursive (mainly text-external) elements that constitute the artefacts (e.g. documents), procedures and responsibilities that form part of the professional practices of those involved in business activities such as a negotiation.

More specifically, we can see from the email message analysed in this section that a negotiation of the type represented in it involves:

Documents:

Table 2. Stage 1 in the procedures for building an EDAN

Stage 1: Core data collection		
This stage focuses on a complex human activity (e.g. online communication among members of a geographically dispersed team) to be analysed, and comprises of three steps which are the foundations upon which an EDAN will be built.		
Steps	**Description**	**Example**
Step 1	Select a complex human activity you wish to explore.	Decision-making in collaborate work by geographically dispersed groups.
Step 2	Collect data that you think best represent or illustrate the activity you wish to examine. These data will become the 'core data' in the EDAN.	Recorded on-line discussions of the team working collaboratively
Step 3	Focus on the main issues emerging from a first analysis of the data. You could use coding techniques facilitated by coding software (e.g. Nvivo).	Access to a specific technology, power distribution, members status, etc.
CHECK 1:	Make sure that the emerging issues you decide to focus on are representative of the human activity you wish to explore	

Table 3. Stage 2 in the procedures for building an EDAN

Stage 2: Complementary data selection and analysis/Network building This second stage has two sub-phases: selection and analysis of complementary data and the bringing together of networked data.		
Steps	**Description**	**Example**
Step 4	Based on step 3, decide what networked data you could collect that would throw some new light on the issues being examined. These data will become the complementary data in your EDAN.	Email-based interviews to collect the team members' views on the issues identified, field notes, etc.
Step 5	Design questions and interview the member that you think plays a central role in the activity you wish to explore.	Questions to the team leader
Step 6	Do a preliminary analysis of the answers/narrative provided in the interviews. You could use coding techniques facilitated by coding software (e.g. Nvivo).	How decisions are made, how roles are distributed among the team members
Step 7	Based on step 6, design new questions to interview people who are 'networked' with the person interviewed in step 5.	How other team members view and perceive the issues already identified
Step 8	Analyse their answers in search of supporting as well as contradictory evidence.	How their views and perceptions compare?
Step 9	Collect documents and artefacts that may throw new/different light on the issues investigated.	Organizational documents, pictures, historical/ organizational charts, etc.
Step 10	Use the issues you identified to build up networks around them by using the multidimensional data you have collected so far.	Issue: unbalanced distribution of workload within the team; online interviews (e.g. how roles and responsibility are allocated), documents produced by the team, etc.
CHECK 2: Check for different ways of organizing the core and complementary data. Different organizations may shed new light on the issues being analysed.		

Table 4. Stage 3 in the procedures for building an EDAN

Stage 3: Intertextual and interdiscurse analyses This final stage focuses on the analysis of discourses present in the network by taking intertextual and interdiscursive elements into consideration.		
Steps	**Description**	**Example**
Step 11	Identify intertextual elements (internal to the data) in the network you have built.	Language used in the data (e.g. as for the documents I mentioned at the beginning…)
Step 12	Identify interdiscursive elements (external to the data) in the network you have built.	Discourses that are called upon (e.g. the business, legal, technical discourses).
Step 13	Decide how intertextual and interdiscursive elements in the network help you to throw new light on the issues you have identified when you started your analysis of the data.	How these reflect the issues involved in the complex human activity you wish to explore.
CHECK 3: Go back to your field notes to help you to interpret the data you are analysing. Make sure your interpretation reflects the context you have observed.		

Figure 2. The three central messages in the embedded email

(1) From: FT
(2) Sent: Thursday, November 03, 2005 1:38 PM
(3) To: AG
(4) CC: AS, JH
(5) Subject: RE: Legal info for [name of local partner]

(6) A,
(7) 1) Of course I can provide the two letter signed by AP [the secretary]; but there is no
(8) such thing as a power of Attorney for AP, it is not required under UK law. Please
(9) follow this link to see such law [external link]

(10) 2) We thought about it and to meet the [country where local partner is based]'s
(11) government requirement we can provide:
(12) - an extract from art. 41 of the UK Companies Act stating that that the company
(13) secretary can authenticate documents for legal purpose
(14) - form 288A, which was signed by AP (when she joined [name of UK company])
(15) and sent to the UK Company House, the UK Registration Authority, when she joined
(16) in the capacity of Company Secretary; note that the form is also signed by the
(17) Company Director. Please follow this link to see the whole document [internal
(18) link]. When requested, please use the password I've sent you as this is a password-
(19) protected document.

(20) There is nothing more that either us or Company House could provide to this effect
(21) so we hope this is sufficient.
(22) F _____

(23) From: AG
(24) Sent: 02 November 2005 23:19
(25) To: FT
(26) CC: AS, JH
(27) Subject: RE: Legal info for [name of local partner]

(28) F,
(29) Sorry for the delay in replying.
(30) 1. Regarding the Power of Attorney for AW and CT, [name of local partner] agreed
(31) with your suggestions that a letter from APs stating that AW and CT are authorised
(32) to sign documents by virtue of their titles, roles and responsibilities, will be
(33) enough. Additionally, we will need a Power of Attorney for AP, which already
(34) exists. We will need to notarize and apostille both the letter and AP's PofA.
(35) 2. Regarding the lack of signed versions of the MofA [Memorandum of Association]
(36) and AofA [Articles of Association], signed copies obtained from the UK company
(37) registration authority would be enough, even if the people signing no longer work
(38) at [name of UK company]. Once these signed copies are obtained, they can be
(39) notarized and apostilled as being true copies of the original documents filed with
(40) the UK company registration authority.

(41) Please let me know whether the suggested course of action for 1 and 2 is
acceptable.
(42) Thank you,
(43) A _____

(44) From: FT
(45) Sent: Wednesday, October 26, 2005 12:51 PM
(46) To: AG
(47) CC: AS, JH
(48) Subject: FW: Legal info for [name of local partner]

(49) A,
(50) Please find attached both the Memorandum of Association and the Articles of
(51) Association of [name of UK company].
(52) Both document refer to your request n. 1 i.e. [name of UK company] Bylaws.
(53) As for documents 2 and 3 I have just spoken to JF, who tells me that neither for
(54) AW, who signed the contractual letter, nor for CT, who normally sign the PSA
(55) contract, a specific power of attorney was given. The fact is that both of them, by
(56) virtue of their role or responsibility at [name of UK company], are authorised to
(57) sign such document. Even AH, the company secretary, signs official documents.

(58) Although it is possible to give power of attorney to a [name of UK company]
(59) employee, this is only done in exceptional cases and would require to be agreed by
(60) the Board of [name of global company], the procedure is lengthy and it's never
(61) been done, so we are very reluctant to do it in this case; is there a way in which we
(62) can explain this to JP? Perhaps we can provide as an alternative statement to this
(63) effect, i.e. a letter signed by AP stating that AW and CT are authorised to sign
(64) documents by virtue of their titles, roles and responsibilities?

(65) I enclose again the Certificate of Incorporation on Change of Name.
(66) Let me know.
(67) Cheers, F

- **Letters:** Letters signed by members of the department (e.g. lines 1 and 31), and contractual letters (line 54);
- **Contracts:** PSA [Production Sharing Agreement] contract (line 54);
- **Certificates:** Certificate of Incorporation (line 65);
- **Constitution documents:** Memorandum of Association and Articles of Association (lines 35, 36, 50 and 51);
- **Acts and laws:** UK companies Act (lines 8 and 12), the company Bylaws (line 52), and Power of Attorney (lines 8, 30, 33 and 58).

Procedures and protocols:

- Notarisation (lines 34 and 38);
- Apostille certification (lines 34 and 38);
- Board agreement (lines 58-59).

Agents and their powers:

- Authorisation to sign official company documents (e.g. lines 55-57 and 62-64);
- Authorisation of exceptional cases (e.g. the Board of the company) (lines 59-60);
- Acting as witnesses to legal procedures being discussed (e.g. AS and JH, two legal team members who have been copied into the messages) (lines 4, 26 and 47; narrative 3).

The material elements and the roles of the agents reflected in the embedded email are further illustrated by the interview narratives of a number of key members of the department. Networking data such as emails and the views about the departmental practices reflected in them provides a more in-depth perspective of the professional practices under consideration. This perspective is central to advancing our understanding of human activity in particular settings such as the business

context in this study where communication has become a more complex practice, and of how such contexts are discursively constituted in specific genres like embedded emails.

Three interview narrative excerpts have been chosen to further explore the material elements and roles of the agents mentioned above. The first is provided by James, one of the legal advisers, who talks about the different documents involved in the negotiation presented in the central message of the embedded email. The second excerpt is from the manager of the department who explains the nature of the business of her department. The final excerpt about the role of legal advisers is provided by Frank, a member in Ann's team.

1. "Necessary documents to proceed with the licence application" (James, legal adviser)

...absolutely there is a complex set of documents which we sometimes need to produce in order to apply for a licence. The number of documents will depend on the country in which our business partners are located but it's never an easy thing, there are always complications not to mention differences in the laws and procedures of each country. As you can see in this email, here in the UK we don't need power of attorney for, say, the secretary sign certain documents, they just do it by virtue of their roles. So where there are differences like this, other documents may need to be produced instead such as the memorandum or the articles... all these are necessary documents to proceed with the licence application... in some cases it's kind of standard procedure but in others there's a lot of negotiating going on...

2. "Why we need to do it this way" (Ann, department manager)

...the regulatory and policy department of a company like this one is a central and sometimes neuralgic part of the system. Because so much is at

stake all the time you need to proceed only when you know that's the right thing to do you know you... you need to establish and follow highly regulated procedures and draw on people's expertise and authority coz you know most of what you do is binding, legally binding...

3. "These are our witnesses" (Frank, Ann's team member)

That's right... if there's nothing unusual then that's... they [members of the department who have been copied into messages] may never say anything... write anything... all they do is make sure procedures are followed.... that we do the right thing you know...they are erm... let's say these are our silent witnesses

These excerpts throw some new light on the practices and procedures reflected in the embedded email. Without access to the views provided in these narratives it would be rather difficult to fully understand why the messages in the email

have been composed in this way (e.g. intertextual elements) and, probably more importantly, why procedures and practices are so highly regulated and dependent on the participants' expertise and authority roles (interdiscursive elements).

The actual documents referred to in the message, which are part of the ethnographic network, cannot be reproduced here due to confidentiality issues. However, they serve to lay out the procedures that need to be followed for new licence applications which would allow the corporation to start new business with a local partner, as well as to specify who needs to get involved in each stage of the application.

In a similar vein, the artefacts collected for the study cannot be reproduced to protect the anonymity of the company researched. Instead, Figure 3 shows a reconstruction of the section of the corporation organisational chart where the department sits –see shaded area- and Table 5 describes some of the graphs on the department website.

Figure 3. Reconstructed organisational chart

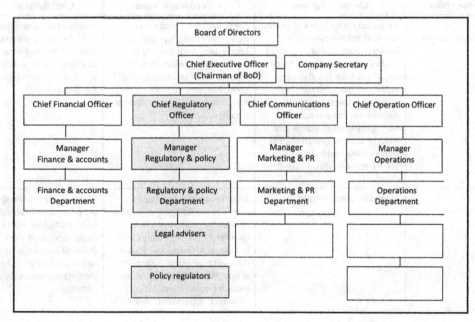

Table 5. Description of graph types on the department website

Website section	Graph description
The regulatory and policy department	*An image of a departmental meeting around a big, oval table and a picture of each member accompanied by a short description of their roles and responsibilities.*
The main activities of the department	*A description of the main activities of the Department with graphs that illustrate these.*

Finally, the observation notes made along the duration of the study also throw some light on the documents associated with the embedded email (connected genres) and procedures and roles involved in the negotiation. Table 6 shows some of the notes made over two of the days when observation instances took place.

THE REPRESENTATIONAL VALUE OF EMAILS

In the contemporary workplace emails are not only a means of communication. They also serve as discursive accounts of professional practice.

As described in the previous part of this section, emails can become windows on the material, social and relational worlds of professionals.

In the particular case of the email reproduced in Figure 2, a wide variety of documents that represent the material world where this group of professionals operate is called upon. To be able to apply for a licence that would allow the multinational to operate in the new country we see that a considerable number of documents have to be produced: letters, contracts, certificates, acts and laws. This 'complex set of documents,' as James describes it in his narrative, represents the complexity of the professional activities carried

Table 6. Sample of observation notes

Day of observation	Connected genres	Procedures & roles	Confidentiality issues
Day 3 (after preliminary analysis of email)	By looking at the types of genres involved and the connection between them, one can see there is obviously a lot at stake being negotiated here. It's also very interesting that each member of the department has a well-defined role and can activate a very specific set of genres (e.g. AH, the company secretary, can sign a contractual letter). I'll ask FT about it when I have the chance.	Every decision –even every move- they make has already been established/decid-ed in the documents which they all seem to know and have agreed upon. But have they? Or do they represent how things are done at the department?	The fact that some issues are 'too confidential' to discuss in my presence is also a clear indication that there's a lot at stake –also in terms of confidentiality'- over this negotiation.
Day 7 (after interviews were finished)	Most documents, emails, etc.	Interviews have confirmed that they all know/are perfectly aware of what they have to do, who they need to consult things with (e.g. legal advisers) and what is the most convenient course of action. Would there ever be any room for agency in this highly structured department? Ask FT?	It's interesting to see that they are progressively abandoning the idea of attaching files to their emails and using more and more (internal and external) links and depending more heavily on their servers where for archiving purposes.

out by the regulatory and policy department of the multinational corporation.

From a discursive perspective, the embedded email displays the intertextual and interdiscursive elements (Bhatia, 2004; 2008; 2010) that have intervened in as well as supported the professional practices of the department. Intertextuality is established between the variety of documents enacted in the email: letters, contracts, certificates, acts and laws, constituting a constellation of genres (Swales, 2004) required to achieve a specific purpose: applying for a new licence. Also, linguistic elements such as "your request n. 1" (line 52), 'As for documents 2 and 3' (line 53), and 'Regarding the lack of signed versions of' (line 35) increase the intertextual quality of the negotiation represented in the embedded email. Interdiscursivity is evidenced by the convergence of three types of discourses: the legal, the business, and the technical discourses. We can thus see that the legal discourse is activated to describe requirements as in "a specific power of attorney was given" (line 55), and brought in line with the business discourse when the agents try to negotiate alternative documents in order to meet the local country's requirements (see, for example, lines 62-64). This is also complemented with examples of the technical discourse in relation to specifications such as "When requested, please use the password I've sent you as this is a password-protected document" (lines 18-19). This exemplifies both the central roles of intertextuality and interdiscursivity in electronic corporate communication as well as the complexity of its nature.

The documents enacted in the email message also reflect the difficulties that the members of the regulatory and policy department encounter when negotiating globally. In this case, the legal systems of different countries (the English law of the UK and the civil law legal system of the country where the multinational wishes to start operating in the case of the present study) contrib-

utes to such difficulty. This adds an extra layer of interdiscursive elements to the embedded email and demonstrates the complexity of the interaction. This complexity is illustrated in instances where the requirements of one legal system do not seem to align with those of the other as is the case of the Authorisation to sign official company documents that the secretary of the multinational has by power of her role and the Power of Attorney requested by the country where the multinational is applying for a new business licence.

Complexity is also revealed in the procedures and protocols enacted in the email negotiation. Notarisation of documents and apostille certificates are rather foreign procedures for the multinational corporation where the validity of a person's signature is given by the nature of their role as discussed above. This also holds true in the case of having to give new powers to employees, exemplifying some of the relational aspects of their professional practice. As seen in the email, the multinational would prefer not to create new relations in their organisational structure and to avoid engaging in procedures that are "lengthy" and are not part of their usual practices: "it's never been done" (lines 60-61). This preference appears to be in line with the highly regulated nature of the department and its professional practices.

Thus, it is clear that the professionals involved in the email exchange in Figure 2 are doing more than just merely negotiating a deal. They are also exchanging professional practices and establishing-or avoiding to establish- new social and relational ones. However, emails by themselves may fail to reveal such complex relations. Combined with other networked data as shown in this chapter, emails can then offer significant insight into the practices of the group of professionals. As proposed in the chapter, multidimensional analytical approaches such as EDANs can further our understanding of the practices, discursive and otherwise, in which professionals get involved.

Without such approaches we run the risk of not only focusing on a single dimension of activity but also providing a rather partial and misleading understanding of the complexity of human interaction in situated practices.

FUTURE RESEARCH DIRECTIONS

Although research in email communication has been conducted for quite some time and the field has reached a significant level of development and maturity, there are still some areas that need further exploration. Two of these seem central to the theme of this volume: new methodologies that help to capture the complexities of electronic discourse, and further examinations of the implications of electronic discourse for the theory and practice of professional communication.

There are a number of existing methodologies that, although not commonly used in researching electronic communication, could provide insightful understandings of this type of discourse. Ethnography[5], with its emphasis on the social and the interpersonal, is taking centre stage in many fields of professional activity. Thus, the opportunities created by combining ethnography with discourse analysis seem quite promising for starting to unpack some of the complexity of electronic communication (Idema & Scheeres, 2009). Coupled with this, 'virtual ethnography,' which suggests cyberspace as an ethnographic site of mediated interaction (Baym, 1995), can offer new methodological tools for researching online corporate communication.

In a similar vein, ethnomethodology (Garfinkel, 1967), which mainly looks at the temporal and sequential details of organizing processes, can help to shed new light on how institutional electronic discourse is typically organized and the meanings of its organization. For those who are interested in the 'management of social institution in interaction' (Heritage, 1997, p. 223), with its focus on turn-taking and sequence organizations, and repairs, conversational analysis can also prove a useful methodology.

Coupled with this, there is the need for both new multidimensional analytical approaches to be developed and for those already being used, such as EDANs, to be applied in different contexts to build a more robust body of findings. In the particular case of EDANs, the analysis presented in this chapter is of a single case. Other cases from different contexts will have to be examined before we can gain a more comprehensive understanding of the advantages and challenges of using EDANs. However, as illustrated in this chapter the results of using EDANs are quite promising in advancing our understanding on online communication in international organisations. Whilst it may be too early to make any general recommendations, it is possible to point to areas of exploration where the networks could produce interesting results. One such area could be collaborative work of geographically dispersed groups where decision-making processes involve complex mechanisms of analysis and decisions, sometimes determined by the status, the location and access to specific technology of the members of the team.

The second research direction relates to the impact of electronic mediated communication (EMC) on the theory and practice of professional communication. Research in this area has already started to attract considerable attention by researchers and practitioners. However, there are questions about EMC that have not yet been answered. One such questions relates to 'virtual identity:' Do users of EMC assume different identities for different media? Or in other words, do different media (email vs. video chat) allow users to display different identities? What implications for the theory and practice of professional communication does online identity display have? Another area worthy of further investigation is the relationship between EMC and institutional power. EMC has been widely perceived as a 'democratic equaliser', but when EMC is part of employees' performance assessment it may feel to some as an imposition rather than an attempt to make things more equal. It would then be interesting to examine the relationship between EMC and performance assessment in contemporary workplaces, especially those that highly depend on technology for conducting their business activities.

These are some of ideas and directions that research in electronic discourse could embrace in the future to further our understanding of this central aspect of contemporary professional communication.

CONCLUSION

This chapter has shown that the complexity of the professional practices of the regulatory and policy department of a multinational corporation as reflected in their email negotiation can only be unpacked if explored in a multidimensional fashion.

Research on email communication has shown significant progress since its beginnings in the late 1990s. The development of analytical methods that would allow us to see the full complexity of email interactions from a discursive perspective has been less promising, however. By the same token, the application of discursive analytical approaches such as ethnography and conversational analysis to the analysis of email communication has not yet been taken fully on board in the literature.

In an attempt to start narrowing this methodological gap, this chapter has proposed using electronic discourse analysis networks (EDANs) which consist of a variety of networked data sets (emails, narratives, documents and artefacts) collected from the same context of interaction.

It is hoped that this chapter will help to generate further discussions and research on email communication as representations of professional practice. In a similar vein, it is hoped that it will serve as the basis for new discourse-oriented

analytical methods which can help us to gain a fuller understanding of the reality of professional online communication.

REFERENCES

Akar, D. (2002). The macro contextual factors shaping business discourse: The Turkish case. *International Review of Applied Linguistics in Language Teaching, 40*(4), 305–322. doi:10.1515/iral.2002.015.

Atkinson, P., Coffey, A., Delamont, S., Lofland, J., & Lofland, L. (Eds.). (2008). *Handbook of ethnography*. London: Sage.

Baron, N. S. (1998). Letters by phone or speech by other means: The linguistics of email. *Language & Communication, 18*(2), 133–170. doi:10.1016/S0271-5309(98)00005-6.

Baym, N. (1995). The emergence of community in computer-mediated communication. In Jones, S. G. (Ed.), *Cybersociety: Computer-mediated communication and community* (pp. 138–163). Thousand Oaks, CA: Sage.

Bhatia, V. K. (2004). *Worlds of written discourse: A genre-based view*. London: Continuum.

Bhatia, V. K. (2008). Towards critical genre analysis. In Bhatia, V. K., Flowerdew, J., & Jones, R. (Eds.), *Advances in discourse studies* (pp. 166–177). London: Routledge.

Bhatia, V. K. (2010). Interdiscursivity in professional communication. *Discourse & Communication, 4*(1), 32–50. doi:10.1177/1750481309351208.

Crystal, D. (2001). *Language and the Internet*. Cambridge: Cambridge University Press. doi:10.1017/CBO9781139164771.

Daft, R. L., & Lengel, R. H. (1986). Organizational information requirements, media richness and structural design. *Management Science, 32*(5), 554–571. doi:10.1287/mnsc.32.5.554.

Fidel, R., Pejtersen, A. M., Cleal, B., & Bruce, H. (2004). A multidimensional approach to the study of human-information interaction: A case study of collaborative information retrieval. *Journal of the American Society for Information Science and Technology*, *55*(11), 939–953. doi:10.1002/asi.20041.

Gains, J. (1999). Electronic-mail - A new style of communication or just a new medium? An investigation into the text features of e-mail. *English for Specific Purposes*, *18*(1), 81–101. doi:10.1016/S0889-4906(97)00051-3.

Garfinkel, H. (1967). *Studies in ethnomethodology*. Malden, MA: Blackwell.

Gimenez, J. (2000). Business e-mail communication: Some emerging tendencies in register. *English for Specific Purposes*, *19*(3), 237–251. doi:10.1016/S0889-4906(98)00030-1.

Gimenez, J. (2002). New media and conflicting realities in multinational corporate communication: A case study. *International Review of Applied Linguistics*, *40*(4), 323–343. doi:10.1515/iral.2002.016.

Gimenez, J. (2005). Unpacking business emails: Message embeddedness in international business email communication. In Gotti, M., & Gillaerts, P. (Eds.), *Genre variation in business letters* (pp. 235–255). Frankfurt: Peter Lang.

Gimenez, J. (2006). Embedded business emails: Meeting new demands in international business communication. *English for Specific Purposes*, *25*(2), 154–172. doi:10.1016/j.esp.2005.04.005.

Gimenez, J. (2010). Narrative analysis in linguistic research. In Litosseliti, L. (Ed.), *Research methods in linguistics* (pp. 198–216). London: Continuum.

Heritage, J. (1997). Conversation analysis and institutional talk: Analyzing data. In Silverman, D. (Ed.), *Qualitative research: Theory, method and practice* (pp. 222–245). London: Sage.

Hinds, P., & Kiesler, S. (1995). Communication across boundaries: Work, structure, and use of communication technologies in a large organization. *Organization Science*, *6*(4), 373–393. doi:10.1287/orsc.6.4.373.

Ho, V. C. K. (2011). A discourse-based study of three communities of practice: How members maintain a harmonious relationship while threatening each other's face via email. *Discourse Studies*, *13*(3), 299–326. doi:10.1177/1461445611400673.

Iedema, R., & Scheeres, H. (2009). Organizational discourse analysis. In Bargiela-Chiappini, F. (Ed.), *The handbook of business discourse* (pp. 80–91). Edinburgh: Edinburgh University Press.

Lamb, R., & Kling, R. (2003). Reconceptualizing users as social actors in information systems research. *Management Information Systems Quarterly*, *27*(2), 197–235.

Lengel, R. H., & Daft, R. L. (1988). The selection of communication media as an executive skill. *The Academy of Management Executive*, *2*(3), 225–232. doi:10.5465/AME.1988.4277259.

Louhiala-Salminen, L. (2002). The fly's perspective: Discourse in the daily routine of a business manager. *English for Specific Purposes*, *21*(3), 211–231. doi:10.1016/S0889-4906(00)00036-3.

Mallon, R., & Oppenheim, C. (2002). Style used in electronic mail. *Aslib Proceedings*, *54*(1), 8–22. doi:10.1108/00012530210697482.

Markus, M. L. (1994). Electronic mail as the medium of managerial choice. *Organization Science*, *5*(4), 502–527. doi:10.1287/orsc.5.4.502.

Mulholland, J. (1999). Email: Uses, issues and problems in an institutional setting. In Bargiela-Chiappini, F., & Nickerson, C. (Eds.), *Writing business: Genres, media and discourses* (pp. 50–84). London: Longman.

Nickerson, C. (2000). *Playing the corporate language game*. Amsterdam and Atlanta, GA: Rodopi.

Orlikowski, W., & Yates, J. A. (1994). Genre repertoire: The structuring of communicative practices in organizations. *Administrative Science Quarterly, 39*(4), 541–574. doi:10.2307/2393771.

Sonnenwald, D. H., Wildemuth, B. M., & Harmon, G. L. (2001). A research method to investigate information seeking using the concept of information horizons: An example from a study of lower socio-economic student's information seeking behaviour. *The New Review of Information Behaviour Research, 2*(1), 65–86.

Swales, J. M. (2004). *Research genres: Explorations and applications*. Cambridge: Cambridge University Press. doi:10.1017/CBO9781139524827.

Turner, J. W., Grube, J. A., Tinsley, C. H., Lee, C., & O'Pell, C. (2006). Exploring the dominant media: How does media use reflect organizational norms and affect performance? *Journal of Business Communication, 43*(3), 220–250. doi:10.1177/0021943606288772.

Turner, J. W., & Reinsch, N. L. (2007). The business communicator as presence allocator: Multicommunicating, equivocality, and status at work. *Journal of Business Communication, 44*(1), 36–58. doi:10.1177/0021943606295779.

Turner, J. W., & Reinsch, N. L. (2009). Successful and unsuccessful multicommunication episodes: Engaging in dialogue or juggling messages? *Information Systems Frontiers, 12*(3), 277–285. doi:10.1007/s10796-009-9175-y.

Turner, J. W., & Reinsch, N. L. (2011). Multicommunicating and episodic presence: Creating new constructs for studying new phenomenon. In Wright, K., & Webb, L. (Eds.), *Computer mediated communication in personal relationships* (pp. 181–193). New York: Peter Lang.

van den Hoof, B., Groot, J., & de Jonge, S. (2005). Situational influences on the use of communication technologies: A meta-analysis and exploratory study. *Journal of Business Communication, 42*(1), 4–27. doi:10.1177/0021943604271192.

Wollman-Bonilla, J. E. (2003). Email as genre: A beginning writer learns the conventions. *Language Arts, 81*(2), 126–134.

ADDITIONAL READING

Bargiela-Chiappini, F. (Ed.). (2009). *The handbook of business discourse*. Edinburgh: Edinburgh University Press.

Bargiela-Chiappini, F., & Nickerson, C. (2002). Business discourse: Old debates, new horizons. *International Review of Applied Linguistics in Language Teaching, 40*(4), 273–286. doi:10.1515/iral.2002.013.

Bargiela-Chiappini, F., Nickerson, C., & Planken, B. (2007). *Business discourse*. Basingstoke: Palgrave.

Berry, G. R. (2011). Enhancing effectiveness on virtual teams: Understanding why traditional team skills are insufficient. *Journal of Business Communication, 48*(2), 186–206. doi:10.1177/0021943610397270.

Boje, D. M. (2001). *Narrative methods for organizational and communication research*. London: Sage.

Curran, K., O'Hara, K., & O'Brien, S. (2011). The role of twitter in the world of business. *International Journal of Business Data Communications and Networking, 7*(3), 1–15. doi:10.4018/jbdcn.2011070101.

Denstadli, J. M., Julsrud, T. E., & Hjorthol, R. J. (2012). Videoconferencing as a mode of communication: A comparative study of the use of videoconferencing and face-to-face meetings. *Journal of Business and Technical Communication*, *26*(1), 65–91. doi:10.1177/1050651911421125.

Derks, D., & Bakker, A. (2010). The impact of e-mail communication on organizational life. *Cyberpsychology: Journal of Psychosocial Research on Cyberspace*, 4, article 1. Retrieved March 02, 2012, from http://cyberpsychology.eu/view.php?cisloclanku=2010052401&article=1

Eid, R., & El-Kassrawy, Y. (2012). The effect of the internet use on customer relations and targeting activities: An empirical study of UK companies. *International Journal of Online Marketing*, *2*(3), 39–51. doi:10.4018/ijom.2012070103.

Forey, G., & Lockwood, J. (Eds.). (2010). *Globalisation, communication and the workplace*. London: Continuum.

Halbe, D. (2012). "Who's there?": Differences in the features of telephone and face-to-face conferences. *Journal of Business Communication*, *49*(1), 48–73. doi:10.1177/0021943611425238.

Hammersley, M., & Atkinson, P. (2007). *Ethnography*. London: Routledge.

Hine, C. (2000). *Virtual ethnography*. London: Sage.

Jensen, A. (2009). Discourse strategies in professional e-mail negotiation: A case study. *English for Specific Purposes*, *28*(1), 4–18. doi:10.1016/j.esp.2008.10.002.

Jones, S. G. (Ed.). (1998). *Cybersociety2.0: Revisiting computer-mediated communication and community*. Thousand Oaks, CA: Sage.

Koester, A. (2010). *Workplace discourse*. London: Continuum.

Kupritz, V. W., & Cowell, E. (2011). Productive management communication online and face-to-face. *Journal of Business Communication*, *48*(1), 54–82. doi:10.1177/0021943610385656.

Reinsch, L. N. Jr, Turner, J. W., & Tinsley, C. (2008). Multicommunicating: A practice whose time has come? *Academy of Management Review*, *33*(2), 391–403. doi:10.5465/AMR.2008.31193450.

Samra-Fredericks, D. (2009). Ethnomethodology. In Bargiela-Chiappini, F. (Ed.), *The handbook of business discourse* (pp. 92–104). Edinburgh: Edinburgh University Press.

Sillince, J. A. (2007). Organizational context and the discursive construction of organizing. *Management Communication Quarterly*, *20*(4), 363–394. doi:10.1177/0893318906298477.

Smith, V. (2008). Ethnographies of work and the work of ethnographers. In Atkinson, P., Coffey, A., Delamont, S., Lofland, J., & Lofland, L. (Eds.), *Handbook of ethnography* (pp. 220–233). London: Sage.

Stephens, K. K., & Davis, J. (2009). The social influences on electronic multitasking in organizational meetings. *Management Communication Quarterly*, *23*(1), 63–83. doi:10.1177/0893318909335417.

Stolley, K. (2009). Integrating social media into existing work environments: The case of delicious. *Journal of Business and Technical Communication*, *23*(3), 350–371. doi:10.1177/1050651909333260.

Zachry, M. (2009). Rhetorical analysis. In Bargiela-Chiappini, F. (Ed.), *The handbook of business discourse* (pp. 68–79). Edinburgh: Edinburgh University Press.

Zemliansky, P., & St. Amant, K. (Eds.). (2008). *Handbook of research on virtual workplaces and the new nature of business practices*. London: Information Science Reference. doi:10.4018/978-1-59904-893-2.

KEY TERMS AND DEFINITIONS

Artefact: A man-made object, such as a graph, a tool or a work of art, that is used as evidence for accomplishing some end. In the context of the study reported on in this chapter, an artefact refers to a flyer, a chart or a website designed for purposes other than the research study.

Core Data: Central data in the networks (the embedded emails in this study) around which the rest of the elements are organised. The core data serve not only to organise the elements in the network but also to guide their collection and analysis.

Electronic Discourse Analysis Networks (EDANs): An analytical framework for investigating electronic discourse that consists of a variety of networked data sets (emails, narratives, documents and artefacts) collected from the same context of interaction in order to provide multidimensional explorations of professional practice.

Electronic Mediated Communication (EMC): An umbrella term used to refer to computer-mediated communication (CMC), the study of the style of online communication and the information it conveys, and information communication technologies (ICTs), the machines themselves, the computers, and mobile phones.

Embedded Business Emails: (Also called 'chain' and 'threaded' emails) An email message that embeds a series of messages generated in response to the initial email. The term 'embedded email' is sometimes preferred to indicate the different status that the different parts of a message have. For example, all the 'reply' messages that constitute the chain depend on or are subordinate to the initial message to make complete communicative sense.

Ethnography: One of the many approaches used in social research which aims at examining cultural phenomena which reproduce the knowledge and system of meanings in the life of a given group. Although initially restricted to anthropology, ethnography has gained wide recognition in fields as varied as sociology, communication studies, health sciences, and history, to mention just a few. Data collection, which normally involves the researcher as a participant in people's daily practices over a considerable period of time, is carried out through observation, interviews, and questionnaires.

Supplementary Data: Data in the networks (the documents, narratives, observation notes, and artefacts in this study) that have been collected, organised, and analysed in relation to the core data.

ENDNOTES

1. A general discussion on the different notions of and approaches to "genre" in the existing literature is beyond this chapter. Readers are referred to Bhatia (2004; 2008; 2010) for detailed discussions of these issues.

2. Names are pseudonyms used to protect the anonymity of the participants.

3. Readers are reminded that they should read emails in the chain in the order they were written, that is, from bottom to top.

4. Notarization is an essential protocol for certifying documents or document copies which may need to be used in countries other than that where the company that produced such documents is registered. An apostille certificate is then attached to the documents by the foreign office of the country where the company is registered.

5. The scope of this chapter does not allow for a lengthy discussion on ethnography but readers may wish to see Atkinson et al.'s (2008) authoritative volume.

Chapter 16

Computer–Aided Deductive Critical Discourse Analysis of a Case Study from Mauritius with ATLAS–ti 6.2

Komalsingh Rambaree
University of Gävle, Sweden

ABSTRACT

This chapter considers computer-aided deductive critical discourse analysis with ATLAS-ti 6.2 using a case study on eco-social work research from Mauritius. Data for this case study were gathered in digital audio format from eight focus group discussions, three semi-structured interviews and various reports from secondary sources. For the analysis, a literature review using ATLAS-ti was first carried out, in order to develop a conceptual/theoretical framework related to eco-social work. Then, the gathered data were directly plugged into ATLAS-ti for a computer-aided deductive critical discourse analysis using the developed eco-social work conceptual/theoretical framework from the literature review. Using the case study as an example, this chapter (a) demonstrates the techniques, and (b) appraises the opportunities, limitations and challenges of computer-aided critical discourse analysis.

INTRODUCTION

Critical discourse analysis (CDA) – where meanings, motivations, ideologies and power are analysed through the deconstruction of text and talk – can be a complex process for novice researchers. When a large volume of research evidence is gathered through the use of new technological tools such as new social media (Facebook, Twitter, Skype, YouTube and so on) and digital recorders (graphics, audio, video), CDA becomes challenging even for experienced researchers. Fortunately, over the last few decades a number of Computer-Aided Qualitative Data Analysis Software (CAQDAS) has been developed allowing more rapid, as well as more rigorous, data analysis (Rambaree, 2007; Rambaree & Faxelid, 2013).

DOI: 10.4018/978-1-4666-4426-7.ch016

CAQDAS packages are designed to aid researchers to interpret qualitative data through the identification, development and exploration of themes, concepts, and processes through coding and management of data. The identification and development of codes, themes, concepts and processes with CAQDAS facilitate the construction of explanations/theories or the testing/expansion of an existing theory (Lewins & Silver, 2007). ATLAS-ti is one among the range of CAQDAS systems currently available in the market, and its use within the field of qualitative research has been growing over the last few years (Konopásek, 2008). Like any other CAQDAS, ATLAS-ti is a tool for supporting the process of qualitative data analysis, particularly through automating and speeding up the coding and linking processes for a more efficient and effective way of exploring gathered data in breadth and depth (Barry, 1998; Rambaree, 2007; Friese, 2012; Stewart, 2012). Comparing some of the CAQDAS, a number of researchers argue that ATLAS-ti is relatively more advanced in terms of software development – with a more complex inter-connected, hypertext structure, and it is also more intuitive and easier to learn, as well as more versatile (Barry, 1998; Lewis, 2004; Stewart, 2012). In relation to data management, ATLAS-ti can be considered user-friendly software, with almost all the essential capabilities for undertaking different types of qualitative analysis, within which different formats of data (text, graphics, audio and video) can be input directly for analysis (Barry, 1998; Lewis, 2004).

It is generally argued that several CAQDAS present a number of features and functions without a clear approach for undertaking different types of qualitative analysis (Stewart, 2012). In addition, most contemporary literature has mainly focused on describing, evaluating and or appreciating the programme functions of the software, rather than providing clear directions for undertaking certain types of qualitative data analysis using

CAQDAS. Within qualitative research discourses, therefore, there is still a noticeable gap in terms of basic guidelines and procedures for how to undertake different types of qualitative analysis (such as Thematic, Narrative, and CDA) using the features and functions of CAQDAS. In a similar vein, Hwang (2008) argues that not many scholarly works have been published to show how to use CAQDAS with actual research cases. Given that CAQDAS, such as ATLAS-ti, provides new possibilities for dealing with data, a systematic and methodological approach for qualitative data analysis needs to be further elaborated, in order to exploit the benefits of such software (Friese, 2012). Moreover, qualitative data tend to be voluminous and vast in nature; therefore, without proper guidance it is easy for researchers to get lost and confused within the data analysis process. In order to discover the benefits of CAQDAS, it is important to have step-by-step procedures for guiding the different types of qualitative data analysis. In particular, a step-by-step guide can provide researchers more insight in understanding, evaluating and appreciating the discovery that could be made by using ATLAS-ti for qualitative data analysis, such as CDA.

In her book, Friese (2012, p. 92) presents '*Notice, Code and Think*' (NCT) as a general model of qualitative data analysis using ATLAS-ti tools. NCT, in fact, represents a very simple model of processing qualitative data (Seidel, 1998). Hence, Friese (2012) calls upon researchers to use this particular simple NCT model to work with ATLAS-ti for reporting what else may be discovered. She provides an interesting analogy stating:

The data material is the terrain that you want to study; the chosen analytic approach is your pathway through it. The tools and functions provided by ATLAS.ti tools are your equipment to examine what there is to discover. (p. 4)

How is the NCT model applied within ATLAS-ti for CDA? What can be discovered when using ATLAS-ti for CDA? Such information is still missing within qualitative research discourses. In this connection, this chapter focuses on demonstrating a step-by-step approach in doing computer-aided CDA with ATLAS-ti (version 6.2) using the case study on eco-social work from Mauritius. The structure of this chapter is as follows. After this brief introduction, the background section starts by considering the broad definitions and discussions of certain terms and concepts that are frequently used in this chapter. In addition, the background section provides a brief introduction of the context of the case study, (which is considered as an example for demonstrating the techniques of computer-aided CDA in this chapter). The section following the background is related to the techniques of computer-aided CDA. Within this section, the steps of doing computer-aided CDA with ATLAS-ti using the case study from Mauritius are demonstrated and explained; and, an appraisal of doing computer-aided CDA with ATLAS-ti is carried out. Then, some future research directions for computer-aided critical discourse analysis using ATLAS-ti are considered. Finally, the conclusion summarises the main points of this chapter and makes some general concluding remarks with regards to CDA with ATLAS-ti.

BACKGROUND

Critical Discourse Analysis

CDA focuses on discourses as a critical way of studying, explaining and understanding social issues, concerns and problems. Discourse is broadly understood as ideas or patterned ways of thinking, reasoning and communicating (Lupton, 1992). A discourse is also regarded as a system of possibilities for the construction of knowledge based on interpretations and understandings (Flax, 1992). Fairclough and Wodak (1997, p.258) posit

that, "discourse is socially constitutive as well as socially conditioned – it constitutes situations, objects of knowledge, and the social identities of and relationships between people and groups of people."

A critical perspective to discourse is considered as having an important role in the (re)-production and challenge of dominance, oppression, and injustices (van Dijk, 1993; 1995). Through the analysis of the gathered discourses from the field, some researchers mainly focus on the disclosure of undemocratic, unjust and inhumane living conditions by which victimised groups are affected (Dirks, 2006). One of the most common prerequisites within CDA is therefore to describe and undertake critical reflection on the social processes and structures that give rise to certain discourses, which in turn provide the basis for understanding and explaining of social issues, concerns and problems (Wodak, 2001). In particular, CDA requires researchers to take a critical and oppositional stance against the powerful and the dominant group in order to explore and explain the implicit, hidden/camouflaged/otherwise not immediately obvious power dominance and underlying ideologies of dominance for oppression (van Dijk, 1995). In a similar manner, Fairclough (2010) states that through CDA, social researchers aim to produce interpretations and explanations of areas of social life which both identify the causes of injustices and inequalities and produce relevant knowledge for correcting such "social wrongs." For van Dijk (2008), CDA is a critical assessment of abusive practices through power resulting in social inequality and calls for guidelines for practical intervention in the interest of the victims and approaches for resistance against illegitimate domination.

Perhaps, it is worth pointing out that CDA is not based upon a single theoretical framework. According to Chouliaraki (2008), two major perspectives influence the notion of power within text and talk in the social sciences. These are: (a) the post-structuralist perspective, which is associated with Foucault's theory of discourse – where language is considered as a constitutive component of the social world with power; and (b) the critical perspective, which is broadly associated with neo-Marxism and with the Frankfurt School – where language and power are believed to be organised around economic and political structures of domination. From a critical perspective, discourse is therefore understood not only as an epiphenomenal product of structural determinants, but also as a constitutive mode/function of power relation (Park, 2005). Within this context, Wodak and Meyer (2009) argue:

...it is important to stress that CDA has never been and has never attempted to be or to provide one single or specific theory. Neither is one specific methodology characteristic of research in CDA... CDA are multifarious, derived from quite different theoretical backgrounds, oriented towards different data and methodologies (p.5).

In sum, CDA is therefore commonly used in social research that intends to contribute towards the rectification of injustice and inequality in society (Jørgensen & Phillips, 2002). Thus, social researchers aim, through CDA, at *"revealing structures of power and unmasking ideologies"* for contributing towards change for a more equal, fair and just society (Wodak & Meyer, 2009, p.8). In particular, CDA researchers study quotations from text and talks to deconstruct meanings, understandings, and ideologies.

Quotations and Codes

Quotations and codes are two of the most essential aspects of CDA (as they are for any other qualitative data analysis). Both quotations and codes help researchers to explore, understand and explain social phenomena from the gathered data. In particular, quotations are segments of data that researchers identify as being central to the research questions for exploring, understand-

ing and explaining the social phenomena being studied. For instance, during the data collection for the case study on eco-social work in Mauritius, one of the respondents in the focus group discussion mentions:

People have the right to know that from the high-tide to the low-tide water mark it is public...but people have to choose either they want money, development ... employment for their children or they want to apply the law... tourists come to Mauritius to have peace and quiet time, not to see Mauritians eating on the beach [sic].

This statement, given as example, is an interesting quotation for CDA. Such quotations are central for grounding the analysis in exploring meanings and power within the discourses used by the respondents in focus group discussions. In CDA, such quotations represent the fundamental part of the analysis in exploring, understanding and explaining how power is expressed by research participants.

In particular, exploration of gathered quotations can be considered as a starting block in CDA. In deductive CDA, quotations provide essential substance that contributes towards the chosen conceptual/theoretical framework. In this connection, Konopásek (2008) opines that quotations are elementary units of analysis that provide meaning to the research, they are accessible to our minds and mental processing and can be physically presented on paper and computers. In deductive CDA, while going through the collected data from the beginning to the end, in an orderly manner, researchers look for quotations that support, contradict, explain, and expand the conceptual and theoretical framework. Such quotations are usually coded for creating linkages and for comparison with other quotations or other codes from different segments of the collected data and/or theoretical explanations.

A code can be considered as a reference given to some part of the gathered qualitative data that directs researchers towards data reduction. A code can be a word, some words or even a few sentences. Coding in qualitative research is hence considered as a data reduction technique, which is the central part of the analysis that sorts, focuses, discards, and organizes the gathered evidence in such a way that conclusions based on the research questions can be drawn and verified (Miles & Huberman, 1994; Rambaree & Faxelid, 2013). In a similar manner, Friese (2012) states that coding in a practical manner refers to the process of assigning codes to parts of the data (usually quotations) that are central to the research objectives. Codes provide pathways for reaching general conclusions on the research objectives based on the research findings. Coding is the process through which the data are described with reference to the quotations and/or the conceptual/theoretical framework (Friese, 2012). Codes that provide meaning and references to the quotations, as well as to the theoretical framework, are therefore created/assigned by exploring the gathered data. Saldana (2009) states:

A code in qualitative inquiry is most often a word or short phrase that symbolically assigns a summative, salient, essence-capturing, and/or evocative attribute for a portion of language-based or visual data. (p. 3)

For instance, from the previously given example of a quotation – "People have the right to know …," researchers can identify different segments that could be coded as follows: "Right to Know," "Choose either money, development … employment for their children or they want to apply the law," "Tourists don't come to see Mauritians eating on the beach." These codes can be regrouped, linked or compared with other similar or contradictory codes. In particular, identified/developed codes provide a basis for understanding and explaining the gathered data in an organised manner.

Reflexivity and Memoing

Birks, Chapman, and Francis (2008, p.69) argue that, "the very nature of qualitative research requires the researcher to assume a reflexive stance in relation to the research situation, participants and data under study." CDA, which forms part of qualitative data analysis, is not an exception. Reflexivity basically means making reflections on the knowledge construction within the research process. Reflexivity is an important part of CDA and it is an active acknowledgement by researchers that their own thinking, actions and decisions will inevitably impact upon the meaning and context of the experience under investigation (Horsburgh, 2003). Such an activity helps researchers to focus their attention to the way in which the subject and the object of the philosophical discourse are mutually constituted for the construction of knowledge within the whole research process (Hammersley, 2012).

Reflexivity is therefore not to be restricted only to the data analysis, but rather it needs to be carried out throughout the whole research process (Mauthner & Doucet, 2003). Friese (2012) opines that reflexivity is essential throughout the entire research project and it helps researchers to be aware of biases. Wodak and Meyer (2009) state:

CDA researchers also attempt to make their own positions and interests explicit while retaining their respective scientific methodologies and while remaining self-reflective of their own research process. (p. 3)

In CDA (as with any other type of qualitative data analysis) reflexive notes are gathered through memos. In particular, qualitative researchers employ two main types of reflexive memos – procedural and analytical (Esterberg, 2002). Procedural memos focus on reflexivity related to the research process and the analytic reflexive memos focus more on how the data are analysed (Myers, 2008).

Basically, memoing serves to assist researchers in making conceptual leaps from raw data to those abstractions that explain research phenomena in the context in which it is examined (Birks et al., 2008). Konopásek (2008) states:

Memos are a special case... In memos we integrate partial observations. The integration is not just an abstract mental operation. It corresponds with the ability of memos to be attached to several codes, quotations and other memos at once. (p. 13)

In deductive CDA, the memoing technique is therefore used to make critical reflections upon noteworthy segments of the data and compare the data with memos from (developed) conceptual/theoretical frameworks. Thus, memoing forms an important and integral part of CDA. Gathered memos can also be analysed and used as a build-

ing blocks for reporting the findings from CDA (Friese, 2012). A memo may "stand alone" or it may refer to and link to quotations, codes, and other memos (ATLAS-ti, 2011). In sum, it is important to note that writing memos throughout the entire research process is vital in qualitative data analysis; and at different phases of the analytic process, different types of reflexive memos can be written (Friese, 2012). An example of a reflective memo from the research project on eco-social work in Mauritius is given as shown in Figure 1.

Eco-Social Work: A Critical Perspective

A critical approach to eco-social work is based on ideas borrowed from the system theory, which focuses on people-environment interactions; and critical theory, that focuses on power, injustices

Figure 1. Example of a reflective memo from the research project on eco-social work in Mauritius with ATLAS-ti

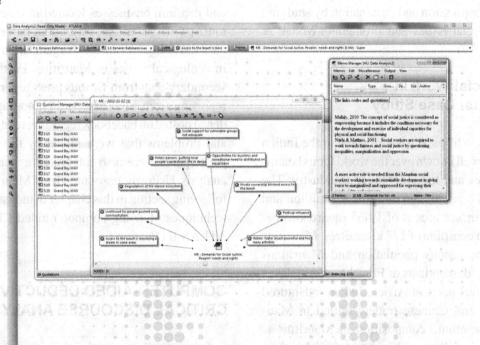

and oppression. In particular, the eco-social work perspective is based on the belief that dominant political and economic systems not only produce ecological problems, but also cause continuously growing social inequality, which exacerbates the ecological crisis (United Nations Development Programme, as referred to in Peeters, 2012, p. 106). An eco-critical perspective also analyses the people-environment relationship through a focus on the impact of forms, speed and influence of globalisation on people's life and livelihood (Coates, 2003; Payne, 2005).

The eco-social work perspective is therefore based on a philosophy of the enhancement of understanding of social processes and structures with a main concern for sustainable development (Närhi & Matthies, 2001; Nähri, 2004; Payne, 2005). Eco-social work researchers therefore often use CDA to analyse societal processes and structures in explaining socio-ecological issues and problems. In particular, CDA allows eco-social work researchers to focus on critical knowledge for enabling the emancipation of people from forms of oppression and domination by studying various social issues and problems (Wodak & Meyer, 2009).

Eco-Social Work in Mauritius: Case Study

Mauritius, a tropical island located in the Indian Ocean, is well known over the world for its beautiful beaches and top class tourism industry. The island has a population of about 1.2 million and the land surface area is of 1,865 square kilometres with a coastline of 177 kilometres. Mauritius has no indigenous population and Mauritians are mainly descendants of French settlers, slaves from various parts of Africa, Indian indentured labourers and Chinese traders settled in Mauritius. The ethnic composition in Mauritius is classified as follows: 52% Hindu, 16% Muslim, 27% Creole (Mauritians of African descent), 3%

Chino-Mauritian, 2% Franco-Mauritian (Central Statistics Office, 2000).

In this chapter, the case study on eco-social work in Mauritius is considered as an example to facilitate the demonstration techniques for doing computer-aided CDA with ATLAS-ti. This case study was undertaken in a country that is being branded as "Maurice Ile Durable" (Sustainable Mauritius) by its current government (Rambaree, 2012). Social workers involved in community development play an important role in mobilising people around ecological initiatives (Dominelli, 2011). Mauritian social workers are therefore regularly engaged in sustainable development programmes through community empowerment and development activities (Rambaree, 2012). The aim of the case study was to carry out a CDA for considering the main implications of eco-social work in Mauritius. The data set for the case study consisted of eight focus group discussions (FGDs) with local inhabitants from eight key coastal villages. In addition, there were three semi-structured face-to-face interviews with two owners of small and medium businesses located in three coastal tourist villages and an influential leader from a national non-governmental organisation engaged in ecological issues in Mauritius. Furthermore, secondary data from various press reports, video reporting from YouTube, and photographic evidence posted on Facebook regarding related issues and problems that were raised by the research participants were also integrated as part of the analysis. Using the case study from Mauritius, the following section in this chapter demonstrates the techniques of doing computer-aided CDA with ATLAS-ti (Version 6.2).

COMPUTER-AIDED DEDUCTIVE CRITICAL DISCOURSE ANALYSIS

Before embarking on the demonstration, there are a couple of important points that are worth mentioning at this stage. Firstly, the demonstration of the steps for the analysis relies to a large extent on the ATLAS-ti 6.2 user guide written by Friese (hereafter referred as ATLAS-ti, 2011). This chapter therefore avoids describing steps for the software features and functions as this kind of information is readily available in ATLAS-ti (2011). Rather, this chapter focuses more on the step-by-step techniques for undertaking CDA with ATLAS-ti software using a case study as an example. Secondly, the analysis undertaken here is of a deductive nature. The vast majority of CDA tends to be deductive rather than inductive in nature (Paulsen, 2010). In particular, the orientation for deductive or inductive or even a combination of both depends on the research questions as well as the researchers assumptions of the phenomena being studied. Given that CDA is highly influenced by critical theory, a deductive orientation usually provides a closed conceptual/theoretical framework for guiding and helping researchers to illustrate their assumptions with a few examples that seem to fit their claims (Wodak & Meyer, 2009).

Analysis of the Case Study with ATLAS-ti 6.2

Step 1: Construction of a Conceptual/Theoretical Framework

The construction of a conceptual/theoretical framework for guiding the deductive CDA is done through a literature review of classical and contemporary publications related to the main subject area of research. For instance, in the case study the main subject area of research was '*Eco-social Work*' and therefore theoretical discussions identified in classical and contemporary publications on '*Eco-social Work*' were used for developing a conceptual framework on eco-social work for CDA of the gathered data. To undertake such task, it is advisable to spend sufficient time using skimming and scanning styles in the reading of the publications, in order to determine the relevance and eventual selection of the material/s for literature review with the help of ATLAS-ti. Once the relevant and appropriate publications are selected and collected in an electronic folder, ATLAS-ti is opened for undertaking a review. The aim of the literature review is mainly to develop a conceptual framework for facilitating and guiding the analysis of the gathered data.

After opening ATLAS-ti, the selected publications in electronic format (text, word, PDF) are assigned as documents to ATLAS-ti (refer to ATLAS-ti, 2011, p. 78). After assigning the publications, a name is given to the project as a 'Hermeneutic Unit' (HU). The HU is like a folder within ATLAS-ti, in which everything that is assigned (for instance for the literature review and data analysis) is kept within the software (Friese, 2012). The assigned publications are all saved as primary documents (P-Docs feature in ATLAS-ti) for literature review with ATLAS-ti[1]. Each publication is opened one at a time to carry out the review in order to identify key theoretical concepts that are used and explained by the respective author/s.

To start with the literature review in ATLAS-ti, theoretical statements in the publications made by the respective author/s are gathered as quotations (Refer to 'Quotations' sections in ATLAS-ti, 2011, pp. 28 and 181). From the quotations, key concepts are identified and coded. There are several coding techniques[2] within ATLAS-ti such as 'Open Coding,' 'Coding in Vivo,' 'Coding by List,' 'Quick Coding.' (Refer to 'Coding Techniques' in ATLAS-ti, 2011, p. 199) which can be used for the coding process within the computer programme. Using ATLAS-ti coding features and techniques, a gathered publication is therefore reviewed for having a repertoire of theoretical and conceptual codes that can be used as a base for developing a structured framework for guiding the intended CDA of the gathered data.

Once a publication has been reviewed and relevant quotations and codes are gathered and saved within ATLAS-ti, it is important to give some order to the collection of codes. Such a task is vital in developing a clear, understandable and easy way to follow the theoretical and conceptual framework. There are several ways to order the codes – the most common are merging codes, code prefixes, super-codes, families, and networks (ATLAS-ti, 2011). After giving order to the codes, an overall review of all the gathered publications is carried out with ATLAS-ti. Using the coding feature of ATLAS-ti, some 'free codes' (see Atlas-ti, 2011, p. 215) are created to facilitate the review of all the gathered publications in a coherent and integrated manner.

For instance, for the 'Eco-social Work' review in the case study, the researcher was interested in looking in the publications for (a) the theoretical basis/stand (b) the situation analysed (c) the causes

of issues/problems/concerns (d) social work interventions proposed in the gathered publications for literature review. Thus, free codes labelled as 'Stand,' 'Situation,' 'Cause' and 'Intervention' were created. A network (a kind of mind-map) is then designed using the networking features in ATLAS-ti (see ATLAS-ti, 6.2, p.32 and p.318), which integrate most of the codes in a structured manner (see Figure 2 as an example of literature review coding and quotation in ATLAS-ti). After reviewing a certain number of publications (let us say around five), it becomes easier to get a sense of the main concepts that could be used as a base for developing a theoretical/conceptual framework for guiding the analysis of the gathered data. The first step – developing a conceptual/ theoretical framework from the literature review with ATLAS-ti – can be regarded as the basis of the *'Noticing'* task within Friese's NCT model (2012). It is usually the developed theoretical/

Figure 2. Example of Coding and networking in literature review with ATLAS-ti

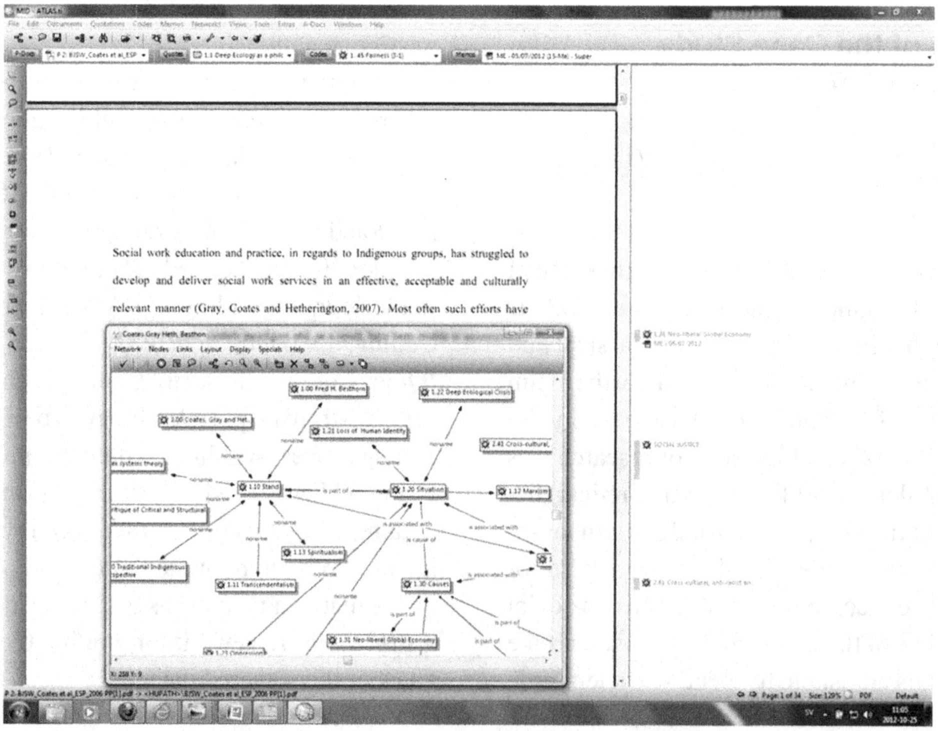

conceptual framework that guides the researcher/s towards noticing important analytical aspects in the gathered empirical data.

At this stage, it is also important that researchers undertake reflexivity with regards to the literature review for developing the conceptual/theoretical framework. A reflexive examination within the literature review obliges researcher/s to consider not only the meaning of the discourses used in context but also the ways that certain discourses are constructed and disseminated as knowledge (Bucholtz, 2001). Such an activity allows the researcher/s to make critical reflections on how conceptual and theoretical knowledge construction for undertaking his/her/their own research has been shaped. To facilitate the task of reflexivity, the 'Edit Comment' and 'Memo' features in ATLAS-ti can be used (Refer to AT-LAS-ti, 2011 for details). After the review is completed, researchers can have a list of concepts – central codes, which are usually dense and grounded in the publications (Refer to ATLAS-ti,

2011 for the meaning of code density and groundedness). The concept linkages can then be used as a conceptual/theoretical framework for analyzing the gathered data. It is advisable to have a simple, clear and well-structured conceptual/theoretical framework that can facilitate the task of data analysis (see Figure 3, as an example of the conceptual/theoretical framework that was designed from the literature review for the data analysis of the case study).

The reflexive activities for the main concepts (or nodes as referred in ATLAS-ti language) and the relations in between the concepts can be saved using the 'Memo' and/or 'Edit Comment' features. For the case study, the 'Edit Comment' feature was used for minor comments as reference for the codes and networks and the 'Memo' feature was used for making some general reflexive notes in relation to the conceptual/theoretical framework. The reflexive memos were mainly targeted at the main concepts (nodes in ATLAS-ti language). For instance, for concepts such as '*Colonisation*'

Figure 3. Example of the conceptual/theoretical framework with ATLAS-ti

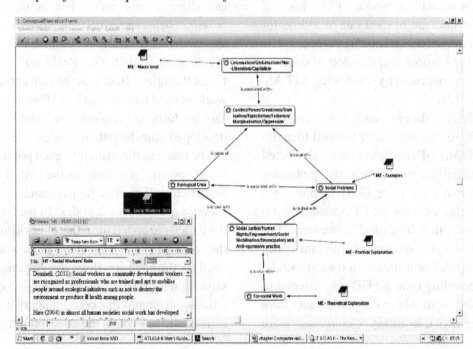

'*Globalisation*,' '*Neo-Liberalism*' and '*Capitalism*,' different memos were written on what different author and ... in different publications have argued and given as examples and so on.

Step 2: Selection of Quotations and Coding of Data

As a second step, the gathered data from the field (which can be of any format – text, graphics, audio and/or video) is then assigned to the HU. After assigning a data set to the HU, the gathered data are explored through the quotations from which codes that are relevant to the developed conceptual/theoretical framework are created/assigned[3]. In the case study that is considered as an example in this chapter, audio recordings from FGDs and interviews were assigned in a similar manner as per the literature review. While assigning the data, it is important to provide clear names that make sense for each individual piece of data. For instance, in this case study, names given to the data were such as '*FGD Grand Bay*' for a FGD carried out in a region called Grand Bay and '*Interview NGOENVCARE*' for an interview carried out with a representative of a Non-Governmental Organisation called Environment Care. Each of the assigned data are opened one at a time for selection of quotations and coding purposes. The selection of quotations and creation of codes is considered the main activity when using ATLAS.ti (Friese, 2012).

For analysis of the case study from Mauritius with ATLAS-ti, the researcher listened to audio recordings from FGDs and interviews and selected the essential quotations. The selected quotations were those that were more likely to provide a 'good fit' (relevance) for the CDA using the developed conceptual/theoretical framework. For each of the selected quotations, relevant codes were developed. For instance, in the case study, an audio recording from a FGD was listened to and the discussions where the participants have been talking about, let us say '*Capitalism*,' were

selected as a quotation in ATLAS-ti. Then, appropriate codes were created to further reduce the data. For instance, from the discussion regarding capitalism, codes such as '*Competitive Businesses*,' '*Greediness*,' '*Over-exploitation*,' '*Cheap Labour*' and so on were created/assigned.

When the selection of the quotations and the creation of the codes were completed for all the gathered data, the researcher proceeded with organising the codes. The 'Merge Code' feature was first used to bundle similar codes under a common appellation. For instance, codes such as '*River Pollution*,' '*Industrial Discharge in River*,' '*Waste Water in the River*,' '*Pesticide in the River*' were bundled together under a single code labelled '*River Pollution*.' Then, the 'Family' feature was used to create codes that could be used in relation to the developed conceptual/theoretical framework. For example, all the codes that were related to capitalism directly or indirectly were assigned under a family named '*Capitalism*,' which was found to be very relevant to the developed theoretical/conceptual framework (see Figure 4, as an example).

It is worth pointing out that different 'Families' can share several codes. For example, a code '*Conflict between Small-scale Businesses*' can be shared by two different 'Families' – such as, '*Capitalism*' and '*Social Problems*' as two different 'families.' Based on the conceptual framework, several families such as '*Power*,' '*Control*' '*Social Justice*,' '*Exploitation*,' and so on were developed from the gathered codes. The 'Families' can be taken as the main reference point for looking at specific quotations as the unit of analysis. In particular, 'Families' help researchers to access specific quotations via codes. In the case study, the data were coded until there was saturation to the conceptual and theoretical framework developed for the analysis. Here, the judgement about saturation is based on having enough codes, quotations and memos that could support, contradict, expand and or explain the conceptual/theoretical

Figure 4. Example of a family (concept) with ATLAS-ti

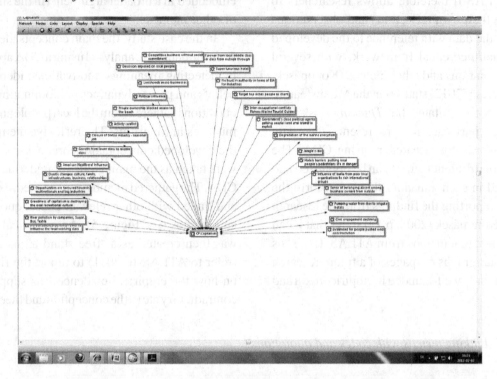

framework with empirical evidence gathered from the research project. For instance, looking at Figure 3, one can easily judge that there are sufficient amounts of coded data and quotations from which a CDA and discussion related to '*Capitalism*' could be carried out.

Once again, the 'Edit Comment' and 'Memo' features were used for reflexivity at this particular stage of data analysis in the case study. As mentioned earlier, the 'Edit Comment' feature was used for some minor reflexive comments relating to the codes and linkages; and, the 'Memo' feature was used for higher levels of reflexive comments, for instance those related to the developed conceptual/theoretical framework. The reflexive memos were then linked with the appropriate quotations and codes. Once quotations were selected, appropriate codes were developed, dense families were created and reflexive memos were written, and housekeeping tasks of putting a structure and organisation to the data were carried out. In other words, similar

codes were merged, quotations were reviewed to ensure their relevance in relation to the codes and network linkages were organised in a way that it would be easy to view and follow.

Step 3: Deductive Critical Discourse Analysis of the Data

The main activity within deductive CDA is to analyse the gathered quotations that support, contradict, explain or expand the conceptual/theoretical framework. The conceptual/theoretical framework developed from the literature review therefore provides the basis and guidance for such analysis. In order to carry out such analysis the 'Memo' feature in ATLAS-ti can be used (See ATLAS-ti, 2011, p. 254; Friese, 2012, p. 133). The Memo feature in ATLAS-ti facilitates researcher/s to write down analytical thinking in a visual and transparent manner that allows the creation of depth within the analysis process. ATLAS-ti therefore allows researchers to integrate their own reflections and observations made on the data with reference to the developed conceptual/theoretical framework, with several codes, quotations and other memos (Konopásek, 2008). Friese (2012) states that the Memo feature in ATLAS-ti facilitates the '*Thinking*' task. The 'thinking' part therefore represents the main analytical task for researchers using CDA. The analysis of different memos can be organized and structured in such a manner that it can form the basis for reporting the findings from the research project. Konopásek (2008, p.12) states that it can be imagined that memos from ATLAS-Ti are "as embryoparagraphs or -pages of a future research report, already well-founded in empirical data and embedded in a broader argument (in the structure of other memos."

In the case study, the main concepts identified from the data were analysed using a CDA approach by detecting meanings, motivations, ideologies, beliefs and power dynamics predominating in the quotations gathered from the local people and communities in Mauritius. The reflexive memos and the developed conceptual/theoretical framework were taken as the main guide for undertaking the CDA. The gathered memos were opened, explored and linked with other relevant codes, quotations and memos (see Figure 5). An analytical memo was then created as a 'free stand alone memo' (refer to ATLAS-ti, 2011) to report the findings on how the empirical evidence was supportive, contradictory etc to the conceptual and theoretical

Figure 5. Linking memos with codes and quotations

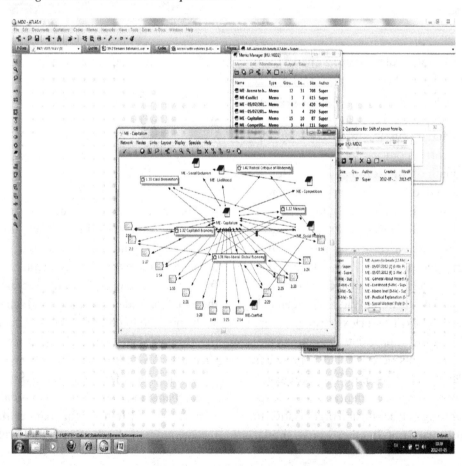

Figure 6. Collection of analytical memos

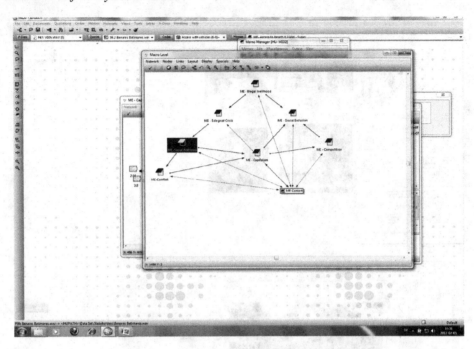

framework developed from the literature review. For instance, looking at the memo and following the codes and quotations, the researcher reported the discourse used by the research participants in explaining, describing and discussing certain concepts such as dominance, oppression, and injustices. The family features for 'Memo' were used to assemble all related memos that could provide a good basis for reporting the analysis (see Figure 6). Exploring the memos, discourses were critically analysed with reference to the conceptual/theoretical framework. The freestanding memos were labelled under different appellations that were used as sub-sections of the research findings report. For example, in the case study, freestanding memos labelled as *'Livelihood,' 'Power,' 'Oppression,' 'Resources,' 'Exploitation'* were used to report the findings of the analysis.

Depth in the discussion of the findings was created using supportive materials gathered from various sources. The supportive materials were identified from local newspapers (PDF), photographic evidence from Facebook and blogs and also videos on YouTube[4] posted by various individuals (see Figure 7). Those gathered materials were then assigned as new primary document (PD) and were linked with relevant codes from the lists and new memos regarding the linkages were written ('Code by List' feature in ATLAS-ti). The final report on a CDA of eco-social work in Mauritius was thus written on the basis of the memos that were based on the gathered data from the field and that were linked to the conceptual/theoretical framework developed from the literature review.

A CAQDAS, like ATLAS-ti, provides researchers with a number of possibilities for future research. Before considering some future research directions, it would be worth mentioning the benefits, limitations and challenges of using a CAQDAS like ATLAS-ti for undertaking qualitative data analysis. ATLAS-ti allows researchers to integrate various types and forms of data. As this case study has demonstrated, it was possible to integrate the literature review (text – PDF) with the primary data collected in audio format (from

Figure 7. Integration of supportive materials from newspapers, Facebook, and YouTube

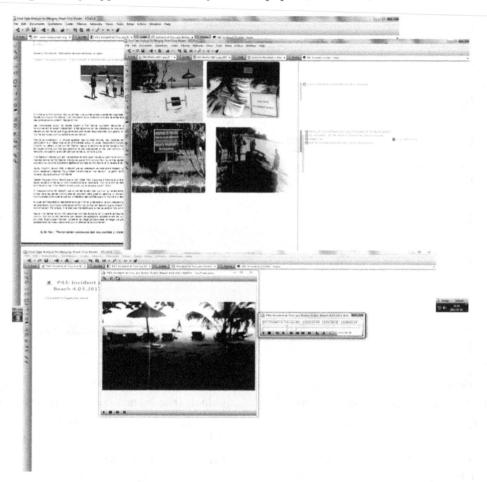

FGDs and interviews) and triangulate with data from secondary sources (text, graphics, video) under the HU (project). Although the integration lead to a large volume of different types and forms of data in the case study, it can be said that ATLAS-ti made it possible to undertake the CDA in a relatively rapid, organized, systematic, effective and efficient manner. In particular, computer-aided techniques for qualitative data analysis offer some shortcuts for coding, sorting, and integrating the data (Charmaz, 2000).

Computer programmes like ATLAS-ti help in creating a *'virtualised environment'* that provides researchers with the possibility of doing more analytical work than they have been traditionally doing (Konopásek, 2008). Using ATLAS-ti for

the case study has allowed the researcher to have a better visualization of the gathered data with the possibility of exploring different ways of analysing, interpreting and presenting empirical evidence from the research. In particular, computer programmes, such as ATLAS-ti, enable a researcher to explore the gathered data more in depth and breadth with the help of a range of new techniques, tools and functions (Rambaree, forthcoming). Before the invention of CAQDAS, analysis of large volumes of qualitative data was not only difficult and time-consuming, but also the possibilities for venturing through new avenues were limited (Richards, 2002; Carcary, 2011). Computer programs, like ATLAS-ti, have made it possible for qualitative data analysts to manage large volumes of textual data and offer an immense improvement in the efficiency and ease with which qualitative data analysis can be done with possibilities for 'Click,' 'Drag,' 'View,' 'Output result' and so on (Smith & Short, 2001, p. 401).

Within this particular context, Barry (1998) states that CAQDAS systems:

... help to automate and thus speed up and liven up the coding process; provide a more complex way of looking at the relationships in the data; provide a formal structure for writing and storing memos to develop the analysis; and, aid more conceptual and theoretical thinking about the data. (p.1)

ATLAS-ti also helps in enhancing rigour in qualitative research. In the case study, ATLAS-ti helps in enhancing rigour not only through data triangulation (primary with secondary data), but also through the coding reliability and reflexivity process. Mays and Pope (1995) state that in qualitative research, rigour in analyzing the data can be achieved by organising an independent assessment by additional skilled qualitative researchers and comparing agreement in the coding process. In the analysis of the case study two types of coding reliability were taken care of. Firstly, the 'intra-coder reliability' check was carried out for consistency between the codes within a single main data coder. Secondly, the inter-coder reliability was meticulously looked at for consistency between the codes when using two or more data coders. In the coding process of the data from the case study, a small section of the gathered data was given to another qualitative researcher for separate coding using the developed conceptual and theoretical framework. A comparison of the coding carried out between the main researcher and with that of the other coder was then made to check the reliability of the codes using a third independent person. The third independent person checked for consistencies, contradictions and agreements on the developed codes. ATLAS-ti provides the possibility for flexibility in mak-

ing the data set and the codes portable and also provides an easy and convenient way of deleting, re-coding, merging codes etc. Such capabilities are of great importance in enhancing reliability in qualitative research (Rambaree, 2007).

Moreover, the 'Memo' feature and the possibilities of linkages in ATLAS-ti provide researchers with the ability to enhance their research process through making critical reflections on their reflexive notes in a transparent manner. In particular, CAQDAS systems not only provide the possibility for making research findings more robust, with higher reliability and validity, but also play an important part in legitimizing qualitative research by making analytic work "transparent" (Fielding, 2012, p. 5). Qualitative researchers are encouraged to reflect on and record their interpretations, and they are reminded that the validity of their interpretations is dependent on being able to demonstrate how they were reached (Mauthner & Doucet, 2003). This sort of reflexive action is vital for rigour in CDA. The reflexive memos also give credibility, confirmability and dependability to the CDA undertaken in a research project. Friese (2011) opines that ATLAS-ti:

...allows qualitative researchers to move out of the black box of analysis and to make the entire analysis process more transparent, thus adding credibility, confirmability and dependability. Credibility involves establishing that the results of qualitative research are credible or believable from the perspective of the participant in the research. The criterion confirmability replaces the conventional criterion of neutrality and objectivity and refers to the degree to which the results can be confirmed or corroborated by others. This can be achieved by documenting the research process, the decisions made during a project and by the presentation of the end product. Dependability substitutes consistency or reliability, which can be for example achieved by a procedure called auditing... (p. 2)

Although CAQDAS have managed to facilitate the process of data analysis, researchers still remain central in designing and deciding how the qualitative data, gathered as evidence from the field, are to be analysed, interpreted and presented (Rambaree, 2007). CAQDAS do not analyse data, they simply help us to manage them. In the analysis of the case study, a lot of critical thinking was required. In particular, CDA requires researchers to think critically, and thinking is what computer programmes cannot do. As Konopásek (2008) puts it:

Software packages such as ATLAS.ti simply cannot do mental work for you. It is always you, as the analyst, who has to do the real analysis. Because only human researchers can think. (p. 2)

Since the case-study research regarding eco-social work in Mauritius was based on a deductive approach, the conceptual/theoretical framework developed from the literature review provided clear guidance towards a structured way of thinking and writing the memos. As a CAQDAS, ATLAS-ti has a number of features and functions, such as '*Memo*,' '*Network*,' '*Family*,' and '*Edit Comment*' etc, that help researchers to make thinking visible in an organised, structured and integrated manner (Konopásek, 2008). The '*Query Tool*,' '*Co-occurrence Explorer*' and '*Network View*' are among the important tools of ATLAS-ti through which certain intelligent work be done by this particular software (Friese, 2012). Hence, ATLAS-ti can be recommended as a CAQDAS for CDA.

FUTURE RESEARCH DIRECTIONS

From the above discussion, one can therefore identify several possibilities for future research directions. Firstly, researchers can focus on the challenges of integrating different formats of qualitative data within ATLAS-ti. As mentioned earlier, within qualitative research discourses, more scholarly works are needed, especially on undertaking different types of qualitative analysis (such as Thematic, Narrative, and CDA) using CAQDAS. This chapter is focused on using ATLAS-ti for CDA; a similar approach can be taken in future studies to report what can be discovered using this particular software for other types of qualitative analysis – for instance, narrative analysis.

Secondly, it would be interesting to have a comparative perspective on the presentation of CDA using the same data set but with two or more CAQDAS. On the basis of the preference for data analysis representation, the researcher/s can decide which CAQDAS to opt for. Thirdly, for novice qualitative researchers, CAQDAS can be deceptive unless and until future research could bring more detailed evidence on how practically rapidity and rigour can be achieved using such software. Thus, more detailed and focused research that clearly demonstrates the steps of enhancing rapidity and rigour using CAQDAS is still needed.

Finally for this article, as there was no previously written guidance on how to undertake CDA with ATLAS-ti, the researcher had to work using trial and error on several occasions when analysing the data. Friese (2012) does present a guide to undertaking qualitative data analysis – albeit in a very general manner – through the 'NCT' analysis model. The method for undertaking a deductive approach in a research project is very different from the method for undertaking an inductive or an abductive approach. Methods of coding for a thematic analysis and for a CDA are different. Thus, it was challenging to explore CDA using ATLAS-ti in the case study research project. Several times, the researcher got carried away in unnecessary tasks and steps. Perhaps, there might be a better and more efficient and effective way of doing CDA using ATLAS-ti. However, given that no precise guidance was available at the time when the research project was undertaken, the researcher hopes to have done justice to CDA with ATLAS-ti. For instance, ATLAS-ti has a feature called 'Flat Code Migration' which is useful when a code list is first developed in starting deductive structural theory work (See ATLAS-ti, 2011, p. 352) and this could be another route. As Friese (2012) states, the tools and functions in ATLAS-ti are there for qualitative researchers to make discoveries. The researcher in the case study has discovered a way and this is reported here. Thus, it would be interesting to see some other ways/routes for undertaking CDA with ATLAS-ti in future research.

CONCLUSION

Emerging technologies and computer programmes are gradually changing the way researchers handle and manage qualitative data. However, not much has been written on the way that CAQDAS, such as ATLAS-ti, can be used to carry out analysis like CDA. This chapter has therefore addressed such a gap within qualitative research discourses by demonstrating how ATLAS-ti can effectively be used for carrying out CDA, taking a case study from Mauritius as an example. In particular, this chapter outlined three steps of CDA using ATLAS-ti: (1) construction of a theoretical/conceptual framework for guiding the deductive CDA; (2) selection of quotations and coding of gathered data with reference to the developed theoretical/conceptual framework; and (3) deductive CDA of the data using the network and memo functions. This chapter also points out that although ATLAS-ti offers a number of possibilities for undertaking a computer-based CDA, such a process can be very challenging. The challenges emanate from limitations including the inability of programmes such as ATLAS-ti to think as humans and the limited guidance and discussions on how computer programmes can be used for CDA. Through this chapter, the author hopes to have addressed an important gap left in qualitative research discourses. However, the author would also like to acknowledge that perhaps there could be other ways (possibly more efficient, effective and rapid) to undertake such analysis. Nevertheless, in an area of limited guidance and discussion, this chapter has set an important path within computer-aided CDA discourses.

REFERENCES

ATLAS-ti. (2011). *ATLAS-ti 6.2: User guide and reference*. Berlin: ATLAS.ti Scientific Software Development GmbH. Retrieved May 14, 2011, from http://www.atlasti.com/uploads/media/miniManual_v6_2011.pdf

Barry, C. A. (1998). Choosing qualitative data analysis software: Atlas-ti and Nudist compared. *Sociological Research Online, 3*(3), 1–17. doi:10.5153/sro.178.

Birks, M., Chapman, Y., & Francis, K. (2008). Memoing in qualitative research: Probing data and processes. *Journal of Research in Nursing, 13*(1), 68–75. doi:10.1177/1744987107081254.

Bucholtz, M. (2001). Reflexivity and critique in discourse analysis. *Critique of Anthropology, 21*(2), 165–183. doi:10.1177/0308275X0102100203.

Carcary, M. (2011). Evidence analysis using CAQDAS: Insights from a qualitative researcher. *The Electronic Journal of Business Research Methods, 9*(1), 10-24. Retrieved May 16, 2011, from http://www.ejbrm.com

Central Statistics Office. (2000). Population census 2000. Retrieved January 14, 2010, from www.gov.mu/portal/sites/ncb/cso/report/.../census5/index.htm

Charmaz, K. (2000). Grounded theory: Objectivist and constructivist methods. In Denzin, N. K., & Lincoln, Y. S. (Eds.), *Handbook of qualitative research* (pp. 249–291). Thousand Oaks: Sage.

Chouliaraki, L. (2008). Discourse analysis. In Bennett, T., & Frow, J. (Eds.), *The SAGE handbook of cultural analysis* (pp. 674–698). London: SAGE Publications. doi:10.4135/9781848608443.n33.

Coates, J. (2003). *Ecology and social work. Toward a new paradigm*. Halifax: Fernwood Publishing.

Dirks, U. (2006). How critical discourse analysis faces the challenge of interpretive explanations from a micro- and macro-theoretical perspective. Review Essay. In G. Weiss & R. Wodak (Eds.), *Critical discourse analysis. Theory and interdisciplinarity*. Retrieved May 18, 2012, from http://nbn-resolving.de/urn:nbn:de:0114-fqs0602261

Dominelli, L. (2011). Climate change: Social workers' roles and contributions to policy debates and interventions. *International Journal of Social Welfare*, *20*(4), 430–438. doi:10.1111/j.1468-2397.2011.00795.x.

Esterberg, K. G. (2002). *Qualitative methods in social research*. Boston: McGraw-Hill.

Fairclough, N. (2010). *Critical discourse analysis: The critical study of language*. London: Routledge.

Fairclough, N., & Wodak, R. (1997). Critical discourse analysis. In van Dijk, T. A. (Ed.), *Introduction to discourse analysis* (pp. 258–284). London: Sage.

Fielding, N. G. (2012). The diverse worlds and research practices of qualitative software [50 paragraphs]. *Forum Qualitative Sozialforschung/ Forum: Qualitative Social Research, 13*(2). Art. 13. Retrieved May 18, 2012, from http://nbn-resolving.de/urn:nbn:de:0114-fqs1202124

Flax, J. (1992). The end of innocence. In Butler, J., & Scott, J. (Eds.), *Feminists theorize the political* (pp. 445–463). New York: Routledge.

Friese, S. (2011). Using ATLAS.ti for analyzing the financial crisis data [67 paragraphs]. *Forum Qualitative Sozialforschung/Forum: Qualitative Social Research, 12*(1), Art. 39. Retrieved May 18, 2012, from http://nbn-resolving.de/urn:nbn:de:0114-fqs1101397

Friese, S. (2012). *Qualitative data analysis with ATLAS.ti*. London: SAGE.

Hammersley, M. (2012). Transcription of speech. In Delamont, S. (Ed.), *Handbook of qualitative research in education* (pp. 439–445). Cheltenham: Edward Elgar Publishing Ltd..

Horsburgh, D. (2003). Evaluation of qualitative research. *Journal of Clinical Nursing*, *12*(2), 307–312. doi:10.1046/j.1365-2702.2003.00683.x PMID:12603565.

Hwang, S. (2008). Utilizing qualitative data analysis software: A review of ATLAS.ti. *Social Science Computer Review*, *26*(4), 519–527. doi:10.1177/0894439307312485.

Jørgensen, M., & Phillips, L. (2002). *Discourse analysis as theory and method*. London: SAGE.

Konopásek, Z. (2008). Making thinking visible with Atlas.ti: Computer assisted qualitative analysis as textual practices [62 paragraphs]. *Forum Qualitative Sozialforschung/Forum: Qualitative Social Research, 9*(2), Art. 12. Retrieved May 19, 2012, from http://nbn-resolving.de/urn:nbn:de:0114-fqs0802124

Lewins, A., & Silver, C. (2007). *Using software in qualitative research: A step-by-step guide*. London: Sage.

Lewis, B. (2004). NVivo 2.0 and ATLAS.ti 5.0: A comparative review of two popular qualitative data-analysis programs. *Field Methods*, *16*(4), 439–469. doi:10.1177/1525822X04269174.

Lupton, D. (1992). Discourse analysis: A new methodology for understanding the ideologies of health and illness. *Australian Journal of Public Health, 16*, 145–150. doi:10.1111/j.1753-6405.1992.tb00043.x PMID:1391155.

Mauthner, N. S., & Doucet, A. (2003). Reflexive accounts and accounts of reflexivity in qualitative data analysis. *Sociology, 37*(3), 413–431. doi:10.1177/00380385030373002.

Mays, N., & Pope, C. (1995). Qualitative research: Rigour and qualitative research. *British Medical Journal, 311*, 09-112.

Miles, M. B., & Huberman, M. A. (1994). *Qualitative data analysis: An expanded sourcebook* (2nd ed.). Thousand Oaks, CA: SAGE.

Myers, M. (2008). *Qualitative research in business and management*. Thousand Oaks, CA: SAGE.

Närhi, K. (2004). *The eco-social approach in social work and the challenges to the expertise of social work*. Jyväskylä, Finland: University of Jyväskylä. Retrieved January 4, 2012, from http://dissertations.jyu.fi/studeduc/9513918343.pdf

Närhi, K., & Matthies, A.-L. (2001). What is the ecological (self-)consciousness of social work? Perspectives on the relationship between social work and ecology. In Matthies, A.-L., Nähri, K., & Ward, D. (Eds.), *The eco-social approach in social work* (pp. 16–53). Jyväskylä, Finland: Sophi.

Park, Y. (2005). Culture as deficit: A critical discourse analysis of the concept of culture in contemporary social work discourse. *Journal of Sociology and Social Welfare*, September, *32*(3) 11-33.

Paulsen, R. (2010). Mediated psychopathy—A critical discourse analysis of newspaper representations of aggression. *KRITIKE, 4*(2), 60–86.

Payne, M. (2005). *Modern social work theory* (3rd ed.). Chicago: Lyceum.

Peeters, J. (2012). Invited commentary: A comment on 'climate change: social workers' roles and contributions to policy debates and interventions. *International Journal of Social Welfare, 21*, 105–107. doi:10.1111/j.1468-2397.2011.00847.x.

Rambaree, K. (2007). Bringing rigour in qualitative social research: The Use of a CAQDAS. *University of Mauritius Research Journal, 13A*(Special Issue), 1–16.

Rambaree, K. (2012). *Social work and sustainable development: Local voices from 'Maurice Ile Durable.'* Paper presented at the 2nd Joint World Conference on Social Work and Social Development held in Stockholm, Sweden from 8-12 June.

Rambaree, K., & Faxelid, E. (2013). Considering Abductive Thematic Network Analysis with ATLAS-ti 6.2. In N. Sappleton (Ed.), *Advancing Research Methods with New Technologies* (pp. 170–186). Hershey, PA: Information Science Reference.

Richards, L. (2002). Qualitative computing—A methods revolution? *International Journal of Social Research Methodology, 5*(3), 236–276. doi:10.1080/13645570210146302.

Saldana, J. (2009). *The coding manual for qualitative researchers*. Los Angeles, CA: SAGE.

Seidel, J. V. (1998). Qualitative data analysis: Ethnograph. Retrieved May 21, 2012, from ftp://ftp.qualisresearch.com/pub/qda.pdf

Smith, C., & Short, P. M. (2001). Integrating technology to improve the efficiency of qualitative data analysis—A note on methods. *Qualitative Sociology, 24*(3), 401–407. doi:10.1023/A:1010643025038.

Stewart, K. (2012). Considering CAQDAS: Using and choosing software. In Delamont, S. (Ed.), *Handbook of qualitative research in education* (pp. 503–511). Cheltenham: Edward Elgar.

van Dijk, T. A. (1993). Principles of critical discourse analysis. *Discourse & Society, 4*(2), 249–283. doi:10.1177/0957926593004002006.

van Dijk, T. A. (1995). Aims of critical discourse analysis. *Japanese Discourse, 1*(1), 17–27.

van Dijk, T.A. (2008). *Discourse and power: Contributions to critical discourse studies*. Houndsmills: Palgrave.

Wodak, R. (2001). What CDA is about – a summary of its history, important concepts and its development. In Wodak, R., & Meyer, M. (Eds.), *Methods of critical discourse analysis* (pp. 1–13). London: SAGE Publications Ltd. doi:10.4135/9780857028020.d3.

Wodak, R., & Meyer, M. (Eds.). (2009). *Methods of critical discourse analysis*. London: SAGE.

ADDITIONAL READING

Banner, D. J., & Albarrran, J. W. (2009). Computer-assisted qualitative data analysis software: A review. *Canadian Journal of Cardiovascular Nursing, 19*(3), 24–31. PMID:19694114.

Baugh, J., Hallcom, A. S., & Harris, M. (2010). Computer assisted qualitative data analysis software: A practical perspective for applied research. *Revista del Instituto Internacional de Costos, 6*, 69-81. Retrieved October 10, 2012, from http://www.revistaiic.org/articulos/num6/articulo4_esp.pdf

Contreras, R. B. (2011). ATLAS.ti-the qualitative data analysis software: Making sense of research data. Retrieved October 10, 2012, from http://downloads.atlasti.com/library/contreras_researchdata.pdf

di Gregorio, S., & Davidson, J. (2008). *Qualitative research for software users*. McGraw Hill, Open University Press.

Drisko, J. (1998). Using qualitative data analysis software. *Computers in Human Services, 15*(1), 1–19. doi:10.1300/J407v15n01_01.

Fairclough, N. (1989). *Language and power*. Harlow: Longman.

Friese, S. (2009). Working effectively with memos in ATLAS.ti. Retrieved October 10, 2012, from http://downloads.atlasti.com/library/Friese_2009-09_1.pdf

Gibbs, G. R., Friese, S., & Mangabeira, W. C. (2002). The use of new technology in qualitative research. *Forum Qualitative Sozialforschung/Forum: Qualitative Social Research, 3*(2), Art. 8. Retrieved October 10, 2012, from http://nbn-resolving.de/urn:nbn:de:0114-fqs020287

Goble, E., Austin, W., Larsen, D., Kreitzer, L., & Brintnell, S. (2012). Habits of mind and the split-mind effect: When computer-assisted qualitative data analysis software is used in phenomenological research [46 paragraphs]. *Forum Qualitative Sozialforschung/Forum: Qualitative Social Research, 13*(2), Art. 2. Retrieved October 10, 2012, from http://nbn-resolving.de/urn:nbn:de:0114-fqs120227

Lee, R. M., & Esterhuizen, L. (2000). Computer software and qualitative analysis: Trends, issues and resources. *International Journal of Social Research Methodology, 3*(3), 231–243. doi:10.1080/13645570050083715.

Lu, C.-J., & Shulman, S. W. (2008). Rigor and flexibility in computer-based qualitative research: Introducing the coding analysis toolkit. *International Journal of Multiple Research Approaches, 2*, 105–117. doi:10.5172/mra.455.2.1.105.

MacMillan, K. (2005). More than just coding? Evaluating CAQDAS in a discourse analysis of new texts. *Forum Qualitative Sozialforschung/Forum: Qualitative Social Research, 6*(3), Art. 25. Retrieved October 10, 2012, from http://nbn-resolving.de/urn:nbn:de:0114-fqs0503257

Morison, M., & Moir, J. (1998). The role of computer software in the analysis of qualitative data: Efficient clerk, research assistant, or Trojan horse? *Journal of Advanced Nursing, 28,* 106–116. doi:10.1046/j.1365-2648.1998.00768.x PMID:9687137.

Rademaker, L. L., Grace, E. J., & Curda, S. K. (2012). Using computer-assisted qualiative data analysis sofware (CAQDAS) to re-examine traditionally analyzed data: Expanding our understanding of the data and of ourselves as scholars. *The Qualitative Report, 17*(Art. 43), 1-11. Retrieved October 10, 2012, from http://www.nova.edu/ssss/QR/QR17/rademaker.pdf

Seale, C. (2000). Using computers to analyse qualitative data. In Silverman, D. (Ed.), *Doing qualitative research: A practical handbook* (pp. 154–174). London: SAGE.

St John, W., & Johnson, P. (2000). The pros and cons of data analysis software for qualitative research. *Journal of Nursing Scholarship, 32*(4), 393–397. doi:10.1111/j.1547-5069.2000.00393.x PMID:11140204.

Thompson, R. (2002). Reporting the results of computer-assisted analysis of qualitative research data [42 paragraphs]. *Forum Qualitative Sozialforschung/Forum: Qualitative Social Research, 3*(2), Art. 25. Retrieved October 10, 2012, from http://nbn-resolving.de/urn:nbn:de:0114-fqs0202252

Udo, K. (Ed.). (1995). *Computer-aided qualitative data analysis: Theory, methods and practice.* London: Sage.

van Dijk, T. A. (1985). *Handbook of discourse analysis.* London: Academic Press.

van Dijk, T. A. (2008). *Discourse and context: A sociocognitive approach.* Cambridge: Cambridge University Press. doi:10.1017/CBO9780511481499.

Webb, C. (1999). Analysing qualitative data: Computerized and other approaches. *Journal of Advanced Nursing, 29*(2), 323–330. doi:10.1046/j.1365-2648.1999.00892.x PMID:10197931.

Wickham, M., & Woods, M. (2005). Reflecting on the strategic use of CAQDAS to manage and report on the qualitative research process. *The Qualitative Report, 10*(4), 687-702. Retrieved October 10, 2012, from http://www.qsrinternational.com/FileResourceHandler.ashx/RelatedDocuments/DocumentFile/73/Reflecting_on_the_strategic_use_of_CAQDAS-Wickham_and_Woods.pdf

Wodak, R. (1989). *Language, power, and ideology. Studies in political discourse.* Amsterdam: J. Benjamins Pub. Co..

Woolf, N. (2007). *A little structure in your codes will make your research a lot easier (Part 1).* Retrieved October 10, 2012, from http://downloads.atlasti.com/library/Woolf_2007-03_12.pdf

Woolf, N. (2007). *A little structure in your codes will make your research a lot easier (Part 2).* Retrieved October 10, 2012, from http://downloads.atlasti.com/library/Woolf_2007-07_13.pdf

Woolf, N. (2008). *How to bring structure to a list of codes Part 3: Networks.* Retrieved October 10, 2012, from http://downloads.atlasti.com/library/Woolf_2008-06_9.pdf

KEY TERMS AND DEFINITIONS

Code: A reference given to some part of the gathered qualitative data that direct researchers towards data reduction. It can be a word, some words or even few sentences.

Concept: Word or words that encompass certain meanings and ideas about particular aspects, issues, problems etc.

Critical Discourse Analysis: A type of qualitative research data analysis where meanings, motivations, ideologies, power and so on are analysed through the deconstruction of text and talk.

Deductive: An approach to social research where theory provides guidance for data analysis.

Eco-Social Work: A holistic critical approach to social work where human-environment interaction is considered in relation to the structural context of a society.

Memo: A written text that helps researchers to relate their position with respect to the research participants, data, theory and so on.

Qualitative Research: A research method that focuses on qualitative aspects such as richness and depth in the analysis of the data.

Quotation: Segment of text or talk that are considered essential for qualitative data analysis.

Social Justice: A concept used for making a call for fairness, equality and respect of human rights.

ENDNOTES

1. Additional publications worth reviewing found during the literature review of a publication (from the reference lists) can also be added.

2. The basic techniques can be found from YouTube. See http://www.youtube.com/watch?v=TUZpXEySp1U.

3. Created for new codes and assigned for the codes that already exist (selection of *'coding by list'* from ATLAS-ti).

4. Additional software is required for downloading videos from YouTube.

Section 3
Future Trends:
Emergent Methods for the New Media

Chapter 17

Conversation Analysis and Electronic Interactions:
Methodological, Analytic and Technical Considerations

Joanne Meredith
Loughborough University, UK

Jonathan Potter
Loughborough University, UK

ABSTRACT

This chapter proposes that, as a method which has engaged with interaction in other contexts, conversation analysis (CA) should be used to analyze electronic interactions. The adoption of CA leads to a number of methodological pointers and this chapter reviews some of these. The authors firstly overview previous research on electronic discourse, including work which has also applied CA to electronic interactions. The authors then describe the main elements of CA, and also briefly discuss the closely related approach of discursive psychology. Using a corpus of quasi-synchronous instant messaging chats, the authors show how data can be collected which captures how users actually conduct online interactions. The authors discuss the ethical issues inherent in collecting such data. Finally, using examples from the corpus, the authors demonstrate the importance of making timed transcripts and working with screen capture data.

INTRODUCTION

This chapter discusses how electronic discourse is inherently interactional; that is, it is designed for a particular recipient or recipients; it unfolds sequentially responding to what has come before and building a context for what comes next; and its intelligibility is centrally related to its role in building and responding to particular actions. To analyze such interactions it is necessary to employ a method which can best explicate how interaction functions. We propose that conversation analysis (CA), which has dealt in great detail with how spoken interactions are managed, is the best method for doing this. Our approach is not merely that CA will allow us to investigate interactions,

DOI: 10.4018/978-1-4666-4426-7.ch017

but also that it will enable a better understanding of the practices of everyday internet use.

Once CA as a method of analysis is adopted, there are a number of methodological and technical considerations to be addressed. Much prior work on electronic discourse has relied upon experimental studies, or has viewed electronic discourse as a way of understanding the people behind the screen. We will discuss the problems with taking such an approach, and - drawing on the work of discursive psychology (Edwards & Potter, 1992; Edwards, 2004a; Potter, 2010) - suggest that electronic discourse should be analyzed as a social practice in its own right. As such, we propose that researchers should aim to collect data which captures how people use the internet, new media and new communicative technologies in their everyday lives. We also propose that both synchronous and asynchronous electronic discourse can be analyzed using CA and discursive psychology.

In order to conduct such an analysis, it is necessary to consider how to collect 'naturalistic' data. We aim to show the benefits of collecting data directly from the internet; that is, through timed transcripts as well as from participants recruited to provide screen capture data. There are a number of technical and ethical issues, which we will consider as part of this chapter.

Our objectives in this chapter are:

- First, to argue that because electronic discourse is interactional, it requires a method of analysis which is used to analyze interaction;
- Second, to introduce CA and discuss its approach to language, as well as demonstrating why it is beginning to be seen as a crucial method for analyzing electronic interactions; and
- Third, to explain why it is necessary to take a particular approach to collecting data, and the ethical implications of this.

We will demonstrate the necessity of taking this approach to data collection through examples from quasi-synchronous instant messaging chats.

BACKGROUND

The study of electronic discourse is a heterogeneous field which is distributed across a range of academic disciplines. Consequently, there are a number of different approaches to studying electronic discourse. One approach is to analyze the way particular *topics* are discussed online (e.g. Brown, 2009; Connor & Wesolowski, 2009; Lynch, 2002; Swan & McCarthy, 2003). While this research analyzes discourse that appears on the internet, the main interest is in the way the topic is treated as opposed to anything specific about the use of new media and the internet. Other approaches examine how electronic discourse impacts upon issues such as developing or maintaining online friendships (e.g. Brunet & Schmidt, 2007; Hinduja & Patchin, 2008; Paine & Joinson, 2008) or using electronic discourse to facilitate learning (e.g. Fitze, 2006; Gleason, 2011; Schulze, 2010). In these kinds of work the concern is with sociological, psychological or educational matters, rather than with investigating the interactional and technological specificity of electronic discourse. However, in order to understand and analyze electronic discourse, it is necessary to move away from treating *internet-data-as-resource* and move towards treating *internet-data-as-topic* (Rapley, 2001). In other words, rather than seeing online discourse as "a way to reach the people behind the screen" (Flinkfeldt, 2011, p. 763), electronic interactions can be analyzed as "social practices in their own right" (Lamerichs & te Molder, 2003, p. 461).

There has been an interest for over a decade in sociolinguistics in how the practices of online discourse differ from spoken discourse. Such research describes and classifies electronic discourse, and how it differs from spoken and written language

(Herring, 2007). It has been suggested that a form of language, known as 'netspeak', has developed online, which is characterized by abbreviations, emoticons and non-standard spellings (Crystal, 2001; Herring, 2007). One of the problems with sociolinguistic research is that it classifies such practices without reference to their local interactional context. Yet practices such as emoticons and abbreviations are often used to respond to other messages, and therefore taking them out of context ignores the ways in which they may be managing the interactional context (Benwell & Stokoe, 2006; Hutchby, 2001).

However, there is a growing body of research which has started to analyze electronic discourse in its interactional context (e.g. Androutsopoulos & Beisswenger, 2008; Antaki, Ardévol, Núñez, & Vayreda, 2005; Gibson, 2009a; Gibson, 2009b; Herring, 1999; Lim & Sudweeks, 2008; Marcoccia, Atifi, & Gauducheau, 2008). This research maintains that electronic discourse is inherently interactive. Even examples such as blog posts that do not appear to have an obvious individual target are recipient designed. Recipient design is fundamental to CA and its key figures sum it up as:

The multitude of respects in which talk by a party in a conversation is constructed or designed in ways which display an orientation and sensitivity to the particular other(s) who are the co-participants. (Sacks, Schegloff, & Jefferson, 1974, p. 727)

We can rephrase this for our current focus:

recipient design is the multitude of respects in which electronic communication is constructed or designed in ways which display an orientation and sensitivity to the particular or more general other(s) who are receiving or co-participating in this electronic communication.

While some electronic discourse, such as forum posts, may have a direct recipient, there will also be 'overhearing' recipients who read, and potentially

respond to, the posts (Goffman, 1981). Even when there is apparently no interaction, the discourse can still be analyzed for how it is 'recipient designed' (see Stokoe, 2011 for example).

A number of studies of electronic interactions draw upon this concept of recipient design when analyzing online forums using discursive psychology (DP). For example, Lamerichs and te Molder (2003) focus on how posters in a forum about depression manage their identities. They argue that identities are not "selected from a pre-established set of potential categories" but rather "are locally constructed in such a way so as to perform all sorts of interactional business" (Lamerichs & te Molder, 2003, p. 461). Similarly, Horne and Wiggins (2009) examine how posters in an online forum present themselves as 'authentically' suicidal. This research, therefore, focuses on "the vast array of interactional business that participants attend to in their everyday online talk" (Lamerichs & te Molder, 2003, p. 469). It emphasises the recipient-design of discourse, but does not always fully analyze the local interactional context, including its textual and visually spatial organization. Most DP research has focused on asynchronous as opposed to synchronous electronic interactions, and has devoted relatively little attention to the potential technological affordances of different forms of online interactions; instead it has tended to model them on everyday interaction (Flinkfeldt, 2011; Lamerichs & te Molder, 2003).

However, a number of researchers have drawn upon CA in order to analyze asynchronous interactions (e.g. Antaki et al., 2005; Smithson et al., 2011; Stommel, 2008; Stommel & Koole, 2010). For example, Gibson's work (2009a; 2009b) addresses how matters such as sequence organization and turn-taking are managed in asynchronous interactions. He notes that using CA is "very useful for looking at online discourse, and the ways that postings are structured in order to produce particular kinds of readings" (Gibson, 2009a, [np]). Similarly, some research has begun to examine the organization of asynchronous e-mail interactions (e.g. McWilliams, 2001). There is, then, a small body of work which uses interactional methods, including CA, to analyze asynchronous interactions.

The resources of CA, with its emphasis on sequential organization, are particularly useful for developing a fuller understanding of how synchronous electronic interactions are managed by users. Research which examines synchronous (or quasi-synchronous) interactions, such as those in chat-rooms (e.g. Elsner & Charniak, 2010; Panyametheekul & Herring, 2003) or in online games (e.g. Collister, 2008; Collister, 2011; Martey & Stromer-Galley, 2007) has often used CA. The focus has been on organizational practices such as sequential and interactional coherence (e.g. Greenfield & Subrahmanyam, 2003; Herring, 1999; Simpson, 2005; Werry, 1996), turn-taking (e.g. Garcia & Jacobs, 1999; Murray, 1989; Panyametheekul & Herring, 2003), openings (Antaki et al., 2005; Rintel, Mulholland, & Pittam, 2001), closings (Pojanapunya & Jaroenkitboworn, 2011; Rintel et al., 2001) and repair (Schönfeldt & Golato, 2003). It is notable that this research has tended to focus on multi-party interactions (e.g. Antaki et al., 2005; Herring, 1999; Stommel, 2009; Vayreda & Antaki, 2009; Werry, 1996), where the users are anonymous and use pseudonyms (Bechar-Israeli, 1995; Stommel, 2007). The data for such studies are collected directly from the websites, and therefore the analysts do not have access to how the users have managed the construction of their messages; in other words, they do not have access to the participants' lived experience of posting on an internet forum.

There are some studies which have analyzed one-to-one interactions, such as those conducted via instant messaging, using CA, (e.g. Berglund, 2009; Marcoccia et al., 2008). Berglund's (2009) study focused on one-to-one instant messaging chats and analyzed disrupted turn-adjacency and the maintenance of coherence in such interactions. This study found that participants used a variety of different interactional resources, including con-

junctions or linking expressions (such as 'unless' and 'or'), lexical substitution and lexical repetition, in order to maintain coherence. However, as with the research on asynchronous interactions, the researcher did not have access to the participants' orientations during the chats. The participants provided transcripts of their chats, but some did not include precise timings of when messages appeared, and some had no timings at all. Thus, the analyst does not have the same information that the participants had, and as will be shown below, timing is highly relevant to the coherence of such interaction.

Similarly, the participants used two different programmes for collecting data, which have different technological affordances. As Berglund (2009) explains:

MSN shares information that the other 'is writing', and if he or she takes a break in the middle of the message, this notification will disappear, making it difficult to distinguish between having taken a pause in typing and having erased the message completely. Gtalk provides information that the other 'is typing', and if the person is idle for a while, the message will change and instead read that the other 'has entered text', indicating that the other participant is still composing the message. (p. 9)

Such differences will clearly have an impact on issues such as turn-taking (if a participant can see that their co-participant is writing or composing a message they may not start composing their own), which will in turn impact upon sequential coherence. Yet Berglund (2009) argues that "it is not an absolute requirement to have access to recordings of the computer screen of the participant, as this information is not available to the other participant in the interaction either" (p. 10). However, this does not take into account the fact that the analyst is missing what *either* participant can see; that is, a participant is able to see, self-evidently, their own computer screen, and therefore is able to see when the other person starts typing.

In order to conduct an analysis using CA it is necessary to be able to fully analyze the participants' orientations, including aspects such as message construction. The analyst must have access to what is 'live' for the participant at that time, and not merely rely upon partial transcripts. In the following sections we will show it is important to ensure that timings are collected. Although adequate research can be done using timed transcripts it is preferential to collect data using screen capture software. As we will show, this provides the analyst with the best access to the participants' orientations and helps us explicate the role of the different technological affordances. We will show, using examples from a corpus of one-to-one chats, the benefits of collecting data in this way.

In this chapter, then, we develop three key points:

1. Electronic discourse should be viewed as electronic *interaction,* and as such it will be necessary to use a method which can explicate this;

2. Such analysis requires an appropriate corpus of materials which capture the analysis of electronic interaction as it faces its participants;

3. Conversation analysis is particularly powerful for the analysis of synchronous electronic interactions.

We will start an overview of key features of CA and DP.

Conversation Analysis

CA offers a method to explicate the "processes of social interaction, shared meaning, mutual understanding, and the coordination of human conduct" (Goodwin & Heritage, 1990, p. 283). It conceptualizes interaction as "a social institution in

its own right" (Heritage, 1995, p. 393), which can be examined in close empirical detail in order to find the normative practices of interaction (Potter, 2012a). CA analyzes interactions as they occur for participants and "puts participants' own orientations at the heart of its analysis" (Potter, 2012a, p. 446). Thus, the aim of CA is to "examine how, through talking, people live their lives, build and maintain relationships and establish who they are to one another" (Stokoe, 2009, p. 81).

CA makes a number of core assumptions about conversation and its role in social action. Firstly, as Edwards (2004b) notes "talk basically does things, accomplishes things, and is a kind of action, rather than represents things, or conveys thought and intentions" (p. 43). In other words, CA finds that talk is *action-oriented.* CA analyzes discourse for "how action is done rather than treating it as a pathway to putative mental objects" (Potter, 2012b, p. 123). These actions occur in a particular context in the interaction (Goodwin & Heritage, 1990), and as such the actions are themselves *situated.*

Actions are situated in three senses (Potter, 2012b). First, they are situated *sequentially,* meaning that they follow on and orient to the immediately prior talk, but also provide the environment for what follows that talk (Potter & Hepburn, 2008). Actions are also situated *institutionally.* They are "generated within, and give sense and structure to, practices such as news interviews, air traffic instructions and family meals" (Potter & Hepburn, 2008, p. 279). Finally actions are situated *rhetorically.* Descriptions can be built to counter actual or potentially alternatives, and also manage attempts to undermine them (Potter, 1996; Potter, 2012b).

CA also finds that "whatever happens in conversation happens within some particular, ultimately unique, context" (Sidnell, 2010, p. 6). Every action within a conversation is "*context-shaped* (in that the framework of action from which it emerges provides primary organization for its production and interpretation) and *context-renewing* (in that it now helps constitute the frame of relevance that will shape subsequent action)" (Goodwin & Heritage, 1990, p. 289). Context is therefore dynamic and renewed at each point in talk (Liddicoat, 2007). In terms of the wider context, this is available for the analyst "as displayed as relevant and consequential to the participants themselves" (Liddicoat, 2007, p. 8).

It is important to note that CA is not a method or a theory of communication, but rather aims to empirically discover patterns of talk (Antaki, 1994). Its focus is not on "conversation" in and of itself, but rather how that conversation illuminates actions, events and objects (Pomerantz & Fehr, 1997). Thus, "the analytic approach of CA is not limited to an explication of talk alone but is amenable to analyses of conduct, practice or praxis in whatever form it is accomplished" (Pomerantz & Fehr, 1997, p. 65). By applying this method to online interactions the aim is *not* to apply some *a priori* approach to how online interactions work, but rather to empirically analyze the practices which occur online. In using CA, there is a wealth of literature about the management of spoken interactions, which can be used as a basis for analysing electronic interactions.

Many of the basic features of CA are built on by discursive psychology (DP) which is an approach to talk-in-interaction which treats it as socially organized and interactional (Edwards & Potter, 1992; Edwards, 1997; Potter, 2011). This approach moves away from treating language as a system of rules and categories, or as a "set of signs for transporting thoughts from one mind to another" (Edwards, Hepburn, & Potter, 2009, p. 1). Rather, DP conceives of talk "as a domain of situated social action, rather than a set of conventions for the expression of intended messages" (Edwards, 2004b, p. 41). Its aim is not to understand talk by reference to "underlying cognitive structures, mental processes or neuronal objects" (Potter & Edwards, 2013, p. 704), but rather to analyze "what people *treat as* meaningful, publicly and for each other" (Potter & Edwards, 2013, p. 703). DP also engages with CA, merging an interest in

how facts are constructed and how actions are made accountable, with an interest in interaction (Potter, 2012b, p. 122).

DATA COLLECTION

Once we understand that electronic discourse is best seen as electronic *interaction*, this leads us to methods of data collection that can capture its interactional features. Much research on electronic interaction is experimental. Participants are often required to interact online under experimental conditions (e.g. Brunet & Schmidt, 2007; Fitze, 2006; Mallen, Day, & Green, 2003). Other research requires participants to respond to pre-prepared vignettes of online interactions (e.g. Derks, Bos, & von Grumbkow, 2007). These experimental conditions attempt to control for extraneous variables in order to focus on the phenomenon of interest, and are most often analyzed by counting and coding combined with performing inferential statistics (e.g. Chen, Chiu, & Wang, 2012).

Experimental work can be important, innovative and sophisticated. We certainly have no objection in principle to its use, particularly in the context of loose, speculative 'qualitative research' in this area. Nevertheless, the sequential context, action formation and recipient design that have been highlighted as central in CA present formidable challenges for those wishing to achieve workable experiments (see Potter, 2012b). Moreover, generalizing from experimental findings to the use of electronic communication in natural settings is particularly difficult without careful studies of what is going on in those settings.

Experimental studies are inevitably flooded with the researcher's own categories and agenda (Hepburn & Potter, 2003; Potter & Hepburn, 2012). In their use of data that is 'got up' by the researcher (Potter, 2004), these methods of analyzing electronic discourse do not provide a clear pathway to understanding how people actually interact on the internet in settings where they may be dealing with a number of communication threads at once, using multiple technologies, and perhaps combining them with face-to-face interaction. Moreover, the type of research often makes assumptions about the importance of online affordances, such as anonymity or the ability to edit posts, with little empirical evidence to back up such assertions or to show that these are relevant for participants (Hutchby, 2003). These are fundamentally problems for experimentalists to manage; for us they are part of the negative push toward doing naturalistic studies of electronic communication. Far more important is the positive pull from the tractability of our suggested approach and its success in throwing light on old issues and opening up new ones.

CA collects interactions as they occur in people's lives, and as they are understood by participants (Mondada, 2013). Rather than asking people about how they live their lives using an interview or an experiment, researchers record the actual events (Potter & Edwards, 2001; Potter, 2004). Data is collected of people actually living their lives, from visiting the doctors, to chatting to friends, to using internet forums. The aim is to reduce researcher involvement, although it is also acknowledged that if participants are to be recorded the researcher "must first obtain the *informed* consent of participants" (Speer, 2002, p. 516; emphasis in original). For this reason, rather than calling this 'natural' data, it is rather qualified as naturalis*tic* "to highlight a sophisticated awareness of the potential for researcher involvement in such material" (Potter, 2012a, p. 438).

Those working within the perspective of CA will want to collect materials from participants' ordinary use of their PC or other devices rather than setting up such materials in laboratory or other formal settings (e.g. Garcia & Jacobs, 1999; Wade & Fauske, 2004). At the same time the focus will be on people's use of their familiar programmes. If a new programme has to be taught for the purposes of data collection this is likely to have an important and not easily explicated impact on the material generated.

Ethical guidelines state that informed consent should be gained from participants who are being recorded for research purposes. There is a continuing debate across academic fields about the necessity of gaining informed consent when collecting data online (e.g. Bassett & O'Riordan, 2002; Eysenbach & Till, 2001; Sharf, 1999). The guidance of professional bodies, such as the British Psychological Society (2007) suggests that:

It is strongly arguable that postings to both synchronous or asynchronous discussion groups, on the other hand, do not automatically count as public activity. When constructing research using discussion groups, any requirement for consent by participants obviously needs to be tempered by a consideration of the nature of the research, the intrusiveness and privacy implications of the data collected, analyzed and reported, and possible harm caused by the research. (p. 5)

While different researchers take different approaches to how to get informed consent from online discussion forums (compare, for example, Stokoe, 2011 and Vayreda & Antaki, 2009), the ethical implications of collecting an individual's private interactions, or collecting screen capture data is more straightforward. Informed consent *must* be obtained, and as with any piece of social research, information should be provided on anonymity, confidentiality, and the right of participants to withdraw from the research. When providing assurances of anonymity it is useful to provide examples of how screen capture data will be anonymized.

When recording private conversations it is also necessary to obtain informed consent from the people that participants are interacting with. There are a number of considerations when getting consent from 'secondary' participants; that is, those whose screens are not being recorded, but who are participating in the private interaction. The researcher will need to decide *who* gets informed consent. If the researcher gets consent they will have to consider how and when to do this, and how to get contact details of these participants. However, if the participant gets consent as part of their interaction, it is important that the researcher ensures that the secondary participants are fully informed about the nature of the research and provided with assurances of their right to refuse to participate. Finally, the researcher will need to consider the ages of the participants and whether their participation requires parental consent.

A Brief Note about Data Used in This Chapter

The data in this chapter come from a corpus of quasi-synchronous one-to-one instant messaging chats conducted using Facebook chat. These were collected by research participants who downloaded a number of pieces of software to their computers, and then continued to use Facebook chat as they normally would. Participants provided both timed transcripts and screen capture videos of their interactions. In this chapter we have discussed both asynchronous and quasi-synchronous electronic interactions. We acknowledge that focusing on just quasi-synchronous interaction may give the impression that CA is most relevant for these interactions. This is not our intention, merely a constraint of the data. Our points about data collection, ethics and method apply to all forms of electronic discourse, although we also suggest that for asynchronous interactions it may be more relevant to also incorporate DP as this "extends more readily to studies of written text" (Potter & Edwards, 2013, p. 702).

Timed Transcripts

It is important that timed transcripts of online interactions are collected. Timing has been a key concern of conversation analysts, particularly with regards to turn-taking systems (Jefferson,

1984; Jefferson, 2004b; Sacks et al., 1974). In spoken interaction transitions from one turn-at-talk to the next tend to occur with no gap and no overlap (Sacks et al., 1974). Jefferson (1989) has suggested that there is a 'maximum tolerance' of around one second for the length of silence in spoken interaction. Silence can, in fact, be a signal that there is some sort of trouble in the interaction (Pomerantz, 1984). Delay in response to an action such as an invitation or request can be an important indication that some 'dispreferred' second action is imminent – a refusal or rejection (Pomerantz & Heritage, 2013).

Online gaps do not need to be as precisely timed as in spoken conversation, where gaps are timed in tenths of seconds (Jefferson, 2004a). However, it is important to ensure that transcripts have precisely measured timings. While it is possible to conduct analysis without timed log-files (e.g. Garcia & Jacobs, 1999; Greenfield & Subrahmanyam, 2003; Simpson, 2005), the issue is that the timings of chat messages are features of the chat that participants have access to. Even when analyzing asynchronous interactions, the timings of responses may be relevant (Smithson et al., 2011). If we are, as conversation analysts, attempting to analyze interactions as they occurred for the participants themselves, not having timed log files means that cues that are available for the participant are missing.

To demonstrate this, consider the following basic transcript of a Facebook chat[1]. Isla has started the interaction by apologising for her drunken behaviour the last time she saw Dave (not shown below). Her turns from lines 6-10 indicate that Isla sees her drunkenness as an accountable matter. Between Isla's turn at line 10 and Dave's turn at line 12 there is a gap of around 25 minutes (although this is displayed in seconds).

At line 16 Isla orients to the length of time it has taken Dave to respond 'you took a while replying there lol'. Dave then provides an account for the gap at line 20 'I know, dinners on lol'. Prior to this Isla has apologised for her drunken

Extract 1. [IS-DA/1b: 6-20]

```
6    Isla:  yeah but you're always sober and here's me
7           always with a glass in my hand!
        (19.0)
9    Isla:  and considering we met on a world junior team
10          at a major champs... haha
   →        (1502.0)
12   Dave:  haah its true, you are terrible ☺
        (9.0)
14   Dave:  but each to their own aye!
        (1.0)
16   Isla:  you took a while replying there lol
        (9.0)
18   Isla:  thought you were off
        (1.0)
20   Dave:  i know, dinners on lol
```

behaviour, and then goes on to orient to Dave's apparent sobriety. In doing so she draws on both of their identities as athletes (lines 9-10). Thus, Isla is doing a form of self-deprecation and in spoken interaction when there is a gap after a self-deprecation it may indicate the coparticipant is going to provide a critical response (Pomerantz, 1984). In this sequential context the lengthy gap could indicate trouble. Note, in fact, that when Dave does respond he provides a critical response, but mitigates it by using an emoticon. However, Isla does not orient to the potential trouble but rather to the notion that Dave may have actually ended the interaction. Most important to note is that the gap becomes relevant to the interaction and to the participants themselves, in that it is an accountable matter.

Extract 1 demonstrates that, firstly, the timing of an internet interaction is an important resource for participants and therefore analysts also need to have this information. Without this information it would be difficult to provide the above analysis as it is impossible to know what 'a while' is (particularly in comparison to spoken interaction). Considering that analysis of spoken interaction

has suggested that pauses and gaps are treated as significant for participants (e.g. Pomerantz, 1984), and that our analysis of online data collected as part of this research has suggested that gaps and pauses are relevant and can become live in an online interaction, we would urge that when collecting data of any online interaction timings are always collected and presented as part of the analysis.

It is worth noting that in spoken interaction, a gap between turns is not timed from "speech-object to speech-object" but rather may be timed as:

some sort of shift in activity, whether it be from silence to an utterance's next word, or from silence to another 'pause filler', or from silence to some non-speech (or pre-speech) sound such as an inbreath or click. (Jefferson, 1989, p. 168)

There is a parallel here with online interaction, in that the gaps indicated in Extract 1 are the gaps between when messages appear on screen. They are *not* the gaps between the turn and when a response is being constructed. Participants in Facebook chat are able to see when their co-participant is writing a message (although not *what* they are writing), and thus even by having timed transcripts we do not have access to all of the participants' orientations. Therefore, we argue that it is important to also collect screen capture data.

Screen Capture

Screen capture software enables participants to record their computer screen whilst engaging in online interactions. There is both free and paid-for software which can be downloaded. The choice of software depends on a number of factors including how good the quality of the recording is; how large the saved files are; and to what extent it affects the performance of the computer. Using screen capture software enables data to be collected about how the participants are using the internet in real time.

Screen capture software provides analysts with potentially relevant information such as when the other person starts typing, whether messages are edited during message construction and what other activities a participant is engaged in whilst chatting online (such as checking e-mail, watching videos on YouTube, or conducting multiple chats). Most importantly, this information is what participants themselves draw on, and can be shown to be relevant for their interactional practices.

Data from online interactions should, therefore, be collected in two formats: a timed transcript and a screen capture recording of the same interactions. It is necessary to work with both forms of data, but, as with recordings of spoken interaction, it will be necessary to transcribe the video recordings. As Hepburn and Bolden (2013) comment, a transcript is:

compact, transportable and reproducible, and provides for easy random access unlike audio or video records. CA transcription is a fundamental resource for data sessions, presentations and journal articles, and, as such, it is often the medium through which analysts encounter and evaluate each other's work. (p. 72)

For the Facebook chat data, a transcription system was developed based on the Jefferson system used for spoken interaction (Jefferson, 2004a). The Jefferson system captures "those features of interaction that are hearably relevant for the ongoing actions for the participants" (Potter, 2012a, p. 444). Similarly, the system developed for transcribing screen capture data includes as much information as possible, so that the transcripts are "detailed enough to facilitate the analyst's quest to discover and describe orderly practices of social action in interaction" (Hepburn & Bolden, 2013, p. 57). The screen capture data is therefore presented below with the transcription symbols in the appendix, although relevant transcription symbols or notations will be explained as part of the analysis.

The extract below provides a simple example of why having the screen capture data is important for analysts. Prior to this extract, Joe and Isla have been discussing Joe's night out, where he has been quite drunk and ended up 'chatting up' a girl, from whom he is now receiving text messages. Joe's turn at lines 147-148 orients to this topic.

In this extract, lines 147-148 and 164 are turns which appear as part of the chat itself. The lines of transcript from 149-163 are not visible to Joe, but are to Isla (who is the participant whose system is collecting data). Of particular interest are lines 156-163, where Isla is constructing the turn which eventually appears at line 164. This turn construction consists of a question ("where were you last night") and an assertion about Joe's behaviour ("I bet you can't remember a thing"). Isla then deletes her original question and assertion, replacing it with an assessment which appears at line 164. However, Joe is unaware of what was originally written, and only sees what is finally sent at line 164 (which is subsequently corrected to "oh dear").

The first thing to note is that the screen capture data provides empirical evidence for the claim that when chatting on the internet users *can* and *do* edit their posts before sending. We can also see

Extract 2. [IS-JO/3f: 147-164]

```
147 09.27 00.26  Joe:   i didnt do anything i dont think but she
148                     isn't even a student
149              I*:    🗨 4.0 chatting to BRM 🗨
150                     ((Switches to chat with FW))
151                     🗨 13.0 chatting to FW 🗨
152                     ((Switches to chat with BRM))
153                     🗨 27.0 chatting to BRM 🗨
154                     ((Switches to chat with Joe))
155                     (3.0)
156                     ✍ holy (.) shit hit (.) s t t st t
157                     hit joe - wherewe ewe e were you
158                     lastnight night night ? ? ? and i bet
159                     you can't remember a thinkg kg glo glo
160                     g g g lol (3.0) i th i th (1.0)
161                     holy shit joe - where were you last
162                     night? and i bet you can't remember
163                     a thing lol (2.0) oh dar ✍
164 10.50 01.23 Isla:  oh dar
```

that there are a number of significant pauses in Isla's message construction at line 160 and 163. In spoken interaction pauses may occur both between turns and during a turn, and those during a turn are 'intra-utterance pauses', which may indicate some trouble with the developing turn (Jefferson, 1989). The screen capture data suggests that there is an equivalent to intra-utterance pauses in on-line interactions, and that these may also suggest trouble in a turn (indicated by the fact that Isla subsequently deletes the entire message).

The availability of screen capture data also enables more detailed analysis of the participants' orientations to their discourse as a social action. The message being constructed by Isla includes two actions, the first being a question - "where were you last night?" – and the second, an assertion about Joe's behaviour - "I bet you can't remember a thing lol." Conversation analysts have found that in spoken interaction, "the action that a speaker might be doing in or with an utterance

may have implications for what action should or might be done in the next turn as a response to it" (Schegloff, 2007, p. 2). If Isla had sent the message which she initially constructed, the relevant next turn would have been for Joe to provide further details of his evening. Isla is therefore effectively working to close down the topic by merely providing an assessment, rather than asking for further information.

Up to now, then, we have seen that having screen capture data can enable analysts to identify trouble in a participants' message construction. Equally, we can provide a richer analysis of the concerns that are live for the participant in the interaction. Finally, we can see that participants make use of the affordances of the internet in order to edit messages before they are sent. Without the screen capture, we would only see the assessment, and would therefore miss Isla's fairly explicit concern with the action-orientation of her original turn.

Figure 1. A Facebook chat window showing that the other participant is constructing a message

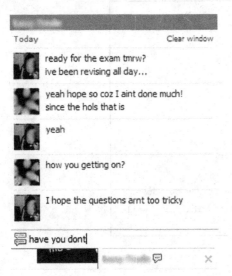

Another point worth noting is that when a message is being constructed, a small writing icon appears for their co-participant, as the Figure 1 shows.

This means that the other person can see that their co-participant has begun to construct a message. While the inter-turn gap between Joe's turn at 147-148 and Isla's at 163 is 1 minute and 23 seconds, from around 47 seconds Joe can see that Isla had begun constructing her turn. Thus, the gap that is indicated by the timed transcript is actually much longer than the *actual* gap. This distinction is only analytically available once we are using screen capture software. It is, of course, available to the participants whether screen capture software is being used or not, and we could question what Joe was doing while Isla was typing this message. It could be that Joe had noticed that Isla was writing for quite a long time, but then only posts 'oh dar'. However, as Joe does not orient to this at all during the subsequent interaction, we have no evidence that Joe had indeed noticed the length of time that Isla had been writing. We do not, then, have empirical evidence that this was a concern for him. Therefore, we do not concern ourselves with what Joe is thinking during this time, but rather we analyze what he *does* in the interaction. In other words, "don't worry about whether they're 'thinking'. Just try to come to terms with how it is that the thing comes off" (Sacks, 1992, p. 11).

The previous example also shows how CA can be used for analyzing electronic interactions. Particularly it demonstrates how CA is concerned with how turns at talk show an orientation to the action being done in the prior talk, and how it then constrains the subsequent talk. In other words, "speakers *display* their *understanding* through the sequential unfolding of their talk" (Potter & Edwards, 2013, p. 709, emphasis in original). As Schegloff (2007) notes "each participant's talk is inspectable, and is inspected, by co-participants to see how it stands to the one that preceded, what sort of response it has accorded the preceding turn" (p. 1).

As a further brief example of this type of analysis from Facebook chat, in the basic transcript depicted in Extract 3a, Isla and Dave are discussing their plans for the following week.

At line 164 Isla questions whether Dave has 'been out recently?', to which Dave responds at line 169 with an answer. Pairs of actions like this (question/answer, invitation/acceptance, and so on) are characterised in CA as adjacency pairs. Once a participant produces the first part of an adjacency pair, such as a question in Extract 3, the next participant "should produce a second pair part of the same pair type" (Schegloff, 2007, p. 14). Thus, Dave's response to Isla's question must be fitted to the form and type of the question. Looking further down the transcript, we see that this sequence is extended and at line 186 Dave issues another question to Isla. At lines 188-190 Isla responds to the question by providing an account for why she might be sober. We can see from this transcript that there is a sequence which involves a question being asked (a first pair part) followed by an answer (a second pair part) which is fitted to the question asked. However, when we

Extract 3a. [IS-DA/2b: 164-190]

164	Isla:	been out recently?
		(8.0)
169	Dave:	Monday
		(5.0)
171	Dave:	going out a bit this week!
182	Isla:	i'll maybe see you sober then ☺
		(11.0)
186 →	Dave:	why would you be sober?
		(5.0)
188 →	Isla:	i got pretty messy on friday so not
189 →		touching the alcoholic drink for a while
190 →		haha

Extract 3b. [IS-DA:2f: 164-190]

164	16.44	0.39	Isla:	been out recently?
165			I*:	((Switch to chat with SW))
166				🕭 5.0 chatting to SW 🗩 ↵
167			D*:	[✎ 2.0 writing ✎]
168			I*:	↵ [🕭 2.0 chatting to SW 🗩] ↵
169	16.52	0.08	Dave:	Monday
170			I*:	↵ 🕭 4.0 chatting to SW 🗩 ↵
171	16.57	0.05	Dave:	going out a bit this week!
172			I*:	↵ 🕭 33.0 chatting to SW 🗩
173				((Switch to chat with Zandro))
174				🕭 23.0 chatting to Zandro 🗩
175				((Switch to chat with SW))
176				🕭 9.0 chatting to SW 🗩
177				((Switch to chat with Gavin))
178				🕭 10.0 chatting to Gavin 🗩
179				((Switch to chat with Dave))
180				(8.0)
181			I*:	✎ i'll maybe see you sober then:-) ✎
182 →	18.26	1.29	Isla:	i'll maybe see you sober then ☺
183			I*:	✎ i got pretty mse se on friday so m m
184				not touching [the alcohol] ‖ ic ‖ ↵
185			D*:	[✎ writing ✎]
186 →	18.37	0.11	Dave:	‖why would you be sober? ‖
187			I*:	↵ (.) drink for a while haha ✎
188 →	18.42	0.05	Isla:	i got pretty messy on friday so not
189 →				touching the alcoholic drink for a while
190 →				Haha

examine the screen capture data, we can see that this sequence is constructed differently to how it appears in the basic transcript.

The relevant lines here are from 182 to 190, which we also saw in the basic transcript. From the basic transcript we saw that Dave had asked a question to which Isla had provided the answer, forming a canonical adjacency pair. In the full transcript, we can see that at line 182 Isla posts "I'll maybe see you sober then." She then *immediately* starts typing the text in line 183 that subsequently appears at lines 188-190. Thus, Isla is typing the 'answer' *before* Dave even issues the question. At line 185 we see that Dave has begun writing and this occurs as Isla is writing 'the alcohol'. As Isla is finishing the word 'alcoholic' Dave posts his question 'why would you be sober?'. In other words, Dave asks the question to which Isla is *already* writing the response.

We can see that while in the basic transcript it appeared that lines 188-190 were the second part of an adjacency pair, once we look at the screen capture data, we can see that this is not the case. Both Dave and Isla are orienting to the accountability of Isla being sober, with Isla immediately starting to construct her account for this. However, the fact that it becomes the second pair part of an adjacency pair is more an accident rather than being designed as such. This extract therefore shows again how CA can be used to analyze participants' orientations (that is, to the accountability of *not* being drunk). It also demonstrates how the affordances of the medium, such as being able to type messages at the same time, can be important for how the interaction proceeds. Finally, it shows the value of having screen capture data as well as timed transcripts.

DISCUSSION AND RECOMMENDATIONS

In this chapter, we have demonstrated that electronic communication can be analyzed as a form of interaction that is designed for a recipient, sequentially organized, and building actions. Whether the data is asynchronous (such as from a forum, or from Twitter for example) or quasi-synchronous (from chat rooms or instant messaging services) it should be analyzed as a social practice. It should not be viewed as a way of getting to the participant behind the screen, but rather as a way of understanding the actions *that* discourse does in *that* particular interactional context. We have tried to show how an approach informed by both CA and DP can be fruitful in explicating participants' orientations and revealing the way in which the varied affordances of specific technology and software are relevant to interaction.

This chapter has also shown that, in order to conduct analysis using CA, it is beneficial to consider the technical requirements of data collection. It is necessary to recruit participants to collect data, rather than simply taking data from the website itself. It is also important that those participants continue to use the internet in the same ways as they normally would throughout the period of data collection. In this way, we are able to capture how electronic interactions are managed in everyday practice. We have shown that, as well as timed transcripts, it is important to collect screen capture data. This allows the analyst access to the same cues that the participant has. Such research will inevitably have to engage with the ethical and technical difficulties that arise. Nevertheless, the benefits to understanding the use of the internet in everyday life, and particularly to understanding the management of electronic interactions, are immense.

FUTURE RESEARCH DIRECTIONS

As research in this field develops it will need to collect records from more than one party simultaneously, maybe having a small community of chat users working with screen capture software. One of the important potentials will be in technically grounding comparative work on different forms of chat, forums, blogs, and so on. This comparative work will be somewhat analogous to work comparing different institutional settings (news interviews, police interviews, research interviews, say).

While screen capture data provides much information that is relevant to the interaction, other research has used digital video recorders to examine how individuals use their computer, and also – if there are others in the room – how they interact with other individuals *and* their computer (e.g. Keating & Sunakawa, 2010; Marcoccia et al., 2008). Further research which records both the user's screen and their environment could provide for further analysis on how individuals manage online interactions.

There has also been interest in how the internet can distract from other tasks, or how it is used during work/study hours (Fox, Rosen, & Crawford, 2009). This could also be a fruitful avenue for research which collects video and screen capture data, as it would enable an empirical, non-experimental study of how participants manage multiple interests whilst interacting with one another. The interaction between technologies and interaction is also of growing interest to CA scholars (e.g. Arminen & Leinonen, 2006; Frohlich, Drew, & Monk, 1994; Laurier, 2000; Richardson & Stokoe, forthcoming), so such research would also add to this literature.

CONCLUSION

The objectives of this chapter were to discuss the interactional nature of electronic discourse. We have described how all talk and text is designed for a recipient, and as such all electronic discourse is in some way interactional. We then introduced CA as a way of approaching interaction, and described how this approach can be applied to both asynchronous and synchronous discourse. Our approach throughout the chapter has been

to show that internet data should be approached as a topic, rather than merely as a resource for understanding the individuals behind the screen. Our final objective was to demonstrate, using empirical evidence, how the adoption of such an approach requires data to be collected in a certain way. By collecting transcripts and screen capture data, the analyst is able to gain a better understanding of how participants use the internet in their everyday lives, and how this is oriented to in their interactions.

REFERENCES

Androutsopoulos, J., & Beisswenger, M. (2008). Introduction: Data and methods in computer-mediated discourse analysis. *Language@Internet, 5,* Article 9. Retrieved October 14, 2012, from www.languageatinternet.de

Antaki, C. (1994). *Explaining and arguing: The social organization of accounts.* London: Sage.

Antaki, C., Ardévol, E., Núñez, F., & Vayreda, A. (2005). "For she who knows who she is": Managing accountability in online forum messages. *Journal of Computer-Mediated Communication, 11*(1). Retrieved November 2, 2010, from http://jcmc.indiana.edu/vol11/issue1/antaki.html

Arminen, I., & Leinonen, M. (2006). Mobile phone call openings: Tailoring answers to personalized summonses. *Discourse Studies, 8*(3), 339–368. doi:10.1177/1461445606061791.

Bassett, E. H., & O'Riordan, K. (2002). Ethics of internet research: Contesting the human subjects research model. *Ethics and Information Technology, 4,* 233–247. doi:10.1023/A:1021319125207.

Bechar-Israeli, H. (1995). From <Bonehead> to <cLoNehEAd>: Nicknames, play and identity on internet relay chat. *Journal of Computer Mediated Communication, 1*(2). Retrieved December 3, 2010, from http://jcmc.indiana.edu/vol1/issue2/bechar.html

Benwell, B., & Stokoe, E. (2006). *Discourse and identity*. Edinburgh: Edinburgh University Press.

Berglund, T. Ö. (2009). Disrupted turn adjacency and coherence maintenance in instant messaging conversations. *Language@Internet, 6*(2). Retrieved December 3, 2010, from www.languageatinternet.de/articles/2009/2106/Berglund.pdf/

British Psychological Society. (2007). *Report of the working party on conducting research on the internet: Guidelines for ethical practice in psychological research online*. (No. 62/06.2007). Retrieved July 30, 2012, from http://www.bps.org.uk/publications/policy-guidelines/research-guidelines-policy-documents/research-guidelines-policy-docum: BPS

Brown, C. (2009). White supremacist discourse on the internet and the construction of whiteness ideology. *The Howard Journal of Communications, 20*(2), 189–208. WWW.HATE.COM doi:10.1080/10646170902869544.

Brunet, P. M., & Schmidt, L. A. (2007). Is shyness context specific? Relation between shyness and online self-disclosure with and without a live webcam in young adults. *Journal of Research in Personality, 41*(4), 938–945. doi:10.1016/j.jrp.2006.09.001.

Chen, G., Chiu, M. M., & Wang, Z. (2012). Social metacognition and the creation of correct, new ideas: A statistical discourse analysis of online mathematics discussions. *Computers in Human Behavior, 28*(3), 868–880. doi:10.1016/j.chb.2011.12.006.

Collister, L. B. (2008). *Virtual discourse structure: An analysis of conversation in World of Warcraft*. (Unpublished MA thesis). University of Pittsburgh.

Collister, L. B. (2011). *-Repair in online discourse. *Journal of Pragmatics, 23*(3), 918–921. doi:10.1016/j.pragma.2010.09.025.

Connor, S. M., & Wesolowski, K. (2009). Posts to online news message boards and public discourse surrounding DUI enforcement. *Traffic Injury Prevention, 10*(6), 546–551. doi:10.1080/15389580903261105 PMID:19916124.

Crystal, D. (2001). *Language and the internet*. Cambridge: Cambridge University Press. doi:10.1017/CBO9781139164771.

Derks, D., Bos, A. E. R., & von Grumbkow, J. (2007). Emoticons and social interaction on the internet: The importance of social context. *Computers in Human Behavior, 23*, 842–849. doi:10.1016/j.chb.2004.11.013.

Edwards, D. (1997). *Discourse and cognition*. London: Sage.

Edwards, D. (2004a). Discursive psychology. In Fitch, K. L., & Sanders, R. E. (Eds.), *Handbook of language and social interaction* (pp. 257–273). Mahwah, NJ: Lawrence Erlbaum.

Edwards, D. (2004b). Shared knowledge as a performative category in conversation. *Rivista Di Psicololinguistica Applicata, 4*(2-3), 41–53.

Edwards, D., Hepburn, A., & Potter, J. (2009). Psychology, sociology and interaction: Disciplinary allegiance or analytic quality? - A response to Housley and Fitzgerald. *Qualitative Research, 9*(1), 119–128. doi:10.1177/1468794108095078.

Edwards, D., & Potter, J. (1992). *Discursive psychology*. London: Sage.

Elsner, M., & Charniak, E. (2010). Disentangling chat. *Computational Linguistics, 36*(3), 389–409. doi:10.1162/coli_a_00003.

Eysenbach, G., & Till, J. E. (2001). Ethical issues in qualitative research on internet communities. *British Medical Journal, 323*, 1103–1105. doi:10.1136/bmj.323.7321.1103 PMID:11701577.

Fitze, M. (2006). Discourse and participation in ESL face-to-face and written electronic conferences. *Language Learning & Technology, 10*(1), 67–86.

Flinkfeldt, M. (2011). 'Filling one's days': Managing sick leave legitimacy in an online forum. *Sociology of Health & Illness, 33*(5), 761–776. doi:10.1111/j.1467-9566.2011.01330.x PMID:21561459.

Fox, A. B., Rosen, J., & Crawford, M. (2009). Distractions, distractions: Does instant messaging affect college students' performance on a concurrent reading comprehension task? *Cyberpsychology & Behavior, 12*(1), 51–53. doi:10.1089/cpb.2008.0107 PMID:19006461.

Frohlich, D., Drew, P., & Monk, A. (1994). The management of repair in human-computer interaction. *Human-Computer Interaction, 9*(3-4), 385–426. doi:10.1207/s15327051hci0903&4_5.

Garcia, A. C., & Jacobs, J. B. (1999). The eyes of the beholder: Understanding the turn-taking system in quasi-synchronous computer-mediated communication. *Research on Language and Social Interaction, 32*(4), 337–367. doi:10.1207/S15327973rls3204_2.

Gibson, W. (2009a). Intercultural communication online: Conversation analysis and the investigation of asynchronous written discourse. *Forum Qualitative Sozialforschung/Forum: Qualitative Social Research, 10*(1). Retrieved November 2, 2010, from http://www.qualitative-research.net/index.php/fqs/article/view/1253

Gibson, W. (2009b). Negotiating textual talk: Conversation analysis, pedagogy and the organisation of online asynchronous discourse. *British Educational Research Journal, 35*(5), 705–721. doi:10.1080/01411920802688754.

Gleason, J. S. (2011). Electronic discourse in language learning and language teaching. *Studies in Second Language Acquisition, 33*(1), 135–137. doi:10.1017/S0272263110000616.

Goffman, E. (1981). *Forms of talk*. Oxford: Basil Blackwell.

Goodwin, C., & Heritage, J. (1990). Conversation analysis. *Annual Review of Anthropology, 19*, 283–307. doi:10.1146/annurev.an.19.100190.001435.

Greenfield, P. M., & Subrahmanyam, K. (2003). Online discourse in a teen chatroom: New codes and new modes of coherence in a visual medium. *Journal of Applied Developmental Psychology, 24*(6), 713–738. doi:10.1016/j.appdev.2003.09.005.

Hepburn, A., & Bolden, G. B. (2013). Transcription. In Stivers, T., & Sidnell, J. (Eds.), *The handbook of conversation analysis* (pp. 57–76). Oxford: Wiley-Blackwell.

Hepburn, A., & Potter, J. (2003). Discourse analytic practice. In Seale, C., Silverman, D., Gubrium, J. F., & Gobo, G. (Eds.), *Qualitative research practice* (pp. 180–196). London: Sage.

Heritage, J. (1995). Conversation analysis: Methodological aspects. In Quasthoff, U. M. (Ed.), *Aspects of oral communication* (pp. 391–418). Berlin, New York: Walter de Gruyter. doi:10.1515/9783110879032.391.

Herring, S. C. (1999). Interactional coherence in CMC. *Journal of Computer-Mediated Communication, 4*(4). Retrieved November 2, 2010, from http://www.ascusc.org/jcmc/vol4/issue4/herring.html

Herring, S. C. (2007). A faceted classification scheme for computer-mediated discourse. *Language@Internet, 1*. Retrieved November 2, 2010, from www.languageatinternet.de

Hinduja, S., & Patchin, J. W. (2008). Social networking and identity construction: Personal information of adolescents on the internet: A quantitative content analysis of MySpace. *Journal of Adolescence, 31*(1), 125–146. doi:10.1016/j.adolescence.2007.05.004 PMID:17604833.

Horne, J., & Wiggins, S. (2009). Doing being 'on the edge': Managing the dilemma of being authentically suicidal in an online forum. *Sociology of Health & Illness, 31*(2), 170–184. doi:10.1111/j.1467-9566.2008.01130.x PMID:18983421.

Hutchby, I. (2001). *Conversation and technology*. Cambridge: Polity Press.

Hutchby, I. (2003). Affordances and the analysis of technologically-mediated interaction. *Sociology, 37*, 581–589. doi:10.1177/00380385030373011.

Jefferson, G. (1984). Notes on some orderliness of overlap onset. In V. d'Urso & P. Leonardi (Eds.), *Discourse analysis and natural rhetorics* (pp. 11-38). Cleup Editore: Padua.

Jefferson, G. (1989). Preliminary notes on a possible metric which provides for a 'standard maximum' silence of approximately one second in conversation. In Roger, D., & Bull, P. (Eds.), *Conversation: An interdisciplinary perspective* (pp. 166–196). Philadelphia: Multilingual Matters.

Jefferson, G. (2004a). Glossary of transcript symbols with an introduction. In Lerner, G. H. (Ed.), *Conversation analysis: Studies from the first generation* (pp. 13–23). Philadelphia: John Benjamins.

Jefferson, G. (2004b). A sketch of some orderly aspects of overlap in natural conversation. In Lerner, G. H. (Ed.), *Conversation analysis: Studies from the first generation* (pp. 43–59). Amsterdam: John Benjamins.

Keating, E., & Sunakawa, C. (2010). Participation cues: Coordinating activity and collaboration in complex online gaming worlds. *Language in Society, 39*(3), 331–356. doi:10.1017/S0047404510000217.

Lamerichs, J., & te Molder, H. F. M. (2003). Computer-mediated communication: From a cognitive to a discursive model. *New Media & Society, 5*(4), 451–473. doi:10.1177/146144480354001.

Laurier, E. (2000). Why people say where they are during mobile phone calls. *Environment and Planning. D, Society & Space, 19*, 485–504. doi:10.1068/d228t.

Liddicoat, A. J. (2007). *An introduction to conversation analysis*. London: Continuum.

Lim, H. L., & Sudweeks, F. (2008). Constructing learning conversations: Discourse and social network analyses of educational chat exchanges. In Kelsey, S., & St. Amant, K. (Eds.), *Handbook of research on computer-mediated communication* (pp. 451–476). London: Information Science Reference. doi:10.4018/978-1-59904-863-5.ch034.

Lynch, M. (2002). Capital punishment as moral imperative: Pro-death-penalty discourse on the internet. *Punishment and Society, 4*(2), 213–236. doi:10.1177/14624740222228554.

Mallen, M. J., Day, S. X., & Green, M. A. (2003). Online versus face-to-face conversations: An examination of relational and discourse variables. *Psychotherapy (Chicago, Ill.), 40*(1-2), 155–163. doi:10.1037/0033-3204.40.1-2.155.

Marcoccia, M., Atifi, H., & Gauducheau, N. (2008). Text-centered versus multimodal analysis of instant messaging conversation. *Language@ Internet, 5*, Article 7. Retrieved October 14, 2012, from www.languageatinternet.de

Martey, R. M., & Stromer-Galley, J. (2007). The digital dollhouse: Context and social norms in The Sims online. *Games and Culture: A Journal of Interactive Media, 2*(4), 314-334.

McWilliams, E. M. (2001). *Social and organizational frames in e-mail: A discourse analysis of e-mail sent at work.* (Unpublished MA thesis). Georgetown University.

Mondada, L. (2013). The conversation analytic approach to data collection. In Stivers, T., & Sidnell, J. (Eds.), *The handbook of conversation analysis* (pp. 32–56). Oxford: Wiley-Blackwell.

Murray, D. E. (1989). When the medium determines turns: Turn-taking in computer conversation. In Coleman, H. (Ed.), *Working with language: A multidisciplinary consideration of language use in work contexts* (pp. 319–338). Berlin, New York: Mouton de Gruyter.

Paine, C. B., & Joinson, A. N. (2008). Privacy, trust and disclosure online. In A. Barak (Ed.), *Psychological aspects of cyberspace: Theory, research, applications* (pp. 13-31). Cambridge, UK: Cambridge University Press.

Panyametheekul, S., & Herring, S. C. (2003). Gender and turn allocation in a Thai chat room. *Journal of Computer Mediated Communication, 9*(1). Retrieved 2 November, 2010, from http://onlinelibrary.wiley.com/doi/10.1111/j.1083-6101.2003.tb00362.x/full

Pojanapunya, P., & Jaroenkitboworn, K. (2011). How to say "good-bye" in second life. *Journal of Pragmatics, 43*, 3591–3602. doi:10.1016/j.pragma.2011.08.010.

Pomerantz, A. M. (1984). Agreeing and disagreeing with assessments: Some features of preferred/dispreferred turn shapes. In Atkinson, J. M., & Heritage, J. (Eds.), *Structures of social action: Studies in conversation analysis* (pp. 57–101). Cambridge: Cambridge University Press.

Pomerantz, A. M., & Fehr, B. J. (1997). Conversation analysis: An approach to the study of social action as sense making practices. In T. A. van Dijk (Ed.), *Discourse studies: A multidisciplinary introduction, volume 2. Discourse as social interaction* (pp. 64-91). London: Sage Publications.

Pomerantz, A. M., & Heritage, J. (2013). Preference. In Stivers, T., & Sidnell, J. (Eds.), *The handbook of conversation analysis* (pp. 210–228). Oxford: Wiley-Blackwell.

Potter, J. (1996). *Representing reality: Discourse, rhetoric and social construction.* London: Sage.

Potter, J. (2004). Discourse analysis as a way of analysing naturally occurring talk. In Silverman, D. (Ed.), *Qualitative research: Theory, method and practice* (pp. 200–221). London: Sage.

Potter, J. (2010). Contemporary discursive psychology: Issues, prospects, and Corcoran's awkward ontology. *The British Journal of Social Psychology, 49*, 691–701. doi:10.1348/014466610X535946 PMID:20178684.

Potter, J. (2011a). Discursive psychology and discourse analysis. In Gee, J. P., & Handford, M. (Eds.), *Routledge handbook of discourse analysis* (pp. 104–119). London: Routledge.

Potter, J. (2012a). Re-reading *Discourse and Social Psychology*: Transforming social psychology. *The British Journal of Social Psychology, 51*(3), 436–455. doi:10.1111/j.2044-8309.2011.02085.x PMID:22168901.

Potter, J. (2012b). Discourse analysis and discursive psychology. In Cooper, H. (Ed.), *APA handbook of research methods in psychology: Vol2. Quantitative, qualitative, neuropsychological and biological* (pp. 111–130). Washington: American Psychological Association. doi:10.1037/13620-008.

Potter, J., & Edwards, D. (2001). Discursive social psychology. In Robinson, P. W., & Giles, H. (Eds.), *The new handbook of language and social psychology* (2nd ed., pp. 103–118). Chichester: Wiley.

Potter, J., & Edwards, D. (2013). Conversation analysis and psychology. In Stivers, T., & Sidnell, J. (Eds.), *The handbook of conversation analysis* (pp. 701–725). London: Routledge.

Potter, J., & Hepburn, A. (2008). Discursive constructionism. In Holstein, J. A., & Gubrium, J. F. (Eds.), *Handbook of constructionist research* (pp. 275–293). New York: Guildford.

Potter, J., & Hepburn, A. (2012). Eight challenges for interview researchers. In Gubrium, J. F., & Holstein, J. A. (Eds.), *Handbook of interview research* (2nd ed., pp. 555–570). London: Sage.

Rapley, T. J. (2001). The art(fulness) of open-ended interviewing: Some considerations on analysing interviews. *Qualitative Research, 1*(3), 303–323. doi:10.1177/146879410100100303.

Richardson, E., & Stokoe, E. (Forthcoming). *The order of ordering: Requests, objects and embodied conduct in a public bar.*

Rintel, E. S., Mulholland, J., & Pittam, J. (2001). First things first: Internet relay chat openings. *Journal of Computer-Mediated Communication, 6*(3). Retrieved from http://onlinelibrary.wiley.com/doi/10.1111/j.1083-6101.2001.tb00125.x/full.

Sacks, H. (1992). *Lectures on conversation* (vols. 1 and 2, edited by Gail Jefferson). Oxford: Blackwell.

Sacks, H., Schegloff, E. A., & Jefferson, G. (1974). A simplest systemstics for the organization of turn-taking in conversation. *Language, 50*(4), 696–735. doi:10.2307/412243.

Schegloff, E. A. (2007). *Sequence organization in interaction: A primer in conversation analysis.* Cambridge: Cambridge University press. doi:10.1017/CBO9780511791208.

Schönfeldt, J., & Golato, A. (2003). Repair in chats: A conversation analytic approach. *Research on Language and Social Interaction, 36*(3), 241–284. doi:10.1207/S15327973RLSI3603_02.

Schulze, M. (2010). Electronic discourse and language learning and language teaching. *Canadian Modern Language Review-Revue Canadienne Des Langues Vivantes, 66*(5), 765–768.

Sharf, B. F. (1999). Beyond netiquette: The ethics of doing naturalistic discourse research on the internet. In Jones, S. (Ed.), *Doing internet research: Critical issues and methods for examining the net* (pp. 243–256). Thousand Oaks, CA: Sage. doi:10.4135/9781452231471.n12.

Sidnell, J. (2010). *Conversation analysis: An introduction.* Chichester, MA: Wiley-Blackwell.

Simpson, J. (2005). Conversational floors in synchronous text-based CMC discourse. *Discourse Studies, 7*(3), 337–361. doi:10.1177/1461445605052190.

Smithson, J., Sharkey, S., Hewis, E., Jones, R., Emmens, T., Ford, T., & Owens, C. (2011). Problem presentation and responses on an online forum for young people who self-harm. *Discourse Studies, 13*(4), 487–501. doi:10.1177/1461445611403356.

Speer, S. A. (2002). 'Natural' and 'contrived' data: A sustainable distinction? *Discourse Studies, 4*, 511–525.

Stokoe, E. (2009). Doing actions with identity categories: Complaints and denials in neighbour disputes. *Text and Talk, 20*(1), 75–97.

Stokoe, E. (2011). 'Girl - woman - sorry!': On the repair and non-repair of consecutive gender categories. In Speer, S. A., & Stokoe, E. (Eds.), *Conversation and gender* (pp. 84–111). Cambridge: Cambridge University Press. doi:10.1017/CBO9780511781032.006.

Stommel, W. (2007). Mein nick bin ich! Nicknames in a German forum on eating disorders. *Journal of Computer Mediated Communication, 13*(1), Article 8. Retrieved from http://jcmc.indiana.edu/vol13/issue1/stommel.html

Stommel, W. (2008). Conversation analysis and community of practice as approaches to studying online community. *Language@Internet, 5,* [np]. Retrieved November 2, 2010, from www.languageatinternet.de

Stommel, W. (2009). *Entering an online support group on eating disorders: A discourse analysis.* Amsterdam: Rodopi.

Stommel, W., & Koole, T. (2010). The online support group as a community: A micro-analysis of the interaction with a new member. *Discourse Studies, 12*(3), 357–378. doi:10.1177/1461445609358518.

Swan, D., & McCarthy, J. C. (2003). Contesting animal rights on the internet: Discourse analysis of the social construction of argument. *Journal of Language and Social Psychology, 22*(3), 297–320. doi:10.1177/0261927X03252279.

Vayreda, A., & Antaki, C. (2009). Social support and unsolicited advice in a bipolar disorder online forum. *Qualitative Health Research, 19*(7), 931–942. doi:10.1177/1049732309338952 PMID:19556400.

Wade, S. E., & Fauske, J. R. (2004). Dialogue online: Prospective teachers' discourse strategies in computer-mediated discussions. *Reading Research Quarterly, 39*(2), 134–160. doi:10.1598/RRQ.39.2.1.

Werry, C. C. (1996). Linguistic and interactional features of internet relay chat. In Herring, S. C. (Ed.), *Computer-mediated communication: Linguistic, social and cross-cultural perspectives* (pp. 47–64). Amsterdam: John Benjamins.

ADDITIONAL READING

Antaki, C. (2004). Conversation analysis. In Becker, S., & Bryman, A. (Eds.), *Understanding research methods for social policy and practice* (pp. 313–317). London: Policy Press.

Antaki, C. (Ed.). (2011). *Applied conversation analysis.* Basingstoke: Palgrave-Macmillan.

Antaki, C., Billig, M., Edwards, D., & Potter, J. (2003). Discourse analysis means doing analysis: A critique of six analytic shortcomings. *Discourse Analysis Online, 1.* Retrieved October 30, 2010, from http://www.shu.ac.uk/daol/articles/v1/n1/a1/antaki2002002-paper.html

Craven, A., & Potter, J. (2010). Directives: Entitlement and contingency in action. *Discourse Studies, 12*(4), 419–442. doi:10.1177/1461445610370126.

Drew, P. (2005). Conversation analysis. In Fitch, K. L., & Sanders, R. E. (Eds.), *Handbook of language and social interaction* (pp. 71–102). Mahwah, NJ: Lawrence Erlbaum.

Drew, P., Raymond, G., & Weinberg, D. (Eds.). (2006). *Talk and interaction in social research methods.* London: Sage Publications.

Edwards, D., & Potter, J. (2005). Discursive psychology, mental states and descriptions. In te Molder, H. F. M., & Potter, J. (Eds.), *Conversation and cognition* (pp. 241–259). Cambridge: Cambridge University Press. doi:10.1017/CBO9780511489990.012.

Hepburn, A. (2004). Crying: Notes on description, transcription and interaction. *Research on Language and Social Interaction, 37*, 251–290. doi:10.1207/s15327973rlsi3703_1.

Hepburn, A., & Wiggins, S. (Eds.). (2007). *Discursive research in practice*. Cambridge: Cambridge University Press. doi:10.1017/CBO9780511611216.

Heritage, J. (1989). Current developments in conversation analysis. In D. Roger & P. Bull (Eds.), Conversation: An interdisciplinary perspective (pp.21-47). Avon: Multilingual Matters.

Heritage, J. (2004). Conversation analysis and institutional talk. In Sanders, R., & Fitch, K. (Eds.), *Handbook of language and social interaction* (pp. 103–146). Mahwah, NJ: Erlbaum.

Heritage, J. (2010). Conversation analysis: Practices and methods. In Silverman, D. (Ed.), *Qualitative sociology* (3rd ed., pp. 208–230). London: Sage.

Heritage, J. (2012). Epistemics in action: Action formation and territories of knowledge. *Research on Language and Social Interaction, 45*, 1–29. doi:10.1080/08351813.2012.646684.

Potter, J., & Hepburn, A. (2003). 'I'm a bit concerned': Call openings on a child protection helpline. *Research on Language and Social Interaction, 36*, 197–240. doi:10.1207/S15327973RLSI3603_01.

Potter, J., & Wetherell, M. (1987). *Discourse and social psychology: Beyond attitudes and behaviour*. London: Sage.

Sacks, H. (1984). Notes on methodology. In Atkinson, J. M., & Heritage, J. (Eds.), *Structures of social action: Studies in conversation analysis* (pp. 21–27). Cambridge: Cambridge University Press.

Sacks, H. (1987). On the preference for agreement and contiguity in sequences in conversation. In Button, G., & Lee, J. R. E. (Eds.), *Talk and social organisation* (pp. 54–69). Clevedon: Multilingual Matters.

Sacks, H., & Schegloff, E. A. (1979). Two preferences in the organization of reference to persons in conversation and their interaction. In Psathas, G. (Ed.), *Everyday language: Studies in ethnomethodology* (pp. 15–21). New York: Irvington Publishers, Inc..

Schegloff, E. A. (1987). Analyzing single episodes of interaction: An exercise in conversation analysis. *Social Psychology Quarterly, 50*(2), 101–114. doi:10.2307/2786745.

Schegloff, E. A. (1990). On the organization of sequences as a source of 'coherence' in talk-in-interaction. In Dorval, B. (Ed.), *Conversational organization and its development* (pp. 51–77). Norwood, New Jersey: Ablex.

Schegloff, E. A., Jefferson, G., & Sacks, H. (1977). The preference for self-correction in the organization of repair in conversation. *Language, 53*(2), 361–382.

Sneiijder, P., & te Molder, H. F. M. (2004). 'Health should not have to be a problem': Talking health and accountability in an internet forum on veganism. *Journal of Health Psychology, 9*(4), 599–616. doi:10.1177/1359105304044046 PMID:15231059.

Sneiijder, P., & te Molder, H. F. M. (2005). Moral logic and logical morality: Attributions of responsibility and blame in online discourse on veganism. *Discourse & Society, 16*(5), 675–696. doi:10.1177/0957926505054941.

Sneijder, P., & te Molder, H. F. M. (2009). Normalizing ideological food choice and eating practices. Identity work in online discussions on veganism. *Appetite, 52*(3), 621–630. doi:10.1016/j.appet.2009.02.012 PMID:19501759.

Stokoe, E. (2008). Dispreferred actions and other interactional breaches as devices for occasioning audience laughter in television 'sitcoms.'. *Social Semiotics*, *18*(3), 289–307. doi:10.1080/10350330802217071.

Stokoe, E., Hepburn, A., & Antaki, C. (2012). Beware the 'Loughborough school' of social psychology? Interaction and the politics of intervention. *The British Journal of Social Psychology*, *51*(3), 486–496. doi:10.1111/j.2044-8309.2011.02088.x PMID:22404636.

ten Have, P. (2007). *Doing conversation analysis: A practical guide* (2nd ed.). London: Sage Publications.

Wilkinson, S., & Kitzinger, C. (2008). Using conversation analysis in feminist and critical research. *Social and Personality Psychology Compass*, *2*(2), 555–573. doi:10.1111/j.1751-9004.2007.00049.x.

KEY TERMS AND DEFINITIONS

Adjacency Pair: A pair of turns, by different speakers, which compose pair types differentiated into first pair parts and second pair parts. On the production of a first pair part the next speaker should produce a relevant second pair part.

Conversation Analysis: A method for explicating everyday practices as it is lived by the participants, through analysing their interactions.

Discursive Psychology: A method for analysing discourse which is concerned with the role of talk and texts as social practices. It focuses on action orientation, situation and construction.

Jefferson Transcription: A method of transcribing spoken interaction which includes all the aspects of the interaction that are hearably relevant for the participants.

Naturalistic Data: Data which is collected with a minimal amount of researcher involvement, and which would have happened without the intervention of the researcher.

Quasi-Synchronous: Online interactions where the construction of turns is separate from the sending of turns, but where the participants do have some feedback on the actions of the other participant.

Sequence Organisation: The organisation of courses of action enacted through turns-at-talk. Sequences are the vehicle for getting some activity accomplished.

ENDNOTES

1. Please note that all transcripts are presented as they appeared for participants, with no spelling or typing errors corrected.

APPENDIX

Transcription Symbols

✍	= Writing
💻	= Surfing
‖	= At the same time as
↔	= Latching
💬	= Talking to someone else
(.)	= Pause shorter than 1 second
(1.0)	= Gap
[ ]	= Overlap
(())	= Descriptions of actions
~~Strikethrough~~	= Deleted
→	= Line or turn of interest

Chapter 18

Positioning Goes to Work:
Computer–Aided Identification of Stance Shifts and Semantic Themes in Electronic Discourse Analysis

Boyd Davis
University of North Carolina – Charlotte, USA

Peyton Mason
Next-Generation Marketing Insights, USA

ABSTRACT

This discussion presents two specific computer-aided techniques that allow researchers to combine quantitative and qualitative approaches to the discourse analysis of electronically-searchable text. It illustrates the application of these techniques and their supporting tools to a range of online interactions, including brief reference to entries in online tourism blogs and Facebook comments, in order to provide nuanced interpretations of electronic discourse: (1) stance-shift analysis, a software-based analysis keyed to tagged parts of speech (POS) to identify when speakers/writers shift among evaluative and affective stances to topic, to prompts, and to other participants in communicative interactions; (2) semantic domain analysis using WMatrix®, an online corpus analysis package including UCREL Semantic Analysis System, which tags words by semantic domains, and uses a log-likelihood calculator to identify significant semantic relationships across texts.

INTRODUCTION

The analysis of interactive electronic discourse, both asynchronous and synchronous, involves the researcher with investigating the presence or absence of "'relational work.' . . the linguistic work that people invest in negotiating relationships" (Locher & Watts, 2005, cited in Langlotz & Locher, 2012). Whether a person is interacting online with a specific and named Other or with an unnamed and presumably unknown group, such as a blog site for travel reviews, some degree of

DOI: 10.4018/978-1-4666-4426-7.ch018

relational work can be posited and identified. Earlier scholarship studied this phenomenon under the construct of presence, an offshoot of social presence theory as expanded by Walther's social information processing perspective, a term Walther (1992, p. 67) credits to Fulk et al. (1987) to describe a "socially constructed model of media choice."

Establishing the social components of e-discourse has not always been simple. Early work on e-discourse was often concerned with the presence or absence of social cues in computer-mediated communication. In flat email text, or verbal-only data, it was assumed that social context cues were largely absent. However, Walther (1992) reviewed email texts in electronic conferences and found that participants were developing impressions of other participants from their communications. These impressions created a sense of intimacy and identification between participants, and even visual projections of what the others might look like, which led to greater perceptions of social presence. From the perspective of positioning theory (Davies & Harré, 1990), such perceptions underscore the social positioning and re-positioning of participants in e-discourse as a key factor in understanding their relational work.

We first present an overview of key concepts of positioning in order to see how stance and affect interact online, and move to incorporate highlights from current theory and work about stance. As participants interact, they negotiate positions or reposition themselves, and as part of that positioning and repositioning, they shift their stances. Their online negotiation will be keyed to the evaluation and affect they bring to the topic and to each other. Given the explosion of interaction on and through the internet, the amount of data that can be analyzed is increasingly large, making manual coding an extensive process. Since automated coding of stance is not only speedy but also allows researchers to diminish bias, we discuss and illustrate two specific computer-aided techniques

that allow researchers to combine quantitative and qualitative approaches to the discourse analysis of electronically-searchable text, which we have found quite helpful. The twelve illustrations are taken from our own work and from work with colleagues in various fields: a reminder that stance, positioning and affect are present in every area of interaction. The two techniques are:

1. *Stance-shift analysis*, a software-based analysis keyed to tagged parts of speech (POS) to identify when speakers/writers shift among evaluative and affective stances to topic, to prompts, and to other participants in communicative interactions;
2. *Semantic domain analysis* using WMatrix®, an online corpus analysis package including UCREL Semantic Analysis System, which tags words by semantic domains, and uses a log-likelihood calculator to identify significant semantic relationships across texts.

BACKGROUND

Positioning theory, according to Harré et al. (2009, p. 5), "is concerned with revealing the explicit and implicit patterns of reasoning that are realized in the ways that people act toward others" as opposed to being only a reaction to a particular social stimulus. Someone with the role of teacher may position herself as a learner or as a collaborator or a coach; focus group moderators may position themselves as facilitators, reporters, moderators. Positions, like roles, "pre-exist" as common knowledge among a family, team, or community, including a community of practice, but they are considerably different from roles. Roles are seen as more static, more fixed, less open to choice. Positions are, on the other hand, "labile, contestable and ephemeral" (Harré, 2004). Luberda (2000, n.p.) explains this as due to the fact that positioning *typically takes place in a conversation; we explain our positions, defend them, alter them. Further, we often try to position others, as, for example: wrong, incompetent, misinformed; or, right, competent, knowledgeable. Finally, these positions tend to be taken up according to an unfolding narrative, as in a tale of a modest infidelity: the guilty party will try to position him or herself as weak-willed, perhaps, or as having been unfaithful in response to some wrong done by the other (http://www.sp.uconn.edu/~jbl00001/positioning/luberda_positioning.htm).*

Linehan and McCarthy (2000, p. 435) see positioning as "an attempt to develop a social psychology of selfhood in which self and other are constituted and reconstituted as people move between discourses." Their effort to apply positioning in combination with practice theory in order to understand "ongoing co-construction, through compliance with or resistance to, organisational storylines" (p. 448), has been taken up by other educators. Dennen (2007), for example, is a widely-cited study coupling theory about presence and positioning in studies of the creation of instructor persona in instructor-student online discussions. She finds positioning theory helpful in understanding how students did or did not attempt to position their instructor as other than their traditional role of expert or leader because it "focuses on the phenomenon of one's position -- what it is relative to others, who constructs it, and whether or not it is accepted" (Dennen, 2006, p. 268).

In applying positioning theory to discourse analysis, Slocum-Bradley (2009) reviews the work of a number of scholars on positioning selves and identities. She includes, for example, Anselm Strauss, who "focuses on how people assume different 'positions,' 'social positions,' 'roles,' 'statuses' or 'masks' . . . to describe the different identities that people assume in the course of interactions. . . ." She then offers a chronological review of the development of positioning theory

by Harré and others. Her goal in so doing is to lay groundwork for a 'positioning diamond' that can graphically display multiple levels for the generation and analysis of meaning: level 1 involves content of a discourse; level 2 looks at the interaction and the identities, rights and duties of the participants in the discourse; and level 3 incorporates larger societal issues and ideologies. In this discussion, we are most interested in positioning as it contributes to the production of discourse stances and their shifts.

Positioning and Stance

There are at least two kinds of positioning in the relational work being carried on in e-discourse: reflexive positioning: how people position themselves; and interactive positioning, in which positioning is negotiated or 'assigned' by other participants in an interaction (Sabat, 2008). Either kind of positioning can produce a particular stance: *as participants negotiate positions or reposition themselves, they shift their stances.* That shift can be identified by computer-based analyses such as quantitative content analysis, and the significant shifts can then be interpreted by conventional qualitative methodologies such as discourse analysis. It is in the constant shifts among stances that attitudes, opinions, and potential choices can be located and interpreted.

Specific stances are often associated with particular parts of speech, such as modal auxiliaries (*might, could*) or stance adverbs. Single-word adverbs, for example, can be adverbs such as *arguably, apparently or unofficially*, to comment on the degree of commitment the speaker/writer has to what is being said. They might comment on the evaluation of a particular proposition, with examples such as *interestingly, preferably* or *significantly*. And they might be used in an illocutionary fashion to comment on or qualify a proposition or action, such as *bluntly, honestly, basically*, or *indeed* (Tseronis, 2009, p. 50).

However, stance more properly describes a meaning or type of meaning, rather than a particular language form (Hunston, 2007, p. 27): just as a golfer addresses the golf ball, so does the speaker address the situation and the content of an utterance. Englebretson (2007, pp.10-11) adds that stance is "a personal belief or attitude" and indicates "a social value;" it is therefore both interactive and indexical of feelings and attitudes. Dubois (2007, p.163) notes that "In taking a stance, the stancetaker (1) evaluates an object, (2) positions a subject (usually the self), and (3) aligns with other subjects." Every time speakers produce utterances, they indicate some kind of stance toward the content or the situation; indeed, as Jaffe (2008, p.10) claims, "Social identity can thus be seen as the cumulation of stances taken over time." She bases this on a reading of how speakers invoke and co-construct stances. According to Jaffe, "Goffman's concept of *footing* and Gumperz's formulation of *contextualization cues* relate to the alignments speakers take up toward themselves and others by managing the production or the reception of an utterance" (2008, p.10). Over time in an electronic interaction, as in face-to-face conversation, stances shift as positionings or footings shift: the identification and analysis of those shifts can reveal information about participants' attitudes, evaluations and feelings.

The approach we take to the analysis of stance shifts is drawn from corpus linguistics, in that it uses computer-assisted coding of a transcript or text to identify where a speaker (or writer) shifts from one stance to another, with the shift relative to the speaker's own mean for each stance. This approach derives from the multidimensional corpus analysis techniques developed by the linguist and lexicographer, Douglas Biber and his colleagues, beginning with his first computer-based analysis of variation across speech and writing (1988). Corpus analysis differs from traditional content analysis in that it works with the co-occurrence of grammatical features as well as words, thus supporting deeper analysis of rhetorical moves across the span

of a text. Rhetorical moves in a particular focus group, for example, might include shifts from an appeal to authority, to a timid demurral, or to a sudden back-pedaling. The analysis of particular moves or themes within a focus group can highlight sections of a transcript of conversational interaction, as well as the changes throughout the whole session (Catterall & MacLaren, 1997).

Linguists working with the analysis of meaning and affect in machine-readable collections of text have initially been drawn from the fields of computational linguistics and, more commonly, as with Biber or Precht, from corpus linguistics. Social psychologists have been prominent, such as James Pennebaker, whose *Linguistic Inquiry and Word Count* program (LIWC; Pennebaker et al., 2001) is widely used in a number of domains. The inexpensive cross-platform version can be downloaded, or the user can upload a text for immediate analysis, leaving the text behind in Pennebaker's data set. LIWC computes the words in a text that are emotion-related, reflect cognitive processes such as causation, social processes and physical issues, and markers of linguistic style. As Pennebaker explains on his website and in his multiple publications, words can fall into content or style: style is created by the use of pronouns, prepositions and articles. This is more formally described by linguists as the distinction between content and function words. Chung and Pennebaker (2007) summarize their primary interest as being

how word use can reflect basic social, personality, cognitive, and biological processes. Relying on computerized text analysis procedures, we are finding that the examination of often-overlooked "junk words" – more formally known as function words or particles – can provide powerful insight into the human psyche. (p. 344)

The original purpose for LIWC was to analyze word use in written texts about traumatic experiences in order to see how affective language provided insight into ways people handled those crises (p. 344).

Affect and emotion are not the same (affect is a conscious experience of emotion; see Panksepp (2000), as cited by Dean (2013) in *PsyBlog*), but discussions of both are beginning to appear in theoretical discussions in a number of fields. A recent linguistic study of emotion as it is involved in the phenomenon of stance-taking presents a fine analysis of issues around affect or emotion (DuBois & Kärkkäinen, 2012):

Emotion can be a motivator of goals and projects of social actors; a trigger of social action; a factor in framing the interactional agenda for as long as the emotion persists; and a determinant of consequences that remain when all has been said and done. (p. 434)

They see affect as one kind of stance and, as do we, they look at how speakers/writers position others. Theoretical justification for looking at stance, affect and positioning is beginning to be more widely discussed; perhaps this will pave the way for wider acceptance of techniques for coding and analysis of electronic collections of discourse.

For example, affect, more recently called sentiment, is a major focus of current political analysis as well as being the Holy Grail for market analysts. Young and Soroka (2012) draw on the *Lexicoder Sentiment Dictionary* (LSD) for the analysis of a set of news content. They compare the LSD's output with results from nine other content-analytic dictionaries and to human coding applied first to 900 articles from the *New York Times* and subsequently to a second set of 1590 articles drawn from the database *Nexis*. To conduct this study, they used the *Lexicoder* cross-platform software, which lets users insert any available machine-readable dictionary to code text automatically for sentiment or any other feature keyed to the particular dictionary. *Lexicoder* was developed at the Media Observatory at the McGill Institute for the Study of Canada; the software is free and available for academic use. Its companion is the *Lexicoder*

Sentiment Dictionary, which was designed to examine sentiment in political texts. Unlike Pennebaker's *LIWC*, prospective users cannot try it out online; they can, however, register and apply to download both for non-commercial use.

Machine-readable dictionaries vary widely with respect to sentiment categories, coding schemes, and scope of coverage. Accordingly, Young and Soroka (2012) focus their work on analyzing current sentiment lexicons, and review current techniques in automated content analysis, beginning with a comparison between supervised and unsupervised machine learning for developing categories of word association. They list a series of psycholinguistic lexicons "coded for basic affective and cognitive dimensions or tagged for valence to categorize the positive and negative connotations they carry" (p. 210), including Pennebaker et al.'s LIWC. However, Young and Soroka (2012, p. 211) note that no single lexicon yet developed can handle diverse corpora. That is, even when limited to political affect, no one size fits all.

Part of the reason is that individual words are slippery, polysemic wrigglers: phrasal context has as much plasticity. Stance can incorporate affect; however, affect can establish stance. We have learned, as we code for stance, to use both words and phrasal patterns in identifying categories for our dictionaries, and to adjust categories to different genres: the factors and weights used to code legal depositions are slightly different from those that we have compiled to examine online focus groups or bulletin boards. Some genres have a greater priority on evaluation, while others prioritize affective interaction. Hyland (2005) proposed a framework incorporating both stance and engagement, derived from his analysis of 240 research articles across eight disciplines. Developed for print media converted into an electronic corpus, and drawing from corpus linguists such as Biber for aspects of interactivity, his work identifies key stance and engagement features by academic discipline, derived from constructs of evidentiality, affect and presence.

Development of Applications of Stance-Shift Analysis

In Biber's first study, the frequencies for roughly 80 parts of speech were able to differentiate dimensions of language use by both genre and register. His multidimensional approach is based on the assumption that "statistical patterns reflect underlying shared communicative functions" (Biber, Conrad, & Reppen, 1998). Drawing on the stance literature for individual parts of speech and using a series of statistical measures, Davis and Mason (2008) were able to reduce Biber's choices for parts of speech to just under two dozen (22) whose multivariate interaction would support frequency analysis in successive standardized segments of a transcript or text.

Our early analyses drew on our corpus of Task-Focused Conversation, collected from 1999-2003. It included online chat groups, interviews and focus groups, and face-to-face conversations, interviews and focus groups. Each of these kinds of interaction has its own characteristics, constrained by both medium and by social situation. We collected the material in ways consistent with the ethics statements of several professional organizations, such as the Association of Internet Researchers (http://www.aoir.org/reports/ethics.pdf).

For example, we logged and immediately anonymized chat from public archives and at rotating hours during the day and night over a four-month period, from open public chats, self-listed on the Internet as available to anyone, sponsored by major commercial portals (Yahoo, MSN, and AOL), and, if the content were in any way sensitive, with the permission of the other participants. Names, nicknames, user-ids, aliases, and the occasional comment which could identify a participant, were deleted from the captured text before being entered into our corpus.

Our Task-Focused Conversation corpus would be considered minute today, as it contained only about 750,000 words, representing several social and geographic varieties of English across a number of topical areas. To ensure a broad base of language usage in different contexts, the full collection held groups and chats on such subjects as: travel, family, friendship, money and finance, music, religion, friendship, health, hobbies (including shopping), book talk, sports and politics. In the online universe of chat groups in the early 2000s, topics served as 'places' where language styles could differ in the same way the different sections of a high school – classroom, auditorium, lunchroom, gym – constrain the way teens choose their words, their tone of voice, even the choice of who speaks to whom. One subset of online focus groups currently has 104,000 words of predominantly North American English. This subset covered topics of finance, travel, fashion and online retail, and included both male and female participants (n=126) from different regions and ages.

We began by highlighting differences in stance between online real-time focus groups and online chat, between online and face-to-face focus groups, and among very different online focus groups such as older adults discussing financial services or teens discussing clothes (Mason, Davis, & Bosley, 2005). The computational approach we developed and later refined, and our basic coding of variables, follows Douglas Biber's earlier multidimensional analyses of text (Biber, 1988). Biber, a corpus linguist, performs statistical operations such as factor and cluster analysis on standardized lengths of machine-readable texts to determine underlying associations across a speaker's – or a group's – language features.

Early Stance-Shift Analysis Methodology

The initial research that was conducted on stance-shift analysis used a collection of off-the-shelf software with a custom Microsoft Visual Basic program to format the data for preparation of the text for use in the analytic software. The early work used depositions, focus group transcripts, and online chat for data. The data was placed in *ansi* text files for cleaning. The cleaning was accomplished by using a combination of Microsoft Word and manual effort. At this point the text was placed in word blocks ready for tagging the POS (Parts-Of-Speech). Tagging was done using a tagger we had developed specifically for this task: we had downloaded, trained and customized the widely-available Brill Tagger. The early research relied upon 2 software products, *Code-A-Text* (Cartwright, 1998) and *NUD*IST*, now part of *NVivo* (QSR) for the majority of the coding, with manual researcher review to ensure proper disambiguation of words. Upon completion of the tagging, the POS were counted for each of the word blocks and the obtained frequencies loaded into a spreadsheet for analysis. A software product, *QDA*, was also experimented with for the tagging of larger data files, but its ability to generate word count frequencies based on multiple usages of the same word was found to be too variable.

The off-the-shelf programs have since been replaced with proprietary software designed specifically for stance-shift analysis. As opposed to continuing the use of software design for the un-ambiguous qualita-tive classification of researcher identified variables, i.e., themes, speakers, key word, etc., that are mutually exclusive; unlike POS. Currently there does not appear to be either a commercial or publicly accessible POS tagger suitable for stance-shift analysis. A dissertation on stance (Precht, 2000) by Kristin Precht, now Kristin Precht-Byrd, was applied in Precht (2008), her article on stance and gender, in which she discussed *StanceSearch*, a program she developed. This program is also briefly discussed in Precht (2003), in which she explains that stance markers are found in lexical verbs, adverbials, adjectives, nouns, and modal verbs), correspond to four main semantic categories: affect, evidentiality, amount, and modality. We have not been able to locate any further discussion of her program which, we assume, remains proprietary and linked to specific data sets.

In our early studies, we prepared the text for analysis in the following manner, and adapted

Code-A-Text © software to code and tabulate the variables. The text was first divided into 200-word units or segments, to standardize for length. The use of this size of unit provided two computer screens of dialogue and allowed some inclusion of infrequently used categories of words or word patterns. We wrote a small program to divide the text into segments. At that time (1999-2005) we used Code-A-Text © to tag the coded variables because it could search for individual words as well as strings of words: that capability is what supports the identification of an array of language features to represent the syntax and semantic possibilities of usage in synchronous online discourse. Frequencies obtained for the tagged variables by segment are placed in a spreadsheet, representing the conversion of focus group text into quantitative units for further data analysis. Segments of a transcript that are statistically significant (1-standard deviation), relative to a writer's/speaker's mean for the full posting or response, are of particular interest.

Although we continue to standardize segment length for more extensive text, such as blogs, we have reduced our number of variables and have compiled our own coding program. Our original set of variables, features used by Biber and other corpus analysts to characterize specific kinds of texts, included 73 categories. However, not all of those variables have significance for isolating and identifying stance. As reported in Mason, Davis, and Bosley (2005), prior to conducting our initial factor analyses, the number of variables was reduced to 49, based on 1) very low frequency of usage (less than 2% of the 104,000 word database), 2) word usage that was not related by the literature to the appraisal or evaluative component of stance, and 3) word usages that were highly correlated and potentially duplicative, such as nouns and definite/indefinite articles. A second factor analysis used only those variables with factor score coefficients greater than .300. This procedure led to the elimination of 26 more variables, resulting in the final 23 language features listed in Table 1.

The 4 factors from the second analysis measure 4 dimensions of stance, keyed to the genre of text being analyzed. Only those factors that exhibit a decline in eigenvalues to the point that the scree plot exhibits a flattening of the plot are used as measures of stance (Park, Dailey, & Lemus, 2002). Those factors are then scaled, as illustrated in Figure 1 (Davis & Mason, 2008).

Examples from Early Applications of Stance-Shift Analysis

1. Online focus group, Large Bank

Tracking how participants changed their stance from topic to topic led to the identification of where and how they wanted immediate response from their bank, and the extent to which they wanted face-to-face contact with bankers as opposed to ATMs. In effect, participants positioned themselves reflexively as bank customers with goals around financial stability, and interactively as concerned consumers who were cutting back on luxuries, eliminating vacations and worrying about the economy. We do not chart the changes

in topic, we chart the changes in stance keyed to those topics and their changes.

2. Online focus group on osteoporosis and menopause

In an example from this focus group (Davis & Mason, 2008), as shown in Table 2, the scales for the first 3 word sections identify significance when participants are 1) giving opinions, 2) telling reasons for those opinions, 3) adding details and feelings, and 4) personalizing what they say. The higher the scale score, the more ownership they take; the lower the number, the more distance they put between themselves and their opinion. Significant scale scores (above 1) have been italicized in Table 2.

The first three (of 27) sections displayed how participants positioned themselves as knowledgeable about symptoms of menopause and willing to share experiences. In the first section, speakers scored above the mean for giving opinions and offering rationalizations for why they thought a specific way, but they presented few details and feelings, and did not personalize their opinions.

Table 1. Variables identifying stance

The variables or language features fall into the following categories, discussed further in *Longman Grammar of English* (Biber et al., 1999); examples of words in categories are italicized:
*   Adverbs: Adverbs/adverbial phrases used as:
    o additive (*also, too*)
    o amplifiers (*completely*)
    o linking (*anyway, however*)
    o emphatics (*really!*)
    o conditional (*if, unless*)
    o downtoners (*barely, only*)
    o time (*afterwards, soon*)
    o hedges (*almost*)
    o degree (*exactly*)
    o discourse particles (*Well*)
    o stance (*actually*)
*   Adjectives: (*bitter, cheap, rich*)
*   Negatives (*not, n't*)
*   Pronouns: First, Second and Third person; indefinite (*anybody*); impersonal (*it*)
*   Verbs: public (observable: *walk*) and private (*anticipate, believe, feel*)
*   Modal verbs: possibility (*can*), necessity (*should*)
Adapted from Mason, Davis, and Bosley (2005, p. 270)

Figure 1. Stance scores, financial focus group

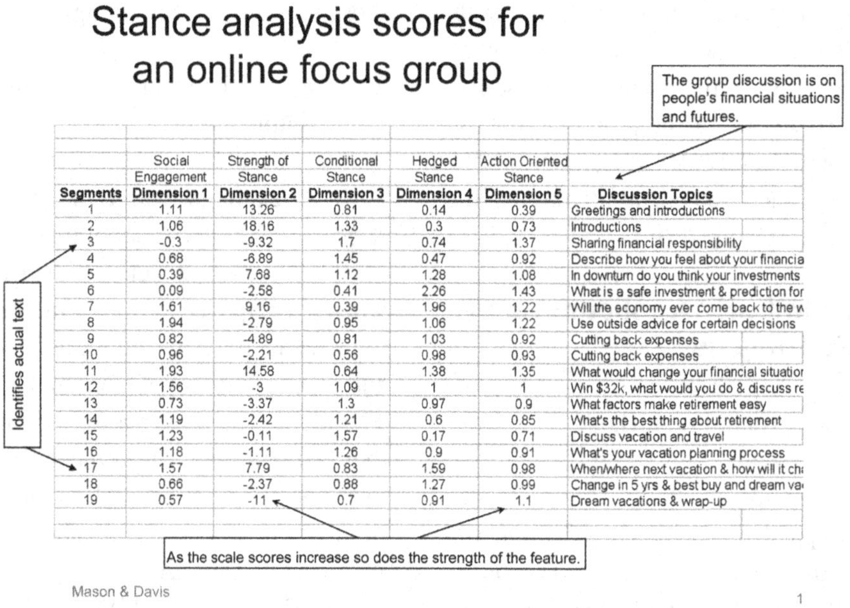

Stance analysis scores for an online focus group

The group discussion is on people's financial situations and futures.

Identifies actual text

Segments	Social Engagement Dimension 1	Strength of Stance Dimension 2	Conditional Stance Dimension 3	Hedged Stance Dimension 4	Action Oriented Stance Dimension 5	Discussion Topics
1	1.11	13.26	0.81	0.14	0.39	Greetings and introductions
2	1.06	18.16	1.33	0.3	0.73	Introductions
3	-0.3	-9.32	1.7	0.74	1.37	Sharing financial responsibility
4	0.68	-6.89	1.45	0.47	0.92	Describe how you feel about your financia
5	0.39	7.68	1.12	1.28	1.08	In downturn do you think your investments
6	0.09	-2.58	0.41	2.26	1.43	What is a safe investment & prediction for
7	1.61	9.16	0.39	1.96	1.22	Will the economy ever come back to the w
8	1.94	-2.79	0.95	1.06	1.22	Use outside advice for certain decisions
9	0.82	-4.89	0.81	1.03	0.92	Cutting back expenses
10	0.96	-2.21	0.56	0.98	0.93	Cutting back expenses
11	1.93	14.58	0.64	1.38	1.35	What would change your financial situatior
12	1.56	-3	1.09	1	1	Win $32k, what would you do & discuss re
13	0.73	-3.37	1.3	0.97	0.9	What factors make retirement easy
14	1.19	-2.42	1.21	0.6	0.85	What's the best thing about retirement
15	1.23	-0.11	1.57	0.17	0.71	Discuss vacation and travel
16	1.18	-1.11	1.26	0.9	0.91	What's your vacation planning process
17	1.57	7.79	0.83	1.59	0.98	When/where next vacation & how will it chi
18	0.66	-2.37	0.88	1.27	0.99	Change in 5 yrs & best buy and dream va
19	0.57	-11	0.7	0.91	1.1	Dream vacations & wrap-up

As the scale scores increase so does the strength of the feature.

Mason & Davis

They continued to emphasize rationales in section 2. By section 3, they began significant personalization:

I don't think I have terrible mood swings or anything like that. So for me, it's just been a kind of hey, no more Tampax. Although you have to carry it around because I know people get their period. Other than the hot flashes and maybe a little insomnia. You're forgetful. You can become forgetful a lot more now than before. I find I do more lists. More lists. Can't sleep at night. You're sleepy; you're tired. Your body is sleepy...

3.   Offender, victim and witness statements: where agency is often deflected

Although stance shift analysis has been successfully employed on a number of depositions and transcripts from investigation, most of them are still privileged content. However, Lord, Davis, and Mason (2008) reported stance shift analysis of oral statements by sex offenders, using the technique to examine how their stances suggested the agency by the speaker in committing sexual offenses, their attribution of blame and on occasion, their assumption of responsibility. In these statements, speakers could present reflexive positioning, where their self-initiated confessional

Table 2. Example, scale score for focus groups

Sections	Scale 1 Opinions	Scale 2 Reasons Why	Scale 3 Details/Feelings	Scale 4 Personalizing
1	*1.50*	*1.67*	-0.60	-0.58
2	0.82	*1.97*	-0.13	0.62
3	0.40	*1.27*	0.53	*1.12*

components assumed personal agency, or inter-active positioning, where they either assumed or reacted against the speech of their interrogators.

For this genre, three scales sufficed to char-acterize recall/disavowal of knowledge about an act, elaboration of affect or action, and agency, in which the speaker points a finger at the person or issue seen as responsible. The third scale for agentive behavior was especially interesting in the statement by a confessed rapist on death row. The analysis of the scales for his significant stance shifts showed that

When he did a murder, he created a Murderer who was then the responsible party and chased down the victim; however, he claimed that her escape effort is what brought about her murder. (Ibid., p. 371)

The offender began with a claim of agency, but quickly deflected personal responsibility to claim that employing aggression, in this case, murder, was reasonable and to be expected. He placed blame on the victim for trying to escape, positioning himself as a rational person who re-sorted to violence only when provoked.

4. A claim of malpractice: positioning and agency as crucial features of depositions

In depositions opened only after the case was settled and the deponent had died, "Mrs. Wil-low" made very clear distinctions between her reports of her speech and that of others (Davis & Mason, 2010):

When she reported that a medical person had said something, she apparently assumed the medical person had delivered information or made a com-ment requiring no action on her part. (p. 278)

She reported herself as accepting personal responsibility for taking action only when a

medical person specifically *told* or *ordered* her to do something:

And she [the nurse] immediately said, "Has your doctor ordered a colonoscopy?" And I started crying and told her that that's the same thing Dr.___ had asked me, and why is this such com-mon knowledge and my doctor hadn't ordered it? (Ibid., p. 279)

Her lack of positive agentive behavior meant that she did not make an appointment for an im-portant medical test, whose findings could pos-sibly have saved her life. Her self-reports show that she had positioned herself as unknowing, dependent, willing to follow orders, but unable to move through the medical system. And that positioning contributed to her death.

5. Reanalysis of educational interaction

In 2009, we collected online data with which to study the construct of cognitive presence in task-oriented student writings from asynchronous online forums for nursing and healthcare and com-munication courses (Davis, Smith, & Tsai, 2010, p. 580). We were particularly interested in writings that (1) were content based, with evaluation at a particular level of cognitive skills or abstraction; (2) used self-disclosure or social commentary in replies to another writer, suggesting a desire to affiliate with that writer, and thereby signaling social presence; and (3) writings which were both content-based and evaluative, and also showed some degree of social presence. Because of our interest in combining content analysis techniques with linguistic approaches (Davis & Thiede, 2008) we followed Schrire (2006) in applying the SOLO taxonomy and the Practical Inquiry Model to locate and analyze cognitive presence in those forums.

The original analysis identified entries that attracted replies in a set from a Nursing course fo-rum, as being personalized with details from "their personal evaluation, their affect, their experience, or their stance on a topic … suggest[ing] that their entry derives from reflection and integration of course content as an aspiring professional as well as a caring person" (Davis, Smith, & Tsai, 2010, p. 587). In the set combining undergraduate and graduate students in a course on language and health, writers received replies if they had presented above-average content, and either directed a question to the group, provided new information about another culture, or included a statement inviting controversy (*Ibid.*, p 588).

Turning to the confluences between positioning and stance, we would now interpret those interactions as representing how the writers positioned themselves as expert and knowledgeable, and as welcoming reciprocal acts of self-disclosure. In other words, rather than seeing the particular entries as being the crucial factor in attracting interest from other participants, it is the stance taken by the entry, and the self-positioning of the writer that elicited alignment from other participants.

Combining Stance-Shift and Semantic Domain Analysis

The rise of social media, including tweets, blogs, and Facebook and Youtube postings, share the responsibility for the explosion of data available on the Internet with the increase in users world-wide, the expansion of mobile devices, and the bandwidth needed to accommodate photos and videos. The phenomenon is reviewed in the 2012 World Economic Forum report, *Big data, big impact: New possibilities for international development* (http://www.weforum.org/reports/big-data-big-impact-new-possibilities-international-development). Storing, managing and mining that data is, of course, the current challenge. Stance shift analysis combined with semantic domain analysis has supported the rapid and nuanced exploration of large quantities of text.

The association of semantics with the identification of domains is a well-known ethnographic technique. According to ethnographer James Spradley, a domain is a "symbolic category that includes other categories," (Spradley, 1979, p. 100); it is "a search for the larger units of cultural knowledge" (*Ibid.*, p. 94) and those units are characterized by specific semantic relationships. The online corpus management software tool *Wmatrix* ® (http://ucrel.lancs.ac.uk/wmatrix/; Rayson, 2009) initiates its identification of semantic relationships by automatic corpus tagging of part-of-speech and semantic field (Rayson, 2008). Rayson uses the USAS tagger to assign a semantic field to each word or multiword expression. USAS stands for U[CREL]Semantic Analysis System; the 21 major domains were originally keyed to McArthur's *Longman Lexicon of Contemporary English* (1981) and is currently expanded into 232 category labels (http://ucrel.lancs.ac.uk/usas/). The keywords of two texts can be compared using the log likelihood statistic, a type of linear regression. The semantic domain tagset can be used to analyze types of documents, types of annotations, spelling variation across time, and even metaphor: according to Koeller (2008, pp.141-2), "semantic domain tagging can be used to identify instances of metaphoric expressions in a lengthy text or corpus with a greater recall than other methods that have previously been used." Bridle (2011) has used the semantic domain component of Wmatrix ® to look at pre- and post-World War II blues lyrics, and Yu-Fang Ho (2011) has used it to explore stylistics in John Fowles' novel, *The Magus.*

Using Combined Applications on Tourist Data: Four Examples

Travellers today will often turn to online word-of-mouth reviews for tourism and hospitality experiences, including hotels.

1.   Hotels compared for customer delight

In one study, stance-shift analysis was used on travel blogs to identify both customer satisfaction and customer delight, an experience which is seen as more emotional and memorable, and may include an element of surprise (Crotts, Mason, & Davis, 2009). 16,000 words of evaluative narrative about three New York hotels were taken (with permission) from TripAdvisor.com, perhaps the best-known travel blog in the hospitality field. The four factors identified *Opinions; Reasons behind Opinions; Feelings and Details;* and *Personalized projection of choices* (*Ibid.*, p 143). Table 3 displays a summary of the language features associated with each factor, and their eigenvalues:

Opinions and rationalization in significant sections of the blog narratives identified Hotel A as providing greater delight by room quality and service/room service. Semantic domains in the blog narratives were analyzed using Wmatrix ® in order to see which semantic concepts were significantly associated with each of the hotels. Hotel A's decor had a patina of age which was seen as attractive (as opposed to old and run-down),

and it also had significantly more positive clusters for drinks and beverages; Hotel C was found to be most delightful for food, especially breakfast. Writers positioned themselves as observant, interested in value received for cash expended, and as seeking satisfaction and delight.

2. Hotels compared for features affecting potential return visits

In a second study designed to elicit rich marketing intelligence from blogger posts, semantic categories were identified by Wmatrix® in 200 guest narratives about hotels in Atlanta, GA, with the narratives again taken from TripAdvisor.com (Crotts et al., 2011). Next, stance shift analysis coded and analysed the texts for underlying patterns of language use that indexed attitudes and opinions. In this data set, four factors identified 4 key stances:

- **Agency:** Assignment of responsibility for actions and choices;

Table 3. Language features by factors (adapted with permission from Crotts et al., 2009, p. 143)

Language Feature	Factor 1	Language Feature	Factor 2
Emphatics	0.744	Degree adverbial	0.665
Stance adverbial	0.687	Amplifier	0.624
Additive adverbial	0.685	Adjective	0.521
Third person pronoun	0.483	Impersonal pronoun	0.482
Linking adverb	0.346	Discourse particle	0.376
Private verb	0.304	Conditional adverbial	−0.345
Time adverbial	−0.307	First person pronoun	−0.446
Language Feature	**Factor 3**	**Language Feature**	**Factor 4**
First person pronoun	0.560	Discourse particle	0.655
Negative analytic	0.518	Time adverbial	0.608
Degree adverbial	0.493	Impersonal pronoun	0.409
Amplifier	0.481	Negative analytic	0.340
Conditional adverbial	0.343	Indefinite pronoun	0.321
Indefinite pronoun	−0.323		
Second person pronoun	−0.358		

- **Opinions:** Information about events and actions;
- **Rationale:** Explanatory reasons and some notion of speaker's confidence;
- **Elaboration:** Details of affect or emotion.

Stance sections were analysed quantitatively to identify the most significant areas of text for interpretation. (As mentioned previously, statistically significant sections are 1 or more standard deviations above a writer's/speaker's mean for the full posting or response). The agency of participants was of particular interest, as positive, significant agency suggested what features would underscore decisions about return visits to a particular hotel. Writers with significant agency positioned themselves as being the persons in the family or group who made decisions, allocated the funds, and considered returning to the destination.

3. Comparison of analytic techniques applied to farm-stay data

To examine reliability in computer-aided stance-shift and semantic domain analysis using WMatrix® as compared with manual coding, Capriello et al. (2011) compiled a corpus of 800 narratives describing farm-stay experiences in Australia, Italy, UK, and USA. Two researchers applied manual coding to the data set, and used an interpretive approach with a cognitive map built from adjectives defining the perfect host, to identify cultural archetypes underscoring the importance of the owner or operator (*Ibid.*, p. 2). Semantic domain analysis using Wmatrix ® discriminated among different national experiences and located areas of consumer expectations which could be addressed prior to the farm-stay experience. Stance shift analysis enabled the researchers to rank countries by effusiveness and locate additional expectations: for example, Italian visitors positioned themselves as serious

about agritourism, expecting special courses at the destination, while Australians positioned themselves as travel-savvy, anticipating interesting animals and unusual locales (p. 5). Similar findings suggest that all three methods produce reliable, if different, results. Manual content coding "allows the identification of recurrent factors and the analysis of innovative themes, but may be inconsistent when compared to computer-assisted analyses;" however, the software must be bought and learned.

4. Stance and density in Facebook comments

A corpus of 8000 Facebook comments on a popular consumer beverage was coded for 15 language features selected from the two dozen used for stance shift analysis. Chosen part-of-speech features comprised two groups: those using idea and lexical density for appraisal (nouns, pronouns, and adjectives), and those signaling agency and affect or sentiment, such as hedges *(maybe)*, boosters *(very)*, modal verbs *(could)* and negation. To measure idea and lexical density, we used CPIDR (*Computerized Propositional Idea Density Rater*), a computer program that determines the propositional idea density (P-density) of an English text automatically on the basis of part-of-speech tags (Brown et al., 2008; Covington, 2007). The construct of propositional idea density is that propositional density can be approximated by the number of verbs, adjectives, adverbs, prepositions, and conjunctions divided by the total number of words in the text. Exploratory factor analyses of the data using Promax rotation identified two factors: these account for 50% of the variation and distinguish between consumer opinions and consumer recommendations. Members of this Facebook 'community' positioned themselves in differing membership categories: as loyal to the brand vs. disinterested in brand identification; as aligned with the brand's stated values vs. being disaffiliated from those values. More investigation of positioning and stance in tweets and Facebook comments should provide better understanding of how customers relate to specific brands, whether they are beverages, basketball teams or political parties.

FUTURE RESEARCH DIRECTIONS

Our future research will look more closely at short asynchronous postings in social media, specifically, in discovering whether there is a relationship between stance-shift and idea density with language features that can characterize how a single comment captures the sender's posture toward the topic. In short responses, the relationship between appraisal and density may be what flags the salience of the topic to the reader. Speakers signal that they are assuming responsibility for an action, idea or opinion, or dodging it, or even attributing responsibility to someone else, by subtle changes in the ways they speak, in order to present themselves and their ideas in different ways. Figure 2 is our working sketch showing components in social media comments that lead to consumer stance, consumer engagement, and ultimately, consumer behavior.

In the single comment postings in Table 4, what indexes 'hot-button' meanings are adjectives, adverbs, and adverbially-used prepositions – not simultaneously, and not to the same degree.

Modifiers, especially adverbs and prepositions used adverbially, are key carriers of meaning,

Figure 2. Components in social media comments

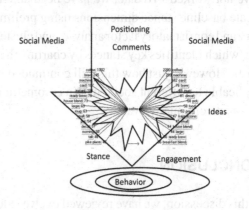

shading the force of the verbs. Although adverbs are content words, they and adverbial prepositions combine constantly in English to suggest style and shade meaning. Participants arrange other types of words around them to signal the direction of the online discussion and the strength of their feelings or opinions. When scaled, the interactions among these patterns can identify the successive stages of the stance a person is taking toward the topic under discussion. In our efforts to date, we think that a short answer analysis will differ from stance-shift analysis in that it is not looking for a *shift* in stance to uncover what is important to the speaker. Instead it scores responses on the presence of concepts, the predominant stance, and the *degree* of engagement that is present in the comment and its positioning by the writer. Also being reviewed: the size of a segment: can a number of very short responses be combined? If so, how can the stances best be identified, particularly if the short responses represent a genre with which we

Table 4. Sample single-comment postings

Weird thing is that today I went to an AT&T store to try out the pre, and of course I tested the keyboard, slider, etc. I then turned on the GPS And opened googe maps, but it wouldn't get a lock, I tried the ##GPS# fix, and that didn't work either. Just like the pre on Veizon
Lol...I've heard mixed reactions to the whole "Droid" sound. Personally I love it and the red eyeball logo, especially considering the boring old Verizon logo that used to show up.
I love my Droid but VZ Navigator worked very well, except maybe in hills. I think it uses cell tower positioning instead of satellite.

have not worked? To date, we have been able to create baseline stance dimensions using preliminary and confirmatory factor analyses and clustering, which identifies key stances by charting their shifts. However, just how this will continue to be applicable to different social media is something we must continually evaluate.

CONCLUSION

In this discussion, we have reviewed twelve studies of the application of two specific computer-assisted softwares to the coding and interpretation of electronic discourse. The first, stance-shift analysis, is an approach developed by the authors, keyed to the burgeoning literature on stance, using techniques derived from corpus analysis, and grounded in positioning theory. We have reviewed the development of that approach, as applied to online chat and focus groups, depositions, and interviews, and we have tried to illustrate not only how to identify shifts among stances, but to reanalyze data in some instances to expand the interconnections between stance, presence and positioning as crucial components of relational work. The second approach, semantic domain analysis, links semantic and syntactic tagging to expand the qualitative what and why of the more quantitative analyses. Sentiment and opinion mining is still developing; the rapid growth of social media makes it imperative that techniques for managing and coding the flood of data be tested and reviewed, and on occasion, revisited.

REFERENCES

Biber, D. (1988). *Variation across speech and writing*. Cambridge: Cambridge University Press. doi:10.1017/CBO9780511621024.

Biber, D., Conrad, S., & Reppen, R. (1998). *Corpus linguistics: Investigating language structure and use*. Cambridge: Cambridge University Press. doi:10.1017/CBO9780511804489.

Biber, D., Johansson, S., Leech, G., Conrad, S., & Finegan, E. (1999). *The Longman grammar of spoken and written English*. London: Longman.

Bridle, M. (2011). *Male Blues Lyrics 1920-1965: A corpus assisted analysis*. (Unpublished masters dissertation). University of Huddersfield, UK.

Brown, C., Snodgrass, T., Kemper, S., Herman, R., & Covington, M. (2008). Automatic measurement of propositional idea density from part-of-speech tagging. *Behavior Research Methods*, *40*, 540–545. doi:10.3758/BRM.40.2.540 PMID:18522065.

Capriello, A., Mason, P., Davis, B., & Crotts, J. (2011). Farm tourism experiences in travel reviews: A cross-comparison of three alternative methods for data analysis. *Journal of Business Research*, 1–8.

Cartwright, A. (1988). *Code-A-Text [Software; Orphaned and unsupported since 2002]*. Retrieved January 10, 2013, from http://micabrera.co.uk/code-a-text/default.aspx

Catterall, C., & Maclaran, P. (1997). Focus group data and qualitative analysis programs: Coding the moving picture as well as the snapshots. *Sociological Research Online, 2*(1). Retrieved July 1, 2011, from http://socresonline.org.uk/socresonline/2/1/6.html

Chung, C., & Pennebaker, J. (2007). The psychological function words. In Fiedler, K. (Ed.), *Social communication* (pp. 343–359). NY: Psychology Press.

Covington, M. (2007). *CPIDR 3 User Manual*. GA: University of Georgia Artificial Intelligence Center. Retrieved December 1, 2011, from http://www.ai.uga.edu/caspr/

Crotts, J., Davis, B., & Mason, P. (2011). Analyzing travel blog content for competitive advantage: Lessons learned in the application of software aided linguistics analysis. In Sigala, M. (Ed.), *Web 2.0 in travel, tourism and hospitality: Theory, practice and cases* (pp. 281–293). Surrey, UK: Ashgate Publishing Ltd..

Crotts, J., Mason, P., & Davis, B. (2009). Measuring guest satisfaction and competitive position: An application of stance shift analysis of blog narratives. *Journal of Travel Research*, *48*(3), 139–151. doi:10.1177/0047287508328795.

Davies, B., & Harre, R. (1990). Positioning the discursive production of selves. *Journal for the Theory of Social Behaviour*, *20*(1), 43–63. doi:10.1111/j.1468-5914.1990.tb00174.x.

Davis, B., & Mason, P. (2008). Stance-shift analysis: Locating presence and positions in online focus group chat. In Kelsey, S., & St Amant, K. (Eds.), *Handbook of research on computer-mediated communication* (pp. 634–646). Hershey, PA: ICI Press. doi:10.4018/978-1-59904-863-5.ch045.

Davis, B., & Mason, P. (2010). Stance shift analysis. In Lord, V., & Cowan, A. (Eds.), *Interviewing in criminal justice* (pp. 273–282). NY: Jones & Bartlett.

Davis, B., Smith, M., & Tsai, S.-C. (2010). When the online conversation is prompted. In Taiwo, R. (Ed.), *Handbook of research in discourse behavior and digital communication: Language structures and social interaction* (pp. 579–591). Hershey, PA: IGI Global. doi:10.4018/978-1-61520-773-2.ch037.

Davis, B., & Thiede, R. (2000). Writing into change: Style-shifting in asynchronous electronic discourse. In Warschaeur, M., & Kern, R. (Eds.), *Network-based teaching: concepts and practice* (pp. 87–120). Cambridge: University Press. doi:10.1017/CBO9781139524735.007.

Dean, J. (n.d). *PsyBlog: Understand your mind.* Retrieved January 8, 2013, from http://www.spring.org.uk

Dennen, V. (2006). Assessing presence: Using positioning theory to examine instructor participation and persona in online discourse. *IADS International Conference on Cognition and Exploratory Learning in a Digital Age (CELDA 2006)*, 267-273. Retrieved July 15, 2012, from http://www.iadisportal.org/digital-library/assessing-presence-using-positioning-theory-to-examine-instructor-participation-and-persona-in-online-discourse

Dennen, V. (2007). *Presence* and *positioning* as components of online instructor persona. *Journal of Research on Technology in Education*, *40*, 95–108.

DuBois, J. (2007). The stance triangle. In Englebretson, R. (Ed.), *Stancetaking in discourse: Subjectivity, evaluation, interaction* (pp. 139–182). Philadelphia: John Benjamins.

DuBois, J., & Kärkkäinen, E. (2012). Taking a stance on emotion: Affect, sequence and intersubjectivity in dialogic interaction. *Text & Talk*, *32*, 433–451.

Englebretson, R. (Ed.). (2007). *Stancetaking in discourse: Subjectivity, evaluation, interaction.* Philadelphia: John Benjamins.

Fulk, J., Steinfield, C., Schmitz, J., & Power, J. (1987). A social information processing model of media use in organizations. *Communication Research*, *14*, 529–552. doi:10.1177/009365087014005005.

Goffman, I. (1974). *Frame analysis.* NY: Harper and Row.

Gumperz, J. (1982). *Discourse strategies.* Cambridge: Cambridge University Press. doi:10.1017/CBO9780511611834.

Harré, R. (2004). *Positioning theory*. Retrieved July 15, 2012, from http://www.massey.ac.nz/~alock/virtual/

Harré, R., Moghaddam, F., Cairnie, T., Rothbart, D., & Sabat, S. (2009). Recent advances in positioning theory. *Theory & Psychology*, *19*, 5–31. doi:10.1177/0959354308101417.

Ho, Y.-F. (2011). *Corpus stylistics in principles and practice: a stylistic exploration of John Fowles' The Magus*. NY: Continuum.

Hunston, S. (2007). Using a corpus to investigate stance quantitatively and qualitatively. In Englebretson, R. (Ed.), *Stance-taking in discourse: Subjectivity, evaluation, interaction* (pp. 27–48). NY: Benjamins.

Hyland, K. (2005). Stance and engagement: A model of interaction in academic discourse. *Discourse Studies*, *7*, 173–192. doi:10.1177/1461445605050365.

Jaffe, A. (Ed.). (2008). *Stance: Sociolinguistic perspectives*. Oxford: Oxford University Press.

Koller, V., Hardie, A., Rayson, P., & Semino, E. (2008). Using a semantic annotation tool for the analysis of metaphor in discourse. *Metaphoric.de*, *15*, 141–160.

Langlotz, A., & Locher, M. (2012). Ways of communicating emotional stance in online disagreements. *Journal of Pragmatics*, *44*, 1591–1606. doi:10.1016/j.pragma.2012.04.002.

Lexicoder 2.0. (2011). *Media Observatory*. McGill Institute for the Study of Canada. Retrieved January 4, 2013, from http://www.lexicoder.com

Lexicoder Semantic Dictionary. (2011). *Media observatory*. McGill Institute for the Study of Canada. Retrieved January 4, 2013, from http://www.lexicoder.com

Linehan, C., & McCarthy, J. (2000). Positioning in practice: Understanding participation in the social world. *Journal for the Theory of Social Behaviour*, *30*, 435–453. doi:10.1111/1468-5914.00139.

Locher, M., & Watts, R. (2005). Politeness theory and relational work. *Journal of Politeness Research*, *1*, 9–33.

Lord, V., Davis, B., & Mason, P. (2008). Stance shifts in rapist discourse: Characteristics and taxonomies. *Psychology, Crime & Law*, *14*, 357–379. doi:10.1080/10683160701770153.

Luberda, J. (2000). *Unassuming positions: Middlemarch, its critics, and positioning theory*. Retrieved August 6, 2012, from http://www.sp.uconn.edu/~jbl00001/positioning/luberda_positioning.htm

Mason, P., Davis, B., & Bosley, D. (2005). Stance analysis: When people talk online. In Krishnamurthy, S. (Ed.), *Innovations in E-Marketing* (Vol. 2, pp. 261–282). Hershey, PA: Idea Group.

Miner, Q. D. A. (2009). Version 3.2.3. Montreal, QC, Canada. Provalis Research, 2414 Bennett Ave.

Moghaddam, R., Harré, R., & Lee, N. (2008). Positioning and conflict: An introduction. In Moghaddam, R., Harré, R., & Lee, N. (Eds.), *Global conflict resolution through positioning theory* (pp. 81–93). NY: Springer. doi:10.1007/978-0-387-72112-5_1.

NUD-IST. (1997). *Version 4.0*. Melbourne, Victoria, Australia: Qualitative Solutions & Research Ltd..

Panksepp, J. (2000). Affective consciousness and the instinctual motor system. In Ellis, R., & Newton, N. (Eds.), *The caldron of consciousness: Motivation, affect and self-organization, advances in consciousness research* (pp. 27–54). Amsterdam: John Benjamins.

Park, H., Dailey, R., & Lemus, D. (2002). The use of exploratory factor analysis and principal components analysis in communication research. *Human Communication Research*, *23*, 562–577. doi:10.1111/j.1468-2958.2002.tb00824.x.

Pennebaker, J., Francis, M., & Booth, R. (2001). *Linguistic inquiry and word count (LIWC): LIWC2001*. Mahwah: Lawrence Erlbaum.

Precht, K. (2000). *Patterns of stance in English*. (Unpublished doctoral dissertation). Northern Arizona University.

Precht, K. (2003). Great vs. lovely: Stance differences in American and British English. In Leistyna, P., & Meyer, C. (Eds.), *Corpus analysis: Language structure and language use* (pp. 133–152). NY: Rodopi.

Precht, K. (2008). Sex similarities and differences in stance in informal American conversation. *Journal of Sociolinguistics*, *12*(1), 89–111. doi:10.1111/j.1467-9841.2008.00354.x.

Rayson, P. (2008). From key words to key semantic domains. *International Journal of Corpus Linguistics*, *13*(4), 519–549. doi:10.1075/ijcl.13.4.06ray.

Rayson, P. (2009). *Wmatrix: A web-based corpus processing environment*. Lancaster University: Computing Department. Retrieved July 1, 2012, from http://ucrel.lancs.ac.uk/wmatrix/

Sabat, S. (2008). Positioning and conflict involving a person with dementia. In Moghaddam, F., Harré, R., & Lee, N. (Eds.), *Global conflict resolution through positioning theory* (pp. 81–93). New York: Springer. doi:10.1007/978-0-387-72112-5_5.

Schrire, S. (2006). Knowledge building in asynchronous discussion groups: Going beyond quantitative analysis. *Computers & Education*, *46*, 49–70. doi:10.1016/j.compedu.2005.04.006.

Slocum-Bradley, N. (2009). The positioning diamond: A trans-disciplinary framework for discourse analysis. *Journal for the Theory of Social Behaviour*, *40*, 79–107. doi:10.1111/j.1468-5914.2009.00418.x.

Spradley, J. (1979). *The ethnographic interview*. *Holt*. NY: Rinehart and Winston.

Walther, J. (1992). Interpersonal effects in computer-mediated interaction: A relational perspective. *Communication Research*, *19*, 52–90. doi:10.1177/009365092019001003.

Walther, J. (1996). Computer-mediated communication: Impersonal, interpersonal, and hyperpersonal interaction. *Communication Research*, *23*, 3–43. doi:10.1177/009365096023001001.

Young, L., & Soroka, S. (2012). Affective news: The automated coding of sentiment in political texts. *Political Communication*, *29*, 205–231. doi:10.1080/10584609.2012.671234.

ADDITIONAL READING

Andersen, G., & Fretheim, T. (2000). *Pragmatic markers and propositional attitude*. Amsterdam: John Benjamins.

Barton, E. (1993). Evidentials, argumentation, and epistemological stance. *College English*, *55*, 745–769. doi:10.2307/378428.

Beach, R., & Anson, C. (1992). Stance and intertextuality in written discourse. *Linguistics and Education*, *4*, 335–357. doi:10.1016/0898-5898(92)90007-J.

Bednarek, M. (2006). Epistemological positioning and evidentiality in English news discourse – a text-driven approach. *Text and Talk*, *6*, 635–660.

Biber, D., & Finegan, F. (1988). Adverbial stance types in English. *Discourse Processes, 11*, 1–34. doi:10.1080/01638538809544689.

Biber, D., & Finegan, E. (1989). Styles of stance in English: Lexical and grammatical marking of evidentiality and affect. *Text, 9*, 93–124. doi:10.1515/text.1.1989.9.1.93.

Chafe, W., & Nichols, J. (1986). *Evidentials: The linguistic coding of epistemology.* Norwood, NJ: Ablex.

Channell, J. (2000). Corpus-based analysis of evaluative lexis. In Hunston, S., & Thompson, G. (Eds.), *Evaluation in text: Authorial stance and the construction of discourse* (pp. 38–55). Oxford: Oxford University Press.

Charles, M. (2003). "This mystery…": A corpus-based study of the use of nouns to construct stance in theses from two contrasting disciplines. *Journal of English for Academic Purposes, 2*, 313–326. doi:10.1016/S1475-1585(03)00048-1.

Conrad, S., & Biber, D. (2000). Adverbial marking of stance in speech and writing. In Hunston, S., & Thompson, G. (Eds.), *Evaluation in text: Authorial stance and the construction of discourse* (pp. 56–73). Oxford: Oxford University Press.

Damari, R. (2009). Stancetaking as identity work: Attributed, accreted, and adjusted stances taken by an intercultural couple. *eVox, 3*, 18-37.

Downing, A. (2001). "Surely you knew!": 'surely' as a marker of evidentiality and stance. *Functions of Language, 8*, 253–285. doi:10.1075/fol.8.2.05dow.

Du Bois, J. (2007). The stance triangle. In Englebretson, R. (Ed.), *Stancetaking in discourse: The intersubjectivity of interaction* (pp. 138–182). Amsterdam: John Benjamins.

Kärkkäinen, E. (2003). "Is she vicious or dense?" Dialogic practices of stance taking in conversation. In Nakayama, T., Ono, T., & Tao, H. (Eds.), *Santa Barbara papers in linguistics 12. Recent studies in empirical approaches to language* (pp. 47–65). Santa Barbara: University of California.

Kärkkäinen, E. (2006). Stance taking in conversation: from subjectivity to intersubjectivity. *Text & Talk, 26*, 699–731. doi:10.1515/TEXT.2006.029.

Kockelman, P. (2004). Stance and subjectivity. *Journal of Linguistic Anthropology, 14*, 127–150. doi:10.1525/jlin.2004.14.2.127.

Lempert, M. (2008). The poetics of stance: Text-metricality, epistemicity, interaction. *Language in Society, 37*(4), 569–592. doi:10.1017/S0047404508080779.

Lempert, M. (2009). On "flip-flopping": Branded stance-taking in U.S. electoral politics. *Journal of Sociolinguistics, 13*, 223–248. doi:10.1111/j.1467-9841.2009.00405.x.

Linde, C. (1997). Evaluation as linguistic structure and social practice. In B. Gunnarsson, P. Linell, & B. Nordberg (Eds.), The construction of professional discourse (151-172). London: Longman.

Martin, J. (2000). Beyond exchange: Appraisal systems in English. In Hunston, S., & Thompson, G. (Eds.), *Evaluation in text: Authorial stance and the construction of discourse* (pp. 142–175). Oxford: OUP.

Martin, J., & White, P. (2005). *The language of evaluation: Appraisal in English.* London, New York: Palgrave Macmillan.

Precht, K. (2003). Stance moods in spoken English: Evidentiality and affect in British and American conversation. *Text, 23*, 239–257. doi:10.1515/text.2003.010.

Reilly, J., Zamora, A., & McGivern, R. (2005). Acquiring perspective in English: The development of stance. *Journal of Pragmatics*, *37*(2), 185–208.

Riddle Harding, J. (2007). Evaluative stance and counterfactuals in language and literature. *Language and Literature*, *16*, 263–280. doi:10.1177/0963947007079109.

Silver, M. (2003). The stance of stance: A critical look at ways stance is expressed and modelled in academic discourse. *Journal of English for Academic Purposes*, *2*, 359–374. doi:10.1016/S1475-1585(03)00051-1.

van Langenhove, L., & Harré, R. (1999). Introducing positioning theory. In van Langenhove, L., & Harré, R. (Eds.), *Positioning theory* (pp. 14–31). Oxford: Blackwell.

White, P. (2003). Beyond modality and hedging: A dialogic view of the language of intersubjective stance. *Text*, *23*, 259–284. doi:10.1515/text.2003.011.

White, P. (2008). Praising and blaming, applauding, and disparaging: Solidarity, audience positioning, and the linguistics of evaluative disposition. In Antos, G., & Ventola, E. (Eds.), *Handbook of interpersonal communication* (pp. 567–594). Berlin: Mouton de Gruyter.

KEY TERMS AND DEFINITIONS

Affect: Affect is the awareness of emotion; as applied to e-text analysis, it typically refers to the emotion expressed or suggested by the writer's word and language pattern choices.

Positioning: Positioning theory seeks to explain how people assume and project the rights and obligations of speaking and acting by how they position themselves and others as they speak. For example: If a person positions herself/himself as the authority on something that happened, then that person has appropriated the right and the obligation to decide whether anyone else can say what happened.

Presence: In technologically-supported environments, presence refers to the awareness of participants in the environment of each other's being there. The term can also refer to the degree of social richness or realism in the environment.

Semantic Domain: A semantic domain is an area, field or place that shares meanings. These meanings could be seen as cognitive or as cultural categories. The words in a semantic field co-occur in texts.

Stance: Stance in language analysis looks at the position a person takes with regard to a topic, an issue, or another conversant.

Stance Shift: People shift stances constantly as their appraisal or evaluation of a situation or topic or other stimulus changes, or as their affect toward the stimulus rises or falls.

WMatrix®: WMatrix is an online corpus processing software package that is hosted at Lancaster University by Paul Rayson. It tags words in a text for each word (or multi-word expression) for part of speech and semantic domain.

Chapter 19
Textuality on the Web:
A Focus on Argumentative Text Types

Chiara Degano
Università degli Studi di Milano, Italy

ABSTRACT

This chapter focuses on computer mediated communication from a linguistic perspective, exploring aspects of textuality which have been impacted by the pervasive spread of the hypertext. Central features in the construction of texts are the notions of cohesion and coherence, originally tailored on linear time-based modes of communication, where both the elements and their sequentiality – fully controlled by the author – contribute to meaning making. In light of the disruption of linear sequentiality brought by the space-based logic of the hypertext, this chapter aims to understand how cohesion and coherence work in the website environment, with specific regard to genres characterised by an argumentative drive, which potentially suffer more than other text types from the loss of the author's control on the linear dispositio of arguments. The analysis identifies different patterns for the construction of cohesion and coherence in argumentative websites, which accommodate traditional standards of textuality into the new environment.

INTRODUCTION

Of all elements characterizing electronic discourse, hypertextuality has probably been the most macroscopic, resulting in a loss of linearity as well as a reduced author's control on text construction, with users gaining 'power' in that respect. Following closely are multimodality, i.e. the coexistence of different semiotic modes (verbal, visual and audio), and in more recent times increased interactivity, marking the transformation of the website from a hypertextual information space to a 'remote software interface' (Garrett, 2000), where the user is increasingly pushed to action. Such a profound innovation has triggered far-reaching change in our conception of discourse, at least as far as its formal aspects are concerned, which – some claim – has started exerting a deep influence on literacy itself and on cognitive processes of meaning formation, whose effects cannot yet be fully grasped (Kress, 2003).

DOI: 10.4018/978-1-4666-4426-7.ch019

A similar scenario certainly poses several important questions from the viewpoint of the adequacy of the tools traditionally employed by discourse analysts. Considering discourse from a linguistic perspective, where the textual component is the privileged object of investigation, this paper addresses a basic concern: in what way are textual realizations on the Web unique? What is the impact of website affordances on the standards of textuality? In particular, attention will be focussed on argumentative discourse, as one which more than others, might suffer from the loss of a rigorous logical progression, jeopardised on the Web by the disruption of linear reading modes.

Indeed, in argumentative discourse it is the logical sequence of reasoning that is fundamental, and arranging arguments in the best possible order (*dispositio* in classical rhetoric) was traditionally seen as a crucial ability of the orator in the pursuit of rhetorical effectiveness. On this ground, argumentation on the web, here epitomized by an NGO's campaign against genetically engineered food, is investigated with a view to understanding how coherence is imposed on the fragmented and multi-linear (Landow, 1992) content of a website.

BACKGROUND

The impact of the hypertextual/web environment on textuality has been investigated both from a linguistic (Fritz, 1998; Tosca, 2000; Bolter, 2001; Askehave & Ellerup Nielsen, 2005; Garzone, 1997; Garzone, Catenaccio, & Poncini, 2007) and a computer-science perspective (for a review of the literature, see Carter, 2000), even though only rarely has the focus been specifically on argumentative discourse (Carter, 2000; 2003; Shauf, 2001; Degano, 2012; Catenaccio, 2012). Salient factors affecting textuality on the web, as emerged from previous research, include multimodality, hypertextuality, co-articulation and interactivity, multiple reading modes and granularity (Garzone, 2007, pp. 20 and ff).[1]

Multimodality refers to the possibility of combining different modes of communication in the same communicative event and is strictly dependent on multi-medianess (Askehave & Ellerup-Nielsen, 2004, pp. 12-13) i.e. the integration of different media into a single environment, which is an inherent characteristic of the Web. The ease with which visual and written semiotic resources, both in their static and dynamic forms, can be combined on a website has certainly contributed to accelerating the process of 'dethronization' of written discourse – which had been dominating western cultures since the seventeenth century (Kress & van Leeuwen, 2006, p. 18) – started with the spread of TV. From the viewpoint of discourse analysis, this has raised the issue of the (in)adequacy of purely linguistic models to grasp the complexity of contemporary discourses.

If multimodality is not exclusive to the web, but only heightened by its affordances, hypertextuality is the very innovative trait of web-textuality.[2] According to a well-known definition by Landow (1992, pp. 3-4), hypertext designates "text composed of blocks of text – what Barthes terms a lexia – and the electronic links that join them." It is the presence of electronic links that disrupts the perception of text as something linear, creating what Landow calls 'multilinear or multisequential' texts. According to the same author the term *hypertextuality* is interchangeable with *hypermediality* as in fact web affordances are such that written text is as easily linked to visual content, sound, animation as to other texts properly intended.

Co-articulation and interactivity denote the reader's concurrence to the construction of the text, as the website architecture offers a number of different paths, but it is the user's action which determines the shape (i.e. the contents and their sequentiality) of the text s/he will actually engage with (Garzone, 2007, p. 23). This is all the more true when website visitors shift from the reading to the navigating mode (Finnemann, 1999), with the former corresponding to traditional sequential reading and the latter allowing the user to choose his/her reading path. According to studies of reading on the web, literacy exerts its influence on how websites are experienced by users as the deep-rooted familiarity with the left-right top-down patterns of reading/writing (as far as western cultures are concerned) induces web users to follow a similar route also on websites, referred to as the 'Gutenberg Z' (Lynch & Horton, 2008). In turn readers' habits influence the design of webpages and content distribution within the page compositional plan. However, compositional aspects are just part of the story, as other elements – among which personal interests – may easily prompt departure from suggested paths, making it virtually impossible to pre-establish with certainty what navigation path will be taken by users.

Finally, granularity refers to the fact that Web texts are generally broken into smaller units (lexias) to facilitate reading on the screen, where too long and wide sequences of linear text would not be easily coped with. On the other hand, a possible drawback of such textual organization could be an over-simplification and a fragmentation of reasoning, as pointed out with regard to other electronic genres where space constraints heavily influence the organization of thoughts, as is the case in slideware presentations (Tufte, 2003).

All these factors have limited the author's control on text composition in general, and on the arrangement of arguments (what in classical rhetoric was known as *dispositio*), thus raising questions as to the effectiveness of argumentation in this environment. In particular this concern rests on the assumption that the notion of *dispositio* as intended in classical rhetoric, cannot be 'transferred' to the Web as such, due to the disruption of linearity. However, as shown by Catenaccio (2012) in a review of the literature on this specific issue, there is a consensus among scholars that *dispositio* is not necessarily to be understood as linear, linearity being a constraint imposed by orality and literacy, both relying on a time-based logic (Tapia, 2003). Rhetoric in the era of the

Web should simply fine-tune its tools to meet the requirements of the space-based logic which dominates the webpage (Shauf, 2001).

Further impinging on the traditional understanding of textuality there is fragmentation, which Carter (2003, p. 7) defines as the isolation of units of meaning from their co-text. If in printed documents it is the norm that paragraphs and chapters form coherent relations with preceding and following textual units, which are crucial for text comprehension, on the webpage textual units are reduced to self-contained 'nodes,' 'islands of meaning' which do not depend on each other for interpretation. Truth to tell, this phenomenon is not exclusive to web-born genres. The news story, for example, in its traditional printed form is characterized by a similar textual structure referred to by means of various metaphors such as the inverted pyramid, the satellite structure (for an account of them, see Clark, 2006), or the instalment structure (van Dijk, 1988, p. 15). Whatever the metaphor, the point is that under the pressure of growingly tight news-production schedules, but also as a result of the fast-paced rhythm of contemporary society leaving people with little time for reading newspapers, news-writing has turned towards a specific structure, with paragraphs 'gravitating' around the nucleus (headline and lead, i.e. the first paragraph containing synthetically all the important information), each adding details on one of the aspects therein mentioned, and not depending on neighbouring text units for coherence. In this way news stories can easily be edited rearranging the order of paragraphs or cutting them without prejudice to global meaning, and readers can quit reading at any point after the nucleus, or selectively scan the text, still retaining the gist of the story.

It is to be noted that in the press the instalment (or satellite, or inverted-pyramid) structure works for news stories which are primarily informative, while comment articles and editorials, which are argumentative, still rely on the establishment of more traditional bounds of coherence between paragraphs, which presuppose thorough linear reading of the text. On the web, different strategies must be used for presenting arguments, if affordances therein provided but also limits imposed by online reading are to be taken into consideration. In this respect, Bolter (1991, p. 119) points out that to cope with the multitude of paths allowed by the navigating mode, a 'structure of possibilities' instead of 'a single argument' must be envisaged. Drawing on previous studies (Hovland, 1957; Kolb, 1997; Bernstein, 1998) Carter identifies two macro strategies. One tries to mitigate the effects of the author's loss of control on *dispositio*, and consists in trying to induce a certain 'reading' path of the hypertextual content by leveraging on the effects of primacy (the first things the user encounters is more likely to draw attention), recency (the last thing encountered tends to be more easily remembered) and repetition, so that different routes would lead to the same message (Carter, 2003, p. 8). The other strategy addresses concerns posed by text fragmentation, and basically suggests avoiding separation of the main parts of the argument,[3] i.e. claim and ground (Toulmin, 1969) or, following the pragmadialectical terminology (van Eemeren & Grotendorst, 1992), standpoint and supporting arguments.

All the considerations above on the peculiarity of textuality on the Web imply an implicit comparison against the norm of traditional textuality. Devised well before the massive spread of electronic discourse, research on the standards of textuality (de Beaugrande & Dressler, 1981) was meant to extend the systematic study of language beyond the level of proposition, to identify those factors influencing the production and reception of texts – the privileged unit of meaning in real-life communication, as opposed to isolated sentences that for such a long time had been the focus of linguistic investigation. Central to such a theoretical frame are the text internal notions of cohesion and coherence (while text external factors include intentionality, acceptability, situationality, informativity and intertextuality), which deserve a mention in this section as they will be brought

to bear on the analysis of electronic discourse carried out in the chapter.

One of the most influential accounts of cohesion is Halliday and Hasan's book-length 1976 study (*Cohesion in English*), in which the concept is in fact used to subsume both cohesion and coherence. Few years later, de Beaugrande and Dressler (1981) drew a distinction among them, defining cohesion as grammatical and lexical ties on the *surface* of the text, and coherence as the mutual relevance of concepts *underlying* the text proper:

A text makes sense because there is continuity of senses[4] among the knowledge activated by the expressions of the text. [...] We would define this continuity of senses as the foundation of coherence, being the mutual access and relevance within a configuration of concepts and relations. (V. 2)[5]

Cohesion provides access to coherence, as when processing a text the receiver starts with "parsing the surface text onto a configuration of grammatical dependencies" (V. 24), which activate concepts and relations among them, forming the starting point for the construction of continuity of sense. However, if the notion of cohesion is closely related to the material sequentiality of elements, otherwise lexico-grammatical dependencies would not hold (e.g. a pronoun cannot occur too far from the noun it refers to), coherence does not rest on a chronological linearity. The very language used by the same authors to talk about coherence, incidentally, makes reference to spatial – rather than temporal – metaphors, as seen in the propositions "text users must build up a configuration of *pathways* among [meanings] to create a *textual world*" (V. 22), and "[coherence is] the result of combining concepts and relations into a *network* composed of *knowledge spaces centred around* main topics" (V. 23).

In light of the above, nothing seems to preclude the possibility of applying the notion of coherence to a hypertextual environment, even though conceptual adjustments may be in order to accommodate the original concept to the new context. Here, the issue is how surface elements – including not only the alphabetical stuff of which texts are traditionally made, but also those compositional elements constituting the 'page-as-text' – can be arranged within and across pages to favour the reconstruction of continuity of sense by the user. In a previous study, Degano (2012) has addressed this concern comparing the strategies adopted by two activists' groups on their websites, which from a preliminary survey stood out as two extreme cases: BabyMilk Action campaign against Nestlé (whose central point is a boycott of the company's products), for its 'malpractice' advertising policies in developing countries, and Greenpeace's campaign against genetically engineered food. The former presents a lack of global coherence among the materials assembled on the website, as a result of concomitant factors, among which information overload, lack of compliance with web-writing norms – many texts being simply an electronic version of a printed counterpart – and a failure in exploiting compositional resources. In particular, lower-level pages, where arguments briefly anticipated on the homepage are actually provided, hardly favour the identification of the 'continuity of senses' which is the foundation of coherence: the different lines of defense are haphazardly pursued, mixing – apparently without any superimposed design – the planes of making a case for the boycott, giving information about the campaign and calling people to action. Borrowing Gray's (1995) words on the nature of troubles that users experience in the construction of meaning from hypertexts, the website presented two orders of problems: "those that result from violations of expectations of coherent linear flow and those that result from violation of relevance assumptions" (p. 628).

On the other hand, Greenpeace's campaign against genetically engineered crops pursued successfully the ideal of a 'dynamic coherence planning' (Storrer, 2002), as pages were compositionally and discursively devised to suggest a pattern of reading which reflects a hierarchical organization of issues, from general to particular, thus providing global coherence. Besides, a 'modular' structure was deployed, where each node synthetically featured the core elements of the campaign genre (expressing the standpoint, supporting it through arguments and calling to action), thus warranting local coherence. Furthermore, the same critical discussion, with slight variations, was repeated in more than one node, so that different navigation patterns would lead to the same message.

STUDY DESIGN

Drawing on text linguistics, multimodality, and works on argumentation on the Web developed within computer science as described in the previous section, the issue of how coherence can be conferred upon argumentative hypertexts will be addressed by focussing on activists' campaigns on the Web. A prototypically argumentative activity, being geared towards getting support for a cause, which, at the same time – being generally excluded from mainstream media – has thrived on the web, this appeared an ideal ground for analysis.

As seen in section 2, existing recommendations on how to establish coherence in hypertextual arguments are formulated in rather general terms, without going into the details of practical realizations. The analysis here carried out contributes to filling this gap, thus setting the basis for the creation of a repertoire, which may be put to use for both scholarly and practical purposes. Due to the preliminary character of the investigation, attention will be focussed on just one website, that of Greenpeace's campaign against genetically engineered food, which from a previous study (Degano, 2012, cf. section 2) qualified as a case of best practice. It complies, indeed, with the few general recommendations available for the construction of arguments on the web, managing to strike a balance between allowing for different reading patterns and orienting access to information, so as to maintain global coherence in spite of surface spatial discontinuity.

Resting on qualitative in-depth analysis, the website will be explored following navigation routes, with a view to identifying patterns of coherence and proposing a tentative systematization of them. The results thus yielded will need to be tested against a larger sample in future research stages.

ANALYSIS

In the following sections different patterns of coherence will be identified and discussed, relying on the methodological assumptions outlined above.

Coherence within the Node

The first pattern will be called the 'nutshell' structure, i.e. a text unit which synthetically contains all the elements of an argument in a limited portion of the page suitable for online reading. An example can be found in Figure 1.

In this lexia, opening Greenpeace's campaign against GE in a previous version of the website (accessed in June 2010), a whole argument is enclosed, including the overarching standpoint ("you should say no to GE"), and arguments

Figure 1. Example of 'nutshell' structure (http://www.greenpeace.org. Used with permission.)

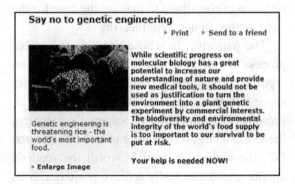

defending it. Reconstructing the text following the pragmadialectical approach (van Eemeren, 2010), it is possible to identify all the four stages of the critical discussion model: the instruction 'say no to genetic engineering' corresponds to the confrontation stage, in which the difference of opinion emerges. The very presence of negation implies that other people do or may take an opposite stand towards the issue. The concessive proposition "While scientific progress on molecular biology has a great potential to increase our understanding of nature and provide new medical tools" pertains to the opening stage, in which a zone of agreement is established between the sender and those receivers who have a positive opinion of GE. Acknowledging that scientific progress on molecular biology may prove valuable for purposes other than the commercialization of genetically engineered food has the function of legitimating the value of scientific research per se, as opposed to research serving commercial interests, thus reducing the space of disagreement to some of the uses to which it is put. Also typical of the opening stage is the establishment of premises which will function as a starting point accepted by both parties to a dispute. Here stating that "the Biodiversity and environmental integrity of the world's food supply is too important to our survival" establishes a premise which will be relied upon in the argumentation stage proper. The argument put forth in support of the standpoint is that genetic engineering puts at risk biodiversity and integrity of the world's food supply (which, as established earlier, are all too important for our survival), an example of the negative pragmatic argument scheme (van Eemeren, Grotendorst, & Snoeck Henkemans, 2002, p. 101), whereby it is claimed that an action should not be taken as it would lead to a certain consequence, and that consequence is undesirable. In this case the scheme is associated also to a rhetorical appeal to fear, as it is claimed that catastrophe would ensue from transforming the environment into a giant genetic experiment, driven by commercial interest. Finally, in light of the elements put forth thus far, the initial point that the addressee should take action against the risks of GE is restated, functioning as a conclusion of a critical discussion meant to resolve the difference of opinion in favor of the protagonist.

This can be considered a maximally coherent *dispositio*, where – as highlighted by the reconstruction above – coherence between the textual components is warranted by adherence to the typical stages of a critical discussion. In other words, the logical relations underpinning global coherence can be expressed as follows: "You should say no to GE *because* it puts biodiversity and environmental integrity at risk, *and* biodiversity and environmental integrity are vital for our survival. *Therefore* your help is needed now."

Cohesive mechanisms are also unproblematic, as the self-containedness of the lexia allows for an easy decoding of internal grammatical and lexical relations. Particularly worthy of notice from the latter point of view is the presence of two opposite semantic areas to which different evaluations are attached, both connected with the field of scientific research. On the one hand there are the positively connoted 'scientific progress,' 'increase understanding of nature,' and 'providing new medical tools, biodiversity and environmental integrity,' and on the other the negatively-assessed 'giant environmental experiment,' and 'commercial interests and risk.' If the notions of cohesion and coherence are extended to include also visual elements, the image accompanying the lexia can be seen as belonging to the positively connoted area, as inferentially the hands of a presumably poor farmer holding rice stand for the simplicity and ancient wisdom of traditional agriculture as opposed to the hazardous genetic engineering experiments driven by the huge commercial interests of multinational corporations in the agricultural industry.

Coherence beyond the Node: The 'Page-as-a-Hub"

All in all, its brevity as well as 'unity of space' (i.e. the arrangement of the content in a single graphical unit) makes the text discussed in section 4.1 similar to its printed, non navigable texts, with lexico-grammatical interdependencies easily processed as they are all retrievable in the lexia. Not so for stretches of text spanning over greater spaces and exploiting hypertextual affordances more fully. An example is provided by Figure 2, which shows the current homepage of the same campaign (last accessed on November 12, 2012).

In this case no main standpoint is explicitly expressed in salient positions: if we consider the headlines of the three lexias featured in the central column ("China says no to genetically engineered rice," "Agriculture campaign" and "Quick facts about agriculture"), none of them has the features of an argumentative thematic-text-base, nor of an instructive one (Werlich, 1983) functioning as a deontic standpoint. The first one, basically an action-recording sentence, qualifies as the text-base of a narrative (for the role of narratives in persuasive discourse see Schubert, 2010), while the second and the third look like the thematic-text-bases of expository text types, in which either a concept is analyzed into its components or discreet elements are related to a superordinate concept. However, alone or jointly with the text associated to them, they all have an argumentative flavor and, on the basis of the user's background knowledge of the campaign as a genre,[6] they can be taken to contribute to making the case for the fight against genetic engineering.

The narrative, in whose headline the verbal process "says [no]" activates the scheme of an argumentative situation, has the function of, so to say, establishing credentials for the campaign: if, presumably as an effect of Greenpeace's campaign, the world's largest consumer of rice has rejected GE, the campaign itself is worth the reader's attention as it can really achieve positive results

Figure 2. Agriculture campaign's homepage (http://www.greenpeace.org. Used with permission.)

(pragmatic argument) and it has already succeeded in persuading a critical portion of public opinion (argument *ad populum*).

In the "Agriculture campaign" box, reading

1. *Greenpeace is campaigning for agriculture that is good for the planet and people. Healthy food grown with the environment — not against it. Farming that helps cope with climate change. Get involved.*

the very concept of campaigning entails a contrast between two social groups, contrast which is further implied by the predicate 'good for the planet and the people,' as under the maxim of relevance (Grice, 1975) this remark will be processed as antithetical to another form of agriculture which is not good for the planet and the people, and by the antithetical structure 'grown with the environment — not against it.'

Here the argument can be reconstructed as "you should get involved in the campaign, because the campaign will lead to a better form of agriculture,

and such a result is desirable," corresponding again to the pragmatic scheme.

Finally, the bullet list beneath, (see excerpt 2), is not factual at all, being in fact the most explicitly confrontational content of the page. What it presents is a list of arguments against genetic engineering and more generally polluting industrial agriculture:

2. *Quick facts about agriculture*
    *   *Ten corporations control nearly 70 percent of the world's seed market. This corporate control of agriculture means farmers have less choice.*
    *   *Genetic Engineering does not feed the world. 99.5 percent of farmers around the world do not grow Genetically Engineered crops.*
    *   *Industrial polluting agriculture uses synthetic fertilizers and toxic chemicals which pollute our water and soils – the very things we need in order to provide healthy food now and in the future.*

- *Excessive use of synthetic fertilizers in industrial polluting agriculture contributes to climate change.*

As one discovers navigating through lower levels in the website architecture, these arguments recur throughout the pages: the concentration of market control in the hands of few corporations, with the consequent reduction of differentiation in the offer, and the massive recourse to chemical fertilizers and pesticides which apart from polluting soil and water negatively affect climate change, are other examples of pragmatic arguments, while the remark about the very limited grasp of GE on farmers world wide is a negative form of *ad pupulum* reasoning: if 99.5% of farmers do not grow GE crops, then GE crops are not valuable per se.

These and other information bits discussed earlier are all related to the overarching standpoint that the commercialization of genetically engineered crops must be stopped – what Storrer (2002, p. 4) calls 'global coherence' – but are not immediately coherent with one another, i.e. in terms of 'local coherence.' For example, the bulleted 'facts' reported in the bottom box do not show high interdependency with the agriculture campaign box above it, contrary to what a conservative approach to web reading, transferring here linearity expectations, might suggest. The reasons against GE are in a way the premises justifying the campaign, but are not the campaign itself, so this part can hardly be seen as a continuation of the preceding lexia. In other words, local coherence does not seem a concern for the website author, who apparently relies on the assumption that the user will make allowances for the loosening of ties between neighbouring parts of a text, provided a tenuous topical continuity is warranted, in so far as expectations of continuity of sense (de Beaugrande & Dressler, 1981, V.1) are met elsewhere in the website, by means of links and navigation buttons. In this sense this page seems to be designed as a 'navigation hub' (a term commonly used in the field of web design, which once again rests on a space-based metaphor), displaying contents which are meant to attract the attention of the reader so as to induce him/her to explore deeper levels of the website. At the same time, the variety of information provided on this first page manages to convey at least some arguments against GE which will reach the user even if s/he decides to quit reading at this point.

From a compositional point of view, the central feature story (China says no to GE rice) has good chances of attracting attention: it is the first meaningful cluster of information the visitor encounters, occupying almost entirely the so-called golden triangle, i.e. the upper-left part of the page which, according to studies of navigation preferences, receives greatest notice in western cultures, due to the deeply-rooted influence of left-to-right, top-down progression of reading and writing.[7] Apart from that, the presence of a large glossy picture, and the possibility for the user to take action, i.e. to click on the link or change picture and story using a progression bar in the bottom-left of the picture, increases its potential as an entry point (cf. Garret, 2000). At the same time the prospect of reading a story may be more enticing than a bullet list of arguments for some readers, especially for those who bump into the website without having a strong stake with the issue.

As already pointed out, the narrative here presented has a function in the overarching argumentative speech act performed by the website. However, formally, the text follows the scheme of a narrative text type, and particularly of the feature article, a press genre typically published in magazines sitting between the news story and the comment article, concerning topics which are not so timely as in news stories, and following a sequential flow of reasoning (Pape & Featherstone, 2006), as opposed to the satellite structure of news stories. More than argumentative texts, narrative forms rely on time as an organizational principle, and in text grammar, the narrative text-type is associated with a focus on phenomena in the temporal context (Werlich, 1983, p. 19). This is not to say that coherence in narrative text types is necessarily linear: suffice it to think of the well established difference between the time of the story and the time of narration, the former being necessarily subject to a chronological order, while the second can depart from it with flashbacks, anticipations, to and from leaks in time. However, it is interesting to observe how a narrative text is embedded in a website whose compositional plan is dominated by space-bound logics. The title on the feature story 'China says no to GE rice' gives access to the page shown in Figure 3.

Like the campaign's homepage discussed above, also this one works as a 'hub' in the information architecture of the website, as it does not itself host the story but contains links to parts of it, which taken together form a complete and coherent unit of meaning, but will have to be accessed singularly to get the whole of it. The current page, however, differs from the previous one as all the modules[8] in the page frame cling together to convey a continuity of sense which makes the sequence highly coherent.

From a compositional point of view, the page accommodates the reading habits of the average western user, as the story starts with the larger module displayed on the left and unfolds throughout the smaller modules on the right. As can be noticed from Figure 3, three alternative entry-points have been designed, all leading to the beginning of the feature story: the headline on the big picture, the identical text repeated in the first module of the right column and the 'read more' link placed at the end of the short lexia below the big picture (whose content can be read in excerpt 3). The latter, like the lead in news stories and the introduction in comment articles, is meant to wet the reader's appetite, so as to induce him/her to continue with the story.

Incidentally, the repetition of the link leading to the beginning of the story in the right column is quite revealing in terms of the rationale behind the general compositional plan: had the aim simply been to provide access to the lower-level content, two entry points would have probably been enough. The repetition of the module in the right column seems thus to serve a different purpose in the new context, namely that of enhancing the perception of continuity and progression of the story, in spite of its being chunked into bits on the surface. On lower-level pages, where the story is actually told, the sense of progression is further conveyed by the bidirectional arrow displayed in Figure 4, which explicitly shows the user what comes before and after the current chunk.

Figure 3. Entry-points to a feature story (http://www.greenpeace.org. Used with permission.)

Figure 4. Graphical indication of sequentiality (http://www.greenpeace.org. Used with permission.)

Besides graphical elements, coherence is imposed on this sequence also through the alphabetical text, although to work effectively this presupposes the reader's familiarity with another genre, i.e. the fairy tale, impinging then on the mediating function of intertextuality (cf. endnote vi). Drawing on Propp's (1928) model of the folk tale structure, the following sequences can be identified here: in module 1 [*How Greenpeace got China to say no to GE rice. The beginning of an epic battle to keep GE rice out*], genetically engineered rice is the complicating element which disrupts the initial calm. Worthy of notice is the use of the hyperbolic expression 'epic battle,' which echoes the hero vs villain antagonistm that lies at the heart of the fairy tale itself. Module 2 and 3 [respectively *Web of deceit. The complex web of player involved in the push to commercialize GE rice* and *When the scientists are the bad guys. In china the bad guys were on a government*

board] correspond to the sections devoted to the difficulties met by the hero and his/her battle against the antagonist. In the latter, familiarity with the fairy-tale mental model is implied also by the use of grammatical reference with the definite article "*the* bad guys" presupposing that someone must fill the 'antagonist' slot in the fairy-tale role scheme. Finally, in cluster 4 [*Better, brighter, GE-free future. Why the next 5-10 years is forecast for sunny days*] the solution comes, thanks to the help of an (unexpected) assistant, order is re-established and a bright future is announced, again in a conscious mimic of the fairy tale happy-end cliché.

Moving to the story itself, text analysis reveals that as well as being highly coherent (both locally and globally) the text presents also a fair degree of cohesion with lexico-grammatical ties stretching across pages.

The very first lines of the story, displayed in the lexia beneath the main picture (see Figure 3) introduce the protagonists of the story – *one* bald guy, *one* determined Swiss woman etc. –, treating them as new information, as signalled by the use of the indeterminate article:

3.   *It took seven years, one bald guy, one determined swiss woman and successive teams of young campaigners but finally late September 2011 Bejing said it was suspending the commercialization of genetically-engineered (GE) rice. Here's a historical look at one of our earliest - and most successful campaigns – in East Asia.*

In the next lower-level page, the battle against GE rice in China, occupying the theme position, is presented as given information, on account of its being introduced in the previous pages, and the protagonist becomes '*the* bald guy,' with the determinate article marking a shift of status in the information structure.

4.   *The fight [given] to keep GE rice out of China is one that can be traced back to the beginnings of Greenpeace in Mainland China itself. And it's a story that encapsulates much of what Greenpeace stands for: Even with the most formidable of opponents, from both government and industry, positive change can be achieved.*
First let's introduce the bald guy [given]. He's 38-year-old Sze Pang Cheung, also known as Kontau (which means bald in Cantonese). He's now the Campaign Director of Greenpeace East Asia.

Apart from creating interdependency with the immediately higher-level content, the page's incipit (excerpt 4) just discussed provides also an anchorage to the macro argumentative speech act accomplished by the campaign's website, making it explicit that the feature story has an exemplary function ("it's a story that encapsulates much of what Greenpeace stands for: Even with the most formidable of opponents, from both government and industry, positive change can be achieved"), and is therefore a variant of the symptomatic argumentative scheme (see van Eemeren et al., 2002, p. 96). The core argumentation structure introduced on the campaign's homepage is thus enriched with a further level of arguments (taking the form of what van Eemeren, Grotendorst, & Snoeck Hankemans, [1996] call subordinate argumentation, where arguments are brought in support of other arguments) which can be reconstructed as seen in Figure 5.

This also leads to a more general consideration on how an argumentation structure builds-up on the web: the core of the critical discussion[9] is immediately conveyed on the home page, consisting of the main standpoint (in the case of NGOs' campaigns an exhortation for the reader to get involved in the campaign, if only by adhering to the positions therein upheld) and at least a general supporting argument (which in the case of NGO's campaigns is likely to rest on the pragmatic argument scheme). Subsequent pages, which

Figure 5. Reconstruction of argumentation

may contain repetitions of the core components, generally add up new elements (starting points or new arguments) which the user, irrespectively of the local position in the website information structure, will remotely connect to the core of the main critical discussion, i.e. standpoint and main argument(s). In this way temporary configurations of interconnected topics come into being only to 'dissolve' with the next click. In other words, each visitor will be espoused to contents generating different argumentative structures, depending on the path followed, but whatever the route, the main idea – al least – is conveyed, and hopefully a residual track of the individual arguments encountered during the website exploration will be retained.

The first part of the story (How Greenpeace got China to say no to GE rice. The beginning of an epic battle to keep GE rice out) concludes with a 'hook' to the next part of it, anticipating the obstacles met by the hero in the pursuit of the final goal, which will be dealt with more extensively in the next section of the story (Web of deceit):

5. *But just as they were about to head south, the team got some bad news. Chinese scientists had applied to commercialize four varieties of Chinese GE rice. [...]*

At the bottom of the page, a box is displayed (Figure 6), which is clearly set apart from the continuity of sense tying up the sections of the story, and provides reasons for taking on genetic engineering.

In argumentation theory this lexia would qualify as a premise, i.e. information that – whether taken for granted of explicitly negotiated – conceptually (and not necessarily sequentially) comes prior to argumentation proper, and has the function of creating a sufficient zone of agreement between the parties to a discussion, on which the subsequent effort to win the other party's adherence of mind will rest. In other words it aims to bridge a possible gap between the writer's and the receiver's knowledge and beliefs system, so as to reach a common starting point. Here of course if someone does not share the view that genetically engineering is dangerous, in no way will s/he commit to (i.e. accept) the claim that the campaign is worth joining. Furthermore, should a user choose this page as the beginning of this path, having ignored the previous ones, the box provides a rationale against which the narrative can make sense.

The Analytic Path

So far the analysis has concerned the creation of coherence among contents occupying a central position on the page. This section will consider a peripheral navigation area, located in the right-hand column, i.e. a navigation menu where each link prompts the display of further links to sub-directories, thus giving rise to a complex hierarchy of contents structured analytically, i.e.

Figure 6. Bottom-page box (http://www.greenpeace.org. Used with permission.)

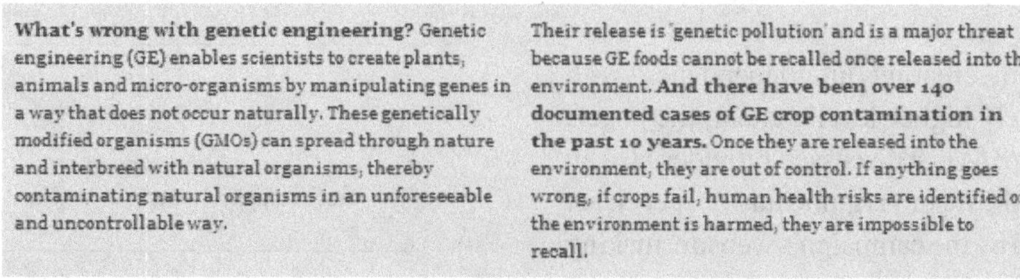

What's wrong with genetic engineering? Genetic engineering (GE) enables scientists to create plants, animals and micro-organisms by manipulating genes in a way that does not occur naturally. These genetically modified organisms (GMOs) can spread through nature and interbreed with natural organisms, thereby contaminating natural organisms in an unforeseeable and uncontrollable way.

Their release is 'genetic pollution' and is a major threat because GE foods cannot be recalled once released into the environment. And there have been over 140 documented cases of GE crop contamination in the past 10 years. Once they are released into the environment, they are out of control. If anything goes wrong, if crops fail, human health risks are identified or the environment is harmed, they are impossible to recall.

Figure 7. Expandable menu (http://www.greenpeace.org. Used with permission.)

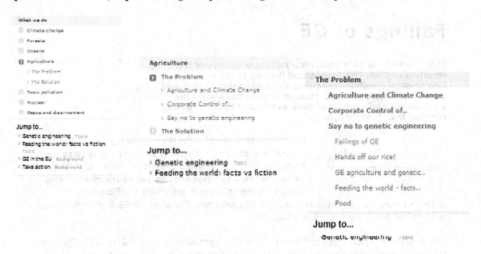

with superordinate concepts divided into smaller constitutive parts (Werlich, 1983). Initially only few links appear (see Figure 7, left column), grouped under the headings *What we do,* which presents the different campaigns promoted by Greenpeace, including the one on Agriculture investigated in this chapter, and *Jump to...* which directs to selected highlights, accessible also from other paths. The 'Agriculture' link is structured in *The problem* and *The solution*, thus explicitly referring to the cognitive function of the argumentative text-type: judging in answer to a problem (Werlich, 1983, p. 40).

The problem is further divided into three navigation links (Figure 7, center column): *Agriculture and climate change, Corporate control of agriculture* and *Say no to genetic engineering,* which restate and expand the arguments presented on the agriculture campaign's homepage against genetic engineering and 'polluting' agriculture in general. Their content is arranged hierarchically in a number of sub-directories, links to which become available as the user descends in the information architecture, as shown in Figure 7 (right column). These links also provide an indication as to the position of the currently dis-

played page in the immediate hypertextual context, thanks to the repetition of the headline, with a function similar to that performed by a table of content in a book or magazine.

"Click-depth," i.e. the number of clicks needed to reach a content (Lynch & Horton, 2008), is here directly proportional to informativity,[10] as it generally takes several clicks to reach the arguments which concludes the defense of the standpoint. For example, if we consider the climate change argument, a causal relation between polluting agriculture and climate change itself is already established on the home page, but it is only several 'clicks' later that one finds a satisfactory explanation for such a relation:

6. *Agriculture and Climate Change: Sources of Pollution*
   What, exactly, are the sources of the human-caused greenhouse gas emissions in agriculture? Apart from deforestation and other land use changes, it is mainly synthetic fertilizers and livestock that emit nitrous oxide and methane, potent greenhouse gases.
   Approximately half of agricultural emissions come from livestock and meat production.

Figure 8. Example of inverted-pyramid structure (http://www.greenpeace.org)

Failings of GE

2003 marked the 50th anniversary of the discovery of the structure of DNA. This highlighted the fact that many fundamental questions regarding the functioning of DNA and genes remain unanswered. Modern science has shown the mechanisms and controls of gene expression to be far more complex than first thought.

On this page
GE Crude and Old Fashioned
GE Chronology
Illustrating the problems of genetic engineering

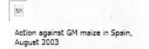

Action against GM maize in Spain,
August 2003

The fundamental basis for genetic engineering (GE) is a theory or 'dogma' that dates from the 1950s and is now considered over-simplistic. GE is a crude and old fashioned technology which has lead to the many surprises and unexpected effects associated with GE organisms. As such the effects of GE crops on the environment and human health cannot be reliably predicted. Therefore, no GE organisms should be released into the environment or the food chain.

This collection of documents was prepared for the DNA anniversary on April 25th 2003. They detail the underlying scientific basis for Greenpeace's campaign to prevent deliberate releases of GE organisms to the environment.

GE Crude and Old Fashioned
This document is a scientific review of changes in the understanding of the complexity of gene

The average amount of fossil-fuel energy needed to produce calories in meat is roughly ten times higher than the energy needed to produce calories in plants.

The website designer's assumption here seems to be that curiosity will push the reader further until s/he finds a satisfactory explanation for what is stated in higher-rank pages, in a sort of delayed disclosure. However, this risks being a somewhat presumptive assumption as the ever-expanding number of subdirectories might discourage the user to get to the 'end of the story,' or more appropriately in this case to the 'killer argument.'

The Inverted-Pyramid Structure

The risk of excessive delay is pre-empted in the structure shown in Figure 8, which introduces the last pattern of coherence discussed in this chapter:

This page's layout is reminiscent of online newspapers, with a headline, a lead (in bold face) and several paragraphs clearly separated from one-another. The main point here is that "many fundamental questions regarding the functioning of DNA and genes remain unanswered" as our understanding of DNA is in too early a stage, in which errors are still very common. Therefore (and this is the unexpressed standpoint, or conclusion) current scientific knowledge on GE crops cannot reliably rule out dangers for the human being and the environment.

This reasoning is already conveyed by the lead, while the first paragraph simply expands on that, making some of the inferences activated in the link explicit: the foundation of genetic engineering (a rephrasing of 'the discovery of DNA' mentioned in the lead) is defined as a dogma more than as a theory, to signify that it has not been demonstrated scientifically. The lack of reliable knowledge has led to "many surprises and unexpected effects associated with GE organisms," and on this ground, the effects of GE organisms on human health and the environment cannot be reliably assessed. In light of all these elements, it is concluded, GE crops must not be released into the environment. Further arguments in support of the ones here presented are made available in pdf documents, leaving to the reader the choice of whether exploring them or not.

It should be noted that this textual organization is similar to the inverted-pyramid structure typical of newspaper stories: the basic information is fed all at once at the very beginning of the story, so that even if reading is quit early, the core message is nonetheless conveyed. While a single example does not warrant generalizations, should further research confirm that this is not an isolated case, the satellite/inverted pyramid structure would cease being exclusive to the news story, marking an important shift in our mental model of how an argumentative piece of writing should be organized on its surface. As for underlying ties pertaining to coherence, no major changes would be implied, as even in linear texts these are imposed independently of what is materially printed out, much resting on inferences which are not linguistically codified.

FUTURE RESEARCH DIRECTIONS

The analysis carried out here and in previous works by the same author (Degano, forth.a; forth.b) contributes to the ongoing debate on the textuality of electronic discourse, which is just in its early stages. Further research may develop into different directions. First of all, the patterns of coherence here tentatively identified should be validated against a larger sample of websites geared to influencing people's beliefs and behaviour by making appeal to their rationality, so as to refine and expand the repertoire of strategies used to compensate for the loss of linearity. Parallel to this descriptive concern, research should aim to test the results of qualitative analysis in experimental settings, in order to gain evidence on how people actually impose coherence on web and other computer-mediated electronic contents, and eventually establish standards of best practice. This latter strand of research presupposes a multidisciplinary approach where discourse analysts work jointly with cognitive psychologists, following in the thread of a similar research endeavour pursued in the Seventies with regard to traditional texts (cf. e.g. Kintch & van Dijk, 1978). Furthermore, the issue of how coherence (and relevance at large) work in electronic discourse should be explored also with regard to more genuinely dialectical genres, where two or more parties are actively involved in deliberation activities.

Following a second thread, investigation may address more squarely the impact of multimodality – the other macroscopic distinguishing trait of Web's textuality – on argumentative discourse, drawing on the existing literature on visual arguments and visual rhetoric at large (Birdsell & Groarke, 1996; Groarke, 2002; Foss, 2005). In so far as images are regaining pace in the digital era, thus determining a new balance between visual and verbal semiotic modes, it is reasonable to expect that argumentative discourse makes no exception. Yet, the possibility of transferring the analytic categories of argumentative discourse from verbal to visual semiotic systems is an issue of debate, which is far from being settled. Furthermore research on this issue may contribute to shedding light on the all too relevant issue of how literacy is changing in contemporary society.

CONCLUSION

Drawing on categories devised for traditional linear textuality as well as on previous works of textuality on the web, the analysis here carried out has explored how coherence is created in the multilinear, user-coarticulated hypertextual and multimodal discourse of the Web.

Focusing in particular on argumentative discourse – here epitomized by an NGO's online campaign – as a text type that more than others have traditionally impinged on the time-based logic of sequential linear flow of reasoning, the study has addressed the issue of how the disruption of such mono-directional progression can be coped with in website argumentation.

In light of the analysis carried out here, it can be concluded that while the mechanisms at work for the construction of coherence on a website are not qualitatively different from those that hold for the construction of coherence in traditional texts (after all the cognitive function presiding over arguing is one and the same, and notions like grammatical interdependency and continuity of sense hold here as well as in printed documents), differences lie in the intensity of relevance ties between physically adjacent contents. These tend to be significantly looser on the web, where relations of mutual accessibility among concepts tend to form 'vertical' threads, activated by the user as s/he navigates through the web, which are 'transversal' (cf. Lemke, 2001) to the levels of the website's information architecture. In the specific case of argumentative discourse such a process of coherence construction is all the more akin to what happens when the structure of argumentation is reconstructed analytically, collocating individual bits of the linear text into a diagram of hierarchically organized relations between standpoints, arguments supporting standpoints, and other arguments that in turn support them.

Caution must be taken by the designer of a website with a prevalently argumentative function as to how elements are distributed within and across pages and levels to favour and guide, as much as possible, the identification of such threads of continuity by users, whatever the route they will follow. In particular, in the course of this analysis, four patterns have been identified for the creation of coherence, accounting for portions of text that range from circumscribed lexias to the page and beyond.

The simplest pattern, referred to as the *nutshell* structure, is a self-contained node which includes a complete though synthetic critical discussion, comprehensive of standpoints and arguments (cf. endnote [iii]), posing no problems at all in terms of coherence reconstruction on the part of the reader.

On the other hand, space constraints impose a trade-off in terms of the quantity of information that can be 'squeezed' into it, thus allowing only for reasoning that is not too complex.

The *page-as-a-hub* pattern is far more complex, characterized as it is by a multitude of contents that are only tenuously related to one another, each establishing in fact a closer dependency with the overarching campaign's standpoint. If it is a homepage that features this structure, it contains only an argumentative core, comprising the main standpoint and at least one supporting argument, while the greatest part of the argumentation develops throughout lower levels. These will add elements to the argumentative structure, which will be directly connected with the argumentative core (thus contributing to the construction of global coherence) and possibly, but not necessarily, to 'neighbouring' parts of the text (local coherence), giving rise to volatile argumentative structures which change as the user moves through the website.

The *analytic* pattern, here found in a peripheral area of the page template, rests on a hierarchy of directories and subdirectories, accessible through a list of logically structured links, in which larger concepts are divided into smaller concepts following a general-to-particular rationale. Here local coherence is quite strong, but so is the risk of excessive distance (measurable in click-depth) between the beginning and the end of the chunked sequence, to the point that the reader might desist from the purpose of getting to the end.

Finally, in the *inverted pyramid* argumentative pattern, content is made available in instalments, following in the track of a well-established practice in news and web writing, where all the basic pieces of information are given at the beginning of the story (in the lead), with details provided in subsequent paragraphs which depend directly on the lead rather than on neighbouring units of meaning. In this analysis such a structure has been identified on lower pages, corresponding to lower arguments in a subordinative argumentation structure, with the point which is being made summarized in a sort of lead, placed at the beginning of the story and in bold face for greater emphasis, and expanded upon in the subsequent paragraphs.

Fundamental is also the role of intertextuality, (the reliance on user's background knowledge of textual organization models) as it exerts a mediating function in the process of imposing coherence on the graphically separated bits of discourse concurring to the global meaning. So, for example, even though no explicit standpoint is formulated on the homepage, where only arguments are present, a user who is familiar with the campaign as an argumentative genre that makes the case against some practice judged dangerous or morally wrong will be able to infer that there must be a standpoint and to relate all the relevant individual bits of content to that.

To conclude, while the repertoire of possible patterns of coherence in argumentative texts presented in this chapter is not meant to be exhaustive, nor does it allow for generalizations, it shows that there are several strategies for constructing argumentatively effective texts on the Web. Further light on the fundamental issue of whether and how computer-mediated communication is changing our discursive competence might come from multidisciplinary research drawing together linguists, cognitivists and web-designers.

REFERENCES

Askehave, I., & Ellerup Nielsen, A. (2004). Web-mediated genres – A challenge to traditional genre theory. *Working Paper nr. 6* (pp. 1-50). Aarhus: Cenre for Virksomhedscommunication.

Askehave, I., & Ellerup Nielsen, A. (2005). Digital genres: A challenge to traditional genre theory. *IT & People, 18*(2), 120–141. doi:10.1108/09593840510601504.

Bernstein, M. (1998). Patterns of hypertext. [Pittsburgh: Association of Computing Machinery.]. *Proceedings of Hypertext, 98*, 21–29.

Birdsell, D., & Groarke, L. (1996). Toward a theory of visual arguments. *Argumentation and Advocacy, 33*, 1–10.

Bolter, J. D. (1991). Topographic writing: Hypertext and the electronic writing space. In Delany, P., & Landow, G. P. (Eds.), *Hypermedia and literary studies* (pp. 105–118). Cambridge, MA: MIT.

Bolter, J. D. (2001). *Writing space: The computer, hypertext, and the history of writing* (2nd ed.). Hillsdale, NJ: Lawrence Erlbaum.

Carter, L. M. (2000). Arguments in hypertext: A rhetorical approach. In F. M. Shipman, P. J. Nürnberg, & D. L. Hicks (Eds.), *Proceedings of the Eleventh ACM on Hypertext and Hypermedia* (pp. 85-91). New York: ACM.

Carter, L. M. (2003). Argument in hypertext: Writing strategies and the problem of order in a non-sequential world. *Computers and Composition, 20*, 3–22. doi:10.1016/S8755-4615(02)00176-7.

Catenaccio, P. (2012). *Networked dispositio: A preliminary investigation of hypermodal resource deployment for argument building on the web*. Paper presented at the ESSE Conference, Istanbul.

Clark, C. (2006). *Views in the news*. Milano: Led Edizioni Universitarie.

De Beaugrande, R. A., & Dressler, W. U. (1981). *An introduction to text linguistics*. London: Longman. Retrieved August 4, 2012, from http://beaugrande.com/introduction_to_text_linguistics.htm

Degano, C. (2012). Argumentative genres on the Web: the case of two NGOs' campaigns. In Campagna, S., Garzone, G., Ilie, C., & Rowley-Jolivet, E. (Eds.), *Evolving genres in Web-mediated communication* (pp. 97–124). Bern: Peter Lang.

Finnemann, N. O. (1999). *Hypertext and the representational capacities of the binary alphabet.* Retrieved February, 2005, from www.hum.au.dk/ckulturf/ pages/publications/nof/hypertext.htm

Foss, S. (2005). *Handbook of visual communication: Theory, methods, and media.* Mahwa, NJ: Lawrence Erlbaum.

Fritz, G. (1998). Coherence in hypertext. In Wolfram, B., Lenk, U., & Ventola, E. (Eds.), *Coherence in spoken and written discourse: How to create it and how to describe it* (pp. 221–234). Amsterdam: John Benjamins.

Garret, J. J. (2000). *The elements of user experience. User-centered design for the web.* New Riders Publishing. Retrieved August 18, 2012, from http://www.jjg.net/elements/

Garzone, G. (1997). Osservazioni sul valore pedagogico dell'ipertesto. In Schena, L., & Garzone, G. (Eds.), *Il computer al servizio degli insegnamenti linguistici, Milano 28.4.1995 - 3.5.1996* (pp. 21–39). Milan: Centro Linguistico Università Bocconi.

Garzone, G. (2007). Genres, multimodality and the world-wide web: Theoretical issues. In Garzone et al., 15-30.

Garzone, G. E., Catenaccio, P., & Poncini, G. (Eds.). (2007). *Multimodality in corporate communication. Web genres and discursive identity.* Milano: Franco Angeli.

Gray, S. H. (1995). Linear coherence and relevance: Logic in computer-human 'conversations.'. *Journal of Pragmatics, 23,* 627–647. doi:10.1016/0378-2166(94)00039-H.

Grice, H. P. (1975). Logic and conversation. In Cole, P., & Morgan, J. L. (Eds.), *Syntax and semantics* (pp. 41–58). New York: Academic Press.

Groarke, L. (2002). Towards a pragma-dialectics of visual arguments. In van Eemeren, F. H. (Ed.), *Advances in pragma-dialectics* (pp. 137–151). Amsterdam: Sic Sat.

Halliday, M. A. K., & Hasan, R. (1976). *Cohesion in English.* London: Longman.

Hovland, C. I. (1957). *The order of presentation in persuasion.* New Haven: Yale UP.

Kintsch, W., & van Dijk, T. A. (1978). Toward a model of text comprehension and production. *Psychological Review, 85*(5), 363–393. doi:10.1037/0033-295X.85.5.363.

Kolb, D. (1997). Scholarly hypertext: Self-represented complexity. In M. Bernstein & L. Carr (Eds.), Proceedings of Hypertext '97 (pp. 247-268). Southhampton: Association of Computing Machinery.

Kress, G. (2003). *Literacy in the media age.* London, New York: Routledge. doi:10.4324/9780203164754.

Kress, G., & van Leeuwen, T. (2006). *Reading images: The grammar of visual design.* New York: Routledge.

Landow, G. P. (1992). *Hypertext: The convergence of contemporary critical theory and technology.* Baltimore: Johns Hopkins University Press.

Lemke, J. L. (2001). *Towards a theory of traversals.* Retrieved August 4, 2012, from http://academic.brooklyn.cuny.edu/education/jlemke/papers/traversals/traversal-theory.htm

Lynch, P., & Horton, S. (2008). *Web style guide online* (3rd ed.). Yale University. Retrieved August 18, 2012, from http://webstyleguide.com/

Nielsen, J. (2006). *F-shaped pattern for reading web content.* Retrieved August 4, 2012, from http://www.useit.com/alertbox/ reading_pattern.html

Pape, S., & Featherstone, S. (2006). *Feature writing. A practical introduction.* London: Sage.

Propp, V. Y. (1928). *Morfologiya skazki*. Leningrad: Akademija.

Schubert, C. (2010). Narrative sequences in political discourse: Forms and functions in speeches and hypertext frameworks. In Hoffmann, C. R. (Ed.), *Narrative revisited. Telling a story in the age of new media* (pp. 143–162). Amsterdam, Philadelphia: John Benjamins.

Shauf, M. (2001). The problem of electronic argument: a humanist's perspective. *Computers and Composition, 18*, 33–37. doi:10.1016/S8755-4615(00)00046-3.

Storrer, A. (2002). Coherence in text and hypertext. (Preprint). Then published in *Document design*. Retrieved May 2009, from http://www.hytext.info

Tapia, A. (2003). Graphic design in the digital era: The rhetoric of hypertext. *Design Issues, 19*(1), 5–24. doi:10.1162/074793603762667665.

Tosca, S. P. (2000). A pragmatics of links. *Journal of Digital Information, 1*(6). Retrieved May 2009, from http://journals.tdl.org/jodi/article/viewArticle/23/24

Toulmin, S. E. (1969). *The uses of argument*. Cambridge: Cambridge University Press.

Tufte, E. R. (2003). *The cognitive style of power point*. Cheshire, CT: Graphics Press LIC.

van Dijk, T. A. (1988). *News analysis*. Hillsdale, London: Lawrence Erlbaum Associates.

van Eemeren, F. H. (2010). *Strategic manoeuvring in argumentative discourse: Extending the pragma-dialectical theory of argumentation*. Amsterdam: John Benjamins.

van Eemeren, F. H., & Grootendorst, R. (1992). *Argumentation, communication, and fallacies: A pragma-dialectical perspective*. Hillsdale, NJ: Lawrence Erlbaum Associates.

van Eemeren, F. H., Grootendorst, R., & Snoeck Henkemans, F. (1996). *Fundamentals of argumentation theory: A handbook of historical background and contemporary developments*. Mahwah, NJ: Erlbaum.

van Eemeren, F. H., Grootendorst, R., & Snoeck Henkemans, F. (2002). *Argumentation: Analysis, evaluation, presentation*. Mahwah, NJ: Lawrence Erlbaum Associates.

Werlich, E. (1983). *A text grammar of English*. Heidelberg: Quelle und Meyer.

ADDITIONAL READING

Aakhus, M., & Jackson, S. (2005). Technology, interaction, and design. In Fitch, K. L., & Sanders, R. E. (Eds.), *Handbook of language and social interaction* (pp. 411–436). Mahwah, NJ: Lawrence Erlbaum.

Chuy, A. M., & Rondelli, F. (2010). Traitement des contraintes linguistiques et cognitives dans la construction de la cohérence textuelle. *Langages, 177*(1), 83–111. doi:10.3917/lang.177.0083.

Graesser, A. C., Singer, M., & Trabasso, T. (1994). Constructing inferences during narrative text comprehension. *Psychological Review, 101*(3), 371–395. doi:10.1037/0033-295X.101.3.371 PMID:7938337.

Hoey, M. (2001). Signalling in discourse: A functional analysis of a common discourse pattern in written and spoken English. In Coulthard, M. (Ed.), *Advances in written text analysis* (pp. 26–45). London: Routledge.

Hoey, M. (2001). *Textual interaction: An introduction to written discourse analysis*. London: Routledge.

Hoffmann, C. (2012). *Cohesive profiling. Meaning and interaction in personal weblogs*. Amsterdam, Philadelphia: Benjamins.

Hutchby, I. (2001). *Conversation and technology: From the telephone to the Internet*. Cambridge, UK: Polity.

Jackson, S. (1998). Disputation by design. *Argumentation*, *12*(2), 183–198. doi:10.1023/A:1007743830491.

Kolb, D. (1997). *Socrates in the labyrinth: Hypertext, argument, philosophy*. Watertown, MA: Eastgate System.

Lemke, J. L. (2002). Travels in hypermodality. *Visual Communication*, *1*(3), 299–325. doi:10.1177/147035720200100303.

Lemke, J. L. (2005). Multimedia genres and traversals. *Folia Linguistica, 39*(1, 2), 45-56.

Martin, J. R. (1994). Macro-genres: The ecology of the page. *Network, 21*, 29–52.

Perleman, C., & Olbrects-Tyteca, L. (1969). The new rhetoric. A treatise on argumentation. Paris: Notre Dame. (original: Traité de l'Argumentation. La nouvelle Rhétorique Paris. Paris: Presses Universitaires de France, 1958).

Petroni, S. (2011). *Language in the multimodal web domain*. Rome: Aracne.

Plantin, C. (1999). Arguing emotions. In F. H. van Eemeren, R. Grotendorst, A. J. Blair, & C. A. Willard (Eds.), *Proceedings of the Fourth International Conference of the International Society for the Study of Argumentation* (pp. 631-638). Amsterdam: SicSat.

Plantin, C. (2004). On the inseparability of reason and emotion in argumentation. In Weigand, E. (Ed.), *Emotion in dialogic interaction* (pp. 269–281). London: Benjamins.

Prakken, H. (2005). AI and law, logic and argumentation schemes. *Argumentation, 19*, 303–320. doi:10.1007/s10503-005-4418-7.

Santini, M. (2007). Characterizing genres of web pages: Genre hybridism and individualization. In *Proceedings of the 40th Hawaii International Conference on System Sciences*. Retrieved September 2, 2012, from http://origin-www.computer.org/csdl/proceedings/hicss/2007/2755/00/27550071.pdf

Snoeck Henkemans, A. F. (1992). *Analysing complex argumentation: The reconstruction of multiple and coordinatively compound argumentation in a critical discussion*. Amsterdam: SicSat.

van Eemeren, F. H. (1990). The study of argumentation as normative pragmatics. *Text: An Interdisciplinary Journal for the Study of Discourse, 10*, 37–44.

van Eemeren, F. H., Grootendorst, R., Jackson, S., & Jacobs, S. (1993). *Reconstructing argumentative discourse. Studies in rhetoric and communication*. Tuscaloosa: The University of Alabama Press.

van Eemeren, F. H., & Houtlosser, P. (2005). Theoretical construction and argumentative reality: An analytic model of critical discussion and conventionalised types of argumentative activity. In D. Hitchcock (Ed.), *The uses of argument: Proceedings of a Conference at Mcmaster University* (pp. 75-84). Hamilton: OSSA.

Verhoeven, L., & Perfetti, C. (2008). Advances in text comprehension: Model, process and development. *Applied Cognitive Psychology, 22*, 293–301. doi:10.1002/acp.1417.

Walton, D., Reed, C., & Macagno, F. (2008). *Argumentation schemes*. Cambridge: Cambridge University Press. doi:10.1017/CBO9780511802034.

Weger, H. Jr, & Aakhus, M. (2003). Arguing in Internet chat rooms: Argumentative adaptations to chat room design and some consequences for public deliberation at a distance. *Argumentation and Advocacy, 40*(1), 23–38.

KEY TERMS AND DEFINITIONS

Activists' Discourse: The expression is used here to refer to the discursive practices of groups and organizations that pursue political or social change, by means of activities geared towards raising audience awareness and changing citizens' behaviour.

Argumentation: Discursive activity meant to defend a standpoint against real or potential criticism by making appeal to rationality.

Coherence: The mutual relevance of concepts underlying the text proper.

Cohesion: Grammatical and lexical ties on the surface of the text. Mechanisms of cohesion include pronouns, conjunctions at phrase, clause and sentence level, lexical repetition, synonymy and paraphrase as well as ellipsis and substitution.

New Literacies: New forms of literacy developed as a consequence of the pervasive spread of digital technologies. Differently from writing-dominated traditional literacy, computer-mediated-communication has enhanced interactivity and the combination of several semiotic resources.

NGOs' Campaigns: Series of actions designed by non-governmental organizations to produce political or social change. These include public information activities and direct action such as boycotts and flashmobs.

Textuality (on the Web): The property of being a text. In Text Linguistics textuality is seen as the resultant of seven standards, two of which are text internal (cohesion and coherence) and five are text external, i.e. depend on contextual factors: intentionality, acceptability, informativity, situationality, intertextuality.

Web Writing: The expression refers to writing conventions on the Web, differing from the traditional writing on account of how people read web pages. Web writing should favour page scanning, an end pursued, for example, by keeping texts short, highlighting keywords, using subheadings, and sticking to the one idea per paragraph style.

ENDNOTES

1. The original model includes more features, as it was devised to account for the impact of the Web on genres, a perspective which is not pursued in this paper.

2. In actual fact hypertext started off-line around the 1960s as a tool for facilitating the search of entries in electronic dictionaries and encyclopaedias (http://www.techterms.com/definition/hypertext).

3. The word 'argument' designates different entities in different traditions within the field of argumentation theory. One designation refers to the whole of 'claim' and 'ground' (with the relevant 'warrant') (Toulmin, 1969), while the other indicates only the propositions backing a thesis. This is the case of pragma-dialectics (van Eemeren & Grotendorst, 1992), which uses the terms 'standpoint' for claim, 'argument' for those utterances meant to back the standpoint, and 'critical discussion' for an argumentative speech act as a whole.

4. 'Sense' refers for the authors to the knowledge which is actually conveyed by an expression in a given text, as opposed to 'meaning' which designates "the potential of a language expression for representing and conveying knowledge" (1981: V. 1).

5. V and 24 refer respectively to the chapter and the paragraph in de Beaugrande and Dressler's digital version of their *Introduction to text linguistics*, which features no page numbers.

6. In text linguistics, and more generally in discourse analysis, this mechanism goes under the name of intertextuality, which refers to "the ways in which the production and reception of a given text depend upon the participants' knowledge of another text" (de Beaugrande & Dressler, 1981, IX.1). Such a relation can be either in the form of an allusion to another text which the

sender presumes the receiver knows, or of familiarity with a matrix (text type, genre, communicative situation) of which a given textual realization is an instance.

7. Quoting from Lynch & Horton (2006) "[e]ye-tracking studies by the Poynter Institute of readers looking at web pages have shown that readers start their scanning with many fixations in the upper left of the page. Their gaze then follows a 'Gutenberg Z' pattern down the page, and only later do typical readers lightly scan the right area of the page. Eye-tracking studies by Jakob Nielsen (2006) show that web pages dominated by text information are scanned in an "F" pattern of intense eye fixations across the top header area, and down the left edge of the text."

8. The term 'module' and the idea of a modular structure for web-pages is drawn from Garret's lexicon, and particularly from her definition of 'wireframes,' i.e. "rough two-dimensional guides to where the major navigation and content elements of your site might appear on the page. They bring a consistent modular structure to the various page forms of your site and provide the fundamental layout and navigation structure for the finished templates to come.

9. In the pragma-dialectical approach to argumentation theory, a 'critical discussion' is meant to solve a difference of opinion on the merits by making appeal to the other party's rationality (van Eemeren & Grotendorst, 1992).

10. Together with cohesion, coherence, intertextuality and others, informativity is one of the standards of textuality posited by de Beaugrande and Dressler (1981). It refers to the extent of unexpectedness of an enunciation: the more unexpected (i.e. unknown), the more informative.

Chapter 20
Learning on the Move
in the Web 2.0:
New Initiatives in M-Learning

Carlos Baladrón
Universidad de Valladolid, Spain

Lorena Calavia
Universidad de Valladolid, Spain

Javier M. Aguiar
Universidad de Valladolid, Spain

Belén Carro
Universidad de Valladolid, Spain

Antonio Sánchez-Esguevillas
Universidad de Valladolid, Spain

ABSTRACT

This work aims at presenting the current state of the art of the m-learning trend, an innovative new approach to teaching focused on taking advantage of mobile devices for learning anytime, anywhere and anyhow, usually employing collaborative tools. However, this new trend is still young, and research and innovation results are still fragmented. This work aims at providing an overview of the state of the art through the analysis of the most interesting initiatives published and reported, studying the different approaches followed, their pros and cons, and their results. And after that, this chapter provides a discussion of where we stand nowadays regarding m-learning, what has been achieved so far, which are the open challenges and where we are heading.

INTRODUCTION

M-learning (or mobile learning) is a growing trend in education extending the concept initiated years ago by e-learning, and can be easily summarized as "learning on the move." Initially, e-learning

meant the introduction of computer networks to facilitate learning, promoting new ways of remotely accessing, managing and acquiring knowledge. However, the advent of mobile technologies resulted in a fast penetration of portable devices like mobile phones, tablets or netbooks,

DOI: 10.4018/978-1-4666-4426-7.ch020

which support anytime/anywhere execution of a wide array of applications. And education and learning applications are no exception.

However, m-learning does not just mean accessing e-learning services on the move. E-learning normally provides services to be consumed statically, like remote access to training material, educational platforms to facilitate course and score tracking by teachers, discussion forums to allow exchanging of knowledge, personalized learning content selection, etc. While it is true that mobile devices are a great way to access these services, it is also true that a whole new array of applications which were completely out of reach for e-learning are now viable thanks to m-learning. Mobile devices are capable of real time interactions and normally pack advanced hardware like cameras or accelerometers, capable of supporting collaborative applications for field experiments, evidence retrieval on the go, real time evaluation of students, context-aware learning clients, etc.

There are a large number of new initiatives offering m-learning solutions for diverse applications, targeting several groups of people (from school students to specialized training). However, the education world is not always receptive to the introduction of new methodologies, with some academic and professional institutions usually being reluctant to abandon well tested, old learning and teaching schemes. The result is that in the current educational landscape there are many emerging m-learning alternatives, but it is hard to find standards, large scale real world applications (deployments and experiments are usually done at small local tests) or widely adopted solutions. Initiatives are usually promoted as research projects instead of deployable products. Even more, the community is still debating whether there are real benefits in m-learning as an educational methodology or it is just a new fashionable technological trend.

This work aims to clarify these questions by offering a synthesized view of the current m-learning landscape, summarizing and analyzing the main features of the most prominent m-learning initiatives, allowing the reader to understand what are the differential features of m-learning applications, their advantages and disadvantages, lessons learned during these experiences, and the results of their application to the real world.

BACKGROUND

While there are some differential concepts and features among them, m-learning and e-learning could be considered technological siblings in some way. Both are trends evolving around the idea of applying new technologies to the educational plane, with e-learning focused on computers and m-learning focused on mobility.

The theoretical fundamentals of m-learning have been widely studied in the literature. For instance, Caudill (2007) presents a detailed theoretical study of the different definitions given traditionally for m-learning (Frohberg, 2006) and the existing differences with e-learning, concluding that m-learning is a new educational method, made possible thanks to mobile computing technologies, but going further than a simple technological change. M-learning allows learning on the move, facilitating many knowledge acquisition applications and methodologies that will remain valid even if the technology is updated and that do not only represent an update of e-learning applications.

The main conclusion at which most authors arrive is that m-learning is always e-learning, but e-learning is not necessarily m-learning, as it is the case that e-learning is always distance learning (d-learning), but d-learning is not necessarily e-learning (Georgiev, Georgieva, & Smrikarov, 2004). The differences between e-learning and d-learning are originated in the application of a new set of technologies to the traditional principles of d-learning, but during its evolution e-learning has become its own paradigm, with its own methodologies and applications. The same is true for m-learning: the differences from e-learning have been originated by a technological breakthrough, but its application has given birth to a new set of tools and methodologies.

This relationship is proved also by the fact that many platforms originally designed for e-learning have been adapted or extended to embrace m-learning applications, as reported in Trifonova et al. (2004), Wang et al. (2005), and Corbeil et al. (2007).

Historically, progress on e-learning has been faster, mainly because requirements over hardware are not as much: m-learning requires normally the same multimedia, communication and processing capabilities as e-learning, but packed in mobile devices which need to be small and light in order to be carried around, and getting all their power from batteries. Therefore, optimal hardware for e-learning was available for the wide public much earlier.

The result is that the current e-learning landscape already presents a set of well-known platforms and initiatives that in some cases could even being considered *de facto* standards, such as Moodle (Dougiamas & Taylor, 2003). Thanks to this coherent technological offer, e-learning is generally well-accepted in educational and academic institutions all around the world as a very valuable tool for supporting learning activities such as content and exercise download, file exchange between teacher and students, quizzes and evaluation support, discussion forums for collaborative learning, remote teacher support, etc. Therefore, the current state of the art, while still progressing at a good pace, could be considered mature (Kahiigi et al., 2008; Andrews & Haythornthwaite, 2007).

The rise of m-learning as a technological trend can be traced back to the end of the nineties, where mobile devices with enough processing power and connectivity solutions began to appear in the market. However, some experiments where already conducted as early as 1991, when the Wireless Coyote (Grant, 1993) project took place. During this initiative directed by Apple

Classrooms of Tomorrow (ACOT), the behaviour of teachers and students was observed while they were confronted with a complex system of mobile computers (connected together using wireless technologies) for carrying out an educational activity in the field. The objective of the activity was to perform a set of nature studies (such as measuring environmental conditions and counting animal and plant species), sharing data in real time with the mobile computers. In order to facilitate these tasks, specifically designed software was installed in the computer to provide real time data sharing, immediate data display, and real time data plotting. Voice communication was also possible by using a set of walkie-talkies.

When confronted with modern day m-learning system, it is easy to realize that the functionalities of this system are basically rough versions of the ones offered today. However, the Wireless Coyote initiative was so ahead of its time with respect to hardware that, for instance, radio modems had to be attached to the mobile computers using duct tape in order to provide wireless communication features. Additionally, these computers and networks were also unable to provide voice transport back in the day, so the equipment had to be completed with the walkie-talkies.

The look of the today's technological landscape in m-learning is quite different from the one presented for e-learning. Currently, there are a large number of small, non-related and isolated initiatives, resulting in a fragmented state of the art where it is difficult to see any prominent platform or standard (UNESCO, 2012; Calavia et al., 2011; Kukulska-Hulme et al., 2011). While there are already some commercial products, they are normally produced *ad hoc*, or are vendor proprietary. Therefore, due to this lack of standardization, a big part of the most interesting work regarding m-learning is still under research.

However, in the recent years the success of online application stores in the world of mobile platforms (most notably Apple's AppStore and Google Play) has represented a big leap forward for m-learning, since it has facilitated the necessary tools for developers around the world to easily enter the mobile application market. The result has been a big increase in the number of small applications devoted to m-learning offered through these popular platforms, normally produced by small studies or even individuals.

CURRENT TECHNOLOGICAL LANDSCAPE OF M-LEARNING

This section presents a selection of the most prominent m-learning initiatives currently available in the state of the art and reported in the literature. The section is divided in four blocks, with the first three devoted to research projects (respectively, projects funded by the European Union –one of the most important and active institutions in research funding around the world-, projects funded by national entities and private initiatives) and the fourth one dealing with market products that are already deployed and used by the general public.

Projects Funded by the European Commission

HandLER

The Handheld Learning Resources Project (HandLER) (Rudman, Sharples, & Baber, 2002; Sharples, 2002) was a mobile learning project launched in 1998 by the School of Engineering's Education Technology Research Group at the University of Birmingham in the UK. The aim of the project was to provide support to lifelong learning regardless the context in which it was carried out. Therefore, several different scenarios and target groups were considered, including school, specialist training (applied to neuroradiology), and personal lifelong learning (Kukulska-Hulme et al., 2011).

For instance, the school scenario was based on provision of learning support for a school field practice targeted at 11-year old children.

For this, a tablet device (with camera and Wi-Fi/telephony network connection) was employed running a specifically designed application that could provide support for the field experiment. Simplicity, usability and user friendliness of the application were high in the priority list, so direct feedback obtained from children (using interviews and questionnaires) was employed for design and development. At the beginning of the 2000's when kids were not as familiar with technology as they are today, this was a critical point.

However, the results of the experience were not as positive as expected. The main conclusion was that hardware was not sufficiently evolved to support this kind of field applications, with interface failures due to low sensitivity, short operation time due to batteries, lack of advanced context information and problems to carry and operate devices due to weight and dimensions. It is important to take into account that this project was carried out at the beginning of the mobility era, thus devices employed were nowhere as optimized as they are today to be operated on the move.

If not capable of delivering a completely successful field experience, in the worst case the project helped to extract conclusions about the main methodological and technological guidelines that m-learning had to follow in subsequent years.

MOBIlearn

Context information has become one of the key resources for mobile applications in the world of Web 2.0 and smartphones. Real time data about users is collected by intelligent devices and made available to local and remote applications, so they can automatically adapt their behaviour to user's context. This computing trend is known as Context Awareness, and it is generally regarded as one of the key aspects of m-learning.

The MOBIlearn project (MOBIlearn, 2002), which was executed with EU funding from 2002 to 2005, represents one of the first attempts of introducing the concept of Context Awareness into the world of m-learning. It brings together partners across Europe, Israel, USA and Australia, including 14 universities, to investigate context sensitive approaches to informal, problem-based, workplace learning. While the main objective of the MOBIlearn project was to create an open framework for the integration of different mobile learning and educational services (so as resources offered by different providers could coexist and collaborate inside this framework) (da Bormida et al., 2003), one of the big advances of MOBIlearn was to develop an integrated context-aware platform for m-learning so as to include context as a key variable for taking automated decisions related to several aspects of the learning experience. Specifically context is used as a driver for content selection and distribution, interface adaptation and interaction among learners. There are also a set of context-aware tools for capturing learning experiences (Calavia et al., 2011).

Therefore, the aim of the project was to build a learning system capable of selecting the most appropriate learning service, content or activity for each specific user situation, and deliver it to the specific terminal the user is employing with the most adequate adapted interface. For instance, this adaptation implies modifying the service operation on the basis of bandwidth available or screen resolution (Lonsdale, Baber, & Sharples, 2004). Additionally, the system stores the results of the learning experience (Vavoula et al., 2004), so as to let users review past experiences and educational progress, and allow the system to better perform content selection and delivery adaptation depending on the results of past experiences.

In order to validate its results, pilots of the MOBIlearn project were designed and deployed in three very different domains (UNESCO, 2012): first, Master of Business Administration (MBA) programmes at partner universities were enriched with mixed approaches merging traditional classroom methodologies with online and mobile components; second, learning services in mobile devices were deployed in museums and galleries

under management of the Firenze Musei association; and third, an application was developed together with the European Resuscitation Council to provide mobile education for management of emergency situations.

MOTFAL

The MOTFAL Project (Mobile Technologies For Ad-Hoc Learning) (MOTFAL, 2004; Malliou et al., 2004) aims at designing, developing, testing and evaluating a learning environment for mobile devices to allow *in situ* learning, maximizing the motivation of learners and optimizing the results of the learning process. The MOTFAL platform was designed to support a variety of activities related to m-learning such as provision of context-aware and personalized learning material, real time content sharing, collaborative learning and quizzes.

The project considered a test scenario focused on history learning, and specifically, a field trip to the Parthenon. During this visit, students were able to download to their PDAs multimedia content that was dynamically adapted to the capabilities of each device, and share it in real time with their colleagues staying at the school. These colleagues could respond with messages and questions.

Technologically, the MOTFAL platform is based on the connected mobile device - Web server paradigm, and is designed to handle several multimedia learning modules. Complex scenarios can be built combining these multimedia modules. The server is also capable of adapting the provided multimedia content to the specific features of each terminal, such as bandwidth or screen resolution.

COLLAGE

COLLAGE (Collaborative Learning Platform Using Game-like Enhancements) (COLLAGE, 2006) was a project funded by the European Commission aimed at building a platform for context-aware collaborative mobile learning in secondary school environments based on educational games.

The platform includes tools for supporting both creation and participation in games.

In order to create games, the creation tools allow the definition of different contextual elements such as locations, paths and territories. Attached to these elements, the game creator is able to define questions. The entire creation process is carried out easily within a browser using a set of predefined forms. Games have to be designed to guide the learning process within a specific site, posing questions that the players have to solve by performing specific actions or understanding elements within the game site.

In order to play the game, each player needs to join the platform with a mobile device. Players are then organized in different teams, with different roles within each team. Then, the paths defined in the game have to be travelled while answering the questions posed along. Interaction is carried out both via mobile browser and SMSs.

eMapps

eMapps (Motivating Active Participation of Primary Schoolchildren in Digital Online Technologies for Creative Opportunities through Multimedia) (eMapps, 2005; Davies, Krizova, & Weiss, 2006) was a project funded by the European Commission between 2005 and 2008 aimed at producing a set of interactive tools to integrate the usage of mobile ICT into learning, and specifically targeting students at the school. Therefore, one of the main objectives for these tools was to be attractive to children, and game-based learning was the chosen approach to cope with this requirement.

The eMapps project developed a platform containing all the necessary tools to create interactive games to be played in real locations, including multimedia content. The designed games are normally alternate reality games that take place in the real word, hosting immersive activities that take place beyond the Internet. The games may include items such as map scenarios or story narratives, and allow the creators to observe and react to players in real time using game control mechanisms, to conduct the flow of the story. The clients allow the students to interact with the system and communicate with each other, allowing multiplayer games to be highly interactive.

The eMapps system is an open platform capable of embracing multiple networks and devices, offering tools such as graphical user interfaces for route editing or podcast/videocast servers, and allows tagging of map zones that can be linked to resources. The tools are designed to be accessed with several devices (including mobile phones, PDAs and tablets), even through the general purpose web browser, and supports several languages and operating systems.

The "desk game" was developed inside the projects as an example of the games that can be played within eMapps. Players have to look for clues to fill up several placeholders that required specific multimedia content. Players upload the multimedia work produced, which is then examined by the teacher playing the role of game master so as to promote students to the next level when the previous one is completed.

The platform was validated with a series of experiments conducted by the partner schools across ten European countries, with each school creating and conducting their own game.

M-Learning

M-Learning (Attewell, 2005) was an EU funded project that was executed between 2001 and 2004, and was specifically conceived for helping young adults (aged from 16 to 24) that had left the ordinary education system. The idea was to offer them an innovative, attractive, and highly interesting alternative for learning that could attract their attention, taking advantage of the natural tendency of youngsters towards new technologies and collaborative games. The usage of mobile technologies was therefore employed to promote creativity, collaboration and peer-to-peer communication, leaving delivery of educational content as a second priority.

The platform designed included clients for mobile phones and a set of authoring tools to let teachers build their own educational materials, including for instance a quiz authoring tool, a media board authoring tool and a PocketPC authoring tool, that allowed teachers to create interactive multimedia quizzes to be delivered dynamically in any device based on the PocketPC operating system.

The project had to face several challenges related to the time during which it was developed, most notably the variety of technologies available to deliver services in mobile devices. While mobile application design today is focused on high level programming frameworks (which is the case for two of the most popular platforms, Apple's iPhone and Google's Android), back in the day there was a wide array of technologies available at several levels: transport layer (GPRS/EDGE, 3G, infrared, WiFi, Bluetooth), delivery layer (SMS, MMS, WAP, email, HTTP), development language (Flash, C, WML, VoiceXML, HTML, XHTML) or platform (PocketPC, Windows, Symbian, Palm OS, J2ME, etc.).

Finally, the project extracted a set of valuable conclusions from the experiences conducted. For instance, it was highlighted that the inclusion of a direct feedback loop with the learner increased the quality and satisfaction of users with the learning materials and systems; that it was necessary to include a software virtualization layer to let the educational content work across all supported platforms; that it is necessary to remember that working with the users' mobile phones is quite close to be inside their personal space, so it is necessary to be careful and minimize intrusiveness; that it is a good idea to train users (students and teachers) in the usage of the system.

CONTSENS

CONTSENS (Cook & Pachler, 2011; Bachmair, Pachler, & Cook, 2010; CONTSENS, 2008) was a project funded by the European Union under the Lifelong Learning programme aimed at developing learning software to be executed in mobile devices in order to enhance the educational experience using context aware and location based adaptation. The project produced different learning applications (some of them enhanced with augmented reality capabilities) that covered four different areas: task based, location and context aware training; museum education; application of context awareness in mobile learning, and application of context awareness in language learning.

Examples of these applications included a field trip for archaeologists to Fountains Abbey in Yorkshire or a guided visit to examine how shops on Holloway Road market themselves to the public.

Nationally Funded Projects

FABULA (Norway)

FABULA (FABULA, 2007; Khan & Matskin, 2009) is an m-learning project funded nationally by the Norwegian government with the aim of building a service oriented framework to allow easy interoperation of different components supporting mobile learning. The system is designed to operate within a city-wide scenario and to facilitate learning of its inhabitants in specific situations.

The FABULA platform works within a layered architecture where everything is a service, embracing a series of agents which operate and interact with each other according to the principles of Multi Agent System (MAS) computing (Khan & Matskin, 2011; Kathayat & Bræk, 2011). Services are grouped in two different sets: passive learning services (or services which provide a learning functionality on request) and active learning services (agents which represent entities interacting with each other and autonomously requesting execution of passive services).

Passive services are distributed along three different layers. The Resource Management layer contains low level services in charge of basic management operations, including for instance discovery, security, information retrieval, or metadata search. The second layer, Basic Learning Services, comprises a set of learning services which are commonly shared among all the different learning applications, such as community management, application composition, user management or event management. Finally, the top layer contains Application Specific learning services such as authoring support, collaboration support, or communication services.

The active learning services are agents designed according to a MAS architecture using the AGORA (Matskin et al., 2001) approach. Agents running in the users' mobile devices and managing lower-level services are examples of AGORA agents in the FABULA context.

The system is validated in a test scenario that takes the shape of a treasure hunt game. In this scenario, a teacher coordinates twenty students that have to search for a set of objects hidden inside the game area. These objects (treasures) have to be found in a sequential order, with a set of clues associated to each treasure that have to be properly understood in order to extract the necessary information. Students are divided in groups of four that collaborate to find the clues and treasures, and to solve the riddles that contain the clues. For that, they can take advantage of the different services offered by the platform, including collaboration, communication and coordination support.

MoLeNET (United Kingdom)

The MoLeNET (Mobile Learning Network) project (UNESCO, 2012; Attewell et al., 2010) was a national UK initiative executed from 2007 to 2010, funded by the UK government with more than 12 million pounds and designed to coordinate a number of smaller initiatives. As such, its objectives were quite wide, defining mobile learning as the exploitation of ubiquitous hand-held technologies and communication networks to support and extend the range of remote teaching and learning. The project comprised several initiatives that took place in very different environments, from classrooms to workplaces and on-the-move scenarios. The project coordinator, the now extinct non-profit organization Learning and Skills Network (LSN) unified all the initiatives providing coherent management and resources such as educational materials, technical and pedagogical support or mentoring programmes.

The analysis of the results showed that across schools, students involved in the MoLeNET initiatives presented higher success rates in their respective programmes than the national average. Additionally, it was found that ICT skills, creativity, and critical thinking were increased, not only in learners, but also in teachers. Additionally, learner-specific benefits included increased focus and retention, also helping in attracting people that were previously considered demotivated students. The researchers finally highlighted that mobile learning has excelled in helping vocational learners and non-full-time students to find their optimal schedule for performing educational tasks.

GIPSY/MANOLO (The Netherlands)

The GIPSY (Geo-Information for Integrating Personal Learning Environments) project (Calavia et al., 2011; UNESCO, 2012; Wentzel et al., 2005) was funded by the government of The Netherlands during 2002 and 2003 with the aim of developing two different courses at university level seamlessly integrating typical classroom tasks with practical field activities that could be carried out with the help of mobile devices. The first course was an introduction to the use of mobile technologies for personal learning, therefore representing an extension of the typical e-learning platforms to embrace the mobile world. However, the second course fostered group learning through field activities such as collecting location data with positioning devices, analyzing and processing the information together with group members and returning to the field to validate the results.

The Manolo project (Calavia et al., 2011; UNESCO, 2012; van Lammeren & Molendijk,

2004) was executed during 2004 and 2005 taking the results of GIPSY as an starting point, and advancing research towards finding answers to the questions that the advent of m-learning has posed, such as which tasks better fit the mobile learning paradigm, what is the role of teachers in this scheme and what changes are required in the methodologies and infrastructures to support these new technologies. The results of the project showed that at the time there were still some fundamental technological barriers hindering the wide adoption of the m-learning paradigm (specifically posing a problem to field experiments), such as battery life or connectivity. However, it reaffirmed the fact that m-learning had much more potential than just accessing e-learning contents on the move, specifically as a communication and collaboration framework for interactive educational experiences.

Skills Arena (United States of America)

The objective of the study detailed in Lee et al. (2004) was to determine the real benefits of employing videogames in classes, both from the learner and the teacher perspectives. For that, Skills Arena is a videogame designed for the teaching of mathematics using the GameBoy Advanced platform, a popular gaming console among children. The application provides an attractive, challenge-based graphical environment within which arithmetical problems are posed to the user with increased difficulty. The application is enriched with a set of tools, such as activity logging, progress tracking and scoring, tools to modify preferences and problems posed, etc.

The application was employed to execute a field test with a group of 39 second grade students, divided in two classes directed by two different teachers that followed two different approaches for the introduction of the experience. While one class had a daily session with Skills Arena before an ordinary mathematics lesson, the other teacher employed the application as a part of a rewarding system, in which students were allowed to play

when they completed some tasks. The most interesting result of the study was that students solved roughly three times more mathematical exercises than they do normally when using traditional exercise books. Students also showed behaviours of extreme interest on the new tool such as exploring on their own parts of the software that were not supposed to be used by them (such as the edition tools). Both facts suggest that motivation and interest are greatly increased thanks to the interactive application.

Mobile Learning for HIV/AIDS Healthcare (Perú)

The work in Zolfo et al. (2010) reports the results of a Peruvian project conducted during 2009/2010 studied the efficiency of m-learning for specialist training in the field of HIV/AIDS healthcare. Healthcare workers in limited resource environments such as Peruvian peri-urban areas could have a difficult access to specialized state-of-the-art medical knowledge, and the system's objective is to bridge this gap by training these workers in the latest procedures available.

The system was designed to train each individual in a set of use cases, known as clinical modules. These use cases simulate five different knowledge domains, such as usage of new drugs (doses, time schedules, procedure of administration, safety or side-effects).

For each use case, multimedia content (including movies and 3D animations) for introducing the simulated patients and conditions of the training situation are provided. Trainees employ the MLE Moodle m-learning platform in their smartphones to support learning events, facilitate progress tracking and allow collaborative learning with medical experts and colleagues involved in the experiment via Facebook.

The usage of m-learning in this project allows the trainees and medical experts to continue with their every day jobs while at the same time conducting the learning program, saving human and economic resources. The results show that, while most participants did not have advanced skills in mobile devices or social networks, in the end 86.6% of the participants were satisfied with the ability to choose their own time schedule for the training program, while 94.4% highlighted that it was very convenient for them to be able to access the educational content without actually requiring a computer.

Private Initiatives

CatchBob!

Even if it is not a pure m-learning initiative, CatchBob! is the typical example of an application that can be easily employed for collaborative learning and training in team work skills by using location aware services (Catchbob, 2006; Nova et al., 2006). CatchBob! is a game in which groups of three people compete against each other for finding a virtual object hidden inside a specific area. The game was designed to study how people interacted together and the way they collaborate, and for that the system records the behaviour of each player.

The game employs a set of mobile devices (tablet computers) equipped with geo-positioning systems. The application interface consists of a map of the game zone showing varied data such as the location of team colleagues or a proximity sensor which gives information about how far the player is located from the hidden object. Additionally, the client implements a communication system to allow message broadcasting and suggestion of search directions to team mates.

MLE Moodle

MLE (Mobile Learning Engine) Moodle (MLE Moodle, 2003) is an open source tool for m-learning which is basically a mobile extension of the popular e-learning platform Moodle (Dougiamas & Taylor, 2003). Currently, work on the platform has been stopped, but the applications are still downloadable and fully operative.

MLE allows access to the Moodle platform using mobile devices either through a JAVA MLE client or just an ordinary internet browser. The feature list offered originally by Moodle (which thanks to MLE is easily accessible with mobile terminals) includes a wide array of different operations that facilitate learning, such as interactive lessons, quiz solving, submission and correction of assignments, creation and management of surveys, forums capable of supporting collaborative learning or creation and maintenance of wikis. All of them are provided together with a collection of wizards and tools that facilitate user interaction.

Additionally the MLE offers a set of m-learning specific features, including for instance a virtual flashcard trainer (a virtual implementation of the traditional learning method based on a set of boxes containing cards with questions and answers that help remembering important items of information, such as language vocabulary), Mobile Learning Objects (a learning item which could combine several features such as questions, quizzes, graphical markup questions, flashcards, etc.) which can be easily created using the built-in editor, Communications and messaging (fully integrated with the standard Moodle messaging platform) or Mobile Tags (a way to implement location based learning scenarios by producing and deploying a set of QR tags around a physical training place directly linking to the appropriate learning resource).

POSIT

The POSIT project (Developing Public Opinions on Science Using Information Technologies) (POSIT, 2006; Rosenbaum et al., 2007) was an initiative developed at the MIT (Massachusetts Institute of Technology) in 2006. The objective was to build a learning application to foster general public involvement in scientific and technological discussions including social and ethical components. For that, the tool designed takes advantage of mobility and augmented reality technologies to promote sharing of ideas and collaboration among people.

The POSIT tool takes the shape of a simulation game run in a museum for groups of visitors during which each player plays a specific role defending a specific position in a given discussion, and before that, retrieve evidence around the place to better understand the situation. The games intend to let visitors to explore complex scientific ideas, examine controversies, engage in discussions using scientific evidence, understand alternative viewpoints through role playing, observe opinion change in themselves and in the group and globally gain a deeper understanding of the relevance of science.

The pilot experience was executed in the MIT and evolved around a simulation scenario in which players had to discuss the controversial question of deciding whether it was a good or a bad idea to build a new biological laboratory of the highest bio-safety level for the treatment of deadly pathogens within the MIT. For that, each player was given a specific role (such as an activist, a biotechnology executive or a city councilor) and an initial background on the simulated situation and the position they have to defend. Then, the players had to move around the campus to gather different evidence with the help of the POSIT tool as a support running in their mobile devices. The game was completed with a set of virtual items and characters (such as other students, nurses, newspaper articles, etc.) that provided information.

The tool provides support for evidence retrieval and management, location aware services (displaying the relevant content of the game depending on the building the player is located), game event notifications and storyline management (such as some players receiving updated information bulletins at fixed times depending on their role),

real time communication (to send messages and specific evidences to other players trying to modify their opinion and/or behaviour) or collaborative evidence and argument rating.

Some lessons learned with the experience and the subsequent feedback retrieval stage includes the fact that every player enjoyed the feeling of being involved in a game, and specifically the storyline development. The rating system was also highlighted by students as a very valuable tool that helped in modifying preconceived opinions and understanding other participants' points of view about a specific matter. And finally, physical interaction with the real world also helped them to understand the implications of each decision to be taken within the simulated scenario.

EvaMovil

The EvaMóvil project (Baladrón et al., 2012) is a mobile application designed for Android-based terminals to allow the remote, real-time evaluation of students. Teachers may publish exams containing series of questions that should be answered online by the students using their own mobile phones. The teacher can then see the responses given and evaluate the results, also using his or her mobile terminal.

EvaMóvil intends to provide a tool for adapting current educational methodologies to the new communication requirements among students and teachers, generated by the collaborative and active learning paradigms which are being introduced in the teaching programs of academic institutions. The project expects to increase interest and implication of students with the subject under study, taking advantage of their affinity for mobile technologies.

Market and Commercial Products

With the advent of the last generation of mobile platforms, specifically the now extremely popular iPhone and Android (which have quickly overcome other systems such as Symbian or Windows mobile), and the popularization of easy development tools and online application markets which greatly facilitate the creation and distribution of new software (AppStore and Google Play), a lot of developers have entered the mobile platforms market, and a plethora of new services are available to customers.

Developers who are also involved with education and learning have quickly realized that these development and distribution platforms are the perfect means for introducing new m-learning applications in the market, and as such, during the last years a large number of this kind of applications have appeared.

One of the most populated areas is the language learning domain, with examples such as *Hello-Hello* (Hello-Hello, 2012), a language learning framework designed in collaboration with the American Council on the Teaching of Foreign Languages (ACTFL) which groups together several functionalities already studied previously in research projects: it allows individual mobile learning through multimedia interactive courses (comprising several areas of language learning such as vocabulary, conversational courses and flashcards), but also provides support for remote teaching and collaborative learning using a communication framework. The basic application is available for 11 languages, but support applications are available as well. This software is available for three of the most important mobile platforms today: Android, iOS and Blackberry.

But mobile learning applications in the online stores are not restricted to the language learning domain. There are also examples of professional-grade m-learning generic platforms designed to allow institutions and teachers to produce their own training and educational courses and deliver them to learners and trainees. *Upside2Go*, for instance, is a generic m-learning platform developed by Upside Learning (Upside2Go, 2012). This platform provides configurable modules for all kinds of m-learning activities, from downloadable content to online evaluation and quizzes, keeping everything under control of the system manager. Upside2Go is again available for Android, iOS and Blackberry.

In addition to these large and medium-sized initiatives there are also many applications designed and developed by smaller teams. A simple search for the word "learning" in Google's Play Store (performed in July 2012) returns as many as 26719 results. It is true that not all these applications will be actual m-learning or suitable for the user (since amateur developers can upload their work freely, some of them may even be demo or unfinished versions), but it gives a first glance impression of the figure under consideration. Again, the language learning area is rich in examples of nice and useful m-learning applications (with for instance services such as *MyWords* or *WordPower*, which cover vocabulary learning for a vast array of languages). Many different applications of different quality levels are available for many learning domains (such as *Kids Reading* to start teaching pre-school children how to read, or *ActPiano: Piano & Sheet Music*, which teaches users how to play the piano and learn music).

These small applications may lack some of the advanced features of the more complex professional solutions or the research initiatives discussed before, but they currently represent the most popular (and probably the only) way for m-learning to start reaching the general public.

Discussion and Recommendations

To facilitate an easy understanding of the current m-learning landscape, after seeing a lot of examples of m-learning initiatives, it is usually possible to classify them in the following groups, as shown in Table 1:

- **Field experiments:** Tools and experiences that involve the creation of specialized software and/or hardware to support a specific set of field experiments and activities.

Table 1. Classification and summary of the studied initiatives

Project Name	Category	Objective	Results	Start Year
HandLER	Personal Lifelong Learning	To provide support to lifelong learning regardless the context in which that learning happens.	Hardware was not sufficiently evolved to support this kind of field applications.	1998
MOBIlearn	Platform	To create an open framework for the integration of different mobile learning and educational services.	Pilots of the MOBIlearn projects were designed and deployed in three different domains.	2002
MOTFAL	Platform	Aimed at designing, developing, testing and evaluating a learning environment for mobile devices to allow *in situ* learning.	Test scenario focused on history learning, and specifically, a field trip to the Parthenon.	2004
COLLAGE	Games	Aimed at building a platform for allowing context-aware collaborative mobile learning in secondary school environments based on educational games.	The prototype was completed and different games were implemented within.	2006
eMapps	Games	Aimed at producing a set of interactive tools to integrate the usage of mobile ICT into learning, and specifically for students at school.	The platform was validated with a series of experiments conducted by the partner schools across ten European countries.	2005
M-Learning	Platform	Conceived for helping young adults that had left the ordinary education system with an innovative, attractive, and highly interesting alternative for learning.	The project extracted a set of valuable conclusions from the experiences conducted related to best practices for m-learning.	2001
CONTSENS	Field Experiments	Aimed at developing learning software (to be executed in mobile devices) capable of enhancing the educational experience using context aware and location based adaptation.	The project produced different learning applications) that covered four different areas: location and context aware training; museum education; application of context awareness in mobile learning, and application of context awareness in language learning.	2008
FABULA	Platform	Aimed at building a service oriented framework to allow easy interoperation of different components for supporting mobile learning.	The system was validated in a specific test scenario that takes the shape of a treasure hunt game.	2007
MoLeNET	Field Experiments	Was designed to coordinate a number of smaller initiatives for defining mobile learning as the exploitation of ubiquitous hand-held technologies and communication networks to support and extend teaching and learning.	The analysis of the results shown that across schools, students involved in the MoLeNET initiatives presented higher success rates in their respective programmes against the national average.	2007
GIPSY/MANOLO	Field Experiments	To develop two different curses at university level seamlessly integrating typical classroom tasks with practical field activities.	The results showed that at the time there were still some fundamental technological barriers hindering the wide adoption of the m-learning paradigm, but reaffirmed the fact that m-learning had much more potential that just accessing e-learning contents on the move.	2002

continued on following page

Table 1. Continued

Project Name	Category	Objective	Results	Start Year
Skills Arena	Field Experiments	To determine the real benefits of employing videogames in the classes, both from the learner and the teacher perspectives.	The most interesting result of the study was that students solved about three times more mathematical exercises than they do normally when using traditional exercise books.	2004
Mobile Learning for HIV/AIDS Healthcare	Specialist Training	To study of the effectiveness of m-learning for specialist training in the field of HIV/AIDS healthcare.	The usage of m-learning in this project allows the trainees and medical experts to continue with their every day jobs while at the same time conducting the learning program, saving human and economic resources. 86.6% of the participants were satisfied with the ability to choose their own time schedule for the training program.	2009
CatchBob!	Games	An application that can be easily employed for collaborative learning and training in team work skills by using location aware services.	The game was helpful to allow studying how people interacted together and the way they collaborate.	2006
MLE Moodle	Platform	Open source tool for m-learning which is basically a mobile extension of the popular e-learning platform Moodle.	MLE gives access to the Moodle platform using mobile devices either through a JAVA MLE client or just using an internet browser.	2003
POSIT	Games, Field Experiment	To build a learning application to foster general public involvement in scientific and technological discussions including social and ethical components	Lessons learned included the fact that every player enjoyed a lot the feeling of being involved in a game (specifically the storyline development) and that physical interaction with the real world also helped to understand the implications of each of the decisions to be taken within the simulated scenario.	2006
EvaMovil	Platform	To build a mobile application to allow remote, real-time evaluation of students.	The expected results include increased interest and implication of the students taking advantage of their affinity for mobile technologies.	2012
Hello-Hello	Platform, Personal Lifelong Learning, Specialist Training	Professional Language Learning platform.	A professional language learning framework designed in collaboration with the American Council on the Teaching of Foreign Languages (ACTFL)	2012
Upside2Go	Platform, Personal Lifelong Learning, Specialist Training	Professional, Generic m-learning platform.	Provides configurable modules for all kinds of m-learning activities.	2012

- **Platforms:** Development of relatively open and generic frameworks and platforms for supporting m-learning across different domains. These platforms normally include, in addition to clients, a set of authoring tools to let teachers personalize the contents, activities, and modules.
- **Games:** Software that supports both development and execution of educational games, normally with a collaborative component.
- **Personal lifelong learning:** Applications and services that help people to perform learning and educational activities outside a specific academic/educational institution/environment, normally with a generic component in mind.
- **Specialist training:** Solutions for providing specialist training to professionals inside a highly specialized institution, like a factory or hospital.

The monitorized experiments studied along this work report several important benefits for the users, both learners and teachers. Most notably, there is an apparent consensus in the literature that m-learning solutions provide a boost to the motivation and interest that learners experience with a subject. This is clearly a consequence of the shift in focus that the m-learning activities produce: they are normally learner-centered, making the learner the protagonist of the educational experience, assuming a very active role and departing from traditional activities associated to other paradigms (even e-learning) in which the learner just passively receives information. While increased interest and motivation is especially notable in young school students, this phenomenon has also been reported for other target audiences, such as young adults who have left the ordinary education system due to a lack of motivation.

Besides this main effect, there are other three very important benefits consistently reported along the literature:

- The first one is that m-learning is a key factor for supporting modern collaborative learning, allowing educational schemes based on team work and knowledge sharing. This is very important taking into account that this kind of paradigms seem to be the future in educative trends. For instance the European Higher Education Area has adopted similar principles (Baladrón et al., 2011). Additionally, in a society which is increasingly permeated by social networks, it will be extremely beneficial to take advantage of this new social computing to foster collaborative learning.
- The second benefit is that m-learning greatly facilitates the learning process for those people that are not full-time students. Usage of mobile devices helps them to find the most suitable schedule compatible with their everyday jobs, even allowing the usage of otherwise lost time gaps (such as travels by bus or train) for learning activities.
- And finally, the third benefit that can be concluded from the analysis of the state of the art is that m-learning is an optimal solution for the integration of specialist training programs within specialized organizations:
  - Allowing the employees to choose their most convenient time table for learning helps them to continue performing well in their work and minimize interferences from the educational process.
  - Allowing an easy expert-knowledge transfer from senior professionals, experts, teachers and trainers towards trainees using a convenient framework that allows real time interaction and communication.
  - Acting as a support framework for helping the trainees in their first real world field experiences.

However, the first idea that comes to mind when performing an analysis of the wide literature available about m-learning projects, initiatives and experiences, is that m-learning is currently still a very fragmented field. Even if the previously mentioned benefits are consistently reported along literature, there is an important lack of "big players" and popular solutions shared among several communities. In the end, every solution is normally built from scratch with a specific purpose in mind. This hinders wide-scale deployment of m-learning for solving real life situations because there is no easy solution for quickly deploying an m-learning application for a specific purpose, and the penetration of m-learning is still small. The perception of potential adopters, such as academic/educational institutions or training professionals in the industry is that m-learning is not a must, but probably just a fancy new trend, and there is no need for making the big investment a personalized solution would require.

In order to overcome this situation, a very important step further has been the popularization of application markets for mobile platforms such as iPhone and Android. This has greatly facilitated implementation of m-learning solutions that, even if small and still fragmented, are starting to hit the society, because they are easy to develop, easy to purchase and easy to use. This is not enough, though, and while research and experiments are quite popular, there are still very few examples of actual integration of m-learning into official curricula and training programmes.

FUTURE RESEARCH DIRECTIONS

As studied during the previous section, m-learning is still not completely adopted by the educational and learning communities for official curricula and real world training tasks, and this is the real challenge for the future. Some clear and important benefits have already been unveiled and demonstrated in the literature and in the media, but still m-learning is seen like an optional and trendy technological concept. Therefore, the main research direction in the upcoming years should be focused not only on technology, but on social aspects in order to facilitate adoption of m-learning among the general public. Real world implementation experiences, not only in reduced, constrained and controlled environments, but also in official curriculums and institutions should be conducted and measured scientifically to promote the complete adoption of m-learning by the society.

Besides, another important challenge is the unification of the current fragmented base of experiences, initiatives and projects. This may be accomplished by some form of standardization, open platform for the integration of different resources, or by the adoption of a *de facto* standard among the currently available solutions. However, some sort of unification is probably required within the community, because currently it is quite difficult for potential users to understand the differences among the existing applications and services, and identify an easy to deploy solution that fits their needs.

Some technological challenges also on the table represent technical directions that m-learning research should investigate and follow in the near future. For instance, application of advanced interfaces, such as gestural interaction provided by current generation gaming consoles (mainly Microsoft's Kinect), augmented reality, seamless integration with social networks to provide continuous support to life-long collaborative learning and knowledge sharing, and convergence with intelligent context awareness that will allow smart adaptation of the learning services to the specific context together with smart tutoring, smart scoring and smart recommendation of contents and exercises.

Finally, it is worth mentioning that, while the devices currently in the market have evolved quickly and the features they provide are normally able to support (with a reasonable degree of user satisfaction) the vast majority of m-learning applications, hardware improvements in battery life, sensor accuracy, screen resolution and responsiveness, or terminal size and dimensions will also result in increased quality of experience for the learners.

CONCLUSION

This chapter has provided an analysis of the current technological landscape in the m-learning world, studying some of the most prominent initiatives and solutions reported in the literature. This has made clear that the paradigm is not fully adopted by society, since these initiatives are usually isolated, carried out in reduced environments, and/or with research purposes. However, the paradigm has proven itself as a useful tool to provide several advantages to the education and academic communities, such as increased motivation and interest in learners or facilitating life-long education to people that are not full-time students.

In order for the paradigm to progress and be more widely adopted, it is necessary for the m-learning community to produce unified and/or standardized tools that could be perceived by potential adopters as viable, beneficial and easy to deploy/use solutions. Thanks to the popularization of online application stores for mobile platforms, this direction is already being explored, with many small m-learning services that are starting to become popular solutions among the people.

Therefore, m-learning is currently in a position where it has already showed and proved the potential benefits it can bring to the learning and academic communities, and even more, the entire society interested in collaborative and life-long learning. Now it is time to develop solutions which can actually deliver these promises to the world.

REFERENCES

Andrews, R., & Haythornthwaite, C. (Eds.). (2007). *The Sage handbook of e-learning research*. London: Sage.

Attewell, J. (2005). From research and development to mobile learning: Tools for education and training providers and their learners. *4th World conference on mLearning (mLearn 2005)*. Cape Town, South Africa.

Attewell, J., Savil-Smith, C., Douch, R., & Parker, G. (2010). *Modernizing education and training: Mobilizing technology for learning*. United Kingdom: LSN.

Bachmair, B., Pachler, N., & Cook, J. (2010). Individualised mobility as cultural resource: Harnessing the 'Mobile Complex' for participatory learning. *German Education Research Association Congress (DGfE 2010)*. Mainz, Germany.

Baladrón, C., Aguiar, J. M., Calavia, L., Carro, B., & Sánchez, A. (2012). Interactive learning application for mobile devices. *4th International Conference on Education and New Learning Technologies (EDULEARN)* (pp. 618-624). Barcelona, Spain: IATED - International Association of Technology, Education and Development.

Baladrón, C., Jiménez, M. I., Aguiar, J. M., Carro, B., & Sánchez-Esguevillas, A. J. (2011). Improving teaching in engineering education: Adjunct enterprise professors programme. *Journal of Intelligent Manufacturing, 2011*, 1–5.

Calavia, L., Aguiar, J. M., Baladrón, C., Carro, B., & Sánchez-Esguevillas, A. J. (2011). New trends in education: M-learning initiatives. *5th International Technology, Education and Development Conference (INTED 2011)* (pp. 895-900). Valencia, Spain: IATED - International Association of Technology, Education and Development.

Catchbob! Project Website. (2006). *Website*. Retrieved July 10, 2012, from http://craftwww.epfl.ch/research/catchbob/

Caudill, J. (2007). The growth of m-learning and the growth of mobile computing: Parallel developments. *International Review of Research in Open and Distance Learning*, 8(2), 1–13.

COLLAGE Project Website. (2006). *Website*. Retrieved July 10, 2012, from http://www.ea.gr/ep/collage

CONTSENS Project Website. (2008). *Website*. Retrieved July 10, 2012, from http://www.ericsson.com/ericsson/corpinfo/programs/using_wireless_technologies_for_context_sensitive_education_and_training/

Cook, J., & Pachler, N. (2011). Appropriation of mobile phones in and across formal and informal learning. *Educational Futures Rethinking Theory and Practice: Digital Difference*, 50(4), 145–158.

Corbeil, R., Pan, C. C., Sullivan, M., & Butler, J. (2007). Enhancing e-learning through m-learning: Are you ready to go mobile? In R. Carlsen et al. (Eds.), *Society for Information Technology & Teacher Education International Conference 2007* (pp. 273-280). Chesapeake, VA: AACE.

Da Bormida, G., Bo, G., Lefrere, P., & Taylor, J. (2003). An open abstract framework for modelling interoperability of mobile learning services. *European Journal of Engineering for Information Society Applications*, 5(1), 1–9.

Davies, R., Krizova, R., & Weiss, D. (2006). eMapps.com: Games and mobile technology in learning. In W. Nejdl & K. Tochtermann (Eds.), Innovative approaches for learning and knowledge sharing (pp. 103-110). Springer Berlin Heidelberg.

Dougiamas, M., & Taylor, P. (2003). Moodle: Using learning communities to create an open source course management system. In D. Lassner & C. McNaught (Eds.), *World conference on educational multimedia, hypermedia and telecommunications* (pp. 171-178). Chesapeake, VA: AACE.

eMapps Project Website. (2005). *Website*. Retrieved July 20, 2012, from http://emapps.info

FABULA Project Website. (2007). *Website*. Retrieved July 20, 2012, from http://www.fabula.idi.ntnu.no

Frohberg, D. (2006). *Mobile learning is coming of age: What we have and what we still miss*. Paper presented at DeLFI 2006, Darmstadt, Germany.

Georgiev, T., Georgieva, E., & Smrikarov, A. (2004). M-Learning - a new stage of e-learning. *5th international conference on Computer systems and technologies*. Rousse, Bulgaria: CompSysTech.

Grant, W.C. (1993). Wireless coyote: A computer-supported field trip. *Communications of the ACM - Special issue on technology in K–12 education*, 36(5), 57-59.

Hello-Hello Product Website. (2012). *Website*. Retrieved July 13, 2012, from http://www.hello-hello.com/

Kahiigi, E., Ekenberg, L., Hansson, H., Tusubira, F., & Danielson, M. (2008). Exploring the e-learning state of art. *Electronic Journal of e-Learning*, 6(2), 149-160.

Kathayat, S. B., & Bræk, R. (2011). Modeling collaborative learning services - A case study. *International Conference on Collaboration Technologies and Systems* (pp. 326-333). Philadelphia, PA: IEEE Press.

Khan, B. A., & Matskin, M. (2009). FABULA platform for active e-learning in mobile networks. *IADIS International Conference Mobile Learning 2009* (pp. 33-41). Barcelona, Spain: IADIS Press.

Khan, B. A., & Matskin, M. (2011). Multiagent system to support place/space based mobile learning in city. In *International Conference on Information Society (i-Society)* (pp. 66-71). London, UK.

Kukulska-Hulme, A., Sharples, M., Milrad, M., Arnedillo-Sanchez, I., & Vavoula, G. (2011). The genesis and development of mobile learning in Europe. In Parsons, D. (Ed.), *Combining e-learning and m-learning: New applications of blended educational resources* (pp. 151–177). Hershey, PA: IGI Global. doi:10.4018/978-1-60960-481-3.ch010.

Lee, J., Luchini, K., Michael, B., Norris, C., & Soloway, E. (2004). *More than just fun and games: Assessing the value of educational video games in the classroom. Extended abstracts on Human factors in computing systems* (pp. 1375–1378). New York, NY: ACM Press.

Lonsdale, P., Baber, C., & Sharples, M. (2004). A context awareness architecture for facilitating mobile learning. In Attewell, J., & Savill-Smith, C. (Eds.), *Learning with mobile devices: Research and development* (pp. 79–85). London: Learning and Skills Development Agency.

Malliou, E., Maounis, F., Miliarakis, A., Savvas, S., Sotiriou, S., & Stratakis, M. (2004). The Motfal project - Mobile technologies for ad-hoc learning. In *IEEE International Conference on Advanced Learning Technologies* (pp. 910-911). Joensuu, Finland.

Matskin, M., Kirkeluten, O., Krossnes, S., Sæle, O., & Wagner, T. (2001). Agora: An infrastructure for cooperative work support in multi-agent systems. In Wagner, T., & Rana, O. (Eds.), *Infrastructure for agents, multi-agent systems, and scalable multi-agent systems* (pp. 28–40). Berlin, Germany: Springer Berlin-Heidelberg.

MOBIlearn project website. (2002). *Website*. Retrieved July 11, 2012, from http://www.mobilearn.org/

Moodle Web Site, M. L. E. (2003). *Website*. Retrieved July 10, 2012, from http://mle.sourceforge.net/

MOTFAL Project Website. (2004). *Website*. Retrieved July 10, 2012, from http://www.ellinogermaniki.gr/ep/motfal/

Nova, N., Girardin, F., Molinari, G., & Dillenbourg, P. (2006). The underwhelming effects of automatic location-awareness on collaboration in a pervasive game. *7th International Conference on the Design of Cooperative Systems* (pp. 224-238). Provence, France.

POSIT Project Website. (2006). *Website*. Retrieved July 11, 2012, from http://icampus.mit.edu/projects/POSIT.shtml

Rosenbaum, E., Klopfer, E., Boughner, B., & Rosenheck, L. (2007). Engaging students in science controversy through an augmented reality role-playing game. *7th International conference on Computer supported collaborative learning, CSCL* (pp. 612-614). New Brunswick, NJ: International Society of the Learning Sciences.

Rudman, P. D., Sharples, M., & Baber, C. (2002). Supporting learning in conversations using personal technologies. *European Workshop on Mobile and Contextual Learning (MLEARN2002)* (pp. 44-46). Birmingham, UK.

Sharples, M. (2002). Disruptive devices: Mobile technology for conversational learning. *International Journal of Continuing Engineering Education and Lifelong Learning, 12*(5-6), 504–520. doi:10.1504/IJCEELL.2002.002148.

Trifonova, A., Knapp, J., Ronchetti, M., & Gamper, J. (2004). Mobile ELDIT: Transition from an e-learning to an m-learning system. *World Conference on Educational Multimedia, Hypermedia and Telecommunications (ED-MEDIA 2004)* (pp. 188-193). Lugano, Switzerland.

UNESCO. (2012). Turning on mobile learning in Europe: Illustrative initiatives and policy implications. *UNESCO Working Paper Series on Mobile Learning*. Retrieved July 10, 2012, from http://unesdoc.unesco.org/images/0021/002161/216165e.pdf

Upside2Go product Website. (2012). Retrieved July 12, 2012, from http://www.upsidelearning.com/mobile-learning-solution-upside2go.asp

Van Lammeren, R. J. A., & Molendijk, M. (2004). *Location based learning: Lessons learned* (p. 10). Amsterdam, The Netherlands: European GIS Education Seminar EUGISES.

Vavoula, G. N., Sharples, M., O'Malley, C., & Taylor, J. (2004). A study of mobile learning as part of everyday learning. In Attewell, J., & Savill-Smith, C. (Eds.), *Mobile learning anytime everywhere: A book of papers from MLEARN 2004* (pp. 211–212). London, UK: Learning and Skills Development Agency.

Wang, H. H., Wu, T. H., Kuo, R., & Heh, J. S. (2005). EM-learning platform: A mobile learning environment integrating e-learning system. In P. Kommers & G. Richards (Eds.), *World Conference on Educational Multimedia, Hypermedia and Telecommunications* (pp. 1437-1443). Chesapeake, VA: AACE.

Wentzel, P., van Lammeren, R. J. A., Molendijk, M., de Bruin, S., & Wagtendonk, A. (2005). *Using mobile technology to enhance students' educational experiences*. Boulder, CO: EDUCAUSE Center for Applied Research.

Zolfo, M., Iglesias, D., Kiyan, C., Echevarria, J., Fucay, L., & Llacsahuanga, E. et al. (2010). Mobile learning for HIV/AIDS healthcare worker training in resource-limited settings. *AIDS Research and Therapy*, *7*(35), 1–6. PMID:20051116.

ADDITIONAL READING

Badusah, J., Mohd Nordin, N., Ab Rahman, H., & Romly, R. (2011). M-learning portal's usage among Malaysian public university students. In Barton, S. et al. (Eds.), *Global learn Asia Pacific* (pp. 152–161). Melbourne, Australia: AACE.

Brown, T. H. (2005). Towards a model for m-learning in Africa. *International Journal on E-Learning*, *4*(3), 299–315.

Chmiliar, L. (2010). Mobile learning - Student perspectives. In J. Sanchez & K. Zhang (Eds.), *World Conference on E-Learning in Corporate, Government, Healthcare, and Higher Education* (pp. 1646-1651). Chesapeake, VA: AACE.

Colazzo, L., Molinari, A., & Ronchetti, M. (2005). Integrating mobile devices in a multi-platform learning management system using web services. In P. Kommers & G. Richards (Eds.), *World conference on educational multimedia, hypermedia and telecommunications* (pp. 1367-1372). Chesapeake, VA: AACE.

Evans, C. (2008). The effectiveness of m-learning in the form of podcast revision lectures in higher education. *Computers & Education*, *50*(2), 491–498. doi:10.1016/j.compedu.2007.09.016.

Fetaji, M. (2008). Devising a strategy for usability testing of m-learning applications. In J. Luca & E. Weippl (Eds.), *World Conference on Educational Multimedia, Hypermedia and Telecommunications* (pp. 1393-1398). Chesapeake, VA: AACE.

Fetaji, M. (2008). Literature review of m-learning issues, m-learning projects and technologies. In C. Bonk et al. (Eds.), *World Conference on E-Learning in Corporate, Government, Healthcare, and Higher Education* (pp. 348-353). Chesapeake, VA: AACE.

Goh, T., & Kinshuk, D. (2004). Getting ready for mobile learning. In L. Cantoni & C. McLoughlin (Eds.), *World Conference on Educational Multimedia, Hypermedia and Telecommunications* (pp. 56-63). Chesapeake, VA: AACE.

Hall, O. (2011). iPad: Assessing the impact of mobile learning technologies on graduate management education. Global TIME (pp. 19-20). AACE.

Keegan, D. (2002). *The future of learning: From eLearning to mLearning*. Retrieved July 10, 2012, from http://learning.ericsson.net/mlearning2/project_one/book.html

Kim, S. H., Mims, C., & Holmes, K. P. (2006). An introduction to current trends and benefits of mobile wireless technology use in higher education. *AACE Journal, 14*(1), 77–100.

Kirsti, A., Redecker, C., Punie, Y., Ferrari, A., Cachia, R., & Centeno, C. (2010). The future of learning: European teachers' visions. Report on a foresight consultation at the 2010 eTwinning Conference. Sevilla, Spain.

Looi, C., So, H., Toh, Y., & Chen, W. (2011). The Singapore experience: Synergy of national policy, classroom practice and design research. *International Journal of Computer-Supported Collaborative Learning, 8*(1), 9–37. doi:10.1007/s11412-010-9102-8.

Lucey, K., & Heo, M. (2011). Educational web portals: Moving forward to web 2.0 and m-learning. In M. Koehler & P. Mishra (Eds.), *Society for Information Technology & Teacher Education International Conference* (pp. 3080-3086). Chesapeake, VA: AACE.

Maniar, N. (2007). M-learning to teach university students. In C. Montgomerie & J. Seale (Eds.), *World Conference on Educational Multimedia, Hypermedia and Telecommunications* (pp. 881-887). Chesapeake, VA: AACE.

Miller, R., Shapiro, H., & Hilding-Haman, K. E. (2008). *School's over: Learning spaces in Europe in 2020: An imagining exercise on the future of learning*. Seville, Spain: Joint Research Centre, Institute for Prospective Technological Studies. Retrieved July 8, 2012, from http://ftp.jrc.es/EURdoc/JRC47412.pdf

Neumann, G. (2007). No time for learning? Methodological and technological support to training-on-the-job. In C. Montgomerie & J. Seale (Eds.), *World Conference on Educational Multimedia, Hypermedia and Telecommunications* (pp. 345-352). Chesapeake, VA: AACE.

Nischelwitzer, A., & Meisenberger, M. (2005). Mobile phones as a challenge for m-learning: Examples for mobile interactive learning objects (MILOs). In D. Tavangarian (Ed.), *Third IEEE International Conference on Pervasive Computing and Communications Workshops (PerCom 2005 Workshops)* (pp. 307-311), Hawaii, USA.

Nyiri, K. (2002). Towards a philosophy of m-learning. *IEEE International Workshop on Wireless and Mobile Technologies in Education (WMTE' 02)* (pp. 121-124). Växjö, Sweden.

O'Shea, C., Lillis, D., O'Shea, S., & Collins, P. (2005). The application of e-learning and m-learning technology in the context of life long learning in Irish Higher Education. In P. Kommers & G. Richards (Eds.), *World Conference on Educational Multimedia, Hypermedia and Telecommunications* (pp. 568-572). Chesapeake, VA: AACE.

Parsons, D. Hokyoung Ryu, & Cranshaw, M. (2006). A study of design requirements for mobile learning environments. In *Sixth International Conference on Advanced Learning Technologies (ICALT'06)* (pp. 96-100). Kerkrade, The Netherlands: IEEE Computer Society.

Trifonova, A., & Ronchetti, M. (2003). Where is mobile learning going? In A. Rossett (Ed.), *World Conference on E-Learning in Corporate, Government, Healthcare, and Higher Education 2003* (pp. 1794-1801). Chesapeake, VA: AACE.

Wen, J. Chuang, M.K., Cheng, K.M., & Kuo, S.H. (2010). M-learning incorporated into the elementary school English teaching. In Z. Abas et al. (Eds.), Global Learn Asia Pacific (pp. 224-229). Penang, Malaysia: AACE.

Wong, Y. H., & Csete, J. (2004). Mobile learning framework: A cross-reference of m-commerce experience. In L. Cantoni & C. McLoughlin (Eds.), *World Conference on Educational Multimedia, Hypermedia and Telecommunications* (pp. 223-230). Chesapeake, VA: AACE.

Yuen, S., & Wang, S. (2004). M-learning: Mobility in learning. In J. Nall & R. Robson (Eds.), *World Conference on E-Learning in Corporate, Government, Healthcare, and Higher Education* (pp. 2248-2252). Chesapeake, VA: AACE.

KEY TERMS AND DEFINITIONS

Context-Awareness: Computing trend in which services and applications adapt their behaviour autonomously to the preferences and surrounding conditions of the user.

Distance Learning (D-Learning): A field of education focused on facilitating learning for students who do not share a physical and/or temporal space with the teacher or the sources of information.

E-Learning: Computing trend based on the application of new communication and information technologies to learning and education.

M-Learning: Computing trend based on the application of mobile technologies to learning and education.

Mobile Computing: A computing trend in which information processing capabilities are embedded in small devices which can be carried around and operated on the move.

Pervasive (Ubiquitous) Computing: A model of human-machine interaction in which intelligence and information processing features have been included into several connected devices surrounding each individual's everyday life, resulting in a constant exchange of information between the person and the terminals which facilitates the conclusion of several human tasks.

Web 2.0: A new incarnation of the World Wide Web defined by the rise of collaborative applications and information sharing tools (such as blogs, social networks, wikis, etc.) that allow a symmetric communication paradigm instead of the old content provider (site owner) – content consumer relationship.

Compilation of References

Abercrombie, N., & Longhurst, B. (1998). *Audiences: A sociological theory of performance and imagination.* London: Sage.

Abrilian, S., Devillers, L., Buisine, S., & Martin, J. C. (2005). EmoTV1: Annotation of real-life emotions for the specification of multimodal affective interfaces. In *Proceedings of the 11th International Conference on Human-Computer Interaction (HCII'2005)* (pp. 1-11). Las Vegas, Nevada, USA, 22–27 July 2005.

Adar, E., Zhang, L., Adamic, L. A., & Lukose, R. M. (2004). *Implicit structure and the dynamics of blogspace.* Paper presented at the Workshop on the Weblogging Ecosystem, 13th World Wide Web Conference (WWW 2004), New York, NY.

Ahn, J. (2010). *The influence of social networking sites on high school students' social and academic development.* (Unpublished doctoral dissertation). University of Southern California, Los Angeles. Retrieved July 30, 2012, from http://gateway.proquest.com/openurl?url_ver=Z39.88-2004&rft_ val_fmt=info:ofi/fmt:kev:mtx:dissertation&res_dat= xri:pqdiss&rft _dat=xri:pqdiss:3417985

Akar, D. (2002). The macro contextual factors shaping business discourse: The Turkish case. *International Review of Applied Linguistics in Language Teaching, 40*(4), 305–322. doi:10.1515/iral.2002.015.

Al-Jarf, R. (2007). Online instruction and creative writing by Saudi EFL freshman students. *The Asian EFL Journal Professional Teaching Articles, 22*(August). Retrieved July 30, 2012, from http://www.asian-efl-journal.com/pta_Aug_07_rajl.php

Allen, J., & Core, M. (1997). *Draft of DAMSL: Dialog act markup in several layers.* Philadelphia, PA: University of Pennsylvania.

Alonso, C. (1992). *Análisis y diagnóstico de los estilos de aprendizaje en estudiantes universitarios.* (Unpublished doctoral dissertation). Tomo I. Madrid: Colección Tesis Doctorales. Editorial de la Universidad Complutense.

Alzoubi, O., D'Mello, S. K., & Calvo, R. A. (2012). Detecting naturalistic expressions of nonbasic affect using physiological signals. *IEEE Transactions on Affective Computing, 3*(3), 298–310. doi:10.1109/T-AFFC.2012.4.

Amer-Yahia, S., Doan, A., Kleinberg, J., Koudas, N., & Franklin, M. (2010). Crowds, clouds, and algorithms: Exploring the human side of "big data" applications. In A. K. Elmagarmid & D. Agrawal (Eds.), *Proceedings of SIGMOD International Conference on Management of data* (pp. 1259-1260). Indianapolis, IN, USA.

Andrews, R., & Haythornthwaite, C. (Eds.). (2007). *The Sage handbook of e-learning research.* London: Sage.

Androutsopoulos, J., & Beisswenger, M. (2008). Introduction: Data and methods in computer-mediated discourse analysis. *Language@Internet, 5,* Article 9. Retrieved October 14, 2012, from www.languageatinternet.de

Angouri, J., & Tseliga, T. (2010). "You have no idea what you are talking about!" From e-disagreement to e-impoliteness in two online fora. *Journal of Politeness Research. Language, Behaviour. Culture (Canadian Ethnology Society), 6*(1), 57–82.

Antaki, C., Ardévol, E., Núñez, F., & Vayreda, A. (2005). "For she who knows who she is": Managing accountability in online forum messages. *Journal of Computer-Mediated Communication, 11*(1). Retrieved November 2, 2010, from http://jcmc.indiana.edu/vol11/issue1/antaki.html

Antaki, C. (1994). *Explaining and arguing: The social organization of accounts.* London: Sage.

Antaki, C., & Widdicombe, S. (Eds.). (1998). *Identities in talk*. London: Sage Publications.

Arminen, I., & Leinonen, M. (2006). Mobile phone call openings: Tailoring answers to personalized summonses. *Discourse Studies*, 8(3), 339–368. doi:10.1177/1461445606061791.

Arnold, N., & Paulus, T. (2010). Using a social networking site for experiential learning: Appropriating, lurking, modeling and community building. *The Internet and Higher Education*, 13(4), 188–196. doi:10.1016/j.iheduc.2010.04.002.

Aronson, E. (1995). *The social animal*. New York, NY: W.H. Freeman and Co..

Arroyo, I., Cooper, D. G., Burleson, W., Woolf, B. P., Muldner, K., & Christopherson, R. (2009). Emotion sensors go to school. In Dimitrova, V., Mizoguchi, R., du Boulay, B., & Grasser, A. (Eds.), *Artificial intelligence in education. Building learning systems that care: From knowledge representation to affective modeling. Vol. Frontiers in Artificial Intelligence and Applications* (pp. 17–24). Amsterdam: IOS Press.

Asher, N., Benamara, F., & Mathieu, Y. Y. (2009). Appraisal of opinion expressions in discourse. *Lingvisticae Investigationes*, 32(2), 279–292. doi:10.1075/li.32.2.10ash.

Askehave, I., & Ellerup Nielsen, A. (2004). Webmediated genres – A challenge to traditional genre theory. *Working Paper nr. 6* (pp. 1-50). Aarhus: Centre for Virksomhedscommunication.

Askehave, I., & Ellerup Nielsen, A. (2005). Digital genres: A challenge to traditional genre theory. *IT & People*, 18(2), 120–141. doi:10.1108/09593840510601504.

Assaker, G., Vinzi, V.E., & O'Connor, P. (2010). Structural equation modeling in tourism demand forecasting: A critical review. *Journal of Travel and Tourism Research*, Spring/Fall 2010, 1-27.

Atkinson, P., Coffey, A., Delamont, S., Lofland, J., & Lofland, L. (Eds.). (2008). *Handbook of ethnography*. London: Sage.

ATLAS-ti. (2011). *ATLAS-ti 6.2: User guide and reference*. Berlin: ATLAS.ti Scientific Software Development GmbH. Retrieved May 14, 2011, from http://www.atlasti.com/uploads/media/miniManual_v6_2011.pdf

Attardo, S. (2001). *Humorous texts: A semantic and pragmatic analysis*. Berlin, Germany: Mouton de Gruyter. doi:10.1515/9783110887969.

Attewell, J. (2005). From research and development to mobile learning: Tools for education and training providers and their learners. *4th World conference on mLearning (mLearn 2005)*. Cape Town, South Africa.

Attewell, J., Savil-Smith, C., Douch, R., & Parker, G. (2010). *Modernizing education and training: Mobilizing technology for learning*. United Kingdom: LSN.

Audiradio. (2009). *Dati Audiradio annuale 2009*. Retrieved October 10, 2010, from http://www.audiradio.it/upload/File/Dati%20Audiradio%20annuale%202009.pdf

Aumayr, E., Chan, J., & Hayes, C. (2011). *Reconstruction of threaded conversations in online discussion forums*. Paper presented at the Fifth International Conference on Weblogs and Social Media - AAAI ICWSM 2011.

Austin, J. L. (1962). *How to do things with words*. Cambridge, MA: Harvard University Press.

Bachmair, B., Pachler, N., & Cook, J. (2010). Individualised mobility as cultural resource: Harnessing the 'Mobile Complex' for participatory learning. *German Education Research Association Congress (DGfE 2010)*. Mainz, Germany.

Baker, A. J. (2005). *Double click: Romance and commitment among online couples*. Cresskill, NJ: Hampton Press.

Baker, P. (2006). *Using corpora in discourse analysis*. London: Continuum International Publishing Group.

Bakhtin, M. M. (1981). *The dialogic imagination: Four essays*. Austin, TX: University of Texas Press.

Bakhtin, M. M. (1986). *Speech genres and other late essays*. Austin, TX: University of Texas Press.

Bakhtin, M. M. (1986). The problem of speech genres. In Emerson, C., & Holquist, M. (Eds.), *Speech genres and other late essays* (pp. 60–102). (McGee, V. W., Trans.). Austin: University of Texas Press.

Baladrón, C., Aguiar, J. M., Calavia, L., Carro, B., & Sánchez, A. (2012). Interactive learning application for mobile devices. *4th International Conference on Education and New Learning Technologies (EDULEARN)* (pp. 618-624). Barcelona, Spain: IATED - International Association of Technology, Education and Development.

Baladrón, C., Jiménez, M. I., Aguiar, J. M., Carro, B., & Sánchez-Esguevillas, A. J. (2011). Improving teaching in engineering education: Adjunct enterprise professors programme. *Journal of Intelligent Manufacturing, 2011*, 1–5.

Balahur, A., Hermida, J. M., & Montoyo, A. (2012). Building and exploiting emotinet, a knowledge base for emotion detection based on the appraisal theory model. *IEEE Transactions on Affective Computing, 3*(1), 88–101. doi:10.1109/T-AFFC.2011.33.

Ballano, S. (2011). *Evaluación de un sistema multimodal de reconocimiento de emociones*. (Unpublished master's thesis). Universidad de Zaragoza, Zaragoza.

Bandura, A. (1997). *Self-efficacy: The exercise of control*. New York: Freeman.

Barab, S. A., Dodge, T., Ingram-Goble, A., Volk, C., Peppler, K., & Pettyjohn, P. et al. (2009). Pedagogical dramas and transformational play: Narratively-rich games for education. In Lurgel, I. A., Zagalo, N., & Petta, P. (Eds.), *Interactive storytelling* (pp. 332–335). Berlin: Springer. doi:10.1007/978-3-642-10643-9_42.

Barab, S. A., Thomas, M., Dodge, T., Carteaux, R., & Tuzun, H. (2005). Making learning fun: Quest Atlantis, a game without guns. *Educational Technology Research and Development, 53*(1), 86–107. doi:10.1007/BF02504859.

Baron, N. S. (2010). Discourse structures in Instant Messaging: The case of utterance breaks *Language@Internet, 7*. Retrieved October 11, 2012, from http://www.languageatinternet.org/articles/2010/2651

Baron, N. S. (1998). Letters by phone or speech by other means: The linguistics of email. *Language & Communication, 18*(2), 133–170. doi:10.1016/S0271-5309(98)00005-6.

Barry, C. A. (1998). Choosing qualitative data analysis software: Atlas-ti and Nudist compared. *Sociological Research Online, 3*(3), 1–17. doi:10.5153/sro.178.

Barthes, R. (1971). *Mythologies*. London, England: Jonathan Cape.

Barthes, R. (1974). *S/Z* (Miller, R., Trans.). Farrar, Straus & Giroux.

Barton, D., & Tusting, K. (2005). *Beyond communities of practice: Language, power, and social context*. New York: Cambridge University Press. doi:10.1017/CBO9780511610554.

Bartscher, M., Lawler, K., Ramirez, A., & Schinault, K. (2001). *Improving student's writing ability through journals and creative writing exercises*. ERIC Document Reproduction Service No. ED455525.

Barzilay, R., & Elhadad, M. (1997). *Using lexical chains for text summarization*. In Proceedings of the ACL Workshop on Intelligent Scalable Text Summarization, Madrid, Spain.

Bassett, E. H., & O'Riordan, K. (2002). Ethics of internet research: Contesting the human subjects research model. *Ethics and Information Technology, 4*, 233–247. doi:10.1023/A:1021319125207.

Bateman, J., Delin, J., & Allen, P. (2000). Constraints on layout in multimodal document generation. In *Proceedings of the First International Natural Language Generation Conference. Workshop on Coherence in Generated Multimedia* (pp. 7-14). Mitzpe Ramon, Israel.

Baym, N. (1995). The emergence of community in computer-mediated communication. In Jones, S. G. (Ed.), *Cybersociety: Computer-mediated communication and community* (pp. 138–163). Thousand Oaks, CA: Sage.

Baym, N. (2006). Interpersonal life online. In Livingstone, S., & Lievrouw, L. (Eds.), *The handbook of new media* (pp. 62–76). London, UK: Sage Publications.

Bazarova, N., & Walther, J. B. (2008). Attributions in virtual groups: Distances and behavioral variations in computer-mediated discussions. *Small Group Research, 40*(2), 138–162. doi:10.1177/1046496408328490.

Beach, R., & Doerr-Stevens, C. (2011). Using social networking for online role-plays to develop students' argumentative strategies. *Journal of Educational Computing Research, 45*(2), 165–181. doi:10.2190/EC.45.2.c.

Beale, R., & Creed, C. (2009). Affective interaction: How emotional agents affect users. *International Journal of Human-Computer Studies, 67*(9), 755–776. doi:10.1016/j.ijhcs.2009.05.001.

Bechar-Israeli, H. (1995). From <Bonehead> to <cLoNe-hEAd>: Nicknames, play and identity on internet relay chat. *Journal of Computer Mediated Communication, 1*(2). Retrieved December 3, 2010, from http://jcmc.indiana.edu/vol1/issue2/bechar.html

Beck, I. L., McKeown, M. G., Hamilton, R. L., & Kucan, L. (1997). *Questioning the author: An approach for enhancing student engagement in text*. Newark, DE: International Reading Association.

Beltrán Llera, J. (1993). *Procesos, estrategias y técnicas de aprendizaje*. Madrid. Editorial Síntesis, S.A.

Benjamini, Y., Krieger, A. M., & Yekutieli, D. (2006). Adaptive linear step-up procedures that control the false discovery rate. *Biometrika, 93*, 491–507. doi:10.1093/biomet/93.3.491.

Bentley, J., & Bourret, R. (1991). *Using emerging technology to improve instruction in college transfer*. ERIC Document Reproduction Service No. ED405011.

Benwell, B., & Stokoe, E. (2006). *Discourse and identity*. Edinburgh: Edinburgh University Press.

Benwell, B., & Stokoe, E. (2010). Analysing identity in interaction: Contrasting discourse, genealogical, narrative, and conversation analysis. In Wetherell, M., & Mohanty, C. T. (Eds.), *The Sage handbook of identities* (pp. 82–103). Los Angeles: Sage Publications. doi:10.4135/9781446200889.n6.

Bereiter, C. (1994). Implications of postmodernism for science, or, science as progressive discourse. *Educational Psychologist, 29*(1), 3–12. doi:10.1207/s15326985ep2901_1.

Bereiter, C. (2002). *Education and mind in the knowledge age*. Hillsdale: LEA.

Bereiter, C., & Scardamalia, M. (2003). Learning to work creatively with knowledge. In De Corte, E., Verschaffel, L., Entwistle, N., & van Merriënboer, J. (Eds.), *Powerful learning environments: Unravelling basic components and dimension* (pp. 55–68). Oxford: Elsevier Science.

Bereiter, C., & Scardamalia, M. (2006). Education for the knowledge age: Design-centered models of teaching and instruction. In Alexander, P. A., & Winne, P. H. (Eds.), *Handbook of educational psychology* (2nd ed., pp. 695–713). Mahwah, NJ: Lawrence Erlbaum.

Bereiter, C., Scardamalia, M., Cassells, C., & Hewitt, J. (1997). Postmodernism, knowledge building, and elementary science. *The Elementary School Journal, 97*, 329–340. doi:10.1086/461869.

Berglund, T. Ö. (2009). Disrupted turn adjacency and coherence maintenance in instant messaging conversations. *Language@Internet, 6*(2). Retrieved December 3, 2010, from www.languageatinternet.de/articles/2009/2106/Berglund.pdf/

Bernstein, J., Cohen, M., Murveit, H., Rtischev, D., & Weintraub, M. (1990). Automatic evaluation and training in English pronunciation.[Kobe, Japan.]. *Proceedings ICSLP, 90*, 1185–1188.

Bernstein, M. (1998). Patterns of hypertext.[Pittsburgh: Association of Computing Machinery.]. *Proceedings of Hypertext, 98*, 21–29.

Berzsenyi, C. (1999). Teaching interlocutor relationships in electronic classrooms. *Computers and Composition, 16*(2), 229–246. doi:10.1016/S8755-4615(99)00004-3.

Beyer, Y., Enli, G. S., Maasø, A. J., & Ytreberg, E. (2007). Small talk makes a big difference: Recent developments in interactive, SMS-based television. *Television & New Media, 8*(3), 213–234. doi:10.1177/1527476407301642.

Bhatia, V. K. (2004). *Worlds of written discourse: A genre-based view*. London: Continuum.

Bhatia, V. K. (2008). Towards critical genre analysis. In Bhatia, V. K., Flowerdew, J., & Jones, R. (Eds.), *Advances in discourse studies* (pp. 166–177). London: Routledge.

Bhatia, V. K. (2010). Interdiscursivity in professional communication. *Discourse & Communication, 4*(1), 32–50. doi:10.1177/1750481309351208.

Biber, D. (1988). *Variation across speech and writing*. Cambridge: Cambridge University Press. doi:10.1017/CBO9780511621024.

Biber, D., Conrad, S., & Reppen, R. (1998). *Corpus linguistics: Investigating language structure and use*. Cambridge: Cambridge University Press. doi:10.1017/CBO9780511804489.

Biber, D., Johansson, S., Leech, G., Conrad, S., & Finegan, E. (1999). *The Longman grammar of spoken and written English*. London: Longman.

Biesenbach-Lucas, S., & Weasenforth, D. (2001). E-Mail and word processing in the ESL classroom: How the medium affects the message. *Language Learning & Technology*, 5(1), 135–165.

Bigelow, M., delMas, R., Hansen, K., & Tarone, E. (2006). Literacy and the processing of oral recasts in SLA. *TESOL Quarterly*, 40(4), 665–685. doi:10.2307/40264303.

Birdsell, D., & Groarke, L. (1996). Toward a theory of visual arguments. *Argumentation and Advocacy*, 33, 1–10.

Birks, M., Chapman, Y., & Francis, K. (2008). Memoing in qualitative research: Probing data and processes. *Journal of Research in Nursing*, 13(1), 68–75. doi:10.1177/1744987107081254.

Blei, D. M., Ng, A. Y., & Jordan, M. I. (2003). Latent dirichlet allocation. *Journal of Machine Learning Research*, 3, 993–1022.

Blimes, J. (1988). The concept of preference in conversation analysis. *Language in Society*, 17(2), 161–181. doi:10.1017/S0047404500012744.

Blumenfeld, P. C., Marx, R. W., Soloway, E., & Krajcik, J. (1996). Learning with peers: From small group cooperation to collaborative communities. *Educational Research*, 25(8), 37–40.

Blythe, M., & Cairns, P. (2009). Critical methods and user generated content: The iPhone on YouTube. In *Proceedings of the 27th international conference on Human factors in computing systems*. Boston, MA, USA.

Bodnar, S., Cucchiarini, C., & Strik, H. (2011). Computer-assisted grammar practice for oral communication. *Proceedings of the 3rd International Conference on Computer Supported Education (CSEDU)* (pp. 355-361). Noordwijkerhout, The Netherlands.

Bodnar, S., Penning de Vries, B., Cucchiarini, C., Strik, H., & van Hout, R. (2011). Feedback in an ASR-based CALL system for L2 syntax: A feasibility study. *Proceedings of the SLaTE-2011 workshop* (pp. 1-4). Venice, Italy.

Boggio, C. (2010). Automobile advertising for cultural elites: A multimodal analysis. In Evangelisti Allori, P., & Garzoni, G. (Eds.), *Discourse, identities and genres in corporate communication* (pp. 145–161). Bern: Peter Lang.

Bolin, G. (2010). Digitalization, multiplatform texts, and audience reception. *Popular Communication*, 8(1), 72–83. doi:10.1080/15405700903502353.

Bolter, J. D. (1991). Topographic writing: Hypertext and the electronic writing space. In Delany, P., & Landow, G. P. (Eds.), *Hypermedia and literary studies* (pp. 105–118). Cambridge, MA: MIT.

Bolter, J. D. (2001). *Writing space: The computer, hypertext, and the history of writing* (2nd ed.). Hillsdale, NJ: Lawrence Erlbaum.

Bou-Franch, P., Lorenzo-Dus, N., & Blitvich, P. G.-C. (2012). Social interaction in YouTube text-based polylogues: A study of coherence. *Journal of Computer-Mediated Communication*, 17(4), 501–521. doi:10.1111/j.1083-6101.2012.01579.x.

Bourdieu, P. (1984). *Distinction: A social critique of the judgment of taste*. Cambridge, MA: Harvard University Press.

Boyd, D., Golder, S., & Lotan, G. (2010, January). *Tweet, tweet, retweet: Conversational aspects of retweeting on Twitter*. Paper presented at the Hawaii International Conference on System Sciences (HICSS-43), Kauai, HI.

Boyd, S. (2003). Are you ready for social software? *Darwin Magazine (IDG)*. Retrieved June 11, 2012, from http://stoweboyd.com/post/2325281845/are-you-ready-for-social-software

Boyer, K. E., Phillips, R., Ha, E. Y., Wallis, M. D., Vouk, M. A., & Lester, J. C. (2009). *Modeling dialogue structure with adjacency pair analysis and hidden Markov models*. Paper presented at the Human Language Technologies: The 2009 Annual Conference of the North American Chapter of the Association for Computational Linguistics.

Bransford, J. D., Brown, A. L., & Cocking, R. R. (1999). *How people learn: Brain, mind, experience, and school*. Washington, DC: National Academy Press.

Braun, H. I., Jones, D. H., Rubin, D. B., & Thayer, D. T. (1983). Empirical Bayes estimation of coefficients in the general linear model from data of deficient rank. *Psychometrika*, 489(2), 171–181. doi:10.1007/BF02294013.

Brave, S., & Nass, C. (2002). Emotion in human computer interaction. In Jacko, J., & Sears, A. (Eds.), *The human-computer interaction handbook: Fundamentals, evolving technologies and emerging applications* (pp. 91–96). Hillsdale, NJ: Lawrence Erlbaum Associates.

Bridle, M. (2011). *Male Blues Lyrics 1920-1965: A corpus assisted analysis.* (Unpublished masters dissertation). University of Huddersfield, UK.

British Psychological Society. (2007). *Report of the working party on conducting research on the internet: Guidelines for ethical practice in psychological research online.* (No. 62/06.2007). Retrieved July 30, 2012, from http://www.bps.org.uk/publications/policy-guidelines/research-guidelines-policy-documents/research-guidelines-policy-docum: BPS

Brown, C. (2009). White supremacist discourse on the internet and the construction of whiteness ideology. *The Howard Journal of Communications, 20*(2), 189–208. WWW.HATE.COM doi:10.1080/10646170902869544.

Brown, C., Snodgrass, T., Kemper, S., Herman, R., & Covington, M. (2008). Automatic measurement of propositional idea density from part-of-speech tagging. *Behavior Research Methods, 40,* 540–545. doi:10.3758/BRM.40.2.540 PMID:18522065.

Brown, P., & Levinson, S. C. (1987). *Politeness.* New York: Cambridge University Press.

Brunet, P. M., & Schmidt, L. A. (2007). Is shyness context specific? Relation between shyness and online self-disclosure with and without a live webcam in young adults. *Journal of Research in Personality, 41*(4), 938–945. doi:10.1016/j.jrp.2006.09.001.

Bruno, M. (2002). *Creative writing: The warm-up.* ERIC Document Reproduction Service No. ED464335.

Bruns, A. (2010). *Blogs, Wikipedia, Second life, and beyond: From production to produsage.* New York: Peter Lang Publishing.

Bryk, A. S., & Raudenbush, S. W. (1992). *Hierarchical linear models.* London: Sage.

Brynjolfsson, E., & McAfee, A. (2012). *Race against the machine: How the digital revolution is accelerating innovation, driving productivity, and irreversibly transforming employment and the economy.* Lexington, MA: Digital Frontier Press.

Bucholtz, M. (2001). Reflexivity and critique in discourse analysis. *Critique of Anthropology, 21*(2), 165–183. doi:10.1177/0308275X0102100203.

Bucholtz, M. (2007). Shop talk: Branding, consumption, and gender in American middle-class youth interaction. In McElhinny, B. S. (Ed.), *Words, worlds, and material girls: Language, gender, globalization* (pp. 371–402). Berlin: Mouton de Gruyter. doi:10.1515/9783110198805.4.371.

Bucholtz, M., & Hall, K. (2005). Identity and interaction: A sociocultural linguistic approach. *Discourse Studies, 7*(4-5), 585–614. doi:10.1177/1461445605054407.

Budanitsky, A., & Hirst, G. (2006). Evaluating Word-Net-based measures of lexical semantic relatedness. *Computational Linguistics, 32*(1), 13–47. doi:10.1162/coli.2006.32.1.13.

Buehl, D. (2001). *Classroom strategies for interactive learning.* Newark, DE: International Reading Association.

Bullen, M. (1997). *A case study of participation and critical thinking in a University-level course delivered by computer conferencing.* (Unpublished doctoral dissertation). University of British Columbia, Vancouver, Canada.

Burbules, N. C. (1993). *Dialogue in teaching: Theory and practice.* New York: Teachers College Press.

Burgos, P., Cucchiarini, C., van Hout, R., Strik, H. (in press). *Phonology acquisition in Spanish learners of Dutch: Error patterns in pronunciation.*

Busby, R. (2009). *Marketing the populist politician: The demotic democrat.* London, England: Palgrave Macmillan. doi:10.1057/9780230244283.

Cacciamani, S., & Ferrini, T. (2007). Costruire conoscenza in un corso universitario on line: è davvero possibile? [Knowledge building in an online university course: Is it really possible?] In *Tecnologie didattiche, 40,* 28-35.

Calavia, L., Aguiar, J. M., Baladrón, C., Carro, B., & Sánchez-Esguevillas, A. J. (2011). New trends in education: M-learning initiatives. *5th International Technology, Education and Development Conference (INTED 2011)* (pp. 895-900). Valencia, Spain: IATED - International Association of Technology, Education and Development. Catchbob! Project Website. (2006). *Website*. Retrieved July 10, 2012, from http://craftwww.epfl.ch/research/catchbob/

Calvo, R. (2009). Incorporating affect into educational design patterns and technologies. In *Proceedings of the 9th IEEE international conference on advanced learning technologies* (pp. 1-5). Riga, Latvia. Retrieved February 5, 2013, from http://sydney.edu.au/engineering/latte/docs/Calvo09-Icalt.pdf

Calvo, R. A., & D'Mello, S. K. (2010). Affect detection: An interdisciplinary review of models, methods, and their applications. *IEEE Transactions on Affective Computing*, *1*(1), 18–37. doi:10.1109/T-AFFC.2010.1.

Capriello, A., Mason, P., Davis, B., & Crotts, J. (2011). Farm tourism experiences in travel reviews: A cross-comparison of three alternative methods for data analysis. *Journal of Business Research*, 1–8.

Carcary, M. (2011). Evidence analysis using CAQDAS: Insights from a qualitative researcher. *The Electronic Journal of Business Research Methods, 9*(1), 10-24. Retrieved May 16, 2011, from http://www.ejbrm.com

Carpentier, N. (2007). Participation, access, and interaction: Changing perspectives. In V. Nightingale & T. Dwyer (Eds.), New media worlds: Challenges for convergence (pp. 214-231). New York: Oxford.

Carrillo de Albornoz, J. (2011). *Un Modelo Lingüístico-Semántico Basado en Emociones para la Clasificación de Textos según su Polaridad e Intensidad*. (Doctoral Thesis). Universidad Complutense de Madrid, Spain.

Carroll, S., & Swain, M. (1993). Explicit and implicit negative feedback: An empirical study of the learning of linguistic generalizations. *Studies in Second Language Acquisition*, *15*, 357–386. doi:10.1017/S0272263100012158.

Carter, L. M. (2000). Arguments in hypertext: A rhetorical approach. In F. M. Shipman, P. J. Nürnberg, & D. L. Hicks (Eds.), *Proceedings of the Eleventh ACM on Hypertext and Hypermedia* (pp. 85-91). New York: ACM.

Carter, L. M. (2003). Argument in hypertext: Writing strategies and the problem of order in a nonsequential world. *Computers and Composition*, *20*, 3–22. doi:10.1016/S8755-4615(02)00176-7.

Cartwright, A. (1988). *Code-A-Text [Software; Orphaned and unsupported since 2002]*. Retrieved January 10, 2013, from http://micabrera.co.uk/code-a-text/default.aspx

Casella, V. (1989). Poetry and word processing inspire good writing. *Instructor*, *98*(9), 28.

Castells, M. (2000). *The rise of the network society*. London, England: Blackwell.

Caswell, B., & Bielaczyc, K. (2002). Knowledge forum: Altering the relationship between students and scientific knowledge. *Education Communication and Information*, *1*(3), 281–305. doi:10.1080/146363102753535240.

Catenaccio, P. (2012). *Networked dispositio: A preliminary investigation of hypermodal resource deployment for argument building on the web*. Paper presented at the ESSE Conference, Istanbul.

Catterall, C., & Maclaran, P. (1997). Focus group data and qualitative analysis programs: Coding the moving picture as well as the snapshots. *Sociological Research Online*, *2*(1). Retrieved July 1, 2011, from http://socresonline.org.uk/socresonlin e/2/1/6.html

Caudill, J. (2007). The growth of m-learning and the growth of mobile computing: Parallel developments. *International Review of Research in Open and Distance Learning*, *8*(2), 1–13.

Celce-Murcia, M., & Olshtain, E. (2000). *Discourse and context in language teaching*. New York: Cambridge University Press.

Central Statistics Office. (2000). Population census 2000. Retrieved January 14, 2010, from www.gov.mu/portal/sites/ncb/cso/report/.../census5/index.htm

Chafe, W. (1982). Integration and involvement in speaking, writing, and oral literature. In Tannen, D. (Ed.), *Spoken and written language: Exploring orality and literacy* (pp. 35–54). Norwood, NJ: Ablex.

Chafe, W. (1985). Linguistic differences produced by differences between speaking and writing. In Olson, D. R., Hildyard, A., & Torrance, N. (Eds.), *Literacy, language, and learning: The nature and consequences of reading and writing* (pp. 105–123). Cambridge: Cambridge University Press.

Chafe, W. (1994). *Discourse, consciousness, and time: The flow and displacement of conscious experience in speaking and writing.* Chicago: University of Chicago Press.

Chafe, W., & Danielewicz, J. (1987). Properties of spoken and written language. In Horowitz, R., & Samuels, F. J. (Eds.), *Comprehending oral and written language.* New York: Academic Press.

Chan, C. K. K., & Van Aalst, J. (2004). Learning, assessment, and collaboration in computer-supported collaborative learning. In Strijbos, J. W., Kirschner, P., & Martens, R. (Eds.), *What we know about CSCL: And implementing it in higher education* (pp. 87–112). Kluwer Academic Publishers. doi:10.1007/1-4020-7921-4_4.

Charmaz, K. (2000). Grounded theory: Objectivist and constructivist methods. In Denzin, N. K., & Lincoln, Y. S. (Eds.), *Handbook of qualitative research* (pp. 249–291). Thousand Oaks: Sage.

Chaudron, C. (1988). *Second language classrooms.* New York: Cambridge University Press. doi:10.1017/CBO9781139524469.

Chen, G., & Chiu, M. M. (2008). Online discussion processes: Effects of earlier messages' evaluations, knowledge content, social cues and personal information on later messages. *Computers & Education, 50*(3), 678–692. doi:10.1016/j.compedu.2006.07.007.

Chen, G., Chiu, M. M., & Wang, Z. (2012). Social metacognition and the creation of correct, new ideas: A statistical discourse analysis. *Computers in Human Behavior, 28*(3), 868–880. doi:10.1016/j.chb.2011.12.006.

Chen, G., Chiu, M. M., & Wang, Z. (2012). Predicting social cues during online discussions: Effects of evaluations and knowledge content. *Computers in Human Behavior, 28*(4), 1497–1509. doi:10.1016/j.chb.2012.03.017.

Cherny, L. (1999). *Conversation and community: Chat in a virtual world.* Stanford, CA: CSLI Publications.

Cheung, W., Tse, S., & Tsang, H. (2003). Teaching creative writing skills to primary school children in Hong Kong: Discordance between the views and practices of language teachers. *The Journal of Creative Behavior, 37*(2), 77–98. doi:10.1002/j.2162-6057.2003.tb00827.x.

Chevalier, S., & Cao, Z. (2008). Application and evaluation of speech technologies in language learning: Experiments with the Saybot Player.[Brisbane, Australia.]. *Proceedings of Interspeech, 2008*, 2811–2814.

Chinn, C. A., O'Donnell, A. M., & Jinks, T. S. (2000). The structure of discourse in collaborative learning. *Journal of Experimental Education, 69*(1), 77–97. doi:10.1080/00220970009600650.

Chiu, M. M. (2000). Group problem solving processes: Social interactions and individual actions. *Journal for the Theory of Social Behaviour, 30*(1), 27–50. doi:10.1111/1468-5914.00118.

Chiu, M. M. (2008). Flowing toward correct contributions during group problem solving. *Journal of the Learning Sciences, 17*(3), 415–463. doi:10.1080/10508400802224830.

Chiu, M. M. (2008). Effects of argumentation on group micro-creativity. *Contemporary Educational Psychology, 33*, 383–402. doi:10.1016/j.cedpsych.2008.05.001.

Chiu, M. M., & Khoo, L. (2003). Rudeness and status effects during group problem solving: Do they bias evaluations and reduce the likelihood of correct solutions? *Journal of Educational Psychology, 95*, 506–523. doi:10.1037/0022-0663.95.3.506.

Chiu, M. M., & Khoo, L. (2005). A new method for analyzing sequential processes: Dynamic multi-level analysis. *Small Group Research, 36*, 1–32. doi:10.1177/1046496405279309.

Chouliaraki, L. (2008). Discourse analysis. In Bennett, T., & Frow, J. (Eds.), *The SAGE handbook of cultural analysis* (pp. 674–698). London: SAGE Publications. doi:10.4135/9781848608443.n33.

Choy, D., Wong, A., & Gao, P. (2008). *Singapore's pre-service teachers perspectives in integrating information and communication technology (ICT) during practicum.* Paper presented at the AARE 2008. Retrieved from http://www.aare.edu.au/08pap/cho08326.pdf.

Chung, C., & Pennebaker, J. (2007). The psychological function words. In Fiedler, K. (Ed.), *Social communication* (pp. 343–359). NY: Psychology Press.

Ciccarese, P., Wu, E., Wong, G., Ocana, M., Kinoshita, J., & Ruttenberg, A. et al. (2008). The SWAN biomedical discourse ontology. *Journal of Biomedical Informatics*, *41*(5), 739–751. doi:10.1016/j.jbi.2008.04.010.

Cilibrasi, R. L., & Vitanyi, P. M. B. (2007). The Google similarity distance. *IEEE Transactions on Knowledge and Data Engineering*, *19*(3), 370–383. doi:10.1109/TKDE.2007.48.

Clarà, M., & Mauri, T. (2010). Toward a dialectic relation between the results in CSCL: Three critical methodological aspects of content analysis schemes. *International Journal of Computer-Supported Collaborative Learning*, *5*(1), 117–136. doi:10.1007/s11412-009-9078-4.

Clark, C. (2006). *Views in the news*. Milano: Led Edizioni Universitarie.

Clark, H., & Schaefer, E. (1989). Contributing to discourse. *Cognitive Science*, *13*, 259–294. doi:10.1207/s15516709cog1302_7.

Coates, J. (2003). *Ecology and social work. Toward a new paradigm*. Halifax: Fernwood Publishing.

Cole, M. (1996). *Cultural psychology*. Cambridge, MA.

Collaborative for Academic. Social and Emotional Learning. (2006). *About CASEL*. Retrieved May 28, 2012, from http://www.casel.org/about/index.php

COLLAGE Project Website. (2006). *Website*. Retrieved July10, 2012, from http://www.ea.gr/ep/collage

Collins, M. (1992). *Flaming: The relationship between social context cues and uninhibited verbal behavior in computer-mediated communication*. Retrieved December 15, 2010, from http://www.mediensprache.net/archiv/pubs/2842.htm

Collister, L. B. (2008). *Virtual discourse structure: An analysis of conversation in World of Warcraft*. (Unpublished MA thesis). University of Pittsburgh.

Collister, L. B. (2011). *-Repair in online discourse. *Journal of Pragmatics*, *23*(3), 918–921. doi:10.1016/j.pragma.2010.09.025.

Coniam, D. (1999). Voice recognition software accuracy with second language speakers of English. *System*, *27*, 49–64. doi:10.1016/S0346-251X(98)00049-9.

Connor, S. M., & Wesolowski, K. (2009). Posts to online news message boards and public discourse surrounding DUI enforcement. *Traffic Injury Prevention*, *10*(6), 546–551. doi:10.1080/15389580903261105 PMID:19916124.

Conole, G., Galley, R., & Culver, J. (2011). Frameworks for understanding the nature of interactions, networking, and community in a social networking site for academic practice. *International Review of Research in Open and Distance Learning*, *12*(3), 119–138.

ConsumerSearch. (2012, February). Online dating: Comparing the top sites. Retrieved June 10, 2012, from http://www.consumersearch.com/online-dating/review

CONTSENS Project Website. (2008). *Website*. Retrieved July 10, 2012, from http://www.ericsson.com/ericsson/corpinfo/programs/using_wireless_technologies_for_context_sensitive_education_and_training/

Cook, J., & Pachler, N. (2011). Appropriation of mobile phones in and across formal and informal learning. *Educational Futures Rethinking Theory and Practice: Digital Difference*, *50*(4), 145–158.

Corbeil, R., Pan, C. C., Sullivan, M., & Butler, J. (2007). Enhancing e-learning through m-learning: Are you ready to go mobile? In R. Carlsen et al. (Eds.), *Society for Information Technology & Teacher Education International Conference 2007* (pp. 273-280). Chesapeake, VA: AACE.

Cornelius, L. L., & Herrenkohl, L. R. (2004). Power in the classroom: How the classroom environment shapes students' relationships with each other and with concepts. *Cognition and Instruction*, *22*, 467–498. doi:10.1207/s1532690Xci2204_4.

Covington, M. (2007). *CPIDR 3 User Manual*. GA: University of Georgia Artificial Intelligence Center. Retrieved December 1, 2011, from http://www.ai.uga.edu/caspr/

Coxhead, A. (2000). A new academic word list. *TESOL Quarterly*, *34*(2), 213–238. doi:10.2307/3587951.

Cox, R. (2007). Technology-enhanced research: Educational ICT systems as research instruments. *Technology, Pedagogy and Education*, *16*(3), 337–356. doi:10.1080/14759390701614470.

Cramer, I., & Finthammer, M. (2008). *An evaluation procedure for word net based lexical chaining: Methods and issues*. Paper presented at the Global WordNet Conference 2008, Szeged, Hungary.

Creto, J. (2004). Cold plums and the old men in the water: Let children read and write great poetry. *The Reading Teacher*, *58*(3), 266–271. doi:10.1598/RT.58.3.4.

Crotts, J., Davis, B., & Mason, P. (2011). Analyzing travel blog content for competitive advantage: Lessons learned in the application of software aided linguistics analysis. In Sigala, M. (Ed.), *Web 2.0 in travel, tourism and hospitality: Theory, practice and cases* (pp. 281–293). Surrey, UK: Ashgate Publishing Ltd..

Crotts, J., Mason, P., & Davis, B. (2009). Measuring guest satisfaction and competitive position: An application of stance shift analysis of blog narratives. *Journal of Travel Research*, *48*(3), 139–151. doi:10.1177/0047287508328795.

Crowe, A. R., & Berry, A. (2007). Teaching prospective teachers about learning to think like a teacher: Articulating *our* principles of practice. In Russell, T., & Loughran, J. (Eds.), *Enacting a pedagogy of teacher education: Values, relationships, and practices* (pp. 153–189). London: Routledge.

Crystal, D. (2001). *Language and the Internet*. Cambridge: Cambridge University Press. doi:10.1017/CBO9781139164771.

Crystal, D. (2006). *Language and the Internet*. Cambridge, UK: Cambridge University Press. doi:10.1017/CBO9780511487002.

Csikszentmihalyi, M. (1990). *Flow: The psychology of optimal experience*. New York: Harper and Row Publishers Inc..

Cucchiarini, C., van Doremalen, J., & Strik, H. (2012). *Practice and feedback in L2 speaking: An evaluation of the DISCO CALL system*. Paper presented at Interspeech 2012. Portland, Oregon.

Cucchiarini, C., Neri, A., & Strik, H. (2009). Oral proficiency training in Dutch L2: The contribution of ASR-based corrective feedback. *Speech Communication*, *51*(10), 853–863. doi:10.1016/j.specom.2009.03.003.

Cucchiarini, C., Strik, H., & Boves, L. (1997). Automatic assessment of foreign speakers' pronunciation of Dutch.[Rhodes, Greece.]. *Proceedings Eurospeech*, *1997*, 713–716.

Cucchiarini, C., Strik, H., & Boves, L. (2000). Different aspects of expert pronunciation quality ratings and their relation to scores produced by speech recognition algorithm. *Speech Communication*, *30*(2-3), 109–119. doi:10.1016/S0167-6393(99)00040-0.

Cucchiarini, C., Strik, H., & Boves, L. (2000). Quantitative assessment of second language learners' fluency. *The Journal of the Acoustical Society of America*, *107*(2), 989–999. doi:10.1121/1.428279 PMID:10687708.

Cucchiarini, C., Strik, H., & Boves, L. (2002). Quantitative assessment of second language learners' fluency: Comparisons between read and spontaneous speech. *The Journal of the Acoustical Society of America*, *111*(6), 2862–2873. doi:10.1121/1.1471894 PMID:12083220.

Cucchiarini, C., van den Heuvel, H., Sanders, E., & Strik, H. (2011). Error selection for ASR-based English pronunciation training in 'My Pronunciation Coach.'[Florence, Italy.]. *Proceedings Interspeech*, *2011*, 1165–1168.

Culpeper, J. (1996). Towards an anatomy of impoliteness. *Journal of Pragmatics*, *25*, 349–367. doi:10.1016/0378-2166(95)00014-3.

Da Bormida, G., Bo, G., Lefrere, P., & Taylor, J. (2003). An open abstract framework for modelling interoperability of mobile learning services. *European Journal of Engineering for Information Society Applications*, *5*(1), 1–9.

Daft, R. L., & Lengel, R. H. (1986). Organizational information requirements, media richness and structural design. *Management Science*, *32*(5), 554–571. doi:10.1287/mnsc.32.5.554.

Dana, N. F., & Yendol-Hoppey, D. (2009). *The reflective educator's guide to classroom research: Learning to teach and teaching to learn through practitioner inquiry*. Thousand Oaks, CA: Corwin Press.

Daradoumis, T. (1995). Using rhetorical relations in building a coherent conversational teaching session. In Beun, R. J., Baker, M. J., & Reiner, M. (Eds.), *Dialogue and instruction* (pp. 56–71). Heidelberg, Berlin: Springer-Verlag. doi:10.1007/978-3-642-57827-4_5.

Daradoumis, T., Martinez-Mones, A., & Xhafa, F. (2004). In De Vreede, G., Guerrero, L. A., & Raventós, G. M. (Eds.), *An integrated approach for analyzing and assessing the performance of virtual learning groups* (pp. 289–304). Lecture notes in computer scienceNew York: Springer, Berlin Heidelberg. doi:10.1007/978-3-540-30112-7_25.

Das, A. (2010). Social interaction process analysis of Bengalis' on Orkut. In Taiwo, R. (Ed.), *Handbook of research on discourse behavior and digital communication: Language structures and social interaction* (pp. 66–87). Hershey, PA: Information Science Reference. doi:10.4018/978-1-61520-773-2.ch004.

Davies, R., Krizova, R., & Weiss, D. (2006). eMapps. com: Games and mobile technology in learning. In W. Nejdl & K. Tochtermann (Eds.), Innovative approaches for learning and knowledge sharing (pp. 103–110). Springer Berlin Heidelberg.

Davies, B., & Harre, R. (1990). Positioning the discursive production of selves. *Journal for the Theory of Social Behaviour, 20*(1), 43–63. doi:10.1111/j.1468-5914.1990.tb00174.x.

Davies, J., & Merchant, G. (2007). Looking from the inside out: Academic blogging as new literacy. In Lankshear, C., & Knobel, M. (Eds.), *A new literacies sampler* (pp. 167–198). New York, NY: Peter Lang.

Davis, B., & Mason, P. (2008). Stance-shift analysis: Locating presence and positions in online focus group chat. In Kelsey, S., & St Amant, K. (Eds.), *Handbook of research on computer-mediated communication* (pp. 634–646). Hershey, PA: ICI Press. doi:10.4018/978-1-59904-863-5.ch045.

Davis, B., & Mason, P. (2010). Stance shift analysis. In Lord, V., & Cowan, A. (Eds.), *Interviewing in criminal justice* (pp. 273–282). NY: Jones & Bartlett.

Davis, B., Smith, M., & Tsai, S.-C. (2010). When the online conversation is prompted. In Taiwo, R. (Ed.), *Handbook of research in discourse behavior and digital communication: Language structures and social interaction* (pp. 579–591). Hershey, PA: IGI Global. doi:10.4018/978-1-61520-773-2.ch037.

Davis, B., & Thiede, R. (2000). Writing into change: Style-shifting in asynchronous electronic discourse. In Warschaeur, M., & Kern, R. (Eds.), *Network-based teaching: concepts and practice* (pp. 87–120). Cambridge: University Press. doi:10.1017/CBO9781139524735.007.

Dawkins, R. (2008). *The Oxford book of modern science writing*. Oxford, UK: Oxford University Press.

Day, E. M., & Shapson, M. (2001). Integrating formal and functional approaches to language teaching in French immersion: An experimental study. *Language Learning, 51*, 47–80. doi:10.1111/j.1467-1770.2001.tb00014.x.

De Beaugrande, R. A., & Dressler, W. U. (1981). *An introduction to text linguistics*. London: Longman. Retrieved August 4, 2012, from http://beaugrande.com/introduction_to_text_linguistics.htm

De Bot, K. (1996). The psycholinguistics of the output hypothesis. *Language Learning, 46*, 529–555. doi:10.1111/j.1467-1770.1996.tb01246.x.

de Freitas, S., & Neumann, T. (2009). The use of 'exploratory learning' for supporting immersive learning in virtual environments. *Computers & Education, 52*(2), 343–352. doi:10.1016/j.compedu.2008.09.010.

de Freitas, S., & Oliver, M. (2006). How can exploratory learning with games and simulations within the curriculum be most effectively evaluated? *Computers & Education, 46*(3), 249–264. doi:10.1016/j.compedu.2005.11.007.

De Laat, M. F., Lally, V., Lipponen, L., & Simons, R. J. (2007). Investigating patterns of interaction in networked learning and computer-supported collaborative learning: A role for social network analysis. *International Journal of Computer-Supported Collaborative Learning, 2*, 87–103. doi:10.1007/s11412-007-9006-4.

de Leeuw, J. (2001). Reproducible research: The bottom line. *Department of Statistics Papers*. Department of Statistics, UCLA. Retrieved September 14, 2011, from http://repositories.cdlib.org/uclastat/papers/2001031101

de Wever, B., Schellens, T., Valcke, M., & van Keer, H. (2006). Content analysis schemes to analyze transcripts of online asynchronous discussion groups: A review. *Computers & Education, 46*(1), 6–28. doi:10.1016/j.compedu.2005.04.005.

Dean, J. (n.d). *PsyBlog: Understand your mind.* Retrieved January 8, 2013, from http://www.spring.org.uk

Dede, C., Clarke, J., Ketelhut, D. J., Nelson, B., & Bowman, C. (2005). *Fostering motivation, learning and transfer in multi-user virtual environments.* Paper presented at the American Educational Research Association. Retrieved from http://muve.gse.harvard.edu/rivercityproject/research-publications.htm#2005.

Deerwester, S., Dumais, S. T., Furnas, G. W., Landauer, T. K., & Harshman, R. (1990). Indexing by latent semantic analysis. *Journal of the American Society for Information Science American Society for Information Science, 41*(6), 391–407. doi:10.1002/(SICI)1097-4571(199009)41:6<391::AID-ASI1>3.0.CO;2-9.

Degano, C. (2012). Argumentative genres on the Web: the case of two NGOs' campaigns. In Campagna, S., Garzone, G., Ilie, C., & Rowley-Jolivet, E. (Eds.), *Evolving genres in Web-mediated communication* (pp. 97–124). Bern: Peter Lang.

DeKeyser, R. (2007). *Practice in a second language. Perspectives from applied linguistics and cognitive psychology.* UK: Cambridge University Press.

DeKeyser, R. M., & Sokalski, K. J. (1996). The differential role of comprehension and production practice. *Language Learning, 46*(4), 613–642. doi:10.1111/j.1467-1770.1996.tb01354.x.

Delahunty, J. (2012). "Who am I?:" Exploring identity in online discussion forums. *International Journal of Educational Research, 53*, 407–420. doi:10.1016/j.ijer.2012.05.005.

Demo, D. (2001). *Discourse analysis for language teachers. ERIC Digest. ERIC Clearinghouse on Languages and linguistics.* Washington, DC: Center for Applied Linguistics.

Dennen, V. (2006). Assessing presence: Using positioning theory to examine instructor participation and persona in online discourse. *IADS International Conference on Cognition and Exploratory Learning in a Digital Age (CELDA 2006)*, 267-273. Retrieved July 15, 2012, from http://www.iadisportal.org/digital-library/assessing-presence-using-positioning-theory-to-examine-instructor-participation-and-persona-in-online-discourse

Dennen, V. (2007). *Presence* and *positioning* as components of online instructor persona. *Journal of Research on Technology in Education, 40*, 95–108.

Dennen, V., & Pashnyak, T. (2008). Finding community in the comments: The role of reader and blogger responses in a weblog community of practice. *International Journal of Web Based Communities, 4*(3), 272–283. doi:10.1504/IJWBC.2008.019189.

Department for education and skills, UK. (2005). *Social and emotional aspects of learning... improving behaviour... improving learning.* Retrieved May 3, 2012, from http://webarchive.nationalarchives.gov.uk/20110809101133/nsonline.org.uk/node/87009

Department for education and skills, UK. (2005). *Excellence and enjoyment: Social and emotional aspects of learning guidance.* Retrieved May 3, 2007, from http://public.merlin.swgfl.org.uk/establishments/803/QandS/Wellbeing/SealResourcesCD/data_folder/docs.html

Derks, D., Bos, A. E. R., & von Grumbkow, J. (2007). Emoticons and social interaction on the internet: The importance of social context. *Computers in Human Behavior, 23*, 842–849. doi:10.1016/j.chb.2004.11.013.

Derks, D., Fischer, A. H., & Bos, A. E. R. (2008). The role of emotion in computer-mediated communication: A review. *Computers in Human Behavior, 24*, 766–785. doi:10.1016/j.chb.2007.04.004.

Derwing, T. M., Munro, M. J., & Carbonaro, M. (2000). Does popular speech recognition software work with ESL speech? *TESOL Quarterly, 34*, 592–603. doi:10.2307/3587748.

Dewey, J. (1938). *Experience and education.* New York: Simon & Schuster.

D'Hertefelt, S. (2000). *Emerging and future usability challenges: Designing user experiences and user communities.* Netherlands: InteractiveArchtecture.com. Retrieved May 3, 2012, from http://users.skynet.be/fa250900/future/vision20000202shd.htm

Dhillon, R., Bhagat, S., Carvey, H., & Shriberg, E. (2004). *Meeting recorder project: Dialog act labeling guide.*

Dickey, M. D. (2004). The impact of web-logs (blogs) on student perceptions of isolation and alienation in a web-based distance-learning environment. *Open Learning*, *19*(3), 279–291. doi:10.1080/0268051042000280138.

Dickinson, M., Eom, S., Kang, Y., Lee, C. M., & Sachs, R. (2008). A balancing act: How can intelligent computer-generated feedback be provided in learner-to-learner interactions? *Computer Assisted Language Learning*, *21*(4), 369–382. doi:10.1080/09588220802343702.

Dillon, A. (2002). Beyond usability: Process, outcome and affect in human-computer interactions. *Canadian Journal of Library and Information Science*, *26*(4), 57–69.

Dimitracopoulou, A. (2005). Designing collaborative learning systems: Current trends and future research agenda. In T. Koschmann, D. Suthers, & T. Chan (Eds.), *Computer supported collaborative learning. The next 10 years! Proceedings of CSCL 2005* (pp. 115-124). Mahwah, NJ: Lawrence Erlbaum Associates.

Ding, N. (2009). Visualizing the sequential process of knowledge elaboration in computer-supported collaborative problem solving. *Computers & Education*, *52*, 509–519. doi:10.1016/j.compedu.2008.10.009.

Dirks, U. (2006). How critical discourse analysis faces the challenge of interpretive explanations from a micro- and macro-theoretical perspective. Review Essay. In G. Weiss & R. Wodak (Eds.), *Critical discourse analysis. Theory and interdisciplinarity*. Retrieved May 18, 2012, from http://nbn-resolving.de/urn:nbn:de:0114-fqs0602261

Djajadiningrat, J. P., Overbeeke, C. J., & Wensveen, S. A. G. (2000). Augmenting fun and beauty: A pamphlet. In *Proceedings of DARE 2000 on Designing Augmented Reality Environments* (pp. 131-134). Elsinore, Denmark.

Dlaska, A., & Krekeler, C. (2008). Self-assessment of pronunciation. *System*, *36*, 506–516. doi:10.1016/j.system.2008.03.003.

Dominelli, L. (2011). Climate change: Social workers' roles and contributions to policy debates and interventions. *International Journal of Social Welfare*, *20*(4), 430–438. doi:10.1111/j.1468-2397.2011.00795.x.

Donath, J. (2002). A semantic approach to visualizing online conversations. *Communications of the ACM*, *45*(4), 45–49. doi:10.1145/505248.505271.

Dong, A. (2004). *Quantifying coherent thinking in design: A computational linguistics approach*. Paper presented at the Design Computing and Cognition 2004.

Dong, A. (2006). Concept formation as knowledge accumulation: A computational linguistics study. *Artificial Intelligence for Engineering Design, Analysis and Manufacturing*, *20*(1), 35–53. doi:10.1017/S0890060406060033.

Donmoyer, R. (1990). Generalizability and the single-case study. In Eisner, E., & Peshkin, A. (Eds.), *Qualitative inquiry in education: The continuing debate* (pp. 175–200). New York: Teachers College Press.

Donoho, D. L., & Huo, X. (2005). BeamLab and reproducible research. *International Journal of Wavelets, Multresolution, and Information Processing*, *2*(4), 391–414. doi:10.1142/S0219691304000615.

Doughty, C. J., & Long, M. H. (2003). Optimal psycholinguistic environments for distance foreign language learning. *Language Learning & Technology*, *7*(3), 50–80.

Dougiamas, M., & Taylor, P. (2003). Moodle: Using learning communities to create an open source course management system. In D. Lassner & C. McNaught (Eds.), *World conference on educational multimedia, hypermedia and telecommunications* (pp. 171-178). Chesapeake, VA: AACE.

Doyle, G. (2010). From television to multi-platform. *Convergence: The International Journal of Research into New Media Technologies*, *16*(4), 431–449. doi:10.1177/1354856510375145.

Dresner, E., & Herring, S. C. (2012). Emoticons and illocutionary force. In Riesenfel, D., & Scarafile, G. (Eds.), *Philosophical dialogue: Writings in honor of Marcelo Dascal* (pp. 59–70). London, UK: College Publication.

DuBois, J. (2007). The stance triangle. In Englebretson, R. (Ed.), *Stancetaking in discourse: Subjectivity, evaluation, interaction* (pp. 139–182). Philadelphia: John Benjamins.

DuBois, J., & Kärkkäinen, E. (2012). Taking a stance on emotion: Affect, sequence and intersubjectivity in dialogic interaction. *Text & Talk*, *32*, 433–451.

DuFour, R., Dufour, R., Eaker, R., & Many, T. W. (2009). *Collaborative teams in professional learning communities at work: Learning by doing*. Bloomington, MA: Solution Tree.

Duke, N., & Pearson, P. D. (2002). Effective practices for developing reading comprehension. In Farstrup, A. E., & Samuels, S. J. (Eds.), *What research has to say about reading instruction* (pp. 205–242). Newark, DE: International Reading Association.

Dyke, G., Lund, K., Jeong, H., Medina, R., Suthers, D. D., van Aalst, J., et al. (2011). *Technological affordances for productive multivocality in analysis*. In 9th International Conference on Computer Supported Collaborative Learning. CSCL2011: Connecting computer supported collaborative learning to policy and practice (pp. 454–461). Hong Kong, 4–8 July.

Echeverría, A., García-Campo, C., Nussbaum, M., Gil, F., Villalta, M., & Améstica, M. et al. (2011). A framework for the design and integration of collaborative classroom games. *Computers & Education*, *57*(1), 1127–1136. doi:10.1016/j.compedu.2010.12.010.

Edwards, D. (1997). *Discourse and cognition*. London: Sage.

Edwards, D. (2004). Discursive psychology. In Fitch, K. L., & Sanders, R. E. (Eds.), *Handbook of language and social interaction* (pp. 257–273). Mahwah, NJ: Lawrence Erlbaum.

Edwards, D. (2004). Shared knowledge as a performative category in conversation. *Rivista Di Psicololinguistica Applicata*, *4*(2-3), 41–53.

Edwards, D., Hepburn, A., & Potter, J. (2009). Psychology, sociology and interaction: Disciplinary allegiance or analytic quality? - A response to Housley and Fitzgerald. *Qualitative Research*, *9*(1), 119–128. doi:10.1177/1468794108095078.

Edwards, D., & Potter, J. (1992). *Discursive psychology*. London: Sage.

Efimova, L., & de Moor, A. (2005). Beyond personal web-publishing: An exploratory study of conversational blogging practices. In *Proceedings of the 38th Annual Hawaii International Conference on System Sciences (HICSS'05)*. Retrieved May 5, 2012, from http://origin-www.computer.org/csdl/proceedings/hicss/2005/2268/04/22680107a.pdf

Eggins, S., & Slade, S. D. (1997). *Analysing casual conversation*. London, UK: Cassell.

Ekman, P. (1970). Universal facial expressions of emotion. *California Mental Health Research Digest, 8(4)*, 151-158. Retrieved April 24, 2012, from http://www.paulekman.com/wp-content/uploads/2009/02/Universal-Facial-Expressions-of-Emotions1.pdf

Ekman, P., & Friesen, W. V. (1971). Constants across culture in the face and emotion. *Journal of Personality and Social Psychology*, *17*(2), 124–129. doi:10.1037/h0030377.

El Tatawi, M. (2002). Corrective feedback in second language acquisition. *Working papers in TESOL and Applied Linguistics, 2*, 1-19.

Ellis, N. C., & Bogart, P. S. H. (2007). Speech and language technology in education: The perspective from SLA research and practice. *Proceedings SLaTE* (pp. 1-8). Farmington, PA.

Ellis, N. C. (2008). Optimizing the input: Frequency and sampling in usage-based and form-focused learning. In Long, M. H., & Doughty, C. (Eds.), *Handbook of language teaching* (pp. 139–158). Oxford: Blackwell.

Ellis, N., & Larsen-Freeman, D. (2006). Language emergence: Implications for applied Linguistics. *Applied Linguistics*, *27*(4), 558–589. doi:10.1093/applin/aml028.

Ellison, N. B., Heino, R. D., & Gibbs, J. L. (2006). Managing impressions online: Self-presentation processes in the online dating environment. *Journal of Computer-Mediated Communication*, *11*(2), 152–177. doi:10.1111/j.1083-6101.2006.00020.x.

Ellis, R., Loewen, S., & Erlam, R. (2006). Implicit and explicit corrective feedback and the acquisition of L2 grammar. *Studies in Second Language Acquisition*, *28*, 339–368. doi:10.1017/S0272263106060141.

Ellis, R., & Sheen, Y. (2006). Reexamining the role of recasts in second language acquisition. *Studies in Second Language Acquisition*, *28*, 575–601. doi:10.1017/S027226310606027X.

Elsner, M., & Charniak, E. (2008). You talking to me? A corpus and algorithm for conversation disentanglement. In *Proceedings of the 2008 Meeting of the Association for Computational Linguistics (ACL 2008)* (pp. 834-842). Columbus, OH.

Elsner, M., & Charniak, E. (2010). Disentangling chat. *Computational Linguistics*, *36*(3), 389–409. doi:10.1162/coli_a_00003.

eMapps Project Website. (2005). *Website*. Retrieved July 20, 2012, from http://emapps.info

Engeström, Y., Miettinen, R., & Punamäki, R. L. (1999). *Perspectives on activity theory*. Cambridge University Press. doi:10.1017/CBO9780511812774.

Englebretson, R. (Ed.). (2007). *Stancetaking in discourse: Subjectivity, evaluation, interaction*. Philadelphia: John Benjamins.

Engle, R. A., & Conant, F. R. (2002). Guiding principles for fostering productive disciplinary engagement: Explaining an emergent argument in a community of learners classroom. *Cognition and Instruction*, *20*, 399–484. doi:10.1207/S1532690XCI2004_1.

Enli, G. S. (2007). Gate-keeping in the new media age: A case study of the selection of text-messages in a current affairs programme. *Javnost - The public*, *14*(2), 47-62.

Enli, G. S., & Syvertsen, T. (2007). Participation, play and socializing in new media environments. In Dwyer, T., & Nightingale, V. (Eds.), *New media worlds: Challenges for convergence* (pp. 147–162). South Melbourne: Oxford University Press.

Erkens, G., & Janssen, J. J. H. M. (2008). Automatic coding of dialogue acts in collaboration protocols. *International Journal of Computer-Supported Collaborative Learning*, *3*(4), 447–470. doi:10.1007/s11412-008-9052-6.

Eskenazi, M., Kennedy, A., Ketchum, C., Olszewski, R., & Pelton, G. (2007). The NativeaccentTM pronunciation tutor: Measuring success in the real world. *Proceedings of the SLaTE-2007 workshop*, Farmington (pp. 124-127). PA, USA.

Eskenazi, M. (1996). Detection of foreign speakers' pronunciation errors for second language training – preliminary results.[Philadelphia, Pennsylvania.]. *Proceedings ICSLP*, *96*, 1465–1468.

Eskenazi, M. (2009). An overview of spoken language technology for education. *Speech Communication*, *51*, 832–844. doi:10.1016/j.specom.2009.04.005.

Essex, C. (1996). *Teaching creative writing in the elementary school*. ERIC Document Reproduction Service No. ED391182.

Esterberg, K. G. (2002). *Qualitative methods in social research*. Boston: McGraw-Hill.

Esuli, A., & Sebastiani, F. (2006). SentiWordNet: A publicly available lexical resource for opinion mining. In *Proceedings of the 5th Conference on Language Resources and Evaluation (LREC-2006)* (pp. 417-422). Genova, Italy.

Evans, M. A., Feenstra, E., Ryon, E., & McNeill, D. (2011). A multimodal approach to coding discourse: Collaboration, distributed cognition, and geometric reasoning. *International Journal of Computer-Supported Collaborative Learning*, *6*(2), 253–278. doi:10.1007/s11412-011-9113-0.

Eysenbach, G., & Till, J. E. (2001). Ethical issues in qualitative research on internet communities. *British Medical Journal*, *323*, 1103–1105. doi:10.1136/bmj.323.7321.1103 PMID:11701577.

FABULA Project Website. (2007). *Website*. Retrieved July 20, 2012, from http://www.fabula.idi.ntnu.no

Fairclough, N. (1989). *Language and power*. London, England: Longmans.

Fairclough, N. (1992). *Discourse and social change*. Malden, MA: Blackwell.

Fairclough, N. (1995). *Critical discourse analysis: The critical study of language*. London: Longman.

Fairclough, N. (1995). *Media discourse*. London, UK: Arnold.

Fairclough, N. (2001). The discourse of New Labour: Critical discourse analysis. In Wetherell, M., Taylor, S., & Yates, S. J. (Eds.), *Discourse as data: A guide for analysis* (pp. 229–266). London: The Open University/Sage.

Fairclough, N. (2010). *Critical discourse analysis: The critical study of language*. London: Routledge.

Fairclough, N., & Wodak, R. (1997). Critical discourse analysis. In van Dijk, T. A. (Ed.), *Introduction to discourse analysis* (pp. 258–284). London: Sage.

Faust, E. (2012, April 16). *Definition of online dating*. In eHow. Retrieved November 04, 2012, from http://www.ehow.com/about_6679610_definition-online-dating.html

Fawcett, R. P., & Davies, B. L. (1992). Monologue as a turn in dialogue: Towards an integration of exchange structure and rhetorical structure theory. In Dale, R., Hovy, E., Rösner, D., & Stock, O. (Eds.), *Aspects of automated language generation* (pp. 151–166). Berlin: Springer. doi:10.1007/3-540-55399-1_11.

Fehr, B., & Russell, J. A. (1984). Concept of emotion viewed from a prototype perspective. *Journal of Experimental Psychology. General, 113*, 464–486. doi:10.1037/0096-3445.113.3.464.

Feidakis, M., & Daradoumis, T. (2010). A five-layer approach in collaborative learning systems design with respect to emotion. In F. Xhafa et al. (Eds.), *2nd International Conference on Intelligent Networking and Collaborative Systems (INCOS 2010)* (pp. 290-296). Washington, DC: IEEE Computer Society.

Feidakis, M., Daradoumis, T., & Caballé, S. (2011). Endowing e-learning systems with emotion awareness. In L. Barolli et al. (Eds.), *3rd International Conference on Networking and Collaborative Systems (INCOS 2011)* (pp. 68-75). Washington, DC: IEEE Computer Society.

Feinberg, J. (2009). *Wordle*. Retrieved September 23, 2010, from http://www.wordle.net

Ferguson, C. (2010). *Online social networking goes to college: Two case studies of higher education institutions that implemented college-created social networking sites for recruiting undergraduate students*. ERIC Document Reproduction Service No. ED516904.

Feuer, A. (2011). Developing foreign language skills, competence and identity through a collaborative creative writing project. *Language, Culture and Curriculum, 24*(2), 125–139. doi:10.1080/07908318.2011.582873.

Fidel, R., Pejtersen, A. M., Cleal, B., & Bruce, H. (2004). A multidimensional approach to the study of human-information interaction: A case study of collaborative information retrieval. *Journal of the American Society for Information Science and Technology, 55*(11), 939–953. doi:10.1002/asi.20041.

Fielding, N. G. (2012). The diverse worlds and research practices of qualitative software [50 paragraphs]. *Forum Qualitative Sozialforschung/Forum: Qualitative Social Research, 13*(2). Art. 13. Retrieved May 18, 2012, from http://nbn-resolving.de/urn:nbn:de:0114-fqs1202124

Finnemann, N. O. (1999). *Hypertext and the representational capacities of the binary alphabet*. Retrieved February, 2005, from www.hum.au.dk/ckulturf/ pages/publications/nof/hypertext.htm

Fitze, M. (2006). Discourse and participation in ESL face-to-face and written electronic conferences. *Language Learning & Technology, 10*(1), 67–86.

Fitzgerald, P. (1998). The EyeCue system: A prototype for the next generation of educational technology. *Meridian Computer Technologies Journal, 1*(2). Retrieved June 13, 2012 from http://www.ncsu.edu/meridian/jun98/june98.pdf

Fjeld, M., Lauche, K., Bichsel, M., Voorhorst, F., Krueger, H., & Rauterberg, M. (2002). Physical and virtual tools: Activity theory applied to the design of groupware. *The Journal of Collaborative Computing – Special Issue of CSCW on Activity Theory and the Practice of Design, 11*(1-2), 153-180.

Flavell, J. H. (1976). Metacognitive aspects of problem solving. In Resnick, L. B. (Ed.), *The nature of intelligence* (pp. 231–236). Hillsdale, NJ: Erlbaum.

Flax, J. (1992). The end of innocence. In Butler, J., & Scott, J. (Eds.), *Feminists theorize the political* (pp. 445–463). New York: Routledge.

Flinkfeldt, M. (2011). 'Filling one's days': Managing sick leave legitimacy in an online forum. *Sociology of Health & Illness, 33*(5), 761–776. doi:10.1111/j.1467-9566.2011.01330.x PMID:21561459.

Flyvbjerg, B. (2006). Five misunderstandings about case-study research. *Qualitative Inquiry, 12*, 219–245. doi:10.1177/1077800405284363.

Foss, S. (2005). *Handbook of visual communication: Theory, methods, and media*. Mahwa, NJ: Lawrence Erlbaum.

Foucault, M. (1972). Orders of discourse. *Social Sciences Information. Information Sur les Sciences Sociales, 10*(2), 7–30. doi:10.1177/053901847101000201.

Fowler, R., Hodge, B., Kress, G., & Trew, T. (1979). *Language and control*. London, England: Routledge.

Fox, A. B., Rosen, J., & Crawford, M. (2009). Distractions, distractions: Does instant messaging affect college students' performance on a concurrent reading comprehension task? *Cyberpsychology & Behavior, 12*(1), 51–53. doi:10.1089/cpb.2008.0107 PMID:19006461.

Franco, H., Abrash, V., Precoda, K., Bratt, H., Rao, R., & Butzberger, J. et al. (2000). The SRI Eduspeak system: Recognition and pronunciation scoring for language learning.[Dundee Scotland.]. *Proceedings ESCA ETRW INSTi, L2000*, 123–128.

Franco, H., Neumeyer, L., Digalakis, V., & Ronen, O. (2000). Combination of machine scores for automatic grading of pronunciation quality. *Speech Communication, 30*, 121–130. doi:10.1016/S0167-6393(99)00045-X.

Fraser, D. (2006). The creative potential of metaphorical writing in the literacy classroom. *English Teaching: Practice and Critique, 5*(2), 93–108.

Frasson, C., & Chalfoun, P. (2010). Managing learner's affective states in intelligent tutoring systems. In Nkambou, R., Mizoguchi, R., & Bourdeau, J. (Eds.), *Advances in intelligent tutoring systems* (pp. 339–358). Springer-Verlag. doi:10.1007/978-3-642-14363-2_17.

Friend Wise, A., & Chiu, M. M. (2011). *Knowledge construction patterns in online conversation: A statistical discourse analysis of a role-based discussion forum*. In 9th International Conference on Computer Supported Collaborative Learning. CSCL2011: Connecting computer supported collaborative learning to policy and practice (pp. 64-71). Hong Kong, 4–8 July.

Friend Wise, A., Hsiao, Y.-T., Marbouti, F., Speer, J., & Perera, N. (2012). Initial validation of "Listening" behavior typologies for online discussions using microanalytic case studies. In J. van Aalst, K. Thompson, M. J. Jacobson, & P. Reimann (Ed.), *The future of learning: Proceedings of the 10ᵗʰ International Conference of the Learning Sciences (ICLS 2012)* (Vol. 1, pp. 56-63). Sydney, Australia: International Conference of the Learning Sciences.

Friese, S. (2011). Using ATLAS.ti for analyzing the financial crisis data [67 paragraphs]. *Forum Qualitative Sozialforschung/Forum: Qualitative Social Research, 12*(1), Art. 39. Retrieved May 18, 2012, from http://nbn-resolving.de/urn:nbn:de:0114-fqs1101397

Friese, S. (2012). *Qualitative data analysis with ATLAS.ti*. London: SAGE.

Fritz, G. (1998). Coherence in hypertext. In Wolfram, B., Lenk, U., & Ventola, E. (Eds.), *Coherence in spoken and written discourse: How to create it and how to describe it* (pp. 221–234). Amsterdam: John Benjamins.

Frohberg, D. (2006). *Mobile learning is coming of age: What we have and what we still miss*. Paper presented at DeLFI 2006, Darmstadt, Germany.

Frohlich, D., Drew, P., & Monk, A. (1994). The management of repair in human-computer interaction. *Human-Computer Interaction, 9*(3-4), 385–426. doi:10.1207/s15327051hci0903&4_5.

Fruchterman, T. M., & Reingold, E. M. (1991). Graph drawing by force-directed placement. *Software, Practice & Experience, 21*(11), 1129–1164. doi:10.1002/spe.4380211102.

Fulk, J., Steinfield, C., Schmitz, J., & Power, J. (1987). A social information processing model of media use in organizations. *Communication Research, 14*, 529–552. doi:10.1177/009365087014005005.

Gabrilovich, E., & Markovitch, S. (2007). *Computing semantic relatedness using Wikipedia-based explicit semantic analysis*. Paper presented at the 20th international joint conference on Artifical intelligence.

Gains, J. (1999). Electronic-mail - A new style of communication or just a new medium? An investigation into the text features of e-mail. *English for Specific Purposes, 18*(1), 81–101. doi:10.1016/S0889-4906(97)00051-3.

Galley, M., McKeown, K., Fosler-Lussier, E., & Jing, H. (2003). *Discourse segmentation of multi-party conversation*. In *Proceedings of the 41st Annual Meeting on Association for Computational Linguistics - Volume 1*.

Gammon, G. (1989). You won't lay an egg with the bald headed chicken. *B. C. The Journal of Special Education, 13*(2), 183–187.

Gangemi, A., Guarino, N., Masolo, C., & Oltramari, A. (2003). Sweetening WORDNET with DOLCE. *AI Magazine, 24*(3), 13–24.

García Cué, J. L. (2006). *Los estilos de aprendizaje y las tecnologías de la información y la comunicación en la formación del profesorado.* UNED, España. Dirigida por: Catalina M. Alonso García. Disponible en: http://www.estilosdeaprendizaje.es/JLGCue.pdf

Garcia, A. C., & Jacobs, J. B. (1999). The eyes of the beholder: Understanding the turn-taking system in quasi-synchronous computer-mediated communication. *Research on Language and Social Interaction, 32*(4), 337–367. doi:10.1207/S15327973rls3204_2.

Gardner, H. (2006). *Multiple intelligences: New horizons.* New York: Basic Books.

Garfinkel, H. (1967). *Studies in ethnomethodology.* Malden, MA: Blackwell.

Garret, J. J. (2000). *The elements of user experience. User-centered design for the web.* New Riders Publishing. Retrieved August 18, 2012, from http://www.jjg.net/elements/

Garrison, D. R., & Anderson, T. (2003). [*ˢᵗ century: A framework for research and practice.* London: Routledge Falmer.]. *E-learning,* 21.

Garrison, D. R., Anderson, T., & Archer, W. (2001). Critical thinking, cognitive presence, and computer conferencing in distance education. *American Journal of Distance Education, 15*(1), 7–23. doi:10.1080/08923640109527071.

Garzone, G. (2007). Genres, multimodality and the worldwide web: Theoretical issues. In Garzone et al., 15-30.

Garzone, G. (1997). Osservazioni sul valore pedagogico dell'ipertesto. In Schena, L., & Garzone, G. (Eds.), *Il computer al servizio degli insegnamenti linguistici, Milano 28.4.1995 - 3.5.1996* (pp. 21–39). Milan: Centro Linguistico Università Bocconi.

Garzone, G. E., Catenaccio, P., & Poncini, G. (Eds.). (2007). *Multimodality in corporate communication. Web genres and discursive identity.* Milano: Franco Angeli.

Gee, J. P. (2005). Good video games and good learning. *Phi Kappa Phi Forum, 85*(2), 33-37.

Gee, J. P. (1996). *Social linguistics and literacies: Ideology in discourses.* New York: Routledge Falmer Press.

Gee, J. P. (1999). *An introduction to discourse analysis: Theory and method.* New York: Routledge & Kegan Paul.

Gee, J. P. (2004). What is critical about critical discourse analysis? In Roger, R. (Ed.), *An introduction to critical analysis* (pp. 19–50). Mahwah, NJ: Lawrence Erlbaum.

Gentleman, R. (2005). Applying reproducible research in scientific discovery. *BioSilico,* Retrieved September 14, 2011, from http://web.archive.org/web/20090530044050/http://gentleman.fhcrc.org/Fld-talks/RGRepRes.pdf

Georgiev, T., Georgieva, E., & Smrikarov, A. (2004). M-Learning - a new stage of e-learning. *5th international conference on Computer systems and technologies.* Rousse, Bulgaria: CompSysTech.

Gibbs, J. L., Ellison, N. B., & Heino, R. D. (2006). Self-presentation in online personals: The role of anticipated future interaction, self-disclosure, and perceived success in Internet dating. *Communication Research, 33*(2), 152–177. doi:10.1177/0093650205285368.

Gibson, W. (2009). Intercultural communication online: Conversation analysis and the investigation of asynchronous written discourse. *Forum Qualitative Sozialforschung/Forum: Qualitative Social Research, 10*(1). Retrieved November 2, 2010, from http://www.qualitative-research.net/index.php/fqs/article/view/1253

Gibson, W. (2009). Negotiating textual talk: Conversation analysis, pedagogy and the organisation of online asynchronous discourse. *British Educational Research Journal, 35*(5), 705–721. doi:10.1080/01411920802688754.

Gill, L., & Dalgarno, B. (2008). *Influences on pre-service teachers' preparedness to use ICTs in the classroom.* Paper presented at the Hello! Where are you in the landscape of educational technology, ascilite., Melbourne.

Gimenez, J. (2000). Business e-mail communication: Some emerging tendencies in register. *English for Specific Purposes, 19*(3), 237–251. doi:10.1016/S0889-4906(98)00030-1.

Gimenez, J. (2002). New media and conflicting realities in multinational corporate communication: A case study. *International Review of Applied Linguistics, 40*(4), 323–343. doi:10.1515/iral.2002.016.

Gimenez, J. (2005). Unpacking business emails: Message embeddedness in international business email communication. In Gotti, M., & Gillaerts, P. (Eds.), *Genre variation in business letters* (pp. 235–255). Frankfurt: Peter Lang.

Gimenez, J. (2006). Embedded business emails: Meeting new demands in international business communication. *English for Specific Purposes, 25*(2), 154–172. doi:10.1016/j.esp.2005.04.005.

Gimenez, J. (2010). Narrative analysis in linguistic research. In Litosseliti, L. (Ed.), *Research methods in linguistics* (pp. 198–216). London: Continuum.

Gipps, C. (2002). Socio-cultural perspectives on assessment. In Wells, G., & Claxton, G. (Eds.), *Learning for life in the 21st century* (pp. 73–83). Malden, MA: Blackwell Publishers. doi:10.1002/9780470753545.ch6.

Girolami, M., & An, A. K. (2003). *On an equivalence between PLSI and LDA.* Paper presented at SIGIR 2003.

Gleason, J. S. (2011). Electronic discourse in language learning and language teaching. *Studies in Second Language Acquisition, 33*(1), 135–137. doi:10.1017/S0272263110000616.

Goffman, E. (1959). *The presentation of self in everyday life.* NY: Double Day Anchor Books.

Goffman, E. (1981). *Forms of talk.* Oxford: Basil Blackwell.

Goffman, I. (1974). *Frame analysis.* NY: Harper and Row.

Goldstein, H. (1995). *Multi-level statistical models.* Sydney: Edward Arnold.

Goldstein, H., Healy, M., & Rasbash, J. (1994). Multilevel models with applications to repeated measures data. *Statistics in Medicine, 13*, 1643–1655. doi:10.1002/sim.4780131605 PMID:7973240.

Goleman, D. (1995). *Emotional intelligence.* New York: Bantam Books.

Gomez, L. M., Sherin, M. G., Griesdorn, J., & Finn, L.-E. (2008). Creating social relationships: The role of technology in preservice teacher preparation. *Journal of Teacher Education, 59*(2), 117–131. doi:10.1177/0022487107314001.

Goodwin, C., & Heritage, J. (1990). Conversation analysis. *Annual Review of Anthropology, 19*, 283–307. doi:10.1146/annurev.an.19.100190.001435.

Goodyear, P., Jones, C., & Thompson, K. (forthcoming). Computer-supported collaborative learning: Instructional approaches, group processes and educational designs. In Spector, M., Merrill, D., Elan, J., & Bishop, M. J. (Eds.), *Handbook of research on educational communications and technology.* Springer.

Goos, M., Galbraith, P., & Renshaw, P. (2002). Socially mediated metacognition: Creating collaborative zones of proximal development in small group problem solving. *Educational Studies in Mathematics, 49*(2), 193–223. doi:10.1023/A:1016209010120.

Gorman, J. C., Amazeen, P. G., & Cooke, N. J. (2010). Team coordination dynamics. *Nonlinear Dynamics Psychology and Life Sciences, 14*, 265–289. PMID:20587302.

Gottman, J. M., & Krokoff, L. J. (1989). The relationship between marital interaction and marital satisfaction: A longitudinal view. *Journal of Consulting and Clinical Psychology, 57*, 47–52. doi:10.1037/0022-006X.57.1.47 PMID:2487031.

Graesser, A. C., D'Mello, S., Hu, X., Cai, Z., Olney, A., & Morgan, B. (2012). AutoTutor. In McCarthy, P., & Boonthum-Denecke, C. (Eds.), *Applied natural language processing: Identification, investigation and resolution* (pp. 169–187). Hershey, PA: Information Science Reference.

Graesser, A. C., & Person, N. (1994). Question asking during tutoring. *American Educational Research Journal, 31*, 104–137.

Grant, W.C. (1993). Wireless coyote: A computer-supported field trip. *Communications of the ACM - Special issue on technology in K–12 education, 36*(5), 57-59.

Gravano, A., Hirschberg, A., & Beňuš, Š. (2012). Affirmative cue words in task-oriented dialogue. *Computational Linguistics*, *38*(1), 1–39. doi:10.1162/COLI_a_00083.

Gray, S. H. (1995). Linear coherence and relevance: Logic in computer-human 'conversations.'. *Journal of Pragmatics*, *23*, 627–647. doi:10.1016/0378-2166(94)00039-H.

Greenfield, P. M., & Subrahmanyam, K. (2003). Online discourse in a teen chatroom: New codes and new modes of coherence in a visual medium. *Journal of Applied Developmental Psychology*, *24*(6), 713–738. doi:10.1016/j.appdev.2003.09.005.

Green, P. J. (2003). Diversities of gifts, but the same spirit.[The Statistician]. *Journal of the Royal Statistical Society: Series D*, *52*(4), 423–438. doi:10.1046/j.1467-9884.2003.02060.x.

Gress, C. L. Z., Fior, M., Hadwin, A. F., & Winne, P. H. (2008). Measurement and assessment in computer-supported collaborative learning. *Computers in Human Behavior*, *26*, 806–814. doi:10.1016/j.chb.2007.05.012.

Grice, H. P. (1975). Logic and conversation. In Cole, P., & Morgan, J. L. (Eds.), *Syntax and semantics* (pp. 41–58). New York: Academic Press.

Groarke, L. (2002). Towards a pragma-dialectics of visual arguments. In van Eemeren, F. H. (Ed.), *Advances in pragma-dialectics* (pp. 137–151). Amsterdam: Sic Sat.

Gros, B., & Silva, J. (2005). La formación del profesorado para su labor docente en espacios virtuales de aprendizaje. *Revista Iberoamericana de Educación, 36*(1). Retrieved May 24, 2012, from http://www.campus-oei.org/revista/tec_edu32.htm

Grosz, B. J., Weinstein, S., & Joshi, A. K. (1995). Centering: A framework for modeling the local coherence of discourse. *Computational Linguistics*, *21*(2), 203–225.

Grosz, B., & Sidner, C. (1986). Attention, intentions, and the structure of discourse. *Computational Linguistics*, *12*(3), 175–204.

Grote, B., Hagen, E., Stein, A., & Teich, E. (1997). Speech production in human-machine dialogue: A natural language generation perspective. In Maier, E., Mast, M., & Luperfoy, S. (Eds.), *Dialogue processing in spoken language systems* (pp. 70–85). Berlin: Springer. doi:10.1007/3-540-63175-5_38.

Grote, B., Lenke, N., & Stede, M. (1997). Ma(r)king concessions in English and German. *Discourse Processes*, *24*, 87–117. doi:10.1080/01638539709545008.

Gumperz, J. (1982). *Discourse strategies*. Cambridge: Cambridge University Press. doi:10.1017/CBO9780511611834.

Gunawardena, C. N., Hermans, M. B., Sanchez, D., Richmond, C., Boley, M., & Tuttle, R. (2009). A theoretical framework for building online communities of practice with social networking tools. *Educational Media International*, *46*(1), 3–16. doi:10.1080/09523980802588626.

Gunes, A., Inal, A., Adak, M. S., Bagci, E. G., Cicek, N., & Eraslan, F. (2008). Effect of drought stress implemented at pre – or post – anthesis stage on some physiological parameters as screening criteria in chickpea cultivars. *Russian Journal of Plant Physiology: a Comprehensive Russian Journal on Modern Phytophysiology*, *55*(1), 59–67. doi:10.1134/S102144370801007X.

Gurak, L. J. (1997). *Persuasion and privacy in cyberspace: the online protests over lotus marketplace and the clipper chip*. New Haven, CT: Yale University Press.

Guzzetti, B. J., Snyder, T. E., Glass, G. V., & Gamas, W. S. (1993). Promoting conceptual change in science: A comparative meta-analysis of instructional interventions from reading and science education. *Reading Research Quarterly*, *28*(2), 117–155. doi:10.2307/747886.

Guzzetti, B., & Gamboa, M. (2005). Online journaling: The informal writings of two adolescent girls. *Research in the Teaching of English*, *40*(2), 168–206.

Gwinnell, E. (1998). *Online seductions: Falling in love with strangers on the Internet*. New York, NY: Kodansha America, Inc..

Hakkarainen, K. (2012 in press). Expertise, collective creativity, and shared knowledge practices. In Gaunt, H., & Westerlund, H. (Eds.), *Collaborative learning in higher music education: Why, what, and how*. Ashgate.

Hakkarainen, K., Lipponen, L., & Järvelä, S. (2002). Epistemology of inquiry and computer supported collaborative learning. In Koschmann, T., Miyake, N., & Hall, R. (Eds.), *CSCL2: Carrying forward the conversation* (pp. 129–156). Mahwah, NJ: Erlbaum.

Halliday, M. A. K. (1978). *Language as a social semiotic*. London: Edward Arnold.

Halliday, M. A. K. (1994). *Introduction to functional grammar*. London: Arnold.

Halliday, M. A. K., & Hasan, R. (1976). *Cohesion in English*. London: Longman.

Hammersley, M. (2012). Transcription of speech. In Delamont, S. (Ed.), *Handbook of qualitative research in education* (pp. 439–445). Cheltenham: Edward Elgar Publishing Ltd..

Han, Z. (2002). A study of the impact of recasts on tense consistency in L2 output. *TESOL Quarterly, 36*, 542–572. doi:10.2307/3588240.

Hara, N., Bonk, C. J., & Angeli, C. (2000). Content analysis of online discussion in an applied educational psychology course. *Instructional Science, 28*, 115–152. doi:10.1023/A:1003764722829.

Harasim, L., Hiltz, R. S., Teles, L., & Turoff, M. (1995). *Learning network: A field guide to teaching and learning online*. Cambridge: The MIT Press.

Harasim, L., Hiltz, S. R., Teles, L., & Turoff, M. (1995). Network learning: A paradigm for the twenty-first century. In *Learning networks: A field guide to teaching and learning online* (pp. 271–278). Cambridge, MA: MIT Press.

Hård af Segerstad, Y. (2005). Language use in Swedish mobile text messaging. *Mobile Communications* (Vol. 31, pp. 313-333). Springer: London.

Harré, R. (2004). *Positioning theory*. Retrieved July 15, 2012, from http://www.massey.ac.nz/~alock/virtual/

Harré, R., Moghaddam, F., Cairnie, T., Rothbart, D., & Sabat, S. (2009). Recent advances in positioning theory. *Theory & Psychology, 19*, 5–31. doi:10.1177/0959354308101417.

Hartcher, P. (2010, June 26). Dark clouds that spelt doom for a prime minister. *The Sydney Morning Herald*. Retrieved from http://www.smh.com.au

Hascher, T. (2010). Learning and emotion: Perspectives for theory and research. *European Educational Research Journal, 9*, 13–28. doi:10.2304/eerj.2010.9.1.13.

Havranek, G. (2002). When is corrective feedback most likely to succeed? *International Journal of Educational Research, 37*, 255–270. doi:10.1016/S0883-0355(03)00004-1.

Haythornthwaite, C. (1996). Social network analysis: An approach and technique for the study of information exchange. *Library & Information Science Research, 18*(4), 323–342. doi:10.1016/S0740-8188(96)90003-1.

Heift, T., & Schulze, M. (2007). *Errors and intelligence in computer-assisted language learning: Parsers and pedagogues*. New York: Routledge.

Heino, R. D., Ellison, N. B., & Gibbs, J. L. (2010). Relationshopping: Investigating the market metaphor in online dating. *Journal of Social and Personal Relationships, 27*(4), 427–447. doi:10.1177/0265407510361614.

Hello-Hello Product Website. (2012). *Website*. Retrieved July 13, 2012, from http://www.hello-hello.com/

Henry, L. (2003). *Creative writing through wordless picture books*. ERIC Document Reproduction Service No. ED477997.

Hepburn, A., & Bolden, G. B. (2013). Transcription. In Stivers, T., & Sidnell, J. (Eds.), *The handbook of conversation analysis* (pp. 57–76). Oxford: Wiley-Blackwell.

Hepburn, A., & Potter, J. (2003). Discourse analytic practice. In Seale, C., Silverman, D., Gubrium, J. F., & Gobo, G. (Eds.), *Qualitative research practice* (pp. 180–196). London: Sage.

Heritage, J. (1995). Conversation analysis: Methodological aspects. In Quasthoff, U. M. (Ed.), *Aspects of oral communication* (pp. 391–418). Berlin, New York: Walter de Gruyter. doi:10.1515/9783110879032.391.

Heritage, J. (1997). Conversation analysis and institutional talk: Analyzing data. In Silverman, D. (Ed.), *Qualitative research: Theory, method and practice* (pp. 222–245). London: Sage.

Heritage, J., & Clayman, S. (2010). *Talk in action: Interactions, identities, and institutions*. West Sussex, UK: Wiley-Blackwell.

Heritage, J., & Raymond, G. (2005). The terms of agreement: Indexing epistemic authority and subordination in talk-in-interaction. *Social Psychology Quarterly, 68*(1), 15–38. doi:10.1177/019027250506800103.

Herring, S. C. (1994). Politeness in computer culture: Why women thank and men flame. In *Cultural performances: Proceedings of the third Berkeley women and language conference* (pp. 278-294). Berkeley, CA: Berkeley Women and Language Group.

Herring, S. C. (1999). Interactional coherence in CMC. *Journal of Computer-Mediated Communication, 4*(4). Retrieved November 2, 2010, from http://www.ascusc.org/jcmc/vol4/issue4/herring.html

Herring, S. C. (2007). A faceted classification scheme for computer-mediated discourse. *Language@Internet, 4.* Retrieved December 24, 2012, from http://www.languageatinternet.org/articles/2007/761

Herring, S. C. (2009). *Convergent media computer-mediated communication: Introduction and theory. Panel on Convergent Media Computer-Mediated Communication.* Paper presented at the Internet Research 10.0, Milwaukee, WI.

Herring, S. C. (2011). Computer-mediated conversation, Part II. Special issue. *Language@Internet, 8.*

Herring, S. C. (2001). Computer-mediated discourse. In Schiffrin, D., Tannen, D., & Hamilton, H. (Eds.), *The Handbook of discourse analysis* (pp. 612–634). Oxford: Blackwell Publishers.

Herring, S. C. (2004). Computer-mediated discourse analysis: An approach to researching online behavior. In Barab, S. A., Kling, R., & Gray, J. H. (Eds.), *Designing for virtual communities in the service of learning* (pp. 338–376). New York: Cambridge University Press. doi:10.1017/CBO9780511805080.016.

Herring, S. C. (2010). Web content analysis: Expanding the paradigm. In Hunsinger, J., Allen, M., & Klastrup, L. (Eds.), *The International handbook of Internet research* (pp. 233–249). Berlin, Germany: Springer Verlag.

Herring, S. C. (2013). Discourse in Web 2.0: Familiar, reconfigured, and emergent. In Tannen, D., & Tester, A. M. (Eds.), *Georgetown University round table on languages and linguistics 2011: Discourse 2.0: Language and new media* (pp. 1–25). Washington, DC: Georgetown University Press.

Herring, S., & Zelenkauskaite, A. (2009). Symbolic capital in a virtual heterosexual market: Abbreviation and insertion in Italian iTV SMS. *Written Communication, 26*(1), 5–31. doi:10.1177/0741088308327911.

Hesse, D. (2010). The place of creative writing in composition studies. *College Composition and Communication, 62*(1), 31–52.

Hewitt, J. (2005). Toward an understanding of how threads die in asynchronous computer conferences. *Journal of the Learning Sciences, 14*(4), 567–589. doi:10.1207/s15327809jls1404_4.

Higgins, J. P. T., & Thompson, S. G. (2002). Quantifying heterogeneity in a meta-analysis. *Statistics in Medicine, 21,* 1539–1558. doi:10.1002/sim.1186 PMID:12111919.

Hinds, P., & Kiesler, S. (1995). Communication across boundaries: Work, structure, and use of communication technologies in a large organization. *Organization Science, 6*(4), 373–393. doi:10.1287/orsc.6.4.373.

Hinduja, S., & Patchin, J. W. (2008). Social networking and identity construction: Personal information of adolescents on the internet: A quantitative content analysis of MySpace. *Journal of Adolescence, 31*(1), 125–146. doi:10.1016/j.adolescence.2007.05.004 PMID:17604833.

Hirst, G., & St Onge, D. (1998). *Lexical chains as representation of context for the detection and correction malapropisms. WordNet: An electronic lexical database (Language, Speech, and Communication).* Cambridge, MA: The MIT Press.

Hodge, B., & Kress, G. (1974). Transformations, models and processes: Towards a usable linguistics. *Journal of Literary Semantics, 4*(1), 4–18.

Hodge, B., & Kress, G. (1988). *Social semiotics.* Oxford, England: Polity Press.

Hodge, B., & Matthews, I. (2011). New media for old bottles: Linear thinking and the 2012 Australian election. *Communication. Politics and Culture, 44*(2), 95–111.

Hodges, B. (1999). Electronic books: Presentation software makes writing more fun. *Learning and Leading with Technology, 27*(1), 18–21.

Hodsdon-Champeon, C. (2010). Conversations within conversations: Intertextuality in racially antagonistic online discourse. *Language@Internet, 7,* article 10. Retrieved May 11, 2012, from http://www.languageatinternet.org/articles/2010/2820.

Holsti, O. R. (1969). *Content analysis for the social sciences and humanities*. Reading, MA: Addison Wesley.

Honeycutt, C., & Herring, S. C. (2009). Beyond microblogging: Convesation and collaboration via Twitter. In *Proceedings of the Forty-Second Hawai'I International Conference on System Sciences* (pp. 1-10). Los Alamitos, CA: IEEE Press.

Horne, J., & Wiggins, S. (2009). Doing being 'on the edge': Managing the dilemma of being authentically suicidal in an online forum. *Sociology of Health & Illness, 31*(2), 170–184. doi:10.1111/j.1467-9566.2008.01130.x PMID:18983421.

Horsburgh, D. (2003). Evaluation of qualitative research. *Journal of Clinical Nursing, 12*(2), 307–312. doi:10.1046/j.1365-2702.2003.00683.x PMID:12603565.

Ho, V. C. K. (2011). A discourse-based study of three communities of practice: How members maintain a harmonious relationship while threatening each other's face via email. *Discourse Studies, 13*(3), 299–326. doi:10.1177/1461445611400673.

Hovland, C. I. (1957). *The order of presentation in persuasion*. New Haven: Yale UP.

Hovy, E. H., & Arens, Y. (1991). Automatic generation of formatted text. In *Proceedings of the 9th AAAI National Conference on Artificial Intelligence* (pp. 92-96). Anaheim, California.

Howard, T. (1997). *The rhetoric of electronic communities. New Directions in Computers and Composition Studies Series*. Greenwich, CT: Ablex Publishing Corporation.

Howarth, P. (2007). Creative writing and Schiller's aesthetic education. *Journal of Aesthetic Education, 41*(3), 41–58. doi:10.1353/jae.2007.0025.

Howe, J. (2007). *To save themselves, US newspapers put readers to work*. Retrieved August 17, 2012, from http://www.wired.com/techbiz/media/magazine/15-08/ff_gannett?currentPage=all

Ho, Y.-F. (2011). *Corpus stylistics in principles and practice: a stylistic exploration of John Fowles' The Magus*. NY: Continuum.

Huedo-Medina, T. B., Sanchez-Meca, J., Marin-Martinez, F., & Botella, J. (2006). Assessing heterogeneity in meta-analysis. *Psychological Methods, 11,* 193–206. doi:10.1037/1082-989X.11.2.193 PMID:16784338.

Hulstijn, J. (2002). Towards a unified account of the representation, processing and acquisition of second language knowledge. *Second Language Research, 18*(3), 193–223. doi:10.1191/0267658302sr207oa.

Hung, H., & Yuen, S. (2010). Educational use of social networking technology in higher education. *Teaching in Higher Education, 15*(6), 703–714. doi:10.1080/13562517.2010.507307.

Hunston, S. (2005). Conflict and consensus. Constructing opposition in Applied Linguistics. In Tognini-Bonelli, E., & Lungo Camiciotti, G. (Eds.), *Strategies in academic discourse* (pp. 1–16). Amsterdam: John Benjamins.

Hunston, S. (2007). Using a corpus to investigate stance quantitatively and qualitatively. In Englebretson, R. (Ed.), *Stance-taking in discourse: Subjectivity, evaluation, interaction* (pp. 27–48). NY: Benjamins.

Hutchby, I. (1996). Power in discourse: The case of arguments on a British talk radio show. *Discourse & Society, 7*(4), 481–497. doi:10.1177/0957926596007004003.

Hutchby, I. (2001). *Conversation and technology*. Cambridge: Polity Press.

Hutchby, I. (2003). Affordances and the analysis of technologically-mediated interaction. *Sociology, 37,* 581–589. doi:10.1177/00380385030373011.

Hwang, S. (2008). Utilizing qualitative data analysis software: A review of ATLAS.ti. *Social Science Computer Review, 26*(4), 519–527. doi:10.1177/0894439307312485.

Hyland, K. (1993). ESL computer writers: What can we do to help? *System, 2*(1), 21–30. doi:10.1016/0346-251X(93)90004-Z.

Hyland, K. (2000). *Disciplinary discourses: Social interactions in academic writing*. Harlow, UK: Pearson Education Limited.

Hyland, K. (2005). Stance and engagement: A model of interaction in academic discourse. *Discourse Studies, 7*, 173–192. doi:10.1177/1461445605050365.

Hyland, K. (2008). Persuasion, interaction and the construction of knowledge: Representing self and others in research writing. *International Journal of English Studies, 8*(2), 8–18.

Iba, T., Nemoto, K., Peters, B., & Gloor, P. A. (2010). Analyzing the creative editing behavior of Wikipedia editors: Through dynamic social network analysis. Social and Behavioral Sciences, 2(4), 6441-6456.

Iedema, R. (2001). Analysing film and television: A social semiotic account of hospital: An unhealthy business. In van Leeuwen, T., & Jewitt, C. (Eds.), *Handbook of visual analysis* (pp. 183–204). London: Sage Publications.

Iedema, R., & Scheeres, H. (2009). Organizational discourse analysis. In Bargiela-Chiappini, F. (Ed.), *The handbook of business discourse* (pp. 80–91). Edinburgh: Edinburgh University Press.

Imm, K., & Stylianou, D. A. (2012). Talking mathematically: An analysis of discourse communities. *The Journal of Mathematical Behavior, 31*(1), 130–148. doi:10.1016/j.jmathb.2011.10.001.

Ireland, M. E., & Pennebaker, J. W. (2010). Language style matching in writing: Synchrony in essays, correspondence, and poetry. *Journal of Personality and Social Psychology, 99*(3), 549–571. doi:10.1037/a0020386 PMID:20804263.

ISLE 1.4. (1999). Pronunciation training: Requirements and solutions. ISLE Deliverable 1.4. Retrieved February 27, 2002, from http://nats-www.informatik.uni-hamburg.de/~isle/public/D14/D14.html

Ivanič, R. (1998). *Writing and identity: The discoursal construction of identity in academic writing*. Amsterdam: John Benjamins.

Iwashita, N. (2003). Negative feedback and positive evidence in task-based interaction: Differential, effects on L2 development. *Studies in Second Language Acquisition, 25*, 1–36. doi:10.1017/S0272263103000019.

Izard, C. E. (1971). *The face of emotions*. New York: Appleton-Century-Crofts.

Izard, C. E. (1977). *Human emotions*. New York: Plenum Press.

Jackson, H., & Stockwell, P. (2011). *An introduction to the nature and functions of language* (2nd ed.). London: Continuum International Publishing Group.

Jacobson, M. J., Lim, S. H., Lee, J., & Low, S.-H. (2007). *Virtual Singapura: Design considerations for an intelligent agent augmented multi-user virtual environment for learning science inquiry.* 15th International Conference on Computers in Education.

Jaffe, A. (Ed.). (2008). *Stance: Sociolinguistic perspectives*. Oxford: Oxford University Press.

James, D. (2008). A short take on evaluation and creative writing. *Community College Enterprise, 14*(1), 79–82.

Jaques, P., & Vicari, R. M. (2007). A BDI approach to infer student's emotions in an intelligent learning environment. *Computers & Education, 49*(2), 360–384. doi:10.1016/j.compedu.2005.09.002.

Jefferson, G. (1984). Notes of some orderliness of overlap onset. In V. d'Urso & P. Leonardi (Eds.), Discourse analysis and natural rhetorics (pp. 11-38). Cleup Editore: Padua.

Jefferson, G. (1989). Preliminary notes on a possible metric which provides for a 'standard maximum' silence of approximately one second in conversation. In Roger, D., & Bull, P. (Eds.), *Conversation: An interdisciplinary perspective* (pp. 166–196). Philadelphia: Multilingual Matters.

Jefferson, G. (2004). Glossary of transcript symbols with an introduction. In Lerner, G. H. (Ed.), *Conversation analysis: Studies from the first generation* (pp. 13–23). Philadelphia: John Benjamins.

Jefferson, G. (2004). A sketch of some orderly aspects of overlap in natural conversation. In Lerner, G. H. (Ed.), *Conversation analysis: Studies from the first generation* (pp. 43–59). Amsterdam: John Benjamins.

Jenkins, H. (2006). *Convergence culture: Where old and new media collide*. New York: University Press.

Jeong, H., & Chi, M. (2007). Knowledge convergence and collaborative learning. *Instructional Science, 35*(4), 287–315. doi:10.1007/s11251-006-9008-z.

Jewitt, C., & Oyama, R. (2001). Visual meaning: A social semiotic approach. In van Leeuwen, T., & Jewitt, C. (Eds.), *Handbook of visual analysis* (pp. 134–156). London: Sage Publications.

Jiang, J. J., & Conrath, D. W. (1997). Semantic similarity based on corpus statistics and lexical taxonomy. *CoRR*.

Johnson, W. L., Beal, C. R., Fowles-Winkler, A., Lauper, U., Marsella, S., Narayanan, S., & Papachristou, D. (2004). Tactical language training system: An interim report. *Intelligent Tutoring Systems*, 336-345.

Johnstone, B. (2007). Linking identity and dialect through stancetaking. In Englebretson, R. (Ed.), *Stancetaking in discourse: Subjectivity, evaluation, and interaction* (pp. 49–68). Amsterdam: John Benjamins.

Jonassen, D. H. (1991). Evaluating constructivist learning. *Educational Technology*, *31*(9), 28–33.

Jonesa, A., & Issroffb, K. (2005). Learning technologies: Affective and social issues in computer-supported collaborative learning. *Computers & Education*, *44*(4), 395–408. doi:10.1016/j.compedu.2004.04.004.

Jones, R. H. (2009). "Inter-activity:" How new media can help us to understand old media. In Rowe, C., & Wyss, E. L. (Eds.), *Language and new media: Linguistic, cultural and technological evolutions* (pp. 13–31). Cresskill, NJ: Hampton Press.

Jordan, P. W. (1998). Human factors for pleasure in product use. *Applied Ergonomics*, *29*(1), 25–33. doi:10.1016/S0003-6870(97)00022-7.

Jørgensen, M., & Phillips, L. (2002). *Discourse analysis as theory and method*. London: SAGE.

Judge, G. G., Griffiths, W. E., Hill, R. C., Lutkepohl, H., & Lee, T. C. (1985). *The theory and practice of econometrics* (2nd ed.). New York: Wiley.

Kahiigi, E., Ekenberg, L., Hansson, H., Tusubira, F., & Danielson, M. (2008). Exploring the e-learning state of art. *Electronic Journal of e-Learning*, *6*(2), 149-160.

Kanters, S., Cucchiarini, C., & Strik, H. (2009). The goodness of pronunciation algorithm: A detailed performance study. *Proceedings SLaTE-2009 workshop* (pp. 1-4). Warwickshire, England.

Kapoor, A., Burleson, W., & Picard, R. W. (2007). Automatic prediction of frustration. *International Journal of Human-Computer Studies*, *65*(8), 724–736. doi:10.1016/j.ijhcs.2007.02.003.

Kapur, M. (2011). Temporality matters: Advancing a method for analyzing problem-solving processes in a computer-supported collaborative environment. *International Journal of Computer-Supported Collaborative Learning*, *6*(1), 39–56. doi:10.1007/s11412-011-9109-9.

Kapur, M., & Kinzer, C. K. (2009). Productive failure in CSCL groups. *International Journal of Computer-Supported Learning*, *4*(1), 21–46. doi:10.1007/s11412-008-9059-z.

Karlsen, F., Sundet, V. S., Syvertsen, T., & Ytreberg, E. (2009). Non-professional activity on television in a time of digitalization: More fun for elite or new opportunities for ordinary people. *Nordicom Review*, *30*(1), 19–36.

Kathayat, S. B., & Bræk, R. (2011). Modeling collaborative learning services - A case study. *International Conference on Collaboration Technologies and Systems* (pp. 326-333). Philadelphia, PA: IEEE Press.

Katz, J. L. (2010). *Comparing and contrasting web services and open source*. (Unpublished doctoral dissertation). Massachusetts Institute of Technology, US.

Kaufman, J., Gentile, C., & Baer, J. (2005). Do gifted student writers and creative writing experts rate creativity the same way? *Gifted Child Quarterly*, *49*(3), 260. doi:10.1177/001698620504900307.

Keating, E., & Sunakawa, C. (2010). Participation cues: Coordinating activity and collaboration in complex online gaming worlds. *Language in Society*, *39*(3), 331–356. doi:10.1017/S0047404510000217.

Keefe, J. W. (1988). *Profiling and utilizing learning style*. Reston, VA: National Association of Secondary School Principals.

Keiner, J. (1996). *Real audiences-worldwide: A case study of the impact of WWW publication on a child writer's development*. ERIC Document Reproduction Service No. ED427664.

Kennedy, R. C. (2008). *Fat, fatter, fattest: Microsoft's kings of bloat*. Retrieved August 23, 2012, from http://www.infoworld.com/t/applications/fat-fatter-fattest-microsofts-kings-bloat-278

Kennedy-Clark, S., Thompson, K., & Richards, D. (2011). *Collaborative problem solving processes in a scenario-based multi-user environment*. In 9th International Conference on Computer Supported Collaborative Learning. CSCL2011: Connecting computer supported collaborative learning to policy and practice (pp. 706–710). Hong Kong, 4–8 July.

Kennedy-Clark, S. (2011). Pre-service teachers' perspectives on using scenario-based virtual worlds. *Computers & Education, 57*, 2224–2235. doi:10.1016/j.compedu.2011.05.015.

Kennedy-Clark, S., & Thompson, K. (2011). Using game-based inquiry learning in the study of disease epidemics. *Journal of Virtual Worlds Research. History and Heritage in Virtual Worlds, 6*(6), 1–25.

Kennedy-Clark, S., & Thompson, K. (2013). Between the lines: The use of discourse analysis in a virtual inquiry to inform learning design. *International Journal of Virtual and Personal Learning Environments*.

Kennedy, P. (2008). *A guide to econometrics*. Cambridge, MA: MIT Press.

Ketelhut, D. J., & Dede, C. (2006). Assessing inquiry learning. Retrieved from *Harvard Graduate School of Education* http://muve.gse.harvard.edu/rivercityproject/documents/lettersnarst2006paper.pdf

Ketelhut, D. J., Clarke, J., & Nelson, B. (2010). The development of River City, a multi-user virtual environment-based scientific inquiry curriculum: Historical and design evolutions. In M. J. Jacobson & P. Reimann (Eds.), Designs for learning environments of the future (pp. 89-110). New York: Springer Science + Business Media.

Ketelhut, D. J. (2007). The impact of student self-efficacy on scientific inquiry skills: An exploratory investigation in River City, a multi-user virtual environment. *Journal of Science Education and Technology, 16*(1), 99–111. doi:10.1007/s10956-006-9038-y.

Khan, B. A., & Matskin, M. (2009). FABULA platform for active e-learning in mobile networks. *IADIS International Conference Mobile Learning 2009* (pp. 33-41). Barcelona, Spain: IADIS Press.

Khan, B. A., & Matskin, M. (2011). Multiagent system to support place/space based mobile learning in city. In *International Conference on Information Society (i-Society)* (pp. 66-71). London, UK.

Khan, F. M., Fisher, T. A., Shuler, L., Wu, T., & Pottenger, W. M. (2002). *Mining chat-room conversations for social and semantic interactions*.

Kiesler, S., Siegel, J., & McGuire, T. W. (1984). Social psychological aspects of computer-mediated communication. *The American Psychologist, 39*, 1123–1134. doi:10.1037/0003-066X.39.10.1123.

Kim, M. S., & Raja, N. S. (1991). *Verbal aggression and self-disclosure on computer bulletin boards*. Paper presented at the Annual Meeting of the International Communication Association, Chicago, IL, May.

Kim, Y., Franco, H., & Neumeyer, L. (1997). *Automatic pronunciation scoring of specific phone segments for language instruction. Proceedings of Eurospeech* (pp. 645–648). Greece: Rhodes.

King, A. (1999). Discourse patterns for mediating peer learning. In O'Donnell, A. M., & King, A. (Eds.), *Cognitive perspectives on peer learning* (pp. 87–117). Mahwah, NJ: Erlbaum.

King, G., & Zeng, L. (2001). Logistic regression in rare events data. *Political Analysis, 9*, 137–163. doi:10.1093/oxfordjournals.pan.a004868.

Kintsch, W., & van Dijk, T. A. (1978). Toward a model of text comprehension and production. *Psychological Review, 85*(5), 363–393. doi:10.1037/0033-295X.85.5.363.

Klein, B. (2009). Contrasting interactivities: BBC radio message boards and listener participation. *The Radio Journal: International Studies in Broadcast and Audio Media, 7*(1), 11–26. doi:10.1386/rajo.7.1.11/1.

Kleinke, S. (2008). Emotional commitment in public political Internet message boards. *Journal of Language and Social Psychology, 27*(4), 409–421. doi:10.1177/0261927X08322483.

Klein, N. (2000). *No logo*. New York: Picador.

Koenker, R., & Zeileis, A. (2007). Reproducible econometric research (A Critical Review of the State of the Art). In Research Report Series, 60, Department of Statistics and Mathematics, Wirtschaftsuni-versität Wien.

Kolb, D. (1997). Scholarly hypertext: Self-represented complexity. In M. Bernstein & L. Carr (Eds.), Proceedings of Hypertext '97 (pp. 247-268). Southhampton: Association of Computing Machinery.

Koller, V., Hardie, A., Rayson, P., & Semino, E. (2008). Using a semantic annotation tool for the analysis of metaphor in discourse. *Metaphoric.de, 15*, 141–160.

Konopásek, Z. (2008). Making thinking visible with Atlas.ti: Computer assisted qualitative analysis as textual practices [62 paragraphs]. *Forum Qualitative Sozialforschung/Forum: Qualitative Social Research, 9*(2), Art. 12. Retrieved May 19, 2012, from http://nbn-resolving.de/urn:nbn:de:0114-fqs0802124

Kort, B., & Reilly, R. (2002). Analytical models of emotions, learning and relationships: Towards an affect sensitive cognitive machine. In *Proceedings of the International Conference on Virtual Worlds and Simulation (VWSim 2002)* (pp. 1-15). San Antonio, Texas. Retrieved February 15, 2013, from http://affect.media.mit.edu/projectpages/lc/vworlds.pdf

Koschmann, T. (1999). *Toward a dialogic theory of learning: Bakhtin's contribution to understanding learning in settings of collaboration*. Paper presented at the Computer Support for Collaborative Learning (CSCL'99), Palo Alto.

Kreijns, K., Kirschner, P. J., & Jochems, W. (2002). The sociability of computer-supported collaborative learning environments. *Journal of Educational Technology & Society, 5*(1), 8–22.

Kress, G. (2003). *Literacy in the media age*. London, New York: Routledge. doi:10.4324/9780203164754.

Kress, G., & Hodge, B. (1979). *Language as ideology*. London, England: Routledge.

Kress, G., & van Leeuwen, T. (1996). *Reading images: The grammar of visual design*. London: Routledge.

Kress, G., & van Leeuwen, T. (2006). *Reading images: The grammar of visual design*. New York: Routledge.

Kress, G., & Van Leeuwen, T. (Eds.). (2001). *Multimodal discourse: The modes and media of contemporary communication*. London, England: Bloomsbury Academic.

Krippendorff, K. (2004). *Content analysis: An introduction to its methodology*. Thousand Oaks: Sage.

Kristeva, J. (1980). *Desire in language: A semiotic approach to literature and art*. New York, NY: Columbia University Press.

Kukulska-Hulme, A., Sharples, M., Milrad, M., Arnedillo-Sanchez, I., & Vavoula, G. (2011). The genesis and development of mobile learning in Europe. In Parsons, D. (Ed.), *Combining e-learning and m-learning: New applications of blended educational resources* (pp. 151–177). Hershey, PA: IGI Global. doi:10.4018/978-1-60960-481-3.ch010.

Kumar, R., Mahdian, M., & McGlohon, M. (2010). *Dynamics of conversations*. Paper presented at the 16th ACM SIGKDD international conference on Knowledge discovery and data mining.

Kuzu, A. (2007). Views of pre-service teachers on blog use for instruction and social interaction. *Turkish Online Journal of Education, 8*(3), 34–51.

Lamb, R., & Kling, R. (2003). Reconceptualizing users as social actors in information systems research. *Management Information Systems Quarterly, 27*(2), 197–235.

Lamerichs, J., & te Molder, H. F. M. (2003). Computer-mediated communication: From a cognitive to a discursive model. *New Media & Society, 5*(4), 451–473. doi:10.1177/146144480354001.

Lampa, G. (2004). Imagining the blogosphere: An introduction to the imagined community of instant publishing. In L. J. Gurak, S. Antonijevic, L. Johnson, C. Ratliff, & J. Reyman (Eds.), *Into the blogosphere: Rhetoric, community, and culture of weblogs*. Retrieved May 5, 2012, from http://blog.lib.umn.edu/blogosphere/imagining_the_blogosphere.html

Landauer, T. K., & Dumais, S. T. (1997). A solution to Plato's problem: The Latent Semantic Analysis theory of acquisition, induction and representation of knowledge. *Psychological Review, 104*(2), 211–240. doi:10.1037/0033-295X.104.2.211.

Landow, G. (2001). Hypertext and critical theory. In Trend, D. (Ed.), *Reading digital culture* (pp. 98–108). Oxford, UK: Blackwell Publishers.

Landow, G. P. (1992). *Hypertext: The convergence of contemporary critical theory and technology*. Baltimore: Johns Hopkins University Press.

Langlotz, A., & Locher, M. (2012). Ways of communicating emotional stance in online disagreements. *Journal of Pragmatics*, *44*, 1591–1606. doi:10.1016/j.pragma.2012.04.002.

Larsen-Freeman, D., & Cameron, L. (2008). Research methodology on language development from a complex systems perspective. *Modern Language Journal*, *92*, 200–213. doi:10.1111/j.1540-4781.2008.00714.x.

Lather, P. (2001). Validity as an incitement to discourse: Qualitative research and the crisis of legitimation. In Richardson, V. (Ed.), *Handbook of research on teaching* (4th ed., pp. 241–250). Washington, DC: American Educational Research Association.

Laureano-Cruces, A. (2004). Agentes Pedagógicos. In *En el XVII Congreso Nacional y III Congreso Internacional de Informática y Computación de la ANIEI* (pp. 1-10). Tepic, Nayarit.

Laureano-Cruces, A. (2006). Emociones Sintéticas y Avatars. División de Ciencias y Artes para el Diseño (Ed.), *Reflexión a la Acción* (pp. 251-255). Retrieved April 24, 2012, from http://ce.azc.uam.mx/profesores/clc/04_proyecto_de_inv/comp_suave/EmocionesSint.pdf

Laureano-Cruces, A., Terán-Gilmore, A., & Rodríguez-Aguilar, R. M. (2005). Cognitive and affective interaction in a pedagogical agent. In *XVIII Congreso Nacional y IV Congreso Internacional de Informática y Computación de la ANIEI* (pp. 1-7).Torreón, Coah.

Laurier, E. (2000). Why people say where they are during mobile phone calls. *Environment and Planning. D, Society & Space*, *19*, 485–504. doi:10.1068/d228t.

Law, N., & Wong, O.-W. (2013). Exploring pivotal moments in students' knowledge building progress using participation and discourse marker indicators as heuristic guides. In Suthers, D., Lund, K., Rosé, C., Law, N., & Teplovs, C. (Eds.), *Productive multivocality in the analysis of group interactions*. New York: Springer.

Lawson, H. M., & Leck, K. (2012). Dynamics of Internet dating. *Social Science Computer Review*, *24*(2), 189–208. doi:10.1177/0894439305283402.

Leary, M. R. (1995). *Impression management and interpersonal behavior*. Madison, WI: Brown and Benchmark Publishers.

LeCompte, M. D., & Preissle, J. (2003). *Ethnography and qualitative design in educational research* (2nd ed.). San Diego, CA: Academic Press.

Lee, E. Y. C., Chan, C. K. K., & van Aalst, J. (2006). Students assessing their own collaborative knowledge building. *International Journal of Computer-Supported Collaborative Learning*, *1*, 103–125.

Lee, J., Luchini, K., Michael, B., Norris, C., & Soloway, E. (2004). *More than just fun and games: Assessing the value of educational video games in the classroom. Extended abstracts on Human factors in computing systems* (pp. 1375–1378). New York, NY: ACM Press.

Lehmann-Willenbrock, N., & Kauffeld, S. (2010). The downside of communication: Complaining cycles in group discussions. In Schuman, S. (Ed.), *The handbook for working with difficult groups* (pp. 33–54). San Francisco: Jossey-Bass/Wiley.

Leisch, F. (2003). Sweave and beyond: Computations on text documents. In K. Hornik, F. Leisch, & A. Zeileis (Eds.), *Proceedings of the 3ʳᵈ International Workshop on Distributed Statistical Computing* (pp. 1-15). Technische Universität Wien, Austria.

Lemke, J. L. (2001). *Towards a theory of traversals*. Retrieved August 4, 2012, from http://academic.brooklyn.cuny.edu/education/jlemke/papers/traversals/traversal-theory.htm

Lemke, J. (1989). Semantics and social values. *Word*, *40*(1-2), 37–50.

Lengel, R. H., & Daft, R. L. (1988). The selection of communication media as an executive skill. *The Academy of Management Executive*, *2*(3), 225–232. doi:10.5465/AME.1988.4277259.

Lesk, M. (1986). *Automatic sense disambiguation using machine readable dictionaries: How to tell a pine cone from an ice cream cone*. Paper presented at the 5th annual international conference on Systems documentation.

Lester, J., & Stone, B. (1997). Increasing believability in animated pedagogical agents. In Memories Autonomous Agents '97 (pp. 16-21). Marina del Rey, California.

Levine, A., Winkler, C., & Petersen, S. (2010). The CUNY young adult program--utilizing social networking to foster interdisciplinary and cross-cohort student communication during workforce training. *Journal of Asynchronous Learning Networks, 14*(3), 74–80.

Levinson, S. C. (1983). *Pragmatics*. Cambridge: Cambridge University Press.

Lewins, A., & Silver, C. (2007). *Using software in qualitative research: A step-by-step guide*. London: Sage.

Lewis, B. (2004). NVivo 2.0 and ATLAS.ti 5.0: A comparative review of two popular qualitative data-analysis programs. *Field Methods, 16*(4), 439–469. doi:10.1177/1525822X04269174.

Lexicoder 2.0. (2011). *Media Observatory*. McGill Institute for the Study of Canada. Retrieved January 4, 2013, from http://www.lexicoder.com

Lexicoder Semantic Dictionary. (2011). *Media observatory*. McGill Institute for the Study of Canada. Retrieved January 4, 2013, from http://www.lexicoder.com

Li, D., & Lim, C. P. (2007). Scaffolding online historical inquiry tasks: A case study of two secondary school classrooms. *Computers & Education, 50*, 1394–1410. doi:10.1016/j.compedu.2006.12.013.

Liddicoat, A. J. (2007). *An introduction to conversation analysis*. London: Continuum.

Ligorio, M. B., & Cucchiara, S. (2011). Blended Collaborative Constructive Participation (BCCP): A model for teaching in higher education. In eLearning Papers 27th Edition "Transforming education through technology" (pp. 1-9). Barcelona, Spain: elearningeuropa.info.

Ligorio, M. B. (2001). Integrating communication formats: Synchronous versus asynchronous and text-based versus visual. *Computers & Education, 37*(2), 103–125. doi:10.1016/S0360-1315(01)00039-2.

Ligorio, M. B., Loperfido, F. F., Sansone, N., & Spadaro, P. F. (2010). Blending educational models to design blended activities. In Persico, D., & Pozzi, F. (Eds.), *Techniques for fostering collaboration in online learning communities: Theoretical and practical perspectives* (pp. 64–81). Hershey, PA: IGI Global. doi:10.4018/978-1-61692-898-8.ch005.

Lim, H. L., & Sudweeks, F. (2008). Constructing learning conversations: Discourse and social network analyses of educational chat exchanges. In Kelsey, S., & St. Amant, K. (Eds.), *Handbook of research on computer-mediated communication* (pp. 451–476). London: Information Science Reference. doi:10.4018/978-1-59904-863-5.ch034.

Lin, D. (1998). *An information-theoretic definition of similarity*. Paper presented at the Fifteenth International Conference on Machine Learning.

Linehan, C., & McCarthy, J. (2000). Positioning in practice: Understanding participation in the social world. *Journal for the Theory of Social Behaviour, 30*, 435–453. doi:10.1111/1468-5914.00139.

Ling, R., & Baron, N. S. (2007). Text messaging and IM: Linguistic comparison of American college data. *Journal of Language and Social Psychology, 26*(3), 291–298. doi:10.1177/0261927X06303480.

Lintean, M., Rus, V., Cai, Z., Witherspoon-Johnson, A., Graesser, A. C., & Azevedo, R. (2012). Computational aspects of the intelligent tutoring system MetaTutor. In McCarthy, P., & Boonthum-Denecke, C. (Eds.), *Applied natural language processing: Identification, investigation and resolution* (pp. 247–260). Hershey, PA: Information Science Reference.

Liu, B. (2012). *Sentiment analysis & opinion mining. Synthesis Lectures on Human Language Technologies*. Morgan & Claypool Publishers.

Livingstone, S. (1999). New media, new audiences? *New Media & Society, 1*(1), 59–66. doi:10.1177/146144489 9001001010.

Livingstone, S. (2004). The challenge of changing audiences: Or, what is the audience researcher to do in the age of the internet? *European Journal of Communication*, *19*(1), 75–86. doi:10.1177/0267323104040695.

Ljung, G., & Box, G. (1979). On a measure of lack of fit in time series models. *Biometrika, 66*, 265–270. doi:10.1093/biomet/66.2.265.

Lloyd, S. L. (2004). Using comprehension strategies as a springboard for student talk. *Journal of Adolescent & Adult Literacy, 48*(4), 114–124. doi:10.1598/JAAL.48.2.3.

Locher, M., & Watts, R. (2005). Politeness theory and relational work. *Journal of Politeness Research, 1*, 9–33.

Loewen, S., & Philp, J. (2006). Recasts in the adult English L2 classroom: Characteristics, explicitness, and effectiveness. *Modern Language Journal, 90*, 536–556. doi:10.1111/j.1540-4781.2006.00465.x.

Lombard, M., Snyder-Duch, J., & Bracken, C. C. (2002). Content analysis in mass communication: Assessment and reporting of intercoder reliability. *Human Communication Research, 28*(4), 587–604. doi:10.1111/j.1468-2958.2002.tb00826.x.

Lonsdale, P., Baber, C., & Sharples, M. (2004). A context awareness architecture for facilitating mobile learning. In Attewell, J., & Savill-Smith, C. (Eds.), *Learning with mobile devices: Research and development* (pp. 79–85). London: Learning and Skills Development Agency.

Lord, V., Davis, B., & Mason, P. (2008). Stance shifts in rapist discourse: Characteristics and taxonomies. *Psychology, Crime & Law, 14*, 357–379. doi:10.1080/10683160701770153.

Lorenzo-Dus, N., Garcés-Conejos, P., & Bou-Franch, P. (2011). On-line polylogues and impoliteness: The case of postings sent in response to the Obama Reggaeton YouTube video. *Journal of Pragmatics, 43*, 2578–2593. doi:10.1016/j.pragma.2011.03.005.

Louhiala-Salminen, L. (2002). The fly's perspective: Discourse in the daily routine of a business manager. *English for Specific Purposes, 21*(3), 211–231. doi:10.1016/S0889-4906(00)00036-3.

Lowrey, W., & Mackay, J. (2008). Journalism and blogging: A test of a model of occupational competition. *Journalism Practice, 2*, 64–81. doi:10.1080/17512780701768527.

Lowrey, W., & Woo, C. W. (2010). The news organization in uncertain times: Business or institution? *Journalism & Mass Communication Quarterly, 87*(1), 41–61. doi:10.1177/107769901008700103.

Luberda, J. (2000). *Unassuming positions: Middlemarch, its critics, and positioning theory*. Retrieved August 6, 2012, from http://www.sp.uconn.edu/~jbl00001/positioning/luberda_positioning.htm

Lu, J., Chiu, M. M., & Law, N. W. (2011). Collaborative argumentation and justifications: A statistical discourse analysis of online discussions. *Computers in Human Behavior, 27*(2), 946–955. doi:10.1016/j.chb.2010.11.021.

Lupton, D. (1992). Discourse analysis: A new methodology for understanding the ideologies of health and illness. *Australian Journal of Public Health, 16*, 145–150. doi:10.1111/j.1753-6405.1992.tb00043.x PMID:1391155.

Lury, C. (1996). *Consumer culture*. New Brunswick, NJ: Rutgers University Press.

Luzón, M. J. (2011). "Interesting post, but I disagree:" Social presence and antisocial behaviour in academic weblogs. *Applied Linguistics, 32*(5), 517–540. doi:10.1093/applin/amr021.

Lynch, P., & Horton, S. (2008). *Web style guide online* (3rd ed.). Yale University. Retrieved August 18, 2012, from http://webstyleguide.com/

Lynch, M. (2002). Capital punishment as moral imperative: Pro-death-penalty discourse on the internet. *Punishment and Society, 4*(2), 213–236. doi:10.1177/14624740222228554.

Lyster, R. (1998). Negotiation of form, recasts, and explicit correction in relation to error types and learner repair in immersion classrooms. *Language Learning, 48*, 183–218. doi:10.1111/1467-9922.00039.

Lyster, R., & Ranta, L. (1997). Corrective feedback and learner uptake. *Studies in Second Language Acquisition, 19*, 37–66. doi:10.1017/S0272263197001034.

Lyster, R., & Saito, K. (2010). Oral feedback in classroom SLA: A meta-analysis. *Studies in Second Language Acquisition, 32*, 265–302. doi:10.1017/S0272263109990520.

Mabry, E. A. (1997). Framing flames: The structure of argumentative messages on the net. *Journal of Computer Mediated Communication, 2*(4). Retrieved February 29, 2012 from http://jcmc.indiana.edu/vol2/issue4/mabry.html

Macdonell, D. (1986). *Theories of discourse: An introduction*. Oxford, England: Blackwell.

MacGregor, P. (2007). Tracking the online audience: Metric data start a subtle revolution. *Journalism Studies, 8*, 280–298. doi:10.1080/14616700601148879.

Machin, D., & van Leeuwen, T. (2007). *Global media discourse: A critical introduction*. London: Routledge.

Mackey, A., & Philp, J. (1998). Conversational interaction and second language development: Recasts, responses, and red herrings. *Modern Language Journal, 82*, 338–356. doi:10.1111/j.1540-4781.1998.tb01211.x.

MacKinnon, D. P., Lockwood, C. M., & Williams, J. (2004). Confidence limits for the indirect effect: Distribution of the product and resampling methods. *Multivariate Behavioral Research, 39*, 99–128. doi:10.1207/s15327906mbr3901_4 PMID:20157642.

Mafé, C. R., Blas, S. S., & Tavera-Mesías, J. F. (2010). A comparative study of mobile messaging services acceptance to participate in television programmes. *Journal of Service Management, 21*(1), 69–102. doi:10.1108/09564231011025128.

Mak, B., Siu, M., Ng, M., Tam, Y.-C., Chan, Y.-C., & Chan, K.-W. (2003). PLASER: Pronunciation learning via automatic speech recognition. *Proceedings of the HLT-NAACL 2003 Workshop on Building Educational Applications using Natural Language Processing* (pp. 23-29). Edmonton, Canada.

Makri, K., & Kynigos, C. (2007). The role of blogs in studying the discourse and social practices of mathematics teachers. *Journal of Educational Technology & Society, 10*(1), 73–84.

Maks, I., & Vossen, P. (2012). A lexicon model for deep sentiment analysis and opinion mining applications. *Decision Support Systems, 53*(4), 680–688. doi:10.1016/j.dss.2012.05.025.

Malesky, L., & Peters, C. (2012). Defining appropriate professional behavior for faculty and university students on social networking websites. *Higher Education: The International Journal of Higher Education and Educational Planning, 63*(1), 135–151.

Mallen, M. J., Day, S. X., & Green, M. A. (2003). Online versus face-to-face conversations: An examination of relational and discourse variables. *Psychotherapy (Chicago, Ill.), 40*(1-2), 155–163. doi:10.1037/0033-3204.40.1-2.155.

Malliou, E., Maounis, F., Miliarakis, A., Savvas, S., Sotiriou, S., & Stratakis, M. (2004). The Motfal project - Mobile technologies for ad-hoc learning. In *IEEE International Conference on Advanced Learning Technologies* (pp. 910-911). Joensuu, Finland.

Mallon, R., & Oppenheim, C. (2002). Style used in electronic mail. *Aslib Proceedings, 54*(1), 8–22. doi:10.1108/00012530210697482.

Manabu, O., & Takeo, H. (1994). *Word sense disambiguation and text segmentation based on lexical cohesion*. Paper presented at the 15th conference on Computational linguistics - Volume 2.

Mann, W. C., & Thompson, S. A. (1987). *Rhetorical structure theory: A theory of text organization*. Los Angeles, CA: University of Southern California, Information Sciences Institute.

Mann, W. C., & Thompson, S. A. (1988). Rhetorical structure theory: Toward a functional theory of text organization.[from http://www.sfu.ca/rst/index.html]. *Text, 8*(3), 243–281. Retrieved February 4, 2013 doi:10.1515/text.1.1988.8.3.243.

Many Eyes. (*n.d.*). Word cloud generator guide. Retrieved December 22, 2012, from http://www-958.ibm.com/software/data/cognos/manyeyes/page/Word_Cloud_Generator.html

Marcoccia, M., Atifi, H., & Gauducheau, N. (2008). Text-centered versus multimodal analysis of instant messaging conversation. *Language@Internet, 5*, Article 7. Retrieved October 14, 2012, from www.languageatinternet.de

Markauskaite, L. (2007). Exploring the structure of trainee teachers' ICT literacy: The main components of, and relationships between, general cognitive and technical capabilities. *Educational Technology Research and Development, 55*, 547–572. doi:10.1007/s11423-007-9043-8.

Markus, M. L. (1994). Electronic mail as the medium of managerial choice. *Organization Science, 5*(4), 502–527. doi:10.1287/orsc.5.4.502.

Martey, R. M., & Stromer-Galley, J. (2007). The digital dollhouse: Context and social norms in The Sims online. *Games and Culture: A Journal of Interactive Media, 2*(4), 314-334.

Martin, B. (2011). Debating vaccination: Understanding the attack on the Australian Vaccination Network. *Living Wisdom, 8*, 14–40.

Martinez, A., Dimitriadis, Y., Gomez, E., Jorrin, I., Rubia, B., & Marcos, J. A. (2006). Studying participation networks in collaboration using mixed methods. *International Journal of Computer-Supported Collaborative Learning, 1*(3), 383–408. doi:10.1007/s11412-006-8705-6.

Martinez, R., Yacef, K., Kay, J., & Schwendimann, B. (2012). *An interactive teacher's dashboard for monitoring multiple groups in a multi-tabletop learning environment. In Proceedings of Intelligent Tutoring Systems* (pp. 482–492). Springer.

Martin, J. R. (1992). *English text: Systems and structure*. Amsterdam: Benjamin Press.

Martin, J. R., & Rose, D. (2007). *Working with discourse: Meaning beyond the clause* (2nd ed.). London: Continuum International.

Martin, J. R., & White, P. R. (2005). *The language of evaluation: Appraisal in English*. Basingstoke, New York: Palgrave Macmillan.

Marx, K., & Engels, F. (1975). Manifesto of the Communist party. In *Collected works* (*Vol. 6*, pp. 1845–1848). London: Lawrence and Wishart.

Mason, P., Davis, B., & Bosley, D. (2005). Stance analysis: When people talk online. In Krishnamurthy, S. (Ed.), *Innovations in E-Marketing* (*Vol. 2*, pp. 261–282). Hershey, PA: Idea Group.

Matskin, M., Kirkeluten, O., Krossnes, S., Sæle, O., & Wagner, T. (2001). Agora: An infrastructure for cooperative work support in multi-agent systems. In Wagner, T., & Rana, O. (Eds.), *Infrastructure for agents, multi-agent systems, and scalable multi-agent systems* (pp. 28–40). Berlin, Germany: Springer Berlin-Heidelberg.

Matsuzawa, Y., Oshima, J., Oshima, R., Niihara, Y., & Saki, S. (2011). KBDeX: A platform for exploring discourse in collaborative learning. *Procedia: Social and Behavioral Sciences, 26*(1), 198–207. doi:10.1016/j.sbspro.2011.10.576.

Matthiessen, C., Zeng, L., Cross, M., Kobayashi, I., Teruya, K., & Wu, C. (1998). The Multex generator and its environment: Application and development. In *Proceedings of ACL Workshop on Natural Language Generation* (pp. 228–37). Montréal, Canada.

Matuszek, C., Cabral, J., Witbrock, M., & Deoliveira, J. (2006). *An introduction to the syntax and content of Cyc.* Paper presented at the 2006 AAAI Spring Symposium on Formalizing and Compiling Background Knowledge and Its Applications to Knowledge Representation and Question Answering.

Mauthner, N. S., & Doucet, A. (2003). Reflexive accounts and accounts of reflexivity in qualitative data analysis. *Sociology, 37*(3), 413–431. doi:10.1177/00380385030373002.

Mayes, P. (2010). Corporate culture in a global age: Starbucks' "social responsibility" and the merging of corporate and personal interests. In Trosborg, A. (Ed.), *Pragmatics across cultures* (pp. 597–628). Berlin: De Gruyter Mouton.

Mays, N., & Pope, C. (1995). Qualitative research: Rigour and qualitative research. *British Medical Journal, 311*, 09-112.

Mazur, J., & Lio, C. (2004). *Learner articulation in an immersive visualization environment*. Paper presented at the Conference on Human Factors in Computing Systems, Vienna, Austria.

Mazur, J. (2004). Conversation analysis for educational technologists: Theoretical and methodological issues for researching the structures, processes and meaning of on-line talk. In Jonassen, D. (Ed.), *Handbook of research for educational communications and technology*. New York: MacMillian.

McCarthy, M. (1992). *Discourse analysis for language teachers*. New York: Cambridge University Press.

McCarthy, M., & Carter, R. (1994). *Language as discourse: Perspectives for language teachers*. New York: Longman.

McDaniel, S. E., Olson, G. M., & Magee, J. C. (1996). *Identifying and analyzing multiple threads in computer-mediated and face-to-face conversations*. Paper presented at the 1996 ACM conference on Computer supported cooperative work.

McKee, H. (2002). "YOUR VIEWS SHOWED TRUE IGNORANCE!!!": (Mis)Communication in an online interracial discussion forum. *Computers and Composition, 19*, 411–434. doi:10.1016/S8755-4615(02)00143-3.

McKenzie, C. T., Lowrey, W., Hays, H., Chung, J. Y., & Woo, C. W. (2012). Listening to news audiences: The impact of community structure and economic factors. *Mass Communication & Society, 14*(3), 375–395. doi:10.1080/15205436.2010.491934.

McLuhan, M. (1964). *Understanding media: The extensions of man*. London, England: Routledge.

McPherson, A. (2009). *Introduction to macromolecular crystallography* (2nd ed.). New Jersey: Wiley-Blackwell. doi:10.1002/9780470391518.

McQuail, D. (1997). *Audience analysis*. Thousand Oaks, London, New Delhi: Sage Publications.

McQuail, D. (2005). *Mcquail's mass communication theory* (5th ed.). London: Sage Publications.

McWilliams, E. M. (2001). *Social and organizational frames in e-mail: A discourse analysis of e-mail sent at work*. (Unpublished MA thesis). Georgetown University.

Menzel, W., Herron, D., Bonaventura, P., & Morton, R. (2000). Automatic detection and correction of non-native English pronunciations.[Dundee, Scotland.]. *Proceedings of InSTIL, L2000*, 49–56.

Mercer, N. (2008). The seeds of time: Why classroom dialogue needs a temporal analysis. *Journal of the Learning Sciences, 17*, 33–59. doi:10.1080/10508400701793182.

Mihalcea, R., Corley, C., & Strapparava, C. (2006). *Corpus-based and knowledge-based measures of text semantic similarity*. Paper presented at the 21st national conference on Artificial intelligence - Volume 1.

Miles, M. B., & Huberman, M. A. (1994). *Qualitative data analysis: An expanded sourcebook* (2nd ed.). Thousand Oaks, CA: SAGE.

Miller, G. A. (1995). WordNet: A lexical database for English. *Communications of the ACM, 38*(11), 39–41. doi:10.1145/219717.219748.

Miller, G. A., & Isard, S. (1963). Some perceptual consequences of linguistic rules. *Journal of Verbal Learning and Verbal Behavior, 2*(3), 217–228. doi:10.1016/S0022-5371(63)80087-0.

Mills, N. (2011). Situated learning through social networking communities: The development of joint enterprise, mutual engagement, and a shared repertoire. *CALICO Journal, 28*(2), 345–368.

Miner, Q. D. A. (2009). Version 3.2.3. Montreal, QC, Canada. Provalis Research, 2414 Bennett Ave.

Misztal, J. (2001). Young children's literacy practices in a virtual world: Establishing an inline interaction order. *Reading Research Quarterly, 46*(2), 101–118.

MOBIlearn project website. (2002). *Website*. Retrieved July 11, 2012, from http://www.mobilearn.org/

Moghaddam, R., Harré, R., & Lee, N. (2008). Positioning and conflict: An introduction. In Moghaddam, R., Harré, R., & Lee, N. (Eds.), *Global conflict resolution through positioning theory* (pp. 81–93). NY: Springer. doi:10.1007/978-0-387-72112-5_1.

Mondada, L. (2013). The conversation analytic approach to data collection. In Stivers, T., & Sidnell, J. (Eds.), *The handbook of conversation analysis* (pp. 32–56). Oxford: Wiley-Blackwell.

Moodle Web Site, M. L. E. (2003). *Website.* Retrieved July 10, 2012, from http://mle.sourceforge.net/

Moor, P. J., Heuvelman, A., & Verleur, R. (2010). Flaming on YouTube. *Computers in Human Behavior, 26*(6), 1536–1546. doi:10.1016/j.chb.2010.05.023.

Moreante, R., & Sporleder, C. (2012). Modality and negation: An introduction to the special issue. *Computational Linguistics, 38*(2), 223–260. doi:10.1162/COLI_a_00095.

Morgan, W. (2006). Poetry makes nothing happen: Creative writing and the English classroom. *English Teaching: Practice and Critique, 5*(2), 17–33.

Morris, M., & Ogan, C. (1996). The Internet as mass medium. *Journal of Computer-Mediated Communication, 1*(4). Retrieved May 10, 2012, from http://jcmc.indiana.edu/vol1/issue4/morris.html

Morris, J., & Hirst, G. (1991). Lexical cohesion computed by thesaural relations as an indicator of the structure of text. *Computational Linguistics, 17*(1), 21–48.

Mortensen, T., & Walker, J. (2002). Blogging thoughts: Personal publication as an online research tool. In A. Morrison (Ed.), Researching ICTs in context (pp. 249-279). Oslo, Norway: InterMedia Report.

Moshtagh, M. (2009). *The development of controversies: From the Early Modern Period to online discussion forums.* Bern, Switzerland: Peter Lang.

MOTFAL Project Website. (2004). *Website.* Retrieved July 10, 2012, from http://www.ellinogermaniki.gr/ep/motfal/

Muhlpfordt, M., & Wessner, M. (2005). *Explicit referencing in chat supports collaborative learning.* Paper presented at the Proceedings of the 2005 Conference on Computer support for collaborative learning: learning 2005: The next 10 years!

Mulholland, J. (1999). Email: Uses, issues and problems in an institutional setting. In Bargiela-Chiappini, F., & Nickerson, C. (Eds.), *Writing business: Genres, media and discourses* (pp. 50–84). London: Longman.

Murray, D. E. (1989). When the medium determines turns: Turn-taking in computer conversation. In Coleman, H. (Ed.), *Working with language: A multidisciplinary consideration of language use in work contexts* (pp. 319–338). Berlin, New York: Mouton de Gruyter.

Myers, M. (2008). *Qualitative research in business and management.* Thousand Oaks, CA: SAGE.

Närhi, K. (2004). *The eco-social approach in social work and the challenges to the expertise of social work.* Jyväskylä, Finland: University of Jyväskylä. Retrieved January 4, 2012, from http://dissertations.jyu.fi/studeduc/9513918343.pdf

Närhi, K., & Matthies, A.-L. (2001). What is the ecological (self-)consciousness of social work? Perspectives on the relationship between social work and ecology. In Matthies, A.-L., Nähri, K., & Ward, D. (Eds.), *The eco-social approach in social work* (pp. 16–53). Jyväskylä, Finland: Sophi.

Nelson, T. H. (1965). *Complex information processing: A file structure for the complex, the changing and the indeterminate.* Paper presented at the Proceedings of the 1965 20th national conference.

Nelson, T. H. (1981). *Literary machines: The report on, and of, project xanadu concerning word processing, electronic publishing, hypertext, thinkertoys, tomorrow's intellectual revolution, and certain other topics including knowledge, education and freedom.* Self-published.

Neri, A., Cucchiarini, C., & Strik, H. (2006). Selecting segmental errors in L2 Dutch for optimal pronunciation training. *IRAL -. International Review of Applied Linguistics in Language Teaching, 44*, 357–404. doi:10.1515/IRAL.2006.016.

Neri, A., Cucchiarini, C., & Strik, H. (2008). The effectiveness of computer-based speech corrective feedback for improving segmental quality in L2 Dutch. *ReCALL, 20*(2), 225–243. doi:10.1017/S0958344008000724.

Neri, A., Cucchiarini, C., Strik, H., & Boves, L. (2002). The pedagogy technology interface in computer assisted pronunciation training. *Computer Assisted Language Learning, 15*, 441–467. doi:10.1076/call.15.5.441.13473.

Neumeyer, L., Franco, H., Digalakis, V., & Weintraub, M. (2000). Automatic scoring of pronunciation quality. *Speech Communication, 30*(2), 83–93. doi:10.1016/S0167-6393(99)00046-1.

Neumeyer, L., Franco, H., Weintraub, M., & Price, P. (1996). Automatic text independent pronunciation scoring of foreign language student speech.[Philadelphia, Pennsylvania.]. *Proceedings ICSLP, 96*, 1457–1460.

Newman, D. R., Johnson, C., Webb, B., & Cochrane, C. (1996). Evaluating the quality of learning in Computer Supported Co-operative Learning. *Journal of the American Society for Information Science American Society for Information Science*, *48*(6), 484–494. doi:10.1002/(SICI)1097-4571(199706)48:6<484::AID-ASI2>3.0.CO;2-Q.

Nicholas, H., Lightbown, P. M., & Spada, N. (2001). Recasts as feedback to language learners. *Language Learning*, *51*, 719–758. doi:10.1111/0023-8333.00172.

Nickerson, C. (2000). *Playing the corporate language game*. Amsterdam and Atlanta, GA: Rodopi.

Nielsen, J. (2006). *F-shaped pattern for reading web content*. Retrieved August 4, 2012, from http://www.useit.com/alertbox/ reading_pattern.html

Niles, I., & Pease, A. (2001). *Towards a standard upper ontology*. Paper presented at the international conference on Formal Ontology in Information Systems - Volume 2001.

Nilsson, M., van Laere, J., Susi, T., & Ziemke, T. (2012). Information fusion in practice: A distributed cognition perspective on the active role of users. *Information Fusion*, *13*(1), 60–78. doi:10.1016/j.inffus.2011.01.005.

Nivre, J., Allwood, J., & Ahlsen, E. (1999). *Interactive communication management: Coding manual V1.0*. Gotyeborg University.

Norman, D. A. (2002). Emotion and design: Attractive things work better. *Interactions Magazine*, *ix*(4), 36-42. Retrieved February 4, 2013, from http://www.jnd.org/dn.mss/emotion_design_at.html

Norris, J. M., & Ortega, L. (2000). Effectiveness of L2 instruction: A research synthesis and quantitative meta-analysis. *Language Learning*, *50*, 417–528. doi:10.1111/0023-8333.00136.

Nova, N., Girardin, F., Molinari, G., & Dillenbourg, P. (2006). The underwhelming effects of automatic location-awareness on collaboration in a pervasive game. *7th International Conference on the Design of Cooperative Systems* (pp. 224-238). Provence, France.

Noy, N. F. (2004). Semantic integration: A survey of ontology-based approaches. *SIGMOD Record*, *33*(4), 65–70. doi:10.1145/1041410.1041421.

NUD-IST. (1997). *Version 4.0*. Melbourne, Victoria, Australia: Qualitative Solutions & Research Ltd..

Nüssli, M., Jermann, P., Sangin, M., & Dillenbourg, P. (2009). Collaboration and abstract representations: Towards predictive models based on raw speech and eye-tracking data. *Proceedings of the 9th international conference on Computer supported collaborative learning* (pp.78-82). Rhodes, Greece, 8 - 13 June.

O'Leary, Z. (2004). *The essential guide to doing research*. London, England: Sage.

Ochs, E. (1979). Planned and unplanned discourse. In T. Givón (Ed.), Discourse and syntax (Syntax and semantics, Vol. 12). New York: Academic Press.

O'Day, S. (2006). *Setting the stage for creative writing: Plot scaffolds for beginning and intermediate writers*. ERIC Document Reproduction Service No. ED493378.

O'Donnell, M. (2000). RSTTool 2.4 - A markup tool for rhetorical structure theory. In *Proceedings of the International Natural Language Generation Conference (INLG'2000* (pp. 253-256). Mitzpe Ramon, Israel.

Ogura, K., Ishizaki, M., Nishimoto, K., Negoita, M., Howlett, R., & Jain, L. (2004). A method of extracting topic threads towards facilitating knowledge creation in chat conversations. Knowledge-based intelligent information and engineering systems (Vol. 3213, pp. 330-336). Springer Berlin/Heidelberg.

Olson, D. R. (1977). From utterance to text: The bias of language in speech and writing. *Harvard Educational Review*, *47*, 257–281.

Ong, W. (1982). *Orality and literacy: The technologizing of the word*. London: Methuen. doi:10.4324/9780203328064.

Ong, W. (1988). *Orality and literacy: The technologizing of the Word*. New York: Methuen.

Orlikowski, W., & Yates, J. A. (1994). Genre repertoire: The structuring of communicative practices in organizations. *Administrative Science Quarterly*, *39*(4), 541–574. doi:10.2307/2393771.

Orr, A. (2004). *Meeting, mating, and cheating: Sex, love, and the new world of online dating*. Upper Saddle River, NJ: Reuters Prentice Hall.

Ortega, F., Gonzalez-Barahona, J. M., & Robles, G. (2008). On the inequality of contributions to Wikipedia. In *Proceedings of the 41st Annual Hawaii International Conference on System Sciences*. Waikoloa, HI, USA.

Ortony, A., Clore, G., & Collins, A. (1988). *The cognitive structure of emotions*. Cambridge: Cambridge University Press. doi:10.1017/CBO9780511571299.

Osgood, C. E., Suci, G., & Tannenbaum, P. (1957). *The measurement of meaning*. University of Illinois Press.

Owen, T. (1995). Poems that change the world: Canada's wired writers. *English Journal*, *84*(6), 48–52. doi:10.2307/820891.

Paine, C. B., & Joinson, A. N. (2008). Privacy, trust, and disclosure online. In A. Barak (Ed.), *Psychological aspects of cyberspace: Theory, research, applications* (pp. 13-31). Cambridge, UK: Cambridge University Press.

Palincsar, A. S., & Brown, A. L. (1984). Reciprocal teaching of comprehension-fostering, comprehension-monitoring activities. *Cognition and Instruction*, *1*(2), 117–175. doi:10.1207/s1532690xci0102_1.

Palincsar, A. S., & Herrenkohl, L. (2002). Designing collaborative learning contexts. *Theory into Practice*, *41*, 26–32. doi:10.1207/s15430421tip4101_5.

Pang, B., & Lee, L. (2008). Opinion mining and sentiment analysis. *Foundations and Trends in Information Retrieval*, *2*(1–2), 1–135. Retrieved July 10, 2012, from http://www.cs.cornell.edu/home/llee/omsa/omsa-published.pdf

Panksepp, J. (2000). Affective consciousness and the instinctual motor system. In Ellis, R., & Newton, N. (Eds.), *The caldron of consciousness: Motivation, affect and self-organization, advances in consciousness research* (pp. 27–54). Amsterdam: John Benjamins.

Panova, I., & Lyster, R. (2002). Patterns of corrective feedback and uptake in an adult ESL classroom. *TESOL Quarterly*, *36*, 573–595. doi:10.2307/3588241.

Panyametheekul, S., & Herring, S. C. (2003). Gender and turn allocation in a Thai chat room. *Journal of Computer Mediated Communication, 9*(1). Retrieved 2 November, 2010, from http://onlinelibrary.wiley.com/doi/10.1111/j.1083-6101.2003.tb00362.x/full

Paolillo, J. C. (2008). Structure and network in the YouTube core. In *Proceedings of the 41st Annual Hawaii International Conference on System Sciences*. Waikoloa, HI, USA.

Pape, S., & Featherstone, S. (2006). *Feature writing. A practical introduction*. London: Sage.

Park, Y. (2005). Culture as deficit: A critical discourse analysis of the concept of culture in contemporary social work discourse. *Journal of Sociology and Social Welfare*, September, *32*(3) 11-33.

Park-Fuller, L. M. (1986). Voices: Bakhtin's heteroglossia and polyphony, and the performance of narrative literature. *Literature and Performance*, *7*(1), 1–12. doi:10.1080/10462938609391621.

Park, H., Dailey, R., & Lemus, D. (2002). The use of exploratory factor analysis and principal components analysis in communication research. *Human Communication Research*, *23*, 562–577. doi:10.1111/j.1468-2958.2002.tb00824.x.

Parks, K. A., & Fals-Stewart, W. (2004). The temporal relationship between college women's alcohol consumption and victimization experiences. *Alcoholism, Clinical and Experimental Research*, *28*(4), 625–629. doi:10.1097/01.ALC.0000122105.56109.70 PMID:15100614.

Paulsen, R. (2010). Mediated psychopathy—A critical discourse analysis of newspaper representations of aggression. *KRITIKE*, *4*(2), 60–86.

Paus, E., Werner, C. S., & Jucks, R. (2012). Learning through online peer discourse: Structural equation modeling points to the role of discourse activities in individual understanding. *Computers & Education*, *58*(4), 1127–1137. doi:10.1016/j.compedu.2011.12.008.

Pawan, F., Paulus, T. M., Yalcin, S., & Chang, C.-F. (2003). Online learning: Patterns of engagement and interaction among in-service teachers. *Language Learning & Technology*, *7*(3), 119–140.

Pawley, A., & Syder, F. (1983). Natural selection in syntax: Notes on adaptive variation and change in vernacular and literary grammar. *Journal of Pragmatics*, *7*, 551–579. doi:10.1016/0378-2166(83)90081-4.

Payne, J. S., & Ross, B. M. (2005). Synchronous CMC, working memory, and L2 oral proficiency development. *Language Learning & Technology*, *9*(3), 35–54.

Payne, J. S., & Whitney, P. J. (2002). Developing L2 oral proficiency through synchronous CMC: Output, working memory, and interlanguage development. *CALICO Journal*, *20*(1), 7–32.

Payne, M. (2005). *Modern social work theory* (3rd ed.). Chicago: Lyceum.

Peeters, J. (2012). Invited commentary: A comment on 'climate change: social workers' roles and contributions to policy debates and interventions. *International Journal of Social Welfare, 21*, 105–107. doi:10.1111/j.1468-2397.2011.00847.x.

Peirce, C. (1958). *Values in a universe of chance: Selected writings of Charles S. Peirce (1839-1914)*. Garden City, NY: Doubleday.

Peng, R. D., Dominici, F., & Zeger, S. L. (2006). Reproducible epidemiologic research. *American Journal of Epidemiology, 163*(9), 783–789. doi:10.1093/aje/kwj093 PMID:16510544.

Pennebaker, J. W., & Graybeal, A. (2001). Patterns of natural language use: Disclosure, personality, and social integration. *Current Directions in Psychological Science, 10*(3), 90–93. doi:10.1111/1467-8721.00123.

Pennebaker, J., Francis, M., & Booth, R. (2001). *Linguistic inquiry and word count (LIWC): LIWC2001*. Mahwah: Lawrence Erlbaum.

Penning de Vries, B., Cucchiarini, C., Strik, H., & Van Hout, R. (2011). Adaptive corrective feedback in second language learning. In De Wannemacker, S., Clarebout, G., & De Causmaecker, P. (Eds.), *Interdisciplinary approaches to adaptive learning. A look at the neighbors, Communications in Computer and Information Science series* (pp. 1–14). Heidelberg: Springer Verlag. doi:10.1007/978-3-642-20074-8_1.

Peugh, J. L., & Enders, C. K. (2004). Missing data in educational research. *Review of Educational Research, 74*, 525–556. doi:10.3102/00346543074004525.

Pevalin, D. J., & Ermisch, J. (2004). Cohabitating unions, repartnering and mental health. *Psychological Medicine, 34*, 1553–1559. doi:10.1017/S0033291704002570 PMID:15724885.

Pew Institute. (2010). *Social media and internet use among teens and young adults*. Retrieved June 10, 2012, from http://pewinternet.org/Reports/2010/Social-Media-and-Young-Adults.aspx

Pew Institute. (2011). *Social networking and our lives*. Retrieved June 10, 2012, from http://pewinternet.org/Reports/2011/Technology-and-social-networks.aspx

Peyton, J., & Rigg, P. (1999). *Poetry in the adult ESL classroom*. ERIC Document Reproduction Service No. ED439626.

Philip, D. N. (2010). Social network analysis to examine interaction patterns in knowledge building communities. *Canadian Journal of Learning and Technology, 36*(1), 1–19.

Piaget, J. (1997). *La representación del mundo en el niño*. Madrid: Morata.

Picard, R. W., & Klein, J. (2002). Computers that recognise and respond to user emotion: Theoretical and practical implications. *Interacting with Computers, 14*(2), 141–169. doi:10.1016/S0953-5438(01)00055-8.

Plutchik, R. (1980). *Emotion: A psychoevolutionary synthesis*. New York: Harper & Row.

Poelmans, S., Wessa, P., Milis, K., & van Stee, E. (2009). Modeling educational technology acceptance and satisfaction. In L. Gómez Chova, D. Martí Belenguer, & I. Candel Torres (Eds.), *Proceedings of EDULEARN09 Conference* (pp. 5882-5889). US: IATED.

Pojanapunya, P., & Jaroenkitboworn, K. (2011). How to say "good-bye" in second life. *Journal of Pragmatics, 43*, 3591–3602. doi:10.1016/j.pragma.2011.08.010.

Pomerantz, A. M., & Fehr, B. J. (1997). Conversation analysis: An approach to the study of social action as sense making practices. In T. A. van Dijk (Ed.), *Discourse studies: A multidisciplinary introduction, volume 2. Discourse as social interaction* (pp. 64-91). London: Sage Publications.

Pomerantz, A. M. (1984). Agreeing and disagreeing with assessments: Some features of preferred/dispreferred turn shapes. In Atkinson, J. M., & Heritage, J. (Eds.), *Structures of social action: Studies in conversation analysis* (pp. 57–101). Cambridge: Cambridge University Press.

Pomerantz, A. M., & Heritage, J. (2013). Preference. In Stivers, T., & Sidnell, J. (Eds.), *The handbook of conversation analysis* (pp. 210–228). Oxford: Wiley-Blackwell.

Pontecorvo, C. (1997). Classroom discourse for the facilitation of learning. Encyclopedia of language and education, 3, 169-178.

Poole, M. S., & Holmes, M. E. (1995). Decision development in computer assisted group decision making. *Human Communication Research*, 22(1), 90–127. doi:10.1111/j.1468-2958.1995.tb00363.x.

Porter, J. (1998). *Rhetorical ethics and internetworked writing*. Greenwich, CT: Albex.

POSIT Project Website. (2006). *Website*. Retrieved July 11, 2012, from http://icampus.mit.edu/projects/POSIT.shtml

Potter, J. (1996). *Representing reality: Discourse, rhetoric and social construction*. London: Sage.

Potter, J. (2004). Discourse analysis as a way of analysing naturally occurring talk. In Silverman, D. (Ed.), *Qualitative research: Theory, method and practice* (pp. 200–221). London: Sage.

Potter, J. (2010). Contemporary discursive psychology: Issues, prospects, and Corcoran's awkward ontology. *The British Journal of Social Psychology*, 49, 691–701. doi:10.1348/014466610X535946 PMID:20178684.

Potter, J. (2011). Discursive psychology and discourse analysis. In Gee, J. P., & Handford, M. (Eds.), *Routledge handbook of discourse analysis* (pp. 104–119). London: Routledge.

Potter, J. (2012). Re-reading *Discourse and Social Psychology*: Transforming social psychology. *The British Journal of Social Psychology*, 51(3), 436–455. doi:10.1111/j.2044-8309.2011.02085.x PMID:22168901.

Potter, J. (2012). Discourse analysis and discursive psychology. In Cooper, H. (Ed.), *APA handbook of research methods in psychology: Vol2. Quantitative, qualitative, neuropsychological and biological* (pp. 111–130). Washington: American Psychological Association. doi:10.1037/13620-008.

Potter, J., & Edwards, D. (2001). Discursive social psychology. In Robinson, P. W., & Giles, H. (Eds.), *The new handbook of language and social psychology* (2nd ed., pp. 103–118). Chichester: Wiley.

Potter, J., & Edwards, D. (2013). Conversation analysis and psychology. In Stivers, T., & Sidnell, J. (Eds.), *The handbook of conversation analysis* (pp. 701–725). London: Routledge.

Potter, J., & Hepburn, A. (2008). Discursive constructionism. In Holstein, J. A., & Gubrium, J. F. (Eds.), *Handbook of constructionist research* (pp. 275–293). New York: Guildford.

Potter, J., & Hepburn, A. (2012). Eight challenges for interview researchers. In Gubrium, J. F., & Holstein, J. A. (Eds.), *Handbook of interview research* (2nd ed., pp. 555–570). London: Sage.

Precht, K. (2000). *Patterns of stance in English*. (Unpublished doctoral dissertation). Northern Arizona University.

Precht, K. (2003). Great vs. lovely: Stance differences in American and British English. In Leistyna, P., & Meyer, C. (Eds.), *Corpus analysis: Language structure and language use* (pp. 133–152). NY: Rodopi.

Precht, K. (2008). Sex similarities and differences in stance in informal American conversation. *Journal of Sociolinguistics*, 12(1), 89–111. doi:10.1111/j.1467-9841.2008.00354.x.

Propp, V. Y. (1928). *Morfologiya skazki*. Leningrad: Akademija.

Provalis. (2012). *Provalis research*. Retrieved November 5, 2012, from http://provalisresearch.com/products/content-analysis-software/

Rafaeli, S., Ravid, G., & Soroka, V. (2004). De-lurking in virtual communities: A social communication network approach to measuring the effects of social and cultural capital. In *Proceedings of the 37th Hawaii International Conference on System Sciences*. Los Alamitos, CA: IEEE Press. Retrieved December 24, 2012, from http://www.languageatinternet.org/articles/2011

Rafaeli, S. (1986). The electronic bulletin board: A computer driven mass medium. *Computers and the Social Sciences*, 2(3), 123–136. doi:10.1177/089443938600200302.

Rafaeli, S. (1988). Interactivity: From new media to communication. In Hawkins, R. P., Wiemann, J. M., & Pingree, S. (Eds.), *Sage annual review of communication research: Advancing communication science* (Vol. *16*, pp. 110–134). Beverly Hills, CA: Sage.

Rafaeli, S. (1989). Interacting with media: Para-social interaction and real interaction. In Ruben, B. D., & Lievrouw, L. A. (Eds.), *Mediation, information, and communication* (Vol. *3*, pp. 125–184). New Brunswick, NJ: Transaction Publishers.

Rafaeli, S., & Sudweeks, F. (1998). Interactivity on the nets. In Sudweeks, F., McLaughlin, M., & Rafaeli, S. (Eds.), *Network and netplay: Virtual groups on the Internet* (pp. 173–189). Cambridge, MA: MIT Press.

Rambaree, K. (2012). *Social work and sustainable development: Local voices from 'Maurice Ile Durable.'* Paper presented at the 2nd Joint World Conference on Social Work and Social Development held in Stockholm, Sweden from 8-12 June.

Rambaree, K. (2007). Bringing rigour in qualitative social research: The Use of a CAQDAS. *University of Mauritius Research Journal, 13A*(Special Issue), 1–16.

Rambaree, K., & Faxelid, E. (2013). Considering Abductive Thematic Network Analysis with ATLAS-ti 6.2. In N. Sappleton (Ed.), *Advancing Research Methods with New Technologies* (pp. 170–186). Hershey, PA: Information Science Reference.

Rambe, P. (2011). Exploring the impacts of social networking sites on academic relations in the university. *Journal of Information Technology Education, 10*, 271–293.

Rapley, T. J. (2001). The art(fulness) of open-ended interviewing: Some considerations on analysing interviews. *Qualitative Research, 1*(3), 303–323. doi:10.1177/1468 79410100100303.

Raymond, G., & Heritage, J. (2006). The epistemics of social relations: Owning grandchildren. *Language in Society, 35*, 677–705. doi:10.1017/S0047404506060325.

Rayson, P. (2009). *Wmatrix: A web-based corpus processing environment.* Lancaster University: Computing Department. Retrieved July 1, 2012, from http://ucrel. lancs.ac.uk/wmatrix/

Rayson, P. (2008). From key words to key semantic domains. *International Journal of Corpus Linguistics, 13*(4), 519–549. doi:10.1075/ijcl.13.4.06ray.

Rebedea, T., Dascalu, M., Trausan-Matu, S., Armitt, G., & Chiru, C. (2011). Automatic assessment of collaborative chat conversations with PolyCAFe. In EC-TEL 2011 - Towards ubiquitous learning (Vol. Lecture Notes in Computer Science, pp. 299-312). Berlin: Springer Verlag.

Rebedea, T., Dascalu, M., Trausan-Matu, S., Banica, D., Gartner, A., Chiru, C., & Mihaila, D. (2010). Overview and preliminary results of using PolyCAFe for collaboration analysis and feedback generation. In M. Wolpers, P. Kirschner, M. Scheffel, S. Lindstaedt, & V. Dimitrova (Eds.), Sustaining TEL: From innovation to learning and practice (Vol. 6383, pp. 420-425). Springer Berlin/ Heidelberg.

Reffay, C., & Chanier, T. (2002). Social network analysis used for modelling collaboration in distance learning groups. In S.A. Cerri, G. Guarderes, & F. Paraguaco (Eds.), Lecture Notes in Computer Science (LNCS), 2363, 31-40.

Reicher, S., Spears, R., & Postmes, T. (1995). A social identity model of deindividuation phenomena. In Stroebe, W., & Hewstone, M. (Eds.), *European Review of Social Psychology* (Vol. *6*). Chichester, UK: Wiley. doi:10.1080/14792779443000049.

Reimann, P., Frerejan, J., & Thompson, K. (2009). Using process mining to identify models of group decision making in chat data. In C. O'Malley, D. Suthers, P. Reimann, & A. Dimitracopoulou (Eds.), *9th International Conference on Computer Supported Collaborative Learning (CSCL2009)* (pp. 98-107). Rhodes, Greece, 8-13 June 2009.

Reimann, P. (2009). Time is precious. *International Journal of Computer-Supported Collaborative Learning, 4*(3), 239–257. doi:10.1007/s11412-009-9070-z.

Reinhardt, J., & Zander, V. (2011). Social networking in an intensive English program classroom: A language socialization perspective. *CALICO Journal, 28*(2), 326–344.

Reinig, B., & Mejias, R. (2004). The effects of national culture and anonymity on flaming and criticalness in GSS-supported discussions. *Small Group Research, 21*(6), 698–723. doi:10.1177/1046496404266773.

Resnick, L. B., Levine, J. M., & Teasley, S. D. (1991). *Perspectives on socially shared cognition*. Washington, DC: American Psychological Association. doi:10.1037/10096-000.

Resnik, P. (1995). *Using information content to evaluate semantic similarity in a taxonomy*. Paper presented at the Proceedings of the 14th international joint conference on Artificial intelligence - Volume 1.

Rezende, F., & Castells, M. (2010). Interanimation of voices and argumentative strategies in collaborative knowledge building of physics teachers in an asynchronous discussion group. *Revista Electrónica de Enseñanza de las Ciencias, 9*(2).

Richards, L. (2002). Qualitative computing—A methods revolution? *International Journal of Social Research Methodology, 5*(3), 236–276. doi:10.1080/13645570210146302.

Richardson, E., & Stokoe, E. (Forthcoming). *The order of ordering: Requests, objects and embodied conduct in a public bar*.

Riggenbach, H. (1999). Discourse analysis in the language classroom: *Vol. 1. The spoken language*. Ann Arbor, MI: University of Michigan Press.

Rintel, E. S., Mulholland, J., & Pittam, J. (2001). First things first: Internet relay chat openings. *Journal of Computer-Mediated Communication, 6*(3). Retrieved from http://onlinelibrary.wiley.com/doi/10.1111/j.1083-6101.2001.tb00125.x/full.

Rodriguez, P., Ortigosa, A., & Carro, R. M. (2012). Extracting emotions from texts in e-learning environments. In *Proceedings of the 6th International Conference on Complex, Intelligent & Software Intensive Systems* (pp. 887-893). Palermo, Italy: IEEE Computer Society.

Rogers, R. (2010). Internet research: The question of method. *Journal of Information Technology & Politics, 7*(2–3), 241–260. doi:10.1080/19331681003753438.

Rogoff, B., Matusov, E., & White, C. (1996). Models of teaching and learning: Participating in a community of learners. In Olson, D. R., & Torrance, N. (Eds.), *Handbook of education and human development* (pp. 338–414). Malden, MA: Blackwell Publishing.

Rohde, D., & Plaut, D. (1999). Language acquisition in the absence of explicit negative evidence: How important is starting small? *Cognition, 72*, 67–109. doi:10.1016/S0010-0277(99)00031-1 PMID:10520565.

Romagnoli, C., & Valdés, A. M. (2007). *Relevancia y beneficios del desarrollo de habilidades emocionales, sociales y éticas en la escuela*. Documento Valoras UC.

Rosé, C. P., Wang, Y. C., Arguello, J., Stegmann, K., Weinberger, A., & Fischer, F. (2008). Analyzing collaborative learning processes automatically. *International Journal of Computer-Supported Collaborative Learning, 3*(3), 237–271. doi:10.1007/s11412-007-9034-0.

Rosenbaum, E., Klopfer, E., Boughner, B., & Rosenheck, L. (2007). Engaging students in science controversy through an augmented reality role-playing game. *7th International conference on Computer supported collaborative learning, CSCL* (pp. 612-614). New Brunswick, NJ: International Society of the Learning Sciences.

Rourke, L., Anderson, T., Garrison, D. R., & Archer, W. (1999). Assessing social presence in asynchronous, text-based computer conferencing. *Journal of Distance Education, 14*(3), 51–70.

Rourke, L., Anderson, T., Garrison, D. R., & Archer, W. (2001). Methodological issues in the content analysis of computer conference transcripts. *International Journal of Artificial Intelligence in Education, 12*, 8–22.

Rubin, R. (1996). Moral distancing and the use of information technologies: The seven temptations. In Kizza, J. M. (Ed.), *Social and ethical effects of the computer revolution* (pp. 124–135). Jefferson, NC: McFarland & Company, Inc. Publishers.

Rudman, P. D., Sharples, M., & Baber, C. (2002). Supporting learning in conversations using personal technologies. *European Workshop on Mobile and Contextual Learning (MLEARN2002)* (pp. 44-46). Birmingham, UK.

Ruppenhofer, J., Ellsworth, M., Petruck, M., Johnson, C., & Scheffzcyk, J. (2010). *Framenet II: Theory and practice* (e-book). Retrieved May 25, 2012, from http://framenet2.icsi.berkeley.edu/docs/r1.5/book.pdf

Russel, J., & Spada, N. (2006). The effectiveness of corrective feedback for second language acquisition: A meta-analysis of the research. In Norris, J., & Ortega, L. (Eds.), *Synthesizing research on language learning and teaching* (pp. 131–164). Amsterdam: John Benjamins Publishing Company.

Russell, J. A. (1983). Pancultural aspects of human conceptual organization of emotion. *Journal of Personality and Social Psychology, 45*, 1281–1288. doi:10.1037/0022-3514.45.6.1281.

Sabat, S. (2008). Positioning and conflict involving a person with dementia. In Moghaddam, F., Harré, R., & Lee, N. (Eds.), *Global conflict resolution through positioning theory* (pp. 81–93). New York: Springer. doi:10.1007/978-0-387-72112-5_5.

Sacks, H. (1992). Lectures on conversation (vols. 1 and 2, edited by Gail Jefferson). Oxford: Blackwell.

Sacks, H., Schegloff, E. A., & Jefferson, G. (1974). A simplest systemstics for the organization of turn-taking in conversation. *Language, 50*(4), 696–735. doi:10.2307/412243.

Sahbaz, N., & Duran, G. (2011). The efficiency of cluster method in improving the creative writing skill of 6th grade students of primary school. *Educational Research Review, 6*(11), 702–709.

Salager-Meyer, F. (2001). From self-highlightedness to self-effacement: A genre based study of the socio-pragmatic function of criticism in medical discourse. *LSP and Professional Communication, 1*(2), 63–84.

Saldana, J. (2009). *The coding manual for qualitative researchers*. Los Angeles, CA: SAGE.

Sanders, T. J. M., Spooren, W. P. M., & Noordman, L. G. M. (1992). Toward a taxonomy of coherence relations. *Discourse Processes, 15*(1), 1–35. doi:10.1080/01638539209544800.

Sawyer, K. (2006). Analyzing collaborative discourse. In Sawyer, K. (Ed.), *The Cambridge handbook of the learning sciences* (pp. 187–204). Cambridge: Cambridge University Press.

Scardamalia, M., & Bereiter, C. (2003). Knowledge building. In J. W. Guthrie (Ed.), Encyclopedia of education, (2nd ed., pp.1370–1373). New York: Macmillan Reference, USA.

Scardamalia, M. (2002). Collective cognitive responsibility for the advancement of knowledge. In Smith, B. (Ed.), *Liberal education in a knowledge society* (pp. 76–98). Chicago: Open Court.

Scardamalia, M., & Bereiter, C. (1994). Computer support for knowledge-building communities. *Journal of the Learning Sciences, 3*(3), 265–283. doi:10.1207/s15327809jls0303_3.

Scardamalia, M., & Bereiter, C. (2006). Knowledge building: Theory, pedagogy, and technology. In Sawyer, K. (Ed.), *Cambridge handbook of the learning sciences* (pp. 97–118). New York: Cambridge University Press.

Scardamalia, M., Bransford, J., Kozma, B., & Quellmalz, E. (2012). New assessments and environments for knowledge building. In Griffin, P., McGaw, B., & Care, E. (Eds.), *Assessment & Teaching of 21st Century Skills* (pp. 231–300). New York: Springer. doi:10.1007/978-94-007-2324-5_5.

Schegloff, E. A. (2007). *Sequence organization in interaction: A primer in conversation analysis*. Cambridge: Cambridge University press. doi:10.1017/CBO9780511791208.

Schegloff, E. A., & Sacks, H. (1973). Opening up closings. *Semiotica, 8*, 289–327. doi:10.1515/semi.1973.8.4.289.

Schlenker, B. R. (1998). Identification and self-identification. In Schlenker, B. R. (Ed.), *The self and social life* (pp. 65–99). NY: McGraw-Hill Book Company.

Schmidt, J. (2007). Blogging practices: An analytical framework. *Journal of Computer-Mediated Communication 12*(4), article 13. Retrieved March 15, 2012, from http://jcmc.indiana.edu/vol12/issue4/schmidt.html

Schmidt, R. W. (1990). The role of consciousness in second language learning. *Applied Linguistics, 11*, 129–158. doi:10.1093/applin/11.2.129.

Schönfeldt, J., & Golato, A. (2003). Repair in chats: A conversation analytic approach. *Research on Language and Social Interaction, 36*(3), 241–284. doi:10.1207/S15327973RLSI3603_02.

Schrire, S. (2004). Interaction and cognition in asynchronous computer conferencing. *Instructional Science, 32*(6), 475–502. doi:10.1007/s11251-004-2518-7.

Schrire, S. (2006). Knowledge building in asynchronous discussion groups: Going beyond quantitative analysis. *Computers & Education, 46*, 49–70. doi:10.1016/j.compedu.2005.04.006.

Schubert, C. (2010). Narrative sequences in political discourse: Forms and functions in speeches and hypertext frameworks. In Hoffmann, C. R. (Ed.), *Narrative revisited. Telling a story in the age of new media* (pp. 143–162). Amsterdam, Philadelphia: John Benjamins.

Schulze, M. (2010). Electronic discourse and language learning and language teaching. *Canadian Modern Language Review-Revue Canadienne Des Langues Vivantes, 66*(5), 765–768.

Schwab, M., Karrenbach, N., & Claerbout, J. (2000). Making scientific computations reproducible. *Computing in Science & Engineering, 2*(6), 61–67. doi:10.1109/5992.881708.

Schwartz, J. (2000). *The complete idiot's guide to online dating and relating*. Indianapolis, IN: Que Corporation.

Scott, D., & de Souza, C. S. (1990). Getting the message across in RST-based text generation. In Dale, R., Mellish, C., & Zock, M. (Eds.), *Current research in natural language generation* (pp. 47–73). London: Academic Press.

Scott, J. (1997). *Social network analysis*. Newbury Park, CA: Sage.

Scott, P., & Mortimer, E. (2005). Meaning making in high school science classrooms: A framework for analysing meaning making interactions. In Boersma, K., Goedhart, M., Jong, O., & Eijkelhof, H. (Eds.), *Research and the quality of science education* (pp. 395–406). Springer. doi:10.1007/1-4020-3673-6_31.

Scott, V. (1990). Task-oriented creative writing with systeme-D. *CALICO Journal, 7*(3), 58–67.

Seidel, J. V. (1998). Qualitative data analysis: Ethnograph. Retrieved May 21, 2012, from ftp://ftp.qualisresearch.com/pub/qda.pdf

Selfe, C. L. (1999). *Technology and literacy in the twenty-first century: The importance of paying attention*. Urbana, IL: National Council of Teachers of English.

Severinson, E. K. (2010). To quote or not to quote: Setting the context for computer-mediated dialogues. *Language@Internet, 7*, article 5. Retrieved May 11, 2012, from http://www.languageatinternet.org/articles/2010/2820

Sha, L., & Van Aalst, J. (2003). *An application of social network analysis to knowledge building*. Paper presented at the American Educational Research Association, Chicago, April 21-25, 2003.

Shana, Z. (2009). Learning with technology: Using discussion forums to augment a traditional-style class. *Journal of Educational Technology & Society, 12*(3), 214–228.

Sharf, B. F. (1999). Beyond netiquette: The ethics of doing naturalistic discourse research on the internet. In Jones, S. (Ed.), *Doing internet research: Critical issues and methods for examining the net* (pp. 243–256). Thousand Oaks, CA: Sage. doi:10.4135/9781452231471.n12.

Sharples, M. (2002). Disruptive devices: Mobile technology for conversational learning. *International Journal of Continuing Engineering Education and Lifelong Learning, 12*(5-6), 504–520. doi:10.1504/IJCEELL.2002.002148.

Sharrock, W. (1989). Ethnomethodology. *The British Journal of Sociology, 40*(4), 657–677. doi:10.2307/590893.

Shauf, M. (2001). The problem of electronic argument: a humanist's perspective. *Computers and Composition, 18*, 33–37. doi:10.1016/S8755-4615(00)00046-3.

Sheen, Y. (2004). Corrective feedback and learner uptake in communicative classrooms across instructional settings. *Language Teaching Research, 8*, 263–300. doi:10.1191/1362168804lr146oa.

Shen, D., Yang, Q., Sun, J.-T., & Chen, Z. (2006). *Thread detection in dynamic text message streams*. Paper presented at the Proceedings of the 29th annual international ACM SIGIR conference on Research and development in information retrieval.

Short, J., Williams, E., & Christie, B. (1976). *The psychology of telecommunication*. London, UK: Wiley.

Shriberg, E., Dhillon, R., Bhagat, S., Ang, J., & Carvey, H. (2004). *The ICSI meeting recorder dialog act (MRDA) corpus*. Paper presented at the Proceedings of the 5th SIGdial Workshop on Discourse and Dialogue.

Sidnell, J. (2010). *Conversation analysis: An introduction*. Chichester, MA: Wiley-Blackwell.

Silber, H. G., & McCoy, K. F. (2002). Efficiently computed lexical chains as an intermediate representation for automatic text summarization. *Computational Linguistics*, *28*(4), 487–496. doi:10.1162/089120102762671954.

Silva, B., Cruz, E., & Laureano- Cruces, A. (2006). Análisis para identificar los Estilos de Aprendizaje para el modelado del Dominio del Conocimiento. Paper presented at the XIX *Congreso Nacional y V Congreso Internacional de Informática y Computación de la ANIEI*. Tuxtla Gutiérrez, Chiapas.

Simon, B. (2004). *Identity in modern society: A social psychological perspective*. Oxford, UK: Blackwell. doi:10.1002/9780470773437.

Simpson, J. (2005). Conversational floors in synchronous text-based CMC discourse. *Discourse Studies*, *7*(3), 337–361. doi:10.1177/1461445605052190.

Slocum-Bradley, N. (2009). The positioning diamond: A trans-disciplinary framework for discourse analysis. *Journal for the Theory of Social Behaviour*, *40*, 79–107. doi:10.1111/j.1468-5914.2009.00418.x.

Smith, M., Cadiz, J. J., & Burkhalter, B. (2000). *Conversation trees and threaded chats*. Paper presented at the Proceedings of the 2000 ACM conference on Computer supported cooperative work.

Smith, A., & Humphreys, M. (2006). Evaluation of unsupervised mapping of natural language with Leximancer concept mapping. *Behavior Research Methods*, *38*(2), 26–79. doi:10.3758/BF03192778 PMID:16956103.

Smith, C., & Short, P. M. (2001). Integrating technology to improve the efficiency of qualitative data analysis—A note on methods. *Qualitative Sociology*, *24*(3), 401–407. doi:10.1023/A:1010643025038.

Smithson, J., Sharkey, S., Hewis, E., Jones, R., Emmens, T., Ford, T., & Owens, C. (2011). Problem presentation and responses on an online forum for young people who self-harm. *Discourse Studies*, *13*(4), 487–501. doi:10.1177/1461445611403356.

Sonnenwald, D. H., Wildemuth, B. M., & Harmon, G. L. (2001). A research method to investigate information seeking using the concept of information horizons: An example from a study of lower socio-economic student's information seeking behaviour. *The New Review of Information Behaviour Research*, *2*(1), 65–86.

Soter, A. O., Wilkinson, I. A., Murphy, P. K., Rudge, L., Reninger, K., & Edwards, M. (2008). What the discourse tells us: Talk and indicators of high-level comprehension. *International Journal of Educational Research*, *47*(6), 372–391. doi:10.1016/j.ijer.2009.01.001.

Spagnolli, A., & Gamberini, L. (2007). Interacting via SMS: Practices of social closeness and reciprocation. *The British Journal of Social Psychology*, *46*(2), 343–364. doi:10.1348/014466606X120482 PMID:17565786.

Spears, R., & Lea, M. (1994). Panacea or panopticon? The hidden power in computer-mediated communication. *Communication Research*, *21*(4), 427–459. doi:10.1177/009365094021004001.

Speer, S. A. (2002). 'Natural' and 'contrived' data: A sustainable distinction? *Discourse Studies*, *4*, 511–525.

Spiegel, D. (2001). *Coterie: A visualization of the conversational dynamics within IRC*. Massachusetts Institute of Technology.

Spradley, J. (1979). *The ethnographic interview*. Holt. NY: Rinehart and Winston.

Spradley, J. P., & McCurdy, D. W. (Eds.). (1972). *The cultural experience: Ethnography in complex society*. Chicago, IL: Science Research Associates.

Sproull, L., & Kiesler, S. (1986). Reducing social context cues: Electronic mail in organizational communication. *Management Science*, *32*, 1492–1512. doi:10.1287/mnsc.32.11.1492.

Squire, K. D., Barnett, M., Grant, J. M., & Higginbottom, T. (2004). *Electromagentism supercharged! Learning physics with digital simulation games*. Paper presented at the International Conference of the Learning Sciences. Retrieved from http://www.educationarcade.org/files/articles/Supercharged/SuperchargedResearch.pdf

Stachowski, A. A., Kaplan, S. A., & Waller, M. J. (2009). The benefits of flexible team interaction during crises. *The Journal of Applied Psychology*, *94*, 1536–1543. doi:10.1037/a0016903 PMID:19916660.

Stahl, G. (2006). *Group cognition: Computer support for building collaborative knowledge*. Cambridge, MA: The MIT Press.

Stake, R. E. (1995). *The art of case study research*. Thousand Oaks, CA: Sage Publications.

Stebick, D. M., & Dain, J. M. (2007). *Comprehension strategies for your K-6 literacy classroom: Thinking before, during, and after reading.* Thousand Oaks, CA: Corwin Press.

Steinkuehler, C. A. (2006). Massively multiplayer online video gaming as participation in a discourse. *Mind, Culture, and Activity, 13*(1), 38–52. doi:10.1207/s15327884mca1301_4.

Stewart, C. (2009). Socio-scientific controversies: A theoretical and methodological framework. *Communication Theory, 19*, 124–145. doi:10.1111/j.1468-2885.2009.01338.x.

Stewart, K. (2012). Considering CAQDAS: Using and choosing software. In Delamont, S. (Ed.), *Handbook of qualitative research in education* (pp. 503–511). Cheltenham: Edward Elgar.

Stokoe, E. (2009). Doing actions with identity categories: Complaints and denials in neighbour disputes. *Text and Talk, 20*(1), 75–97.

Stokoe, E. (2011). 'Girl - woman - sorry!': On the repair and non-repair of consecutive gender categories. In Speer, S. A., & Stokoe, E. (Eds.), *Conversation and gender* (pp. 84–111). Cambridge: Cambridge University Press. doi:10.1017/CBO9780511781032.006.

Stommel, W. (2007). Mein nick bin ich! Nicknames in a German forum on eating disorders. *Journal of Computer Mediated Communication, 13*(1), Article 8. Retrieved from http://jcmc.indiana.edu/vol13/issue1/stommel.html

Stommel, W. (2008). Conversation analysis and community of practice as approaches to studying online community. *Language@Internet, 5*, [np]. Retrieved November 2, 2010, from www.languageatinternet.de

Stommel, W. (2009). *Entering an online support group on eating disorders: A discourse analysis.* Amsterdam: Rodopi.

Stommel, W., & Koole, T. (2010). The online support group as a community: A micro-analysis of the interaction with a new member. *Discourse Studies, 12*(3), 357–378. doi:10.1177/1461445609358518.

Storrer, A. (2002). Coherence in text and hypertext. (Preprint). Then published in *Document design.* Retrieved May 2009, from http://www.hytext.info

Strapparava, C., & Valitutti, A. (2004). WordNet-affect: An affective extension of WordNet. In *Proceedings of the 4th International Conference on Language Resources and Evaluation (LREC 2004)* (pp. 1083-1086). Lisbon, Portugal.

Strik, H., Colpaert, J., van Doremalen, J., & Cucchiarini, C. (2012). The DISCO ASR-based CALL system: Practicing L2 oral skills and beyond. *Proceedings of the Conference on International Language Resources and Evaluation (LREC 2012)* (pp. 2702-2707). Istanbul, Turkey.

Strik, H., Cornillie, F., Colpaert, J., van Doremalen, J., & Cucchiarini, C. (2009). Developing a CALL system for practicing oral proficiency: How to design for speech technology, pedagogy and learners. *Proceedings of the SLaTE-2009 workshop* (pp.1-4). Warwickshire, England.

Strik, H., van de Loo, J., van Doremalen, J., & Cucchiarini, C. (2010). Practicing syntax in spoken interaction: Automatic detection of syntactic errors in non-native utterances. *Proceedings of the SLaTE-2010 workshop* (pp.1-4). Tokyo, Japan.

Strik, H., van Doremalen, J., van de Loo, J., & Cucchiarini, C. (2011). Improving ASR processing of ungrammatical utterances through grammatical error modeling. *Proceedings of the SLaTE-2011 workshop* (pp.1-4). Venice, Italy.

Strik, H., Truong, K., de Wet, F., & Cucchiarini, C. (2007). Comparing classifiers for pronunciation error detection. [Antwerp, Belgium.]. *Proceedings of Interspeech, 2007*, 1837–1840.

Strik, H., Truong, K., de Wet, F., & Cucchiarini, C. (2009). Comparing different approaches for automatic pronunciation error detection. *Speech Communication, 51*(10), 845–852. doi:10.1016/j.specom.2009.05.007.

Suthers, D. D., Lund, K., Rose, C., Dyke, G., Law, N., Teplovs, C., et al. (2011). *Towards productive multivocality in the analysis of collaborative learning.* Paper presented at the Connecting computer-supported collaborative learning to policy and practice.

Suthers, D., Dwyer, N., Medina, R., & Vatrapu, R. (2010). A framework for conceptualizing, representing, and analyzing distributed interaction. *International Journal of Computer-Supported Collaborative Learning, 5*(1), 5–42. doi:10.1007/s11412-009-9081-9.

Swain, M. (1985). Communicative competence: Some roles of comprehensible input and comprehensible output in its development. In Gass, M. A., & Madden, C. G. (Eds.), *Input in second language acquisition* (pp. 235–253). Rowley, MA: Newbury House.

Swales, J. M. (1990). *Genre analysis: English in academic and research settings*. Great Britain: Cambridge University Press.

Swales, J. M. (2004). *Research genres: Explorations and applications*. Cambridge: Cambridge University Press. doi:10.1017/CBO9781139524827.

Swan, D., & McCarthy, J. C. (2003). Contesting animal rights on the internet: Discourse analysis of the social construction of argument. *Journal of Language and Social Psychology*, 22(3), 297–320. doi:10.1177/0261927X03252279.

Swan, K., & Shih, L. F. (2005). On the nature and development of social presence in online course discussions. *Journal of Asynchronous Learning Networks*, 9(3), 115–136.

Taboada, M., & Mann, W. C. (2006). Rhetorical structure theory: Looking back and moving ahead. *Discourse Studies*, 8(3), 423–459. doi:10.1177/1461445606061881.

Tajfel, H., & Turner, J. (1986). An integrative theory of intergroup conflict. In Worchel, S., & Austin, G. W. (Eds.), *The social psychology of intergroup relations* (pp. 33–47). Monterey, CA: Brooks/Cole.

Tallent-Runnels, M. K., Thomas, J. A., Lan, W. Y., Cooper, S., Ahern, T. C., Shaw, S. M., & Liu, X. (2006). Teaching courses online. *Review of Educational Research*, 76(1), 93–135. doi:10.3102/00346543076001093.

Tannen, D. (1982). Oral and literate strategies in spoken and written language. *Language*, 58, 1–21. doi:10.2307/413530.

Tannen, D. (Ed.). (1982). *Spoken and written language: Exploring orality and literacy*. Norwood, NJ: Ablex.

Tapia, A. (2007). *El arbol de la retorica*. Retrieved May 24, 2012, from http://elarboldelaretorica.blogspot.com.es/2007/05/emocin-y-cognicin.html

Tapia, A. (2003). Graphic design in the digital era: The rhetoric of hypertext. *Design Issues*, 19(1), 5–24. doi:10.1162/074793603762667665.

Taylor, T. L. (2003). Multiple pleasures: Women and online gaming. *Convergence: The International Journal of Research into New Technologies*, 9(1), 21–46. doi:10.1177/135485650300900103.

Tedeschi, J. T., & Riess, M. (1981). Identities, the phenomenal self, and laboratory research. In Tedeschi, J. T. (Ed.), *Impression management theory and social psychological research* (pp. 3–22). NY: Academic Press, Inc..

Tenenhaus, M., Vinzi, V. E., Chatelin, Y., & Lauro, C. (2005). PLS path modeling. *Computational Statistics & Data Analysis*, 48(1), 159–205. doi:10.1016/j.csda.2004.03.005.

Teplovs, C. (2008). The knowledge space visualizer: A tool for visualizing online discourse. In G. Kanselaar, V. Jonker, P. A. Kirschner, & F. J. Prins (Eds.), *Proceedings of the International Conference of the Learning Sciences 2008: Cre8 a learning world* (pp.1-12). Utrecht, NL: International Society of the Learning.

Teplovs, C., & Scardmalia, M. (2007). *Visualizations for knowledge building assessment*. Paper presented at the AgileViz workshop, Computer-Supported Collaborative Learning Conference 2007. New Brunswick, NJ.

Thagard, P. (1989). Explanatory coherence. *The Behavioral and Brain Sciences*, (12): 435–502. doi:10.1017/S0140525X00057046.

Thomas, M. J. W. (2002). Learning within incoherent structures: The space of online discussion forums. *Journal of Computer Assisted Learning*, 18, 351–366. doi:10.1046/j.0266-4909.2002.03800.x.

Thompson, K., & Kelly, N. (2012). *Processes of decision-making with adaptive combinations of wiki and chat tools*. In J. van Aalst, K. Thompson, M. J. Jacobson, & P. Reimann (Ed.), *The future of learning: Proceedings of the 10th International Conference of the Learning Sciences (ICLS 2012)* (Vol. 1, pp. 459-466). Sydney, Australia.

Thompson, K., Kennedy-Clark, S., Markauskaite, L., & Southavilay, V. (2011). Capturing and analysing the processes and patterns of learning in collaborative learning environments. In *9th International Conference on Computer Supported Collaborative Learning. CSCL2011: Connecting computer supported collaborative learning to policy and practice* (pp. 596–600). Hong Kong, 4–8 July.

Thompson, J. B. (1984). *Studies in the theory of ideology*. Cambridge, England: Polity Press.

Thompson, K., & Reimann, P. (2010). Patterns of use of an agent-based model and a system dynamics model: The application of patterns of use and the impacts on learning outcomes. *Computers & Education, 54*(2), 392–403. doi:10.1016/j.compedu.2009.08.020.

Tin, T. (2011). Language creativity and co-emergence of form and meaning in creative writing tasks. *Applied Linguistics, 32*(2), 215–235. doi:10.1093/applin/amq050.

Tong, S. T., & Walther, J. B. (2011). Relational maintenance and computer-mediated communication. In Wright, K. B., & Webb, L. M. (Eds.), *Computer-mediated communication in personal relationships* (pp. 98–118). New York, NY: Peter Lang Publishing.

Tosca, S. P. (2000). A pragmatics of links. *Journal of Digital Information, 1*(6). Retrieved May 2009, from http://journals.tdl.org/jodi/article/ viewArticle/23/24

Toulmin, S. E. (1969). *The uses of argument*. Cambridge: Cambridge University Press.

Tracy, K., & Tracy, S. J. (1998). Rudeness at 911: Reconceptualizing face and face attack. *Human Communication Research, 25*, 225–251. doi:10.1111/j.1468-2958.1998. tb00444.x.

Trausan-Matu, S., Stahl, G., & Sarmiento, J. (2007). Supporting polyphonic collaborative learning. *e-Service Journal, 6*(1), 59-74.

Trausan-Matu, S., & Rebedea, T. (2009). Polyphonic inter-animation of voices in VMT. In Stahl, G. (Ed.), *Studying virtual math teams* (pp. 451–473). New York: Springer. doi:10.1007/978-1-4419-0228-3_24.

Trausan-Matu, S., & Rebedea, T. (2010). A polyphonic model and system for inter-animation analysis in chat conversations with multiple participants. In Gelbukh, A. (Ed.), *Computational linguistics and intelligent text processing* (*Vol. 6008*, pp. 354–363). Springer. doi:10.1007/978-3-642-12116-6_29.

Trausan-Matu, S., Rebedea, T., & Dascalu, M. (2010). Analysis of discourse in collaborative learning chat conversations with multiple participants. In Tufis, D., & Forascu, C. (Eds.), *Multilinguality and interoperability in language processing with emphasis on Romanian* (pp. 313–330). Editura Academiei.

Trausan-Matu, S., Rebedea, T., Dragan, A., & Alexandru, C. (2007). Visualisation of learners' contributions in chat conversations. In Fong, J., & Wang, F. L. (Eds.), *Blended learning*. Addison-Wesley.

Trifonova, A., Knapp, J., Ronchetti, M., & Gamper, J. (2004). Mobile ELDIT: Transition from an e-learning to an m-learning system. *World Conference on Educational Multimedia, Hypermedia and Telecommunications (ED-MEDIA 2004)* (pp. 188-193). Lugano, Switzerland.

Tufte, E. R. (2003). *The cognitive style of power point*. Cheshire, CT: Graphics Press LIC.

Turkle, S. (1995). *Life on the screen: Identity in the age of the Internet*. New York, NY: Simon and Schuster.

Turner, J. W., Grube, J. A., Tinsley, C. H., Lee, C., & O'Pell, C. (2006). Exploring the dominant media: How does media use reflect organizational norms and affect performance? *Journal of Business Communication, 43*(3), 220–250. doi:10.1177/0021943606288772.

Turner, J. W., & Reinsch, N. L. (2007). The business communicator as presence allocator: Multicommunicating, equivocality, and status at work. *Journal of Business Communication, 44*(1), 36–58. doi:10.1177/0021943606295779.

Turner, J. W., & Reinsch, N. L. (2009). Successful and unsuccessful multicommunication episodes: Engaging in dialogue or juggling messages? *Information Systems Frontiers, 12*(3), 277–285. doi:10.1007/s10796-009-9175-y.

Turner, J. W., & Reinsch, N. L. (2011). Multicommunicating and episodic presence: Creating new constructs for studying new phenomenon. In Wright, K., & Webb, L. (Eds.), *Computer mediated communication in personal relationships* (pp. 181–193). New York: Peter Lang.

UNESCO. (2012). Turning on mobile learning in Europe: Illustrative initiatives and policy implications. *UNESCO Working Paper Series on Mobile Learning*. Retrieved July 10, 2012, from http://unesdoc.unesco.org/images/0021/002161/216165e.pdf

Upadhyay, S. (2010). Identity and impoliteness in computer-mediated reader responses. *Journal of Politeness Research. Language, Behaviour. Culture (Canadian Ethnology Society), 6*(1), 105–127.

Upside2Go product Website. (2012). Retrieved July 12, 2012, from http://www.upsidelearning.com/mobile-learning-solution-upside2go.asp

Valitutti, C., Strapparava, C., & Stock, O. (2004). Developing affective lexical resources. *PsychNology Journal*, 2(1), 61–83.

van Aalst, J. (2009). Distinguishing knowledge-sharing, knowledge-construction, and knowledge-creation discourses. *International Journal of Computer-Supported Collaborative Learning*, 4, 259–287. doi:10.1007/s11412-009-9069-5.

van den Hoof, B., Groot, J., & de Jonge, S. (2005). Situational influences on the use of communication technologies: A meta-analysis and exploratory study. *Journal of Business Communication*, 42(1), 4–27. doi:10.1177/0021943604271192.

van Dijk, T.A. (2008). *Discourse and power: Contributions to critical discourse studies*. Houndsmills: Palgrave.

van Dijk, T. A. (1988). *News analysis*. Hillsdale, London: Lawrence Erlbaum Associates.

van Dijk, T. A. (1993). Principles of critical discourse analysis. *Discourse & Society*, 4(2), 249–283. doi:10.1177/0957926593004002006.

van Dijk, T. A. (1995). Aims of critical discourse analysis. *Japanese Discourse*, 1(1), 17–27.

van Doremalen, J., Strik, H., & Cucchiarini, C. (2009). Utterance verification in language learning applications. *Proceedings of the SLaTE-2009 workshop* (pp.1-4). Warwickshire, England.

van Doremalen, J., Cucchiarini, C., & Strik, H. (2010). Optimizing automatic speech recognition for low-proficient non-native speakers. *EURASIP Journal on Audio, Speech, and Music Processing*, 2010, 1–13. doi:10.1155/2010/973954.

van Doremalen, J., Cucchiarini, C., & Strik, H. (2010). Using non-native error patterns to improve pronunciation verification.[Tokyo, Japan.]. *Proceedings of Interspeech*, 2010, 1–4.

van Doremalen, J., Cucchiarini, C., & Strik, H. (2011). Speech technology in CALL: The essential role of adaptation. In De Wannemacker, S., Clarebout, G., & De Causmaecker, P. (Eds.), *Interdisciplinary approaches to adaptive learning. A look at the neighbors, Communications in Computer and Information Science series, 26* (pp. 56–69). Heidelberg: Springer Verlag. doi:10.1007/978-3-642-20074-8_5.

van Eemeren, F. H. (2010). *Strategic manoeuvring in argumentative discourse: Extending the pragma-dialectical theory of argumentation*. Amsterdam: John Benjamins.

van Eemeren, F. H., & Grootendorst, R. (1992). *Argumentation, communication, and fallacies: A pragma-dialectical perspective*. Hillsdale, NJ: Lawrence Erlbaum Associates.

van Eemeren, F. H., Grootendorst, R., & Snoeck Henkemans, F. (1996). *Fundamentals of argumentation theory: A handbook of historical background and contemporary developments*. Mahwah, NJ: Erlbaum.

van Eemeren, F. H., Grootendorst, R., & Snoeck Henkemans, F. (2002). *Argumentation: Analysis, evaluation, presentation*. Mahwah, NJ: Lawrence Erlbaum Associates.

Van Lammeren, R. J. A., & Molendijk, M. (2004). *Location based learning: Lessons learned* (p. 10). Amsterdam, The Netherlands: European GIS Education Seminar EUGISES.

van Leeuwen, T. (1985). Rhythmic structure of the film text. In T. A. van Dijk (Ed.), Discourse and communication – New approaches to the analysis of mass media discourse and communication (pp. 216-232). Berlin: de Gruyter.

van Leeuwen, T. (2005). *Introducing social semiotics*. London: Routledge.

van Leeuwen, T., & Jewitt, C. (Eds.). (2001). *Handbook of visual analysis*. London: Sage Publications.

Vass, E. (2002). Friendship and collaborative creative writing in the primary classroom. *Journal of Computer Assisted Learning*, 18(1), 102–110. doi:10.1046/j.0266-4909.2001.00216.x.

Vass, E. (2007). Exploring processes of collaborative creativity--The role of emotions in children's joint creative writing. *Thinking Skills and Creativity*, *2*(2), 107–117. doi:10.1016/j.tsc.2007.06.001.

Vass, E., Littleton, K., Miell, D., & Jones, A. (2008). The discourse of collaborative creative writing: Peer collaboration as a context for mutual inspiration. *Thinking Skills and Creativity*, *3*(3), 192–202. doi:10.1016/j.tsc.2008.09.001.

Vavoula, G. N., Sharples, M., O'Malley, C., & Taylor, J. (2004). A study of mobile learning as part of everyday learning. In Attewell, J., & Savill-Smith, C. (Eds.), *Mobile learning anytime everywhere: A book of papers from MLEARN 2004* (pp. 211–212). London, UK: Learning and Skills Development Agency.

Vayreda, A., & Antaki, C. (2009). Social support and unsolicited advice in a bipolar disorder online forum. *Qualitative Health Research*, *19*(7), 931–942. doi:10.1177/1049732309338952 PMID:19556400.

Viégas, F., Wattenberg, M., Kriss, J., & Ham, F. V. (2007). Talk before you type: Coordination in Wikipedia. In *Proceeedings of the 40th Annual Hawaii International Conference on System Sciences*. Los Alamitos, CA: IEEE Press.

Vinagre, M. (2008). Politeness strategies in collaborative e-mail exchanges. *Computers & Education*, *50*, 1022–1036. doi:10.1016/j.compedu.2006.10.002.

Vitzthum, V. (2007). *I love you, let's meet: Adventures in online dating*. New York, NY: Little Brown and Company.

Vygotsky, L. A. (1978). *Mind in society: The development of higher psychological processes*. Cambridge, MA: Harvard University Press.

Wade, S. E., & Fauske, J. R. (2004). Dialogue online: Prospective teachers' discourse strategies in computer-mediated discussions. *Reading Research Quarterly*, *39*(2), 134–160. doi:10.1598/RRQ.39.2.1.

Walker, J. (2006). Blogging from inside the ivory tower. In Bruns, A., & Jacobs, J. (Eds.), *Uses of blogs* (pp. 127–138). New York, NY: Peter Lang Publishing.

Walther, J. (1992). Interpersonal effects in computer-mediated interaction: A relational perspective. *Communication Research*, *19*, 52–90. doi:10.1177/009365092019001003.

Walther, J. (1996). Computer-mediated communication: Impersonal, interpersonal, and hyperpersonal interaction. *Communication Research*, *23*, 3–43. doi:10.1177/009365096023001001.

Walther, J. B. (2007). Selective self-presentation in computer-mediated communication: Hyperpersonal dimensions of technology, language, and cognition. *Computers in Human Behavior*, *23*, 2538–2557. doi:10.1016/j.chb.2006.05.002.

Walther, J. B. (2010). Computer-mediated communication. In Berger, C. R., Roloff, M. E., & Roskos-Ewoldsen, D. R. (Eds.), *Handbook of communication science* (2nd ed., pp. 489–505). Thousand Oaks, CA: Sage. doi:10.4135/9781412982818.n28.

Walther, J. B. (2011). Theories of computer-mediated communication and interpersonal relations. In Knapp, M. L., & Daly, J. A. (Eds.), *The handbook of interpersonal communication* (4th ed., pp. 443–479). Thousand Oaks, CA: Sage.

Wang, H. (1996). Flaming: More than a necessary evil for academic mailing lists. *The Electronic Journal of Communication, 6*. Retrieved May 11, 2012, from http://www.cios.org/EJCPUBLIC/006/1/00612.HTML

Wang, H. H., Wu, T. H., Kuo, R., & Heh, J. S. (2005). EM-learning platform: A mobile learning environment integrating e-learning system. In P. Kommers & G. Richards (Eds.), *World Conference on Educational Multimedia, Hypermedia and Telecommunications* (pp. 1437-1443). Chesapeake, VA: AACE.

Wang, Y.-C., Joshi, M., Cohen, W., & Rose, C. P. (2008). *Recovering implicit thread structure in newsgroup style conversations*. Paper presented at the International Conference on Weblogs and Social Media, Seattle, Washington.

Warnock, J. (1984). The writing process. In Moran, M. G., & Lunsford, R. F. (Eds.), *Research in composition and rhetoric* (pp. 3–26). Westport, CT: Greenwood Press.

Wasswerman, S., & Faust, K. (1994). *Social network analysis. Methods and applications*. Cambridge: Cambridge University Press. doi:10.1017/CBO9780511815478.

Watson, W. R., Mong, C. J., & Harris, C. A. (2011). A case study of the in-class use of a video game for teaching high school history. *Computers & Education*, *56*, 466–474. doi:10.1016/j.compedu.2010.09.007.

Webb, N. M., & Farivar, S. (1999). Developing productive group interaction in middle-school mathematics. In O'Donnell, A. M., & King, A. (Eds.), *Cognitive perspectives on peer learning* (pp. 117–150). Mahwah, NJ: Erlbaum.

Wegerif, R. (2006). A dialogic understanding of the relationship between CSCL and teaching thinking skills. *International Journal of Computer-Supported Collaborative Learning*, *1*, 143–157. doi:10.1007/s11412-006-6840-8.

Wegerif, R. (2008). Dialogic or dialectic? The significance of ontological assumptions in research on educational dialogue. *British Educational Research Journal*, *34*(3), 347–361. doi:10.1080/01411920701532228.

Weinberger, A., & Fischer, F. (2006). A framework to analyze argumentative knowledge construction in computer-supported collaborative learning. *Computers & Education*, *46*, 71–95. doi:10.1016/j.compedu.2005.04.003.

Wenger, E. (1998). *Communities of practice: Learning, meaning, and identity*. Cambridge, UK: Cambridge University Press.

Wentzel, P., van Lammeren, R. J. A., Molendijk, M., de Bruin, S., & Wagtendonk, A. (2005). *Using mobile technology to enhance students' educational experiences*. Boulder, CO: EDUCAUSE Center for Applied Research.

Werlich, E. (1983). *A text grammar of English*. Heidelberg: Quelle und Meyer.

Werry, C. C. (1996). Linguistic and interactional features of internet relay chat. In Herring, S. C. (Ed.), *Computer-mediated communication: Linguistic, social and cross-cultural perspectives* (pp. 47–64). Amsterdam: John Benjamins.

Wessa, P. (2009). Exploring social networks in reproducible computing and collaborative assignments. In F. Salajan (Ed.), *Proceedings of the 4th International Conference on E-Learning* (pp. 486-492). University of Toronto, Canada.

Wessa, P., & Baesens, B. (2009). Fraud detection in statistics education based on the compendium platform and reproducible computing. In *Proceedings of the 2009 WRI World Congress on Computer Science and Information Engineering* (pp. 50-54). IEEE Computer Society.

Wessa, P. (2009). A framework for statistical software development, maintenance, and publishing within an open-access business model. *Computational Statistics*, *24*(2), 183–193. doi:10.1007/s00180-008-0107-y.

Wessa, P. (2009). Reproducible computing: A new technology for statistics education and educational research. In Ao, S. (Ed.), *IAENG transactions on engineering technologies* (pp. 86–97). American Institute of Physics. doi:10.1063/1.3146201.

Wessa, P., De Rycker, A., & Holliday, I. E. (2011). Content-based VLE designs improve learning efficiency in constructivist statistics education. *PLoS ONE*, *6*(10), e25363. doi:10.1371/journal.pone.0025363 PMID:21998652.

Wessa, P., & Holliday, I. E. (2012). Does reviewing lead to better learning and decision making? Answers from a Randomized Stock Market Experiment. *PLoS ONE*, *7*(5), e37719. doi:10.1371/journal.pone.0037719 PMID:22666385.

Wetherell, M., Taylor, S., & Yates, S. (Eds.). (2001). *Discourse theory and practice: A reader*. London, England: Sage.

Whissell, C. M. (1989). The dictionary of affect in language. In R. Pultchik & H. Kellerman (Eds.), Emotion-theory, research and experience, Vol. 4, The measurement of emotions (pp. 113-131). New York, NY: Academic Press, Inc.

Widdicombe, S. (1998). Identity as an analysts' and a participants' resource. In Antaki, C., & Widdicombe, S. (Eds.), *Identities in talk* (pp. 191–206). London: Sage Publications.

Widdicombe, S., & Wooffitt, R. (1995). *The language of youth subcultures: Social identity in action*. New York: Harvester Wheatsheaf.

Wilson, P. (2011). Creative writing and critical response in the university literature class. *Innovations in Education and Teaching International*, *48*(4), 439–446. doi:10.1080/14703297.2011.617091.

Wise, A. F., & Chiu, M. M. (2011). Analyzing temporal patterns of knowledge construction in a role-based online discussion. *International Journal of Computer-Supported Collaborative Learning*, *6*(3), 445–470. doi:10.1007/s11412-011-9120-1.

Witt, S. (1999). *Use of speech recognition in computer assisted language learning.* (Unpublished doctoral dissertation). University of Cambridge, UK.

Witt, S. (2012). Automatic error detection in pronunciation training: Where we are and where we need to go. *Proceedings IS ADEPT* (pp. 1-8). Stockholm, Sweden.

Witt, S., & Young, S. (1997). Language learning based on non-native speech recognition.[Rhodes, Greece.]. *Proceedings Eurospeech, 1997*, 633–636.

Witty, P., & Labrant, L. (1946). *Teaching the people's language.* New York: Hinds, Hayden & Eldredge. Retrieved July 30, from http://archive.org/stream/teachingpeoplesl00witt#page/n3/mode/2up

Wodak, R. (2001). What CDA is about – a summary of its history, important concepts and its development. In Wodak, R., & Meyer, M. (Eds.), *Methods of critical discourse analysis* (pp. 1–13). London: SAGE Publications Ltd. doi:10.4135/9780857028020.d3.

Wodak, R., & Meyer, M. (Eds.). (2009). *Methods of critical discourse analysis.* London: SAGE.

Wollman-Bonilla, J. E. (2003). Email as genre: A beginning writer learns the conventions. *Language Arts, 81*(2), 126–134.

Wouters, P., van Oostendorp, H., Boonekamp, R., & van der Spek, E. (2011). The role of game discourse analysis and curiosity in creating engaging and effective serious games by implementing a back story and foreshadowing. *Interacting with Computers, 23*(4), 329–336. doi:10.1016/j.intcom.2011.05.001.

Young, D. J. (1990). An investigation of students' perspectives on anxiety and speaking. *Foreign Language Annals, 23*, 539–553. doi:10.1111/j.1944-9720.1990.tb00424.x.

Young, L., & Soroka, S. (2012). Affective news: The automated coding of sentiment in political texts. *Political Communication, 29*, 205–231. doi:10.1080/10584609.2012.671234.

Your Dictionary. (2012). Retrieved July 30, 2012, from http://reference.yourdictionary.com/word-definitions/definition-of-creativewriting.html

Zelenkauskaite, A., & Herring, S. C. (2008). Television-mediated conversation: Coherence in Italian iTV SMS chat. In *Proceedings of the Forty-First Hawai'i International Conference on System Sciences.* Los Alamitos, CA: IEEE Press.

Zelenkauskaite, A., & Massa, P. (2011). Digital libraries and social web: Insights from Wikipedia users' activities. In *IADIS Multiconference on Computer Science and Information Systems* (pp. 39-47). Rome, Italy.

Zelenkauskaite, A., & Herring, S. C. (2008). Gender differences in personal advertisements in Lithuanian iTV SMS. In Sudweeks, F., Hrachovec, H., & Ess, C. (Eds.), *Proceedings of Cultural Attitudes Towards Technology and Communication 2008* (pp. 462–476). Murdoch, Australia: School of Information Technology, Murdoch University.

Zhang, J., Scardamalia, M., Reeve, R., & Messina, R. (2009). Designs for collective cognitive responsibility in knowledge building communities. *Journal of the Learning Sciences, 18*(1), 7–44. doi:10.1080/10508400802581676.

Zhu, E. (2006). Interaction and cognitive engagement: An analysis of four asynchronous online discussions. *Instructional Science, 34*(6), 451–480. doi:10.1007/s11251-006-0004-0.

Zolfo, M., Iglesias, D., Kiyan, C., Echevarria, J., Fucay, L., & Llacsahuanga, E. et al. (2010). Mobile learning for HIV/AIDS healthcare worker training in resource-limited settings. *AIDS Research and Therapy, 7*(35), 1–6. PMID:20051116.

About the Contributors

Hwee Ling Lim is an Associate Professor at The Petroleum Institute in Abu Dhabi, United Arab Emirates (UAE). She obtained her Bachelor, Master degrees and a Diploma in Education from The National University of Singapore (Singapore). She has a Doctor of Philosophy (Information Technology) from Murdoch University, Perth, Australia. Her areas of research include educational technology, computer-mediated communication, electronic discourse analysis and more recently, engineering education and human resource management. She has published over 37 works that included books, book chapters, journal papers and conference proceedings. She received an award for best research paper at the 2007 Computer Science and Information Technology Education Conference (CSITED). Lim is an Editorial Review Board member for the *Journal of Information Technology Education: Research*, and *Journal of Information Technology Education: Innovations in Practice*. She is a regular reviewer for annual international conferences that include *Advances in Social Networks Analysis and Mining* (ASO-NAM); *Computers and Advanced Technology in Education* (CATE); and *Conference on Computer Supported Education* (CSEDU). Lim has recently given invited talks on engineering education in Doha (Qatar) and Abu Dhabi (UAE).

Fay Sudweeks is Emerita Associate Professor at Murdoch University, Perth, Australia. She has a Bachelor of Arts (Psychology and Sociology), Master of Cognitive Science and Doctor of Philosophy (Communication Studies). Her current research interests are social and cultural aspects of communication, group dynamics and e-learning. Fay has been nominated for the Vice Chancellor's *Excellence in Teaching Award* and has been nominated twice for the *Excellence in Research Supervision Award*. She has published 7 authored or edited books, 17 edited proceedings, and more than 80 papers in journals, books and conference proceedings. She is on the editorial board of 6 international journals: *Journal of Computer-Mediated Communication, Human Communication Research, New Media and Society, International Journal of e-Learning, Open Communication Journal,* and *International Journal of Information Systems in the Service Sector.* With Charles Ess, Fay has co-chaired eight international and interdisciplinary conferences on *Cultural Attitudes towards Technology and Communication* (CATaC). Fay has given invited talks in numerous countries including the USA, South Africa, Russia, Germany, Israel, and Sweden.

* * *

Javier M. Aguiar holds a PhD in Telecommunications and Telecommunications Engineer from Universidad de Valladolid, Spain. Currently he is professor of the Higher Technical School of Telecommunications Engineering in the Universidad de Valladolid and his research is focused on Next Generation

Networks and Services. He participated in IST FP5 (ICEBERGS), IST FP6 (MEDIANET, SATSIX, OPUCE), EUREKA-CELTIC (MaCS, QUAR2, IMAGES, PABIOS, HuSIMS), ESA (AO4694), managing technical activities in National and European research projects, as well as cooperation with relevant companies of the telecommunication sector. Furthermore, he has contributed in the standardization field as expert in the Specialist Task Force 294 at the European Telecommunications Standards Institute.

Reima Al-Jarf has worked as a professor of EFL at King Saud University, Riyadh, Saudi Arabia for 26 years. She has published 6 books, 145 book chapters, encyclopedia and journal articles in peer-reviewed International and national journals and conference proceedings, in addition to 150 translated articles, magazine and newspaper articles, course material, teaching and learning guides and reports. She has given 255 conference presentations and 40 workshops in 58 countries. Since the year 2000, she has integrated online discussion forums, blogs, podcasts, MP3 lessons, mind-maps, Text-to-Speech software, mobile Apps and online courses using Blackboard, WebCT, Moodle, Nicenet, and RCampus in teaching EFL to college students. She is a reviewer for numerous international journals, grant and conference proposals, translated books, international research projects, textbooks, language programs and dissertations. She is a winner of three Excellence in Teaching Awards and the Best Faculty Website Award at her university, college and department levels.

Carlos Baladrón holds a Ph.D. in communications and information technologies, and an M.Eng. in telecommunications engineering from the Universidad de Valladolid, where he works as a researcher for the Communication Networks and Services (SRC) laboratory. He has been involved in several Spanish and European projects (including for instance IST FP6 OPUCE, where he performed the role of Technical Manager, and IST FP6 SATSIX) covering topics such as satellite communications, voice encoding, applied artificial intelligence, NGNs, VoIP, context awareness, service engineering, SOA systems, etc., fields in which he has published numerous works in top-level peer-reviewed journals, conferences, white papers and books.

Christyne A. Berzsenyi, Ph.D. is currently an Associate Professor of English and Women's Studies at Penn State University, Wilkes-Barre campus in the United States of America. Her primary areas of scholarship are in rhetoric and written communications in mass media upon which interlocutor identities and relationships are constructed, defined, and sustained through discursive actions and texts with ethical implications. Christyne Berzsenyi has publications in other subjects that include computers, composition, and pedagogy. She teaches courses with computer-assisted, hybrid, and web instructional delivery in composition, professional writing, web writing, science fiction and detective literature, and women in the arts and humanities.

Lorena Calavia holds a M. Eng. Degree in Telecommunications Engineering from the Universidad de Valladolid, Spain, where she is also a Ph.D. candidate in the Department of Signal Theory, Communications and Telematics Engineering and works as a researcher since 2007. For all this time she has been working in several National and European investigation projects financed by different institutions, including IST FP6 OPUCE project, the CELTIC project HuSIMS and the national projects VISION, mIO!, WIMSAT and V-ER. Her research area is mainly focused on Next Generation Networks, service engineering, context-aware services, SOA, Web Service technologies, semantic characterization and inference and applied Artificial Intelligence (clustering, neural networks, genetic algorithms, etc.).

Belén Carro has a PhD in Telecommunications and Telecommunications Engineer. She is professor of the Telecommunications School in the Universidad de Valladolid. She also collaborates with the non-profit technological centre Cedetel in management and development of R&D innovative projects dealing with Systems, Networks and Services for the Information Society. Her research is focused on broadband access networks and advanced QoS topics. She was in charge of IST FP5 ICEBERGS, IST FP6 MEDI-ANET and OPUCE and several CELTIC Initiative projects (MaCS, QUAR2, IMAGES and HuSIMS). She has also managed other R&D projects related to broadband access networks performance and services, including National research projects and collaboration with key telecommunication companies.

Gaowei Chen is a postdoctoral researcher in the Learning Research and Development Center, University of Pittsburgh and Pittsburgh Science of Learning Center (PSLC). He received a BS from Xi'an Jiaotong University, and an MS in educational technology from Peking University. He received his PhD in educational psychology from The Chinese University of Hong Kong. His current research focuses on the interactions among teachers and students. By applying statistical and machine learning methods to the study of both online and classroom discussions, he examines how teacher-student and student-student interactions help produce strong effects on learning. His articles appear in journals such as Computers & Education and Computers in Human Behavior.

Costin Chiru, PhD is a lecturer at the Computer Science Department from University Politehnica of Bucharest. He teaches Logical Programming, Symbolic and Statistical Learning, Human Computer Interface, Algorithm Design, Natural Language Processing (NLP). He has a MSc in Advanced Internet Applications and a PhD awarded in 2011. His thesis was on using NLP for discourse analysis and for Computer Supported Collaborative Learning (CSCL). His interests are Technology-Enhanced Learning, Machine Learning, NLP and Discourse Analysis. In 2006, he worked as a researcher in the field of NLP at Human Language Technology Research Institute from Dallas. He had published papers on NLP and CSCL. He had participated in several national and international projects (LTfLL, ERRIC, COOPER, K-TEAMS, PALIROM).

Ming Ming Chiu is Professor of learning and instruction at the University at Buffalo, State University of New York (UB). He invented statistics methods to analyze conversations (statistical discourse analysis [SDA]) and to analyze how ideas spread through a population (multilevel diffusion analysis [MDA]). He applies these methods to analyze classroom conversations, academic achievement of over 500,000 students in 65 countries, and corruption in the music and banking industries. He has modeled how students influence one another during group problem solving by monitoring and controlling one another's knowledge, emotions, and actions (*social metacognition*). Beyond the classroom, Chiu developed an *ecological* model of how attributes of students, their families, their schools and their countries affect their learning and academic performance on international tests. His publications include journal articles in Journal of Family Psychology, Journal of Educational Psychology, Social Forces, American Educational Research Journal, etc.

Stefania Cucchiara is a postdoctoral research assistant at the University of Bari (Italy). Her doctoral thesis focused on the assessment of knowledge building process in online discussions. Her research interest is in technology-mediated knowledge processes. Her expertise is in psycho-social aspects, such as sense of community, identity, social structure, group management and evaluation practices in virtual communities and blended learning settings. She authored several publications in books and scientific journals. She serves as a member of the Executive Committee of the Collaborative Knowledge Building Group and Editor-in-Chief of the scientific journal Qwerty. Her current research interests are the development of dialogic identity, multiculturalism and career counseling supported by Social Networks.

Catia Cucchiarini obtained her Ph.D. in phonetics from the University of Nijmegen. She worked at the Centre for Language and Education of K.U. Leuven (Belgium), and has been working at the University of Nijmegen on various projects on language learning and testing, and the application of ASR to second language training and testing. She has supervised PhD students and has published in international journals and proceedings. Since 1999, she also works part-time for 'de Nederlandse Taalunie' (Dutch Language Union) as a senior project manager for language policy and Human Language Technologies, where she has led user requirement surveys in the field of language and speech technology applications for education and communicative disabilities. Currently, she is a member of the editorial board of the international journal Computer Assisted Language Learning, of the Flemish FWO (Fonds Wetenschappelijk Onderzoek) Expertpanel Cult1-Languages, and of the ISCA SIG SLaTE.

Thanasis Daradoumis is Associate Professor, Department of Cultural Technology and Communication, University of the Aegean, Greece and Joint Professor, Department of Computer Science, Multimedia and Telecommunications, Open University of Catalonia, Spain. He is also Collaborating Professor at Hellenic Open University. He holds a PhD in Computer Science from the Polytechnic University of Catalonia-Spain, Master of Science from the University of Illinois, and Bachelor in Mathematics from the University of Thessaloniki-Greece. His research focuses on e-learning, e-collaboration, e-learning communities, e-learning content-design, e-course design, synchronous and asynchronous communication, interaction analysis, e-assessment, e-monitoring, scaffolding, computer supported collaborative learning (CSCL), adaptive learning, emotional and affective learning. He serves in the editorial board of several international conferences and journals, and he has coordinated or participated in various European and International R&D projects. He is co-director of the DPCS (Distributed Parallel and Collaborative Systems) Research Laboratory [http://dpcs.uoc.es/]. Finally, he has written over 100 papers.

Boyd Davis received a Ph.D. in Linguistics from University of North Carolina (Chapel Hill). She is the Bonnie E. Cone Professor of Teaching in Applied Linguistics at University of North Carolina, Charlotte. Her areas of interest include narrative, pragmatics and stance in medical and online discourse, and digital collections of speech. Her most recent books are *Alzheimer talk, text and context* (Palgrave 2008; 2005) and *Fillers, Pauses and Placeholders* (Benjamins 2010, with N. Amiridze, M. Maclagan). Her fifteen-year longitudinal collection of conversations with persons with Alzheimer's disease is one cohort in the digital *Carolinas Conversations Collection*, sponsored by the National Libraries of Medicine, of which she is co-Principal Investigator.

Chiara Degano (PhD) is a Tenured Researcher in English Linguistics and Translation at Università degli Studi di Milano, Italy. Her research is centred on discourse analysis, which she has integrated with the quantitative approach of corpus linguistics and with aspects of argumentation theory (she is a member of ILIAS - International Learned Institute for Argumentation Studies, and CLAVIER - Corpus and Language Variation in English Research Group). Within this framework she has pursued a twofold line of research, focusing on the representation of international conflicts in the media, and on professional (corporate, institutional and legal) discourse. In this latter strand of research, her interests include also a reflection on how textuality is changing in electronic genres, with a focus on websites and slideware academic presentations.

Nobuko Fujita is an Assistant Professor, E-Learning in the Faculty of Education at the University of Windsor, Canada. A graduate of the PhD program in the Department of Curriculum, Teaching and Learning at the Ontario Institute for Studies in Education of the University of Toronto, she completed a postdoc at the Copenhagen Business School working on an Integrated Project in the ICT challenge of the 7th framework programme of the European Commission, Next Generation Teaching, Education and Learning for Life. She serves as an editor of *Qwerty – Interdisciplinary Journal of Technology, Culture and Education*. Her research interests include learning and knowledge building in computer-supported collaborative learning environments, assessment, design-based research, teacher education, e-learning, social media, and ICTs in K-12 contexts.

Julio Gimenez is a lecturer at the School of Education, The University of Nottingham, UK, where he teaches and researches academic literacies and communication in the workplace. His work has been published in several international journals such as the International Review of Applied Linguistics, English for Specific Purposes, the Journal of English for Academic Purposes, Higher Education, the Journal of Language and International Business, and the European Journal of Engineering Education, among others and in many edited collections. Julio sits on the editorial board of a number of international journals and is the Reviews Editor of the Journal of English for Academic Purposes (Elsevier).

Bob Hodge is a Fellow of the Australian Academy of Humanities, and Research Professor in Humanities at the Institute for Culture and Society, University of Western Sydney, where he is co-ordinator of the Theme Group in Digital Social and Cultural Research. He received his doctorate from Cambridge University, where he was Research Fellow at Churchill College. He has published seminal works in Critical Linguistics (*Language as Ideology*, 1993, with G Kress) and Social Semiotics (*Social Semiotics* 1988, with G Kress), as well as Cultural Studies works applied to Australia, China and Mexico. His current work explores issues at the interface between language, culture and the digital revolution.

Ian Holliday graduated in Physics from Imperial College, University of London (UK), from where he also obtained his PhD. His main research work has focussed on human vision, both normal and abnormal, using psychophysical methods, MEG and fMRI. Some of his research interests are: MEG investigations of pattern processing, motion perception, computer simulation about MEG signals, and the application of MEG to clinical conditions. Having become aware of the general problem of reproducibility in science and its implications for his research, his interest in Reproducible Computing was spurred when he took up teaching responsibilities on advanced statistics at Aston University (UK).

Shannon Kennedy-Clark is a Senior Lecturer in Academic Development at the Australian Catholic University. Shannon has held a number of academic positions both in Australia and overseas. Her main teaching areas are academic communication and using information and communication technologies in education. Shannon has worked on a number of projects in the field of Technology Enhanced Learning and academic communication. Her PhD centered on the use of collaborative game-based learning to develop inquiry skills. Her current research studies are on the use of collaborative design to develop pre-service teachers TPACK, design-based research in higher education, video capture pedagogy and embedding academic literacy in higher education.

Marta María Arguedas Lafuente has been a Lecturer at the program of Technical Engineering in Computer Systems of La Almunia Polytechnic University School ascribed to the University of Zaragoza, Spain, involved in the areas of Computer Architecture and Technology as well as Computer Languages and Systems until September 2012. She holds a Bachelor's degree in Technical Engineering in Computer Systems from La Almunia Polytechnic University School and a Masters in Education and ICT (e-learning) from the Open University of Catalonia, Spain. Currently, she is developing her thesis at the eLearn Center of the Open University of Catalonia, Spain, in the area of emotional learning and intelligent (affective) tutoring systems.

Maria Beatrice Ligorio is an Associate Professor at the University of Bari (Italy) where she teaches educational Psychology and E-learning. She has a PhD in Psychology of Communication. In 1993 she was a recipient of a NATO fellowship at the University of Berkeley, and in the 1999 she received a Marie Curie grant to develop virtual educational environments at the University of Nijmegen (NL). Her main research interests are educational technology, digital identity, dialogical learning, blended communities, intersubjectivity, and learning organization. She is the main editor of a journal *Qwerty* and she is in the editorial board of the *Learning, Culture and Social Interaction*. She participated in many international and national projects. She had published over 60 articles in national and international journals.

María José Luzón is a Senior Lecturer at the University of Zaragoza, Spain. She has a PhD in English Philology and has published papers on academic and professional discourse and on language teaching and learning in the field of English for Specific Purposes. Her current research interests include the study of the discursive and rhetorical features of online academic genres, especially academic weblogs. She has explored them from an interdiscursive perspective, focusing on their medium-afforded features and on the features shared with other academic genres. She is especially interested in the strategic use of social and antisocial behaviour in academic blogs.

Peyton Mason is the President of Next-Generation Marketing Insights. He obtained his Ph.D. in Sociology from Case Western Reserve University, specializing in survey research. He takes a quantitative approach to market research and the analysis of consumers' language. Prior to developing language analytic techniques, he provided over 20 years of research leadership to launch new products, turn around lagging sales and to move businesses forward. He had worked for Unilever (Lipton), Anheuser-Busch, Kellogg's and Bank of America. Abstracts for his trade and academic articles are at http://linguistic-insights.com.

Patricia Mayes is an Associate Professor of Linguistics in the English Department at the University of Wisconsin – Milwaukee. Her research focuses on how language is used to accomplish social action in various contexts, and includes such disparate topics as examining the functions of reported speech in conversational English, analyzing the construction of similar genres in Japanese and English, and studying the functions of particular grammatical forms in discourse. Her current research involves investigating the relationship between constructs such as *identity*, *agency* and *epistemic stance*, as mediated through language use in institutional contexts. She is also working to develop a framework for analyzing the micro-level construction of power relations through social interaction in face-to-face and electronically mediated discourses and, more generally, to contribute to the development of an overarching framework, incorporating the idea that all modes of communication are inherently dialogic and interactive.

Jo Meredith is a doctoral student in the Department of Social Sciences at Loughborough University. She is interested in the empirical differences between spoken interactions and online, written interactions. Her doctoral research focuses on using conversation analysis to analyze one-to-one online interactions conducted using Facebook chat.

Mary Paxton, Ed.D, is an Assistant Professor in the Teacher Education Department in Shippensburg University, Shippensburg, PA, USA. Dr. Paxton teaches pre-service teachers in reading and language arts courses and graduate students in the Reading Master's Program at the university. She had been an elementary classroom teacher, an elementary principal, and a district level administrator before joining the university faculty. She has provided continuing education training programs for faculty in local school districts and implemented a set of Literacy Coaching training modules based on a statewide grant in one district. Dr. Paxton has collaborated in research based on the mentoring of first year teachers. Her research interests include identifying and applying best practices in literacy education.

Stephan Poelmans holds a PhD degree in Applied Economics (KULeuven, 2002), an advanced masters' degree in Management Information Systems (K.U.Leuven), as well as a masters' degree in Applied Economics (UFSIA, Antwerp). From 2002 to 2008, Stephan worked as an Assistant Professor at the Vlaamse Ekonomische Hogeschool (Vlekho). From September 2008, Stephan is engaged as an Associate Professor at the University-College Brussels (HUB). Stephan is interested in both the design, the usability, and the effects of enterprise systems (in particular Business Process Management and ERP systems). Lately, his research efforts have also been directed towards the deployment and evaluation of e-learning systems, game-based learning applications and the educational use of the new social media. Stephan has done or guided research projects and case studies in several companies and governmental agencies. He published in several international journals and conferences.

Jonathan Potter is Professor of Discourse Analysis and Dean of the School of Social, Political and Geographical Sciences at Loughborough University. He has studied racism, argumentation, fact construction, and topics in social science theory and method. His most recent books include: Representing Reality, which attempted to provide a systematic overview, integration and critique of constructionist research in social psychology, postmodernism, rhetoric and ethnomethodology and Conversation and Cognition (with Hedwig te Molder) in which a range of different researchers consider the implication of studies of interaction for understanding cognition. He is one of the founders of discursive psychology.

Komalsingh Rambaree is currently a senior lecturer in social work and social policy at the University of Gävle in Sweden. He has a PhD in social work and social policy from the University of Manchester in England. Dr Rambaree has worked as a part-time lecturer at the Manchester Metropolitan University and as a teaching assistant at The University of Manchester, in England from 2002-2004. From 2004 to 2009, he worked at the University of Mauritius as a full time lecturer in social work and social policy. His research areas include areas such as eco-social work, qualitative research, internet, and sexuality.

Traian Rebedea, PhD is a lecturer and researcher at the Computer Science Department, University Politehnica of Bucharest. He has recently defended his PhD thesis which proposes the use of the inter-animation framework, a computational linguistics method derived from Bakhtin's dialogism theory, for the analysis of online conversations with multiple participants and parallel discussion threads. His research interests and specializations are Computer-Supported Collaborative Learning (CSCL), Machine Learning, Natural Language Processing (NLP), Discourse Analysis and Information Retrieval. Currently, he is working on using NLP and Social Network Analysis techniques in order to support and provide feedback for chat conversations and discussion forums used for CSCL tasks. Moreover, he is studying the discovery, formation and evolution of opinions in large volumes of social data. He has been involved in research projects (e.g. FP7 LTfLL and ERRIC) and has published several papers related to NLP and CSCL.

Antonio Sánchez holds a Telecommunications Engineer and PhD Degree from Universidad de Valladolid (both with national awards). He collaborated on research projects of the University with internships from the University and the Ministry of Education. Following he worked as Researcher for Acotec, Cedetel and Euroconsulting Informatico and joined Telefonica R&D as a Network Engineer where he was involved in several projects related to the IP-Network/Infovia Plus, deployed in Spain and other countries of South America. Later he joined the VoIP division where he lead several international projects related to IP services. He has very broad experience in European innovation programmes: EC (TEN-TELECOM/eTen, FP5-IST, FP6-IST, FP6-Aerospace), Eureka (Celtic, Itea, Medea+) and ESA; a total of 7 projects as coordinator and more than 20 as main researcher.

Divonna M. Stebick, Ph.D. is an Assistant Professor in the Education Department at Gettysburg College, Gettysburg, PA, USA. Dr. Stebick teaches pre-service teachers in reading and language arts, assessment, education psychology and special education courses. She had been an elementary classroom teacher, an intervention specialist, a reading specialist, and a literacy coach before joining the College faculty. She has provided continuing education training programs for faculty in school districts and academia across the U.S. Dr. Stebick has collaborated in research based on the mentoring of first year teachers, teacher inquiry, digital literacy, best practices, and information literacy. Her research interests include identifying and applying best practices in literacy and special education.

Helmer Strik received his Ph.D. in physics (topic: voice source modeling) from the University of Nijmegen, where he is now Associate Professor in Speech Science and Technology. His research activities address speech processing, automatic speech recognition, spoken dialogue systems, and computer assisted language learning (CALL). He has published over 150 refereed papers in international journals, books, magazines and proceedings, has coordinated several national and international projects, was invited as a panelist and/or keynote speaker at international conferences and symposia, has supervised PhD theses, and has been a member of Ph.D. committees in the Netherlands and abroad. He is a member of the scientific committee of the International Speech Communication Association Special Interest Group (ISCA SIG) on Speech and Language Technology in Education (SLaTE, www.sigslate.org).

Kate Thompson is a Postdoctoral Research Associate at the Centre for Computer Supported Learning and Cognition (CoCo) at the University of Sydney. Her PhD examined the intersection of learning sciences theory (multiple representations, CSCL) with simulation model use, and sparked an interest in user-specific scaffolds and strategies for the interrogation of simulation models. Kate's background in environmental science has led her to a systems perspective, and work on environmental education programs has involved mobile learning as well as virtual worlds and more recently *learning by design*. Currently, Kate's research focuses on developing methods for visualizing and analysing collaborative processes using complex datasets, as well as design for learning more generally.

Stefan Trausan-Matu, PhD is a full professor at the Computer Science Department of the University Politehnica of Bucharest, and principal researcher at the Institute of Artificial Intelligence of the Romanian Academy (http://www.racai.ro/~trausan/). He teaches Human-Computer Interaction, Natural Language Processing, Adaptive and Collaborative Systems, Algorithms Analysis and Design, Semantic Web. Professor Trausan-Matu was a Fulbright post-doc at Drexel University, Philadelphia, USA, was an invited professor and lectured in USA, Netherlands, France, Germany, San Marino, Puerto Rico, etc. His research interests are: Computer-Supported Collaborative Learning, e-Learning, Human-Computer Interaction, Discourse Analysis, and Philosophy. He was Director of research projects for the Romanian part in international EU funded research projects (PEKADS, LarFLaST, IKF, Inf3S, SkyNurse, LTfLL), participated in others (PAIL, BalkaNet, Poirot, EU-NCIT, COOPER, ERRIC, TOWNTOLOGY, MUMIA, etc.) and coordinated many national ones. Prof Trausan-Matu has authored or edited 17 books, 25 book chapters and more than 200 peer-reviewed papers.

Patrick Wessa is a statistician (PhD, Institute for Statistics and Econometrics, University of Basel, CH) with a strong interest in information technology. His research is located at the Leuven Institute for Research on Information Systems (LIRIS, University of Leuven, Belgium) and is mainly focused on multidisciplinary, scientific questions that can be studied through reproducible statistics and information technology. His innovations have been made freely accessible through a series of web applications that have become increasingly popular among academics and have been cited in a large number of scholarly articles. In recent years, he disseminated his findings through a variety of publication outlets in the domains of software engineering (IJ of Computers, Communication and Control), statistics (Computational Statistics), education (J of E-Learning), and multidisciplinary science (PLoS ONE).

Asta Zelenkauskaite is an Assistant Professor of Communication in the Department of Culture and Communication at Drexel University (USA). She earned her doctoral degree (Ph.D.) in Mass Communication from Indiana University, Bloomington (USA) with two minor specializations in the fields of Information Science and Linguistics. Her main research areas focus on the ways in which communication practices are shaped by new communication technologies such as computer network environments as well as mobile telephony. She is also interested in collaborative process in online environment. Dr. Zelenkauskaite analyzes the changes that social media bring to the mass media landscape. She researches these phenomena from a multi-method approach to analyze the changing understanding of content, audiences, and media companies. Her research has been featured in Written Communication, Journal of Communication, Newspaper Research Journal, Journal of Broadcasting and Electronic Media.

Index